Policymakers face enormous challenges during financial crises. Empirical evidence is scant, which seriously limits the power of econometrics, and, moreover, appropriate policies are, in many instances, unconventional or downright heterodox. This makes reaching political consensus much more difficult than usual. Thus, adding and summarizing new knowledge on these issues—which this book superbly does—is highly valuable. This book's timeliness is remarkable because the world is still undergoing a major crisis. It offers a comprehensive discussion of several central issues related to financial crises, going from crisis prevention to remedies, if crisis occurs; and it covers at great length topics like banking crises and sovereign debt. The reader will find answers and, when not available, a discussion of the nature and relevance of the unanswered questions. The book should take a place of honor in the library of every policymaker, and anyone wanting to have up-to-date knowledge on these issues.

Guillermo Calvo
Professor of International and Public Affairs, Columbia University

Financial Crises

Causes, Consequences, and Policy Responses

EDITORS

Stijn Claessens, M. Ayhan Kose,
Luc Laeven, and Fabián Valencia

INTERNATIONAL MONETARY FUND

Cover design: IMF Multimedia Services Division

Cataloging-in-Publication Data
Joint Bank-Fund Library

Financial crises : causes, consequences, and policy responses/Stijn Claessens ...
[et al.]. – Washington, D.C. : International Monetary Fund, 2013.
     p. ; cm.
Includes bibliographical references and index.
ISBN 978-1-47554-340-7

1. Financial crises. I. Claessens, Stijn. II. International Monetary Fund.

HB3722.F554 2013

Please send orders to:
International Monetary Fund, Publication Services
P.O. Box 92780, Washington, DC 20090, U.S.A.
Tel.: (202) 623-7430   Fax: (202) 623-7201
E-mail: publications@imf.org
Internet: www.elibrary.imf.org
www.imfbookstore.org

Contents

Foreword

Financial crises are damaging and contagious, prompting calls for swift policy responses when they happen, and justifying much effort to avoid them. As seen in recent years, crises can result in deep and long-lasting recessions and, in some cases, can trigger sharp current account reversals. Unsustainable macroeconomic policies, excessive credit booms, large capital inflows, and balance sheet fragilities appear prominently as common patterns before financial crises. However, not all crises are preceded by such events. Some crises can be contagious and rapidly spread to other countries with no apparent vulnerabilities.

The quest for knowledge on the best predictors of, and the best policy responses to, financial crises is ongoing. Extensive research has been conducted on various aspects of crises, including analyses of centuries-old episodes. The IMF has been closely involved in the resolution of crises and in mitigating their macroeconomic impact. In addition, the IMF has pursued a comprehensive research agenda over the years to analyze the causes and consequences of financial crises, to develop best measures to prevent crises, and to formulate strategies for coping with their consequences. Moreover, the IMF has been a major international forum for researchers and policymakers to debate and exchange their views on these issues.

As a result of these collective efforts in academia and policy institutions, much knowledge has been accumulated on the causes, evolution, and resolution of various types of crises. Despite the progress so far, these issues remain topics of intense policy discussions, as ongoing events clearly remind us every day. Therefore, there is much value in having leading researchers in the field of financial crises provide their cutting-edge perspectives on the topic, combining their contributions with those of economists at the IMF, and disseminating these insights broadly. This book exactly serves this purpose.

Prevention is always better than a cure, so the book includes a detailed analysis of the key factors leading up to financial crises. For example, credit booms are a particular characteristic that comes up as one of the most powerful predictors of crises over the decades, as Alan Taylor's contribution (Chapter 6) makes clear. Increases in leverage and rapid credit growth are seen time and again. The contribution by Carmen Reinhart and Kenneth Rogoff (Chapter 3), building on their studies of crises over a very long history, makes this pattern quite evident. In addition, funding fragility shows up prominently, particularly during the 2007–09 crisis, as Hyun Shin's contribution documents (Chapter 4).

The book has valuable lessons on how countries can better monitor their economies and financial systems. However, rapid changes in financial systems and growing linkages among economies mean that it is still quite difficult to find robust patterns that can help us to predict crises accurately. Given the developments witnessed during the 2007–09 episodes, the view that only emerging markets are prone to crises is surely wrong. Advanced economies were at the epicenter of the crisis, whereas many emerging markets proved relatively resilient. In his contribution (Chapter 5), José De Gregorio provides an elegant perspective on the sources of this resilience in emerging markets in Latin America, and explores the potential lessons for other emerging markets and advanced economies.

In addition to the chapters by these eminent scholars, a number of contributions from researchers at the IMF are presented in the book. These chapters focus on the causes and consequences of financial crises, and on the best policies for their resolution. They reflect that IMF research and policy activities are geared toward improving the institution's crisis prevention and resolution toolkits, encompassing surveillance, technical assistance, policy design, and emergency lending.

Recent work on credit booms and banking crises conducted by IMF researchers confirms academic research on the critical role of rapid credit expansion before crises. This work has found that one in three boom episodes ends in a crisis. Although it is difficult to differentiate a good credit boom from a bad one beforehand, this research shows that bad booms tend to be longer. Specifically, roughly half of the booms lasting longer than six years ended in a crisis.

Research conducted at the IMF also documents that cross-border financial linkages have intensified and become more complex. Increased linkages promote risk diversification by reducing exposure to local shocks, but global financial networks also transmit shocks and can make the sudden elevation of systemic risk more likely. When such risks materialize and turn into systemic crises, they affect a large number of countries, including "bystanders," that is, those countries with relatively strong fundamentals that are less vulnerable to idiosyncratic crises.

As research advances, we hope to further improve early detection of vulnerabilities. As we learn more about incentives and factors that lead to financial fragility, we will be able to design better policies, including macroprudential ones, and improve the institutional infrastructure and strengthen supervision, thereby reducing the incidence of crises. Having said this, I am realistic enough to realize that there is a long road ahead in having the knowledge and tools, combined with the necessary political will, to prevent all financial crises.

Political economy considerations are often at the core of the challenges policymakers face in preventing and coping with financial crises. In the past they hampered the design of efficient policy responses and they have been present in recent crises. Much needs to be explored to design effective regulatory and supervisory interventions when the signs of excessive risk taking demand strong actions. The flourishing research on macroprudential policies can help provide some answers toward the better design of such interventions.

The findings presented are not just important for crisis prevention, but can also guide the appropriate design of international lending instruments and safety nets, including those of the IMF. For example, to reduce the incidence and scale of crises brought on by contagion, resources should be pooled globally, thus proactively helping to provide the necessary liquidity to avoid self-reinforcing crises and reduce the risk of contagion. In turn, policy space would be provided for innocent bystanders. The IMF has internalized this lesson, quadrupling its resources and revamping its lending toolkit by giving greater emphasis to crisis insurance.

Although further research in this area can help in many dimensions, there are challenges ahead and crises will inevitably happen again. Therefore, the global policy community should also continue to devote efforts to buttressing our understanding of crisis resolution policies. As chapters in this book show, designing a strategy for resolving a crisis and formulating policies to accelerate economic recovery involve many trade-offs. Resolution policies that transfer wealth from savers to borrowers can help restart productive investment, but can create moral hazard. It is clear now that adequate implementation requires arrangements that properly align incentives. Open bank assistance without proper restructuring and recapitalization is not an efficient way to deal with an ailing banking system. Moreover, excessive liquidity support and guarantees cannot substitute for proper restructuring and recapitalization. After all, most crises involve solvency problems, not just liquidity shortfalls.

The book highlights the macroeconomic challenges and consequences of crises. Resolution itself, especially if not properly designed, may result in large fiscal costs. And a weak fiscal position can be a major constraint to implementing the necessary restructuring measures. The book highlights that better outcomes will be achieved, including lower real and fiscal costs, the sooner that restructuring policies are implemented. An aggressive strategy removes residual uncertainties that lead to precautionary contractions in consumption and investment, further exacerbating recessions. Delayed economic recoveries are nevertheless common in financial crises and result in substantial medium-term output losses. These and other challenges emphasize the need for further research on crisis resolution.

The collection of research in this book provides an excellent overview of these critical policy areas. However, because many challenges in the prevention and resolution of crises are yet to be addressed, the topic of financial crises remains a fertile area for future research.

David Lipton
First Deputy Managing Director
International Monetary Fund

Acknowledgments

The editors are grateful to Olivier Blanchard and Prakash Loungani for their constant support of this book project. They would also like to thank Helen Hwang of the Research Department for administrative assistance, and Sean Culhane, Joanne Johnson, and Patricia Loo of the Communications Department for their help in coordinating the publication of this volume.

Introduction

STIJN CLAESSENS, M. AYHAN KOSE, LUC LAEVEN,
AND FABIÁN VALENCIA

By now, the tectonic damage left by the global financial crisis of 2007–09 has been well documented. Global per capita output, which typically expands by about 2.2 percent annually, contracted by 1.8 percent in 2009, the largest contraction the global economy has experienced since World War II. During the crisis, markets around the world experienced colossal disruptions in asset and credit markets, massive erosions of wealth, and unprecedented numbers of bankruptcies. Five years after the crisis began, its lingering effects are still all too visible in advanced economies and emerging markets alike: the global recession left in its wake a worldwide increase of 30 million people unemployed. These are painful reminders of why the understanding of financial crises needs to be improved. This book serves this purpose by bringing together a number of innovative studies on the causes and consequences of financial crises and policy responses to them.

Although there is a rich literature on financial crises, no publication since the 2007–09 crisis has provided a broad overview of this research and distilled its policy lessons. This book fills this critical gap. It covers a wide range of crises, including banking, balance of payments, and sovereign debt crises. It reviews the typical patterns that precede crises and considers lessons on their antecedents, analyzes the evolution of crises and examines various policy responses—macroeconomic policies and the restructuring of banks, households, financial institutions, and sovereigns—and studies their aftermath, including short- and medium-term growth impacts and financial and fiscal consequences. This volume includes contributions from outstanding scholars engaged in research on financial crises and a select set of chapters produced by researchers at the IMF. The book's audience includes researchers, academics, and graduate students working on financial crises. Because it shows that applied research can provide lessons, it is also an excellent reference for policymakers.

SIMILARITIES BETWEEN CRISES ABOUND

As the book documents, lessons from past crises are insightful because many similarities across crisis episodes can be detected, even when the exact triggers for and timing of crises vary. Although the relative importance of the sources of the 2007–09 crisis will be debated for some time, the run-up to this episode shares at least four major features with earlier episodes: rapid increases in asset prices, credit booms, a dramatic expansion in marginal loans, and regulation and supervision that failed to keep up with developments. Combined, these factors sharply increased the risk of a financial crisis, as they had in earlier episodes.

Asset Price Bubbles

Although the specific sector experiencing a boom can vary across crises, asset price booms are common. In the 2007–09 crisis, it was house prices that sharply increased before the meltdown, including in Iceland, Ireland, Spain, the United Kingdom, the United States, and other markets that subsequently ran into problems. The patterns of house price increases are reminiscent of those in earlier major crisis episodes. The overall size of the housing booms and their dynamics—including house prices rising in excess of 30 percent in the five years preceding the crisis and peaking just before the beginning of the crisis—are remarkably similar to developments that preceded previous banking crises in advanced economies, as observed by Reinhart and Rogoff (2008). These booms were generally fueled by quickly rising credit resulting in sharp increases in household leverage. As happened so often before, the rapid house price increases and the buildup in leverage turned out to be a dangerous combination.

Credit Booms

As in most earlier crises, the rapid expansion of credit played a large role in the run-up to the 2007–09 crisis. Credit aggregates grew very fast in Iceland, Ireland, Spain, the United Kingdom, and several eastern European countries, often fueling real estate booms. Rapid credit growth episodes generally coincide, as they did again this time, with large cyclical fluctuations in economic activity. Although aggregate credit growth was less pronounced, reflecting slower corporate credit expansion, household indebtedness in the United States rose rapidly after 2000, driven largely by increased mortgage financing, along with contributions from historically low interest rates and financial innovation. And in spite of low interest rates, debt service relative to disposable income reached record highs.

Historically, not all credit booms end up in crises, but the probability of a crisis increases with a boom, especially the larger its size and the longer its duration. The mechanisms linking credit booms to crises include increases in the leverage of borrowers and lenders and a decline in lending standards. In the 2007–09 episode, both channels were at work. Increased leverage, in part attributable to inadequate oversight, left households vulnerable to a decline in house prices, a tightening in credit conditions, and a slowdown in economic activity. Not only did the correction harm consumers as they ran into debt-servicing problems, it also led to systemic risks. And default rates were higher where credit growth had been more rapid; this pattern extended to other countries caught in crises.

Marginal Loans and Systemic Risk

Credit booms or, more generally, rapid growth in financial markets, are often associated with a deterioration in lending standards. They often mean the creation of marginal assets that are viable only as long as favorable economic conditions last. In the United States and elsewhere, a large portion of the mortgage expansion consisted of loans extended to borrowers with limited credit and employment histories, and often on terms poorly suited to the borrowers' conditions. Debt servicing and repayment were vulnerable to economic downturns and changes in credit and monetary conditions. This situation maximized default correlations across loans, generating portfolios highly exposed to declines in house prices—confirmed afterward by the large fraction of nonperforming loans.

In other countries, the same pattern meant large portions of credit denominated in foreign currency. Similar exposures had been common before, for example, in the corporate and financial sectors before the Asian crisis of the late 1990s. In the 2007–09 crisis, large portions of credit (including to households) in several Eastern European economies were denominated in foreign currency (euros, Swiss francs, and yen). Although interest rates lower than those on local currency loans increased affordability, borrowers' ability to service those loans depended on continued exchange rate stability. Again, this meant high default risk correlations across loans and systemic exposure to macroeconomic shocks.

Risky liability structures in financial intermediaries typically add to vulnerabilities. The importance of wholesale bank funding, which in the past often took the form of foreign liabilities, especially in emerging market crises, manifested itself this time in the nonbank financial system, particularly in the United States. Moreover, commercial banks and investment banks in many advanced economies sharply increased their leverage. As a result of buoyant housing and corporate financing markets, favorable conditions spurred the emergence of large-scale derivatives markets, such as those for mortgage-backed securities and collateralized debt obligations with payoffs that depended in complex ways on underlying asset prices. The corporate credit default swap market also expanded dramatically because of favorable spreads and low volatility. The pricing of these instruments was often based on a continuation of increasing or high asset prices.

Poorly Designed Liberalization, Ineffective Regulation and Supervision, and Inadequate Interventions

Crises often follow expansions triggered by badly sequenced regulatory reforms and financial liberalization. Poorly developed domestic financial systems have often been unable to intermediate large capital inflows in the wake of capital account liberalization. Deficiencies in oversight often led to currency and maturity mismatches and to large and concentrated credit risks. In the 2007–09 crisis as well, although perhaps in more subtle forms, regulatory approaches and prudential oversight were insufficient to restrict excessive risk taking.

As in the past, financial institutions, merchant banks, investment banks, and off-balance-sheet vehicles of commercial banks operated—to varying degrees—outside the regulatory perimeter. The shadow banking system was able to grow without much oversight, eventually becoming a systemic risk. Derivatives markets were largely unregulated and poorly overseen, creating the potential for chain reactions leading to systemic risk. The international activities of financial institutions were not monitored properly. Market discipline was not effective in halting the buildup of systemic risks. Markets, rating agencies, and regulators underestimated the conflicts of interest and information problems associated with the originate-to-distribute model.

As happened in earlier episodes, prevention and early intervention mechanisms also proved to be insufficient. Before the crisis, the focus of authorities remained primarily on the liquidity and solvency of individual institutions, rather than on the resilience of the financial system as a whole. This lapse led to an underestimation of the probability and costs of systemic risk. In addition, as has been common in previous episodes, intervention came late in many countries, significantly raising the real and fiscal costs, and hampering the postcrisis recovery. At the international level, insufficient coordination among regulators and supervisors and the absence of clear procedures for the resolution of global financial institutions hindered efforts to prevent the cross-border transmission of the crisis.

DIFFERENCES DO EXIST

Despite the similarities described above, crises continue to occur partly because the economic and financial conditions before each batch of crises have their own unique features, making people think "this time is different" as succinctly described by Carmen Reinhart and Kenneth Rogoff (2009). In addition to presenting a careful study of the similarities, the book also covers the features that distinguish the 2007–09 crisis from earlier episodes. In particular, many chapters in the book consider four major differentiating elements: benign macroeconomic conditions before the crisis, the opaqueness of financial transactions and the large role of nonbank financial institutions, the high degree of international financial integration, and the major roles played by advanced economies.

Remarkably Benign Macroeconomic Conditions

One of the most significant differences was that the buildup of risks around the world occurred within relatively benign macroeconomic conditions in most countries, with solid economic growth, low inflation, and few financial crises. These circumstances created a sense of exuberance in financial markets and a feeling of accomplishment among policymakers. Historically low real interest rates helped foster increased leverage across a wide range of agents—notably financial institutions and households—and markets. The high degree of leverage, however, limited the ability of borrowers and the financial system to absorb even small shocks, leading to a quick erosion of capital buffers, a rapid decline in confidence, and an escalation of counterparty risk early on in the crisis. These weak spots, in turn, triggered a liquidity crisis with global ramifications.

Opaqueness of Financial Transactions and the Role of Nonbanks

Although the originate-to-distribute model in the United States seemed to be a good template for risk allocation, it turned out to undermine incentives for properly assessing risks and led to a buildup of tail risks. The model also caused serious difficulties for assessing the true value of assets as the crisis unraveled. This lack of understanding quickly turned a liquidity crisis into a solvency crisis. Indeed, the financial turmoil began in those countries in which nonbanks (including money market funds, investment banks, and special-purpose vehicles) played important roles in financial intermediation. Because these nonbanks typically did not fall within the formal financial regulatory perimeter, the risk of runs became more likely.

The complex interdependencies between the regulated and unregulated parts of the financial system also made responses more difficult than when the financial system consisted primarily of traditional banks (as in many earlier crises). The restructuring of assets became far more complicated because homeowners in many countries were directly involved. There are no established best practices for dealing with large-scale household defaults and the associated moral hazard problems and equity and distribution issues. Restoring household balance sheets proved to be very complex and prolonged the recovery from the crisis.

High Degree of International Financial Integration

A significant fraction of financial instruments originated in the United States were held in other advanced economies and by the official sector in emerging markets. Large cross-border banks, exceeding many countries' GDP in size, had extensive, complex exposures in and across many markets. International financial integration more generally had increased dramatically in the decades before the crisis, with global finance no longer involving just a few large players, but many from various markets and different countries. Although this structural evolution undoubtedly had many benefits, it quickly turned turmoil in a few, large countries into a global crisis. The cross-border linkages across institutions and markets meant that disturbances spread quickly, made globally coordinated solutions much more difficult to implement, and worsened confidence in many ways.

The Role of Advanced Economies

The 2007–09 episode was concentrated in advanced economies, in contrast to past crises, which often took place in emerging markets and developing economies. This concentration led to significant contagion effects from financial institutions in advanced economies to other countries, through both financial and trade channels. After all, the crisis countries were not only home to the main intermediaries of global capital but also the main importers of goods and services. Differences in institutional and economic settings, including the typically larger size of advanced economies' financial systems, required different policy responses, both macroeconomic and financial. Whereas emerging markets, for example, typically tightened monetary policy following a crisis to stem capital outflows, advanced economies were able to resort to expansionary monetary policies to support their financial systems and to boost activity, including through fiscal policy, without considering the implications of these policies for capital flows. This strategy had its benefits, but also had costs, because the necessary restructuring was more easily postponed in the presence of expansionary policies.

SYNOPSIS

The remainder of this introduction presents detailed summaries of the chapters in the book. Part I of the book provides an overview of the various types of crises and introduces a comprehensive database of crises. Part II reviews broad lessons on crisis prevention and management. Part III discusses the short-term economic effects of crises, recessions, and recoveries. Part IV analyzes the medium-term effects of financial crises on economic growth. Part V reviews the use of policy measures to prevent booms, mitigate busts, and avoid crises. Finally, Part VI reviews the policy measures for mitigating the adverse impact of crises and examines how to restructure banks, households, and sovereigns.

Part I: Introduction and Description of Financial Crises

The book starts with a review of financial crises, including their origins and macroeconomic consequences, and an overview of the policy responses that countries tend to resort to when dealing with major banking crises. In Chapter 1, Claessens and Kose provide a comprehensive review of the literature on financial crises. They focus on currency crises, sudden stops in capital flows, debt crises, and banking crises. The chapter begins with a general overview of the common elements that precede different types of crises, including asset price bubbles, credit booms, buildups of leverage, and large capital inflows. These can, of course, turn into asset price crashes, credit crunches, deleveraging spirals, sudden capital outflows, or sovereign defaults during financial crises.

They also present a brief discussion of the determinants of crises and document the differences in models developed to explain different types of episodes. Over the years, for example, various generations of models have been developed to explain currency crises, whereas the modeling of systemic banking crises is relatively less advanced. The chapter also reviews the causes identified in empirical work. Despite much overlap, causes can vary depending on the type of crisis. Changes in terms of trade, capital flows, and international interest rates, for example, have been found to be important triggers for currency and foreign debt crises, whereas fundamentals, policy failures, and domestic or external shocks have been shown to be important triggers for banking crises.

The authors discuss the identification of crises in practice, a key challenge for empirical studies. Using existing databases, they show that, although often associated with emerging markets, crises have been universal phenomena. Crises also often overlap and come in waves, indicating the significance of global factors in driving these episodes. In addition, the authors provide a review of the macroeconomic implications of crises. Output losses are almost universal, and consumption, investment, and industrial production follow qualitatively similar declines, although severity and duration vary.

In Chapter 2, Laeven and Valencia provide a detailed database of the starting dates of financial crises and of the resolution policies and fiscal costs associated with resolving crises. Their focus is on banking crises, although information on currency crises and sovereign debt crises is also provided. Using the data, they show that countries typically resort to a mix of policies to contain and resolve banking crises, ranging from macroeconomic stabilization to financial sector restructuring policies and institutional reform.

In addition to offering the most comprehensive and up-to-date available database on banking crises, Laeven and Valencia also point out that, despite the numerous commonalities among crisis origins, many attempted crisis-management strategies have met with mixed success. Successful crisis resolutions have been characterized by transparency and steadfastness in resolving insolvent institutions, thereby removing uncertainty surrounding the viability of financial institutions. This strategy requires a triage of strong and weak institutions, with full disclosure of bad assets and recognition of losses, followed by the recapitalization of viable institutions and the removal of bad assets and unviable institutions from the system.

Conventional wisdom would have it that advanced economies, with their stronger macroeconomic frameworks and institutional settings, have an edge in crisis resolution, but the record thus far supports the opposite: advanced economies have been slow to resolve banking crises, with the average crisis lasting about twice as long as in developing and emerging market economies.

Although differences in initial shocks and financial system size surely contribute to these different outcomes, the authors suggest that the greater reliance by advanced economies on macroeconomic policies as crisis-management tools may delay the needed financial restructuring, thereby prolonging the crisis. This is not to say that macroeconomic policies should not be used to support the broader economy during a crisis. Macroeconomic policies can be the first line of defense. They stimulate aggregate demand and sustain asset prices, thus supporting output and employment, and indirectly a country's financial system. This support helps prevent disorderly deleveraging and provides room for balance sheet repair, buying time to address solvency problems head-on. However, by masking financial institutions' and borrowers' balance sheet problems, macroeconomic policies may also reduce incentives for financial restructuring, with the risk of dampening growth and prolonging the crisis.

Part II: Lessons in Crisis Prevention and Management

The chapters in the second part of the book provide elegant analyses of the lessons learned about the warning signals ahead of crises and the management of such episodes. These specially commissioned papers were presented at a conference held at the IMF on September 14, 2012. Chapter 3, by Reinhart and Rogoff, is based on the keynote address Carmen Reinhart delivered at the conference.

The chapter makes a convincing case that the 2007–09 crisis, which began with the unraveling of the U.S. subprime mortgage market, is far from over and is on a scale that has not been seen in advanced economies since the 1930s and the defaults on World War I debt.

Reinhart and Rogoff draw four thought-provoking lessons from the 2007–09 crisis. First, policymakers have often been better at managing crises than at preventing them, which was also true in the 2007–09 episode. They speculate that this is unlikely to change anytime soon. Second, they argue that significant differences between advanced economies and emerging market economies are not clear with respect to the likelihood of experiencing a crisis. Specifically, they provide a reminder that although crises were the domain of emerging markets in the last half of the 20th century, before 1940, advanced economies were involved in many crises. Third, both the diagnosis and understanding of the scope and depth of the risks and magnitudes of various debts are still incomplete. Observers tend to forget that domestic and external debt are not created equal, that public debt is different from private debt, and that the stock of debt is usually much larger than ever estimated.

Finally, Reinhart and Rogoff show a recurring pattern following global crises, in which governments have resorted to subtly restructuring their debt, rather than defaulting or formally reworking repayment terms. The techniques, part of which they call financial repression, include keeping interest rates low, which lowers debt-servicing costs and liquidates the real value of government debt. Many advanced economies have also used public debt restructurings and conversions of high-yield, short-term debt into low-yield, long-term debt. Other techniques include directed lending to governments by captive domestic savers such as pension funds, regulation of cross-border flows of funds, and a generally tighter relationship between banks and government. The end result is that funds that would otherwise go to nongovernment borrowers are directed to government use, usually at below-market rates. In light of this history, they suggest an increasing likelihood of debt restructurings and conversions to ease sovereign repayments in some of the stressed economies in Europe.

The global financial crisis of 2007–09 caught most economists and policymakers flat-footed, so the search for predictors of such crises has been a major area of research in recent years. Chapters 4, 5, and 6 ask a fundamental question: what are the best warning signals of financial crises?

In Chapter 4, Shin observes that finding a set of early warning indicators that can flag vulnerability to financial turmoil is an extremely challenging task. Shin focuses on three sets of indicators: those based on market prices; the ratio of credit to GDP—to assess whether credit is expanding excessively; and the behavior of banking sector liabilities, such as monetary aggregates. His results suggest that those indicators based on market prices, such as spreads on credit default swaps, do not give sufficient warning of a crisis. Judging the extent to which the ratio of credit to GDP diverges from its long-term trend is more useful, but determining the long-term trend is difficult until after the crisis. He claims that the behavior of bank liabilities has the most promise, simply because banks must borrow to lend. When credit demand is high, banks tend to exhaust their normal, or core, sources of funds and turn to noncore sources, the defining characteristics of which can vary by institution and financial system. A spike in the ratio of noncore to core liabilities is a good indicator that a boom is under way. However, he also notes that it can be difficult to differentiate between core and noncore liabilities before a crisis.

In past global crises, emerging market economies often suffered more than advanced economies did. The reverse was true in the 2007–09 global financial crisis. Whereas advanced economies suffered—and continue to suffer five years later—emerging market economies, including in Latin America, had shorter recessions and quicker recoveries. In Chapter 5, De Gregorio claims that a number of factors contributed to the better performance of emerging markets in the recent financial crisis. Sound macroeconomic policies before the crisis permitted emerging markets in Latin America to undertake sizable monetary and fiscal stimulus to offset the recession. Countries also allowed their currencies to depreciate sharply, which dampened speculation about further declines.

Financial systems were also generally sound, well capitalized, and regulated, and not prone to accumulating risky financial instruments, such as structured securities, that disabled financial systems in advanced economies. Good luck also helped—commodity prices were high before the crisis and, after a sharp contraction in international trade in 2009, rebounded sharply in 2010. In addition, De Gregorio's chapter documents that countries maintained high levels of international reserves, which served dual roles—as a form of self-insurance to be tapped in case of a sudden cessation of foreign capital inflow and as a bulwark against currency speculation.

Taylor argues in Chapter 6 that unusually high, sustained rates of credit growth, so-called credit booms, tend to be the main precursors to financial crises. Before the global financial crisis of 2007–09, many prominent policymakers and economists focused on the turmoil-producing potential of large current account imbalances, in which some major deficit countries, such as the United States, faced possible "jarring shocks" if surplus countries, such as China, ceased financing their deficits. Although external imbalances can play a role in creating credit booms, his chapter documents that it is the credit boom itself, not its source, that policymakers should watch for as a sign of an impending financial crisis. Although economies can have credit booms fueled by external imbalances, most credit booms are homegrown and unrelated to shifts in the current account.

Together with other contributions in the book, these chapters also provide some lessons for crisis management, notably for advanced economies today and with regard to banking crises. The response during the 2007–09 global financial crisis, dominated by advanced economies, relied heavily on the use of monetary and fiscal policies. Advanced economies were generally well placed to resort to such policies without being overly concerned about the impact on their exchange rates, inflation, or public debt. Advanced economies typically benefit from well-anchored inflation expectations, and their reserve currencies benefit from flight-to-quality effects during financial crises. Emerging market economies, conversely, often do not have the fiscal space or the access to external finance to support accommodative fiscal policy, and excessive monetary expansion quickly translates into inflation and large declines in the value of the currency, further impairing balance sheets in the presence of currency mismatches.

In comparison with past episodes in emerging markets, advanced economies used a much broader range of policy measures, including unconventional asset purchases and guarantees, and significant fiscal stimulus packages. These policies were combined with substantial government guarantees on nondeposit bank liabilities and ample liquidity support for banks, often at concessional rates and with reduced collateral requirements. Liquidity support was particularly large in the euro area, indicating the significant role played by the Eurosystem in managing the crisis, compensating in part for the absence of a common fiscal authority.

The lack of deeper restructuring also reflected the limited nature of the available tools. Initially, countries' responses to the crisis were limited to tools that were on hand and did not require institutional reforms or parliamentary approval. For example, many advanced economies did not have the tools in place to resolve complex financial institutions, including nonbanks, before the crisis. Restructuring often involved budgetary approval for government programs to purchase assets or recapitalize financial institutions, causing delays or inadequate funds. Given the lack of cross-border resolution frameworks and often complex burden-sharing challenges, interventions in ailing institutions with international spillovers were often poor.

Political economy considerations, in addition to economic conditions, can also favor the use of such policies over deep financial restructuring using tools such as bank recapitalization. The latter are generally seen by the public as enriching bankers. Accommodative monetary policy, although less targeted to the underlying problems, is more likely to garner broad-based support: low interest rates will support asset prices for investors and house prices for homeowners, and will lower the debt burden for mortgage holders and other debtors. Taken together, as the chapters stress, these actions mitigated the financial turmoil, contained the crisis, and avoided an even sharper contraction in economic activity. However, they also discouraged more active financial restructuring.

The net result appears to be that much of the cost of the 2007–09 crisis has been transferred to the future, in the form of higher public debt and possibly an anemic economic recovery caused by residual uncertainty about the health of banks and continued high private sector indebtedness. The lingering effects stemming from bad assets and uncertainty about the health of financial institutions risk prolonging the crisis and depressing growth for an extended period. Thus, the broader lesson of this part is that macroeconomic stabilization policies should supplement and support, but not displace or delay, necessary financial restructuring.

Part III: Short-Term Effects: Crises, Recessions, and Recoveries

The next part of the book considers the short-term effects of financial crises as seen in the evolution of macroeconomic and financial variables. The chapters in this part show that recessions associated with financial crises tend to be unusually severe, and their recoveries are typically slow as Kannan, Scott, and Terrones discuss in Chapter 8. The recent bout of crises took a particularly heavy toll on the real economy. However, as Claessens, Kose, and Terrones show in Chapter 7, this might not have been a surprising outcome. Recessions associated with financial crises tend to be unusually severe, resulting in much larger declines in real economic activity, and their recoveries tend to be slow. Similarly, globally synchronized recessions are often long and deep, and recoveries from these recessions are generally weak.

These studies also consider the effectiveness of policies during crises. Countercyclical monetary policy can help shorten recessions, but its effectiveness is limited in financial crises. By contrast, expansionary fiscal policy seems particularly effective in shortening recessions associated with financial crises and boosting recoveries. However, its effectiveness is a decreasing function of the level of public debt. These findings are consistent with the long and severe impacts of the 2007–09 financial crisis as well as the ongoing sluggish recovery. However, strong countercyclical policy action, combined with the restoration of confidence in the financial sector, could help move the recovery forward.

Claessens, Kose, and Terrones also present a brief analysis of the similarities and differences between the 2007–09 crisis and previous episodes. They show that the buildup to the crisis had four major features similar to earlier episodes: First, asset prices increased rapidly in a number of countries before the crisis. Second, a number of key economies experienced credit booms ahead of the crisis. Third, there was a dramatic expansion in marginal loans, particularly in the mortgage markets of several advanced economies, which led to a sharp increase in systemic risk. Fourth, the supervision of financial institutions failed to keep up with the development of new financial instruments. These combined factors sharply increased the risk of a financial crisis.

The authors also claim that four new dimensions played important roles in the severity and global scale of the crisis that included surprising disruptions and breakdowns of several markets in fall 2008. First, there was widespread use of complex and opaque financial instruments. Second, the interconnectedness among financial markets, nationally and internationally, with the United States at the core, had increased dramatically in a short time. Third, the degree of leverage of financial institutions accelerated sharply. Fourth, the household sector played a central role. These new elements combined to create unprecedented complications in late 2008, ultimately resulting in the global financial crisis.

Part IV: Medium-Term Effects: Economic Growth

This part of the book considers the medium-term effects of financial crises on the real economy. In Chapter 9, Abiad, Balakrishnan, Koeva Brooks, Leigh, and Tytell examine the medium-term output performance following 88 banking crises since 1970 across a wide range of economies, as well as the behavior of world output following major financial crises going back to the nineteenth century. They find that output tends to be depressed substantially and persistently following banking crises, with no rebound, on average, to the precrisis trend in the medium term. However, growth eventually returns to its precrisis rate for most economies. The depressed output path tends to result from long-lasting reductions of roughly equal proportions in the employment rate, the capital-to-labor ratio, and total factor productivity. In the short term, the output loss is mainly accounted for by total factor productivity losses, but, unlike the employment rate and capital-to-labor ratio, the level of total factor productivity recovers somewhat to its precrisis trend in the medium term. In contrast, capital and employment suffer enduring losses relative to trend.

Surprisingly, a large number of recoveries from crises occur in the absence of credit growth, labeled "creditless recoveries" by Abiad, Dell'Ariccia, and Li in Chapter 10. They show that such recoveries are not rare: about one in five recoveries is creditless, but average growth during these episodes is about a third lower than during normal recoveries. Aggregate and sectoral data suggest that impaired financial intermediation is the culprit. Creditless recoveries are more common after banking crises and credit booms. Furthermore, sectors more dependent on external finance grow relatively less, and more financially dependent activities (such as investment) are curtailed more, during creditless recoveries.

Part V: Policy Measures to Prevent Booms, Mitigate Busts, and Avoid Financial Crises

This part studies the effectiveness of policies in curbing credit booms and busts, with the aim of preventing or managing financial crises. Chapters 11 (Dell'Ariccia, Igan, Laeven, and Tong) and 12 (Crowe, Dell'Ariccia, Igan, and Rabanal) study the effectiveness of macroeconomic and macroprudential policies in reducing the risks associated with real estate credit booms. Both chapters find that well-targeted macroprudential policies, such as caps on loan-to-value ratios; capital requirements that increase during boom times; and to a lesser extent macroeconomic policies, if properly designed, have some success in curbing excessive credit growth and mitigating the consequences of credit crunches and asset price busts.

Financial sector policies need not be used in isolation to address financial sector problems, but can be complemented with and supported by macroeconomic policies. This is evident in Chapters 13 and 14. Laeven and Valencia (Chapter 13) show that the direct fiscal costs of supporting the financial sector were smaller during the 2007–09 crisis than during earlier crises as a consequence of swift policy actions and significant indirect support from expansionary monetary and fiscal policy, the widespread use of guarantees on liabilities, and direct purchases of assets (such as mortgage securities by central banks). Baldacci, Gupta, and Mulas-Granados (Chapter 14) show that timely countercyclical fiscal measures can contribute to shortening the length of crisis episodes by stimulating aggregate demand, with fiscal expansions that rely mostly on measures to support government consumption proving to be more effective in shortening crisis duration than those based on cuts in public investment or income taxes.

Of course, although these policies reduce the real impact of crises, they concurrently increase the burden of public debt and the size of government contingent liabilities, raising concerns about fiscal sustainability in some countries. In fact, the results in Chapter 14 do not hold for countries with limited fiscal space, where fiscal expansions are prevented by funding constraints. The composition of countercyclical fiscal responses matters as well for output recovery after a crisis, with public investment yielding the strongest impact on growth. These results suggest a potential trade-off between short-term aggregate demand support and medium-term productivity growth objectives in fiscal stimulus packages adopted in times of distress, with the trade-off affected by the depth of financial restructuring.

Part VI: Policy Measures to Mitigate the Impact of Crises; and the Restructuring of Banks and of Household and Sovereign Debt

The final part of the book considers policies for dealing with the restructuring of banks and of debt overhang in the public or private sectors of the economy, specifically the restructuring of household debt and sovereign debt.

Claessens, Pazarbasioglu, Laeven, Dobler, Valencia, Nedelescu, and Seal, in Chapter 15, compare policy choices in recent and past crises and argue that the overall asset restructuring and balance sheet repair of financial institutions during the 2007–09 crisis did not advance as rapidly as they should have, and as a result moral hazard may have increased. Consequently, vulnerabilities in the global financial system remain considerable and continue to threaten the sustainability of the recovery. They call for more aggressive asset restructuring to complete the much-needed financial sector repair and reform process.

In Chapter 16, Landier and Ueda argue that the optimal design of a bank-restructuring program depends on the payoffs and incentives for the various key stakeholders, including shareholders, debt holders, and government; and that the benefits and costs of financial sector interventions should be compared with those of alternative government interventions to support the economy. At the same time, time is of the essence.

The historically high levels of household debt in many crisis-hit countries heightened demands for government intervention. If unaddressed, household debt distress can be a drain on the economy and even lead to social unrest. Well-designed and well-executed government interventions may be more efficient than leaving debt restructuring to the marketplace and standard court-based resolution tools. In Chapter 17, Laeven and Laryea make the case for government intervention in household debt restructuring. They propose, in addition to targeted legal reforms, a template for government-supported household debt-restructuring programs designed to reverse nonperforming loans, which could be adapted to individual country circumstances.

The case for household debt restructuring is also made in Chapter 18 by Igan, Leigh, Simon, and Topalova, who show that housing busts and recessions preceded by larger run-ups in household debt tend to be more severe and protracted. These patterns are consistent with the predictions of recent theoretical models. Based on case studies, they show that government policies can help prevent prolonged contractions in economic activity by addressing the problem of excessive household debt. In particular, bold household debt-restructuring programs such as those implemented in the United States in the 1930s and in Iceland in the aftermath of the global crisis can significantly reduce debt-repayment burdens and the number of household defaults and foreclosures. Therefore, such policies can help avert self-reinforcing cycles of household default, further house price declines, and additional contractions in output.

Finally, Das, Papaioannou, and Trebesch provide a comprehensive survey of issues pertinent to sovereign debt restructuring, based on a newly constructed database covering 185 debt exchanges with foreign banks and bondholders since the 1950s, and 447 bilateral debt agreements with the Paris Club. In Chapter 19, they present new stylized facts on the outcome and process of debt restructurings, including the size of haircuts, creditor participation, and the role of legal conditions. They also discuss ongoing debates about crisis resolution mechanisms, credit default swaps, and the role of collective action clauses. Their chapter shows that rapid restructuring can have many benefits.

REFERENCES

Reinhart, Carmen M., and Kenneth S. Rogoff, 2008, "Is the 2007 U.S. Subprime Crisis So Different? An International Historical Comparison," *American Economic Review*, Vol. 98, No. 2, pp. 339–44.

————, 2009, *This Time Is Different: Eight Centuries of Financial Folly* (Princeton, New Jersey: Princeton University Press).

Terrones, Marco E., Alasdair Scott, and Prakash Kannan, 2009, "From Recession to Recovery: How Soon and How Strong?" *World Economic Outlook*, April (Washington: International Monetary Fund).

Contributors

Abdul Abiad is Deputy Division Chief in the Research Department of the International Monetary Fund.

Ravi Balakrishnan is a Resident Representative in Singapore of the International Monetary Fund.

Emanuele Baldacci is Head of the Italian Statistical Institute (Istat).

Petya Koeva Brooks is Advisor in the European Department of the International Monetary Fund.

Stijn Claessens is Assistant Director in the Research Department of the International Monetary Fund.

Christopher Crowe is an economist in the Research Department of the International Monetary Fund, currently on leave and working in the financial sector in London.

Udaibir S. Das is Assistant Director in the Monetary and Capital Markets Department of the International Monetary Fund.

José De Gregorio is Professor of Economics at Universidad de Chile. Between 2007 and 2011, he served as president of the Central Bank of Chile, as vice president between 2003 and 2007, and as an advisor between 2001 and 2003. He was also tri-minister of Economics, Mining, and Energy between 2000 and 2001.

Giovanni Dell'Ariccia is Assistant Director in the Research Department of the International Monetary Fund.

Marc Dobler is Senior Financial Sector Expert in the Monetary and Capital Markets Department of the International Monetary Fund.

Sanjeev Gupta is Deputy Director in the Fiscal Affairs Department of the International Monetary Fund.

Deniz Igan is Senior Economist in the Western Hemisphere Department of the International Monetary Fund.

Prakash Kannan is a vice president at the Government of Singapore Investment Corporation.

M. Ayhan Kose is Assistant to the Director in the Research Department of the International Monetary Fund.

Luc Laeven is Lead Economist in the Research Department of the International Monetary Fund.

Augustin Landier is Professor of Economics at Toulouse 1 University Capitole, France.

Thomas Laryea is a partner at SNR Denton in Washington, DC.

Daniel Leigh is Senior Economist in the Research Department of the International Monetary Fund.

Bin Li is an economist in the Research Department of the International Monetary Fund.

Carlos Mulas-Granados is a Technical Assistance Advisor in the Fiscal Affairs Department of the International Monetary Fund.

Oana Nedelescu is Senior Financial Sector Expert in the Monetary and Capital Markets Department of the International Monetary Fund.

Michael G. Papaioannou is Deputy Division Chief in the Monetary and Capital Markets Department of the International Monetary Fund.

Ceyla Pazarbasioglu is Deputy Director in the Monetary and Capital Markets Department of the International Monetary Fund.

Pau Rabanal is Senior Economist in the Institute for Capacity Development of the International Monetary Fund.

Carmen Reinhart is the Minos A. Zombanakis Professor of the International Financial System at Harvard Kennedy School. Previously she was the Dennis Weatherstone Senior Fellow at the Peterson Institute for International Economics and professor of economics and Director of the Center for International Economics at the University of Maryland.

Kenneth Rogoff is Professor of Economics at Harvard University. Previously he held positions at Princeton University, University of California at Berkeley, University of Wisconsin-Madison, and the Board of Governors of the Federal Reserve System.

Alasdair Scott is Senior Economist in the European Department of the International Monetary Fund.

Katharine Seal is Senior Financial Sector Expert in the Monetary and Capital Markets Department of the International Monetary Fund.

Hyun Song Shin is the Hughes-Rogers Professor of Economics at Princeton University. Previously, he held academic positions at Oxford and the London School of Economics.

John Simon is Senior Economist in the Research Department of the International Monetary Fund.

Alan M. Taylor is Professor of Economics at the University of California, Davis.

Hui Tong is an economist in the Research Department of the International Monetary Fund.

Marco E. Terrones is Assistant to the Director in the Research Department of the International Monetary Fund.

Christoph Trebesch is Assistant Professor, Department of Economics, University of Munich.

Irina Tytell is Senior Economist in the European Department of the International Monetary Fund.

Petia Topalova is Senior Economist in the Research Department of the International Monetary Fund.

Kenichi Ueda is Senior Economist in the Monetary and Capital Markets Department of the International Monetary Fund.

Fabián Valencia is Senior Economist in the Research Department of the International Monetary Fund.

Abbreviations

3S	systemic sudden stop
AMC	asset management company
AUC	area under curve
BAC	bank advisory committee
BMA	Bayesian model averaging
CAC	collective action clause
CCF	Correct Classification Frontier
CDS	credit default swap
DTI	debt to income
EM	emerging market
EU	European Union
Fannie Mae	U.S. Federal National Mortgage Association
FDIC	U.S. Federal Deposit Insurance Corporation
Fed	U.S. Federal Reserve
FHA	U.S. Federal Housing Administration
Freddie Mac	U.S. Federal Home Loan Mortgage Corporation
GDP	gross domestic product
GNP	gross national product
GSE	government-sponsored entity
HAMP	Home Affordable Modification Program
HARP	Home Affordable Refinance Program
HIPC	Heavily Indebted Poor Countries
HOLC	Home Owners' Loan Corporation
H-P	Hodrick-Prescott
IFS	*International Financial Statistics*
LIC	low-income country
LTV	loan to value
M2	broad money
MBS	mortgage-backed security
MDRI	Multilateral Debt Relief Initiative
MHA	Making Home Affordable
NPL	nonperforming loan

OECD	Organization for Economic Cooperation and Development
OLS	ordinary least squares
SAR	Special Administrative Region
TARP	Troubled Asset Relief Program
WDI	*World Development Indicators*
WEO	*World Economic Outlook*

PART I

Introduction and Description of Financial Crises

CHAPTER 1

Financial Crises: Explanations, Types, and Implications

STIJN CLAESSENS AND M. AYHAN KOSE

The 2007–09 global financial crisis and its aftermath have been painful reminders of the multifaceted nature of crises. They hit small and large countries as well as poor and rich ones. As fittingly described by Reinhart and Rogoff (forthcoming), crises "are an equal opportunity menace."[1] They can have domestic or external origins, and stem from private or public sectors. They come in different shapes and sizes, evolve into different forms, and can rapidly spread across borders. They often require immediate and comprehensive policy responses, call for major changes in financial sector and fiscal policies, and can compel global coordination of policies.

The widespread impact of the 2007–09 global financial crisis underlines the importance of having a solid understanding of crises. As the latest episode has vividly shown, the implications of financial turmoil can be substantial and greatly affect the conduct of economic and financial policies. A thorough analysis of the consequences of and best responses to crises has become an integral part of current policy debates as the lingering effects of the latest crisis are still being felt around the world.

This chapter provides a selected survey of the literature on financial crises.[2] Crises are, at a certain level, extreme manifestations of the interactions between the financial sector and the real economy. As such, understanding financial crises requires an understanding of macro-financial linkages, a truly complex challenge in itself. The objective of this chapter is more modest: it presents a focused survey considering three specific questions. First, what are the main factors explaining financial crises? Second, what are the major types of financial crises? Third, what are the real sector and financial sector implications of crises? The chapter also briefly reviews the literature on the prediction of crises and the evolution of early-warning models.

The first section reviews the main factors explaining financial crises. A financial crisis is often an amalgam of events, including substantial changes in credit

---

[1] Reinhart and Rogoff (forthcoming) use this phrase in the context of banking crises, but it also applies to a wider range of crises.

[2] For further reading on financial crises, the starting point is the authoritative study by Reinhart and Rogoff (2009b). Classical references are Minsky (1975) and Kindleberger (1978). See also, IMF (1998); Eichengreen (2002); Tirole (2002); Allen and Gale (2007); Allen, Babus, and Carletti (2009); Allen (2010); and Gorton (2012) for reviews of the causes and consequences of financial crises.

volume and asset prices; severe disruptions in financial intermediation, notably the supply of external financing; large-scale balance sheet problems; and the need for large-scale government support. Although these events can be driven by a variety of factors, financial crises often are preceded by asset and credit booms that then turn into busts. Thus, many theories focusing on the sources of financial crises have recognized the importance of sharp movements in asset and credit markets. In light of this, this section briefly reviews theoretical and empirical studies analyzing developments in asset and credit markets around financial crises.

The second section classifies the types of financial crises identified in many studies into four main groups: currency crises, sudden stop (or capital account or balance of payments) crises, debt crises, and banking crises. This section summarizes the findings of the literature on the analytical causes and empirical determinants of each type of crisis.

The identification of crises is discussed in the third section. Theories designed to explain crises are used to guide the literature on the identification of crises. However, transforming the predictions of the theories into practice has been difficult. Although it is easy to design quantitative methods for identifying currency (and inflation) crises and sudden stops, the identification of debt and banking crises is typically based on qualitative and judgmental analyses. Irrespective of the classification used, different types of crises are likely to overlap. Many banking crises, for example, are also associated with sudden stop episodes and currency crises. The coincidence of multiple types of crises leads to further challenges of identification. The literature, therefore, employs a wide range of methods to identify and classify crises. The section considers various identification approaches and reviews the frequency of crises over time and across different groups of countries.

The fourth section analyzes the implications of financial crises. The macroeconomic and financial implications of crises are typically severe and share many common features across various types. Large output losses are common to many crises, and other macroeconomic variables typically register significant declines. Financial variables, such as asset prices and credit, usually follow qualitatively similar patterns across crises, albeit with variations in severity and duration of declines. The section examines the short- and medium-term effects of crises and presents a set of stylized facts with respect to their macroeconomic and financial implications.

The fifth section summarizes the main methods used for predicting crises. Predicting the timing of crises has been a challenge. Financial markets with high leverage can easily be subject to crises of confidence, making it the main reason that the exact timing of crises is so difficult to predict. Moreover, the nature of crises changes over time as economic and financial structures evolve. Not surprisingly, early-warning tools can quickly become obsolete or inadequate. This section presents a summary of the evolution of different types of prediction models and considers the current state of early-warning models.

The last section first summarizes the major lessons from this literature review, then considers the most relevant issues for research in light of these lessons, including that future research should be geared toward eliminating the "this-time-is-different" syndrome. However, this is a very broad task requiring that two major issues be addressed: How can financial crises be prevented? And, can their costs be mitigated when they take place? In addition, more intensive efforts are required to collect the necessary data and to develop new methods to guide both empirical and theoretical studies.

EXPLAINING FINANCIAL CRISES

Financial crises have common elements, but they come in many forms. A financial crisis is often associated with one or more of the following phenomena: substantial changes in asset prices and credit volume; severe disruptions in financial intermediation and the supply of external financing to various actors in the economy; large-scale balance sheet problems (of firms, households, financial intermediaries, and sovereigns); and large-scale government support (in the form of liquidity support and recapitalization). Financial crises are typically multidimensional events and can be hard to characterize using a single indicator.

The literature has clarified some of the factors driving crises, but definitively identifying their deeper causes remains a challenge. Many theories have been developed regarding the underlying causes of crises. Although fundamental factors—macroeconomic imbalances, internal or external shocks—are often observed, many questions remain about the exact causes of crises. Financial crises sometimes appear to be driven by "irrational" factors, including sudden runs on banks; contagion and spillovers among financial markets; limits to arbitrage during times of stress; the emergence of asset busts, credit crunches, and fire sales; and other aspects of financial turmoil. Indeed, the idea of "animal spirits" (as a source of financial market movements) has long occupied a significant space in the literature attempting to explain crises (Keynes, 1930; Minsky, 1975; and Kindleberger, 1976).[3]

Financial crises are often preceded by asset and credit booms that eventually turn into busts. Many theories focusing on the sources of crises have recognized the importance of booms in asset and credit markets. However, explaining why asset price bubbles or credit booms are allowed to continue and eventually become unsustainable and turn into busts or crunches has been challenging. This naturally requires answering why neither financial market participants nor policymakers foresee the risks and attempt to slow down the increase in asset prices or the expansion of credit.

The dynamics of macroeconomic and financial variables around crises have been extensively studied. Empirical studies have documented the various phases

---

[3] Related are such concepts as "reflexivity" (Soros, 1987), "irrational exuberance" (Greenspan, 1996), and "collective cognition" (de la Torre and Ize, 2011).

of financial crises, from initial, small-scale financial disruptions to large-scale national, regional, or even global crises. They have also described how, in the aftermath of financial crises, asset prices and credit growth can remain depressed for a long time and how crises can have long-lasting consequences for the real economy. Given their central roles, the chapter next briefly discusses developments in asset and credit markets around financial crises.

Asset Price Booms and Busts

Sharp increases in asset prices, sometimes called bubbles, and often followed by crashes, have been experienced for centuries. Asset prices sometimes seem to deviate from what fundamentals would suggest and exhibit patterns different from predictions of standard models with perfect financial markets. A bubble, an extreme form of such deviation, can be defined as "the part of asset price movement that is unexplainable based on what we call fundamentals" (Garber, 2000, p. 4). Patterns of exuberant increases in asset prices, often followed by crashes, figure prominently in many accounts of financial instability, for both advanced economies and emerging market economies, going back millennia.[4]

Some asset price bubbles and crashes are well known. Such historical cases include the Dutch Tulip Mania from 1634 to 1637, the French Mississippi Bubble in 1719–20, and the South Sea Bubble in the United Kingdom in 1720 (Kindleberger, 1986; and Garber, 2000). During some of these periods, certain asset prices increased very rapidly in a short time, followed by sharp corrections. These cases are extreme, but not unique. In the 2007–09 financial crisis, for example, house prices in a number of countries followed this inverse U-shaped pattern (Figure 1.1).

What Explains Asset Price Bubbles?

Formal models attempting to explain asset price bubbles have been available for some time. Some of these models consider how individual episodes of rational behavior can lead to collective mispricing, which in turn can result in bubbles. Others rely on microeconomic distortions that can lead to mispricing. Some others assume "irrationality" on the part of investors. Despite parallels, explaining asset price busts (such as fire sales) often requires accounting for different factors than does explaining bubbles.

Some models using rational investors can explain bubbles without distortions. These models consider asset price bubbles as agents' justified expectations about future returns. For example, in Blanchard and Watson (1982), under rational expectations, the asset price does not need to equal its fundamental value, leading to "rational" bubbles. Thus, observed prices, although exhibiting extremely large fluctuations, are not necessarily excessive or irrational. These models have been applied relatively successfully to explain the Internet bubble of the late 1990s. Pastor and Veronesi (2006) show how a standard model can reproduce the valu-

---

[4] For detailed reviews of models of asset price bubbles, see Garber (2000); Evanoff, Kaufman, and Malliaris (2012); and Scherbina (2013).

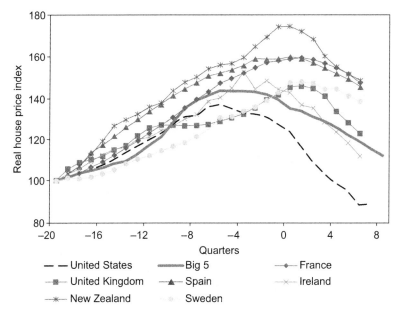

Figure 1.1 Evolution of House Prices during Financial Crises

Sources: Bank for International Settlements; Haver Analytics; and Organization for Economic Co-operation and Development.

Note: The real house price index is equal to 100 five years before each banking crisis. For the 2007–09 crisis, the beginning date is assumed to be 2007:Q3. "Big 5" refers to the average of the house price indices for five major banking crises: Spain in 1977, Norway in 1987, Finland in 1991, Sweden in 1991, and Japan in 1992.

ation and volatility of Internet stocks in the late 1990s, thus arguing that there is no reason to refer to a "dot-com bubble." Branch and Evans (2008), employing a theory of learning in which investors use the most recent (instead of past) data, find that shocks to fundamentals may increase return expectations. This may cause stock prices to rise above levels consistent with fundamentals. As prices increase, investors' perceptions of riskiness decline until the bubble bursts.[5] More generally, theories suggest that bubbles can appear without distortions, uncertainty, speculation, or bounded rationality.

But both micro distortions and macro factors can also lead to bubbles. Bubbles may relate to agency issues (Allen and Gale, 2007). For example, as a result of risk shifting—when agents borrow to invest (e.g., margin lending for stocks, mortgages for housing), but can default if rates of return are not sufficiently high— prices can escalate rapidly. Fund managers who are rewarded on the upside more than on the downside (somewhat analogous to the limited liability of financial institutions) bias their portfolios toward risky assets, which may trigger a bubble

---

[5] Wang and Wen (2012) argue that systemic risk, commonly perceived as changes in the bubble's probability of bursting, can produce asset price movements many times more volatile than the economy's fundamentals and generate boom-bust cycles in the context of a dynamic stochastic general equilibrium model.

(Rajan, 2005).[6] Other microeconomic factors (e.g., interest rate deductibility for household mortgages and corporate debt) can exacerbate this risk-taking, possibly leading to bubbles.[7]

Investors' behavior can also drive asset prices away from fundamentals, at least temporarily. Frictions in financial markets (notably those associated with information asymmetries) and institutional factors can affect asset prices. Theory suggests, for example, that differences of information and opinions among investors (related to disagreements about valuation of assets), short sales constraints, and other limits to arbitrage are possible reasons for asset prices to deviate from fundamentals.[8] Mechanisms such as herding among financial market players, informational cascades, and market sentiment can affect asset prices. Virtuous feedback loops—rising asset prices and increasing net worth positions that allow financial intermediaries to leverage up and buy more of the same assets—play a significant role in driving the evolution of bubbles. The phenomenon of contagion, that is, spillovers beyond what fundamentals would suggest, may have similar roots. Brunnermeier (2001) reviews these models and shows how they can help explain bubbles, crashes, and other market inefficiencies and frictions. Empirical work confirms some of these channels, but formal econometric tests are most often not powerful enough to separate bubbles from rational increases in prices, let alone to detect the causes of bubbles (Gürkaynak, 2008).[9]

Bubbles may also be the result of the same factors that are argued to lead to asset price anomalies. Many deviations of asset prices from the predictions of efficient-market models, on a small scale with no systemic implications, have been documented (Fama, 1998; Lo and MacKinlay, 2001; and Schwert, 2003).[10] Although some of these deviations have diminished over time, possibly as investors have implemented strategies to exploit them, others, even though documented extensively, persist today. Furthermore, deviations have similarly been found across various markets, time periods, and institutional contexts. Thus, anomalies cannot easily be attributed to specific, institution-related distortions. Rather, they appear to reflect factors intrinsic to financial markets. Studies under the rubric of behavioral finance have tried to explain these patterns, with some success (Shleifer, 2000;

---

[6] In Rajan's (2005) "alpha-seeking" argument, firms, asset managers, and traders take more risk to improve returns, with private rewards in the short term. See Gorton and He (2008) and Dell'Ariccia and Marquez (2006) for theories linking credit booms to the quality of lending standards and competition.

[7] See BIS (2002) for a general review and IMF (2009) for a review of debt and other biases in tax policy with respect to the 2007–09 financial crisis.

[8] Models include Harrison and Kreps (1978); Chen, Hong, and Stein (2002); Scheinkman and Xiong (2003); and Hong, Scheinkman, and Xiong (2008).

[9] Empirical studies include Abreu and Brunnermeier (2003); Diether, Malloy, and Scherbina (2002); Lamont and Thaler (2003); Ofek and Richardson (2003); and Shleifer and Vishny (1997).

[10] For example, stocks of small firms get higher rates of return than other stocks do, even after adjusting for risk, liquidity, and other factors. Spreads on lower-rated corporate bonds appear to have a relatively larger compensation for default risk than higher-rated bonds do. Mutual funds whose assets cannot be liquidated when investors sell the funds (so-called closed-end funds) can trade at prices different from those implied by the intrinsic value of their assets.

and Barberis and Thaler, 2003).[11] Of course, "evidence of irrationality" may reflect a misspecified model, that is, irrational behavior is not easily falsifiable.

What Triggers Asset Price Busts?

Busts following bubbles can be triggered by small shocks. Asset prices may experience small declines due to changes in either fundamental values or sentiment. Changes in international financial and economic conditions, for example, may drive prices down. The channels by which small declines in asset prices can trigger a crisis are well understood now. Given information asymmetries, for example, a small shock can lead to market freezes. Adverse feedback loops may then arise, in which asset prices exhibit rapid declines and downward spirals. Notably, a drop in prices can trigger a fire sale as financial institutions experiencing a decline in asset values struggle to attract short-term financing. Such sudden stops can lead to a cascade of forced sales and liquidations of assets, and further declines in prices, with consequences for the real economy.

Flight to quality can further intensify financial turmoil. Relationships among financial intermediaries are multiple and complex. Information asymmetries are prevalent among intermediaries and in financial markets. These problems can easily lead to financial turmoil. They can be aggravated by preferences of investors to hold debt claims (Gorton, 2008). Specifically, debt claims are "low information intensive" in normal states of the world; because the risk of default is remote, little analysis of the underlying asset value is required. They become "high information intensive," however, in times of financial turmoil as risks increase, requiring investors to assess default risks, a complex task involving a multitude of information problems. This situation puts a premium on safety and can create perverse spirals. As investors turn to quality assets, for example, government bonds, they avoid some lower-quality types of debt claims, leading to sharper drops in the prices of those debt claims (Gorton and Ordonez, 2012).

Credit Booms and Busts

A rapid increase in credit is another common thread running through the narratives of events that precede financial crises. Leverage buildups and greater risk taking through rapid credit expansion, in concert with increases in asset prices, often precede crises (albeit typically only recognized with the benefit of hindsight). Both distant and more recent crisis episodes typically witnessed a period of significant growth in credit (and external financing), followed by busts in credit

---

[11] For example, firms tend to issue new stock when prices (and firm profitability) are high. Another example is that the market's reaction to initial public offerings can be "hot" or "cold." Both examples contradict the assumption that firms seek external financing only when they need to (because of a lack of internal funds while growth opportunities are good). Many individual investors also appear to diversify their assets insufficiently (or naively) and rebalance their portfolios too infrequently. At the same time, some investors respond too quickly to price movements, and sell winners too early and hold on to losers too long. These patterns have been "explained" by various behavioral factors.

markets along with sharp corrections in asset prices. In many respects, the descriptions of the Australian boom and bust of the 1880–90s, for example, fit the more recent episodes of financial instability. Likewise, the patterns before the East Asian financial crisis in the late 1990s resembled those of the earlier ones in Nordic countries as banking systems collapsed following periods of rapid credit growth related to investment in real estate. The experience of the United States in the late 1920s and early 1930s exhibits some features similar to the run-up to the 2007–09 global financial crisis with, in addition to rapid growth in asset prices and land speculation, a sharp increase in (household) leverage. The literature has also documented common patterns in various other macroeconomic and financial variables around these episodes.

What Macroeconomic Factors Explain Credit Booms?

Credit booms can be triggered by a wide range of factors, including shocks and structural changes in markets.[12] Shocks that can lead to credit booms include changes in productivity, economic policies, and capital flows. Some credit booms tend to be associated with positive productivity shocks. These booms generally start during or after periods of buoyant economic growth. Dell'Ariccia and others (Chapter 11, this volume) find that lagged GDP growth is positively associated with the probability of a credit boom: in the three-year period preceding a boom, the average real GDP growth rate reaches 5.1 percent, compared with 3.4 percent during a tranquil three-year period.

Sharp increases in international financial flows can amplify credit booms. Most national financial markets are affected by global conditions, even more so today, so asset bubbles can easily spill across borders. Fluctuations in capital flows can amplify movements in local financial markets when inflows lead to a significant increase in the funds available to banks, relaxing credit constraints for corporations and households (Claessens and others, 2010). Rapid expansion of credit and sharp growth in house and other asset prices were indeed associated with large capital inflows in many countries before the 2007–09 financial crisis.

Accommodative monetary policies, especially when in place for extended periods, have been linked to credit booms and excessive risk taking. The channel works as follows: Interest rates affect asset prices and borrowers' net worth, in turn affecting lending conditions. Analytical models, including of the relationship between agency problems and interest rates (e.g., Stiglitz and Weiss, 1983), suggest more risk taking when interest rates decline and a flight to quality when interest rates rise, with consequent effects on the availability of external financing. Empirical evidence (e.g., for Spain and others, 2009; and Maddaloni and Peydró, 2010) supports such a channel because credit standards tend to loosen when policy rates decline.

---

[12] For reviews of factors associated with the onset of credit booms, see Mendoza and Terrones (2008, 2012); Magud, Reinhart, and Vesperoni (2012); and Dell'Ariccia and others (Chapter 11, this volume).

The relatively low interest rates in the United States during 2001–04 are often mentioned as a main factor behind the rapid increases in house prices and household leverage (Lansing, 2008; Hirata and others, 2012).[13]

What Structural Factors Explain Credit Booms?

Structural factors include financial liberalization and innovation. Financial liberalization, especially when poorly designed or sequenced, and financial innovation can trigger credit booms and lead to excessive increases in leverage by facilitating more risk taking. Financial liberalization has been found to often precede crises in empirical studies (Kaminsky and Reinhart, 1999; and Demirgüç-Kunt and Detragiache, 2005). Dell'Ariccia and others (Chapter 11, this volume) report that roughly a third of booms they identified follow or coincide with financial liberalization episodes.

The mechanisms involved include institutional weaknesses as well as the perverse effects of competition. Regulation, supervision, and market discipline seem to be slow to catch up with greater competition and innovation (possibly set in motion by shocks or liberalization). Vulnerabilities in credit markets can naturally arise. Another mechanism commonly linking booms to crises is a decline in lending standards. Greater competition in financial services, although generally enhancing efficiency and stability in the long term, can contribute to financial fragility over shorter periods. This was evident in the higher delinquency rates in those metropolitan areas in the United States with higher growth in loan origination before the onset of the crisis, with the deterioration in lending standards appearing to be related, in part, to increases in competition (Dell'Ariccia, Igan, and Laeven, 2012).

Impact of Asset Price and Credit Busts

Movements in asset and credit markets during financial crises are much sharper than those observed over the course of a normal business cycle. Booms in credit and asset markets, defined as those upturns in the uppermost quartile of all upturns, are shorter, stronger, and faster than other upturns. For example, booms often take place over relatively shorter periods than do other upturns and are associated with much faster increases in the financial variables (Figure 1.2a). The slope of a typical boom, that is, the average increase in the financial variable in each quarter, is two to three times larger than that of regular upturns. And crunches and busts are longer, deeper, and more violent than other downturns.

---

[13] However, whether and how monetary policy affects risk taking, and thereby asset prices and leverage, remains a subject for further research (see de Nicolo and others, 2010, for recent analysis and review). The extent of bank capitalization appears to be an important factor given that it affects incentives: when facing a lower interest rate, a well-capitalized bank decreases its monitoring and takes more risk, whereas a highly levered, poorly capitalized bank does the opposite (see Dell'Ariccia, Laeven, and Marquez, 2011).

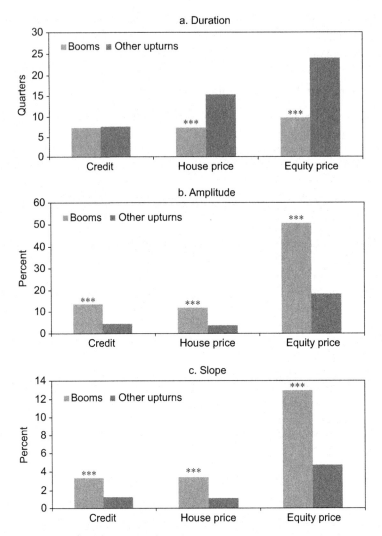

Figure 1.2.A. Credit and Asset Price Booms

Source: Authors' calculations.

Note: The sample includes data for 23 advanced economies and covers 1960–2011. Amplitude and slope correspond to sample median, and duration corresponds to sample mean. Duration is the time it takes to attain the level of the previous peak after the trough. Amplitude is calculated as the one-year change in each respective variable after the trough. Slope is the amplitude from peak to trough divided by the duration. Booms are the top 25 percent of upturns calculated by the amplitude.

*** indicates that the difference between corresponding financial boom and other upturns is statistically significant at the 1 percent level.

Credit crunches and asset price busts have much larger declines than do other downturns (Figure 1.2b). Specifically, credit crunches and house price busts, respectively, lead to roughly 10 and 15 times larger drops than do other downturns, whereas equity busts are more than 2.5 times as large. These episodes also last longer, some two times longer, than other downturns, with house price busts

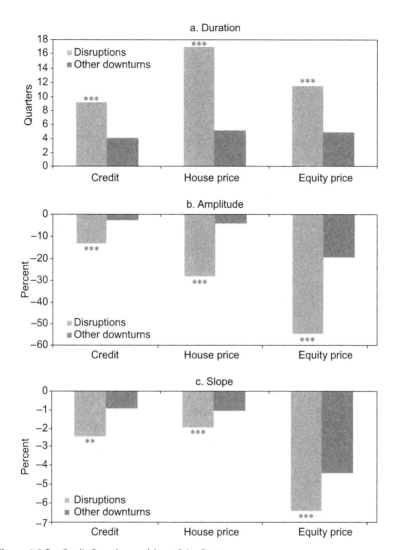

Figure 1.2.B Credit Crunches and Asset Price Busts

Source: Authors' calculations.

Note: The sample includes data for 23 advanced economies and covers 1960–2011. Amplitude and slope correspond to sample median, and duration corresponds to sample mean. Duration is the number of quarters between peak and trough. Amplitude is calculated as the decline in each respective variable during the downturn. Slope is the amplitude from peak to trough divided by the duration. Crunches and busts are the worst 25 percent of downturns calculated by the amplitude.

***, ** indicate that the difference between the corresponding disruptions and other downturns is statistically significant at the 1 and 5 percent levels, respectively.

the longest of all, about 18 quarters, whereas credit crunches and equity busts last about 10–12 quarters. Moreover, disruptions are more violent, as evidenced by higher slope coefficients, with busts in equity prices being three times more violent than those in credit and house prices (Claessens, Kose, and Terrones, 2010a).

Asset price busts and credit crunches typically have adverse effects on the real economy.[14] Asset price busts can affect bank lending and other financial institutions' investment decisions and, in turn, the real economy through two channels. First, when borrowing and lending is collateralized and the market price of collateral falls, the ability of firms to rely on assets as collateral for new loans and financial institutions' ability to extend new credit become impaired, which in turn adversely affect investment. Second, the prospect of large price dislocations arising from fire sales and related financial turmoil distorts financial institutions' decisions to lend or invest, prompting them (among other actions) to hoard cash. Through these channels, fire sales can trigger a credit crunch and cause a severe contraction in real activity.

Those asset price booms supported by leveraged financing and involving financial intermediaries appear to entail larger risks for the economy. Evidence from past episodes suggests that whether excessive movements in asset prices lead to severe misallocations of resources depends in large part on the nature of the boom and how it is financed. Booms largely involving equity market activities appear to have lower risks of adverse consequences. The burst of the Internet bubble of the late 1990s, which mainly involved only equity markets, was not very costly for the real economy. When banks are involved in financing asset price booms, however, as in real estate mortgage and corporate sector financing, risks of adverse consequences from a subsequent asset bust are typically much higher. These booms involve leverage and banks, meaning that the flow of credit to the economy is interrupted when a bust occurs.

The burst of the latest bubble—financed by banks (and the shadow banking system) and involving housing—has been very costly. For the 2007–09 episode, Crow and others (Chapter 12, this volume) report that, in a 40-country sample, almost all the countries with "twin booms" in real estate and credit markets (21 out of 23) ended up suffering from either a crisis or a severe drop in the GDP growth rate relative to the country's performance in the 2003–07 period (Figure 1.3). Eleven of these countries actually suffered both financial sector damage and a sharp drop in economic activity. In contrast, of the seven countries that experienced a real estate boom but not a credit boom, only two went through a systemic crisis and, on average, had relatively mild recessions. A broader discussion of the real and financial implications of financial crises and disruptions is presented in the section below titled "Real and Financial Implications of Crises."

---

[14] Some economists used to be sanguine about the costs of busts in credit and asset markets. Until the 2007–09 crisis, for example, the economic cost of bubbles was dismissed by some analysts. For example, Roger W. Ferguson, then Vice Chairman of the U.S. Federal Reserve Board, argued in January 2005 that "recessions that follow swings in asset prices are not necessarily longer, deeper, and associated with a greater decline in output and investment than other recessions" (Ferguson, 2005, p. 16). There are also theories in which even fully irrational asset bubbles are not necessarily harmful or could even be beneficial (Kocherlakota, 2009). Bubbles can allow for a store of value (collateral) and thereby enhance overall financial intermediation through facilitating exchanges, thus improving overall economic performance. As such, the presence of bubbles per se, whether rational or irrational, need not necessarily be a cause for concern.

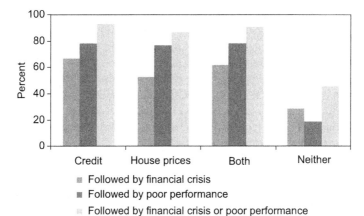

Figure 1.3 Coincidence of Financial Booms and Crises: 1960–2011

Source: Crow and others (Chapter 12 in this volume).
Note: The sample consists of 40 countries. The bars, except "Neither," show the percentage of the cases in which a crisis or poor macroeconomic performance happened after a boom was observed (out of the total number of cases in which a boom occurred).

TYPES OF FINANCIAL CRISES

Financial crises can take various shapes and forms, but two broad types can be distinguished. Reinhart and Rogoff (2009b) describe two types of crises: those classified using strictly quantitative definitions, and those dependent largely on qualitative and judgmental analysis. The first group mainly includes *currency* and *sudden stop* crises, and the second group contains *debt* and *banking* crises. Regardless, definitions are strongly influenced by the theories trying to explain crises.

The literature has been able to arrive at concrete definitions of many types of crises. For example, a *currency* crisis involves a speculative attack on the currency resulting in a devaluation (or sharp depreciation); or forces the authorities to defend the currency by expending large amounts of international reserves, or sharply raising interest rates, or imposing capital controls. A *sudden stop* (or capital account or balance of payments crisis) can be defined as a large (and often unexpected) decline in international capital inflows or a sharp reversal in aggregate capital flows to a country, likely taking place in conjunction with a sharp rise in its credit spreads. Because these are measurable variables, they lend themselves to the use of quantitative methodologies.

Other crises are associated with adverse debt dynamics or banking system turmoil. A *foreign debt* crisis takes place when a country cannot (or does not want to) service its foreign debt, sovereign, private, or both. A *domestic public debt* crisis takes place when a country does not honor its domestic fiscal obligations in real terms, either by defaulting explicitly, or by inflating or otherwise debasing its currency, or by employing other forms of financial repression. In a *systemic banking* crisis, actual or potential bank runs and failures can induce banks to suspend the convertibility of their liabilities, or compel the government to intervene to prevent them from doing so by extending liquidity and capital assistance on a large scale. Because these variables are not so easily measured, these crises lend themselves more to the use of qualitative methodologies.

Other classifications are possible, but the types of crises are still likely to overlap. A number of banking crises, for example, are associated with sudden stop episodes and currency crises. This section examines analytical causes and empirical determinants of each type of crisis. The identification, dating, and frequency of crises are considered in the next section.

Currency Crises

Theories of currency crises, often more precisely articulated than theories for other types of crisis, have evolved as the nature of such crises has changed. In particular, the literature has changed from a focus on the fundamental causes of currency crises, to emphasizing the scope for multiple equilibria, and to stressing the role of financial variables, especially changes in balance sheets, in triggering currency crises (and other types of financial turmoil). Three generations of models are typically used to explain currency crises that took place during the past four decades.

The first generation of models, largely motivated by the collapse in the price of gold, an important nominal anchor before the floating of exchange rates in the 1970s, was often applied to currency devaluations in Latin America and other developing countries (Claessens, 1991). These models are from seminal papers by Krugman (1979) and Flood and Garber (1984), and hence called "KFG" models.[15] They show that a sudden speculative attack on a fixed or pegged currency can result from rational behavior by investors who correctly foresee that a government has been running excessive deficits financed with central bank credit. Investors continue to hold the currency as long as they expect the exchange rate regime to remain intact, but they start dumping it when they anticipate that the peg is about to end. This run leads the central bank to quickly lose its liquid assets or hard foreign currency supporting the exchange rate. The currency then collapses.

The second-generation models stress the importance of multiple equilibria. These models show that doubts about whether a government is willing to maintain its exchange rate peg could lead to multiple equilibria and currency crises (Obstfeld, 1986). In these models, self-fulfilling prophecies are possible, in which the reason investors attack the currency is simply that they expect other investors to attack the currency. As discussed in Flood and Marion (1997), policies before the attack in the first-generation models can translate into a crisis, whereas changes in policies in response to a possible attack (even if these policies are compatible with macroeconomic fundamentals) can lead to an attack and be the trigger of a crisis in the second generation of models. The second-generation

---

[15] Earlier versions of the canonical crisis model were Salant and Henderson (1978) and Salant (1983).

models are, in part, motivated by episodes like the European Exchange Rate Mechanism crisis, in which countries like the United Kingdom came under pressure in 1992 and ended up devaluing, even though other outcomes (that were consistent with macroeconomic fundamentals) were possible too (Eichengreen, Rose, and Wyplosz, 1995).

The third-generation crisis models explore how rapid deteriorations of balance sheets associated with fluctuations in asset prices, including exchange rates, can lead to currency crises. These models were largely motivated by the Asian crises of the late 1990s. In the Asian countries, macroeconomic imbalances were small before the crisis—fiscal positions were often in surplus and current account deficits appeared to be manageable, but vulnerabilities associated with financial and corporate sectors were large. The models show how balance sheet mismatches in these sectors can give rise to currency crises. For example, Chang and Velasco (2000) show how local banks with large debts outstanding that are denominated in foreign currency may lead to a banking and currency crisis.[16]

This generation of models also considers the roles played by banks and the self-fulfilling nature of crises. McKinnon and Pill (1996), Krugman (1999), and Corsetti, Pesenti, and Roubini (1998) suggest that overborrowing by banks can arise as the result of government subsidies (to the extent that governments would bail out failing banks). In turn, vulnerabilities stemming from overborrowing can trigger currency crises. Burnside, Eichenbaum, and Rebelo (2001, 2004) argue that crises can be self-fulfilling because of fiscal concerns and volatile real exchange rate movements (when the banking system has such a government guarantee, a good or a bad equilibrium can result). Radelet and Sachs (1998) argue more generally that self-fulfilling panics hitting financial intermediaries can force a liquidation of assets, which then confirms the panic and leads to a currency crisis.

Empirical research has not been able to determine which generation of these models provides the best characterization of currency crises. Early work had good success with the KFG model. Blanco and Garber (1986), for example, applied the KFG model to the Mexican devaluations in 1976 and 1981–82 and showed that crisis probabilities had built to peaks just before the devaluations (Cumby and van Wijnbergen, 1989; and Klein and Marion, 1994). However, although the KFG model worked well in cases in which macroeconomic fundamentals grew explosively, it was not successful if fundamentals were merely highly volatile and money demand was unstable.

Later empirical work moved away from explicit tests of structural models. Some studies used censored dependent variable models, for example, logit models, to estimate crisis probabilities based on a wide range of lagged variables (Eichengreen, Rose, and Wyploz, 1995; Frankel and Rose, 1996; and Kumar,

---

[16] Hallwood and MacDonald (2000) provide a detailed summary of the first- and second-generation models and consider their extensions to different contexts. Krugman (1999), in an attempt to explain the Asian financial crisis, also provides a similar mechanism operating through firms' balance sheets, with investment as a function of net worth.

Moorthy, and Perraudin, 2003). Others, such as Kaminsky, Lizondo, and Reinhart (1998) and Kaminsky and Reinhart (1999), employed signaling models to evaluate the usefulness of several variables in signaling an impending crisis. This literature found that certain indicators tend to be associated with crises, but the outcomes have nevertheless been disappointing, with the timing of crises very hard to predict.[17] The issue of crisis prediction will be revisited later.

Sudden Stops

Models with sudden stops are more closely associated with disruptions in the supply of external financing. These models resemble the third generation of currency crisis models in that they also focus on balance sheet mismatches—notably currency, but also maturity—in financial and corporate sectors (Calvo, Izquierdo, and Mejía, 2004). They tend to give greater weight, however, to the role of international factors (as captured, for example, by changes in international interest rates or spreads on risky assets) in causing sudden stops in capital flows. These models can account for the current account reversals and the real exchange rate depreciation typically observed during crises in emerging markets. The models explain less well the typical sharp drops in output and total factor productivity.

To match data better, more-recent sudden stop models introduce various frictions. Although counterintuitive, in most models, a sudden stop or currency crisis generates an increase in output rather than a drop. This increase in output happens through an abrupt increase in net exports resulting from the currency depreciation. This theory has led to various arguments explaining why sudden stops in capital flows are associated with large output losses, as is often the case. Models typically include Fisherian channels and financial accelerator mechanisms, or frictions in labor markets, to generate an output drop during a sudden stop, without losing the ability to account for the movements of other variables.

Closely following the literature on domestic financial intermediation, models with financial frictions help to account better for the dynamics of output and productivity in sudden stops. With frictions, for example, when firms must borrow in advance to pay for inputs (e.g., wages, foreign inputs), a decline in credit—the sudden stop combined with rising external financing premiums—reduces aggregate demand and causes a decline in output (Calvo and Reinhart, 2000). Or as a result of collateral constraints in lending, a sudden stop can lead to a debt-deflation spiral of declines in credit, prices, and quantity of collateral assets, resulting in a decline in output. Like the domestic financial accelerator mechanism, financial distress and bankruptcies cause negative externalities, because banks become more cautious and reduce new lending, in turn, inducing a further decline in credit, and thereby contributing to a recession (Calvo, 2000).

---

[17] See Kaminsky, Lizondo, and Reinhart (1998) for an early review; Kaminsky (2003) for an update; and Frankel and Saravelos (2012) for an extensive recent survey up to the 2000s.

These types of amplification mechanisms can make small shocks cause sudden stops. Relatively small shocks—to imported input prices, the world interest rate, or productivity—can trigger collateral constraints on debt and working capital, especially when borrowing levels are high relative to asset values. Fisher's debt-deflation mechanisms can then cause sudden stops through a spiraling decline in asset prices and holdings of collateral assets (Fisher, 1933). This chain of events immediately affects output and demand. Mendoza (2010) shows how a business cycle model with collateral constraints can be consistent with the key features of sudden stops. Korinek (2011) provides a model analyzing the adverse implications of large movements in capital flows on real activity.

Sudden stops often take place in countries with relatively small tradable sectors and large foreign exchange liabilities. Sudden stops have affected countries with widely disparate levels of per capita GDP, levels of financial development, and exchange rate regimes, as well as countries with different levels of reserve coverage. However, most episodes share two elements, as Calvo, Izquierdo, and Mejía (2008) document: a small supply of tradable goods relative to domestic absorption—a proxy for potential changes in the real exchange rate—and a domestic banking system with large foreign exchange–denominated liabilities, raising the probability of a "perverse" cycle.

Empirical studies find that many sudden stops have been associated with global shocks. For a number of emerging markets, for example, those in Latin America and Asia in the 1990s and in Central and Eastern Europe in the 2000s, after a period of large capital inflows, a sharp retrenchment or reversal of capital flows occurred, triggered by global shocks (such as increases in interest rates or changes in commodity prices). Sudden stops are more likely with large cross-border financial linkages. Milesi-Ferretti and Tille (2011) document that rapid changes in capital flows were important triggers of local crises during the 2007–09 crisis. Others, such as Rose and Spiegel (2011), however, find little role for international factors, including capital flows, in the spread of the 2007–09 crisis.

Foreign and Domestic Debt Crises

Theories on foreign debt crises and default are closely linked to those explaining sovereign lending. Absent military action, lenders cannot seize collateral from another country, or at least from a sovereign, when it refuses to honor its debt obligations. Without an enforcement mechanism—the analogue to domestic bankruptcy—economic reasons, instead of legal arguments, are needed to explain why international (sovereign) lending exists at all.

As a gross simplification, models so far rely on either intertemporal or intratemporal sanctions. Intertemporal sanctions arise because of the threat that future lending will be cut off if a country defaults (Eaton and Gersovitz, 1981). With no access to credit (forever or for some time), the country would no longer be able to smooth idiosyncratic income shocks using international financial markets. This cost can induce the country to continue making its debt payments today, even without any immediate, direct costs to default. Intratemporal sanctions can arise from the inability to earn foreign exchange today because trading partners impose sanctions or otherwise shut the country out of international markets, again forever or for some time (Bulow and Rogoff, 1989). Both types of cost can support a certain volume of sovereign lending (Eaton and Fernandez, 1995; and Panizza, Sturzenegger, and Zettelmeyer, 2009).

These models imply that inability or unwillingness to pay, that is, default, can result from different factors. The incentives governments face in repaying debt differ from those for domestic corporations and households. They also vary across models. In the intertemporal model, a country defaults when the opportunity cost of not being able to borrow ever again is low, one such case presumably being when the terms of trade are good and are expected to remain so (Kletzer and Wright, 2000). In the intratemporal sanctions model, in contrast, the costs of a cutoff from trade may be the least when the terms of trade are bad. Aguiar and Gopinath (2006) demonstrate how in a model with persistent shocks, countries default in bad times to smooth consumption. The models thus also have different implications with respect to a country's borrowing capacity.

However, these models are unable to fully account for why sovereigns default and why creditors lend as much as they do. Many models actually assume that default does not happen in equilibrium because creditors and debtors want to avoid the dead-weight costs of default and renegotiation of debt payments. Although some models have been calibrated to match actual experiences of default, models often still underpredict the likelihood of actual defaults. Notably, countries do not always default when times are bad, as most models predict: Tomz and Wright (2007) report that output was below trend in only 62 percent of default cases. Models also underestimate the willingness of investors to lend to countries in spite of large default risk. Moreover, changes in the institutional environment, such as those implemented after the debt crises of the 1980s, do not appear to have modified the relationship between economic and political variables and the probability of a debt default. Together, these factors suggest that models still fail to capture all aspects necessary to explain defaults (Panizza, Sturzenegger, and Zettelmeyer, 2009).

Although domestic debt crises have occurred throughout history, these episodes received only limited attention in the literature until recently. Economic theory assigns a trivial role to domestic debt crises because models often assume that governments always honor their domestic debt obligations—the typical assumption is of "risk-free" government assets. Models also often assume Ricardian equivalence, making government debt less relevant. However, recent reviews of history (Reinhart and Rogoff, 2009b) show that few countries were able to escape default on domestic debt, with often adverse economic consequences.

Government default on domestic debt often happens through bouts of high inflation caused by abuse of the government monopoly on currency issuance. One such episode was when the United States experienced an inflation rate of close to 200 percent in the late 1770s. The periods of hyperinflation in some European countries following World War II were also in this category. Debt defaults in the form of inflation are often followed by currency crashes. In the past, countries would often "debase" their currency by reducing the metal content of coins or switching to another metal. This tactic reduced the real value of government debt and thus provided fiscal relief. There have also been other forms of debt "default," including through financial repression (Reinhart, Kirkegaard, and Sbrancia, 2011). After inflation or debasing crises, it takes a long time to convince the public to start using the currency again. This, in turn, significantly increases the fiscal costs of inflation stabilization, leading to large negative real effects of high inflation and associated currency crashes.

Debt intolerance tends to be associated with the extreme duress many emerging market economies experience at levels of external debt that would often be easily managed by advanced economies. Empirical studies on debt intolerance and serial default suggest that, although safe debt thresholds hinge on country-specific factors, such as a country's record of default and inflation, when the external debt level of an emerging economy is greater than 30–35 percent of GNP, the likelihood of an external debt crisis rises substantially (Reinhart and Rogoff, 2009a). More important, when an emerging market economy becomes a serial defaulter on its external debt, its debt intolerance increases, making it very difficult to graduate to the club of countries that have continuous access to global capital markets.

Many challenges remain with regard to modeling the ability of countries to sustain various types of domestic and external debt. An important challenge is that the form of financing countries use is endogenous. Jeanne (2003) argues that short-term (foreign exchange) debt can be a useful commitment device for countries to employ good macroeconomic policies. Diamond and Rajan (2001) posit that banks in developing countries have little choice but to borrow short term to finance illiquid projects given the low-quality institutional environments in which they operate. Eichengreen and Hausmann (1999) propose the "original sin" argument, explaining how countries with unfavorable conditions have no choice but to rely mostly on short-term, foreign currency–denominated debt as their main source of capital. More generally, although short-term debt can increase vulnerabilities, especially when the domestic financial system is underdeveloped, poorly supervised, and subject to governance problems, it also may be the only source of (external) financing for a capital-poor country with limited access to equity or foreign direct investment inflows. Thus, the country's accumulation of short-term debt and increasing vulnerability to crises are simultaneous outcomes.

More generally, the deeper causes behind debt crises are hard to separate from the proximate causes. Many of the vulnerabilities raising the risk of a debt crisis can result from factors related to financial integration, political economy, and institutional environments. Opening up to capital flows can make countries with profligate governments and weakly supervised financial sectors more vulnerable to shocks. McKinnon and Pill (1996, 1998) describe how moral hazard and inadequate supervision combined with unrestricted capital flows can lead to crises as banks incur currency risks. Debt crises are also likely to involve sudden stops or currency or banking crises (or various combinations), making it hard to identify the initial cause. Empirical studies of the identification of causes are thus subject to the usual problems of omitted variables, endogeneity, and simultaneity. For example, although using short-term (foreign currency) debt as a crisis predictor may work, it does not constitute a proof of the root cause of the crisis. The difficulty of identifying the deeper causes is more generally reflected in the fact that debt crises have occurred throughout history.

Banking Crises

Banking crises are quite common, but perhaps the least understood type of crisis. Banks are inherently fragile, making them subject to runs by depositors. Moreover, the problems of individual banks can quickly spread to the whole banking system. Although public safety nets, including deposit insurance, can limit this risk, public support comes with distortions that can actually increase the likelihood of a crisis. Institutional weaknesses can also elevate the risk of a crisis. For example, banks depend heavily on the informational, legal, and judicial environments to make prudent investment decisions and collect on their loans. With institutional weaknesses, risks can be higher. Although banking crises have occurred over the centuries and exhibited some common patterns, their timing remains hard to predict empirically.

Bank Runs and Banking Crises

Financial institutions are inherently fragile entities, giving rise to many possible coordination problems. Because of their roles in maturity transformation and liquidity creation, financial institutions operate with highly leveraged balance sheets. Hence, banking and other similar forms of financial intermediation can be precarious undertakings. Fragility makes coordination, or lack thereof, a major challenge in financial markets. Coordination problems arise when investors or institutions take actions—like withdrawing liquidity or capital—merely out of fear that others will also take such actions. Given this fragility, a crisis can easily occur in which large amounts of liquidity or capital are withdrawn because of a self-fulfilling belief: it happens because investors fear it will happen. Small shocks, whether real or financial, can translate into turmoil in markets and even a financial crisis.

A simple example of a coordination problem is a bank run. It is a truism that banks borrow short and lend long. This maturity transformation reflects the preferences of consumers and borrowers. However, it makes banks vulnerable to sudden demands for liquidity, that is, runs (the seminal reference here is Diamond and Dybvig, 1983). A run occurs when a large number of customers withdraw their deposits because they believe the bank is, or might become, insolvent. As a bank run proceeds, it generates its own momentum, leading to a self-fulfilling prophecy (or perverse feedback loop): as more people withdraw their deposits, the likelihood of default increases, encouraging further withdrawals. This sequence can destabilize the bank to the point that it faces bankruptcy because it cannot liquidate assets fast enough to cover its short-term liabilities.

These fragilities have long been recognized, and markets, institutions, and policymakers have developed many coping mechanisms (Dewatripont and Tirole, 1994). Market discipline encourages institutions to limit vulnerabilities. At the firm level, intermediaries have adopted risk-management strategies to reduce their fragility. Furthermore, microprudential regulation, with supervision to enforce rules, is designed to reduce the risky behavior of individual financial institutions and can help engineer stability. Deposit insurance can eliminate the concerns of small depositors and can help reduce coordination problems. Lender-of-last-resort facilities (i.e., central banks) can provide short-term liquidity to banks during periods of elevated financial stress. Policy intervention by the public sector, such as public guarantees, capital support, and purchases of nonperforming assets, can mitigate systemic risk when financial turmoil hits.

Although regulation and safety net measures can help, when poorly designed or implemented these measures can increase the likelihood of a banking crisis. Regulations aim to reduce fragility (for example, limits on balance sheet mismatches stemming from interest rate, exchange rate, or maturity mismatches, or certain activities of financial institutions). Regulation and supervision, however, often find themselves playing catch-up with innovation. And they may be poorly designed or implemented. Support from the public sector can also have distortionary effects (Barth, Caprio, and Levine, 2006). Moral hazard caused by a state guarantee (e.g., explicit or implicit deposit insurance) may, for example, lead banks to assume too much leverage. Institutions that know they are too big to fail or unwind can take excessive risks, thereby creating systemic vulnerabilities.[18] More generally, fragilities in the banking system can arise because of policies at both the micro and macro levels (Laeven, 2011).

History of Bank Runs

Runs have occurred in many countries throughout history. In the United States, bank runs were common during the banking panics of the 1800s and in the early 1900s (during the Great Depression). Only with the introduction of deposit insurance in 1933 did most runs stop in the United States (Calomiris and Gorton, 1991). Widespread runs also happened frequently in emerging markets and developing countries in the later decades of the twentieth century, such as in Indonesia during the 1997 Asian financial crisis. Runs occurred more rarely in

---

[18] Ranciere and Tornell (2011) model how financial innovations can allow institutions to maximize a systemic bailout guarantee, and report evidence supporting this mechanism in the context of the 2007 U.S. financial crisis.

other advanced economies, and have occurred even less so in the first decade of the 2000s, in part as a result of the widespread availability of deposit insurance.[19] Yet, Northern Rock, a bank specializing in housing finance in the United Kingdom, provides a very recent example of a bank run in an advanced country (Shin, 2009). Rapid withdrawals of wholesale market funding also took place during the 2007–09 financial crisis, when several investment banks and some commercial banks faced large liquidity demands from investors.

Widespread runs can also take place in nonbank financial markets. For example, in the United States during the fall of 2008, some mutual funds "broke the buck," that is, their net asset value fell below par. This triggered sharp outflows from individual investors and many other mutual funds (Wermers, 2012). This "run," in turn, led the government to provide a guarantee against further declines. These guarantees are a continued source of fiscal risk because the government might be forced to step in to prevent a run again. Other investment vehicles specializing in specific asset classes (such as emerging markets) also experienced sharp outflows because there was a general flight to safety (i.e., more demand for advanced economies' government bonds and treasury bills). More generally, the 2007–09 crisis has been interpreted by many as a widespread liquidity run (Gorton, 2009).

Deeper Causes of Banking Crises

Although funding and liquidity problems can be triggers or proximate causes, a broader perspective shows that banking crises often relate to problems in asset markets. Banking crises may appear to originate from the liability side, but they typically reflect solvency issues. Banks often run into problems when many of their loans go sour or when securities quickly lose their value. This happened in crises as diverse as the Nordic banking crises in the late 1980s, the crisis in Japan in the late 1990s, and the crises in Europe in the 2010s. In all of these episodes, no large-scale deposit runs on banks occurred, but large-scale problems arising from real estate loans resulted in undercapitalization in many banks and required government support. Problems in asset markets, such as those related to the subprime and other mortgage loans, also played a major role during the 2007–09 crisis. These types of problems can go undetected for some time, and a banking crisis often comes into the open through the emergence of funding difficulties among a large fraction of banks.

Although the exact causes are often hard to identify, and risks can be difficult to foresee, in hindsight, banking crises and other financial panics are rarely random events. Banking panics more likely to occur near the peak of the business cycle, with recessions on the horizon, because of concerns that loans will not be

---

[19] Deposit insurance, first introduced in the United States in 1933, was adopted following World War II by many advanced economies, and has since been employed by developing countries (Demirgüç-Kunt, Kane, and Laeven, 2008). Although deposit insurance can reduce the risk of bank runs, it can have severe negative side effects, including increased moral hazard, leading to more risk taking.

repaid (Gorton, 1988; and Gorton and Winton, 2003). Depositors, noticing the risks, demand cash from the banks. Because banks cannot immediately satisfy all requests, a panic may occur. The large-scale bank distress in the 1930s in the United States was traced back to shocks in the real sector. In many emerging markets, banking crises were triggered by external developments, such as sharp movements in capital flows, global interest rates, and commodity prices, which, in turn, led to an increase in nonperforming loans.

Panics can also be policy induced. Panics can take place when some banks experience difficulties and governments intervene in an ad hoc manner, without providing clear signals about the status of other institutions. The banking panic in Indonesia in 1997 has been attributed to poorly managed early interventions.[20] Runs can also be directly triggered by government actions: the runs on banks in Argentina in 2001 occurred when the government imposed a limit on withdrawals, making depositors question the soundness of the entire banking system. The 2007–09 financial crisis in advanced economies has, in part, been attributed to the lack of consistency across government interventions and other policy measures (Calomiris, 2009).

Structural problems can also lead to banking crises. Studies have identified some common, structural characteristics related to banking crises (e.g., Lindgren, Garcia; and Saal, 1996; Barth, Caprio, and Levine, 2006; and many others). These include notably poor market discipline caused by moral hazard and excessive deposit insurance; limited disclosure; weak corporate governance frameworks; and poor supervision, in part due to conflicts of interest.[21] Other structural aspects found to increase the risk of a crisis include large state ownership and limited competition in the financial system, including restricted entry from abroad; and an undiversified financial system, for example, a dominance of banks (World Bank, 2001).

Because the financial sector receives many forms of public support, policy distortions that can lead to crises easily arise. In the context of the 2007–09 financial crisis in the United States, large government support for housing finance (through the government-sponsored enterprises Fannie Mae and Freddie Mac) has been argued to lead to excessive risk taking. The tendency to pursue accommodative monetary and fiscal policies following crises, at least in some advanced economies, can also be interpreted as a form of ex post systemic bailout, which,

---

[20] See Honohan and Laeven (2007) for this and other case studies.

[21] Failures in regulation and supervision remain the most mentioned cause for crises, despite significant upgrading of regulations, supervisory capacity, and expertise. For analysis of how weaknesses in regulation and supervision contributed to the 2007–09 crisis, see Čihák and others (2012). Analysis suggests, though, that the design of regulation matters for the risk of financial distress. Barth, Caprio, and Levine (2006, 2012), for example, suggest not relying solely on regulation and supervision. Rather, they advocate, among other actions, an active but carefully balanced mix of market discipline and official regulation and supervision. This should all be supported by institutional infrastructure that protects property rights; allows for competition, including engagement with global finance; and ensures adequate information. The wider threats to financial stability, including those arising from political economy and corruption, should be kept at bay.

in turn, distorts ex ante incentives and can lead to excessive risk taking (Farhi and Tirole, 2012). Another often-cited problem has been "connected lending," which leads to perverse incentives, because politically connected firms and individuals borrow too much from banks, which can cause a buildup of systemic risk. Some well-studied cases of this phenomenon include Mexico (La Porta, López-de-Silanes, and Zammaripa, 2003; and Haber, 2005), the Russian Federation (Laeven, 2001), and Indonesia (Fisman, 2001).

Systemic banking panics still require further study because many puzzles remain, especially about how contagion arises. The individual importance of the factors listed above in contributing to crises is not known, in part because many of them tend to be observed at the same time. Fragilities remain inherent to the process of financial intermediation, with the causes for panics often difficult to understand. For reasons usually unknown, small shocks can result in significant problems for the entire financial system. Similarly, shocks may spill over from one market to another or from one country to others, leading to financial crises.

The 2007–09 financial crisis had many elements common to other crises. Much has been written about the causes of the 2007–09 crisis (Calomiris, 2009; Gorton, 2009; Claessens and others, 2012a; and many others). Although observers differ on the exact weights, the list of factors common to previous crises is generally similar. Four features often mentioned in common are asset price increases that turned out to be unsustainable, credit booms that led to excessive debt burdens, buildups of marginal loans and systemic risk, and the failure of regulation and supervision to keep up with financial innovation and get ahead of the crisis when it erupted.[22]

The global financial crisis was, however, also rooted in some new factors. Four key new aspects often mentioned are the widespread use of complex and opaque financial instruments; the increased interconnectedness among financial markets, nationally and internationally, with the United States at the core; the high degree of leverage of financial institutions; and the central role of the household sector. These factors, in combination with those common to other crises, and fueled at times by poor government interventions during different stages, led to the worst financial crisis since the Great Depression. It required massive government outlays and guarantees to restore confidence in financial systems. The consequences of the crisis are still being felt in many advanced economies and as of 2013 the crisis is still ongoing in some European countries.

---

[22] Specifically, there was an increase in real estate prices in many markets around the world, paralleled by a run-up in other asset prices, especially in equity. Reinhart and Rogoff (2008) demonstrate that the appreciation of equity and house prices in the United States before the crisis was even more dramatic than appreciations experienced before the "Big Five" post-World War II debt crises. As the global crisis unfolded, those countries that had experienced the greatest increases in equity and house prices during the boom found themselves most vulnerable (Feldstein, 2009). Unfortunately, the similarity in crises patterns was, as is often the case, only recognized after the fact.

IDENTIFICATION, DATING, AND FREQUENCY OF CRISES

A large body of work has been devoted to the identification and dating of crises, but ambiguities remain. Methodologies based on the main theories explaining various types of crises can be used to identify and classify crises.[23] In practice, however, this classification is not so straightforward. Although currency and inflation crises and sudden stops lend themselves to quantitative approaches, the dating of debt and banking crises is typically based on qualitative and judgmental analyses. Irrespective of type, variations in methodologies can lead to differences in the start and end dates of crises. And, as noted, various types of crises can overlap in a single episode, creating possible ambiguities about how to classify the episode. In practice, a wide range of quantitative and qualitative methods involving judgment are used to identify and classify crises.

The difficulties arise, in part, because the frequency and types of financial crises have evolved. For example, currency crises were dominant during the 1980s, whereas banking crises and sudden stops became more prevalent in the 1990s and the first decade of the 2000s. This section begins with a summary of common identification and dating methods (IMF, 1998; Laeven and Valencia, 2008, and Chapter 2, this volume; and Reinhard and Rogoff, 2009b). It then provides a summary of the frequency of crises over time and across groups of countries, and of the overlap among types of crises.

Identification and Dating

Because *currency crises* involve large changes in exchange rates, and related inflation crises, they are relatively easy to identify. Reinhart and Rogoff (2009b) distinguish these episodes by assigning threshold values for the relevant variables. For currency crises, they consider an exchange rate depreciation in excess of 15 percent per year to be a crisis, whereas for inflation, they adopt a threshold of 20 percent per year.[24] A currency crisis is defined in Frankel and Rose (1996) as a cumulative depreciation of at least 25 percent over a 12-month period, and at least 10 percentage points greater than in the preceding 12 months. The dates identified are obviously sensitive to the thresholds used. These thresholds can be universal, specific to the sample of countries under study, or country specific (as

---

[23] Dating does not, of course, establish causes, including whether the event was a rational outcome of some other "cause" (e.g., a crash in an asset price may be rational in response to a real shock).

[24] Their comprehensive analysis includes the period 1258–1799, during which the principal means of exchange was metallic coins. During this earlier era, instead of modern inflation and currency crises, there were a number of episodes of currency debasements, which were associated with a reduction in the metallic content of coins in circulation in excess of 5 percent. They also consider the introduction of a brand new currency replacing a much-depreciated earlier currency in circulation as another form of currency debasement, which is still practiced in the modern era.

when the threshold is adjusted for the country's "normal" exchange rate variations).

A measurement issue naturally arises if no significant adjustment in the currency occurred despite pressures or attacks. Movements in international reserves or adjustments in interest rates can absorb exchange rate pressures and prevent or moderate the fluctuations in the rate. However, episodes involving such pressures or attacks are also important to document and study. To address this issue, starting with Eichengreen, Rose, and Wyplosz (1995), different methodologies have been employed. A composite index of speculative pressure is often constructed based on actual exchange rate changes and movements in international reserves and interest rates, with weights chosen to equalize the variance of the components, thereby preventing one component from dominating the index. Thresholds are then set to date the currency events, including both large exchange rate movements and periods of pressure.[25]

Sudden stops and balance of payments crises can also be objectively classified. Calvo, Izquierdo, and Mejía (2004) define systemic sudden stop events as episodes with output collapses that coincide with large reversals in capital flows. Calvo, Izquierdo, and Mejía (2008) expand on these criteria in two ways: first, the period contains one or more year-over-year declines in capital flows that are at least two standard deviations below its sample mean (thus addressing the "unexpected" requirement of a sudden stop); second, it starts (ends) when the annual change in capital flows falls (exceeds) one standard deviation below (above) its mean (Mauro and Becker, 2006).

Because methodologies vary, various samples of events follow. Calvo, Izquierdo, and Mejía (2004) identified 33 sudden stop events with large and mild output collapses in a sample of 31 emerging market economies. Although studies use different cutoff criteria (Calvo and Reinhart, 2000; Milesi-Ferretti and Razin, 2000; and Calvo, Izquierdo, and Loo-Kung, 2006), the datings of events are very similar. Some studies also require a decline in output, but later studies excluded this requirement (since a decline may be endogenous) and replaced it with the requirement of large spikes in the Emerging Markets Bond Index spread, indicating a shift in the supply of foreign capital (Calvo, Izquierdo, and Mejía, 2008). Cardarelli, Elekdag, and Kose (2010) consider a large capital inflow episode to end "abruptly" if the ratio of net private capital inflows to GDP in the year after the episode terminates is more than 5 percentage points lower than at the end of the episode—closely following the definition of sudden stops in the literature. An episode is also considered to finish abruptly if its end coincides with a currency crisis.

Balance of payments crises can similarly be identified using capital flow data. Despite some differences in approach (e.g., how reserve losses are treated) and statistical variations across studies (e.g., whether the same current account deficit threshold is used for all countries or whether country-specific thresholds are

---

[25] See Frankel and Saravelos (2012) and Glick and Hutchison (2012) for reviews; and Cardarelli, Elekdag, and Kose (2010) for applications.

used), many of them point to similar samples of actual events. Forbes and Warnock (2011) analyze a large set of countries' gross flows instead of the more typical net capital flows (or current account). They identify episodes of extreme capital flow movements using quarterly data, differentiating activity by foreigners and domestics. They classify episodes as "surge," "stop," "flight," or "retrenchment," with surges and stops related, respectively, to periods of large gross capital in- or outflows by foreigners, and flights and retrenchments, respectively, related to periods of large capital out- or inflows by domestic residents.

External sovereign debt crises are generally easy to identify as well, although differences in classifications across studies remain. Sovereign defaults are relatively easy to identify because they involve a unique event, the default on payments. Typical dating of such episodes relies on the classification by rating agencies or on information from international financial institutions (see McFadden and others, 1985; and papers summarized in Sturzenegger and Zettelmeyer, 2007). Still, there are choices of methodology. For example, differences arise from considering the magnitude of defaults (whether default has to be widespread or on just one class of claims), default by type of claim (such as bank claims or bond claims, private or public claims), and the length of default (missing a single or several payments). Others look instead at the increases in spreads in sovereign bonds as an indicator of the probability of default (Edwards, 1984).

The end of a default is harder to date. A major issue with dating an episode, including of default and sovereign debt crises, can be identifying its end, that is, when default or crisis is over. Some studies date this as when countries regained access in some form to private financial markets. Others date it as when countries regain a certain credit rating (IMF, 2005; 2011). As a consequence, differences arise as to how long it takes for a country to emerge from a sovereign default.

Domestic debt crises are more difficult to identify. First, consistent historical data on domestic public debt across countries were missing, at least until recently. Furthermore, following a crisis, unrecorded debt obligations can come to light. However, Abbas and others (2011) and Reinhart and Rogoff (2009b) have since made significant progress in putting together historical series on domestic debt. Second, countries can default in many ways: outright direct default, periods of hyper or high inflation, punitive taxation of interest payments, forced interest rate or principal adjustments or conversions, gold clause abrogation, debasing of currency, and forms of financial repression. Reinhart and Rogoff (2009b) describe each of these and make clear that considerable ambiguity remains in classifications of defaults, especially of "inflation-related default" episodes.

Determining start and end dates for *banking crises* can be particularly challenging. Such crises are usually dated by researchers using a qualitative approach on the basis of a combination of events, such as forced closures, mergers, or government takeover of many financial institutions; runs on several banks; or the extension of government assistance to one or more financial institutions. In addition, in-depth assessments of financial conditions are used as a criterion. Another metric is the fiscal cost associated with resolving these episodes. The end of a banking crisis is also difficult to identify, in part, because its effects can linger for some time.

There are large overlaps in the dating of banking crises across different studies. Reinhart and Rogoff (2009b) date the beginning of banking crises by two types of events: First are bank runs that lead to the closure of, merging, or takeover by the public sector of one or more financial institutions. Second, if there are no runs, they check the closure of, merging of, takeover of, or large-scale public assistance to an important financial institution. As they acknowledge, this approach has some obvious drawbacks: it could date crises too late (or too early) and gives no information about the end date of these episodes. Still, the classification of Reinhart and Rogoff (2009b) largely overlaps with that of Laeven and Valencia (Chapter 2, this volume).

Differences remain in the dating of crises, which can affect analyses. One example of a difference is the start of Japan's banking crisis, which is dated by Reinhart and Rogoff (2009b) as 1992 and as 1997 by Laeven and Valencia (Chapter 2, this volume). Another example, with significant implications for analysis, is from Lopez-Salido and Nelson (2010). Analyzing events surrounding financial market difficulties in the United States over the past 60 years, Lopez-Salido and Nelson report three distinct crises: 1973–75; 1982–84; and 1988–91. These differ from Reinhart and Rogoff (2009b), who identify only one crisis (1984–91), and Laeven and Valencia (Chapter 2, this volume) who also identify only one crisis, 1988 in that period (and another in 2007, since that period). In contrast to most claims that recoveries are systematically slower after financial crises, Lopez-Salido and Nelson (2010) argue on the basis of their analysis that crises need not impact the strength of recoveries.[26] These differences clearly show the importance of dating.

Last, asset price and credit booms, busts, and crunches, common to many crises, are relatively easy to classify, but again approaches vary across studies. Asset prices (notably equity and to a lesser degree house prices) and credit volumes are available from standard data sources. Large changes (in nominal or real terms) in these variables can thus easily be identified. Still, because approaches and focus vary, so do the classifications of booms, busts, and crunches. Claessens, Kose, and Terrones (2012) use the classical business cycle approach, looking at the level of real asset prices or credit to identify peaks and troughs in these variables. They then focus on the top and bottom quartiles of these changes to determine the booms, busts, or crunches. Large deviations from trend in real credit growth (Mendoza and Terrones, 2008) and from the credit-to-GDP ratio can also be used to classify credit booms. And Gourinchas, Valdes, and Landerretche (2001) classify 80 booms based on absolute and relative (to the credit-to-GDP ratio) deviation from trend, but rather than setting the thresholds first, they limit the number of episodes to classify.

---

[26] Bordo and Haubrich (2012) and Howard, Martin, and Wilson (2011) also argue that recoveries following financial crises do not appear to be different from typical recoveries.

Different types of crises can overlap and do not necessarily take place as independent events. One type of crisis can lead to another type. Or two crises can take place simultaneously because of common factors. To classify a crisis as only one type can be misleading when one event is really a derivative of another. Crises in emerging markets, for example, have often been combinations of currency and banking crises associated with sudden stops in capital flows, and subsequently turning into sovereign debt crises. Overall, considerable ambiguity remains on the identification and dating of financial crises, which should serve as an important caveat in reviewing the frequency and distribution of crises over time, as is done in the next section.

Frequency and Distribution

Crises have afflicted both emerging market economies and advanced economies throughout centuries. In the three decades before 2007, most crises occurred in emerging markets and included the Latin American crises in the late 1970s and early 1980s, the Mexican crisis in 1995, and the East Asian crises in the mid- to late 1990s. The susceptibility of emerging markets to crises is not new (Reinhart and Rogoff, Chapter 3, this volume). History shows that many countries that are advanced today, including Australia, Spain, the United Kingdom, and the United States, experienced financial crises when they were going through their own emergence processes in the 1800s. For example, France defaulted on its external debt eight times during the period 1550–1800. Some advanced economies experienced crises in recent decades as well, from the Nordic countries in the late 1980s, to Japan in the 1990s. The most recent crises, starting with the U.S. subprime crisis in late 2007 and then spreading to other advanced economies, show (once again) that crises can affect all types of countries.

Some claim that crises have become more frequent. The three decades after World War II were relatively crisis free, whereas the most recent three decades have seen many episodes (Figure 1.4). Some relate this increase to more liberalized financial markets, including floating exchange rates and greater financial integration. Using macroeconomic and financial series for 14 advanced economies for 1870–2008, Jordà, Schularick, and Taylor (2011) report no financial crises during the Bretton Woods period of highly regulated financial markets and capital controls. Also, Bordo and others (2001) argue that the sudden stop problem has become more severe since the abandonment of the gold standard in the early 1970s.

More recent crises seem to have been shorter, but banking crises still last the longest. The median duration of debt-default episodes in the post-World War II period has been much shorter than for the period 1800–1945, possibly because of improvement in policies in the later period, improved international financial markets, or the active involvement of multilateral lending agencies (see further Das, Papaioannou, and Trebesch, 2012). Currency and sudden stop crises are relatively short (almost by definition). With the major caveat that their ends are hard to date, banking crises tend to last the longest, consistent with their large real and fiscal impacts.

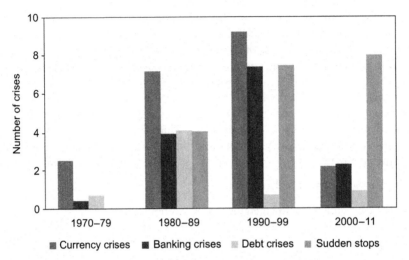

Figure 1.4 Average Number of Financial Crises per Decade

Sources: The dates of banking, currency, and debt crises are from Laeven and Valencia (2008; 2011), and the dates of sudden stops are from Forbes and Warnock (2011).
Note: This figure shows the average number of financial crises in each of the decades.

Financial crises clearly often come in bunches. Sovereign defaults tend to come in waves and in specific regions. Jordà, Schularick, and Taylor (2011) report that there were five major periods when a substantial number of now-advanced economies experienced crises: 1890, 1907, 1921, 1930–31, and 2007–08. Earlier crises bunched around events such as the Napoleonic Wars. Examples of bunches since the 1980s include the Latin America debt crises in the 1980s; in 1992, the European Exchange Rate Mechanism currency crises; in the late 1990s, the East Asian, Russian, and Brazilian financial crisis; the multiple episodes observed in 2007–08; and the crises in Europe still ongoing in 2013. Periods of widespread sovereign defaults often coincide with a sharp rise in the number of countries going through banking crises. These coincidences point toward common factors driving these episodes as well as spillovers of financial crises across borders.

Some types of crises are more frequent than others. Comparisons can be made for the post-Bretton Woods period (although some types of crises have been documented for longer periods, not all have; and currency crises were nonexistent during the fixed exchange rate period; together this necessitates the common, but shorter period). Of the total number of crises Laeven and Valencia (Chapter 2, this volume) report, 147 are banking crises, 217 are currency crises, and 67 are sovereign debt crises during the period 1970–2011. (Note that several countries experienced multiple crises of the same type.)

However, as noted before, the various types of crises overlap to some extent. Currency crises frequently tend to overlap with banking crises, the so-called twin crises (Kaminsky and Reinhart, 1999). In addition, sudden stop crises, not surprisingly, can overlap with currency and balance of payments crises, and sometimes

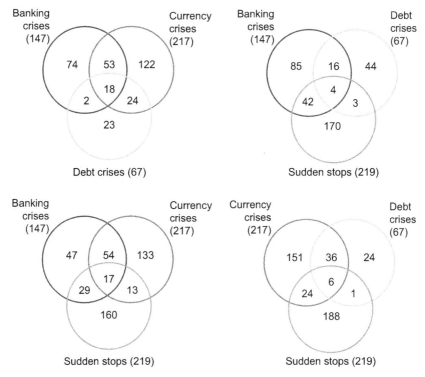

Figure 1.5   Coincidence of Financial Crises: 1970–2011

Sources: The dates of banking, currency, and debt crises are from Laeven and Valencia (2008; 2011) and the dates of sudden stops are from Forbes and Warnock (2011).

Note: A financial crisis starting at time T coincides with another financial crisis if the latter starts at any time between $T-3$ and $T+3$. A financial crisis starting at time T coincides with two other financial crises if the latter two start at any time between $T-3$ and $T+3$, where T stands for year. The sample consists of 181 countries.

sovereign crises (Figure 1.5). Of the 431 banking (147), currency (217), and sovereign (67) crises Laeven and Valencia report in Chapter 2, this volume, they consider 68 to be twin crises, and 8 can be classified as triple crises. There are relative differences in coincidences of these episodes. A systemic banking crisis, for example, often involves a currency crisis, and a sovereign debt crisis sometimes overlaps with other crises—20 out of 67 sovereign debt crises are also banking crises, and 42 are also currency crises.

REAL AND FINANCIAL IMPLICATIONS OF CRISES

Macroeconomic and financial consequences of crises are typically severe and are similar across the various types of crisis. Despite the obvious differences between crises, the macroeconomic variables follow similar patterns. Large output losses are common and other macroeconomic variables (consumption, investment, and industrial production) typically register significant declines. Financial variables like asset prices and credit usually follow qualitatively similar patterns across crises, albeit with variations in duration and severity. This section provides a summary of the literature on the macroeconomic and financial implications of crises.

Real Effects of Crises

Financial crises have large economic costs with large effects on economic activity. Many recessions follow from financial crises (Figure 1.6) (Claessens, Kose, and Terrones, 2009, 2012). And financial crises often tend to make these recessions worse than a "normal" business cycle recession (Figure 1.7). The average duration of a recession associated with a financial crisis is some six quarters, two more than a normal recession. There is also typically a larger output decline in recessions associated with crises than in other recessions. And the cumulative loss of a recession associated with a crisis (computed using lost output relative to the precrisis peak) is also much larger than that of a recession without a crisis.

The real impact of a crisis on output can be computed using various approaches. For a large cross-section of countries and a long period, Claessens, Kose, and Terrones (2012) use the traditional business cycle methodology to identify recessions. They show that recessions associated with credit crunches and housing busts tend to be more costly than those associated with equity price busts. Overall losses can also be estimated by adding up the differences between trend growth and actual growth for a number of years following the crisis or until the time when annual output growth returns to its trend. On this basis, Laeven

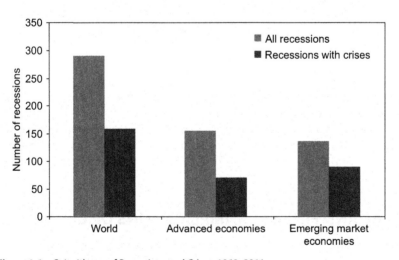

Figure 1.6 Coincidence of Recessions and Crises, 1960–2011

Source: Authors' calculations.

Note: The sample includes data for 23 advanced economies and 38 emerging market economies. A recession is associated with a financial crisis if the financial crisis starts at the same time as the recession or one year before or two years after the peak of the recession.

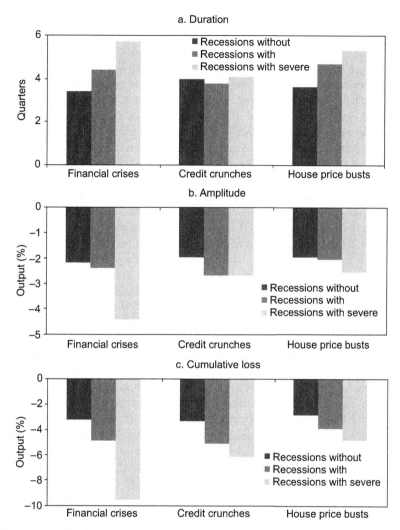

Figure 1.7   Real Implications of Financial Crises, Crunches, and Busts, 1960–2011

Source: Authors' calculations.

Note: The sample includes data for 23 advanced economies and covers 1960–2011. For "Duration" means are shown, for "Cumulative Loss" and "Amplitude" medians are shown. Amplitude is calculated based on the decline in output from peak to trough of a recession, duration is the number of quarters between peak and trough, and cumulative loss combines information about the duration and amplitude to measure overall cost of a recession and is expressed in percent. Disruptions (severe disruptions) are the worst 25 percent (12.5 percent) of downturns calculated by amplitude. A recession is associated with a (severe) credit crunch or a house price bust if the (severe) credit crunch or the house price bust starts at the same time or one quarter before the peak of the recession. A recession is associated with a financial crisis if the financial crisis starts at the same time as the recession or one year before or two years after the peak of the recession. The severe financial crises are the worst 50 percent of financial crises as measured by output decline during the recession.

and Valencia (Chapter 2, this volume) estimate that the cumulative cost of banking crises is, on average, about 23 percent of GDP during the first four years.[27] Regardless of the methodology, losses do vary across countries. Overall losses tend to be larger in emerging markets, but the large losses in recent crises in advanced economies (e.g., both Iceland's and Ireland's output losses exceeded 100 percent) paint a different picture. The median output loss for advanced economies is now about 33 percent, which exceeds that of emerging markets at 26 percent.

Crises are generally associated with significant declines in a wide range of macroeconomic aggregates. Recessions following crises exhibit much larger declines in consumption, investment, industrial production, employment, and exports and imports compared with those recessions without crises. For example, the decline in consumption during recessions associated with financial crises is typically seven to ten times larger than those without such crises in emerging markets. In recessions without crises, the growth rate of consumption slows down but does not fall below zero. In contrast, consumption tends to contract during recessions associated with financial crises, another indication of the significant toll that crises have on overall welfare.

Large declines in global output also occur during financial crisis episodes. The significant cost for the world economy associated with the Great Depression has been documented in many studies. The 2007–09 global financial crisis was associated with the worst recession since World War II, causing a 2 percent decline in world per capita GDP in 2009. In addition to 2009, the world economy experienced a global recession and witnessed crises in multiple countries in two other postwar years (Kose, Loungani, and Terrones, forthcoming). In 1982, a global recession was associated with a host of problems in advanced economies, as well as with the Latin American debt crisis.[28] The global recession in 1991 also coincided with financial crises in many parts of the world, including difficulties in U.S. credit markets, banking and currency crises in Europe, and the burst of the asset price bubble in Japan. Although world per capita GDP grows by about 2 percent in a typical year, it declined by about 0.8 percent in 1982 and 0.2 percent in 1991.

Recent studies also document that recoveries following crises tend to be weak and slow, with long-lasting effects. Kannan, Scott, and Terrones (Chapter 8, this volume) use cross-country data and conclude that recoveries following financial crises have typically been slower, and are associated with weak domestic demand and tight credit conditions. These findings are consistent with those reported in several other studies (Reinhart and Rogoff, 2009b; Jordà, Schularick, and Taylor,

---

[27] These loss numbers rely on an estimated trend growth, typically proxied by the trend in GDP growth up to the year preceding the crisis. These numbers can overstate output losses, however, because the economy could have experienced a growth boom before the crisis or been on an unsustainable growth path.

[28] Mexico's default in August 1982 marked the beginning of the crisis and the region's decade-long stagnation (the lost decade). A number of Latin American countries, including Argentina, Mexico, and Venezuela in 1982, and Brazil and Chile in 1983, experienced debt crises during the period.

2011; Papell and Prudan, 2011; and Claessens, Kose, and Terrones, 2012). Abiad and others (Chapter 9, this volume) analyze the medium-term impact of financial crises and conclude that output tends to be depressed substantially following banking crises. Specifically, seven years after a crisis, the level of output is typically about 10 percent lower relative to the precrisis trend (even though growth tends to return to its precrisis rate eventually). They report that the depressed path of output is associated with long-lasting reductions of roughly equal proportions in the employment rate, the capital-to-labor ratio, and total factor productivity.

From a fiscal perspective, banking crises can be especially costly. Both gross fiscal outlays and net fiscal costs of resolving financial distress and restructuring the financial sector can be very large. For banking crises, Laeven and Valencia (Chapter 2, this volume) estimate that fiscal costs, net of recoveries, associated with crises are on average about 6.8 percent of GDP. These costs can, however, be as high as 57 percent of GDP and in several cases are greater than 40 percent of GDP (for example, Chile and Argentina in the early 1980s, Indonesia in the later 1990s, and Iceland and Ireland in 2008). Net resolution costs for banking crises tend to be higher for emerging markets, at 10 percent of GDP, in contrast to 3.8 percent of GDP for advanced economies. Although gross fiscal outlays can be very large in advanced economies too—as in many of the recent and ongoing cases—the final direct fiscal costs have generally been lower in advanced economies, reflecting better recovery of fiscal outlays.

Debt crises can be costly for the real economy. Borensztein and Panizza (2009), Levy-Yeyati and Panizza (2011), and Furceri and Zdzienicka (2012) document that debt crises are associated with substantial GDP losses. Furceri and Zdzienicka (2012) report that debt crises are more costly than banking and currency crises and are typically associated with output declines of 3–5 percent after one year and 6–12 percent after eight years. Gupta, Mishra, and Sahay (2007) find that currency crises are often contractionary.

The combination of financial system restructuring costs and a slow economy can lead public debt to rise sharply during financial crises. Reinhart and Rogoff (2009a) document that crisis episodes are often associated with substantial declines in tax revenues and significant increases in government spending. For example, government debt rises by 86 percent, on average, during the three years following a banking crisis. Using a larger sample, Laeven and Valencia (Chapter 2, this volume) report the median increase in public debt to be about 12 percent for their sample of 147 systemic banking crises. Including indirect fiscal costs, such as those resulting from expansionary fiscal policy and reduced fiscal revenues as a consequence of a recession, makes the overall fiscal costs of the recent crises in advanced economies actually greater than those in emerging markets, 21.4 percent as compared with 9.1 percent of GDP.[29]

Although empirical work has not been able to pinpoint the exact reasons, sudden stops are especially costly. Using a panel data set for 1975–97 and covering

---

[29] Reinhart and Rogoff (2011) provide further statistical analysis of the links between debt and banking crises.

24 emerging markets, Hutchison and Noy (2006) finds that while a currency crisis typically reduces output by 2–3 percent, a sudden stop reduces output by an additional 6–8 percent in the year of the crisis. The cumulative output loss of a sudden stop is even larger, about 13–15 percent over a three-year period.[30] Edwards (2004) finds sudden stops and current account reversals to be closely related, with reversals, in turn, having a negative effect on real growth, an effect that is more pronounced for emerging markets. Cardarelli, Elekdag, and Kose (2010) examine 109 episodes of large net private capital inflows to 52 countries during 1987–2007 and report that the typical post-inflow decline in GDP growth for episodes that end abruptly is about 3 percentage points lower than during the episode, and about 1 percentage point lower than during the two years before the episode. These fluctuations are also accompanied by a significant deterioration of the current account during the inflow period and a sharp reversal at the end.

Financial Effects of Crises

Crises are associated with large downward corrections in financial variables. A sizable research effort has analyzed the evolution of financial variables around crises. Some of the studies in this literature focus on crisis episodes using the dates identified in other work; others consider the behavior of the financial variables during periods of disruptions, including credit crunches and house and equity price busts. Although results differ across the types of crises, both credit and asset prices tend to decline or grow at much lower rates during crises and disruptions than they do during tranquil periods, confirming the boom-bust cycles in these variables discussed in previous sections (Figure 1.8). In a large sample of advanced economies, credit declines by about 7 percent, house prices fall by about 12 percent, and equity prices drop by more than 15 percent during credit crunches and house and equity price busts, respectively (Claessens, Kose, and Terrones, 2012). Asset prices (exchange rates, equity and house prices) and credit around crises exhibit qualitatively similar properties in their temporal evolution in advanced and emerging market countries, but the duration and amplitude of declines tend to be larger for the latter than for the former.

The most notable drag on the real economy from a financial crisis is the lack of credit from banks and other financial institutions. Dell'Ariccia, Detragiache, and Rajan (2008) and Klingebiel, Kroszner, and Laeven (2007) show how after banking crises, sectors that naturally need more external financing grow more slowly, likely because banks are impaired in their lending capacity. Recoveries in aggregate output and its components following recessions associated with credit crunches tend to take place before the revival of credit growth and turnaround in

---

[30] Of course, this and other analyses can suffer from reverse causality. That is, private agents see events that lead them to predict future drops in a country's output and, as a result, these agents pull their capital from the country. In this view, anticipated output drops drive sudden stops, rather than the reverse. Although possible and reasonable, it is hard to prove or refute this view quantitatively.

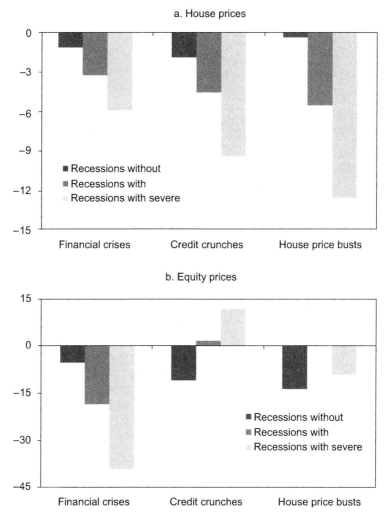

Figure 1.8   Financial Implications of Crises, Crunches, and Busts, 1960–2011

Source: Authors' calculations.

Note: The sample includes data for 23 advanced economies. Each panel shows the median change in respective variable during recessions associated with indicated financial events. Disruptions (severe disruptions) are the worst 25 percent (12.5 percent) of downturns calculated by amplitude. A recession is associated with a (severe) credit crunch or a house price bust if the (severe) credit crunch or house price bust starts at the same time or one quarter before the peak of the recession. A recession is associated with a financial crisis if the crisis starts at the same time as the recession or one year before or two years after the output peak preceding the recession. Severe financial crises are the worst 50 percent of financial crises as measured by output decline during the recession.

house prices (Figure 1.9). These temporal patterns are similar to those for house price busts, that is, economic recoveries start before house prices bottom out during recessions coinciding with sharp drops in house prices.

Both advanced and emerging market countries have experienced the phenomenon of "creditless recoveries." Creditless recoveries are quite common in financial

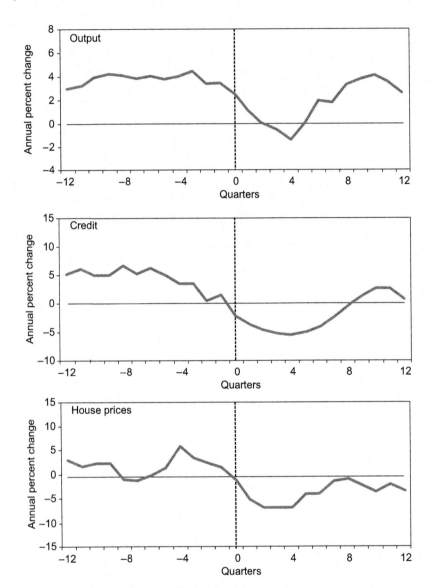

Figure 1.9 Creditless Recoveries, 1960–2011

Source: Authors' calculations.

Note: The sample includes data for 23 advanced economies. Each panel shows the median year-over-year growth rate of the respective variable during recessions associated with credit crunches. Zero is the quarter at which a recession with a credit crunch begins.

crises associated with sudden stops in many emerging market economies (Calvo, Izquierdo, and Talvi, 2006). Abiad, Dell'Ariccia, and Li (Chapter 10, this volume), using a large sample of countries, show that about one out of five recoveries is creditless. Creditless recoveries are, as expected, more common after banking crises and credit booms. The average GDP growth during these episodes is about a third lower than during "normal" recoveries.[31] Furthermore, sectors more dependent on external finance grow relatively less, and more-financially dependent activities (such as investment) are curtailed more (see also Kannan, 2009). Micro evidence for individual countries also shows that financial crises are associated with reductions in investment, research and development, and employment, and firms pass up on growth opportunities.[32] Collectively, these issues suggest that the supply of credit following a financial crisis can constrain economic growth.

PREDICTING FINANCIAL CRISES

It has long been a challenge to predict the timing of crises. Knowing whether and when a crisis may occur would obviously have great benefits: measures can be put in place to prevent a crisis from occurring in the first place or to limit the damage if it does happen. Therefore, much can be gained from better detecting the likelihood of a crisis. Yet, despite significant effort, no single set of indicators can explain the various types of crises, or can do so consistently over time. Periods of turmoil often arise endogenously, with possibilities of multiple equilibria and many nonlinearities.[33] And although it is now easier to document vulnerabilities, such as increasing asset prices and high leverage, predicting the timing of crises with some accuracy remains difficult. This section presents a short review of the evolution of the empirical literature on prediction of crises.[34]

Early-warning models have evolved from the first generation of models that concentrated on macroeconomic imbalances. Early crisis prediction models, mostly aimed at banking and currency crises, focused largely on macroeconomic and financial imbalances, and often in the context of emerging markets. Kaminsky and Reinhart (1999) show that growth rates in money, credit, and several other variables exceeding certain thresholds made a banking crisis more likely. In a comprehensive review, Goldstein, Kaminsky, and Reinhart (2000) report that a wide range of monthly indicators help predict currency crises,

---

[31] The fact that the economy recovers without credit growth and increases in asset prices reflects a combination of factors. First, consumption is typically the key driver of recovery. In particular, private consumption is often the most important contributor to output growth during recoveries. Investment (especially investment other than residential housing) recovers only with a lag, with the contribution of fixed investment growth to recovery often relatively small. Second, firms and households may be able to get external financing from sources other than commercial banks that have been adversely affected by the crisis. These sources are not captured in the aggregate credit series most studies focus on. Third, there can be a switch from more to less credit-intensive sectors in such a way that overall credit does not expand, yet, because of productivity gains, output increases. The aggregate data used in many studies hide such reallocations of credit across sectors, including between corporations and households that vary in their credit intensity.

[32] Campello, Graham, and Harvey (2009) review evidence for the United States.

[33] The slow movement of the financial system from stability to crisis is something for which Hyman Minsky is best known, and the phrase "Minsky moment"—the sudden occurrence of an open financial crisis—refers to this aspect of his work (Minsky, 1992).

[34] Babecky and others (2012) present a detailed review of the empirical studies of early-warning models.

including the appreciation of the real exchange rate (relative to trend), a banking crisis, a decline in equity prices, a decline in exports, a high ratio of broad money (M2) to international reserves, and a recession. Among annual indicators, the two best were both current account indicators, namely, a large current account deficit relative to both GDP and investment. For banking crises, the best monthly indicators (in descending order) were appreciation of the real exchange rate (relative to trend), a decline in equity prices, a rise in the money (M2) multiplier, a decline in real output, a decline in exports, and a rise in the real interest rate. Among eight annual indicators tested, the best were a high ratio of short-term capital flows to GDP and a large current account deficit relative to investment.[35]

In the next generation of models, still largely geared toward external crises, balance sheet variables became more pronounced. Relevant indicators include substantial short-term debt coming due and the level of reserves (Berg, Borensztein, and Pattillo, 2005). The ratio of broad money to international reserves in the year before the crisis was found to be higher (and GDP growth slower) for crises in emerging markets. In these models, fiscal deficit, public debt, inflation, and real broad money growth, however, were often found not to be consistently different between crisis and noncrisis countries before major crises. Neither did interest rate spreads or sovereign credit ratings generally rank high in the list of early-warning indicators of currency and systemic banking crises. Rather, crises were more likely to be preceded by rapid real exchange rate appreciation, current account deficits, domestic credit expansion, and increases in equity prices.

Later models show that a combination of variables can help identify situations of financial stress and vulnerabilities. Frankel and Saravelos (2012) perform a meta analysis based on reviews of crisis prediction models and seven papers published since 2002. The growth rates of credit, foreign exchange reserves, the real exchange rate, GDP, and the current account to GDP ratio are the most frequent significant indicators in the 83 papers reviewed; Lane and Milesi-Ferretti, 2011). Crises are typically preceded by somewhat larger current account deficits relative to historical averages, although credit trends more than external imbalances appear to be the best predictor (Alessi and Detken, 2011; Schularick and Taylor, 2012; and Taylor, Chapter 6, this volume).

Global factors can play important roles in driving sovereign, currency, balance of payments, and sudden stop crises. A variety of global factors are often reported to trigger crises, including deterioration in the terms of trade and shocks to world interest rates and commodity prices. For example, the sharp rise in U.S. interest rates has been identified as a trigger for the Latin American sovereign debt crises of the 1980s. More generally, crises are often preceded by interest rate hikes in advanced economies and by sudden changes in commodity prices, especially oil. But low interest rates can matter as well. For example, Jordà, Schularick, and Taylor (2011) report that global financial crises often take place in an environ-

---

[35] Crespo-Cuaresma and Slacik (2009) report that most of the early-warning variables for currency crises in the literature are quite fragile, whereas the extent of real exchange rate misalignment and financial market indicators appear to be relatively robust determinants of crisis in certain contexts.

ment of low interest rates. Other studies argue that the global imbalances of the 2000s and the 2007–09 crisis are intimately connected (Obstfeld and Rogoff, 2009; and Obstfeld, 2012). International trade and other real linkages can be channels of transmission, and contagion in financial markets is associated with crises (Forbes, 2012). Studies highlight, for example, the role of a common lender in particular in spreading the East Asian financial crisis (Kaminsky and Reinhart, 2001). These global factors can themselves be outcomes, as in the 2007–09 crisis, when interest rates and commodity prices experienced sharp adjustments following the onset of the crisis.

Overall though, rapid growth in credit and asset prices is found to be the factor most reliably related to increases in financial stress and vulnerabilities. Borio and Lowe (2002) document that out of asset price, credit, and investment data, a measure based on credit and asset prices is the most useful: almost 80 percent of crises can be predicted on the basis of a credit boom at a one-year horizon, whereas false positive signals are issued only about 18 percent of the time. Building on this, Elekdag, Cardarelli, and Lall (2009) find that banking crises are typically preceded by sharp increases in credit and house prices. Many others have found the coexistence of unusually rapid increases in credit and asset prices, large booms in residential investment, and deteriorating current account balances, to contribute to the likelihood of credit crunches and asset price busts.

Recent studies confirm that credit growth is the most important, but still imperfect, predictor. Many of the indicators, such as sharp asset price increases, a sustained worsening of the trade balance, and a marked increase in bank leverage, lose predictive significance once one conditions for the presence of a credit boom. Still, there are both Type I and Type II errors. As Bakker and others (Chapter 11, this volume) show, not all booms are associated with crises: only about a third of boom cases end up in financial crises. Others do not lead to busts but are followed by extended periods of below-trend economic growth. And many booms result in permanent financial deepening and benefit long-term economic growth. Although not all booms end up in a crisis, the probability of a crisis increases with a boom. Furthermore, the larger the increase in credit during the boom, the more likely the episode is to result in a crisis. Bakker and others (Chapter 11, this volume) find that half or more of the booms that either lasted longer than six years (4 out of 9), exceeded 25 percent of average annual growth (8 out of 18), or started at an initial credit-to-GDP ratio higher than 60 percent (15 out of 26) ended up in crises.

In practical terms, recent early-warning models typically use a wide array of quantitative leading indicators of vulnerabilities, with a heavy focus on international factors. These indicators capture vulnerabilities that stem from or are centered in the external, public, financial, nonfinancial corporate, or household sectors, and combine these with qualitative inputs (IMF, 2010). Because international financial markets can play multiple roles in transmitting and causing, or at least triggering, various types of crises, as with the 2007–09 crisis, several international linkage measures are typically used. Notably banking system measures, such as exposures to international funding risks and the ratio of noncore to core liabilities, have been found to help signal vulnerabilities (Shin, Chapter 4, this volume).[36] International markets can also help with risk sharing and can reduce volatility, and the empirical evidence is mixed, so the overall relationship of international financial integration and crises is much debated (Kose and others, 2010; and Lane, 2012).

CONCLUSION

This chapter presents a survey of the literature on financial crises to answer three specific questions. First, what main factors explain financial crises? Although the literature has clarified some of these factors, it remains a challenge to definitively identify the causes of crises. Many theories have been developed about the underlying causes of crises. These theories have recognized the importance of booms in asset and credit markets that turned into busts as the driving forces behind most crisis episodes. Given their central roles, the chapter briefly summarizes the theoretical and empirical literature analyzing developments in credit and asset markets around financial crises.

Second, what are the major types of crises? Although financial crises can take various shapes and forms, the literature has focused on four major types: currency crises, sudden stop (or capital account or balance of payments) crises, debt crises, and banking crises. Crises can be classified in other ways, too, but the types still often overlap. A number of banking crises, for example, are also sudden stop episodes and currency crises. The chapter examines the literature on the analytical causes and empirical determinants of each type of crisis. In addition, it reviews studies of various approaches to the identification of crises and their frequency over time and across different groups of countries.

Third, what are the real sector and financial sector implications of crises? Large output losses are common to many crises, and other macroeconomic variables (consumption, investment, and industrial production) typically register significant declines. Financial variables like asset prices and credit usually follow qualitatively similar patterns across crises, albeit with variations in duration and severity. The chapter summarizes the literature on the macroeconomic and financial implications of crises.

The chapter also briefly reviews the literature on the prediction of crises. Although there are many benefits to knowing whether and when a crisis may occur, predicting crises remains a challenge. Vulnerabilities, such as increasing asset prices and high leverage, are easily documented, but it remains difficult to predict with any accuracy the timing of crises. No single set of indicators has proved to predict the various types of crises. The chapter reviews how the empirical literature on the prediction of crises has evolved and analyzes its current state.

---

[36] In Chapter 4, Shin compares the predictive power from price-based measures (credit default swaps and other spreads, implied volatility, value at risk, and others), the gap of the credit-to-GDP ratio from a trend, and monetary aggregates and other bank liability aggregates, and shows that the last group has the most predictive power.

Is This Time Really Different?

One of the main conclusions of the literature on financial crises is that it has been hard to beat the "this-time-is-different" syndrome. This syndrome, as aptly described by Reinhart and Rogoff (2009b), is the belief that "financial crises are things that happen to other people in other countries at other times; crises do not happen to us, here and now. We are doing things better, we are smarter, we have learned from past mistakes" (p. 15). Although often preceded by similar patterns, policymakers tend to ignore the warnings and argue that "the current boom, unlike the many booms that preceded catastrophic collapses in the past (even in our country) is built on sound fundamentals" (p. 15). Leading up to every crisis, claims are made that developments appear to be different from those before earlier episodes. Before the 2007–09 crisis, for example, the extensive diversification of risks and advanced institutional frameworks were used to justify the belief that "this time is different."

As the literature reviewed here makes abundantly clear, there are many similarities in the run-ups to crises. In the 2007–09 crisis, increases in credit and asset prices were similar to those observed in earlier crises. Given these commonalities, it should be possible to prevent crises. Yet, that seems to have been an impossible task. This suggests that future research should be geared to beating the "this-time-is-different" syndrome. This is a very broad task requiring that two major questions be addressed: How can financial crises be prevented? How can their costs be mitigated when they take place? In addition, more intensive efforts are needed to collect the necessary data to guide both empirical and theoretical studies. The rest of this section takes each of these issues in turn and points to future research directions.

How Can Financial Crises Be Prevented?

In light of the lessons from the 2007–09 crisis, asset price bubbles and credit booms can entail substantial costs if they deflate rapidly. Many now agree on a number of issues with respect to asset price bubbles and credit booms. First, rapid increases in asset prices and credit can lead to financial turmoil and crises with significant adverse macroeconomic effects. Second, it is important to monitor vulnerabilities stemming from such sharp increases, and to determine whether they could be followed by large and rapid declines (crashes, busts or crunches, capital outflows). Third, the subsequent busts and crunches are likely to be more harmful if bubbles arise from "distortions." Fourth, even if not caused by distortions, evidence of irrationality can be interpreted as a sign of inefficiency and a potential source of welfare loss. Thus, bubbles and credit booms can warrant intervention.

The challenge for policymakers and researchers is twofold: when to intervene and how to intervene. First, they need to determine when (and to what extent) increases in asset prices and credit represent substantial deviations from those that can be explained by fundamentals. Second, if the behavior of credit and asset markets suggests signs of risk, they need to determine the optimal policy responses to minimize risks and mitigate the adverse effects when risks materialize.

The debate on whether, and how, monetary policy should respond to movements in asset prices and credit remains active. The consensus before the 2007–09 crisis was that the formulation of monetary policy only needed to consider asset prices to the extent that they were relevant for forecasting the economic outlook and inflation, but not otherwise.[37] However, the crisis has made clear (again) that both financial stability and economic activity might be affected by asset price movements, and a view has emerged that monetary policy should take into account, to some degree, developments in asset prices (Bernanke, 2009, 2010; Trichet, 2009; and Blanchard, Dell'Ariccia, and Mauro, 2010, 2013). A way to make this objective operational remains under discussion (Eichengreen, 2011; and Mishkin, 2011). The case for policy intervention is considered to be stronger when the banking system is directly involved in financing the bubble (whereas other asset price bubbles can more justifiably be left to themselves (Crowe and others, Chapter 12, this volume), but the exact adjustment of monetary policy remains unclear (Bean and others, 2010; and King, 2012).

Important lessons are still to be learned about the design of microprudential regulations and institutional structures for the prevention of crises (see also Claessens and others, 2012b). The 2007–09 crisis once again exposed flaws in microprudential regulatory and institutional frameworks. The global nature of the crisis has also shown that financially integrated markets have benefits, but also present risks, because the international financial architecture still is far from institutionally equal to the policy demands of closely integrated financial systems. Elements of existing frameworks provide foundations, but the crisis has forced regulatory policies to be rethought, with many open questions. Although rules calling for well-capitalized and liquid banks that are transparent and adhere to sound accounting standards are being put in place (e.g., Basel III), clarity on how to deal with large, complex financial institutions that operate across many borders is still needed. In addition, what types of changes to the institutional environments—for example, changes in the accounting standards for mark-to-market valuation, adaptations of employee compensation rules, transfers of some derivatives trading to formal exchanges, greater use of central counterparties—would best help to reduce financial markets' procyclicality and the buildup of systemic risks remain elusive. The crisis has also shown that fiscal policies, both micro, such as deductibility of interest payments, and macro, as in the amount of resources available to deal with financial crises, can play a role in creating vulnerabilities, but which adaptations are needed is not always apparent.

Although there is also a call for the use of macroprudential policies, the design of such policies and their interactions with other policies, especially monetary policy, remain unclear. By constraining financial market participants' behavior in advance, macroprudential policies can reduce the impact of externalities and

---

[37] See Mishkin (2008) and Kohn (2008) for reviews, and Campbell (2008) for a collection of papers.

market failures that lead to systemic vulnerabilities. In that way, they can reduce the risks of financial crises and help improve macroeconomic stability (de Nicolò, Favara, and Ratnovski, 2012). But the exact design of such policies is yet to be formulated. Although it is evident that multiple tools are needed, complications abound. Different financial distortions, for example, can lead to different types of risks, which, in turn, imply the use of multiple intermediate targets. Moreover, the relevant distortions can change over time and vary by country circumstances. Excessive leverage among corporations may give way, for example, to excessive leverage in the household sector. Factors such as the development of the financial sector and the exchange rate regime can greatly affect the types of risks economies face. Much is still unknown about these factors and their implications for the formulation of macroprudential policies. As new macroprudential frameworks are established, policymakers have also been increasingly turning their attention to the complex dynamics between macroprudential and monetary policies. These dynamics hinge on the side effects that one policy has on the other, but conceptual models and empirical evidence on these issues are still in the early stages (see IMF, 2013, for an overview).

The review here clearly shows that further analytical research and empirical work on these issues are needed. Macroeconomic models need to reflect the roles of financial intermediaries better. Current models are often limited in the way that they capture financial frictions. With regard to financial stress, they often assume that available instruments can fully offset financial shocks and abstract from effects, such as those of monetary policy on financial stability. More realistic modeling of the channels that give rise to financial instability and the actual transmission of policies and instruments is needed. In particular, the supply side of finance is not well understood and models with realistic calibrations reflecting periods of financial turmoil are still missing (Brunnermeier and Sanikov, 2012). The roles of liquidity and leverage in such periods have yet to be examined using models better suited to addressing the relevant policy questions. More insights, including from empirical studies, are necessary to help calibrate these models and allow the formulation of policy prescriptions that can be adapted to different country circumstances. Only with progress in modeling financial crises can one hope to not only avoid some of these episodes and be prepared with better policies when they occur, but also to minimize their impacts.

From an applied perspective, better early-warning models are needed. An issue extensively discussed in policy forums and receiving substantial attention from international organizations is the need to improve the prediction of the onset of crises (IMF, 2010). As the review in this chapter shows, the predictive power of available models remains limited. The historical record indicates that asset price busts have been especially difficult to predict. Even the best indicator failed to raise an alarm one to three years ahead of roughly one-half of all busts since 1985. This was the case again for the 2007–09 crisis. Although a number of recent papers that analyze the ability of various models to predict the latest crisis come to negative conclusions as well, others have found some predictive patterns. Regardless, there is scope to improve these models.

While known risks are being addressed, new risks can emerge. The limited strength of crisis prediction models arises in part because countries do take steps to reduce vulnerabilities. In response to increased financial globalization and sudden stop risks, many emerging markets increased their international reserves beginning in the late 1990s, which may have helped some countries avoid the impact of the 2007–09 crisis (Kose and Prasad, 2010; and De Gregorio, Chapter 5, this volume). Similarly, improvements in institutional environments that many countries have put in place during the last decades likely helped reduce some vulnerabilities. At the same time, however, new risks have emerged: the explosion of complex financial instruments, greater balance sheet opaqueness, and reliance on wholesale funding in highly integrated global financial markets increased the risks leading to the 2007–09 crisis.

How Can the Costs of Financial Crises Be Mitigated?

Explaining the substantial real costs associated with crises has been a challenge. Various theories attempt to explain the channels by which different types of crises affect the real economy. Many descriptions of the empirical patterns around crisis episodes can also be found. Yet, why crises cause large costs remains an enigma. Many of the channels that lead to macro-financial linkages during normal times also "cause" the adverse effects of crises, but other dynamics are also clearly at work. Normal lending seems undermined for an extended period as evidenced by creditless recoveries following crises. Fiscal policy and public debt dynamics can be affected for decades, in part because governments often end up directly supporting financial systems (by injecting liquidity or providing recapitalization) or suffer from expansionary policies undertaken to mitigate the costs of crises.

The major challenge is to explain the sharp, nonlinear behavior of financial markets in response to "small" shocks. Although the procyclicality of leverage among financial institutions, as highlighted by its increase during the run up to the 2007–09 crisis followed by the sharp deleveraging in its aftermath, has been extensively documented (Adrian and Shin, 2011), the exact causes of this behavior have yet to be identified. Why crises involve liquidity hoarding to such a degree that aggregate liquidity shortages occur and transmission of monetary policy is disrupted remains a puzzle. Although credit crunches are, in part, attributable to capital shortages at financial institutions, shortages do not seem to fully explain the phenomena of lenders becoming overly risk averse following a crisis. This lack of knowledge of the forces shaping the dynamics before and during periods of financial stress greatly complicates the design of proper policy responses.

It is also important to explore why financial spillovers across entities (institutions, markets, countries, and so on) are much more potent than most fundamentals suggest (in other words, why is there so much contagion?). Financial crises often generate effects across markets and have global repercussions. The 2007–09 episode is a case in point; its global reach and depth are without precedent in the post-World War II period. This underscores the value of having a better grasp of the mechanisms through which such episodes spill over to other countries. In addition to trade and cross-border banking linkages, research needs to consider the roles played by new financial channels, such as commercial paper conduits and shadow banking, and new trade channels, such as vertical trade networks, in the transmission of crises across borders. Given their adverse impact, the exact nature of these spillovers matters for the appropriate design of both crisis-mitigation and crisis-management responses. For example, in light of their cross-border implications, pooling resources (regionally or globally) to provide ample liquidity proactively becomes more important because it can prevent liquidity runs from escalating into self-fulfilling solvency crises and help break chains of contagion.

Although many stylized facts are already available, work on the implications of interactions among different crises and sovereign debt defaults is still limited. This review documents that various types of crises can overlap in a single episode, but research on the implications of such overlapping has been lagging. Although default on domestic debt tends to be less frequent than that on external debt, it still takes place quite often, suggesting that the usual assumption of risk-free government debt needs to be revisited. Furthermore, domestic and foreign debt defaults seem to touch on each other. Although domestic debt tends to account for a large share of the total debt stock in both advanced economies and emerging markets, many emerging market economies default on their external debt at seemingly low debt levels. This suggests that, for a given level of unsustainable debt, the cost of defaulting on external debt appears less than the cost of defaulting on domestic debt. More generally, trade-offs that depend on country circumstances likely come into play, maybe because the risk of high inflation varies. With the rising public debt stocks in many advanced economies, more work on this would be very useful.

Many questions are left about the best policy responses to financial crises. The 2007–09 global crisis and associated recessions have shown the limits of policy measures in dealing with financial meltdowns. It has led to an extensive discussion about the ability of macroeconomic and financial sector policies to mitigate the costs stemming from such episodes. Some research shows that countercyclical policies might mitigate the cost and reduce the duration of recessions (Kannan, Scott, and Terrones, Chapter 8, this volume). Others argue that such policies can worsen recession outcomes (Taylor, 2009, 2011). And some others find limited effects associated with expansionary policies (Claessens, Kose, and Terrones, 2009; and Baldacci, Gupta, and Mulas-Granados, Chapter 14, this volume). The discussion on the potency of policies clearly indicates fertile ground for future research as well.

Although valuable lessons have been learned about crisis resolution, countries are still far from adopting the "best" practices to respond to financial turmoil. It is clear now that open bank assistance without proper restructuring and recapitalization is not an efficient way of dealing with an ailing banking system (Laeven and Valencia, Chapter 13, this volume; and Landier and Ueda, Chapter 16, this volume). Excessive liquidity support and guarantees of bank liabilities cannot substitute for proper restructuring and recapitalization either, because most banking crises involve solvency problems, not just liquidity shortfalls. For banking crises, the sooner restructuring is implemented, the better the outcomes will be. Such a strategy removes residual uncertainty that can trigger precautionary contractions in consumption and investment, which, in turn, can further exacerbate recessions. Still, in spite of this understanding, many countries do not adopt these policy responses, including in the crises since 2007 (Claessens and others, Chapter 16, this volume), suggesting that there are deeper factors that research has not been able to uncover or address. Moreover, issues related to restructuring of both household debt and sovereign debt require more sophisticated theoretical and empirical approaches (Laeven and Laryea, Chapter 17, this volume; Das, Papaioannou, and Trebesch, Chapter 19, this volume; and Igan and others, Chapter 18, this volume).

What Additional Data and Methods Are Needed?

As the review in this chapter illustrates, new data series need to be put together and new methodologies need to be designed to gain a better understanding of crisis episodes. The review lists several recent studies that constructed new data series on financial crises. However, more research is clearly needed to collect additional cross-country data on aspects relevant to financial crises. Better data on domestic debt and house prices are urgently needed to provide a richer understanding of domestic debt dynamics and fluctuations in housing markets. Better international data are also needed for both surveillance and early-warning exercises (see Heath, 2013; and Cerutti, Claessens, and McGuire, forthcoming, for data needs). For a deeper understanding of crises and the policy issues surrounding these episodes, another requirement is for new methods to be designed to classify crises more robustly. Moreover, it would be important to examine periods of financial disruptions that are not necessarily crises. Although good luck or adequate policy measures may have prevented financial crises following such disruption episodes, there are lessons to be learned because these are the types of periods that can provide case studies of counterfactuals to analyze the macroeconomic outcomes and implications of policy responses.

REFERENCES

Abbas, S.A., M. Belhocine, A. El Ganainy, and M. Horton, 2011, "Historical Patterns and Dynamics of Public Debt: Evidence from a New Database," *IMF Economic Review*, Vol. 59, No. 4, pp. 717–42.

Abreu, D., and M.K. Brunnermeier, 2003, "Bubbles and Crashes," *Econometrica*, Vol. 71, No.1, pp. 173–204.

Adrian, T., and H.S. Shin, 2011, "Financial Intermediaries and Monetary Economics," in *Handbook of Monetary Economics*, Vol. 3, No. 3, ed. by B. Friedman and M. Woodford (San Diego and Amsterdam: North-Holland) pp. 601–50.

Aguiar, M., and G. Gopinath, 2006, "Defaultable Debt, Interest Rates and the Current Account," *Journal of International Economics*, Vol. 69, No. 1, pp. 64–83.

Alessi, L., and C. Detken, 2011, "Quasi Real Time Early Warning Indicators for Costly Asset Price Boom/Bust Cycles: A Role for Global Liquidity," *European Journal of Political Economy*, Vol. 27, No. 3, pp. 520–33.

Allen, F., A. Babus, and E. Carletti, 2009, "Financial Crises: Theory and Evidence," *Annual Review of Financial Economics*, Vol. 1, No. 1, pp. 97–116.

Allen, F., and D. Gale, 2007, *Understanding Financial Crises,* Clarendon Lectures in Finance (Oxford, United Kingdom: Oxford University Press).

Allen, R.E., 2010, *Financial Crises and Recession in the Global Economy*, 3rd ed. (Cheltenham, United Kingdom: Edward Elgar Publishing).

Babecký, J., T. Havránek, J. Matějů, M. Rusnák, K. Šmídková, and B. Vašíček, 2012, "Banking, Debt and Currency Crises: Early Warning Indicators for Developed Countries," Working Paper No. 1485 (Frankfurt: European Central Bank).

Bank for International Settlements (BIS), 2002, "Turbulence in Asset Markets: The Role of Micro Policies," Report by Contact Group on Asset Prices (Basel).

Barberis, N., and R. Thaler, 2003, "A Survey of Behavioral Finance," in *Handbook of the Economics of Finance*, ed. by G.M. Constantinides, M. Harris, and R. Stulz (Amsterdam: Elsevier B.V.), pp. 1051–121.

Barth, J., G. Caprio, and R. Levine, 2006, *Rethinking Bank Regulation: Till Angels Govern* (New York: Cambridge University Press).

———, 2012, *Guardians of Finance: Making Regulators Work for Us* (Cambridge, Massachusetts: MIT Press).

Bean, C., M. Paustian, A. Penalver, and T. Taylor, 2010, "Monetary Policy after the Fall," Paper presented at the Federal Reserve Bank of Kansas City Annual Conference, Jackson Hole, Wyoming, August 31–September 1.

Berg, A., E. Borensztein, and C. Pattillo, 2005, "Assessing Early Warning Systems: How Have They Worked in Practice?," *IMF Staff Papers*, Vol. 52, No. 3, pp. 462–502.

Bernanke, B., 2009, "Reflections on a Year of Crisis," Speech at the Federal Reserve Bank of Kansas City's Annual Economic Symposium, Jackson Hole, Wyoming, August 31–September 1.

———, 2010, "Monetary Policy and Housing Bubble," Speech at the Annual Meeting of the American Economic Association, Atlanta, Georgia, January 3.

Blanchard O., G. Dell'Ariccia, and P. Mauro, 2010, "Rethinking Macroeconomic Policy," *Journal of Money, Credit and Banking*, Vol. 42, No. s1, pp. 199–215.

———, 2013, "Rethinking Macroeconomic Policy: Getting Granular," IMF Staff Discussion Note No. 13/3 (Washington: International Monetary Fund).

Blanchard, O.J., and M.W. Watson, 1982, "Bubbles, Rational Expectations and Financial Markets," in *Crisis in the Economic and Financial Structure: Bubbles, Bursts, and Shocks*, ed. by P. Wachtel (Lexington, Massachusetts: Lexington Press).

Blanco, H., and P.M. Garber, 1986, "Recurrent Devaluation and Speculative Attacks on the Mexican Peso," *Journal of Political Economy*, Vol. 94, No. 1, pp. 148–66.

Bordo, M., and J. Haubrich, 2012, "Deep Recessions, Fast Recoveries, and Financial Crises: Evidence from the American Record," NBER Working Paper No. 18194 (Cambridge, Massachusetts: National Bureau of Economic Research).

Bordo, M.D., B. Eichengreen, D. Klingebiel, and M.S. Martinez-Peria, 2001, "Is the Crisis Problem Growing More Severe?" *Economic Policy*, Vol. 16, pp. 51–82.

Borensztein, E., and U. Panizza, 2009, "The Costs of Sovereign Default," *IMF Staff Papers*, Vol. 56, No. 4, pp. 683–741.

Borio, C., and P. Lowe, 2002, "Asset Prices, Financial and Monetary Stability: Exploring the Nexus," BIS Working Paper No. 114 (Basel: Bank for International Settlements).

Branch, W., and G.W. Evans, 2008, "Learning about Risk and Return: A Simple Model of Bubbles and Crashes," Working Paper 2008-1 (Eugene, Oregon: University of Oregon Economics Department).

Brunnermeier, M., 2001, *Asset Pricing under Asymmetric Information: Bubbles, Crashes, Technical Analysis and Herding* (Oxford, United Kingdom: Oxford University Press).

———, and Y. Sannikov, 2012, "A Macroeconomic Model with a Financial Sector," 2012 Meeting Papers No. 507 (St. Louis, Missouri: Society for Economic Dynamics).

Bulow, J., and K. Rogoff, 1989, "A Constant Recontracting Model of Sovereign Debt," *Journal of Political Economy*, Vol. 97, No. 1, pp. 155–78.

Burnside, C., M. Eichenbaum, and S. Rebelo, 2001, "On the Fiscal Implications of Twin Crises," Working Paper No. 01-02 (Chicago: Federal Reserve Bank of Chicago).

————, 2004, "Government Guarantees and Self-Fulfilling Speculative Attacks," *Journal of Economic Theory*, Vol. 119, pp. 31–63.

Calomiris, C.W., 2009, "The Subprime Turmoil: What's Old, What's New, and What's Next," *Journal of Structured Finance*, Vol. 15, No. 1, pp. 6–52.

————, and G. Gorton, 1991, "The Origins of Banking Panics: Models, Facts, and Bank Regulation," in *Financial Markets and Financial Crises*, ed. by R.G. Hubbard (Cambridge, Massachusetts: NBER Books), pp. 107–73.

Calvo, G.A., 2000. "Betting against the State: Socially Costly Financial Engineering," *Journal of International Economics*, Vol. 51, No. 1, pp. 5–19.

————, A. Izquierdo, and R. Loo-Kung, 2006, "Relative Price Volatility under Sudden Stops: The Relevance of Balance Sheet Effects," *Journal of International Economics*, Vol. 69, No. 1, pp. 231–54.

Calvo, G., A. Izquierdo, and L.-F. Mejía, 2004, "On the Empirics of Sudden Stops: The Relevance of Balance-Sheet Effects," NBER Working Paper No. 10520 (Cambridge, Massachusetts: National Bureau of Economic Research).

————, 2008, "Systemic Sudden Stops: The Relevance of Balance-Sheet Effects and Financial Integration," NBER Working Paper No. 14026 (Cambridge, Massachusetts: National Bureau of Economic Research).

Calvo, G.A., A. Izquierdo, and E. Talvi, 2006, "Phoenix Miracles in Emerging Markets: Recovering without Credit from Systemic Financial Crises," NBER Working Paper No. 12101 (Cambridge, Massachusetts: National Bureau of Economic Research).

Calvo, G., and C. Reinhart, 1999, "Capital Flow Reversals, the Exchange Rate Debate, and Dollarization," MPRA Paper 8951 (Munich: University of Munich).

————, 2000, "When Capital Inflows Come to a Sudden Stop: Consequences and Policy Options," MPRA Paper 6982 (Munich: University of Munich).

Campbell, J., ed., 2008, *Asset Prices and Monetary Policy*, NBER Conference Report (Chicago: University of Chicago Press).

Campello, M., J. Graham, and C.R. Harvey, 2009, "The Real Effects of Financial Constraints: Evidence from a Financial Crisis," NBER Working Paper No. 15552 (Cambridge, Massachusetts: National Bureau of Economic Research).

Cardarelli, R., S. Elekdag, and M.A. Kose, 2010, "Capital Inflows: Macroeconomic Implications and Policy Responses," *Economic Systems*, Vol. 34, No. 4, pp. 333–56.

Cerutti, E., S. Claessens, and P. McGuire, Forthcoming, "Systemic Risks in Global Banking: What Available Data Can Tell Us and What More Data Are Needed?" in *Risk Topography: Systemic Risk and Macro Modeling*, ed. by M.K. Brunnermeier and A. Krishnamurthy (Chicago: NBER/University of Chicago Press).

Chang, R., and A. Velasco, 2000, "Liquidity Crises in Emerging Markets: Theory and Policy," in *NBER Macroeconomics Annual 1999*, ed. by B.S. Bernanke and J.J. Rotemberg (Cambridge, Massachusetts: MIT Press), pp. 11–78.

Chen, J., H. Hong, and J.C. Stein, 2002, "Breadth of Ownership and Stock Returns," *Journal of Financial Economics*, Vol. 66, No. 2–3, pp. 171–205.

Čihák, M., A. Demirgüç-Kunt, M. Soledad Martínez Pería, and A. Mohseni-Cheraghlou, 2012, "Bank Regulation and Supervision around the World: A Crisis Update," World Bank Policy and Research Working Paper No. 6286 (Washington: World Bank).

Claessens, S., 1991, "Balance of Payments Crises in an Optimal Portfolio Model," *European Economic Review*, Vol. 35, pp. 81–101.

Claessens, S., G. Dell'Ariccia, D. Igan, and L. Laeven, 2010, "Cross-Country Experience and Policy Implications from the Global Financial Crisis," *Economic Policy*, Vol. 25 (April), pp. 267–93.

————, 2012a, "A Cross-Country Perspective on the Causes of the Global Financial Crisis," in *The Evidence and Impact of Financial Globalization*, ed. by Gerard Caprio (Amsterdam: Elsevier B.V.), pp. 753–61.

————, 2012b, "Lessons and Policy Implications from the Global Financial Crisis," in *The Evidence and Impact of Financial Globalization*, ed. by Gerard Caprio (Amsterdam: Elsevier B.V.), pp. 753–61.

Claessens, S., M.A. Kose, and M.E. Terrones, 2009, "What Happens during Recessions, Crunches and Busts?" *Economic Policy*, Vol. 60, pp. 653–700.

————, 2010a, "Financial Cycles: What? How? When?" in *NBER International Seminar in Macroeconomics 2010*, ed. by Richard Clarida and Francesco Giavazzi (Chicago: University of Chicago Press).

————, 2010b, "The Global Financial Crisis: How Similar? How Different? How Costly?" *Journal of Asian Economics*, Vol. 21, No. 3, pp. 247–64.

————, 2012, "How Do Business and Financial Cycles Interact?" *Journal of International Economics*, Vol. 87, pp. 178–90.

Corsetti, G., P. Pesenti, and N. Roubini, 1998, "Paper Tigers? A Model of the Asian Crises," NBER Working Paper No. 6783 (Cambridge, Massachusetts: National Bureau of Economic Research).

Crespo-Cuaresma, J., and T. Slacik, 2009, "On the Determinants of Currency Crisis: The Role of Model Uncertainty," *Journal of Macroeconomics*, Vol. 31, pp. 621–32.

Cumby, R.E., and S. van Wijnbergen, 1989, "Financial Policy and Speculative Runs with a Crawling Peg: Argentina 1979–1981," *Journal of International Economics*, Vol. 27, No. 1–2, pp. 111–27.

Das, U.S., M.G. Papaioannou, and C. Trebesch, 2012, "Sovereign Debt Restructurings 1950–2010: Literature Survey, Data, and Stylized Facts," IMF Working Paper 12/203 (Washington: International Monetary Fund).

de la Torre, A., and A. Ize, 2011, "Containing Systemic Risk: Paradigm-Based Perspectives on Regulatory Reform," Policy Research Working Paper No. 5523 (Washington: World Bank).

Dell'Ariccia, G., E. Detragiache, and R. Rajan, 2008, "The Real Effect of Banking Crises," *Journal of Financial Intermediation*, Vol. 17, No. 1, pp. 89–112.

Dell'Ariccia, G., D. Igan, and L. Laeven, 2012, "Credit Booms and Lending Standards: Evidence from the Subprime Mortgage Market," *Journal of Money, Credit and Banking*, Vol. 44, No. 3, pp. 367–84.

Dell'Ariccia, G., L. Laeven, and R. Marquez, 2011, "Monetary Policy, Leverage, and Bank Risk-Taking," CEPR Discussion Paper No. 8199 (London: Centre for Economic Policy Research).

Dell'Ariccia, G., and R. Marquez, 2006, "Lending Booms and Lending Standards," *Journal of Finance*, Vol. 61, No. 5, pp. 2511–46.

Demirgüç-Kunt, A., E.J. Kane, and L. Laeven, 2008, "Determinants of Deposit-Insurance Adoption and Design," *Journal of Financial Intermediation*, Vol. 17, No. 3, pp. 407–38.

Demirgüç-Kunt, A., and E. Detragiache, 2005, "Cross-Country Empirical Studies of Systemic Bank Distress: A Survey," *National Institute Economic Review*, Vol. 192, pp. 68–83.

de Nicolò, G., G. Dell'Ariccia, L. Laeven, and F. Valencia, 2010, "Monetary Policy and Bank Risk-Taking," IMF Staff Position Note 10/09 (Washington: International Monetary Fund).

de Nicolò, G., G. Favara, and L. Ratnovski, 2012, "Externalities and Macroprudential Policy," IMF Staff Discussion Note 12/05 (Washington: International Monetary Fund).

Dewatripont, M., and J. Tirole, 1994, *The Prudential Regulation of Banks* (Cambridge, Massachusetts: MIT Press).

Diamond, Douglas, and P. Dybvig, 1983, "Bank Runs, Deposit Insurance, and Liquidity," *Journal of Political Economics*, Vol. 91, pp. 401–19.

Diamond, Douglas, and R. Rajan, 2001, "Banks, Short-Term Debt and Financial Crises: Theory, Policy Implications and Applications," *Carnegie-Rochester Conference Series*, Vol. 54, pp. 37–71.

Diether, K., C.J. Malloy, and A. Scherbina, 2002, "Differences of Opinion and the Cross-Section of Stock Returns," *Journal of Finance*, Vol. 57, No. 5, pp. 2113–41.

Eaton, J., and R. Fernandez, 1995, "Sovereign Debt," in *Handbook of International Economics*, Vol. 3, ed. by G.M. Grossman and K. Rogoff (Amsterdam: Elsevier B.V.), pp. 2031–77.

Eaton, J., and M. Gersovitz, 1981, "Debt with Potential Repudiation: Theoretical and Empirical Analysis," *Review of Economic Studies*, Vol. 48, No. 2, pp. 289–309.

Edwards, S., 1984, "The Demand for International Reserves and Monetary Equilibrium: Some Evidence from Developing Countries," *Review of Economics and Statistics*, Vol. 66, No. 3, pp. 495–500.

———, 2004, "Financial Openness, Sudden Stops, and Current-Account Reversals," *American Economic Review*, Vol. 94, No. 2, pp. 59–64.

Eichengreen, B., 2002, *Financial Crises: And What to Do about Them* (Oxford, United Kingdom: Oxford University Press).

———, 2011, "The Great Recession and the Great Depression: Reflections and Lessons," *Economía Chilena*, Vol. 13, No. 2, pp. 5–10.

———, and R. Hausmann, 1999, "Exchange Rates and Financial Fragility," NBER Working Paper No. 7418 (Cambridge, Massachusetts: National Bureau of Economic Research).

Eichengreen, B., A.K. Rose, and C. Wyplosz, 1995, "Speculative Attacks on Pegged Exchange Rates: An Empirical Exploration with Special Reference to the European Monetary System," *Working Papers in Applied Economic Theory*, No. 95-04 (Federal Reserve Bank of San Francisco).

Elekdag, S., R. Cardarelli, and Subir Lall, 2009, "Financial Stress, Downturns, and Recoveries," IMF Working Paper 09/100 (Washington: International Monetary Fund).

Evanoff, D.D., G.G. Kaufman, and A.G. Malliaris, 2012, *New Perspectives on Asset Price Bubbles* (Oxford, United Kingdom: Oxford University Press).

Fama, E.F., 1998, "Market Efficiency, Long-Term Returns, and Behavioral Finance," *Journal of Financial Economics*, Vol. 49, No. 3, pp. 283–306.

Farhi, E., and Jean Tirole, 2012, "Collective Moral Hazard, Maturity Mismatch, and Systemic Bailouts," *American Economic Review*, Vol. 102, No. 1, pp. 60–93.

Feldstein, M., 2009, "Rethinking the Role of Fiscal Policy," *American Economic Review*, Vol. 99, No. 2, pp. 556–59.

Ferguson, Roger W., 2005, "Recessions and Recoveries Associated with Asset Price Movements: What Do We Know?" Address to the Stanford Institute for Economic Policy Research, Stanford, California, January 12.

Fisher, I., 1933, "The Debt Deflation Theory of Great Depressions," *Econometrica*, Vol. 1, pp. 337–57.

Fisman, R., 2001, "Estimating the Value of Political Connections," *American Economic Review*, Vol. 91, No. 4, pp. 1095–1102.

Flood, R., and P. Garber, 1984, "Collapsing Exchange-Rate Regimes: Some Linear Examples," *Journal of International Economics*, Vol.17, No. 1–2, pp. 1–13.

Flood, R., and N.P. Marion, 1997, "Policy Implications of 'Second-Generation' Crisis Models," IMF Working Paper 97/16 (Washington: International Monetary Fund).

Forbes, K.J., 2012, "The Big 'C': Identifying and Mitigating Contagion," Paper prepared for the Jackson Hole Symposium hosted by the Federal Reserve Bank of Kansas City, August 31–September 1.

———, and F. Warnock, 2011, "Capital Flow Waves: Surges, Stops, Flight, and Retrenchment," NBER Working Paper No. 17351 (Cambridge, Massachusetts: National Bureau of Economic Research).

Frankel, J.A., and A.K. Rose, 1996, "Currency Crashes in Emerging Markets: Empirical Indicators," CEPR Discussion Paper 1349 (London: Centre for Economic Policy Research).

Frankel, J.A., and G. Saravelos, 2012, "Can Leading Indicators Assess Country Vulnerability? Evidence from the 2008–09 Global Financial Crisis," *Journal of International Economics*, Vol. 87, No. 2, pp. 216–31.

Furceri, D., and A. Zdzienicka, 2012, "How Costly Are Debt Crises?" *Journal of International Money and Finance*, Vol. 31, No. 4, pp. 726–42.

Garber, P.M., 2000, *Famous First Bubbles: The Fundamentals of Early Manias* (Cambridge, Massachusetts: MIT Press).

Glick, R., and M. Hutchison, 2012, "Currency Crises," in *Encyclopedia on Financial Globalization* (Amsterdam: Elsevier B.V.).

Goldstein, M., G.L. Kaminsky, and C.M. Reinhart, 2000, *Assessing Financial Vulnerability: An Early Warning System for Emerging Markets* (Washington: Institute for International Economics).

Gorton, G., 1988, "Banking Panics and Business Cycles," *Oxford Economic Papers*, Vol. 40, No. 4, pp. 751–81.

———, 2008, "The Panic of 2007," in *Maintaining Stability in a Changing Financial System, Proceedings of the 2008 Jackson Hole Conference* (Kansas City, Missouri: Federal Reserve Bank of Kansas City).

———, 2009, "Slapped in the Face by the Invisible Hand: Banking and the Panic of 2007," Paper prepared for the Federal Reserve Bank of Atlanta's "2009 Financial Markets Conference: Financial Innovation and Crisis," May 11–13.

———, 2012, *Misunderstanding Financial Crises: Why We Don't See Them Coming* (Oxford, United Kingdom: Oxford University Press).

———, and G. Ordonez, 2012, "Collateral Crises," NBER Working Paper No. 17771 (Cambridge, Massachusetts: National Bureau of Economic Research).

Gorton, G., and P. He, 2008, "Bank Credit Cycles," *Review of Economic Studies*, Vol. 75, No. 4, pp. 1181–214.

Gorton, G., and A. Winton, 2003, "Financial Intermediation," in *Handbook of the Economics of Finance*, Vol 1., ed. by G.M. Constantinides, M. Harris, and R.M. Stulz (Amsterdam: Elsevier), pp. 431–552.

Gourinchas, P.-O., R. Valdés, and O. Landerretche, 2001, "Lending Booms: Latin America and the World," *Economia*, Vol. 1, pp. 47–99.

Greenspan, A., 1996, "The Challenge of Central Banking in a Democratic Society," Speech at the American Enterprise Institute, December 5.

Gupta, P., D. Mishra, and R. Sahay, 2007, "Behavior of Output during Currency Crises," *Journal of International Economics*, Vol. 72, No. 2, pp. 428–50.

Gürkaynak, R.S., 2008, "Econometric Tests of Asset Price Bubbles: Taking Stock," *Journal of Economic Surveys*, Vol. 22, No. 1, pp. 166–86.

Haber, S., 2005, "Banking and Economic Growth in Mexico," Working Paper (Stanford, California: Hoover Institution at Stanford University).

Hallwood, C.P., and R. MacDonald, 2000, *International Money and Finance*, 3rd ed. (Malden, Massachusetts: Blackwell Publishing).

Harrison, J.M., and D.M. Kreps, 1978, "Speculative Investor Behavior in a Stock Market with Heterogeneous Expectations," *Quarterly Journal of Economics*, Vol. 92, No. 2, pp. 323–36.

Heath, R., 2013, "Why Are the G-20 Data Gaps Initiative and the SDDS Plus Relevant for Financial Stability Analysis?" IMF Working Paper 13/6 (Washington: International Monetary Fund).

Hirata, H., M.A. Kose, C. Otrok, and M.E. Terrones, 2012, "Global House Price Fluctuations: Synchronization and Determinants," in *NBER International Seminar on Macroeconomics 2012*, ed. by Francesco Giavazzi and Kenneth West (Cambridge, Massachusetts: National Bureau of Economic Research).

Hong, H., J. Scheinkman, and W. Xiong, 2008, "Advisors and Asset Prices: A Model of the Origins of Bubbles," *Journal of Financial Economics*, Vol. 89, No. 2, pp. 268–87.

Honohan, P., and L. Laeven, eds., 2007, *Systemic Financial Crises* (New York: Cambridge University Press).

Howard, G., R. Martin, and B.A. Wilson, 2011, "Are Recoveries from Banking and Financial Crises Really So Different?" International Finance Discussion Papers, Working Paper Number 1037 (Washington: U.S. Federal Reserve System).

Hutchison, M.M., and I. Noy, 2006, "Sudden Stops and the Mexican Wave: Currency Crises, Capital Flow Reversals and Output Loss in Emerging Markets," *Journal of Development Economics*, Vol. 79, pp. 225–48.

International Monetary Fund (IMF), 1998, *World Economic Outlook*, May (Washington).

————, 2005, "Information Note on Modifications to the Fund's Debt Sustainability Assessment Framework for Market Access Countries" (Washington).

————, 2009, "Debt Bias and Other Distortions: Crisis-Related Issues in Tax Policy," (Washington).

————, 2010, "The IMF-FSB Early Warning Exercise: Design and Methodological Toolkit" (Washington: International Monetary Fund). http://www.imf.org/external/np/pp/eng/2010/090110.pdf.

————, 2011, "Modernizing the Framework for Fiscal Policy and Public Debt Sustainability Analysis," Policy Paper (Washington).

————, 2013, "The Interaction of Monetary and Macroprudential Policies," Board Paper (Washington).

Ioannidou, V., S. Ongena, and J.L. Peydró, 2009, "Monetary Policy, Risk-Taking and Pricing: Evidence from a Quasi-Natural Experiment," Discussion Paper 2009-31 S (Tilburg, Netherlands: University of Tilburg).

Jeanne, O., 2003, "Why Do Emerging Economies Borrow in Foreign Currency?" IMF Working Paper 03/177 (Washington: International Monetary Fund).

Jordà, O., M. Schularick, and A.M. Taylor, 2011, "Financial Crises, Credit Booms, and External Imbalances: 140 Years of Lessons," *IMF Economic Review*, Vol. 59, No. 2, pp. 340–78.

Kaminsky, G., 2003, "Varieties of Currency Crises," NBER Working Paper No. 10193 (Cambridge, Massachusetts: National Bureau of Economic Research).

————, S. Lizondo, and C. Reinhart, 1998, "Leading Indicators of Currency Crisis," *IMF Staff Papers*, Vol. 45, No. 1, pp. 1–48.

Kaminsky, G., and C. Reinhart, 1999, "The Twin Crises: The Causes of Banking and Balance-of-Payments Problems," *American Economic Review*, Vol. 89, No. 3 pp. 473–500.

————, 2001, "Bank Lending and Contagion: Evidence from the Asian Crisis," in *Regional and Global Capital Flows: Macroeconomics Causes and Consequences*, Vol. 10, ed. by Takatoshi Ito and Anne O. Krueger (Chicago: University of Chicago Press), pp. 73–116.

Kannan, P., 2009, "On the Welfare Benefits of an International Currency," *European Economic Review*, Vol. 53, No. 5, pp. 588–606.

Keynes, J.M., 1930, *The Great Slump of 1930* (London: The Nation & Athenæum, issues of December 20 and December 27).

Kindleberger, C., 1978, *Manias, Panics, and Crashes: A History of Financial Crises* (New York: Basic Books, revised and enlarged, 1989; 3rd ed. 1996).

————, 1986, *The World in Depression: 1929–1939* (Berkeley, California: University of California Press).

King, M., 2012, "Twenty Years of Inflation Targeting," Speech given at the Stamp Memorial Lecture, London School of Economics, October 9. http://www.bankofengland.co.uk/publications/Pages/speeches/2012/606.aspx.

Klein, M.W., and N.P. Marion, 1994, "Explaining the Duration of Exchange-Rate Pegs," NBER Working Paper No. 4651 (Cambridge, Massachusetts: National Bureau of Economic Research).

Kletzer, K.M., and B.D. Wright, 2000, "Sovereign Debt as Intertemporal Barter," *American Economic Review*, Vol. 90, No. 3, pp. 621–39.

Klingebiel, D., R. Kroszner, and L. Laeven, 2007, "Banking Crises, Financial Dependence and Growth," *Journal of Financial Economics*, Vol. 84, No. 1, pp. 187–228.

Kocherlakota, N., 2009, "Bursting Bubbles: Consequences and Cures," paper presented at "Macroeconomic and Policy Challenges Following Financial Meltdowns" Conference hosted by International Monetary Fund, April 3.

Kohn, D.L., 2008, "Monetary Policy and Asset Prices Revisited," Speech at the Cato Institute's 26th Annual Monetary Policy Conference, Washington, DC, November 19.

Korinek, A., 2011, "Foreign Currency Debt, Risk Premia and Macroeconomic Volatility," *European Economic Review*, Vol. 55, No. 3. pp. 371–85.

Kose, M.A., P. Loungani, and M. Terrones, forthcoming, "Global Recessions and Recoveries," IMF Working Paper (Washington: International Monetary Fund).

Kose, M.A., and E. Prasad, 2010, *Emerging Markets: Resilience and Growth amid Global Turmoil* (Washington: Brookings Institution Press).

———, K. Rogoff, and S.-J. Wei, 2010, "Financial Globalization and Economic Policies," in *Handbook of Development Economics*, Vol. 5, ed. by Dani Rodrik and Mark Rosenzweig (Amsterdam: Elsevier B.V.), pp. 4283–362.

Krugman, P., 1979. "A Model of Balance-of-Payments Crises," *Journal of Money, Credit and Banking*, Vol. 11, No. 3, pp. 311–25.

———, 1999, "Balance Sheets, the Transfer Problem, and Financial Crises," *International Tax and Public Finance*, Vol. 6, No. 4, pp. 459–72.

Kumar, M., U. Moorthy, and W. Perraudin, 2003, "Predicting Emerging Market Currency Crashes," *Journal of Empirical Finance*, Vol. 10, pp. 427–54.

Laeven, L., 2001, "Insider Lending and Bank Ownership: The Case of Russia," *Journal of Comparative Economics*, Vol. 29, No. 2, pp. 207–29.

———, 2011, "Banking Crises: A Review," *Annual Review of Financial Economics*, Vol. 3, No. 1, pp. 17–40.

———, and F. Valencia, 2008, "Systemic Banking Crises: A New Database," IMF Working Paper 08/224 (Washington: International Monetary Fund).

Laeven, L., and F. Valencia, 2011, "The Real Effects of Financial Sector Intervention During Crises," IMF Working Paper No. 11/45 (Washington: International Monetary Fund).

Lamont, O., and A.R.H. Thaler, 2003, "Can the Market Add and Subtract? Mispricing in Tech Stock Carve-outs," *Journal of Political Economy*, Vol. 111, No. 2, pp. 227–68.

Lane, P.R., 2012, "The European Sovereign Debt Crisis," *Journal of Economic Perspectives*, Vol. 26, No. 3, pp. 49–68.

———, and G.-M. Milesi-Ferretti, 2011, "The Cross-Country Incidence of the Global Crisis," *IMF Economic Review*, Vol. 59, No. 1, pp. 77–110.

Lansing, K.J., 2008, "Speculative Growth and Overreaction to Technology Shocks," Working Paper No. 2008-08 (San Francisco, California: Federal Reserve Bank of San Francisco).

La Porta, R., F. López-de-Silanes, and G. Zammaripa, 2003, "Related Lending," *The Quarterly Journal of Economics*, Vol. 118, No. 1, pp. 231–68.

Levy-Yeyati, E.L., and U. Panizza, 2011, "The Elusive Costs of Sovereign Defaults," *Journal of Development Economics*, Vol. 94, No. 1, pp. 95–105.

Lindgren, C.-J., G. Garcia, and M. Saal, eds., 1996, *Bank Soundness and Macroeconomic Policy* (Washington: International Monetary Fund).

Lo, A.W., and A.C. MacKinlay, 2001, *A Non-Random Walk Down Wall Street* (Princeton, New Jersey: Princeton University Press).

Lopez-Salido, D., and E. Nelson, 2010, "Postwar Financial Crises and Economic Recoveries in the United States," Working Paper (Washington: Federal Reserve Board).

Maddaloni, A., and J.-L. Peydró, 2010, "Bank Risk-Taking, Securitization, Supervision and Low Interest Rates: Evidence from the Euro Area and the U.S. Lending Standards," Working Paper No. 1248 (Frankfurt: European Central Bank).

Mauro, P., and T.I. Becker, 2006, "Output Drops and the Shocks That Matter," IMF Working Papers 06/172 (Washington: International Monetary Fund).

Magud, N.E., C.M. Reinhart, and E.R. Vesperoni, 2012, "Capital Inflows, Exchange Rate Flexibility, and Credit Booms," IMF Working Paper No. 12/41 (Washington: International Monetary Fund).

McKinnon, R., and H. Pill, 1996, "Credible Liberalizations and International Capital Flows: The Overborrowing Syndrome," in *Financial Deregulation and Integration in East Asia*, ed. by T. Ito and A. Krueger (Chicago: University of Chicago Press), pp. 7–42.

———, 1998, "International Overborrowing: A Decomposition of Credit and Currency Risks," *World Development*, Vol. 26, No. 7, pp. 1267–82.

McFadden, D., R. Eckaus, G. Feder, V. Hajivassiliou, and S. O'Connell, 1985, "Is there life after Debt? An Econometric Analysis of the Creditworthiness of Developing Countries," in *International Debt and the Developing Countries*, ed. by Gordon Smith and John Cuddington (Washington: World Bank), pp. 179–209.

Mendoza, E.G., 2010, "Sudden Stops, Financial Crises, and Leverage," *American Economic Review*, Vol. 100, No. 5, pp. 1941–66.

———, and M. Terrones, 2008, "An Anatomy of Credit Booms: Evidence from Macro Aggregates and Micro Data," NBER Working Paper No. 14049 (Cambridge, Massachusetts: National Bureau of Economic Research).

———, 2012, "An Anatomy of Credit Booms and Their Demise," *Journal of Economia Chilena*, Central Bank of Chile, Vol. 15, pp. 4–32.

Milesi-Ferretti, G.-M., and A. Razin, 2000, "Current Account Reversals and Currency Crises, Empirical Regularities," in *Currency Crises*, ed. by Paul Krugman (Cambridge, Massachusetts: National Bureau of Economic Research), pp. 285–326.

Milesi-Ferretti, G.-M., and C. Tille, 2011, "The Great Retrenchment: International Capital Flows during the Global Financial Crisis," *Economic Policy*, Vol. 26, No. 66, pp. 285–342.

Minsky, H.P., 1975, *John Maynard Keynes* (New York: Columbia University Press).

———, 1992, "The Financial Instability Hypothesis," Working Paper No. 74 (Annandale-on-Hudson, New York: Levy Economics Institute of Bard College).

Mishkin, F.S., 2008, "Does Stabilizing Inflation Contribute to Stabilizing Economic Activity?" NBER Working Paper No. 13970 (Cambridge, Massachusetts: National Bureau of Economic Research).

———, 2011, "Monetary Policy Strategies: Lessons from the Crisis," NBER Working Paper No. 16755 (Cambridge, Massachusetts: National Bureau of Economic Research.

Obstfeld, M., 1986, "Rational and Self-Fulfilling Balance-of-Payment Crises," *American Economic Review*, Vol. 76, No. 1, pp. 72–81.

———, 2012, "Financial Flows, Financial Crises, and Global Imbalances," *Journal of International Money and Finance*, Vol. 31, No. 3, pp. 469–80.

———, 2009, "Global Imbalances and the Financial Crisis: Products of Common Causes," CEPR Discussion Paper No. 7606 (London: Centre for Economic Policy Research).

Ofek, E., and M. Richardson, 2003, "DotCom Mania: The Rise and Fall of Internet Stock Prices," *Journal of Finance*, Vol. 58, pp. 1113–37.

Panizza, U., F. Sturzenegger, and J. Zettelmeyer, 2009, "The Economics and Law of Sovereign Debt and Default," *Journal of Economic Literature*, Vol. 47, No. 3, pp. 651–98.

Papell, D.H., and R. Prudan, 2011, "The Statistical Behavior of GDP after Financial Crises and Severe Recessions," Paper prepared for the Federal Reserve Bank of Boston conference on "Long-Term Effects of the Great Recession," October 18–19.

Pastor, L., and P. Veronesi, 2006, "Was There a Nasdaq Bubble in the Late 1990s?" *Journal of Financial Economics*, Vol. 81, No. 1, pp. 61–100.

Radelet, S., and J. Sachs, 1998, "The East Asian Financial Crisis: Diagnosis, Remedies, Prospects," *Brookings Papers on Economic Activity*, Vol. 1, No. 1, pp. 1–74.

Rajan, R.G., 2005, "Has Financial Development Made the World Riskier?" *Proceedings*, Federal Reserve Bank of Kansas City, August, pp. 313–69.

Rancière, R., and A. Tornell, 2011, "Financial Black-Holes: The Interaction of Financial Regulation and Bailout Guarantees," CEPR Discussion Paper 8248 (London: Centre for Economic Policy Research).

Reinhart, C., J. Kirkegaard, and B. Sbrancia, 2011, "Financial Repression Redux," *Finance and Development*, Vol. 48, No. 1.

Reinhart, C.M., and K.S. Rogoff, 2008, "Is the 2007 U.S. Subprime Crisis So Different? An International Historical Comparison," *American Economic Review*, Vol. 98, No. 2, pp. 339–44.

———, 2009a, "The Aftermath of Financial Crises," *American Economic Review*, Vol. 99, pp. 466–72.

———, 2009b, *This Time is Different: Eight Centuries of Financial Folly* (Princeton, New Jersey: Princeton University Press).

———, 2011, "From Financial Crash to Debt Crisis," *American Economic Review*, Vol. 101, No. 5, pp. 1676–706.

———, forthcoming, "Banking Crises: An Equal Opportunity Menace," *Journal of Banking and Finance.*

Rose, A.K., and M.M. Spiegel, 2011, "Cross-Country Causes and Consequences of the 2008 Crisis: Early Warning," *European Economic Review*, Vol. 55, No. 3, pp. 309–24.

Salant, S., 1983, "The Vulnerability of Price Stabilization Schemes to Speculative Attack," *Journal of Political Economy*, Vol. 91, No. 1, pp. 1–38.

———, and D. Henderson, 1978, "Market Anticipations of Government Policies and the Price of Gold," *Journal of Political Economy*, Vol. 86, No. 4, pp. 627–48.

Scheinkman, J.A., and W. Xiong, 2003, "Overconfidence and Speculative Bubbles," *Journal of Political Economy*, Vol. 111, No. 6, pp. 1183–219.

Scherbina, A., 2013, "Asset Price Bubbles: A Selective Survey," IMF Working Paper 13/45 (Washington: International Monetary Fund).

Schularick, M., and A.M. Taylor, 2012, "Credit Booms Gone Bust: Monetary Policy, Leverage Cycles, and Financial Crises, 1870–2008," *American Economic Review*, Vol. 102, No. 2, pp. 1029–61.

Schwert, G.W., 2003, "Anomalies and Market Efficiency," in *Handbook of the Economics of Finance*, Vol. 1, ed. by G.M. Constantinides, M. Harris, and R.M. Stulz (Amsterdam: Elsevier B.V.), pp. 939–74.

Shin, H.S., 2009, "Reflections on Northern Rock: The Bank Run That Heralded the Global Financial Crisis," *Journal of Economic Perspectives*, Vol. 23, No. 1, pp. 101–19.

Shleifer, A., 2000, *Inefficient Markets: An Introduction to Behavioral Finance* (Oxford, United Kingdom: Oxford University Press).

———, and R.W. Vishny, 1997, "The Limits of Arbitrage," *Journal of Finance*, Vol. 52, No. 1, pp. 35–55.

Soros, G., 1987, *The Alchemy of Finance: Reading the Mind of the Market* (New York: Touchstone/Simon & Schuster).

Stiglitz, J., and A. Weiss, 1983, "Alternative Approaches to Analyzing Markets with Asymmetric Information: Reply [The Theory of 'Screening,' Education, and the Distribution of Income]," *American Economic Review*, Vol. 73, No. 1, pp. 246–49.

Sturzenegger, F., and J. Zettelmeyer, 2007, *Debt Defaults and Lessons from a Decade of Crises* (Cambridge, Massachusetts, and London: MIT Press).

Taylor, J.B., 2009, "The Financial Crisis and the Policy Responses: An Empirical Analysis of What Went Wrong," NBER Working Paper No. 14631 (Cambridge, Massachusetts: National Bureau of Economic Research).

———, 2011, "An Empirical Analysis of the Revival of Fiscal Activism in the 2000s," *Journal of Economic Literature*, Vol. 49, No. 3, pp. 686–702.

Tirole, J., 2002, *Financial Crises, Liquidity, and the International Monetary System* (Princeton, New Jersey: Princeton University Press).

Tomz, M., and M.L.J. Wright, 2007, "Do Countries Default in 'Bad Times'?" *Journal of the European Economic Association*, Vol. 5, No. 2–3, pp. 352–60.

Trichet, J.-C., 2009, "Credible Alertness Revisited," speech at the symposium on "Financial Stability and Macroeconomic Policy," sponsored by the Federal Reserve Bank of Kansas City, Jackson Hole, Wyoming, August 22.

Wang, P., and Y. Wen, 2012, "Speculative Bubbles and Financial Crises," *American Economic Journal: Macroeconomics*, Vol. 4, No. 3, pp. 184–221.

Wermers, R., 2012, "Runs on Money Market Mutual Funds," Working Paper (College Park, Maryland: University of Maryland).

World Bank, 2001, *Finance for Growth: Policy Choices in a Volatile World* (Washington: World Bank).

CHAPTER 2

Systemic Banking Crises

LUC LAEVEN AND FABIÁN VALENCIA

Financial crises can be damaging and contagious, prompting calls for swift policy responses. The financial crises of the past have led affected economies into deep recessions and sharp current account reversals. Some crises turned out to be contagious, rapidly spreading to countries with no apparent vulnerabilities. Among the many causes of financial crises have been a combination of unsustainable macroeconomic policies (including large current account deficits and unsustainable public debt), excessive credit booms, large capital inflows, and balance sheet fragilities, combined with policy paralysis caused by a variety of political and economic constraints. In many financial crises, currency and maturity mismatches were a salient feature, while in others off–balance sheet operations of the banking sector were prominent.[1]

Choosing the best way to resolve a financial crisis and accelerate economic recovery is difficult. Little agreement has been found on what constitutes best practice or even good practice. Many approaches have been proposed and tried in attempts to resolve systemic crises more efficiently. This lack of agreement may occur, in part, because the objectives of the policy advice have varied. Some have focused on reducing the fiscal costs of financial crises; others on limiting the economic costs of lost output and on accelerating restructuring; still others on achieving long-term, structural reforms. Trade-offs are likely to arise between these objectives.[2] Governments may, for example, through certain policies consciously incur large fiscal outlays in resolving a banking crisis, with the objective of accelerating recovery. Or structural reforms may only be politically feasible in the context of a severe crisis with large output losses and high fiscal costs.

This chapter introduces and describes a new data set on banking crises, with detailed information about the type of policy responses used to resolve crises in

The authors thank Olivier Blanchard, Eduardo Borensztein, Martin Cihak, Stijn Claessens, Luis Cortavarria-Checkley, Giovanni Dell'Ariccia, David Hoelscher, Simon Johnson, Ashok Mody, Jonathan Ostry, and Bob Traa for comments and discussions, and Ming Ai, Chuling Chen, and Mattia Landoni for excellent research assistance. The views expressed in this chapter are those of the authors and do not necessarily represent those of the IMF or IMF policy.

[1] For a review of the literature on the macro origins of banking crisis, see Lindgren, Garcia, and Saal (1996); Dooley and Frankel (2003); and Collyns and Kincaid (2003).

[2] For an overview of existing literature on how crisis resolution policies have been used and the trade-offs involved, see Claessens, Klingebiel, and Laeven (2003); Hoelscher and Quintyn (2003); and Honohan and Laeven (2005).

different countries. The emphasis is on policy responses to restore the banking system to health. The data set expands Caprio and others' (2005) banking crisis database by including recent banking crises, information on currency and debt crises, and information on crisis containment and resolution measures. The database covers all systemically important banking crises for the period 1970 to 2007, and has detailed information on crisis management strategies for 42 systemic banking crises in 37 countries.

Governments have used a broad range of policies to deal with financial crises. Central to identifying sound policy approaches to financial crises is the recognition that policy responses that reallocate wealth toward banks and debtors and away from taxpayers face a critical trade-off. Such reallocations of wealth can help to restart productive investment, but they have large costs. These costs include taxpayers' wealth that is spent on financial assistance, indirect costs from misallocations of capital, and distortions to incentives that may result from encouraging banks and firms to abuse government protections. Those distortions may worsen capital allocation and risk management after the resolution of the crisis.

Institutional weaknesses typically aggravate crises and complicate crisis resolution. Bankruptcy and restructuring frameworks are often deficient. Disclosure and accounting rules for financial institutions and corporations may be weak. Equity and creditor rights may be poorly defined or weakly enforced. And the judiciary system is often inefficient.

Many financial crises, especially those in countries with fixed exchange rates, turn out to be twin crises with currency depreciation exacerbating banking sector problems through the foreign currency exposures of borrowers or the banks themselves. In such cases, another complicating factor is the conflict between the desire to maintain currency pegs and the need to provide liquidity support to the banking system.

Existing empirical research has shown that providing assistance to banks and their borrowers can be counterproductive, resulting in increased losses to banks, which often abuse forbearance to take unproductive risks at government expense. The typical result of forbearance is a deeper hole in the net worth of banks, a crippling tax burden caused by financing bank bailouts, and an even more severe credit supply contraction and economic decline than would have occurred in the absence of forbearance.[3]

Cross-country analyses to date also show that accommodative policy measures (such as substantial liquidity support, explicit government guarantees on financial institutions' liabilities, and forbearance from prudential regulation) tend to be fiscally costly and that these particular policies do not necessarily accelerate the economic recovery.[4] Of course, the weakness in these findings is

---

[3] For empirical evidence, see Demirgüç-Kunt and Detragiache (2002); Claessens, Klingebiel, and Laeven (2003); and Honohan and Klingebiel (2000).

[4] See the analyses in Honohan and Klingebiel (2000); Claessens, Klingebiel, and Laeven (2005); and Laeven and Valencia (2012).

that a counterfactual to the crisis resolution cannot be observed, therefore, it is difficult to speculate how a crisis would unfold in absence of such policies. Better institutions are, however, uniformly positively associated with faster recoveries.

The remainder of the chapter is organized as follows: The first section presents new data on the timing of banking crises, currency crises, and sovereign debt crises. The second section presents variable definitions of the data collected on crisis management techniques for a subset of systemic banking crises. The third section presents descriptive statistics of data on containment and resolution policies, fiscal costs, and output losses. The fourth section discusses the ongoing (as of 2013) global liquidity crisis that originated within the U.S. subprime crisis of 2007–09.

CRISIS DATES

Banking Crises

This analysis defines a systemic banking crisis as occurring when a country's corporate and financial sectors experience a large number of defaults and financial institutions and corporations face great difficulties repaying contracts on time. As a result, nonperforming loans increase sharply and all or most of the aggregate banking system capital is exhausted. This situation may be accompanied by depressed asset prices (such as equity and real estate prices) on the heels of run-ups before the crisis, sharp increases in real interest rates, and a slowdown or reversal in capital flows. In some cases, the crisis is triggered by depositor runs on banks, though in most cases it is a general realization that systemically important financial institutions are in distress.

Using this broad definition of a systemic banking crisis that combines quantitative data with some subjective assessment of the situation, the starting years of systemic banking crises around the world since 1970 are identified. Unlike previous work (Caprio and Klingebiel, 1996; and Caprio and others, 2005), this chapter excludes banking system distress events that affected isolated banks but were not systemic. As a cross-check on the timing of each crisis, the analysis examines whether the crisis year coincides with deposit runs, the introduction of a deposit freeze or blanket guarantee, or extensive liquidity support or bank interventions,[5] and thus confirms about two-thirds of the crisis dates. Alternatively, it must be apparent that the banking system has a large proportion of nonperforming loans

---

[5] Bank runs are defined as a monthly percentage decline in deposits in excess of 5 percent. Demand deposits (*International Financial Statistics* [IFS] line 24) and time, savings, and foreign currency deposits (IFS line 25) are combined for total deposits in national currencies (except for the United Kingdom, Sweden, and Vietnam, where IFS 25L is used for total deposits). Extensive liquidity support is defined as claims from monetary authorities on commercial banks (IFS line 12E) as a ratio of total deposits of at least 5 percent and at least double the ratio compared with the previous year.

and that most of its capital has been exhausted.[6] This additional requirement applies to the remainder of crisis dates.

In sum, 124 systemic banking crises were identified between 1970 and 2007. This list is an updated, corrected, and expanded version of the Caprio and Klingebiel (1996) and Caprio and others (2005) banking crisis databases. Appendix Table 2A.1 lists the starting year of each banking crisis, as well as background information, including peak nonperforming loans, gross fiscal costs, output loss, and minimum real GDP growth rate. Peak nonperforming loans is the highest level of nonperforming loans as a percentage of total loans during the first five years of the crisis. Gross fiscal costs are computed over the five years following the start of the crisis using data from Hoelscher and Quintyn (2003); Honohan and Laeven (2005) IMF staff reports; and publications from national authorities and institutions. Output losses are computed by extrapolating trend real GDP based on the trend in real GDP growth up to the year preceding the crisis, and taking the sum of the differences between actual real GDP and trend real GDP expressed as a percentage of trend real GDP for the first four years of the crisis (including the crisis year).[7] The minimum real GDP growth rate is the lowest real GDP growth rate during the first three years of the crisis.

Currency Crises

Building on the approach in Frankel and Rose (1996), a "currency crisis" is defined as a nominal depreciation of the currency of at least 30 percent that is also at least a 10 percent increase in the rate of depreciation compared with the previous year. To measure exchange rate depreciation, the percentage change of the end-of-period official nominal bilateral dollar exchange rate from the IMF's World Economic Outlook database is used. For countries that meet the criteria for several continuous years, the first year of each five-year window is used to identify the crisis. This definition yields 208 currency crises during the period 1970–2007. (This list also includes large devaluations by countries that had fixed exchange rate regimes.)

---

[6] In some cases, nonperforming loans are built up slowly and financial sector problems arise gradually rather than suddenly. Japan in the 1990s is a case in point. Although nonperforming loans had been increasing since the early 1990s, they reached crisis proportions only in 1997. Also, initial shocks to the financial sector are often followed by additional shocks, further aggravating the crisis. In such cases, these additional shocks can sometimes be considered as part of the same crisis. For example, Latvia experienced a systemic banking crisis in 1995, which was followed by another stress episode in 1998 related to the Russian Federation's financial crisis.

[7] Note that estimates of output losses are highly dependent on the method chosen and the time period considered. In particular, this measure tends to overstate output losses when there has been a growth boom before the banking crisis. Also, if the banking crisis reflects unsustainable economic developments, output losses need not be attributed to the banking crisis itself.

Sovereign Debt Crises

Episodes of sovereign debt default and restructuring are identified and dated by relying on information from Beim and Calomiris (2001); World Bank (2002); Sturzenegger and Zettelmeyer (2006); and IMF staff reports. The information compiled includes year of sovereign defaults to private lending and year of debt rescheduling. Using this approach, 63 episodes of sovereign debt defaults and restructurings are identified since 1970.

Appendix Table 2A.2 lists the complete set of starting years of systemic banking crises, currency crises, and sovereign debt crises.

Frequency of Crises and Occurrence of Twin Crises

Table 2.1 reports the frequency of different types of crises (banking, currency, and sovereign debt), as well as the occurrence of twin (banking and currency) crises or triple (banking, currency, and debt) crises. A twin crisis in year t is defined as a banking crisis in year t, combined with a currency crisis during the period $t - 1$ through $t + 1$; and a triple crisis in year t is defined as a banking crisis in year t, combined with a currency crisis during the period $t - 1$ through $t + 1$ and a sovereign debt crisis during the period $t - 1$ through $t + 1$.[8]

Banking crises were found to be most frequent during the early 1990s, with the largest number of systemic banking crises, 13, starting in 1995. Currency crises were also common during the first half of the 1990s, with a peak in 1994 of 25 episodes. Sovereign debt crises were also relatively common during the early 1980s, with a peak of 9 debt crises in 1983. In total, 124 banking crises, 208 currency crises, and 63 sovereign debt crises occurred during the period 1970–2007. Several countries experienced multiple crises. Of these 124 banking crises, 26 are considered twin crises and 8 can be classified as triple crises, using the definition above.

CRISIS CONTAINMENT AND RESOLUTION

In reviewing crisis policy responses it is useful to differentiate between the containment and resolution phases of systemic restructuring (Honohan and Laeven, 2005; and Hoelscher and Quintyn, 2003, for further details). During the containment phase, the financial crisis is still unfolding. Governments tend to implement policies aimed at restoring public confidence to minimize the repercussions on the real sector of the loss of confidence by depositors and other investors in the financial system. The resolution phase involves the actual financial, and to a lesser extent operational, restructuring of financial institutions and corporations. Although policy responses to crises naturally divide into immediate reactions during the containment phase of the crisis, and long-term responses toward

---

[8] Throughout this chapter, t is the starting year of a crisis, and time is measured in years, for example, $t - 1$ is the year before the start of a crisis.

TABLE 2.1

	Frequency of Financial Crises				
Year	Banking crises (number)	Currency crises (number)	Sovereign debt crises (number)	Twin crises[1] (number)	Triple crises[2] (number)
1970					
1971		1			
1972		5			
1973		1			
1974					
1975		5			
1976	2	4	1		
1977	2	1	1		
1978		5	3		
1979		3	2		
1980	3	4	3	3	
1981	3	9	6	1	
1982	5	5	9	1	1
1983	7	12	9	2	1
1984	1	10	4		
1985	2	10	3		
1986	1	4	3		
1987	6	6		1	
1988	7	5	1		
1989	4	8	3	1	1
1990	7	10	2		
1991	10	6		1	
1992	8	9	1	1	
1993	7	8		1	
1994	11	25		2	
1995	13	4		2	
1996	4	6		1	
1997	7	6		4	
1998	7	10	2	3	3
1999		8	2		
2000	2	4			
2001	1	3	2	1	1
2002	1	5	4		
2003	1	4	1	1	1
2004		1	1		
2005		1			
2006					
2007	2				
Total	124	208	63	26	8

Source: Authors' calculations.

[1] Twin crisis indicates banking crisis in year t and currency crisis during $t - 1$ through $t + 1$.

[2] Triple crisis indicates banking crisis in year t and currency crisis during $t - 1$ through $t + 1$ and debt crisis during $t - 1$ through $t + 1$.

resolution of the crisis, immediate responses often remain part of the long-term policy response. Poorly chosen containment policies undermine the potential for successful long-term resolution. It is thus useful to recognize the context within which policy responses to financial crises occur.

For a subset of 42 well-documented systemic banking crisis episodes (in 37 countries), detailed data have been collected on crisis containment and resolution policies using a variety of sources, including IMF staff reports, World Bank documents, and working papers from central bank staff and academics. This section explains in detail the type of data collected, and defines the variables in the process, organized by the following categories: initial conditions, containment policies, resolution policies, macroeconomic policies, and outcome variables.

Overview and Initial Conditions

This section starts with information on the initial conditions of the crisis, including whether banking distress coincided with exchange rate pressures and sovereign debt-repayment problems, initial macroeconomic conditions, the state of the banking system, and institutional development of the country.

- CRISIS DATE is the starting date of the banking crisis, including year and month, when available. The timing of the banking crisis follows the approach described in the "Crisis Dates" section of this chapter.

- CURRENCY CRISIS indicates whether a currency crisis occurred during the period $t - 1$ through $t + 1$, where t denotes the starting year of the banking crisis. If the currency experiences a nominal depreciation of at least 30 percent that is also at least a 10 percentage point increase in the rate of depreciation in both years $t - 2$ and $t - 1$, with t the starting year of the banking crisis, year $t - 1$ is treated as the year of the currency crisis for the purposes of creating this variable. YEAR OF CURRENCY CRISIS is also listed.

- SOVEREIGN DEBT CRISIS indicates whether a sovereign debt crisis occurred during the period $t - 1$ through $t + 1$. YEAR OF SOVEREIGN DEBT CRISIS is also listed.

- This is followed by a brief description of the crisis, denoted as BRIEF DESCRIPTION OF CRISIS.

Information on the following macroeconomic variables was collected. Each of these variables are computed at time $t - 1$ using data from the IMF's *International Financial Statistics* (IFS) and *World Economic Outlook*.

- FISCAL BALANCE/GDP is the ratio of the general government balance to GDP for the precrisis year $t - 1$.[9]

- PUBLIC DEBT/GDP is the ratio of the general government gross debt to GDP for the precrisis year $t - 1$.

- INFLATION is the percentage increase in the consumer price index during the precrisis year $t - 1$.

- NET FOREIGN ASSETS (CENTRAL BANK) is the net foreign assets of the central bank in millions of U.S. dollars for the precrisis year $t - 1$.

- NET FOREIGN ASSETS/M2 is the ratio of net foreign assets (central bank) to broad money (M2) for the precrisis year $t - 1$.

---

[9] Whenever general government data were not available, central government data were used.

- DEPOSITS/GDP is the ratio of total deposits at deposit-taking institutions to GDP for the precrisis year $t - 1$.
- GDP GROWTH is real growth in GDP during the precrisis year $t - 1$.
- CURRENT ACCOUNT/GDP is the ratio of the current account to GDP for the precrisis year $t - 1$.

The following information was collected on the state of the banking system.

- PEAK NPL is the peak ratio of nonperforming loans to total loans (percent) during the years t through $t + 5$. This is an estimate using data from Honohan and Laeven (2005) and IMF staff reports. In all cases, the country's definition of nonperforming loans was used.
- GOVERNMENT OWNED is the percentage of banking system assets that are government owned in year $t - 1$. Data are from La Porta, Lopez-De-Silanes, and Shleifer (2002) and refer to the year 1980 or 1995, whichever is closer to the starting date of the crisis, t. When more recent data are available from IMF staff reports, such data is used instead.
- SIGNIFICANT BANK RUNS indicates whether the country's banking system experienced a depositors' run, defined as a one-month percentage drop in total outstanding deposits in excess of 5 percent during the period t through $t + 1$. This variable is constructed using data from the IMF's IFS.
- CREDIT BOOM indicates whether the country experienced a credit boom leading up to the crisis, defined as three-year precrisis average growth in private credit to GDP in excess of 10 percent per year, computed for the period $t - 4$ through $t - 1$. This variable is constructed using data from IFS.

As a proxy for institutional development, data were collected on the degree of protection of creditor rights in the country.

- CREDITOR RIGHTS is an index of protection of creditors' rights from Djankov, McLiesh, and Shleifer (2007). The index ranges from 0 to 4, and higher scores denote better protection of creditor rights. The score from year t is used.

Crisis Containment Policies

Initially, the government's policy options are limited to those policies that do not rely on the formation of new institutions or complex new mechanisms. Immediate policy responses include (1) suspension of convertibility of deposits, which prevents depositors from seeking repayment from banks; (2) regulatory capital forbearance,[10] which allows banks to avoid the cost of regulatory compliance (for example, by allowing banks to overstate their equity capital to avoid the costs of contractions in loan supply); (3) emergency liquidity support to banks; or (4) a

---

[10] Regulatory forbearance often continues into the resolution phase, though it is generally viewed as a crisis containment policy.

government guarantee of depositors. Each of these immediate policy actions are motivated by adverse changes in the condition of banks.

Banks suffering severe losses tend not only to see rising costs but also to experience liability rationing, either because they must contract deposits to satisfy their regulatory equity capital requirement, or because depositors at risk of loss prefer to place funds in more stable intermediaries. Banks, in turn, will transmit those difficulties to their borrowers in the form of a contraction of credit supply (Valencia, forthcoming). Credit will become more costly and financial distress of borrowers and banks more likely.

The appropriate policy response will depend on whether the trigger for the crisis is a loss of depositor confidence (causing a deposit run), regulatory recognition of bank insolvency, or the spillover effects of financial asset market disturbances outside the banking system, including exchange rate and wider macroeconomic pressures.

Deposit withdrawals can be addressed by emergency liquidity loans, usually from the central bank when market sources are insufficient, by an extension of government guarantees of depositors and other bank creditors, or by a temporary suspension of depositor rights in what is often called a bank holiday. Each of these techniques is designed to buy time, and the first two help to restore depositor confidence. The success of each technique will depend on the credibility and creditworthiness of the government.

Preventing the looting of an insolvent or near-insolvent bank requires a different set of containment tools. Administrative intervention, including the temporary assumption of management powers by a regulatory official, may be used. Alternatively, closure could be used, which could include the subsidized compulsory sale of a bank's good assets to a sound bank, together with the assumption by that bank of all or most of the failed entity's banking liabilities; or could simply consist of an assisted merger. The availability of the necessary legal powers is critical, given the incentive for bank insiders to hang on, as well as the customary cognitive gaps causing insiders to deny the failure of their bank.

Most complex of all are the cases in which disruption of banking is part of wider financial and macroeconomic turbulence. In this case, the bankers may be innocent victims of external circumstances, and special care is needed to ensure that regulations do not become part of the problem. Regulatory forbearance on capital and liquid reserve requirements may prove to be appropriate in these conditions.

Adopting the correct approach to an emerging financial crisis calls for a clear understanding of the underlying cause of the crisis, as well as a quick judgment of the likely effectiveness of the alternative tools that are available. The actions taken at this time will have a possibly irreversible impact on the ultimate allocation of losses in the system. In addition, the longer-term implications for future moral hazard need to be taken into account.

All too often, central banks favor stability over cost in the heat of the containment phase: if so, they may extend loans too liberally to an illiquid bank that is almost certain to prove insolvent anyway. Also, closure of a nonviable bank is often delayed for too long, even when there are clear signs of insolvency (Lindgren, 2005). Because bank closures face many obstacles, there is a tendency to rely instead on blanket government guarantees, which, if the government's fiscal and political position makes them credible, can work but at the cost of placing the burden on the budget, typically squeezing future provision of needed public services.

Information was collected on the following crisis containment policies.

First, information was collected on whether the authorities impose deposit freezes, bank holidays, or blanket guarantees to stop or prevent bank runs.

- DEPOSIT FREEZE indicates whether the authorities imposed a freeze on deposits. If a freeze on deposits was implemented, information is collected on the duration of the deposit freeze (in months), and the type of deposits affected.

- BANK HOLIDAY indicates whether the authorities installed a bank holiday. If a bank holiday was introduced, information is collected on its duration (in days).

- BLANKET GUARANTEE indicates whether the authorities introduced a blanket guarantee on deposits (and possibly other liabilities). If a blanket guarantee was introduced, information is collected on the date of introduction and the date of removal, and the duration of the guarantee is calculated (in months). Information is also collected on whether a previous explicit deposit insurance arrangement was in place at the time of the introduction of the blanket guarantee, the name of the administering agency of the blanket guarantee, and the coverage of the guarantee (deposits only or also other liabilities).

- TIMING OF FIRST BANK INTERVENTION indicates the date (month and year) that the authorities intervened for the first time in a bank.

- TIMING OF FIRST LIQUIDITY ASSISTANCE indicates the date (month and year) that the first loan under liquidity assistance was granted to a financial institution.

Next, information is collected on the timing and scope of emergency liquidity support to financial institutions.

- LIQUIDITY SUPPORT indicates whether emergency liquidity support, measured as claims from monetary authorities on commercial banks (IFS line 12E) to total deposits, was at least 5 percent and at least doubled with respect to the previous year during the period t through $t + 3$.

  Information is also collected on whether liquidity support was different across banks, or whether emergency lending was remunerated. If liquidity support was remunerated, information is collected on whether interest was at market rates.

  Information is also collected on the peak of liquidity support (as a percentage of deposits), computed as the maximum value (percent) of the ratio of claims from monetary authorities on commercial banks (IFS line 12E) to total deposits during the period t through $t + 3$.

- LOWERING OF RESERVE REQUIREMENTS denotes whether authorities lowered reserve requirements in response to the crisis.

Crisis Resolution Policies

Once emergency measures have been put in place to contain the crisis, the government faces the long-term challenge of crisis resolution, which means the resumption of a normally functioning credit system and legal system, and the rebuilding of banks' and borrowers' balance sheets.

At this point, the crisis has left banks and nonfinancial firms insolvent and many are in government ownership or under court or regulatory administration. Economic growth is unlikely to resume on a secure basis until productive assets and banking franchises are back in the hands of solvent private entities.

The financial and organizational restructuring of financial and nonfinancial firms during the crisis resolution phase is a large task, typically entailing much detailed implementation work in the bankruptcy courts, as well as the use of informal or ad hoc work-out procedures. There are also important trade-offs, such as that between speed and durability of the subsequent economic recovery on the one hand, and the fiscal costs on the other.

Crisis resolution involves inherently complicated coordination problems between debtors and creditors. The fate of an individual corporation or financial institution and the best course of action for its owners and managers will depend on the actions of many others and the general economic outlook. Because of these coordination problems, as well as a lack of capital and the importance of the financial system to economic growth, governments often take the lead in systemic restructuring, especially of the banking system. In the process, governments can incur large fiscal costs, presumably with the objective of accelerating recovery from the crisis.

The most-asked question arising at this time is whether an overindebted corporate entity should be somehow subsidized or forgiven some of its debt, or whether its assets should be transferred to a new corporate structure and new management. This question applies to undercapitalized banks and to overindebted nonbank corporations alike. The feasibility of making such decisions on a case-by-case basis becomes difficult during a systemic crisis resulting in thousands of insolvencies, so a systematic approach needs to be established. General principles have proved elusive and, as well as depending on the scale of the crisis and the quality of existing legal and other governance institutions, the best answer is likely to depend on the source of the crisis.

If the problem results from an economy-wide crash, the best prospect for future performance of banks and their borrowing customers may be with their existing owners and managers, given the information and other intangible forms of firm- or relationship-specific capital they possess. However, if bank insolvency has been the result of incompetent, reckless, or corrupt banking, or the use of government-controlled banks as quasi-fiscal vehicles or for political purposes, the relevant stock of information and relationship capital is unlikely to be of much social value. Therefore, separating the good assets from their current managers and owners offers better prospects in such circumstances and establishes a better precedent for avoiding moral hazard. Information capital is also likely to be relatively unimportant for real estate ventures, which have been central to many recent banking crises.

The main policy approaches used in the resolution phase of recent crises include (1) conditional government-subsidized, but decentralized, work-outs of distressed loans; (2) debt forgiveness; (3) the establishment of a government-owned asset management company to buy and resolve distressed loans; (4) government-assisted sales of financial institutions to new owners, typically foreign; and (5) government-assisted recapitalization of financial institutions through injection of funds. The latter three deal with bank insolvency, and are thus the focus here.

In an attempt to let the market determine which firms are capable of surviving if given some modest assistance, some official schemes have offered loan subsidies to distressed borrowers conditional on the borrowers' shareholders injecting some new capital. There have also been schemes offering injection of government capital funds for insolvent banks whose shareholders were willing to provide matching funds.

To the extent that they are discretionary, debt-relief schemes for bank borrowers carry the risk of moral hazard because debtors stop trying to repay in the hope of being added to the list of scheme beneficiaries.

Generalized forms of debt relief, such as are effectively provided by inflation and currency depreciation, can be regarded as relationship-friendly in the sense introduced above. Inflation is also a solution that reduces the budgetary burden. After all, if the crisis is big enough, the government's choices may be limited by what it can afford. Its capacity to subsidize borrowers or inject capital into banks is constrained by its ability over time to raise taxes or cut expenditure. These reasons are behind the inflationary solutions or currency devaluations that have been a feature of crises resolutions in the past. It amounts to generalized debt relief and a transfer of the costs of the crisis to money holders and other nominal creditors. In this case, the banks as well as the nonbank debtors receive relief without a climate of debtor delinquency being created. Of course, these are questions of monetary and macroeconomic policy as much as banking policy and must be considered in light of the need to preserve an environment of macroeconomic stability into the future.

In contrast, the carving out of an insolvent bank's bad loan portfolio, and its organizational restructuring under new management and ownership, represents the opposite pole, appropriate if large parts of the bank's information capital was dysfunctional. The bad loan portfolio may be sold back into the market, or disposed of by a government-owned asset management company (AMC). The effectiveness of government-run AMCs has been mixed: better if the assets to be disposed of have been primarily real estate, worse if loans to large, politically connected firms dominated (Klingebiel, 2000).

Government itself often retains control and ownership of troubled banks for much of the duration of the resolution phase. Regardless of whether control of the bank passes into public hands, it should eventually emerge, and it must be adequately capitalized. Depending on how earlier loss allocation decisions were made, the sums of money involved in the recapitalization of the bank so that it can safely be sold into private hands may be huge. Many governments have felt constrained by fiscal and monetary policy considerations from properly doing the financial restructuring. Putting the bank on a sound financial footing should be the priority. Without this, banks will be undercapitalized, whatever the accounts state, and will have an incentive to resume reckless behavior.

Countries typically apply a combination of resolution strategies, including both government-managed programs and market-based mechanisms (Calomiris, Klingebiel, and Laeven, 2005). Both depend for their success on efficient and effective legal, regulatory, supervisory, and political institutions. Furthermore, a lack of attention to incentive problems when designing specific rules governing financial assistance can aggravate moral hazard problems, especially in environments in which these institutions are weak, unnecessarily raising the costs of resolution. Accordingly, policymakers in economies with weak institutions should not expect to achieve the same level of success in financial restructuring as is achieved in more advanced economies, and they should design resolution mechanisms suited to their institutional capacity.

Information on the following crisis resolution policies was collected.

- FORBEARANCE indicates whether there is regulatory forbearance during the years t through $t + 3$. This variable is based on a qualitative assessment of information contained in IMF staff reports. As part of this assessment, information was also collected on whether banks were permitted to continue functioning despite being technically insolvent, and whether prudential regulations (such as for loan classification and loan loss provisioning) were suspended or not fully applied during the first three years of the crisis.

With regard to actual bank restructuring, information was collected on nationalizations, closures, mergers, sales, and recapitalizations.

- LARGE-SCALE GOVERNMENT INTERVENTION indicates whether there was large-scale government intervention in banks, such as nationalizations, closures, mergers, sales, and recapitalizations of large banks, during the years t through $t + 3$.

- INSTITUTIONS CLOSED indicates the share (percentage) of bank assets liquidated or closed during the years t through $t + 3$. Information is also collected on the number of banks in year t and the number of banks in year $t + 3$.

- BANK CLOSURES indicates whether banks were closed during the period t through $t + 3$. Information was also collected on the number of banks closed or liquidated during the period t through $t + 3$.

Information is collected separately on whether financial institutions other than banks were closed (OTHER FI CLOSURES), and on whether shareholders of closed institutions were made whole (SHAREHOLDER PROTECTION).

Information is also collected on whether banks were nationalized (NATIONALIZATIONS), merged (MERGERS), or sold to foreigners (SALES TO FOREIGNERS) during the period t through $t + 5$. For mergers, information was also collected on whether private shareholders or owners of banks injected capital, and for sales to foreigners information was collected on the number of banks sold to foreigners during the period t through $t + 5$.

Next, information is collected on whether a bank-restructuring agency (BANK RESTRUCTURING AGENCY) was set up to deal with bank restructuring, and whether an AMC (ASSET MANAGEMENT COMPANY) was set up to take over and manage distressed assets. If an AMC was set up, information is collected on whether it was centralized or decentralized, the entity in charge, its funding, and the type of assets transferred.

As part of crisis resolution, systemically important (or government-owned) banks are often recapitalized by the government.

- RECAPITALIZATION denotes whether banks were recapitalized by the government during the period t through $t + 3$.

  Banks can be recapitalized using a variety of measures. Information is collected on whether recapitalization occurred in the form of cash, government bonds, subordinated debt, preferred shares, purchase of bad loans, credit lines, assumption of bank liabilities, ordinary shares, or other means.

When available, information is also collected on the targeted recapitalization level of banks (expressed as a percentage of assets) and an estimate was made of the gross recapitalization cost (as a percentage of GDP) to the government during the period t through $t + 5$. The latter variable is denoted as RECAP COST (GROSS).

Next, information was collected on the recovery of recapitalization costs.

- RECOVERY denotes whether the government was able to recover part of the recapitalization cost.

- RECOVERY PROCEEDS denotes the recovery proceeds (as a percentage of GDP) during the period t through $t + 5$.

- RECAP COST (NET) denotes the net recapitalization cost to the government, expressed as a percentage of GDP, computed as the difference between the gross recapitalization cost and recovery proceeds.

For deposit insurance and depositor compensation, the following information was collected from Demirgüç-Kunt, Kane, and Laeven (2008) and IMF staff reports.

- DEPOSIT INSURANCE indicates whether an explicit deposit insurance scheme is in place at the start of the banking crisis. Note that deposit insurance arrangements put in place after the first year of the crisis are ignored.
- FORMATION reports the year that the deposit insurance scheme was introduced.
- COVERAGE LIMIT denotes the coverage limit (in local currency) of insured deposits at the start of the banking crisis. This variable is set to zero if there is no explicit deposit insurance.
- COVERAGE RATIO is the ratio of the coverage limit to per capita GDP at the start of the banking crisis. This variable is set to zero if there is no explicit deposit insurance.
- WERE LOSSES IMPOSED ON DEPOSITORS? denotes whether losses were imposed on depositors of failed banks, and if so, whether these losses were severe (implying large discounts and a substantial number of people affected) was reported.

Macroeconomic Policies

Governments also tend to change macroeconomic policy to manage banking crises and reduce the negative impact on the real sector. Therefore, in addition to crisis containment and resolution policies, information on monetary policy and fiscal stance during the first three years of the crisis is collected. Although these measures are somewhat crude, they serve the purpose of providing some understanding of the policy stance.

- MONETARY POLICY INDEX is an index of monetary policy stance during the years t through $t + 3$. The index indicates whether monetary policy is expansive (+1), if the average percentage change in reserve money during the years t through $t + 3$ is between 1 and 5 percent higher than during the years $t - 4$ through $t - 1$; contractive (−1), if the average percentage change in reserve money during the years t through $t + 3$ is between 1 and 5 percent lower than during the years $t - 4$ through $t - 1$; or neither (0).

    The average change in reserve money (in percent) during the years t through $t + 3$, where t denotes the starting year of the banking crisis, was also reported.

- FISCAL POLICY INDEX is an index of the fiscal policy stance during the years t through $t + 3$, where t denotes the starting year of the crisis. The index indicates whether fiscal policy is expansive (+1), if the average fiscal balance during the years t through $t + 3$ is less than −1.5 percent of GDP; contractionary (−1), if the average fiscal balance during the years t through $t + 3$ is greater than 1.5 percent of GDP; or neither (0).

    The average fiscal balance (as a percentage of GDP) during the years t through $t + 3$ is also reported.

Finally, whether an IMF program was put in place around the time of the banking crisis (IMF PROGRAM) is reported, including the year the program was put in place.

Outcome Variables

Information on fiscal costs and output losses, the outcome variables, was collected.

- FISCAL COST (NET) denotes the net fiscal cost, expressed as a percentage of GDP, during the period t through $t + 5$. The gross fiscal costs are also reported, as are the recovery proceeds during the period t through $t + 5$, which is the difference between the two. Fiscal cost estimates are from Hoelscher and Quintyn (2003), Honohan and Laeven (2005), IMF staff reports, and publications from national authorities and institutions.

- OUTPUT LOSS is computed by extrapolating trend real GDP, based on the trend in real GDP growth up to the year preceding the crisis, and taking the sum of the differences between actual real GDP and trend real GDP expressed as a percentage of trend real GDP for the period t through $t + 3$. A minimum of three precrisis real GDP growth observations were required to compute the trend real GDP numbers.[11]

DESCRIPTIVE STATISTICS

Appendix Table 2A.3 summarizes the data collected on crisis containment and resolution policies for a subset of 42 systemic banking crises. The crisis countries comprise Argentina (four crises), Bolivia, Brazil (two crises), Bulgaria, Chile, Colombia (two crises), Côte d'Ivoire, Croatia, the Czech Republic, the Dominican Republic, Ecuador, Estonia, Finland, Ghana, Indonesia, Jamaica, Japan, the Republic of Korea, Latvia, Lithuania, Malaysia, Mexico, Nicaragua, Norway, Paraguay, the Philippines, the Russian Federation, Sri Lanka, Sweden, Thailand, Turkey, Ukraine, the United Kingdom, the United States, Uruguay, Venezuela, and Vietnam. Note that the financial crises in the United Kingdom and the United States were ongoing at the time of writing of this chapter, so the analysis of crisis containment and resolution policies for these two countries is preliminary and incomplete.

The selection of crisis episodes was determined by the availability of detailed information on applicable policies. A variety of sources were relied upon, including IMF staff reports and working papers, World Bank documents, and central bank and academic publications. The exact sources of the data may be found in the electronic version of the database.[12]

---

[11] As a result, output loss estimates are not available for many transition economies that experienced crises in the early 1990s.

[12] The electronic version of the banking crisis database is available at http://www.imf.org/external/pubs/cat/longres.aspx?sk=22345.0. The electronic version also contains a slightly larger set of variables than described here, including a brief description of each crisis; the name of the administering agency of the blanket guarantee (if introduced) and the coverage of the guarantee; and the name of the entity in charge of the AMC (if set up), its funding, and the type of assets transferred to the AMC.

Initial Conditions

Table 2.2 reports summary statistics for the initial conditions variables. The data show that the selected banking crises tend to coincide with currency crises, whereas they rarely coincide with sovereign debt crises. In 55 percent of the cases, the banking crisis coincides with a currency crisis, but in only 11 percent of cases does the banking crisis coincide with a debt crisis.

Macroeconomic conditions are often weak before a banking crisis. Fiscal balances tend to be negative (–2.1 percent on average), current accounts tend to be in deficit (–3.9 percent), and inflation often runs high (137 percent on average) at the onset of the crisis. However, the role of macroeconomic fundamentals has evolved across generations of crises. Whereas crises such as those in Russia in 1998, Argentina in 2001, and most crises of the 1980s were precipitated by large macroeconomic imbalances, particularly unsustainable fiscal policies, the East Asian crises of the late 1990s had more to do with the maturity composition of debt and foreign exchange risk exposures, rather than the levels of public debt and the fiscal deficit.

Nonperforming loans tend to be high at the onset of a banking crisis, running as high as 75 percent of total loans and averaging about 25 percent of loans. It is not always clear, though, to what extent the sharp rise of nonperforming loans is caused by the crisis itself or whether it reflected the effects of the tightening of prudential requirements during the aftermath of the crisis. In Chile, for instance,

TABLE 2.2

Descriptive Statistics of Initial Conditions of Selected Banking Crises					
Variable	Number of crises	Mean	Standard deviation	Minimum	Maximum
Start year of banking crisis	42	1995	6.100	1980	2007
Currency crisis (Y/N)	42	0.548	0.504	0.000	1.000
Sovereign debt crisis (Y/N)	42	0.119	0.328	0.000	1.000
Fiscal balance/GDP (percent)	42	–0.021	0.045	–0.170	0.056
Debt/GDP (percent)	33	0.464	0.395	0.080	1.913
Inflation (percent)	41	1.371	4.862	–0.007	24.772
Net foreign assets/M2 (percent)	42	0.174	0.189	–0.351	0.576
Deposits/GDP (percent)	42	0.491	0.454	0.062	2.524
GDP growth (percent)	42	0.024	0.045	–0.098	0.100
Current account/GDP (percent)	41	–0.039	0.049	–0.249	0.025
Peak NPLs (percent of total loans)	40	0.252	0.155	0.040	0.750
Government-owned banks (percent of total assets)	42	0.309	0.245	0.000	0.920
Bank runs (Y/N)	42	0.619	0.491	0.000	1.000
Largest one-month drop in deposits to GDP (percent)	26	0.112	0.058	0.056	0.267
Credit boom (Y/N)	33	0.303	0.467	0.000	1.000
Annual growth in private credit to GDP before crisis (percent)	33	0.083	0.098	–0.199	0.341
Creditor rights (index)	41	1.780	1.129	0.000	4.000

Source: Authors' calculations.
Note: M2 = broad money; NPL = nonperforming loan.

nonperforming loans peaked at 36 percent of total loans only in 1986, several years after the start of the crisis. However, part of the unsound banking practices that led to the Chilean banking crisis was the existence of substantial connected loans, which ranged from 12 to 45 percent of banks' total loan portfolios (Sanhueza, 2001).

Government ownership of banks is common in crisis countries, with the government owning about 31 percent of banking assets on average. In many cases, government ownership may have become a vulnerability—problems at state-owned banks have been major contributors to the cost and unfolding of crises, with many exhibiting low asset quality before the onset of a crisis. In Uruguay, for instance, state-owned banks Republica and Hipotecario—accounting for 40 percent of the system's assets—exhibited nonperforming loans rates of 39 percent of total loans as of 2001, compared with 5.6 percent at private banks in Uruguay (IMF, 2003). In Turkey, duty losses at state-owned banks were estimated at 12 percent of GNP as early as in 1999, and state-owned bank Bapindo in Indonesia had experienced important losses as early as 1994, three years before the onset of its crisis (Enoch and others, 2001).

Bank runs are a common feature of banking crises, with 62 percent of crises experiencing momentary sharp reductions in total deposits. The largest one-month drop in the ratio of deposits to GDP for countries experiencing bank runs averaged about 11.2 percent, and was as high as 26.7 percent in one case. Severe runs are often system wide, but it is also common to observe a flight to quality within the system from unsound banks to sound banks, which implies no or moderate systemic outflows. During the Indonesian crisis in 1997, for instance, private national banks lost 35 trillion rupiah in deposits between October and December 1997, whereas state-owned banks and foreign and joint-venture banks gained 12 and 2 trillion rupiah, respectively (Batunanggar, 2002). A similar situation occurred in Paraguay following the interventions in the third and fourth largest banks and the uncovering of unrecorded deposits. Depositors migrated from these banks to those perceived as more solid.

Banking crises are also often preceded by credit booms, with rapid precrisis credit growth in about 30 percent of crises. Average annual growth in the ratio of private credit to GDP before the crisis was about 8.3 percent across crisis countries, and was as high as 34.1 percent in Chile. Credit booms were often preceded by financial liberalization processes, such as the one that led to the crisis in the Nordic countries in the 1990s (Drees and Pazarbasioglu, 1998).

Crisis-affected countries often suffer from weak legal institutions, rendering a speedy resolution of distressed assets hard to accomplish. Scores on the creditor rights index in the selected crisis countries averaged about 1.8, ranging from a low of 0 to a high of 4 (the maximum possible score).

In summary, initial conditions are important because they may shape the market's and policymakers' responses during the containment phase. If macroeconomic conditions are weak, policymakers have limited buffers to cushion the impact of the crisis, and the burden falls on the shoulders of containment and resolution policies. Moreover, sudden changes in market expectations may gather strength rapidly depending on how weak initial conditions in the country are, in particular, the macroeconomic setting, the institutional environment, and the banking sector.

Take, for instance, Turkey in 2000. The trigger of the crisis was the collapse of interbank loans from large banks to a few small banks on November 20, in particular to DemirBank, which depended greatly on overnight funding. Turkey was widely known to have macroeconomic vulnerabilities, with inflation hovering around 80 percent per year during the 1990s, high fiscal deficits, large public debt, high current account deficits, and a weak financial system. Banks had high exposures to the government through large holdings of public securities, and also had sizable maturity and exchange rate risk mismatches, making them highly vulnerable to market risk. When credit lines to DemirBank were cut, several small banks were forced to sell their government securities. This sell-off caused a sharp drop in the price of government securities and triggered panic among foreign investors, a reversal in capital flows, sharp increases in interest rates, and declines in the value of the Turkish lira. Within a few weeks of these developments, the Turkish government announced a blanket guarantee.

An opposite example is Argentina in 1995, where the contagion from the Tequila crisis was weathered successfully with a substantial consolidation of the banking sector and small fiscal costs, in large part due to robust macroeconomic performance during the preceding years.

Crisis Containment

Table 2.3 reports summary statistics for the crisis containment and resolution policies of the 42 selected banking crisis episodes.

The data show that emergency liquidity support and blanket guarantees are two commonly used containment measures. Extensive liquidity support was used in 71 percent of crises considered and blanket guarantees were used in 29 percent of crisis episodes. Deposit freezes and bank holidays to deal with bank runs were less frequently used. In this sample, only five cases (or 12 percent of episodes) used deposit freezes: Argentina in 1989 and 2001, Brazil in 1990, Ecuador in 1999, and Uruguay in 2002. In all but one case—Brazil in 1990—the deposit freeze was preceded by a bank holiday. Bank holidays were used in only 10 percent of crises and only in the cases mentioned above. In all episodes in which holidays and deposit freezes were used, bank runs occurred. Bank holidays typically do not last long, about five days on average. However, deposit freezes last much longer, up to 10 years in one case, and about 41 months on average. The longest freeze corresponded to the Bonex Plan implemented in Argentina in 1989.[13] After the conversion, the bonds traded with a discount of almost

---

[13] The freeze converted time deposits—except for the first US$500, special accounts such as charitable foundations, and funds meant to be used in tax or salary payments—into dollar-denominated bonds at the exchange rate prevailing on December 28, 1989. The measure was announced on January 1, 1990, after the exchange rate dropped from 1,800 to more than 3,000 australs per dollar between December 28 and 31, 1989.

TABLE 2.3

Descriptive Statistics of Crisis Resolution Policies of Selected Banking Crisis Episodes					
Variable	Number of crises	Mean	Standard deviation	Minimum	Maximum
Deposit freeze (Y/N)	42	0.119	0.328	0	1
Duration of deposit freeze (months)	5	40.600	46.030	6	120
Coverage of deposit freeze: time deposits only? (Y/N)	5	0.400	0.548	0	1
Bank holiday (Y/N)	42	0.095	0.297	0	1
Duration of bank holiday (days)	4	4.750	0.500	4	5
Blanket guarantee (Y/N)	42	0.286	0.457	0	1
Duration of guarantee (months)	14	53.071	33.992	11	109
Previous explicit deposit insurance arrangement (Y/N)	42	0.524	0.505	0	1
Liquidity support or emergency lending (Y/N)	42	0.714	0.457	0	1
Liquidity support different across banks? (Y/N)	18	0.500	0.514	0	1
Collateral required for liquidity provision	15	0.467	0.516	0	1
Collateral provided is remunerated (Y/N)	13	0.846	0.376	0	1
If remunerated, interest at market rates (Y/N)	11	0.636	0.505	0	1
Peak liquidity support (fraction of deposits)	41	0.277	0.497	0	3
Lowering of reserve requirements (Y/N)	41	0.366	0.488	0	1
Forbearance (Y/N)	42	0.667	0.477	0	1
Banks not intervened in despite being technically insolvent	37	0.351	0.484	0	1
Prudential regulations suspended or not fully applied	37	0.730	0.450	0	1
Large-scale government intervention in banks (Y/N)	42	0.857	0.354	0	1
Fraction of financial institutions closed	39	0.083	0.117	0	0.500
Bank closures (Y/N)	42	0.667	0.477	0	1
Other financial institution closures (Y/N)	34	0.500	0.508	0	1
Were shareholders made whole? (Y/N)	30	0.067	0.254	0	1
Nationalizations (Y/N)	42	0.571	0.501	0	1
Mergers (Y/N)	41	0.610	0.494	0	1
Did private bank shareholders inject fresh capital? (Y/N)	24	0.667	0.482	0	1
Sales to foreigners (Y/N)	37	0.514	0.507	0	1
Bank-restructuring agency (Y/N)	40	0.475	0.506	0	1
Asset management company (Y/N)	42	0.595	0.497	0	1
Centralized asset management company (Y/N)	25	0.840	0.374	0	1
Recapitalization of banks (Y/N)	42	0.762	0.431	0	1
Recap level (percent)	13	0.078	0.020	0.040	0.100
Recap cost to government (gross) (fraction of GDP)	32	0.078	0.096	0.002	0.373
Recovery of recap expense (Y/N)	31	0.516	0.508	0	1
Recovery proceeds (fraction of GDP)	31	0.019	0.053	0	0.279
Recap cost to government (net) (fraction of GDP)	32	0.060	0.079	0	0.373
Deposit insurance (Y/N)	42	0.524	0.505	0	1
Coverage limit to per capita GDP	35	1.142	1.730	0	7.180
Were losses imposed on depositors? (Y/N)	42	0.310	0.468	0	1
Monetary policy index	40	−0.050	0.815	−1	1
Change in reserve money (rate)	35	1.681	4.562	−0.070	20.47

(Continued)

TABLE 2.3 (*Continued*)

Variable	Number of crises	Mean	Standard deviation	Minimum	Maximum
Fiscal index	40	0.600	0.709	−1	1
Fiscal balance (share of GDP)	40	−0.036	0.030	−0.127	0.008
IMF program put in place (Y/N)	42	0.524	0.505	0	1
Fiscal cost net (share of GDP)	40	0.130	0.133	0	0.551
Gross fiscal cost (share of GDP)	40	0.157	0.150	0	0.568
Recovery of fiscal expense	40	0.027	0.048	0	0.261
Output loss (share of GDP)	40	0.201	0.260	0	0.977

Source: Authors' calculations.

two-thirds and recovered to about 50 percent within a few months. Similarly, in Ecuador, depositors received certificates of reprogrammed deposits, which traded at significant discounts depending on the perceived solvency of the issuing bank. Moreover, bank runs resumed as soon as the unfreezing began (Jacome, 2004). It seems that at least in these cases, deposit freezes were highly disruptive, imposing severe losses on depositors, and therefore should be considered only in extreme circumstances. Bank holidays, however, may be used to buy time until a clear strategy is laid out; they were also used in the United States during the Great Depression in the 1930s.

Unlike the Bonex Plan in Argentina in 1989 and the deposit freeze in Uruguay in 2002—both of which covered dollar-denominated time deposits at public banks—the other episodes in which this instrument was used also covered deposits other than time deposits. The 2001 freeze in Argentina, for example, began with the *corralito*, which limited withdrawals to up to US$250 a week, prohibited transfers abroad unless trade related, introduced marginal reserve requirements, and limited transactions that could reduce deposits. However, soon after the corralito, the *corralon* was implemented, which reprogrammed time deposits over a five-year horizon. Similarly, in Brazil in 1990, the freeze included M2 plus federal securities in the hands of the public, except balances below 50,000 Brazilian cruzados novos (NCz$) for checking accounts and NCz$25,000 for savings accounts or 20 percent of the balance (whichever was larger) for deposits in the overnight domestic debt market, and 20 percent of the balance for mutual funds. The broadest freeze recorded in the sample was implemented by Ecuador, and included savings deposits up to US$500, half of checking account balances, repurchase agreements, and all time deposits.

Blanket guarantees also tend to be in place for a long period, about 53 months on average. A blanket guarantee is another policy tool that—if successful—may buy some time for policymakers to implement a credible policy package. Using the data set presented in this chapter, Laeven and Valencia (2012) examine the effectiveness of blanket guarantees in restoring depositor confidence and find that they are often successful. However, they also find that outflows by foreign

TABLE 2.4

Selected Bank-Specific Guarantee Announcements		
Country	Date	Coverage
Chile	Jan. 1983	Explicit guarantee announced to depositors of intervened-in banks.
Czech Republic	Jun. 1996	Deposit insurance coverage was raised substantially (from 100,000 Czech koruny to 4,000,000 Czech koruny) for 18 banks that had entered restructuring programs.
Dominican Republic	Apr. 2003	In their intervention, the authorities announced that all legitimate deposits of Baninter would be honored with central bank certificates. Later, the same treatment was applied in the resolution of two other banks.
Lithuania	Dec. 1995	The government passed a law extending full coverage to two closed banks.
Paraguay	Jul. 1995	All recorded deposits in intervened in banks (unrecorded deposits were initially excluded, though in May 1996 a law was passed to compensate these, too).
United Kingdom	Sep. 2007	All liabilities of Northern Rock outstanding as of September16, 2007.

Sources: IMF Staff reports; and country authorities' reports.

creditors are virtually unresponsive to the announcement of such guarantees, despite being covered in most cases. They find that such guarantees tend to have high fiscal costs, confirming earlier results by Honohan and Klingebiel (2000), but argue that this correlation is driven mainly by the fact that guarantees are usually adopted in conjunction with extensive liquidity support and when crises are severe.

Peak liquidity support tends to be sizable and averaged about 28 percent of total deposits across the 42 crisis episodes considered. Liquidity support is clearly the most common first line of response in systemic crisis episodes, even in Argentina in 1995 when a currency board was in place. This was made possible by an amendment of the charter of the Central Bank of Argentina in February 1995, allowing it to lengthen the maturities of its swap and rediscount facilities, with the possibility of monthly renewal, and in amounts exceeding the net worth of the borrowing bank.

In severe crises, a positive correlation of about 30 percent between the provision of extensive liquidity support and the use of blanket guarantees is observed. Blanket guarantees are often introduced to restore confidence, even when previous explicit deposit insurance arrangements are already in place (this is so in about 52 percent of crises in which blanket guarantees are introduced). In some cases, guarantees were introduced to cover only a segment of the market, not all banks. Examples of such partial guarantees are provided in Table 2.4.

Crisis Resolution

Table 2.3 reports summary statistics for the crisis resolution policies of the 42 selected banking crisis episodes.

Regulatory forbearance is a common feature of crisis management. The policy objective aims at a gradual recovery of the banking system, or a gradual transitioning toward stricter prudential requirements. The latter is a common outcome whenever modifications to the regulatory framework are introduced. In Ecuador, for instance, banks were given two years to comply fully with new loan classification rules, among other requirements. In the 2001 crisis in Argentina, the authorities granted regulatory forbearance, which included a new valuation mechanism for government bonds and loans, allowing for gradual convergence to market value. Banks were also allowed to temporarily decrease their capital charge on interest rate risk, and losses stemming from court injunctions[14] could be booked as assets to be amortized over 60 months. Prolonged forbearance occurred in about 67 percent of crisis episodes. In 35 percent of the episodes, forbearance took the form of banks not being intervened despite being technically insolvent, and in 73 percent of cases prudential regulations were suspended or not fully applied.

Forbearance, however, does not really solve the problems; therefore, a key component of almost every systemic banking crisis is a bank-restructuring plan. In 86 percent of cases, large-scale government intervention in banks took place as bank closures, nationalizations, or assisted mergers. The system survived a crisis without having at least significant bank closures in only a handful of episodes. For instance, in Latvia, banks holding 40 percent of assets were closed, but no further intervention by the government was implemented. In Argentina, in the 1995 episode, 15 institutions ran into problems: 5 of them were liquidated (with 0.6 percent of the system's assets), 6 were resolved under a purchase and assumption scheme (with 1.9 percent of the system's assets), and 4 were absorbed by healthier institutions. However, a significant consolidation process also took place through 14 mergers involving 47 financial institutions. Shareholders often lost money when banks were closed and were often forced to inject new capital in the banks they owned.

Closures were not limited to banks but included nonbank financial institutions. In Thailand, for instance, the problem began with liquidity problems at finance companies as early as March 1997, and 56 finance companies (accounting for 11 percent of the financial system's assets) were closed. In Jamaica, a large component of the financial problem was in the insurance sector, whose restructuring cost reached 11 percent of GDP.

Sales to foreigners is often seen as a last resort before bank restructuring, though it has become common in recent crises. On average, sales of banks to foreigners occurred in 51 percent of the crisis episodes.

Bank closures seem to be associated with larger fiscal costs, with a positive correlation of 22 percent. However, bank closures are negatively associated with

---

[14] In 2002, the Argentine government introduced an asymmetric pesification of assets and liabilities of banks. However, the exchange rate used for deposits—1.4 Argentine pesos per US$1—was substantially below market rates. Depositors initiated legal proceedings and some obtained additional compensation through court injunctions.

the issuance of a blanket guarantee, with a correlation of –22 percent. Because guarantees entail a sizable fiscal contingency, once the guarantee is in place, governments may try to refrain from closing banks to avoid activating the guarantee. Bank closures also seem to be positively associated with peak nonperforming loans, with a correlation of about 25 percent. One potential contributing factor to this correlation is that once a bank is closed, its asset quality may deteriorate because in the process of closing, any value attached to bank relationships with customers may be destroyed. Borrowers may delay payments, or the collection of loans may become less effective than before, which may also contribute to higher fiscal costs.

Special bank-restructuring agencies are often set up to restructure distressed banks (in 48 percent of crises), and AMCs were set up in 60 percent of crises to manage distressed assets. AMCs tend to be centralized rather than decentralized. Examining the cases in which AMCs were used shows that the use of AMCs is positively correlated with peak nonperforming loans and fiscal costs, with correlation coefficients of about 15 percent in both cases. These correlations may suggest some degree of ineffectiveness in AMCs, at least in those episodes in which AMCs were established. In line with these simple correlations, Klingebiel (2000), who studied seven crises in which AMCs were used, concludes that they were largely ineffective.

Another important policy used in the resolution phase of banking crises is recapitalization of banks. In 33 out of the 42 selected crisis episodes, banks were recapitalized by the government. Recapitalization costs constitute the largest fraction of the fiscal costs of banking crises and takes many forms. In 12 crises, recapitalization took place in cash; in 14 crises, in government bonds; in 11 episodes subordinated debt was used; in 6 crises, preferred shares were used; in 7 crises, it took place through the purchase of bad loans; in 4 crises, the government purchased ordinary shares of banks; in 3 crises, the government assumed bank liabilities; and in 2 crises, a government credit line was extended to banks. In some cases, a combination of these methods was used. Recapitalization usually entails writing off losses against shareholders' equity and injecting either Tier 1 or Tier 2 capital or both. Recapitalization programs are usually accompanied by some conditionality. For instance, in Chile, a nonperforming loans purchase program was implemented, and during this period banks could not distribute dividends and all profits and recoveries had to be used to repurchase the loans. In Mexico, PROCAPTE (a temporary recapitalization program) had FOBAPROA (a deposit insurance fund) purchase subordinated debt from qualifying banks, but the resources had to be deposited at the central bank, bearing the same interest rate as the subordinated bonds. Banks could redeem the bonds if their capital adequacy ratio rose above 9 percent, but FOBAPROA had the option to convert the bonds into stocks after five years or if a bank's Tier 1 capital ratio fell below 2 percent.

Similar conditions were applied to recapitalization programs in Turkey in 2000 and Thailand in 1997. In the former, SDIF (the Turkish deposit insurance fund) matched owners' contributions to bring banks' Tier 1 capital to 5 percent, but only for banks with a market share of at least 1 percent. SDIF could also contribute to Tier 2 capital through subordinated debt, to all banks with Tier 1 capital greater or equal to 5 percent. Similar to Mexico, if Tier 1 capital fell below 4 percent, the subordinated debt would convert to stocks. In Thailand, the recapitalization plan involved Tier 1 capital injections, with the government matching private contributions and the requirement that the financial institution make full provisions up front, in line with new regulations. Additionally, the government and the new investors had the right to change the board of directors and management of each participating financial institution. The government also had the right to appoint at least one board member to each financial institution. The program also included Tier 2 capital injections equal to a minimum of the total writedown exceeding previous provisioning or 20 percent of the net increase in lending to the private sector, among other criteria.

On average, the net recapitalization cost to the government (after deducting recovery proceeds from the sale of assets) amounted to 6.0 percent of GDP across crisis countries in the sample, though in the case of Indonesia it reached as high as 37.3 percent of GDP.

It is interesting that about half the countries that experienced a systemic banking crisis had an explicit deposit insurance scheme in place at the outbreak of the crisis (and several countries adopted deposit insurance during the crisis). Losses were imposed on depositors in a minority of cases. Table 2.5 provides brief descriptions of those circumstances in which depositors faced losses. Simple correlations show that episodes in which losses were imposed on depositors faced higher output losses, with a correlation of about 8 percent.

Monetary policy tended to be fairly neutral during crisis episodes, whereas the fiscal stance tended to be expansive, arguably to support the financial and real sectors, and to accommodate bank-restructuring and debt-restructuring programs. On average, the fiscal balance was about –3.6 percent of GDP during the initial years of a banking crisis.

The IMF participated in programs in about 52 percent of the episodes considered.

Fiscal Costs and Real Effects of Banking Crises

Fiscal costs, net of recoveries, associated with crisis management can be substantial, averaging about 13.3 percent of GDP, and can be as high as 55.1 percent of GDP. Recoveries of fiscal outlays vary widely as well, with the average recovery rate reaching 18.2 percent of gross fiscal costs. Although countries that used AMCs seemed to achieve slightly higher recovery rates, the correlation is very small, at about 10 percent.

Finally, output losses (measured as deviations from trend GDP) of systemic banking crises can be large, averaging about 20 percent of GDP during the first four years of the crisis, and ranging from a low of 0 percent to a high of 98 percent of GDP.

TABLE 2.5

Episodes with Losses Imposed on Depositors			
Country	Crisis year	Loss severity	Description
Argentina	1989	Large	Bonex Plan converted time deposits into long-term bonds at an exchange rate below that prevailing on the market.
Argentina	2001	Large	Dollar deposits were converted into domestic currency at Arg$1.4, which was below the prevailing market rate.
Bolivia	1994	Minor to moderate	Large depositors of the two closed banks received as compensation non-interest bearing bonds.
Chile	1981	Minor to moderate	In 1983, depositors at banks forced into liquidation were paid 70 percent of face value.
Côte d'Ivoire	1988	Large	In the liquidation of BDN, 85 percent of depositors were compensated fully.
Ecuador	1998	Large	Frozen deposits were significantly eroded by accelerating inflation and depreciation of the currency, and some payments to depositors are still pending (despite the blanket guarantee)
Estonia	1992	Large	Depositors of Tartu Commercial Bank were partially paid.
Latvia	1995	Large	With the collapse of Baltija Bank the government compensated depositors for LVL 500 ($1,000) per depositor (LVL 200 in 1995 and LVL 100 over next three years).
Lithuania	1995	Minor to moderate	Depositors of Litimpex Bank had their deposits turned into equity. Furthermore, depositors of Innovation Bank received some cash (LTL 4,000 in 1997 and LTL 4,000 in 1998 per person) and the difference in five-year, non-interest-bearing government bonds; legal entities received ten-year, non-tradable, non-interest bearing notes for the entire claim; certain public organizations, embassies, charities, and the like received cash during 1998; other creditors received their pari passu share of residual funds left from collection of Innovation Bank's assets. Public sector deposits were written off.
Russia	1998	Minor to moderate	Some depositors (those whose savings were not transferred to Sberbank) sustained losses at insolvent banks. Even those who benefited from the transfer faced some losses because the exchange rate used in the transaction was less than half of the market exchange rate prevailing at the time.
Thailand	1997	Minor to moderate	Depositors of the closed finance companies received certificates yielding below-market interest rates.
Ukraine	1998	Large	Depositors were not fully compensated.
Venezuela	1994	Minor to moderate	Depositors at Banco Latino with more than 10 million bolivars received long-term nonnegotiable bonds with interest rate below market, for the amount exceeding the 10 million.

Sources: IMF staff reports; and country authorities' reports.
Note: Arg$ = Argentine peso; LTL = Lithuanian litas; LVL= Latvian lats.

GLOBAL LIQUIDITY CRISIS OF 2007–08

During the course of 2007, U.S. subprime mortgage markets melted down and global money markets were under pressure. The U.S. subprime mortgage crisis manifested itself first through liquidity issues in the banking system owing to a sharp decline in demand for asset-backed securities. Hard-to-value structured products and other instruments created during a boom of financial innovation had to be severely marked down because of the newly implemented fair value accounting and credit rating downgrades. Credit losses and asset writedowns worsened with declining house prices and accelerating mortgage foreclosures, which increased in late 2006 and degenerated further in 2007 and 2008. Profits at U.S. banks declined to $5.8 billion from $35.2 billion (83.5 percent) during the fourth quarter of 2007 compared with the previous year as a result of provisions for loan losses. As of August 2008, subprime-related and other credit losses or writedowns by global financial institutions stood at about US$500 billion.

This section briefly compares the ongoing global liquidity crisis and its policy responses to the other crises included in the database. Given that the global liquidity crisis is still very much unfolding at the time of this writing, this analysis is obviously preliminary and incomplete.

Initial Conditions

The underlying causes of the global 2007–08 financial crisis are still being debated, and most likely can be attributed to a combination of factors. However, from the perspective of describing its initial conditions, it is useful to classify the underlying factors into two groups: macroeconomic and microeconomic.

The macroeconomic context is characterized by a prolonged period of excess global liquidity induced, in part, by relatively low interest rates set by the U.S. Federal Reserve Bank and other central banks following the 2001 recession in the United States. The excess liquidity fueled domestic demand, particularly residential investment, triggering a significant increase in house prices, which more than doubled in nominal terms between 2000 and mid-2006.[15] During this period, the U.S. economy faced high current account deficits, reaching 7 percent of GDP in the last quarter of 2005, induced primarily by household expenditure but also by sizable fiscal deficits.

However, microeconomic factors related to financial regulation (and lack thereof) and industry practices by financial institutions also appear to have played a crucial role in the buildup of the bubble. The "originate-and-distribute" lending model (see Bhatia 2007 for a description) adopted by many financial institutions during this period seems to have exacerbated the problem. Under this approach, banks made loans primarily to sell them on to other financial institutions, which, in turn, would pool them to issue asset-backed securities. The underlying rationale for these loan sales was to transfer risk to the ultimate buyer of the security backed by the underlying mortgage loans. These securities could then be pooled again and new instruments would be created and so forth.

A mispricing of risk of mortgage-backed securities linked to subprime loans led the market to believe that there was an arbitrage opportunity. This market perception fueled demand for these instruments and contributed to a deterioration in underwriting standards by banks in an attempt to increase the supply of loans to meet the demand for securitized instruments. Regulatory oversight

---

[15] Measured as the percentage change in the Case-Shiller 20-city composite index between January 2000 and its peak in July 2006.

missed the buildup of vulnerabilities induced by this process because the risks were being transferred to the unregulated segment of the market. The premise was that heavily regulated banks would only be originators, and the ultimate holders of securities were beyond the scope of regulation. In this process, however, spill-over effects and systemic risks seem to have been neglected by regulators, and the regulated segment ended up being significantly affected. The crisis reached a global dimension as it became apparent that foreign banks, mainly European, had also played a significant role in the demand for mortgage-related (particular sub-prime mortgage–linked) securities. For U.K. banks, this shock coincided with a homegrown house price bubble.

In addition to a move toward the originate-and-distribute lending model, many banks, particularly in the United Kingdom, increasingly relied on wholesale funding. As the crisis unfolded, banks that relied heavily on wholesale markets for their funding, such as Northern Rock in the United Kingdom, were hit particu-larly badly, causing stress in global money markets. Given ongoing concerns with counterparty risk, notably regarding adequacy of banks' capital, money market strains have continued.

At first glance, the buildup of this crisis episode in the United States and the United Kingdom does not seem to differ significantly from the traditional boom-bust cycles observed in the other crisis countries in this database. Many of these historical crisis episodes experienced buildups of asset price bubbles, especially real estate bubbles, often originating from financial liberalization. In many cases, deregulation of financial systems led to rapid expansion of credit, but with deficiencies in risk management and pricing as the financial system was evolving and prone to abuse. In the United States, it was not financial liberalization in the conventional sense, but innovation of financial instruments that the market and regulators did not fully understand. Supported by these new financial products and asset securitization, mortgage credit markets expanded rapidly but then virtually collapsed in some segments as the financial crisis unfolded. In 30 percent of the episodes included in the database in this chapter, the crisis was preceded by a credit boom. In the United States and the United Kingdom, however, although credit rose rapidly—mortgage lending, in particular—the pace of expansion did not satisfy the criteria to be labeled as a credit boom in this chapter.

What is different from many previous financial crises, especially in developing countries, is that the United States and the United Kingdom have thus far not suffered from a sudden stop of capital flows, which has caused major economic stress in other countries. The dollar did depreciate against the euro in the years preceding the 2007 turmoil, but demand for U.S. assets did not contract sharply, possibly because of the dollar's use as a reserve currency. Also, the speed and breadth with which stress in U.S. mortgage markets spread to other continents, financial institutions (especially securities firms), and financial markets (notably money markets) seem to have been fueled by uncertainty about the unfolding of the subprime crisis, as it became more clear that risk had been mispriced and exposures had not been transparent.

Containment

Average house prices in the United States reached a peak in mid-2006 and began to decline after the initial signs that a financial crisis could be around the corner. Losses at financial institutions began to appear as early as February 2007 with HSBC Finance, the U.S. mortgage unit of HSBC, reporting more than US$10 billion in losses from its U.S. mortgage lending business. Bad news continued in April 2007 with the bankruptcy filing of New Century Financial, one of the biggest subprime lenders in the United States, followed by the rescue of two Bear Stearns hedge funds in June 2007. Problems intensified when, on August 16, 2007, Countrywide Financial, the largest mortgage lender in the United States, ran into liquidity problems because of the decline in value of securitized mortgage obligations, triggering a deposit run on the bank. The Federal Reserve Bank "intervened" by lowering the discount rate by 0.5 percentage point and by accepting $17.2 billion in repurchase agreements for mortgage-backed securities to aid in liquidity. On January 11, 2008, Bank of America bought Countrywide for US$4 billion. Up to this point, containment policy in the United States was limited to alleviating liquidity pressures through the use of existing tools.

During this time, the United Kingdom experienced its own banking sector problems, in light of tight conditions in money markets. In September 2007, Northern Rock, a mid-sized U.K. mortgage lender, received a liquidity support facility from the Bank of England, following funding problems related to turmoil in the credit markets caused by the U.S. subprime mortgage financial crisis. Starting on September 14, 2007, Northern Rock experienced a bank run, until a government blanket guarantee—covering only Northern Rock—was issued on September 17, 2007. The run on Northern Rock highlighted weaknesses in the U.K. financial sector regulatory framework, including the maintenance of adequate capital by financial institutions, bank resolution procedures, and deposit insurance (IMF, 2008). Commercial banks in the United States did not seem to have experienced runs among retail customers, but as mentioned earlier, many institutions faced significant stress in wholesale markets. The blanket guarantee issued on Northern Rock was perhaps the first significant step away from the usual tools used to resolve liquidity problems. However, unlike in other episodes in which blanket guarantees were used, it was introduced at an early stage. In the sample in this chapter, 29 percent of episodes used a blanket guarantee. However, in the majority of them, they were put in place in the midst of a financial meltdown.[16] In the Asian countries, for instance, blanket guarantees were announced when markets were under significant stress and the crisis was already of systemic proportions with widespread runs throughout the financial system.

The next significant policy measure adopted by authorities in both countries was an increase in the range of tools available to provide liquidity. The Federal

---

[16] Mexico is one example in which an implicit blanket guarantee was already in place before the crisis, beginning end-1993. However, the guarantee was reaffirmed at end-1994, during the burst of the Tequila crisis.

Reserve introduced the Term Securities Lending facility in March 2008 by which it could lend up to US$200 billion of treasury securities to primary dealers secured for a term of 28 days (rather than overnight, as in the program in place at the time) by a pledge of other securities, including federal agency debt, federal agency residential mortgage-backed securities (MBS), and nonagency AAA/Aaa-rated private-label residential MBS. Similarly, it increased its currency swap lines with other central banks in an attempt to reestablish calm in money markets. The Bank of England took similar steps on April 21, 2008, when it announced it would accept a broad range of MBS under the new Special Liquidity Scheme and swap those for government paper for a period of one year to aid banks with liquidity problems. The new scheme enabled banks to temporarily swap high-quality but illiquid mortgage-backed assets and other securities. These steps are common measures in other documented episodes. Central banks usually increase the tools for providing the system with additional liquidity at both longer and more flexible terms.

Following the Fed's announcement of the expansion of liquidity facilities, a major event took place: the collapse of Bear Stearns, the fifth largest investment bank at the time. Mounting losses caused by its mortgage exposure triggered a run on the bank requiring emergency financial assistance from the government. Bear Stearns was to be purchased by JP Morgan Chase with federal guarantees on its liabilities in March 2008. It was a controversial measure because Bear Stearns was not subject to regulation by the Fed, yet the Fed's guarantee on its liabilities was crucial to prevent Bear Stearns' bankruptcy. To some extent the case is similar to the failures of Sanyo Securities and Yamaichi Securities in the Japanese crises (Nakaso, 2001). Neither fell under the scope of the deposit insurance system but were supervised by the Ministry of Finance. However, the collapse of Sanyo caused the first default ever in the Japanese interbank market, resulting in a sharp deterioration in market sentiment. However, Yamaichi was unwound gradually. Because of large counterparty risks, it was believed that an intervention was justified in the case of Bear Stearns, perhaps to avoid a disruption similar to the one that followed the collapse of Sanyo. Although there was no explicit blanket guarantee announced for Bear Stearns, there was a de facto protection of all its creditors. Shareholders of Bear Stearns, however, suffered significant losses.

The containment measures used thus far by U.S. and U.K. authorities to deal with the ongoing financial turmoil were not that different from those used in previous crisis episodes. Almost all crises have used generous liquidity support to deal with illiquid banks. What is different in this episode is that liquidity support has been extended not only to commercial banks but also to investment banks. Blanket guarantees are also not uncommon, although thus far they have mainly been used in developing countries to deal with systemic financial crises in which depositors have lost confidence in the ability of banks to repay depositors.

Resolution

As of the time of this writing, it is too early to discuss how exactly the crisis will be resolved because it is still ongoing and its consequences have not fully materialized. However, some insights can be extracted from the events that have taken place so far.

The vast majority of bank failures observed in the United States since the start of the crisis have been handled through traditional purchase and assumption schemes. This, of course, is no different from what has been done in bank failures in the past. A large fraction of failures included in the database were handled this way, with only 31 percent of episodes imposing losses on depositors.

The most notable failures so far, however, have been those of three major U.S. investment banks: Bear Stearns, Lehman Brothers, and Merrill Lynch. Bear Stearns collapsed on March 16, 2007, after facing major liquidity problems, and was sold to JP Morgan Chase after the Federal Reserve Bank of New York agreed to take over Bear Stearns' US$30 billion portfolio of MBS. Lehman Brothers filed for Chapter 11 bankruptcy protection on September 14, 2008, after failed attempts to sell the bank to private parties. Merrill Lynch was acquired by Bank of America on September 15, 2008.

Another significant event was the placement under conservatorship of Fannie Mae and Freddie Mac, the two largest U.S. housing government-sponsored entities (GSEs). As part of the plan announced on September 7, 2008, the Federal Housing Finance Authority (FHFA) was granted direct oversight of the GSEs, the U.S. Treasury was given authority to inject capital into the GSEs in the form of senior preferred shares and warrants (while dividends on existing common and preferred stock were suspended), and senior management and the boards of directors at both enterprises were dismissed. Effectively, this resulted in nationalization of the two entities. The treasury was also granted temporary authority to purchase agency-backed MBSs, and a short-term credit facility was established for the housing GSEs. The rescue of Fannie and Freddie came shortly after legislation was approved in late July 2008 that gave the U.S. Treasury the power to use public funds to recapitalize them. The bill also contained a tax break of as much as $7,500 for first-time homebuyers, created a new regulator to oversee Fannie Mae and Freddie Mac, and allowed the federal government to insure up to US$300 billion in refinanced mortgages. These measures came after severe declines in the stock prices of Fannie and Freddie following market perceptions of a significant capital shortfall.

Recapitalization measures have been widely used, with 76 percent of episodes in the data set implementing them, but in most cases such measures were implemented only after major insolvency problems at banks. In the United States, gross recapitalization costs reached, as of 2012, 4.5 percent of GDP while those for the United Kingdom, 8.8 percent of GDP.

The crisis at Northern Rock, which was triggered by illiquidity, but in which solvency concerns led to a loss of depositor confidence, was contained at first through a government guarantee on deposits, but when a private sector solution on acceptable terms was not identified by the government, the bank was nationalized on February 22, 2008. Nationalizations are last-resort measures commonly used in previous crises, with 57 percent of episodes in the sample using them. However, they have been more common in developing countries where it may be hard to find new owners for failed banks. In developed economies such as the United Kingdom, where capital is abundant, nationalizations are rare and generally considered something to be avoided. Other U.K. banks that have reported major losses have sought private sector solutions to restore bank capital, mostly by attracting new capital from existing shareholders through rights issues, but also through asset sales and reductions in dividends. Another mortgage lender that experienced stress, Alliance & Leicester, was bought in July 2008 by the Spanish bank Banco Santander.

A noteworthy difference from previous crisis episodes is the role that sovereign wealth funds have played in the 2007–09 crisis in providing new capital to restore the health of banks' capital positions. Globalization in conjunction with asset securitization provided an international dimension to this crisis by allowing many investors around the world to take a piece of the U.S. mortgage pie. Sovereign wealth funds injected capital in major banks in both the United States and the United Kingdom as part of their recapitalization efforts.

CONCLUSION

This chapter presents a new database of information on the timing and resolution of banking crises. The data show that fiscal costs associated with banking crises can be substantial and that output losses are large. Although countries have adopted a variety of crisis management strategies, emergency liquidity support and blanket guarantees have frequently been used to contain crises and restore confidence, though not always with success.

Policy responses to financial crises normally depend on the nature of the crises, and some unsettled issues remain. First, fiscal tightening may be needed when unsustainable fiscal policies are the trigger of the crises, though crises are typically attacked with expansionary fiscal policies. Second, tight monetary policy could help contain financial market pressures. However, in crises characterized by liquidity and solvency problems, the central bank should stand ready to provide liquidity support to illiquid banks. In the event of systemic bank runs, liquidity support may need to be complemented by depositor protection (including through a blanket government guarantee) to restore depositor confidence, although such accommodative policies tend to be very costly and will not necessarily speed up economic recovery. All too often, intervention is delayed because regulatory forbearance and liquidity support are used for too long to deal with insolvent financial institutions in the hope that they will recover, ultimately increasing the stress on the financial system and the real economy.

The preliminary analysis based on partial correlations indicates that some resolution measures are more effective than others in restoring the banking system to health and containing the fallout on the real economy. Above all, speed appears of the essence. As soon as a large part of the financial system is deemed insolvent and has reached systemic crisis proportions, bank losses should be recognized, the scale of the problem should be established, and steps should be taken to ensure that financial institutions are adequately capitalized. A successful bank recapitalization program tends to be selective in its financial assistance to banks, specifies clear quantifiable rules that limit access to preferred stock assistance, and enacts capital regulation that establishes meaningful standards for risk-based capital. Government-owned AMCs appear largely ineffective at resolving distressed assets, largely because of political and legal constraints.

Next, the adverse impact of the stress on the real economy needs to be contained. To relieve indebted corporations and households from financial stress and restore their balance sheets to health, intervention in the form of targeted debt-relief programs for distressed borrowers and corporate restructuring programs appear most successful. Such programs typically require public funds, and tend to be most effective when they are well targeted with adequate safeguards attached.

Future research based on this data set needs to discuss in more detail how policymakers should respond to financial system stress in a way that ensures that the financial system is restored to health while containing the fallout on the economy. Such research should establish to what extent fiscal costs incurred by accommodative policy measures (such as substantial liquidity support, explicit government guarantees, and forbearance from prudential regulations) help to reduce output losses and to accelerate the speed of economic recovery, and identify crisis resolution policies that mitigate moral hazard problems.

APPENDIX TABLE 2A.1

Timing of Systemic Banking Crises

Country	Systemic banking crisis (starting date)	Share of NPLs at peak (%)	Gross fiscal cost (% of GDP)	Output loss (% of GDP)	Minimum real GDP growth rate (%)	Comments
Albania	1994	26.8	—	—	−7.2	Rapid growth in NPLs, reaching 26.8 percent of total loans in 1994, following the creation of a two-tier commercial banking system in 1992.
Algeria	1990	30	—	6.7	−2.1	In 1989, five government-owned banks were granted managerial and financial autonomy from the central government. In the transition to a market economy, NPLs (about 30 percent of total loans) created problems for some banks in 1990, and the central bank had to provide discount financing to these banks.
Argentina	1980	9	55.1	10.8	−5.7	In March 1980, a number of financial institutions were forced to rely heavily on central bank financial assistance when faced with deposit withdrawals. Failed institutions included the largest investment bank and the second largest private commercial bank. More than 70 institutions (accounting for 16 percent of commercial bank assets and 35 percent of finance company assets) were liquidated or subjected to intervention between 1980 and 1982.
Argentina	1989	27	6	10.7	−7.0	During the 1980s, a decline in the availability of external resources led to increased recourse to domestic financing. To fund its credit operations the central bank imposed reserve and investment requirements on deposits. They were replaced by frozen deposits at the central bank in August 1988. Central bank debt grew through the issuance of short-term paper (CEDEPS) to financial entities for purposes of monetary control. The central bank accelerated its placement of CEDEPS, which by midyear were being issued to finance interest payments on the central bank's own debt. By mid-1989 the quasi-fiscal deficit of the central bank reached almost 30 percent of GDP, although most of it was reversed by year-end. On January 1, 1990, the government announced the bond conversion of time deposits and public sector debt coming due in 1990 (Bonex 89). The central bank kept liquidity tight and by end-February interest rates reached more than 1,000 percent a month for seven-day term deposits.
Argentina	1995	17	2	7.1	−2.8	After the Mexican devaluation, a small bond trader experienced a liquidity squeeze pushing it to closure by mid-January 1995. This development persuaded most banks to cut credit to bond traders, which, in turn, affected banks with large bond and open trading positions. Furthermore, provincial banks were having difficulties raising funds and people started moving funds to larger banks, particularly foreign banks that were perceived as more solvent, and by March 1995 capital flight intensified. Several measures were implemented to alleviate liquidity pressures. Eight banks were suspended and three banks collapsed. Out of the 205 banks in existence as of end-1994, 63 exited the market through mergers, absorptions, or liquidation by end-1997.

Country	Year					Description
Argentina	2001	20.1	9.6	42.7	−10.9	In March 2001, a bank run began caused by increasing doubts about the sustainability of the currency board, strong opposition from the public to the new fiscal austerity package sent to the Congress, the resignation of the president of the central bank, and the amendment to the convertibility law (change in parity from being pegged to the U.S. dollar, to being pegged to a basket composed of the U.S. dollar and the euro). During the second half of 2001, bank runs intensified. On December 3, 2001, as several banks were on the verge of collapsing, partial withdrawal restrictions (*corralito*) were imposed on transactional accounts while fixed-term deposits (CDs) were reprogrammed (*corralon*) to stop outflows from banks. On February 4, 2002, bank assets were asymmetrically pesified, adversely affecting the solvency of the banking system. In 2002, two voluntary swaps of deposits for government bonds were offered but received little interest by the public. In December 2002, the corralito was lifted. By August 2003, one bank had been closed, three banks nationalized, and many others had reduced their staff and branches.
Armenia	1994	—	—	—	3.3	Starting in August 1994, the central bank closed half of active banks. Large banks continued to suffer from high NPLs. The savings banks were financially weak.
Azerbaijan	1995	—	—	—	−13.0	Twelve private banks were closed; three large state-owned banks were deemed insolvent; one large state-owned bank faced serious liquidity problems.
Bangladesh	1987	20	—	34.7	2.4	In 1987, four banks accounting for 70 percent of credit had NPLs of 20 percent. From the late 1980s, the entire private and public banking system was technically insolvent.
Belarus	1995	—	—	—	−11.3	Many banks were undercapitalized; forced mergers burdened some banks with poor loan portfolios.
Benin	1988	80	17	1.9	−2.8	All three commercial banks collapsed.
Bolivia	1986	30	—	0	−2.6	Five banks were liquidated. Banking system NPLs reached 30 percent in 1987; in mid-1988 reported arrears stood at 92 percent of commercial banks' net worth.
Bolivia	1994	6.2	6	0	4.4	Two banks with 11 percent of banking system assets were closed in 1994. In 1995, 4 of 15 domestic banks, accounting for 30 percent of banking system assets, experienced liquidity problems and suffered high NPLs.
Bosnia and Herzegovina	1992	—	—	—	−6.4	Banking system suffered from high NPLs caused by the breakup of the former Yugoslavia and the civil war.
Brazil	1990	—	0	12.2	−4.2	Deposits were converted to bonds. Liquidity assistance was provided to public financial institutions.

(Continued)

TABLE 2A.1 (*Continued*)

Country	Systemic banking crisis (starting date)	Share of NPLs at peak (%)	Gross fiscal cost (% of GDP)	Output loss (% of GDP)	Minimum real GDP growth rate (%)	Comments
Brazil	1994	16	13.2	0	2.1	The Brazilian economy entered a new phase with the implementation of the "Plan *Real*" in July 1994. The plan triggered major structural changes, which aimed primarily at lowering inflation. With this process, remonetization of the economy took place and with it, liabilities and assets of banks expanded rapidly—loans to the private sector grew by 60 percent during the first year of the plan—despite higher reserve requirements. At the same time, a sharp deterioration in the trade account took place, to which the central bank responded by raising interest rates and imposing credit restrictions. The financial situation of banks weakened as bad loans increased noticeably and also because the banks lost their inflation revenues. The problems were particularly acute at public banks. For federal banks, the ratio of loans in arrears and in liquidation to total loans increased from 15.4 percent in June 1994 to 22.4 percent at end-1995, and to slightly more than 30 percent in October 1996. For government-owned banks, the ratio increased from 8 percent to almost 12 percent and more than 14 percent for the same dates. For privately held banks, the ratio increased from 5 percent in June 1994 to 9 percent in December 1995. The problems in the banking sector triggered a restructuring of government-owned banks and the resolution of private institutions. Most of the closures were small to medium banks, while large banks were resolved under a "good bank/ bad bank" approach, which separating the performing assets, good bank, from the rest, bad bank.
Bulgaria	1996	75	14	1.3	−8.0	The 1996 banking crisis had its roots in bad loans made during 1991–95, but the deepening insolvency of the system was not reflected in sustained liquidity problems until the second half of 1994. Two ailing state banks required ongoing refinancing from the Bulgarian National Bank (BNB) and the State Savings Bank (SSB) until they were bailed out in mid-1995. The public began to lose confidence in banks after the collapse of pyramid schemes in some cities, and in response to reports about the ill health of other banks. In late 1995, withdrawals of deposits, especially from First Private Bank (the largest private bank), were reflected in substantial BNB refinancing and falling foreign reserves. By early 1996, the sector had a negative net worth equal to 13 percent of GDP. The banking system experienced a run in early 1996. The government then stopped providing bailouts, prompting the closure of 19 banks accounting for one-third of sector assets. Surviving banks were recapitalized by 1997.

Country	Year				Description
Burkina Faso	1990	16	—	45.2	−0.6	In 1989, the system of sectoral credit ratios was abolished, and deposit and lending rates were partially liberalized. During 1990, the financial condition of the banking sector deteriorated sharply. NPLs increased to 23 percent of total credit, and commercial banks' deposits in the money market declined sharply. Three major commercial banks urgently needed restructuring, and two other large banks continued to experience liquidity problems. In 1991, the government merged these three major commercial banks into one bank with minority government participation and rehabilitated the two other banks, while assuming their nonperforming assets.
Burundi	1994	25	—	66.3	−8.0	In 1995 one bank was liquidated.
Cameroon	1987	65	—	118.1	−7.9	Five commercial banks were closed and three banks were restructured.
Cameroon	1995	30	—	0	3.3	Three banks were restructured and two were closed.
Cape Verde	1993	30	—	0	6.7	In 1993, the former monobank was split into a central bank and a commercial bank with 90 percent of banking system deposits. The commercial bank had accumulated a large fraction of nonperforming assets and was recapitalized by the government in 1994 by converting its portfolio of NPLs into interest-bearing notes equivalent to 17.5 percent of GDP. All commercial banking interest rates were liberalized in 1994, with the exception of one benchmark interest rate on time deposits.
Central African Republic	1976	—	—	0	2.5	Four banks were liquidated.
Central African Republic	1995	40	—	1.1	−8.1	The two largest banks, accounting for 90 percent of assets, were restructured.
Chad	1983	—	—	0	5.3	All banking offices closed in 1979 and 1980 when N'Djamena was the scene of heavy fighting. The banking sector experienced solvency problems. With the collapse of world cotton prices in 1985, Cotontchad's revenues dropped, and foreign exchange flowing into Chad declined. As a result, the Bank of Central African State's (BEAC's) exchange reserves dropped precipitously in 1986. Operations in the banking sector ground to a halt as Cotontchad fell into arrears on repayments of its short-term debt. In late 1986, the BEAC negotiated a rescheduling of some three-fourths of the short-term debt, allowing a ten-year maturity, including a five-year grace period with an interest rate of 6 percent. In 1983, the government imposed a five-year moratorium that froze all deposits and outstanding credits before 1980. The moratorium's purpose was to prevent a run on banks and to staunch capital flight when banks restored operations in early 1983 under the new government.

(Continued)

TABLE 2A.1 (Continued)

Country	Systemic banking crisis (starting date)	Share of NPLs at peak (%)	Gross fiscal cost (% of GDP)	Output loss (% of GDP)	Minimum real GDP growth rate (%)	Comments
Chad	1992	35	—	37.2	−2.1	The Chadian banking system came close to collapse in 1992, owing mainly to the vulnerable state of the economy and an expansionary credit policy. To avoid a major financial crisis, the monetary authorities embarked on a comprehensive rehabilitation program of the banking system, involving enhancement of central bank supervision through the Commission Bancaire de l'Afrique Centrale, and the liberalization of banking activity. In addition, they eased the liquidity crisis of the commercial banks in 1993 by consolidating into a long-term loan to the government the rediscounted commercial bank loans that had been extended mainly to public enterprises. Credit policy was tightened; the amount of direct advances to the treasury by the central bank was stabilized; and the Banque Internationale pour le Commerce et l'Industrie du Tchad was liquidated. As a result, the net foreign assets position of the banking system was strengthened and the liquidity position of the banks was gradually restored.
Chile	1976	—	—	0	3.5	Entire mortgage system was insolvent.
Chile	1981	35.6	42.9	92.4	−13.6	By the end of 1981, a six-year expansionary period ended abruptly. High international interest rates, a world recession, lower copper prices, and an abrupt cut of voluntary foreign credit to Latin America pushed Chile into a costly economic crisis. The problems were aggravated by unsound financial practices among banks, which included substantial connected lending ranging from 12 percent to 45 percent of the total loans portfolio. The financial system was affected in two waves. The first wave in 1981–82 included 11 liquidations (banks and finance companies), and all depositors were protected. The second wave was in 1983 and involved liquidations and rehabilitations. For the liquidations, domestic depositors were compensated only partially. Although foreign creditors were offered the same compensation, they threatened to cut trade credit lines and their claims were ultimately restructured under the external debt-restructuring plan.
China	1998	20	18	36.8	7.6	At the end of 1998, China's four large state-owned commercial banks, accounting for 68 percent of banking system assets, were deemed insolvent. Banking system NPLs in 2002 and 2003 were 20 percent and 15 percent, respectively, of total loans. The restructuring costs are estimated to have reached about 1.8 trillion yuan based on estimates of capital injections and loans to AMCs to purchase assets, or 18 percent of 2002 GDP.

Country	Year					Description
Colombia	1982	4.1	5	15.1	0.9	During the early 1980s, an economic downturn affected the profitability of the banks. They came under pressure as the 1981 recession intensified. This, in turn, caused a sharp deterioration in asset quality through an increase in defaults. Colombia began experiencing widespread decline in public confidence, which led to a massive government intervention. The central bank intervened in six banks accounting for 25 percent of banking system assets, and in eight finance companies.
Colombia	1998	14	6.3	33.5	–4.2	A capital account reversal during the first half of 1998 triggered by pressures in emerging markets led to a response from the central bank oriented toward defending the currency. As a result, interest rates increased in real terms, harming the quality of banks' loan portfolios and putting downward pressure on asset prices and hence on the value of collateral, especially real estate. The already-weak large public banks faced severe asset quality deterioration, which spread to private banks and other financial entities.
Congo, Dem. Republic of	1983	—	—	0	0.5	Banking sector experienced solvency problems.
Congo, Dem. Republic of	1991	—	—	81.0	–13.5	Four state-owned banks were insolvent; a fifth bank was recapitalized with private participation.
Congo, Dem. Republic of	1994	75	—	0	–5.4	Two state-owned banks were liquidated and two other state banks privatized. In 1997, 12 banks were having serious financial difficulties.
Congo, Republic of	1992	—	—	63.2	–5.5	Two large banks were restructured and privatized. The remaining insolvent bank was liquidated. The situation was aggravated by the civil war.
Costa Rica	1987	—	—	0	3.4	In 1987, public banks accounting for 90 percent of total banking system loans were in financial distress because 32 percent of their loans were considered uncollectible. Implied losses were at least twice capital plus reserves. Pressure was put on the banks to negotiate a "Brady-type" settlement of foreign debt; settlement was reached in November 1989 at 16 cents on the dollar. Budgetary relief to the government enabled restructuring of state bank debts.
Costa Rica	1994	32	—	1.6	0.9	One large state-owned commercial bank with 17 percent of deposits was closed in December 1994. The ratio of overdue loans (net of provisions) to net worth in state commercial banks exceeded 100 percent in June 1995. Implied losses were at least twice capital plus reserves.
Côte d'Ivoire	1988	50	25	0	–1.1	The recession of 1987 and problems with the cocoa and coffee markets (the country's main exports) substantially increased the private sector's NPLs. These problems were aggravated by a large amount of NPLs in the public enterprise sectors, the large accumulation of government payment arrears, the substantial decline in public and private deposits in the banking system, reduction in credit lines from abroad, and poor management in some banks. Four large banks were affected, accounting for 90 percent of banking system loans; three definitely and one possibly insolvent. Six government banks closed.

(Continued)

TABLE 2A.1 (*Continued*)

Country	Systemic banking crisis (starting date)	Share of NPLs at peak (%)	Gross fiscal cost (% of GDP)	Output loss (% of GDP)	Minimum real GDP growth rate (%)	Comments
Croatia	1998	10.5	6.9	0	−0.9	The introduction of a market-oriented legal framework in the early 1990s led to significant progress in establishing a modern banking system. The banking sector expanded vigorously until end-1997. Meanwhile, the incentives for sound bank behavior had not yet been fully established, and bad debt problems had been inherited from the old regime. These weaknesses were in part addressed with the Bank Rehabilitation Plan (Law of 1994) implemented in 1996–97. Four state-owned banks, accounting for 46 percent of total bank assets (as of 1995) entered rehabilitation, with an overall cost of 6.1 percent of GDP. However, a new wave of problems began in March 1998 with the failure of the fifth largest bank, Dubrovacka (5 percent of total assets). Problems at this bank triggered political turmoil, which, in turn, induced runs at other banks, perceived to be indirectly related to Dubrovacka. In July 1998, the sixth largest bank ran into problems and several small and medium institutions experienced liquidity difficulties in the fall of 1998 and early 1999.
Czech Republic	1996	18	6.8	—	−0.8	In 1994, a small bank (Banka Bohemia) failed because of fraud. Although all depositors were covered, partial deposit insurance coverage was introduced shortly after this first failure. The likelihood of facing material losses triggered runs at other small banks; by the end of 1995, two small banks failed (Ceska and AB Banka), which triggered a second phase of bank restructuring starting in 1996, aimed at 18 small banks (9 percent of industry assets).
Djibouti	1991	—	—	22.6	−6.7	Two of six commercial banks ceased operations in 1991–92; other banks experienced difficulties.
Dominican Republic	2003	9	22	15.5	−1.9	In April 2003, the central bank took over Baninter (Banco Intercontinental), which declared bankruptcy in May and dissolved in July. Baninter's liabilities exceeded its assets by 55 billion pesos (US$2.2 billion) and 15 percent of GDP. The central bank had been providing liquidity support to Baninter since September 2002. Two other banks, Bancredito and Banco Mercantil, were also given liquidity support from the central bank to deal with deposit withdrawals.
Ecuador	1982	—	—	13.6	−2.8	A program was implemented that exchanged domestic for foreign debt to bail out the banking system.
Ecuador	1998	40	21.7	6.5	−6.3	Seven financial institutions, accounting for 25–30 percent of commercial banking assets, were closed in 1998–99. In March 1999, bank deposits were frozen for six months. By January 2000, 16 financial institutions accounting for 65 percent of system assets had either been closed (12) or taken over (4) by the government. All deposits were unfrozen by March 2000. In 2002, the blanket guarantee was lifted.

Country	Year					Description
Egypt	1980	—	—	38.1	2.2	The government closed several large investment companies.
El Salvador	1989	37	—	0	1.0	Nine state-owned commercial banks had NPLs averaging 37 percent.
Equatorial Guinea	1983	—	—	0	-2.3	Two of the country's largest banks were liquidated.
Eritrea	1993	—	—		2.3	Most of the banking system was insolvent.
Estonia	1992	7	1.9		-21.6	Banking problems surfaced in November 1992 when the state-owned North Estonian Bank, the Union Baltic Bank, and the Tartu Commercial Bank exhibited serious liquidity problems and delayed payments by three weeks. A second stress episode took place in early 1994, when the government reduced the level of its deposits from the Social Bank. The Social Bank, which controlled 10 percent of financial system assets, failed. Five banks' licenses were revoked, and two major banks were merged and nationalized. Two other large banks were merged and converted to a loan recovery agency.
Finland	1991	13	12.8	59.1	-6.2	The three Nordic countries went through a financial liberalization process that led to a lending boom. However, they also suffered the adverse consequences of higher German interest rates. In Finland, the problems were exacerbated by the collapse of exports to the former Soviet Union. The first bank in trouble was Skopbank, which was taken over by the central bank in September 1991. Savings banks were badly affected; the government took control of three banks that together accounted for 31 percent of system deposits.
Georgia	1991	33	—	—	-44.9	Largest banks virtually insolvent.
Ghana	1982	35	6	15.8	-6.9	During most of the 1980s Ghana suffered severe structural imbalances related to the cumulative impact of large budgetary deficits, rapid increases in domestic bank credit, a fixed exchange rate, and high inflation, which authorities aimed to control through price controls. The effects of these policies were exacerbated by a deterioration of capital equipment and inadequate price incentives in the agricultural and export sectors. As a result, real output in 1981 was 15 percent lower than its 1974 level. The situation deteriorated further toward the second half of the 1980s because of high fiscal deficits, financed primarily through domestic credit; directed credit policies (since 1981 banks had been obliged to lend at least 20 percent of their portfolios to the agricultural sector); a deterioration in cocoa exports; and a large depreciation of the currency (a 1,173 percent depreciation took place in 1983). Banks experienced liquidity pressures, but there were also deficiencies in banking supervision and regulation. As a result, 7 out of the 11 banks were insolvent and the problems were addressed by recapitalization and purchase of NPLs.
Guinea	1985	—	3	0	3.1	Six banks—accounting for 99 percent of system deposits—deemed insolvent. Repayment of deposits amounted to 3 percent of 1986 GDP.
Guinea	1993	45	—	0	4.0	Two banks were deemed insolvent; one other bank had serious financial difficulties.

(Continued)

TABLE 2A.1 (Continued)

Country	Systemic banking crisis (starting date)	Share of NPLs at peak (%)	Gross fiscal cost (% of GDP)	Output loss (% of GDP)	Minimum real GDP growth rate (%)	Comments
Guinea-Bissau	1995	45	—	22.8	−27.2	At end-1996, the central bank had a negative capital position and Guinea-Bissau's two commercial banks had substantial NPLs. In March–April 1997, the treasury recapitalized the central bank.
Guyana	1993	—	—	0	5.1	Before financial reforms started in 1989, directed credit programs had resulted in investments with low rates of return and large NPLs for the banks. State-owned banks were merged in May 1995 and a state-owned loan-recovery institution was subsequently established to recover the NPLs of the merged bank.
Haiti	1994	—	—	9.3	−11.6	The central bank registered considerable losses because the majority of its assets, represented by credit to the government, were nonperforming.
Hungary	1991	23	10		−11.9	In the second half of 1993, eight banks (25 percent of financial system assets) were deemed insolvent.
India	1993	20	—	3.1	4.9	Nonperforming assets reached 11 percent in 1993–94. Nonperforming assets of the 27 public banks were estimated to be 20 percent in 1995. At the end of 1998, NPLs were estimated to be 16 percent and at the end of 2001 they decreased to 12.4 percent.
Indonesia	1997	32.5	56.8	67.9	−13.1	Through May 2002, Bank Indonesia had closed 70 banks and nationalized 13, of a total of 237. Official NPLs for the banking system were estimated to be 32.5 percent of total loans at the peak of crisis.
Israel	1977	—	30	0	1.0	Almost the entire banking sector was affected, representing 60 percent of stock market capitalization. The stock exchange closed for 18 days, and bank share prices fell more than 40 percent.
Jamaica	1996	28.9	43.9	30.1	−1.2	In 1994, a merchant banking group was closed. In 1996, Financial Sector Adjustment Company, a government resolution agency, provided assistance to five banks, five life insurance companies, two building societies, and nine merchant banks. The government recapitalized 21 troubled institutions using nontradable government-guaranteed bonds. By June 30, 2000, outstanding recap bonds were estimated to account for 44 percent of GDP.
Japan	1997	35	14	17.6	−2.0	Banks suffered from sharp declines in stock market and real estate prices. In 1995, the official estimate of NPLs was 40 trillion yen (US$469 billion, or 10 percent of GDP). An unofficial estimate put NPLs at US$1 trillion, equivalent to 25 percent of GDP. Banks made provisions for some bad loans. At the end of 1998, banking system NPLs were estimated at 88 trillion yen (US$725 billion, or 18 percent of GDP). In 1999, Hakkaido Takushodu Bank was closed, the Long Term Credit Bank was nationalized, Yatsuda Trust was merged with Fuji Bank, and Mitsui Trust was merged with Chuo Trust. In 2002, NPLs were 35 percent of total loans; a total of 7 banks had been nationalized, 61 financial institutions closed, and 28 institutions merged. In 1996, rescue costs were estimated to be more than US$100 billion. In 1998, the government announced the Obuchi Plan, which provided 60 trillion yen (US$500 billion, or 12 percent of GDP) in public funds for loan losses, bank recapitalizations, and depositor protection. Fiscal cost rose to 14 percent of GDP.

Country	Year					Notes
Jordan	1989	—	10	66.6	−10.7	The third largest bank failed in August 1989. The central bank provided overdrafts equivalent to 10 percent of GDP to meet a run on deposits and allowed banks to settle foreign obligations.
Kenya	1985	—	—	0	4.1	Four banks and 24 nonbank financial institutions—accounting for 15 percent of financial system liabilities—faced liquidity and solvency problems.
Kenya	1992	—	—	23.0	−1.1	Intervention occurred in two local banks.
Korea, Republic of	1997	35	31.2	50.1	−6.9	The devaluation of the Thai baht in July 1997, the subsequent regional contagion, and the crash of the Hong Kong stock market sent shock waves through the Korean financial system. Korea's exchange rate remained broadly stable through October 1997. However, the high level of short-term debt and the low level of usable international reserves made the economy increasingly vulnerable to shifts in market sentiment. Although macroeconomic fundamentals continued to be favorable, the growing awareness of problems in the financial sector and in industrial groups led to increasing difficulties for the banks in rolling over their short-term borrowing. Through May 2002, five banks were forced to exit the market through purchase and assumption and 303 financial institutions were shut down (215 were credit unions); another four banks were nationalized.
Kuwait	1982	40	—	0	−9.5	Share dealings using postdated checks created a huge unregulated expansion of credit. The crash of the unofficial stock market finally came in 1982, when a dealer presented a postdated check for payment and it bounced. A house of cards collapsed. An official investigation revealed that total outstanding checks amounted to the equivalent of US$94 billion from about 6,000 investors. Kuwait's financial sector was badly shaken by the crash, as was the entire economy. The crash prompted a recession that rippled through the society as individual families were disrupted by the investment risks taken by particular family members using family credit. The debts from the crash left all but one bank in Kuwait technically insolvent, which survived only because of support from the central bank. Only the National Bank of Kuwait, the largest commercial bank, survived the crisis intact. In the end, the government stepped in, devising a complicated set of policies embodied in the Difficult Credit Facilities Resettlement Program. The implementation of the program was still incomplete in 1990 when the Iraqi invasion changed the entire financial picture.
Kyrgyz Republic	1995	85	—	—	−5.8	In 1995, more than half the commercial banks had a negative net worth. The public lost confidence in the banking system, and many people withdrew their funds, causing many of the banks to go out of business. The licenses of five small banks were withdrawn in 1994–95. Two banks were closed in 1999, following the Russian crisis.
Latvia	1995	20	3	—	−2.1	Between 1994 and 1999, 35 banks saw their license revoked, were closed, or ceased operations. In 1995, the negative net worth of the banking system was estimated at US$320 million, or 7 percent of 1995 GDP. Aggregate banking system losses in 1998 were estimated to be 100 million lats (US$172 million), about 3 percent of GDP.

(Continued)

TABLE 2A.1 (Continued)

Country	Systemic banking crisis (starting date)	Share of NPLs at peak (%)	Gross fiscal cost (% of GDP)	Output loss (% of GDP)	Minimum real GDP growth rate (%)	Comments
Lebanon	1990	—	—	4.2	−13.4	Four small and medium banks became insolvent and 11 had to resort to significant central bank lending. Bank of Lebanon claims on commercial banks reached 31 percent of reserve money in September 1990.
Liberia	1991	—	—	—	0	Seven of eleven banks were not operational; in mid-1995, their assets accounted for 64 percent of bank assets.
Lithuania	1995	32.2	3.1	—	1.2	In 1995, of 25 banks, 12 small banks were liquidated, 3 private banks (accounting for 29 percent of banking system deposits) failed, and 3 state-owned banks were deemed insolvent.
Macedonia, former Yugoslav Republic of	1993	70	32	—	−7.5	The government took over banks' foreign debts and closed the second largest bank. The costs of banking system rehabilitation, obligations from assumption of external debt, liabilities for frozen foreign exchange, and contingent liabilities in banks together were estimated to be 32 percent of GDP.
Madagascar	1988	25	—	0	−6.3	After the formal abandonment in 1985 of the previous policy of bank specialization and the appointment in 1986 of separate boards of directors to replace the single board that was shared by all commercial banks, the rehabilitation of the banking system gained speed with the enactment in 1988 of a new banking law, which opened the system to private capital, and the decision in 1989 to write off most of the NPLs of the existing banks.
Malaysia	1997	30	16.4	50.0	−7.4	The persistent pace of credit expansion to the private sector at an annual rate of nearly 30 percent, particularly to the property sector and for the purchase of stocks and shares, exposed the financial system to potential risks from price declines in property and other assets that occurred in 1997. In the wake of market turbulence and contagion effects in the second half of 1997, concerns among market participants about the true condition and resilience of the financial system increasingly became a central issue, highlighted by the known fragilities among finance companies. The finance company sector was restructured, and the number of finance companies was reduced from 39 to 10 through mergers. Two finance companies, including the largest independent finance company, were taken over by the central bank. Two banks were deemed insolvent—accounting for 14 percent of financial system assets—and were merged with other banks. NPLs peaked between 25 percent and 35 percent of banking system assets and fell to 10.8 percent by March 2002.

Country	Year					Description
Mali	1987	75	—	5.7	-0.3	Mali's economic and financial prospects for 1986 and the medium term changed significantly because of the collapse in late 1985 of the world market price of cotton, Mali's major export commodity. In 1987, although the government undertook some corrective measures, the economic and financial situation deteriorated rapidly. The expansion of credit was significantly higher than programmed, and as a result, NPLs at banks increased rapidly. Owing primarily to the overexposure of the largest commercial bank in its loans and guaranteed letters of credit, a liquidity crunch emerged in the banking system. The financial situation of the largest commercial bank deteriorated further in 1987, reflecting the heavy losses of the public enterprise sector that it had financed over the years, defaults by the private sector on unsecured loans, and inappropriate management. By mid-November 1997, the bank had become virtually illiquid and ceased functioning normally. Its NPLs amounted to some 70 percent of its outstanding credit.
Mauritania	1984	70	15	0	2.0	In 1984, five major banks had nonperforming assets ranging from 45 percent to 70 percent of their portfolios.
Mexico	1981	—	—	51.3	-3.5	The government took over the troubled banking system.
Mexico	1994	18.9	19.3	4.2	-6.2	Of 34 commercial banks in 1994, 9 were intervened in and 11 participated in the loan or purchase recapitalization program. The 9 banks that were intervened in accounted for 19 percent of financial system assets and were deemed insolvent. By 2000, 50 percent of bank assets were held by foreign banks.
Morocco	1980	—	—	29.8	-2.8	The banking sector experienced solvency problems. A debt crisis occurred in 1980–83.
Mozambique	1987	—	—	0	1.0	The main commercial bank experienced solvency problems that became apparent after 1992.
Nepal	1988	29	—	0	4.3	NPLs increased sharply during 1988–89 at the two largest commercial banks. Both banks were majority government owned and together accounted for more than 90 percent of bank assets and deposits. In 1989, loan recovery programs were put in place for these two commercial banks.
Nicaragua	1990	50	—	0	-0.4	During the 1980s, lending rates were subsidized and often set below deposit rates. Deposit rates were for the most part negative in real terms and contributed to a severe contraction of the banks' deposit base. The central bank provided much of the funding for commercial banks, mainly by intermediating foreign loans and donations. Lack of bank supervision and prudential controls resulted in risky lending and contributed to the large percentage of NPLs in banks' portfolios. In 1990, financial sector problems were acknowledged by a new government. In 1992, a financial reform package was announced to confront these problems. The state banking system was recapitalized and reorganized starting in 1992.

(Continued)

TABLE 2A.1 (Continued)

Country	Systemic banking crisis (starting date)	Share of NPLs at peak (%)	Gross fiscal cost (% of GDP)	Output loss (% of GDP)	Minimum real GDP growth rate (%)	Comments
Nicaragua	2000	12.7	13.6	0	0.8	The largest bank in Nicaragua, Interbank, was found to have committed fraud and therefore was intervened in in August 2000. Following the intervention, full protection for its depositors was announced. However, withdrawals continued until the bank was finally resolved in October 2000 through a purchase and assumption. Another institution ran into problems soon after the resolution of Interbank. Runs against other banks occurred in part because the authorities announced limited coverage of its depositors. However, in its resolution a few days later, all depositors were protected. Two additional institutions were resolved a few months later. All banks were resolved under purchase and assumptions and a blanket guarantee was passed by law after the first two failures.
Niger	1983	50	—	122.7	−16.8	In the mid-1980s, banking system NPLs reached 50 percent. Four banks were liquidated and three restructured in the late 1980s. In 2002, a new round of bank restructuring was launched. Four banks were experiencing serious difficulties.
Nigeria	1991	77	—	0.4	−0.6	In 1993, insolvent banks accounted for 20 percent of banking system assets and 22 percent of deposits. In 1995, almost half the banks reported being in financial distress.
Norway	1991	16.4	2.7	0	2.8	Financial deregulation undertaken during 1984–87 led to a credit boom (with real rates of credit growth of 20 percent year-over-year), accompanied by a boom in both residential and nonresidential real estate. In 1985, oil prices fell sharply, turning a 4.8 percent surplus in the current account into a 6.2 percent deficit in 1986 with ensuing pressures on the exchange rate. Meanwhile, rate increases by the Bundesbank following the reunification of Germany forced Norway to keep interest rates high throughout the economic recession, which started in 1988. Problems at small banks that began in 1988 were addressed via mergers and assistance from the guarantee fund, funded by banks. However, by 1990 the fund had been depleted and the financial condition at large banks began to deteriorate. The turmoil reached systemic proportions by October 1991, when the second and fourth largest banks had lost a considerable amount of equity.
Panama	1988	—	—	37.8	−13.4	As a result of severe United States–led economic sanctions, including the freezing of Panamanian assets in U.S. banks, a nine-week bank holiday was declared beginning in March 1988. As a result of these developments, the financial position of most state-owned and private commercial banks was substantially weakened and 15 banks ceased operations.

Country	Year					Description
Paraguay	1995	8.1	12.9	0	0.4	During the early 1990s, the banking system remained undercapitalized and NPLs rose sharply, coupled with insider lending practices. As early as 1989, an assessment by the superintendency revealed that about one-third of the banking system was insolvent. The crisis began in May 1995 when the third and fourth largest banks could not meet clearing obligations and were intervened in. The first line of response was liquidity support. However, as the crisis unfolded, an important amount of unrecorded deposits were discovered. A blanket guarantee covering intervened-in banks was announced, but pressures remained because at first, the guarantee covered only legitimate deposits, although later, all deposits were protected. Through a series of interventions, closures, and substantial liquidity support, the distress period lasted until 1999. In the end, between 1995 and 1999, 15 out of the 19 locally owned banks were either closed or absorbed by stronger institutions. By 1999, banks were predominantly foreign owned.
Peru	1983	—	—	25.5	−9.3	Two large banks failed. The rest of the system suffered from high NPLs and financial disintermediation following the nationalization of the banking system in 1987.
Philippines	1983	19	3	60.1	−7.3	Problems occurred in two public banks accounting for 50 percent of banking system assets, six private banks accounting for 12 percent of banking system assets, 32 thrifts accounting for 53 percent of thrift banking assets, and 128 rural banks.
Philippines	1997	20	13.2	0	−0.6	Since January 1998 one commercial bank, 7 of 88 thrifts, and 40 of 750 rural banks have been placed under receivership. Banking system NPLs reached 12 percent by November 1998, and 20 percent in 1999.
Poland	1992	24	3.5	—	2.0	In 1991, seven of nine treasury-owned commercial banks—accounting for 90 percent of credit—the Bank for Food Economy, and the cooperative banking sector experienced solvency problems.
Romania	1990	30	0.6	—	−12.9	In 1998, NPLs reached 25–30 percent in the six main state-owned banks. The Agricultural Bank was recapitalized on a flow basis. In 1998, the central bank injected US$210 million in Bancorex (0.6 percent of GDP), the largest state bank, and in 1999 another US$60 million.
Russian Federation	1998	40	6	0	−5.3	From mid-1997 to April 1998, the Central Bank of Russia (CBR) was relatively successful in defending the fixed exchange rate policy through a significant tightening of credit. However, the situation became increasingly untenable when significant political turmoil in Russia—starting with the president's dismissal of the government of Prime Minister Chernomyrdin and prolonged by a stalemate over the formation of a new cabinet—cast increasing doubt on the political resolve to come to grips with Russia's fiscal problems. From mid-July, when the Duma refused to pass key fiscal measures, the situation deteriorated rapidly, leading to a unilateral restructuring of ruble-denominated treasury bills and bonds on August 17, 1998. The ruble was allowed to float three days later despite previous

(Continued)

TABLE 2A.1 (Continued)

Country	Systemic banking crisis (starting date)	Share of NPLs at peak (%)	Gross fiscal cost (% of GDP)	Output loss (% of GDP)	Minimum real GDP growth rate (%)	Comments
						announcements that it would not be devalued. A large devaluation in real effective terms (more than 300 percent in nominal terms), loss of access to international capital markets, and massive losses to the banking system ensued. However, well before the crisis, there was widespread recognition that the banking system had a series of weaknesses. In particular, bank reporting and bank supervision were weak, there was excessive exposure to foreign exchange rate risk, connected lending, and poor management. Two key measures implemented were a 90-day moratorium on foreign liabilities of banks and the transfer of a large fraction of deposits from insolvent banks to Sberbank. Nearly 720 banks, or half of those then operating, were deemed insolvent. These banks accounted for 4 percent of sector assets and 32 percent of retail deposits.
São Tomé and Príncipe	1992	90	—	0	0.7	At the end of 1992, 90 percent of the monobank's loans were nonperforming. In 1993, the commercial and development departments of the former monobank were liquidated, as was the only financial institution. At the same time, two new banks were licensed that took over many of the assets of their predecessors. The credit operations of one of the new banks were suspended in 1994.
Senegal	1988	50	17	25.4	–0.7	In 1988, 50 percent of banking system loans were nonperforming. Six commercial banks and one development bank closed, accounting for 20–30 percent of financial system assets.
Sierra Leone	1990	45	—	32.6	–9.6	One bank's license was suspended in 1994.
Slovak Republic	1998	35	—	0	0	In 1998, NPLs reached 35 percent of total loans and a bank-restructuring program was put in place involving the major state-owned banks.
Slovenia	1992	—	14.6	1.0	–5.5	Three banks—accounting for two-thirds of banking system assets—were restructured.
Spain	1977	—	5.6	—	0.2	In 1978–83, 24 institutions were rescued, 4 were liquidated, 4 were merged, and 20 small and medium banks were nationalized. These 52 banks (of 110), representing 20 percent of banking system deposits, were experiencing solvency problems.
Sri Lanka	1989	35	5	2.2	2.3	State-owned banks comprising 70 percent of banking system assets were estimated to have NPLs of about 35 percent. The government recapitalized two large state-owned banks, Bank of Ceylon and the People's Bank, in 1993 (representing two-thirds of banking system assets) to solve their solvency problem caused by high nonperforming assets.
Swaziland	1995	—	—	21.6	2.7	Meridien BIAO Swaziland was taken over by the central bank. The central bank also took over the Swaziland Development and Savings Bank, which faced severe portfolio problems.

Country	Year					Description
Sweden	1991	13	3.6	30.6	−1.2	Nordbanken and Gota Bank, accounting for 22 percent of banking system assets, were insolvent. Sparbanken Foresta, accounting for 24 percent of banking system assets, was intervened. Overall, five of the six largest banks, with more than 70 percent of banking system assets, experienced difficulties.
Tanzania	1987	70	10	0	3.8	In 1987, the main financial institutions had arrears amounting to half their portfolios. In 1995, it was determined that the National Bank of Commerce, which accounted for 95 percent of banking system assets, had been insolvent since at least 1990.
Thailand	1983	—	0.7	9.4	4.6	Authorities intervened in 50 finance and security firms and 5 commercial banks (25 percent of financial system assets); 3 commercial banks were deemed insolvent (accounting for 14 percent of commercial bank assets). The fiscal costs for the 50 finance companies were estimated to be 0.5 percent of GDP; the fiscal cost for subsidized loans amounted to about 0.2 percent of GDP a year.
Thailand	1997	33	43.8	97.7	−10.5	Under the framework of a pegged exchange rate regime, Thailand had enjoyed a decade of robust growth performance, but by late 1996 pressures on the baht emerged. Pressure increased through the first half of 1997 amidst an unsustainable current account deficit; a significant appreciation of the real effective exchange rate; rising short-term foreign debt; a deteriorating fiscal balance; and increasingly visible financial sector weaknesses, including large exposure to the real estate sector, exchange rate risk, and liquidity risk. Finance companies had a disproportionately large exposure to the property sector and were the first institutions affected by the economic downturn. Following mounting exchange rate pressures and ineffective interventions to alleviate these pressures, the baht was floated on July 2, 1997. In light of weak supportive policies, the baht depreciated by 20 percent against the U.S. dollar in July. By May 2002, the Bank of Thailand had closed 59 (of 91) financial companies that in total accounted for 13 percent of financial system assets and 72 percent of finance company assets. It closed 1 (out of 15) domestic banks and nationalized 4 banks. A publicly owned AMC held 29.7 percent of financial system assets as of March 2002. NPLs peaked at 33 percent of total loans and were reduced to 10.3 percent of total loans in February 2002.
Togo	1993	—	—	27.7	−16.3	The banking sector experienced solvency problems.
Tunisia	1991	—	3	0	2.2	In 1991, most commercial banks were undercapitalized. During 1991–94, the banking system raised equity equivalent to 1.5 percent of GDP and made provisions equivalent to another 1.5 percent.
Turkey	1982	—	2.5	0	3.4	Three banks were merged with the state-owned Agriculture Bank and then liquidated; two large banks were restructured.

(Continued)

TABLE 2A.1 (*Continued*)

Country	Systemic banking crisis (starting date)	Share of NPLs at peak (%)	Gross fiscal cost (% of GDP)	Output loss (% of GDP)	Minimum real GDP growth rate (%)	Comments
Turkey	2000	27.6	32	5.4	−5.7	Banks had high exposures to the government through large holdings of public securities and sizable maturity and exchange rate risk mismatches, making them highly vulnerable to market risk. In November 2000, interbank credits to some banks holding long-term government paper were cut, forcing them to liquidate the paper, which caused a sharp drop in the price of such securities, triggering a reversal in capital flows, a sharp increase in interest rates, and a decline in the value of the currency. Two banks closed and 19 banks were taken over by the Savings Deposit Insurance Fund.
Uganda	1994	—	—	0	5.5	Between 1994 and 1998, half of the banking system faced solvency problems. In 1998, two banks were closed and one was recapitalized and privatized. In 1999, two banks were closed. In 2002, one small bank was intervened in and two other banks were experiencing difficulties.
Ukraine	1998	62.4	0	0	−1.9	Between 1995 and 1997, 32 of 195 banks were liquidated, and 25 others were undergoing financial rehabilitation. Bad loans accounted for 50–65 percent of assets even in some leading banks. In 1998, banks were further hit by the government's decision to restructure government debt following the Russian debt crisis.
United Kingdom	2007	—	—	—	—	On September 14, 2007, Northern Rock, a mid-sized U.K. mortgage lender, received a liquidity support facility from the Bank of England, following funding problems related to global turmoil in credit markets caused by the U.S. subprime mortgage financial crisis. Starting on September 14, 2007, Northern Rock experienced a bank run, until a government blanket guarantee—covering only Northern Rock—was issued on September 17, 2007. On February 22, 2008, the bank was nationalized, following two unsuccessful bids to take it over. On April 21, 2008, the Bank of England announced it would accept a broad range of mortgage-backed securities and swap those for government paper for a period of one year to aid banks with liquidity problems. The scheme enabled banks to temporarily swap high quality but illiquid mortgage-backed assets and other securities for treasury bills for one year.
United States	1988	4.1	3.7	4.1	−0.2	More than 1,400 savings and loan institutions and 1,300 banks failed. Cleaning up savings and loan institutions cost $180 billion, or 3.7 percent of GDP.

Country	Year					Notes
United States	2007	—	—	—	—	During the course of 2007, U.S. subprime mortgage markets melted down and global money markets were under pressure. The U.S. subprime mortgage crisis manifested itself first through liquidity issues in the banking system owing to a sharp decline in demand for asset-backed securities. Hard-to-value structured products and other instruments created during a boom of financial innovation had to be severely marked down because of the newly implemented fair value accounting. Credit losses and asset writedowns got worse with accelerating mortgage foreclosures, which increased in late 2006 and worsened further in 2007 and 2008. On August 16, 2007, Countrywide Financial ran into liquidity problems because of the decline in value of securitized mortgage obligations, triggering a deposit run on the bank. The Federal Reserve Bank intervened by lowering the discount rate by 0.5 percentage points and by accepting $17.2 billion in repurchase agreements for mortgage-backed securities to aid in liquidity. On January 11, 2008, Bank of America bought Countrywide for US$4 billion. Bear Stearns, the fifth largest investment bank at the time, required an emergency government bailout and was purchased by JP Morgan Chase with federal guarantees on its liabilities in March 2008. Profits at U.S. banks declined to $5.8 billion from $35.2 (an 83.5 percent decline) during the fourth quarter of 2007 compared with the previous year, due to provisions for loan losses. By June 2008, subprime-related and other credit losses or writedowns by global financial institutions hovered around $400 billion. The Fed introduced the Term Securities Lending facility to swap a broad range of mortgage-backed securities for treasury notes for a period of one month. On September 7, 2008, mortgage giants Fannie Mae and Freddie Mac were placed under conservatorship.
Uruguay	1981	—	31.2	87.5	-9.3	Affected institutions accounted for 30 percent of financial system assets; insolvent banks accounted for 20 percent of financial system deposits.
Uruguay	2002	36.3	20	28.8	-11.0	The introduction of capital controls and deposit freezes in Argentina in December 2001 triggered liquidity problems at the two largest private banks, Banco Galicia Uruguay (BGU) and Banco Comercial (BC) (with combined assets of 20 percent of the system total), as a result of their high level of exposure to the Argentinean economy. In January 2002 alone, BGU lost 15 percent of deposits. BGU was intervened in in February and later suspended. A second wave of deposit withdrawals ensued in April 2002, following Uruguay's downgrade from investment-grade status. By May, the runs expanded to the public banks (Republica and Hipotecario), accounting for 40 percent of the system's assets, which were in a weak condition with NPLs of 39 percent as of 2001 (compared with 6 percent at private banks).
Venezuela	1994	24	15	9.6	-2.3	Insolvent banks accounted for 35 percent of financial system deposits. In 1994, the authorities intervened in 17 of 47 banks that held 50 percent of deposits and nationalized 9 banks and closed 7 others. The government intervened in another five banks in 1995.

(Continued)

TABLE 2A.1 (Continued)

Country	Systemic banking crisis (starting date)	Share of NPLs at peak (%)	Gross fiscal cost (% of GDP)	Output loss (% of GDP)	Minimum real GDP growth rate (%)	Comments
Vietnam	1997	35	10	19.7	4.8	Two of the four large state-owned commercial banks—accounting for 51 percent of banking system loans—were deemed insolvent; the other two experienced significant solvency problems. Several joint stock banks were in severe financial distress. Banking system NPLs reached 18 percent in late 1998.
Yemen, Republic of	1996	—	—	2.4	3.8	Banks suffered from extensive NPLs and heavy foreign currency exposure, leaving many banks technically insolvent. The 1994 civil war drained Yemen's economy leading to a financial crisis in 1996.
Zambia	1995	—	1.4	0.5	-2.8	Meridian Bank, accounting for 13 percent of commercial bank assets, became insolvent.
Zimbabwe	1995	—	—	2.4	0.1	Two of five commercial banks had high NPLs.

Sources: IMF Staff reports; country authorities' reports; and newspaper articles.

Note: — = not available; AMC = asset management company; NPL = nonperforming loan.

APPENDIX TABLE 2A.2

Timing of Financial Crises

Country	Systemic banking crisis (starting date)	Currency crisis (year)	Debt crisis (default date)	Debt restructuring (year)
Albania	1994	1997	1990	1992
Algeria	1990	1988, 1994		
Angola		1991, 1996	1988	1992
Argentina	1980, 1989, 1995, 2001	1975, 1981, 1987, 2002	1982, 2001	1993, 2005
Armenia	1994	1994		
Azerbaijan	1995	1994		
Bangladesh	1987	1976		
Belarus	1995	1994, 1999		
Benin	1988	1994		
Bolivia	1986, 1994	1973, 1981	1980	1992
Bosnia and Herzegovina	1992			
Botswana		1984		
Brazil	1990, 1994	1976, 1982, 1987, 1992, 1999	1983	1994
Bulgaria	1996	1996	1990	1994
Burkina Faso	1990	1994		
Burundi	1994			
Cambodia		1971, 1992		
Cameroon	1987, 1995	1994	1989	1992
Cape Verde	1993			
Central African Republic	1976, 1995	1994		
Chad	1983, 1992	1994		
Chile	1976, 1981	1972, 1982	1983	1990
China	1998			
Colombia	1982, 1998	1985		
Comoros		1994		
Congo, Dem. Republic of	1983, 1991, 1994	1976, 1983, 1989, 1994, 1999	1976	1989
Congo, Rep. of	1992	1994	1986	1992
Costa Rica	1987, 1994	1981, 1991	1981	1990

(Continued)

APPENDIX TABLE 2A.2 (*Continued*)

Country	Systemic banking crisis (starting date)	Currency crisis (year)	Debt crisis (default date)	Debt restructuring (year)
Côte d'Ivoire	1988	1994	1984, 2001	1997, n.a.
Croatia	1998			
Czech Republic	1996			
Djibouti	1991			
Dominica				n.a.
Dominican Republic	2003	1985, 1990, 2003	2002	1994, 2005
Ecuador	1982, 1998	1982, 1999	1982, 2003	1995, 2000
Egypt	1980	1979, 1990	1982, 1999	1992
El Salvador	1989	1986	1984	
Equatorial Guinea	1983	1980, 1994		
Eritrea	1993			
Estonia	1992	1992		
Ethiopia		1993		
Fiji		1998		
Finland	1991	1993		
Gabon		1994	1986, 2002	1994
Gambia, The		1985, 2003	1986	1988
Georgia	1991	1992, 1999		
Ghana	1982	1978, 1983, 1993, 2000		
Greece		1983		
Grenada			2004	2005
Guatemala		1986		
Guinea	1985, 1993	1982, 2005	1985	1992
Guinea-Bissau	1995	1980, 1994		
Guyana	1993	1987	1982	1992
Haiti	1994	1992, 2003		
Honduras		1990	1981	1992
Hungary	1991			
Iceland		1975, 1981, 1989		
India	1993			

Indonesia	1997	1979, 1998	1999	2002
Iran		1985, 1993, 2000	1992	1994
Israel	1977	1975, 1980, 1985		
Italy		1981		
Jamaica	1996	1978, 1983, 1991	1978	1990
Japan	1997			
Jordan	1989	1989	1989	1993
Kazakhstan		1999		
Kenya	1985, 1992	1993		
Korea, Republic of	1997	1998		
Kuwait	1982			
Kyrgyz Republic	1995	1997		
Lao P. D. R.		1972, 1978, 1986, 1997		
Latvia	1995	1992		
Lebanon	1990	1984, 1990		
Lesotho		1985		
Liberia	1991		1980	n.a.
Libya		2002		
Lithuania	1995	1992		
Macedonia, former Yugoslav Rep. of	1993			
Madagascar	1988	1984, 1994, 2004	1981	1992
Malawi		1994		
Malaysia	1997	1998		
Maldives		1975		
Mali	1987	1994		
Mauritania	1984	1993	1982	1988
Mexico	1981, 1994	1977, 1982, 1995	1982	1990
Moldova		1999	2002	2002
Mongolia		1990, 1997		
Morocco	1980	1981	1983	1990
Mozambique	1987	1987	1984	1991
Myanmar		1975, 1990, 1996, 2001, 2007		
Namibia		1984		

(Continued)

APPENDIX TABLE 2A.2 (Continued)

Country	Systemic banking crisis (starting date)	Currency crisis (year)	Debt crisis (default date)	Debt restructuring (year)
Nepal	1988	1984, 1992		
New Caledonia		1981		
New Zealand		1975, 1984		
Nicaragua	1990, 2000	1979, 1985, 1990	1980	1995
Niger	1983	1994	1983	1991
Nigeria	1991	1983, 1989, 1997	1983	1992
Norway	1991			
Pakistan		1972		
Panama	1988		1983	1996
Papua New Guinea		1995		
Paraguay	1995	1984, 1989, 2002	1982	1992
Peru	1983	1976, 1981, 1988	1978	1996
Philippines	1983, 1997	1983, 1998	1983	1992
Poland	1992		1981	1994
Portugal		1983		
Romania	1990	1996	1982	1987
Russian Federation	1998	1998	1998	2000
Rwanda		1991		
São Tomé and Príncipe	1992	1987, 1992, 1997		
Senegal	1988	1994	1981	1996
Serbia, Republic of		2000		
Sierra Leone	1990	1983, 1989, 1998	1977	1995
Slovak Republic	1998			
Slovenia	1992			
South Africa		1984	1985	1993
Spain	1977	1983		
Sri Lanka	1989	1978		
Sudan		1981, 1988, 1994	1979	1985
Suriname		1990, 1995, 2001		
Swaziland	1995	1985		

Country	Banking	Currency	Sovereign debt
Sweden	1991	1993	
Syrian Arab Republic		1988	
Tajikistan		1999	1992
Tanzania	1987	1985, 1990	1984
Thailand	1983, 1997	1998	1997
Togo	1993	1994	1979
Trinidad and Tobago		1986	1989
Tunisia	1991		
Turkey	1982, 2000	1978, 1984, 1991, 1996, 2001	1978, 1982
Turkmenistan		1993	1993
Uganda	1994	1980, 1988	1981
Ukraine	1998	1998	1998
United Kingdom	2007		
United States	1988, 2007		
Uruguay	1981, 2002	1972, 1983, 1990, 2002	1983, 2002
Uzbekistan		1994, 2000	
Venezuela	1994	1984, 1989, 1994, 2002	1982
Vietnam	1997	1972, 1981, 1987	1985
Yemen, Republic of	1996	1985, 1995	
Yugoslavia, SFR		1983, 1989, 1996	1983
Zambia	1995	1983, 1991, 1998, 2003	1983
Zimbabwe	1995		1991, 2003

Source: Authors' calculations.

Note: No entry implies no crisis; SFR = Socialist Federal Republic.

APPENDIX TABLE 2A.3

Crisis Containment and Resolution Policies for Selected Banking Crises

	Argentina	Argentina	Argentina	Argentina	Bolivia	Brazil	Brazil	Bulgaria
Banking crisis date (year and month)	Mar. 1980	Dec. 1989	Jan. 1995	Dec. 2001	Nov. 1994	Feb. 1990	Dec. 1994	Jan. 1996
Currency crisis (Y/N) $t-1$ through $t+1$	Y	Y	N	Y	N	Y	Y	Y
Year of currency crisis	1981	1988		2002		1989	1993	1996
Sovereign debt crisis (Y/N) $t-1$ through $t+1$	N	N	N	Y	N	N	N	N
Year of sovereign debt crisis				2001				
Initial conditions								
Fiscal balance/GDP at $t-1$ (percent)	−2.65	−4.42	0.03	−3.61	−3.00	0.00	0.27	−5.63
Public sector debt/GDP at $t-1$ (percent)	10.20	89.80	33.70	50.80	76.00	22.20	23.00	106.40
Inflation at $t-1$ (percent)	139.74	387.81	3.85	−0.73	8.52	1,972.91	2,477.15	32.66
Net foreign assets/M2 at $t-1$ (percent)	34.21	−16.99	25.90	24.16	7.89	0.01	22.69	9.66
Deposits/GDP at $t-1$ (percent)	22.24	21.25	14.96	28.22	34.87	133.25	101.43	59.81
GDP growth at $t-1$ (percent)	7.10	−1.96	6.25	−0.79	4.67	3.20	4.93	−1.60
Current account/GDP at $t-1$ (percent)	0.55	−1.23	−2.83	−3.15	−3.99	0.21	−0.12	−0.20
Peak NPLs (percentage of total loans)	9.00	27.00	17.00	20.10	6.20		16.00	75.00
Government-owned bank (percentage of assets) at $t-1$	71.94	60.50	41.00	30.00	0.00	31.70	31.70	85.68
Significant bank runs (Y/N)	Y	Y	Y	Y	Y	Y	Y	Y
Largest one-month percentage drop in deposits (>5%), t through $t+1$	13.76	26.65	8.36	6.84	7.01	14.63	9.25	9.44
Credit boom (Y/N)	Y	N	Y	N	Y	—	N	—
Annual growth in private credit to GDP, $t-4$ through $t-1$ (percent)	23.62	−1.70	18.90	6.10	22.50	—	5.80	
Creditor rights in year t	1	1	1	1	2	1	1	1
Containment phase								
Deposit freeze (Y/N)	N	Y	N	Y	N	Y	N	N
Introduction of deposit freeze		1989		2001		1990		
Duration of deposit freeze (in months)		120		12		29		
Coverage of deposit freeze (time deposits only? Y/N)		Y		N		N		
Bank holiday (Y/N)	N	Y	N	Y	N	N	N	N
Introduction of bank holiday		1990		2001				

	(1)	(2)	(3)	(4)	(5)	(6)	(7)	(8)
Duration of bank holiday (days)		4		5				
Blanket guarantee (Y/N)	N	N	N	N	N	N	N	N
Date of introduction								
Date of removal								
Duration of guarantee (months)								
Previous explicit deposit insurance arrangement (Y/N)	Y	Y	N	Y	Y		N	Y
Timing of first bank intervention	Mar. 1980	Feb. 1989	Jan. 1995	Apr. 2002	Nov. 1994	Feb. 1990	Jul. 1994	Early 1996
Timing of first liquidity assistance								
Significant liquidity support or emergency lending (Y/N)	Y	Y	N	Y	Y	Y	Y	Y
Support different across banks? (Y/N)	Y	N	N	Y	Y	Y	Y	Y
Collateral required		Y	N	Y		Y		N
Remunerated (Y/N)		Y	N	Y		Y		Y
If remunerated, interest at market rates (Y/N)						Y		
Peak support (percent of deposits)	15.60	300.00	4.15	24.30	13.90	5.00	23.20	22.90
Lowering of reserve requirements (Y/N)	Y	N	Y	N	Y	N	N	N
Resolution phase								
Forbearance(Y/N)	Y	N	N	Y	Y	N	Y	Y
Banks not intervened in despite being technically insolvent	N		N	Y	Y		Y	Y
Prudential regulations suspended or not fully applied	Y	N	N	Y	Y		Y	Y
Large-scale government intervention (Y/N)	Y	N	N	Y	Y	N	Y	Y
Institutions closed (percent of banks assets)	16		0.62	0	11.00	0	small	24.00
Number of banks in t	214	177	205	84	17	229	246	45
Number of banks in t + 3	203	165	143	73	14	245	238	34
Bank closures (Y/N)	Y	Y	Y	N	Y	N	Y	Y
Number of bank closures during t through t + 3	21	28	5		2		41	16
Other financial institution closures (Y/N)	Y	Y	N	N	N	N	Y	—
Shareholder protection (shareholders made whole? Y/N)	N	N	N		N		N	N
Nationalizations (Y/N)	Y	Y	Y	Y	Y	N	Y	Y
Mergers (Y/N)	Y	Y	Y	N	N	N	Y	N
Did bank shareholders inject new capital? (Y/N)			Y		Y	—		—
Sales to foreigners (Y/N)	Y	N	Y	N	Y	N	Y	Y
Number of banks sold to foreigners during t to t + 5	1	0		0	4	0	3	4

(Continued)

APPENDIX TABLE 2A.3 (*Continued*)

	Argentina	Argentina	Argentina	Argentina	Argentina	Bolivia	Brazil	Brazil	Bulgaria
Bank-restructuring agency (Y/N)	N	N	N	N	Y	Y	N	N	—
Asset management company (Y/N)	N	N	N	N	N	Y	N	N	Y
Centralized (Y); Decentralized (N)						Y			N
Recapitalization (Y/N)	N	N	Y	Y	Y	Y	N	Y	Y
Recap measures									
Cash								Y	
Government bonds					Y			Y	Y
Subordinated debt			Y		Y	Y			
Preferred shares									
Purchase of bad loans						Y			
Credit line									
Assumption of bank liabilities									
Ordinary shares									
Recap level (percent)			—	0.28	—	8.00		—	4.00
Recap cost (gross) (percentage of GDP)			0.28	9.58	0.95	4.98	2.31
Recovery (Y/N)			N	N	Y	N	N
Recovery proceeds during *t* to *t* + 5					0.95		
Recap cost (net) (percentage of GDP)			0.28	9.58	0.00	4.98	2.31
Deposit insurance (Y/N)	Y	Y	Y	Y	N	N	Y
Formation	1979	1979	1979	1979			1996
Coverage limit (in local currency) at *t*	Full	Full	30,000	30,000			5,000
Coverage ratio (coverage limit to GDP per capita) at *t*		4.04	4.19			2.37
Were losses imposed on depositors? (Y/N)	N	Y	N	Y	Y	Y	N	N	N
If yes, severe = 1 and moderate = 2		1		1	1	2	
Macro policies									
Monetary policy index	1	1		0	−1	0	1	−1	1
Average change in reserve money during *t* through *t* + 3 (percent)	324.16	2,046.85			36.28	18.80	1,673.69	939.63	245.13
Fiscal policy index	1	1		1	1	1	−1	1	1
Average fiscal balance during *t* through *t* + 3 (percent)	−6.82	−3.86		−2.24	−7.23	−3.02	0.27	−5.14	−3.09

	Chile	Colombia	Colombia	Côte d'Ivoire	Croatia	Czech Republic	Dominican Republic	Ecuador
IMF program (Y/N)	Y	Y	Y	Y	N	Y	N	Y
IMF program put in place (year)	1983	1990	1995	2000		1989		1996
Outcome variables								
Fiscal cost net (percentage of GDP)								
Gross (percent)	55.10	6.00	2.00	9.58	2.65	0.00	10.20	13.90
Recovery during t through t + 5 (percent)	55.10	6.00	2.00	9.58	6.03	0.00	13.20	14.00
	0	0	0	0	3.37	0.00	3.00	0.10
Output loss								
Output loss during t through t + 3 (percent)	10.81	10.70	7.13	42.65	0.00	12.23	0.00	1.30
Banking crisis date (year and month)	Nov. 1981	Jul. 1982	Jun. 1998	1988	Mar. 1998	1996	Apr. 2003	Aug. 1998
Currency crisis (Y/N) t – 1 through t + 1	Y	N	N	N	N	N	Y	Y
Year of currency crisis	1982						2003	1999
Sovereign debt crisis (Y/N) t – 1 through t + 1	N	N	N	N	N	N	Y	Y
Year of sovereign debt crisis							2003	1999
Initial conditions								
Fiscal balance/GDP at t – 1 (percent)	4.99	-2.26	-3.95	-7.19	-2.01	-1.29	-1.37	-3.02
Public sector debt/GDP at t – 1 (percent)	—	—	30.19	—	26.70	12.47	26.80	61.75
Inflation at t – 1 (percent)	31.24	26.33	17.68	7.48	5.01	107.86	10.51	30.67
Net foreign assets/M2 at t – 1 (percent)	42.17	45.95	31.12	-35.05	28.67	32.51	-1.03	8.35
Deposits/GDP at t – 1 (percent)	26.62	24.78	36.14	20.57	41.42	62.24	34.80	23.25
GDP growth at t – 1 (percent)	7.94	2.28	3.43	-0.50	6.80	6.36	4.43	4.05
Current account/GDP at t – 1 (percent)	-6.35	-4.06	-5.39	-14.93	-12.61	-0.09	-3.69	-3.02
Peak NPLs (percentage of total loans)	35.60	4.10	14.00	50.00	10.50	18.00	9.00	40.00
Government-owned bank (percentage of assets) at t – 1	19.72	57.67	53.62	20.60	1.04	52.00	15.50	9.00
Significant bank runs (Y/N)	Y	N	N	N	Y	Y	N	Y
Largest one-month percentage drop in deposits (>5%), t through t + 1	8.48				6.11	5.67		11.09
Credit boom (Y/N)	Y	N	N	N	N	—	N	N

(Continued)

APPENDIX TABLE 2A.3 (*Continued*)

	Chile	Colombia	Colombia	Côte d'Ivoire	Croatia	Czech Republic	Dominican Republic	Ecuador
Annual growth in private credit to GDP, t − 4 through t − 1 (percent)	34.10	5.40	7.00	0.00	7.60	—	7.70	9.40
Creditor rights in year t	2	0	0	0	3	3	2	0
Containment phase								
Deposit freeze (Y/N)	N	N	N	N	N	N	N	Y
Introduction of deposit freeze								1999
Duration of deposit freeze (in months)								6
Coverage of deposit freeze (time deposits only? Y/N)								N
Bank holiday (Y/N)	N	N	N	N	N	N	N	Y
Introduction of bank holiday								1999
Duration of bank holiday (in days)								5
Blanket guarantee (Y/N)	N	N	N	N	N	Y	N	Y
Date of introduction						Mid-1996		Dec. 1998
Date of removal						Jan. 1998		Jan. 2002
Duration of guarantee (months)						18		37
Previous explicit deposit insurance arrangement (Y/N)	N	N	Y	N	Y	Y	N	Y
Timing of first bank intervention	Nov. 1981	Jul. 1982		1988	Apr. 1998	Dec. 1995	Apr. 2003	Apr. 1998
Timing of first liquidity assistance								
Significant liquidity support or emergency lending (Y/N)	Y	Y	Y	Y	N	N	Y	Y
Support different across banks? (Y/N)	N	—	Y	—			N	—
Collateral required	N	—	—	—			N	—
Remunerated (Y/N)	—	—	—	Y			N	—
If remunerated, interest at market rates (Y/N)	—	—	—	N			N	—
Peak support (percentage of deposits)	124.00	14.90	9.20	59.00	1.70	2.30	61.60	15.30
Lowering of reserve requirements (Y/N)	Y	Y	N	N	Y	N	N	N
Resolution phase								
Forbearance (Y/N)	Y	N	Y	Y	Y	N	Y	Y
Banks not intervened in despite being technically insolvent	N	N	N	Y	N	N	N	Y
Prudential regulations suspended or not fully applied	Y	N	Y	Y	Y	N	Y	Y

Large-scale government intervention (Y/N)	Y	Y	Y	Y	Y	Y	Y	Y
Institutions closed (percentage of banks assets)	20.00	0	9.90	—	7.06	1.50	0.00	50.20
Number of banks in t	61		39	20	60	55	14	40
Number of banks in t + 3	45		27	14	43	45	11	22
Bank closures (Y/N)	Y	N	Y	Y	Y	Y	N	Y
Number of bank closures during t through t + 3	8		12	6	11	4		14
Other financial institution closures (Y/N)	Y	N	Y	Y	N	N	N	Y
Shareholder protection (shareholders made whole? Y/N)	—		N	N	N	N	N	N
Nationalizations (Y/N)	N	N	Y	N	Y	Y	N	Y
Mergers (Y/N)	Y	Y	Y	N	Y	Y	N	Y
Did bank shareholders inject new capital? (Y/N)	Y	—	Y	Y	Y	Y	N	N
Sales to foreigners (Y/N)	Y	N	N	—	Y	Y	N	N
Number of banks sold to foreigners during t through t + 5	1			—	5	5	2	—
Bank-restructuring agency (Y/N)	N	N	Y	Y	Y	Y	Y	Y
Asset management company (Y/N)	N	N	Y	Y	Y	Y	Y	Y
Centralized (Y); Decentralized (N)	Y		Y	Y	Y	Y	Y	Y
Recapitalization (Y/N)	Y	Y	Y	Y	Y	Y	N	Y
Recap measures								
Cash	Y	Y	Y		Y	Y		Y
Government bonds	Y	Y	Y	Y	Y	Y		Y
Subordinated debt				Y				
Preferred shares								
Purchase of bad loans						Y		
Credit line	Y		Y					
Assumption of bank liabilities								
Ordinary shares								
Recap level (percent)	—	—	10.00	—	—	—		9.00
Recap cost (gross) (percentage of GDP)	34.33	1.87	4.26	—	3.20	0.98	—	1.90
Recovery (Y/N)	Y	N	Y	N	N	N		Y
Recovery proceeds during t through t + 5 (percent)	27.87		1.56	—				0.30
Recap cost (net) (percentage of GDP)	6.46	1.87	2.70	—	3.20	0.98		1.60
Deposit insurance(Y/N)	N	N	Y	N	Y	Y	N	Y
Formation			1988		1997	1994		1998

(Continued)

APPENDIX TABLE 2A.3 (Continued)

	Chile	Colombia	Colombia	Côte d'Ivoire	Croatia	Czech Republic	Dominican Republic	Ecuador
Coverage limit (in local currency) at t			10,000,000		50,000	100,000		7,416
Coverage ratio (coverage limit to GDP per capita) at t			3.29		1.8	0.75		3.81
Were losses imposed on depositors? (Y/N)	Y	N	N	Y	N	N	N	Y
If yes, severe = 1 and moderate = 2	2			1				1
Macro policies								
Monetary policy index	-1	0	0	-1	-1	-1	1	1
Average change in reserve money during t through t + 3 (percent)	9.97	21.00	11.97	-6.57	23.19	7.99	45.95	
Fiscal policy index	-1	1	1	1	1	1	1	0
Average fiscal balance during t through t + 3 (percent)	0.81	-3.93	-4.28	-12.69	-5.19	-3.35	-6.45	-0.66
IMF program (Y/N)	Y	N	N	Y	N	N	Y	Y
IMF program put in place (year)	1983			1985			2004	2000
Outcome variables								
Fiscal cost net (percentage of GDP)	16.80	5.00	2.54	25.00	6.90	5.80	20.80	16.26
Gross (percent)	42.90	5.00	6.28	25.00	6.90	6.80	22.00	21.70
Recovery during t through t + 5 (percent)	26.10	0	3.74	0.00	0.00	1.00	1.20	5.44
Output loss								
Output loss during t through t + 3 (percent)	92.35	15.11	33.52	0.00	0.00	—	15.51	6.49

	Estonia	Finland	Ghana	Indonesia	Jamaica	Japan	Korea	Latvia
Banking crisis date (year and month)	Nov. 1992	Sep. 1991	1982	Nov. 1997	Dec. 1996	Nov. 1997	Aug. 1997	Apr. 1995
Currency crisis (Y/N) t − 1 through t + 1	Y	N	Y	Y	Y	N	Y	N
Year of currency crisis	1991		1983	1998	1995		1998	
Sovereign debt crisis (Y/N) t − 1 through t + 1	N	N	N	N	N	N	N	N
Year of sovereign debt crisis								
Initial conditions								
Fiscal balance/GDP at t − 1 (percent)	5.25	5.56	-0.12	-1.13	1.99	-5.13	0.24	-3.86

Public sector debt/GDP at t − 1 (percent)	—	14.04	—	26.40	90.89	100.48	8.80	14.89
Inflation at t − 1 (percent)	—	4.88	16.79	6.04	25.55	0.60	4.93	26.27
Net foreign assets/M2 at t − 1 (percent)	57.63	12.73	-0.06	21.58	19.07	1.62	15.62	36.32
Deposits/GDP at t − 1 (percent)	72.33	52.28	6.20	44.74	40.73	252.41	36.55	21.15
GDP growth at t − 1 (percent)	-7.91	0.08	-6.91	7.82	1.01	2.75	7.00	2.20
Current account/GDP at t − 1 (percent)	59.70	-4.91	-0.32	-2.91	-4.37	1.42	-4.14	-3.61
Peak NPLs (percentage of total loans)	7.00	13.00	35.00	32.50	28.90	35.00	35.00	20.00
Government-owned bank (percentage of assets) at t − 1	25.70	13.40	60.00	42.30	0.00	0.00	23.41	9.90
Significant bank runs (Y/N)	Y	N	Y	Y	N	N	Y	Y
Largest one-month percentage drop in deposits (>5%), t through t + 1	19.94	11.74	—	22.60	—	—	12.00	5.81
Credit boom (Y/N)	—	—	N	N	N	N	N	—
Annual growth in private credit to GDP t − 4 through t − 1 (percent)	—	8.00	-19.90	4.50	-3.10	0.10	1.10	—
Creditor rights in year t	—	3	1	3	2	3	3	3
Containment phase								
Deposit freeze (Y/N)	N	N	N	N	N	N	N	N
Introduction of deposit freeze								
Duration of deposit freeze (in months)								
Coverage of deposit freeze (time deposits only? Y/N)								
Bank holiday (Y/N)	N	N	N	N	N	N	N	N
Introduction of bank holiday								
Duration of bank holiday (in days)								
Blanket guarantee (Y/N)	Y	N	N	Y	Y	Y	Y	N
Date of introduction	Feb. 1993			Jan. 1998	Feb. 1997	Nov. 1997	Nov. 1997	
Date of removal	Dec. 1998			Jul. 2005	Mar. 1998	Apr. 2005	Dec. 2000	
Duration of guarantee (in months)	70			78	11	89	37	
Previous explicit deposit insurance arrangement (Y/N)	Y		N	N	N	Y	Y	N
Timing of first bank intervention	Sep. 1991			Nov. 1997	Dec. 1994	Apr. 1997	Oct. 1997	
Timing of first liquidity assistance	Jun. 2005			Nov. 1997	Dec. 1994	Apr. 1997	May 1995	
Significant liquidity support or emergency lending (Y/N)	Y	Y	Y	N	Y	N	Y	N
Support different across banks? (Y/N)	Y	Y	—	N	N	—	Y	—
Collateral required	—	N	—	N	N	—	—	—

(Continued)

APPENDIX TABLE 2A.3 (Continued)

	Estonia	Finland	Ghana	Indonesia	Jamaica	Japan	Korea	Latvia
Remunerated (Y/N)	—	N		—	Y	Y	—	N
If remunerated, interest at market rates (Y/N)	—	N		—	Y	Y	—	N
Peak support (percentage of deposits)	31.64	5.50	0.00	53.80	12.40	0.40	28.90	3.01
Lowering of reserve requirements (Y/N)	Y	N	Y	N	N	Y	N	Y
Resolution phase								
Forbearance (Y/N)								
Banks not intervened in despite being technically insolvent	Y	Y	Y	Y	N	Y	Y	N
Prudential regulations suspended or not fully applied	N	N	Y	N	N	N	Y	N
	Y	Y	Y	Y	N	Y	N	N
Large-scale government intervention (Y/N)	Y	Y	Y	Y	Y	Y	Y	Y
Institutions closed (percentage of banks' assets)	15.00	0	0	13.50	4.15	0	9.00	40.00
Number of banks in t	21	519	11	238	36	—	59	56
Number of banks in $t + 3$	18	347	11	165	20	—	31	42
Bank closures (Y/N)	Y	N	N	Y	Y	N	Y	Y
Number of bank closures during t through $t + 3$	11	0	0	66	1	0	22	14
Other financial institution closures (Y/N)	Y	N	N	N	Y	Y	Y	—
Shareholder protection (shareholders made whole? Y/N)	N	Y	—	N	N	N	N	—
Nationalizations (Y/N)	Y	Y	N	Y	Y	Y	Y	N
Mergers (Y/N)	Y	Y	N	Y	Y	Y	Y	N
Did bank shareholders inject new capital? (Y/N)	N	N	N	—	N	Y	Y	—
Sales to foreigners (Y/N)	N	—	N	Y	Y	Y	Y	—
Number of banks sold to foreigners during t through $t + 5$	—	—	—	—	2	1	8	N
Bank-restructuring agency (Y/N)	N	Y	N	Y	Y	Y	Y	N
Asset management company (Y/N)	Y	Y	Y	Y	Y	Y	Y	N
Centralized (Y); Decentralized (N)	N	Y	Y	Y	Y	Y	Y	
Recapitalization (Y/N)	Y	Y	Y	Y	Y	Y	Y	N
Recap measures								
Cash	Y			Y			Y	
Government bonds	Y	Y		Y			Y	
Subordinated debt		Y	Y			Y	Y	

	C1	C2	C3	C4	C5	C6	C7
Preferred shares						Y	
Purchase of bad loans		Y					Y
Credit line						Y	Y
Assumption of bank liabilities	Y					Y	
Ordinary shares		Y				Y	Y
Recap level (percent)			6.00	4.00			
Recap cost (gross) (percentage of GDP)	1.26	8.63	6.00	37.30	13.90	6.61	19.31
Recovery (Y/N)	Y	Y	N	N	Y	Y	Y
Recovery proceeds during t to t + 5	0.27	1.72	6.00		4.95	0.09	3.50
Recap cost (net) (percentage of GDP)	0.99	6.91	6.00	37.30	8.95	6.52	15.81
Deposit insurance (Y/N)	N	Y	N	N	N	Y	Y
Formation		1969				1971	1996
Coverage limit (in local currency) at t		Full				Full	20,000,000
Coverage ratio (coverage limit to GDP per capita) at t							2.18
Were losses imposed on depositors? (Y/N)	Y	N	N	N	N	N	Y
If yes, severe = 1 and moderate = 2	1						1
Macro policies							
Monetary policy index	0	−1	0	1	0	0	−1
Average change in reserve money during t through t + 3 (percent)	—	1.75	46.93	47.66	19.35	8.88	4.05
Fiscal policy index	0	1	−1	1	1	1	1
Average fiscal balance during t through t + 3 (percent)	−0.66	−5.07	−0.04	−2.47	−5.71	−6.17	−1.66
IMF program (Y/N)	Y	N	N	Y	N	N	Y
IMF program put in place (year)	1993	1993	1998	1998		1998	1993
Outcome variables							
Fiscal cost net (percentage of GDP)	1.63	11.08	6.00	52.30	38.95	13.91	23.20
Gross (percent)	1.90	12.80	6.00	56.80	43.90	14.00	31.20
Recovery during t through t + 5 (percent)	0.27	1.72	0	4.60	4.95	0.09	8.00
Output loss							
Output loss during t through t + 3 (percent)	—	59.08	15.79	67.95	30.08	17.56	50.10

(Continued)

APPENDIX TABLE 2A.3 (Continued)

	Lithuania	Malaysia	Mexico	Nicaragua	Norway	Paraguay	Philippines	Russia
Banking crisis date (year and month)	Dec. 1995	Jul. 1997	Dec. 1994	Aug. 2000	Oct. 1991	May 1995	Jul. 1997	Aug. 1998
Currency crisis (Y/N) $t-1$ through $t+1$	N	Y	Y	N	N	N	Y	Y
Year of currency crisis		1998	1995				1998	1998
Sovereign debt crisis (Y/N) $t-1$ through $t+1$	N	N	N	N	N	N	N	Y
Year of sovereign debt crisis								1998
Initial conditions								
Fiscal balance/GDP at $t-1$ (percent)	-4.22	1.98	-2.46	-3.30	2.54	2.73	-0.18	-16.96
Public sector debt/GDP at $t-1$ (percent)	8.00	35.16	27.34	191.31	28.92	15.80	—	52.49
Inflation at $t-1$ (percent)	45.10	3.34	8.01	9.28	4.36	18.31	7.14	11.05
Net foreign assets/M2 at $t-1$ (percent)	39.63	23.20	18.12	-14.10	10.34	38.86	19.03	9.47
Deposits/GDP at $t-1$ (percent)	17.43	119.51	26.82	37.02	54.44	27.68	48.61	14.59
GDP growth at $t-1$ (percent)	-9.77	10.00	1.95	7.00	1.93	3.73	5.85	1.40
Current account/GDP at $t-1$ (percent)	-3.86	-4.36	-5.80	-24.90	2.50	-2.02	-0.18	0.00
Peak NPLs (percentage of total loans)	32.20	30.00	18.90	12.70	16.36	8.10	20.00	40.00
Government-owned bank (percentage of assets) at $t-1$	48.00	9.93	28.16	0.00	43.68	48.02	27.23	32.98
Significant bank runs (Y/N)	Y	Y	Y	N	N	Y	N	Y
Largest one-month percentage drop in deposits (>5%), t through $t+1$	6.26	6.03	14.00			7.68		21.00
Credit boom (Y/N)	—	N	Y	—	N	Y	Y	N
Annual growth in private credit to GDP, $t-4$ through $t-1$ (percent)	—	7.10	22.50	—	2.90	17.60	17.70	9.50
Creditor rights in year t	1	3	0	4	2	1	1	1
Containment phase								
Deposit freeze (Y/N)	N	N	N	N	N	N	N	N
Introduction of deposit freeze								
Duration of deposit freeze (in months)								
Coverage of deposit freeze (time deposits only? Y/N)								

Bank holiday (Y/N)	N	N	N	N	N	N	N	N
Introduction of bank holiday								
Duration of bank holiday (days)								
Blanket guarantee (Y/N)	N	Y	Y	Y	N	Y	N	N
Date of introduction		Jan. 1998	Dec. 1993	Jan. 2001		Jul. 1995		
Date of removal		Aug. 2005	Jan. 2003	Jul. 2002		Jun. 1996		
Duration of guarantee (months)		91	109	14		11		
Previous explicit deposit insurance arrangement (Y/N)	N	N	Y	N	Y	N	Y	N
Timing of first bank intervention	Dec. 1995	None	Nov. 1994	Aug. 2000	Fall 1988	May 1995	—	—
Timing of first liquidity assistance				Aug. 2000			Sep. 1997	Sep. 1998
Significant liquidity support or emergency lending (Y/N)	N	Y	Y	Y	Y	Y	N	Y
Support different across banks? (Y/N)	Y	—	Y	N	Y	Y		Y
Collateral required	—	—	—	N	—	N		Y
Remunerated (Y/N)	—	—	—	Y	—	—		Y
If remunerated, interest at market rates (Y/N)	—	—	—	Y	—	—		N
Peak support (percentage of deposits)	4.60	12.20	67.60	9.60	6.20	20.80	2.50	31.50
Lowering of reserve requirements (Y/N)	Y	N	N	N	N	Y	N	Y
Resolution phase								
Forbearance (Y/N)	Y	Y	Y	N	Y	Y	N	Y
Banks not intervened in despite being technically insolvent	Y	N	N		Y	N		Y
Prudential regulations suspended or not fully applied	Y	Y	Y		Y	Y		Y
Large-scale government intervention (Y/N)	Y	Y	Y	Y	Y	Y	N	Y
Institutions closed (percentage of banks assets)	15.00	0	0	0	1.00	23.00	1.00	4.00
Number of banks in t	28	47	52	12	164	34	1,003	1,476
Number of banks in t + 3	14	43	37	6	153	22	925	1,318
Bank closures (Y/N)	Y	N	N	N	Y	Y	Y	Y
Number of bank closures during t through t + 3	14	0	0	0	2	9	26	399
Other financial institution closures (Y/N)	N	N	N	Y	N	Y	—	—
Shareholder protection (shareholders made whole? Y/N)	Y	N	N	N	N	N	N	N
Nationalizations (Y/N)	N	Y	Y	N	Y	N	N	Y
Mergers (Y/N)	Y	Y	Y	N	Y	N	N	Y
Did bank shareholders inject new capital? (Y/N)	—	—	Y	N	Y	Y	N	Y

(Continued)

APPENDIX TABLE 2A.3 (Continued)

	Lithuania	Malaysia	Mexico	Nicaragua	Norway	Paraguay	Philippines	Russia
Sales to foreigners (Y/N)	N	N	Y	N	—	Y	N	N
Number of banks sold to foreigners during t through t + 5			4					
Bank-restructuring agency (Y/N)	Y	Y	Y	N	—	N	N	Y
Asset management company (Y/N)	Y	Y	N	Y	Y	N	N	Y
Centralized (Y); Decentralized (N)	Y	Y		N	N			Y
Recapitalization (Y/N)	Y	Y	Y	N	Y	Y	Y	N
Recap measures								
Cash	Y							
Government bonds	Y							
Subordinated debt		Y	Y		Y			
Preferred shares					Y			
Purchase of bad loans		Y	Y					
Credit line						Y		
Assumption of bank liabilities								
Ordinary shares					Y			
Recap level (percent)	—	9.00	9.00		8.00	—		
Recap cost (gross) (percentage of GDP)	1.70	16.40	3.80		2.61	1.22	0.20	
Recovery (Y/N)	Y	Y	Y		Y	N	N	
Recovery proceeds during t through t + 5	0.20	11.30	1.30		2.00			
Recap cost (net) (percentage of GDP)	1.50	5.10	2.50		0.61	1.22	0.20	
Deposit insurance (Y/N)	N	N	Y	N	Y	N	Y	N
Formation			1986		1961		1963	
Coverage limit (in local currency) at t			Full		Full		10,000	
Coverage ratio (coverage limit to GDP per capita) at t							3.22	
Were losses imposed on depositors? (Y/N)	Y	N	N	N	N	N	N	Y
If yes, severe = 1 and moderate = 2	2							2
Macro policies								
Monetary policy index	0	–1	1	0	0	–1	–1	1
Average change in reserve money during t through t + 3 (percent)	—	–2.78	22.03	17.63	5.57	24.13	7.03	47.21

	Sri Lanka	Sweden	Thailand	Turkey	Ukraine	United Kingdom	United States	Uruguay	Venezuela	Vietnam
Fiscal policy index			1	0	1	1	0	−1	1	0
Average fiscal balance during t through t + 3 (percent)			−5.05	−1.28	−4.77	−3.80	−0.65	−0.02	−2.75	−1.32
IMF program (Y/N)			N	N	Y	N	N	N	Y	Y
IMF program put in place (year)					1995				1998	1999
Outcome variables										
Fiscal cost net (percentage of GDP)			2.90	5.10	18.00	12.57	0.60	10.00	13.20	6.00
Gross (percent)			3.10	16.40	19.30	13.61	2.70	12.90	13.20	6.00
Recovery during t through t + 5 (percent)			0.20	11.30	1.30	1.04	2.10	2.90	0	0
Output loss										
Output loss during t through t + 3 (percent)			—	50.04	4.25	0.00	0.00	0.00	0.00	0.00
Banking crisis date (year and month)	1989	Sep. 1991	Jul. 1997	Nov. 2000	1998	Aug. 2007	Aug. 2007	Jan. 2002	Jan. 1994	Fall 1997
Currency crisis (Y/N) t − 1 through t + 1	N	Y	N	Y	Y	N	N	Y	Y	N
Year of currency crisis		1992		2001	1998			2002	1993	
Sovereign debt crisis (Y/N) t − 1 through t + 1	N	N	N	N	N	N	N	Y	N	N
Year of sovereign debt crisis								2002		
Initial conditions										
Fiscal balance/GDP at t − 1 (percent)	−8.59	3.39	2.40	−14.97	−5.56	−2.56	−2.61	−0.22	−2.92	−2.36
Public sector debt/GDP at t − 1 (percent)	108.72	—	14.15	51.31	29.88	43.04	60.10	39.05	—	—
Inflation at t − 1 (percent)	15.10	10.94	4.77	68.79	10.12	2.78	2.57	3.59	45.94	4.59
Net foreign assets/M2 at t − 1 (percent)	5.80	4.79	25.13	17.84	−1.68	1.40	0.98	27.15	55.29	24.66
Deposits/GDP at t − 1 (percent)	22.01	40.62	76.91	37.28	6.81	139.66	72.01	75.00	—	8.33
GDP growth at t − 1 (percent)	2.30	1.01	5.90	−3.37	−2.99	2.91	2.87	−3.38	0.28	9.34
Current account/GDP at t − 1 (percent)	−0.23	−2.57	−7.89	−0.55	−2.66	−3.62	−6.15	−2.87	−3.33	−9.86
Peak NPLs (percentage of total loans)	35.00	13.00	33.00	27.60	62.40	—	4.80	36.30	24.00	35.00

(Continued)

APPENDIX TABLE 2A.3 (Continued)

	Sri Lanka	Sweden	Thailand	Turkey	Ukraine	United Kingdom	United States	Uruguay	Venezuela	Vietnam
Government-owned bank (percentage of assets) at t − 1	71.39	23.20	17.09	35.00	12.23	0.00	0.00	40.90	9.80	92.00
Significant bank runs (Y/N)	Y	Y	N	N	N	N	N	Y	Y	N
Largest one-month percentage drop in deposits (>5%), t through t + 1	7.51	5.56						9.12	14.06	
Credit boom (Y/N)	N	—	Y	N	Y	N	N	Y	N	—
Annual growth in private credit to GDP, t − 4 through t − 1 (percent)	1.60	—	10.60	6.10	15.00	6.06	5.22	13.10	0.50	—
Creditor rights in year t	2	2	3	2	3	4	1	2	3	1
Containment phase										
Deposit freeze (Y/N)	N	N	N	N	N	N	N	Y	N	N
Introduction of deposit freeze								2002		
Duration of deposit freeze (in months)								36		
Coverage of deposit freeze (time deposits only? Y/N)								Y		
Bank holiday (Y/N)	N	N	N	N	N	N	N	Y	N	N
Introduction of bank holiday								2002		
Duration of bank holiday (days)								5		
Blanket guarantee (Y/N)	N	Y	Y	Y	N	N	N	N	N	N
Date of introduction		Sep. 1992	Aug. 1997	Dec. 2000		Sep. 2007	Mar. 2008			
Date of removal		Jul. 1996	Jan. 2005	Jul. 2004						
Duration of guarantee (months)		46	89	43						
Previous explicit deposit insurance arrangement (Y/N)	Y	N	N	Y	Y	Y	Y	Y	Y	N
Timing of first bank intervention	None	Sep. 1991	Mar. 1997	Nov. 1997	1995	Sep. 2007	Mar. 2008	Feb. 2002	Jan. 1994	Fall 1998

Timing of first liquidity assistance										
Significant liquidity support or emergency lending (Y/N)	N	Y	Y	Y	N	N	N	N	N	N
Support different across banks? (Y/N)	—	N	—	—	Y	Y	Y	Y	Y	—
Collateral required	—	—	—	—	Y	Y	Y	Y	Y	—
Remunerated (Y/N)	—	—	—	—	Y	Y	Y	Y	Y	—
If remunerated, interest at market rates (Y/N)	—	—	—	—	Y	Y	Y	Y	Y	Y
Peak support (percentage of deposits)	3.10	9.40	25.90	22.16	16.30	—	2.06	31.00	31.20	5.20
Lowering of reserve requirements (Y/N)	N	—	N	N	N	N	N	N	Y	Y
Resolution phase										
Forbearance (Y/N)	Y	Y	Y	Y	Y	Y	Y	Y	Y	Y
Banks not intervened in despite being technically insolvent	Y	N	N		Y				N	Y
Prudential regulations suspended or not fully applied	Y	Y	Y		Y				Y	Y
Large-scale government intervention (Y/N)	Y	Y	Y	Y	Y	N	N	Y	Y	Y
Institutions closed (percentage of banks' assets)	0	0	2.00	8.00	2.00	0	0	18.83	23.00	2.00
Number of banks in t	118	41	80	230				31	51	83
Number of banks in t + 3	103	40	54	178				21	39	—
Bank closures (Y/N)	N	N	Y	Y	N	N	N	Y	Y	Y
Number of bank closures during t through t + 3		1	12	48				5	12	5
Other financial institution closures (Y/N)	Y	—	Y	—	—	N	—	N	Y	—
Shareholder protection (shareholders made whole? (Y/N)	—	Y	—	—	—	N	—	Y	N	N
Nationalizations (Y/N)	N	Y	Y	N	N	Y	N	N	Y	N
Mergers (Y/N)	N	Y	Y	N	N	Y	Y	N	N	Y
Did bank shareholders inject new capital? (Y/N)	N	—	Y	Y	—	Y	Y	Y	Y	—
Sales to foreigners (Y/N)	N	—	Y	Y	N	N	N	Y	Y	—
Number of banks sold to foreigners during t through t + 5		3	2					2	5	—
Bank-restructuring agency (Y/N)	N	Y	Y	Y	N	N	N	N	Y	N

(Continued)

APPENDIX TABLE 2A.3 (Continued)

	Sri Lanka	Sweden	Thailand	Turkey	Ukraine	United Kingdom	United States	Uruguay	Venezuela	Vietnam
Asset management company (Y/N)										
Centralized (Y/N)	N	Y	Y	Y	N	—	Y	Y	N	Y
Recapitalization (Y/N)	Y	Y	Y	Y	N	Y	Y	Y	Y	Y
Recap measures										
Cash								Y		Y
Government bonds	Y		Y	Y					Y	Y
Subordinated debt								Y		
Preferred shares						Y			Y	
Purchase of bad loans										
Credit line						Y				
Assumption of bank liabilities										
Ordinary shares		Y								
Recap level (percent)	8.00		8.50	8.00						10.00
Recap cost (gross) (percentage of GDP)	3.60	1.85	18.80	24.50		0.20		6.18	5.59	5.00
Recovery (Y/N)	N	Y	—	N				Y	N	N
Recovery proceeds during t through $t+5$ (percent)		0.36	—					1.16		
Recap cost (net) (percentage of GDP)	3.60	1.49	18.80	24.50		0.20		5.02	5.59	5.00
Deposit insurance (Y/N)	Y	N	N	Y	Y	Y	Y	Y	Y	N
Formation	1987			1983	1998	2001	1933	2002	1985	
Coverage limit (in local currency) at t	100,000			Full	1,200	35,000	100,000	100,000	250,000	
Coverage ratio (coverage limit to GDP per capita) at t	7.18				0.59	1.9	2.26	1.4	0.96	
Were losses imposed on depositors? (Y/N)	N	N	Y	N	Y	N	N	N	Y	N
If yes, severe = 1 and moderate = 2			2		1				2	
Macro policies										
Monetary policy index	0	1	0	−1	−1			−1	1	1
Average change in reserve money during t through $t+3$ (percent)	15.39	21.63	12.95	33.99	33.26	—	—	17.37	79.32	24.17

Fiscal policy index	1	1	1	1	1	—	—	−1	1	1
Average fiscal balance during t through t + 3 (percent)	−7.67	−7.33	−2.51	−10.55	−2.00	—	—	0.04	−1.64	−2.74
IMF program (Y/N)	N	N	Y	Y	Y	—	—	Y	Y	N
IMF program put in place (year)			1998	2000	1995	—	—	1996	1996	
Outcome variables										
Fiscal cost net (percentage of GDP)	5.00	0.20	34.80	30.70	0.00	—	—	10.83	12.50	10.00
Gross (percent)	5.00	3.60	43.80	32.00	0.00	—	—	20.00	15.00	10.00
Recovery during t through t + 5 (percent)	0	3.40	9.00	1.30	0	—	—	9.17	2.50	0
Output loss										
Output loss during t through t + 3 (percent)	2.20	30.60	97.66	5.35	0.00	—	—	28.79	9.62	19.72

Sources: IMF staff reports; country authorities' reports; newspaper articles; and authors' calculations.

Note: t denotes the starting year of the crisis; NPL = nonperforming loan; M2 = broad money.

REFERENCES

Batunanggar, Sukarela, 2002, "Indonesia's Banking Crisis Resolution: Lessons and the Way Forward" (unpublished; London: Center for Central Banking Studies [CCBS], Bank of England).

Bhatia, Ashok, 2007, "New Landscape, New Challenges: Structural Change and Regulation in the U.S. Financial Sector," IMF Working Paper 07/195 (Washington: International Monetary Fund).

Beim, David, and Charles Calomiris, 2001, *Emerging Financial Markets* (New York: McGraw-Hill/Irwin Publishers).

Calomiris, Charles, Daniela Klingebiel, and Luc Laeven, 2005, "Financial Crisis Policies and Resolution Mechanisms: A Taxonomy from Cross-Country Experience," in *Systemic Financial Crises: Containment and Resolution*, ed. by Patrick Honohan and Luc Laeven (Cambridge, United Kingdom: Cambridge University Press), pp. 25–75.

Caprio, Gerard, and Daniela Klingebiel, 1996, "Bank Insolvencies: Cross-Country Experience," Policy Research Working Paper No. 1620 (Washington: World Bank).

Caprio, Gerard, Daniela Klingebiel, Luc Laeven, and Guillermo Noguera, 2005, "Appendix: Banking Crisis Database," in *Systemic Financial Crises: Containment and Resolution*, ed. by Patrick Honohan and Luc Laeven (Cambridge, United Kingdom: Cambridge University Press), pp. 307–40.

Claessens, Stijn, Daniela Klingebiel, and Luc Laeven, 2003, "Financial Restructuring in Banking and Corporate Sector Crises: What Policies to Pursue?" in *Managing Currency Crises in Emerging Markets*, ed. by Michael Dooley and Jeffrey Frankel (Chicago: University of Chicago Press), pp. 147–80.

———, 2005, "Crisis Resolution, Policies, and Institutions: Empirical Evidence," in *Systemic Financial Crises: Containment and Resolution*, ed. by Patrick Honohan and Luc Laeven (Cambridge, United Kingdom: Cambridge University Press), pp. 169–96.

Collyns, Charles, and G. Russell Kincaid, 2003, "Managing Financial Crises: Recent Experience and Lessons for Latin America," IMF Occasional Paper No. 217 (Washington: International Monetary Fund).

Demirgüç-Kunt, Asli, and Enrica Detragiache, 2002, "Does Deposit Insurance Increase Banking System Stability? An Empirical Investigation," *Journal of Monetary Economics*, Vol. 49, pp. 1373–406.

Demirgüç-Kunt, Asli, Edward Kane, and Luc Laeven, eds., 2008, *Deposit Insurance around the World: Issues of Design and Implementation* (Cambridge, Massachusetts: MIT Press).

Djankov, Simeon, Caralee McLiesh, and Andrei Shleifer, 2007, "Private Credit in 129 Countries," *Journal of Financial Economics*, Vol. 84, No. 2, pp. 299–329.

Dooley, Michael, and Jeffrey Frankel, eds., 2003, *Managing Currency Crises in Emerging Markets*, Proceedings of a National Bureau for Economic Research conference. (Chicago: University of Chicago Press).

Drees, Burkhard, and Ceyla Pazarbasioglu, 1998, "The Nordic Banking Crisis: Pitfalls in Financial Liberalization," IMF Occasional Paper No. 161 (Washington: International Monetary Fund).

Enoch, Charles, Barbara Baldwin, Olivier Frécaut, and Arto Kovanen, 2001, "Indonesia: Anatomy of a Banking Crisis: Two Years of Living Dangerously 1997–1999," IMF Working Paper 01/52 (Washington: International Monetary Fund).

Frankel, Jeffrey, and Andrew Rose, 1996, "Currency Crashes in Emerging Markets: An Empirical Treatment," *Journal of International Economics*, Vol. 41, pp. 351–66.

Hoelscher, David, and Marc Quintyn, 2003, "Managing Systemic Banking Crises," IMF Occasional Paper No. 224 (Washington: International Monetary Fund).

Honohan, Patrick, and Daniela Klingebiel, 2000, "Controlling the Fiscal Costs of Banking Crises," Policy Research Working Paper No. 2441 (Washington: World Bank).

Honohan, Patrick, and Luc Laeven, eds., 2005, *Systemic Financial Crises: Containment and Resolution* (Cambridge, United Kingdom: Cambridge University Press).

————, 2003, "Uruguay—Third Review Under the Stand-By Arrangement and Request for Modification and Waiver of Applicability of Performance Criteria—Report on the 2002 Banking Crisis," Country Report 03/247 (Washington).

————, 2008, "United Kingdom: 2008 Article IV Consultation," Staff Report 08/271 (Washington).

Jácome, Luis, 2004, "The Late 1990s Financial Crisis in Ecuador: Institutional Weaknesses, Fiscal Rigidities, and Financial Dollarization at Work," IMF Working Paper 04/12, (Washington: International Monetary Fund).

Klingebiel, Daniela, 2000, "The Use of Asset Management Companies in the Resolution of Banking Crises," Working Paper No. 2294 (Washington: World Bank).

Laeven, Luc, and Fabian Valencia, 2012, "The Use of Blanket Guarantees in Banking Crises," *Journal of International Money and Finance*, Vol. 31, No. 5, pp. 1220–48.

La Porta, Rafael, Florencio Lopez-De-Silanes, and Andrei Shleifer, 2002, "Government Ownership of Banks," *Journal of Finance*, Vol. 57, pp. 265–301.

Lindgren, Carl-Johan, 2005, "Pitfalls in Managing Closures of Financial Institutions," in *Systemic Financial Crises: Containment and Resolution*, ed. by Patrick Honohan and Luc Laeven (Cambridge, United Kingdom: Cambridge University Press), pp. 76–108.

Lindgren, Carl-Johan, Gillian Garcia, and Matthew I. Saal, 1996, *Bank Soundness and Macroeconomic Policy* (Washington: International Monetary Fund).

Nakaso, Hiroshi, 2001, "The Financial Crisis in Japan During the 1990s: How the Bank of Japan Responded and the Lessons Learnt," BIS Paper No. 6 (Basel: Bank for International Settlements).

Sanhueza, Gonzalo, 2001, "Chilean Banking Crisis of the 1980s: Solutions and Estimation of the Costs," Working Paper 104 (Santiago: Central Bank of Chile).

Sturzenegger, Federico, and Jeromin Zettelmeyer, 2006, *Debt Defaults and Lessons from a Decade of Crises* (Cambridge, Massachusetts: MIT Press).

Valencia, Fabian, forthcoming, "Banks' Precautionary Capital and Credit Crunches," *Macroeconomic Dynamics*.

World Bank, 2002, *Global Development Finance* (Washington: World Bank).

PART II

Lessons in Crisis Prevention and Management

CHAPTER 3

Financial and Sovereign Debt Crises: Some Lessons Learned and Those Forgotten

CARMEN M. REINHART AND KENNETH S. ROGOFF

Even after one of the most severe crises on record (in its fifth year as of 2012) in the advanced world, the received wisdom in policy circles clings to the notion that advanced, wealthy economies are completely different animals from their emerging market counterparts. Until 2007–08, the presumption was that they were not nearly as vulnerable to financial crises.[1] When events disabused the world of that notion, the idea still persisted that if a financial crisis does occur, advanced economies are much better at managing the aftermath, thanks to their ability to vigorously apply countercyclical policy. Even as the recovery consistently proved to be far weaker than most forecasters were expecting, policymakers continued to underestimate the depth and duration of the downturn.

In Europe, where the financial crisis transformed into sovereign debt crises in several countries, the current phase of the denial cycle is marked by an official policy approach predicated on the assumption that normal growth can be restored through a mix of austerity, forbearance, and growth. The claim is that advanced economies do not need to apply the standard toolkit used by emerging markets, including debt restructurings, higher inflation, capital controls, and significant financial repression. Advanced economies do not resort to such gimmicks, policymakers say. To do so would be to give up hard-earned credibility, thereby destabilizing expectations and throwing the economy into a vicious circle. Although the view that advanced country financial crises are completely different, and therefore should be handled completely differently, has been a recurrent refrain, notably in both the European sovereign debt crisis and the U.S. subprime mortgage crisis, this view is at odds with the historical track record of most advanced economies, in which debt restructuring or conversions, financial repres-

---

This chapter was initially written as a paper for the conference "Financial Crises: Causes, Consequences, and Policy Responses," IMF, Washington, DC, September 14, 2012. The authors were asked to ponder the question of what lessons have been learned since the crisis began. We are grateful for National Science Foundation Grant No. 0849224 for financial support.
[1] Reinhart and Rogoff (2008) present evidence to the contrary. Since the early 1800s, the incidence of banking crises is similar for advanced and emerging economies—the post-World War II period is the era when crises visited the wealthy economies with less frequency.

sion, and a tolerance for higher inflation have been integral parts of the resolution of significant debt overhangs.

It is certainly true that policymakers need to manage public expectations. However, by consistently choosing instruments and calibrating responses based on overly optimistic medium-term scenarios, they risk ultimately losing credibility and destabilizing expectations rather than the reverse. Nowhere is the denial problem more acute than in the collective amnesia about advanced economy deleveraging experiences (especially, but not exclusively, before World War II) that involved a variety of sovereign and private restructuring, default, debt conversions, and financial repression. This denial has led to policies that in some cases risk exacerbating the final costs of deleveraging.

This chapter extends earlier work on pre–World War II sovereign defaults by further documenting lesser known domestic default episodes but particularly by delving deeper into the widespread default by both advanced and emerging European nations on World War I debts to the United States during the 1930s. This chapter quantifies this largely forgotten episode of debt forgiveness (the debts were never repaid) in both its incidence across countries (which is relatively well known) and its scale, or orders of magnitude of default, in comparison to the debtor countries' GDP as well as to what it collectively amounted to from the U.S. creditor perspective.

The chapter also illustrates the continuing depth of the debt overhang problem, which remains the overarching obstacle to faster recovery. Research shows that a debt overhang of this size is typically associated with a sustained period of sub-par growth, lasting two decades or more (Reinhart, Reinhart, and Rogoff, 2012, which includes a view of the scholarly literature, including critiques; see also the *World Economic Outlook*, October 2012 and April 2013). In light of this danger, the chapter reviews the possible options, concluding that the endgame to the global financial crisis is likely to require some combination of financial repression (a nontransparent form of debt restructuring), outright restructuring of public and private debt, conversions, somewhat higher inflation, and a variety of capital controls under the umbrella of macroprudential regulation. Although austerity in varying degrees is necessary, in many cases it is not sufficient to cope with record public and private debt overhangs. All these options, understandably anathema to the current generation of advanced country policymakers, are more familiar to their economies than is commonly recognized. This opportunity is used to highlight four basic lessons from the historical track record, as well as those lessons economists, financial market participants, and policymakers seem to have collectively forgotten.

FINANCIAL LIBERALIZATION, FINANCIAL CRISES, AND CRISIS PREVENTION

Lesson 1: On prevention versus crisis management. We have done better at the latter than the former. It is doubtful that this will change as memories of the crisis fade and financial market participants and their regulators become complacent.

Although economists' understanding of financial crises has considerably deep-ened in recent years, periods of huge financial sector growth and development (often accompanied by steeply rising private indebtedness) will probably always generate waves of financial crises. As the late Diaz-Alejandro famously titled his 1985 paper "Good-bye Financial Repression, Hello Financial Crash," many crises are the result of financial liberalization gone amok. Diaz-Alejandro was writing about emerging markets, but he could have said very much the same thing for advanced economies. Figure 3.1 presents a composite index of banking, currency, sovereign default, and inflation crises, and stock market crashes. Countries are weighted by their share of world income, so advanced economies carry propor-tionately higher weights. The figure, and the longer analysis of crises in Reinhart and Rogoff (2009), show that the "financial repression" period, 1950–70 in par-ticular, has markedly fewer crises than earlier.

"Financial repression" includes directed lending to government by captive domestic audiences (such as pension funds), explicit or implicit caps on interest

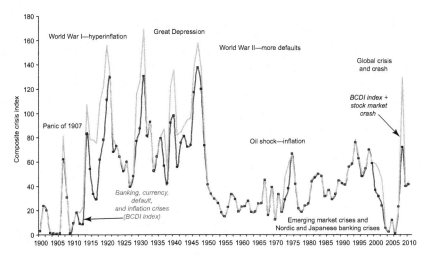

Figure 3.1 Varieties of crises: World aggregate, 1900–2010. *A composite index of banking, cur-rency, sovereign default and, inflation crises, and stock market crashes (weighted by their share of world income)*

Source: Authors' calculations.

Notes: The banking, currency, default (domestic and external), and inflation composite (*BCDI* index—solid line) can take a value between 0 and 5 (for any country in any given year) depending on the varieties of crises taking place in that year. (For instance, in 1998 the index took on a value of 5 for the Russian Federation because there was a currency crash, a banking and inflation crisis, and a sovereign default on both domestic and foreign debt obligations.) The index is then weighted by the country's share in world income. This index is calculated annually for the 66 countries in the sample for 1800–2010 (shown in the figure for 1900 onward). The borderline banking cases identified in Laeven and Valencia (2010) for the period 2007–2010 have been added. In addition, the Barro and Ursua (2009) definition of a stock market crash has been used for the 25 countries in their sample (a subset of the 66-country sample, except for Switzerland) for the period 1864–2006; their crash definition was also updated through June 2010, to compile the *BCDI*+ index. For the United States, for example, the index posts a reading of 2 (banking crisis and stock market crash) in 2008; for Australia and Mexico it also posts a reading of 2 (currency and stock market crash). For each country the reading of the *BCDI*+ index can range from zero crises per year to a maximum of six (banking, currency, inflation, domestic debt crisis, external debt crisis, and equity market crash). As there are 66 countries in the sample, the aggregate world reading can, in principle, reach a maximum value of 396 crises.

rates, regulation of cross-border capital movements, and generally a tighter connection between government and banks. It often masks a subtle type of debt restructuring. Recent work on monetary policy discussed in Brunnermeier and Sannikov (2012) suggests that even in "normal" times, redistribution of wealth between savers and borrowers may be one of the central channels through which monetary policy operates. Periods of monetary tightening and high real interest rates benefit savers, and periods of loose monetary policy benefit borrowers (usually including governments). This redistributive channel, all too often neglected in standard macroeconomic analyses, can become a central one in periods in which governments restrict savers' choices and opportunities. Financial repression is a form of taxation that, like any form of taxation, leads to distortions. However, perhaps because financial repression generally discourages financial excess, it is often associated with reduced frequency of crises as Figure 3.1 illustrates. It is precisely for this reason that the dividing line between prudential regulation and financial repression is not always a sharp one.

TODAY'S MULTIFACETED DEBT OVERHANG

Lesson 2: On diagnosing and understanding the scope and depth of the risks and magnitudes of the debt. What is public and what is private? Domestic and external debt are not created equal. And debt is usually MUCH bigger than what meets the eye.

The magnitude of the overall debt problem facing advanced economies today is difficult to overstate. The mix of an aging society, an expanding social welfare state, and stagnant population growth would be difficult in the best of circumstances. This burden has been significantly compounded by huge increases in government debt in the wake of the crisis, illustrated in Figure 3.2. The figure shows gross central government debt as a percentage of GDP for both advanced economies and emerging markets from 1900 through 2011. As the figure illustrates, the emerging markets actually deleveraged in the decade before the financial crisis whereas advanced economies hit a peak not seen since the end of World War II. In fact, going back to 1800, the current level of central government debt in advanced economies is approaching a two-century high-water mark.

Broader debt measures that include state and local liabilities are unfortunately not available across a long historical period for many countries (Reinhart and Rogoff, 2009), but including them would almost surely make the present public debt burden seem even larger. Similarly, gross government debt is used instead of net government debt because, again, net debt data are not available for nearly as long a period or broad a range of countries. Another reason, however, is that net debt subtracts government old age trust fund holdings of government debt. Including the liability side of old age pensions and medical benefits would only make the overall debt picture much worse today relative to earlier periods.

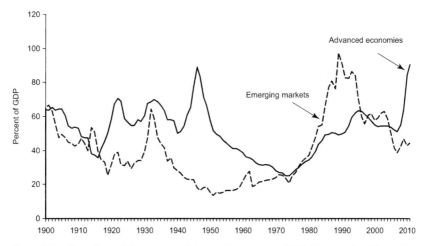

Figure 3.2   Gross Central Government Debt as a Percentage of GDP: Advanced and Emerging Market Economies, 1860–2011 (unweighted average)

Sources: Reinhart and Rogoff (2010); and Reinhart, Reinhart, and Rogoff (2012) and sources cited therein.

External debt is another important marker of overall vulnerability. Figure 3.3 illustrates the level of total external debt, including both public and private, relative to GDP. Again, a picture of deleveraging in emerging markets is clear, as is a dramatic increase in external debt for the advanced economies. Reinhart and Rogoff (2009, 2011) argue that total external debt is an important indicator because the boundaries between public and private debt can become blurred in a crisis. External private debt is one of the forms of "hidden debt" that can come jumping out of the

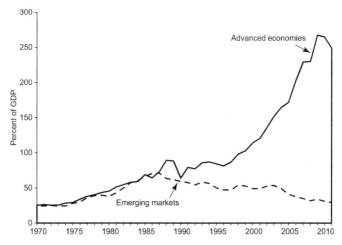

Figure 3.3   Gross Total (public plus private) External Debt as a Percentage of GDP: 22 advanced and 25 emerging market economies, 1970–2011

Sources: Lane and Milesi-Ferretti (2007); Reinhart and Rogoff (2009); Reinhart, Reinhart, and Rogoff (2012), and sources cited therein; World Bank *Quarterly External Debt Statistics*, various years; and World Bank *Global Development Finance*, various years.

woodwork in a crisis. Just as bank balance sheets before the 2007–09 financial crisis did not reflect the true economic risk these institutions faced, official measures of public debt are typically a significant understatement of vulnerability.

Admittedly, a major driving force behind the rise in advanced economy external debt involved the growth in intra-European debt. As the euro area is painfully learning, the lines between national debt and common currency area–wide debt can also become blurred in a financial crisis.

The distinction between external debt and domestic debt can be quite important, and as Reinhart and Rogoff (2009, 2010, 2011) argue, the thresholds for problems in growth and default crises are different for the two types of debt. Domestic debt issued in domestic currency typically offers a far wider range of partial default options than does foreign currency–denominated external debt. Financial repression has already been mentioned; governments can stuff debt into local pension funds and insurance companies, forcing them through regulation to accept far lower rates of return than they might otherwise demand. But domestic debt can also be reduced through inflation. As Reinhart and Sbrancia (2011) show, a mix of financial repression and inflation can be a particularly potent way of reducing domestic-currency debt. The array of options is much narrower for foreign-currency debt,

Finally, Figure 3.4 illustrates the explosion of private sector debt before the financial crisis. Unlike central government debt, for which the series are remarkably stationary over a two-century period, private sector debt shows a marked upward trend due to financial innovation and globalization, punctuated by volatility caused by periods of financial repression and financial liberalization. As the figure shows, the degree of deleveraging after the financial crisis has been limited. In essence, the

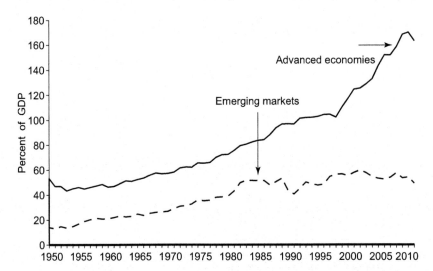

Figure 3.4 Private Domestic Credit as a Percent of GDP, 1950–2011 (22 advanced and 28 emerging market economies)

Sources: IMF, *International Financial Statistics*, and *World Economic Outlook*, various issues; and Reinhart (2010) and sources cited therein.

BOX 3.1 The Elements of Debt Reduction

1. Economic growth
2. Fiscal adjustment and austerity
3. Explicit default or restructuring
4. A sudden surprise burst in inflation
5. A steady dose of financial repression accompanied by an equally steady dose of inflation

advanced economies have exercised the government's capacity to borrow, even after a crisis, to prop up the system. This strategy likely made the initial post-crisis phase less acute. But it also implies that it may take longer to deleverage.

HOW WILL DEBT BE REDUCED?

Lesson 3: On crisis resolution. How different are advanced economies and emerging markets? Not as different as is widely believed.

There are essentially five ways to reduce large debt-to-GDP ratios (Box 3.1). Most historical episodes have involved some combination of these.

The first on the list is relatively rare and the rest are difficult and unpopular.[2] Recent policy discussion has tended to forget options (3) and (5), arguing that advanced economies do not behave that way. In fact, option (5) was used extensively by advanced economies to deal with post-World War II debt (Reinhart and Sbrancia, 2011) and option (3) was common enough before World War II. Given the magnitude of today's debt and the likelihood of a period of very slow growth, it is doubtful that fiscal austerity will be sufficient, even combined with financial repression. Rather, the size of the problem suggests that there will need to be restructurings, particularly, for example, in the periphery of Europe, far beyond anything discussed in public to this point. Of course, mutualization of euro country debt effectively uses northern country taxpayer resources to bail out the periphery and reduces the need for restructuring. But the size of the overall problem is such that mutualization could potentially result in continuing slow growth or even recession in the core countries, magnifying their own already challenging sustainability problems for debt and old age benefit programs.

Historically, periods of high government debt such as the current one have led to marked increases in debt restructurings, as Figure 3.5 illustrates. The figure plots GDP-weighted central government debt against the percentage of countries experiencing inflation higher than 20 percent as well as the share of countries engaged in debt restructuring, from 1826 through 2010. The correlation is strongly statistically significant, and also holds at a more granular level, for example, when dividing the world into regions. Figure 3.6 illustrates the pattern

---

[2] See Reinhart, Rogoff, and Savastano (2003) on the post-World War II experience and Sturzenegger and Zettlemeyer (2006) on the more recent emerging market experiences.

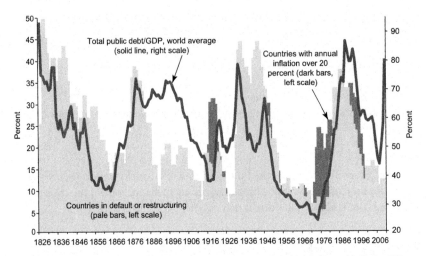

Figure 3.5 Sovereign Default, Total (domestic plus external) Public Debt, and Inflation Crises: World Aggregates, 1826–2010 (debt as a percent of GDP)

Source: Reinhart and Rogoff (2011).

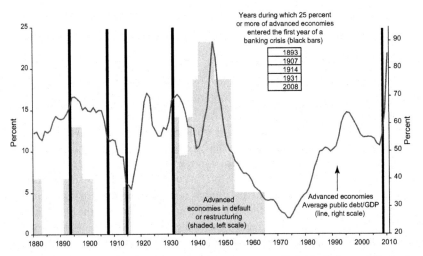

Figure 3.6 Sovereign Default, Total (domestic plus external) Public Debt, and Systemic Banking Crises: Advanced Economies, 1880–2010 (debt as a percent of GDP)

Source: Reinhart and Rogoff (2011).

of waves of sovereign defaults and restructurings that typically follow within a few years of an international wave of banking crises, again a relationship that can be demonstrated statistically, and one that also appears clearly in the individual country histories (as illustrated in Reinhart, 2010). The debt restructurings in Figures 3.5 and 3.6 do not include the numerous less-than-voluntary restructurings, in which domestic debtors were forced to accept inferior terms, or in which the tools of financial repression were used to reduce debt burdens.

Although the connection between indebtedness and default at the aggregate level depicted in Figures 3.5 and 3.6 for both advanced and emerging market economies is highly informative, Table 3.1 presents a selected chronology of domestic and external credit events from the 1920s through the 1960s for the advanced economies. The term "selected" is used not because familiar events are excluded but because, as noted in Reinhart and Rogoff (2009), domestic defaults, restructurings, or conversions are particularly difficult to document and can sometimes be disguised as "voluntary." A broader definition of default would include financial repression and inflation as opaque mechanisms for reducing debt via restrictive regulations and taxes.

As Table 3.1 documents, 13 of 21 advanced economies had at least one credit event involving the sovereign. A number of countries had multiple debt crises and an even larger number than those listed in Table 3.1 had, especially during the 1930s, wholesale private defaults, as evidenced by bank failures and nonfinancial corporate bankruptcies (Reinhart and Rogoff, 2009).

In many of the episodes listed in Table 3.1, it is difficult to document the magnitude of the debt reduction achieved by the credit event in question because

TABLE 3.1

Selected Episodes of Domestic or External Debt Default, Restructuring, or Conversions: Advanced Economies, 1920s–1960s		
Country	**Dates**	**Commentary**
Australia	1931–32	Domestic debt only. The Debt Conversion Agreement Act in 1931/32 appears to have done something similar to the later New Zealand–induced conversion. See New Zealand entry.[1]
Austria	1920–21	Hyperinflation erodes domestic debt.
	1932–33	World War I debt (see Table 3.2); not repaid.
	1934	
	1938	External debt was ultimately settled in 1952.
	1940–52	Domestic default. Restoration of schilling (limit of 150 per person). Remainder placed in blocked accounts. In December 1947, large amounts of previously blocked schillings were invalidated and rendered worthless. Temporary blockage of 50 percent of deposits.
Belgium	1934	World War I debt (see Table 3.2); not repaid.
Canada (Alberta)	April 1935	The only province to default—the default lasted for about 10 years.
France	1934	World War I debt (see Table 3.2); not repaid.
Germany	1923–24	Hyperinflation liquidates domestic currency debt.
	1932–53	External debt. Largest Depression-time default.
	June 20, 1948	Monetary reform setting limit of 40 Deutschmark per person. Partial cancellation and blocking of all accounts.
Greece	1932	Interest on domestic debt was reduced by 75 percent beginning in 1932. Domestic debt was about one-quarter of total public debt.
	1932–64	External arrears not resolved until 1964.
	1934	World War I debt (see Table 3.2); not repaid.
	1941–44	Hyperinflation eroded what little domestic debt there was.

(Continued)

TABLE 3.1 (*Continued*)

Selected Episodes of Domestic or External Debt Default, Restructuring, or Conversions: Advanced Economies, 1920s–1960s		
Country	**Dates**	**Commentary**
Italy	1920	Conversions of domestic debt in the 1920s; multiple attempts
	1924	to reduce the high level of floating rate debt. Unclear how "vol-
	1926	untary" these conversions were; not counted as sovereign
	1930s	defaults.
	1934	World War I debt (see Table 3.2); not repaid.
	1944	Inflation of 500 percent wipes out domestic debt.
	1940–46	External debt in default.
Japan	1942–52	External debt in default.
	1945–47	Inflation of 150–600 percent wipes out domestic debt.
	March 2, 1946–52	After inflation, exchange of all bank notes for new issue (1 to 1) limited to 100 yen per person. Remaining balances were deposited in blocked accounts.
New Zealand	1933	In March 1933, the New Zealand Debt Conversion Act was passed providing for voluntary conversion of internal debt amounting to 113 million pounds to a basis of 4 percent for ordinary debt and 3 percent for tax-free debt. Holders had the option of dissenting but interest in the dissented portion was made subject to an interest tax of 33.3 percent.[1]
Spain	October 1936–April 1939	Interest payments on external debt were suspended; arrears on domestic debt service.
United States	1933	Abrogation of the gold clause in conjunction with a 40 percent reduction in the gold content of the U.S. dollar.
United Kingdom	1934	Most of the outstanding World War I debt was consolidated into a 3.5 percent perpetual annuity. This domestic debt conversion was apparently voluntary. World War I debt to the United States was defaulted on following the end of the Hoover 1931 moratorium. See Table 3.2.

Sources: *New York Times* (1934); United Nations (1948); Bailey (1950); Pick and Sedillot (1971); Lindert and Morton (1989); Dornbusch and Draghi (1990); Reinhart and Rogoff (2009); Redell (2012); and League of Nations, various issues.
[1] See Prichard (1970); Schedvin (1970); and Redell (2012) for accounts of the Australian and New Zealand conversions, respectively, during the Depression. Michael Redell kindly alerted the chapter authors to these episodes and references.

of the opaque nature of the default, restructuring, and renegotiation process; the imprecision of estimated recovery rates; the lack of data; or a combination. The problem is less severe for external default episodes for which the data are better, but even so it is a challenge. Exceptions, of course, are the hyperinflation or very high inflation episodes in which all or nearly all of the existing debt stocks were liquidated (Reinhart and Rogoff, 2009).

An interesting and exceptional episode for which the magnitude of the debt relief provided by default and ultimate debt forgiveness can be estimated with some degree of precision is the World War I debt to the United States (including large-scale borrowing in the immediate aftermath of the war). These defaults came in the summer of 1934, following the end of President Hoover's temporary moratorium on debt payments. Of the 17 countries listed in Table 3.2 as having borrowed from the United States during or right after the war, only Finland repaid its debt. (It is notable that Finland's debt was only 0.2 percent of Finnish GDP compared with burdens two orders of magnitude larger for France and the United Kingdom). The remaining countries received what in today's language is called debt forgiveness of the type usually associated only with highly indebted poor countries.

Table 3.2 presents the amounts of public debt to the United States that were defaulted on and presents information, where nominal GDP data are available, of the magnitude of the default or debt reduction as a percentage of GDP. The magnitude of debt relief is stunning. Perhaps not surprisingly, it is largest for France and the United Kingdom, who enjoyed debt-to-GDP reductions of 20–30 percent. This magnitude is comparable to a number of the emerging market defaults in the post-World War II era, once eventual recovery rates are taken into account. That is, although many emerging market debt burdens ultimately reached 60–100 percent of GDP, creditors typically received significant compensation with recovery rates often in excess of 50 percent, even in cases of dramatic default. By contrast, the defaults on World War I debt to the United States were

TABLE 3.2

Defaults on World War I Debt to the United States in the 1930s: Timing and Magnitude (US$)

Country	Wartime debt	Postwar debt	Total debt (excluding arrears)	Percent of GDP
Armenia	0	11,959,917.49	11,959,917.49	n.a.
Austria	0	24,055,708.92	24,055,708.92	1.7
Belgium	171,780,000.00	207,307,200.43	379,087,200.43	3.3
Czechoslovakia	0	91,879,671.03	91,879,671.03	n.a.
Estonia	0	13,999,145.60	13,999,145.60	n.a.
Finland	0	8,281,926.17	8,281,926.17	0.2
France	1,970,000,000.00	1,434,818,945.01	3,404,818,945.01	24.2
Greece	0	27,167,000.00	27,167,000.00	8.9
Hungary	0	1,685,835.61	1,685,835.61	n.a.
Italy	1,031,000,000.00	617,034,050.90	1,648,034,050.90	19.1
Latvia	0	5,132,287.14	5,132,287.14	n.a.
Lithuania	0	4,981,628.03	4,981,628.03	n.a.
Poland	0	159,666,972.39	159,666,972.39	n.a.
Romania	0	37,911,152.92	37,911,152.92	n.a.
Russia	187,729,750.00	4,871,547.37	192,601,297.37	n.a.
United Kingdom	3,696,000,000.00	581,000,000.00	4,277,000,000.00	22.2
Yugoslavia	10,605,000.00	41,153,486.55	51,758,486.55	n.a.
Total (excluding arrears)	**7,077,114,750.00**	**3,273,364,324.70**	**10,350,479,074.70**	**n.a.**
Percent of U.S. GDP				**15.70**
Memorandum item:				
Total (including arrears)			**11,628,311,614.94**	
Percent of U.S. GDP			**16.9**	

Sources: *New York Times* (June 1934); Bailey (1950); Reinhart and Rogoff, 2009, and sources cited therein.
Note: n.a. = not available.

near total. These estimates in Table 3.2 are conservative, being based on debt levels that do not include interest on arrears, so the effective defaults are in fact even larger.[3]

From the U.S. creditor vantage point, the collective default of World War I debt owed by foreign countries amounted to 15–16 percent of U.S. GDP. In this connection, it must be added that the United States had already defaulted on its sovereign debt in April 1933 to domestic and external creditors alike. The abrogation of the gold clause in conjunction with a 40 percent reduction in the gold content of the U.S. dollar also amounted to a debt haircut of about 16 percent of GDP. The magnitude and incidence of post-World War I default worldwide is also understated by not considering in this exercise war debts owed by countries (other than the United States) to the United Kingdom. For the most part, these debts were also defaulted on and never repaid.

As unpleasant (*New York Times*, June 15, 1934)[4] as these credit events were, it is clear that they played a substantive role in reducing the debt overhang from both World War I and the Great Depression. In light of the historic public and private debt levels discussed above, it is difficult to envision a resolution to the five-year-old crisis that does not involve a greater role for explicit restructuring.

THE RETURN OF FINANCIAL REPRESSION?

Lesson 4: *On international financial architecture after global crises—the return of financial repression.*

Figure 3.7, which extends the schematic in Reinhart and Rogoff (2009), highlights a "prototype" sequence of events after a financial crisis. In the typical sequence, the current stage often ends with some combination of capital controls, financial repression, inflation, and default. This turn of the pendulum from liberalization back to more heavy-handed regulation stems from both the greater aversion to risk that usually accompanies severe financial crises, including the desire to prevent new ones from emerging, as well as from the desire to maintain interest rates as low as possible to facilitate debt financing. Reinhart and Sbrancia (2011) document how, following World War II (when explicit defaults were limited to the losing side), financial repression via negative real interest rates reduced debt to the tune of 2–4 percent a year for the United States, and for the United Kingdom for the years with negative real interest rates.[5] For Italy and Australia, with their higher inflation rates, debt reduction from the financial repression "tax" was on a larger scale and closer to 5 percent per year. As documented in Reinhart (2012), financial repression is well under way in the current post-crisis experience.

---

[3] See memorandum item in Table 3.2.

[4] "Debts Dead, a View in Paris."

[5] Negative real interest rates are a tax on bondholders and effect a transfer or redistribution from savers to borrowers.

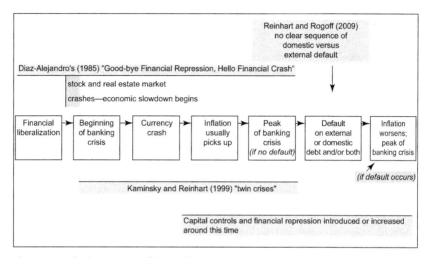

Figure 3.7   The Sequencing of Crises: The Big Picture

Source: Authors' illustration based on prototype sequencing pattern.

FINAL THOUGHTS

Of course, if policymakers are fortunate, economic growth will provide a soft exit, reducing or eliminating the need for painful restructuring, repression, or inflation. The evidence on debt overhangs is not very heartening. Looking just at the public debt overhang, and not taking into account old age support programs, the picture is not encouraging. Reinhart, Reinhart, and Rogoff (2012) consider 26 episodes in which advanced country debt exceeded 90 percent of GDP, encompassing most or all of the episodes since World War II. (They tabulate the small number of cases in which the debt overhang lasted less than five years, but do not include these in their overhang calculations.) They find that debt overhang episodes averaged 1.2 percent lower growth than individual country averages for non-overhang periods. Moreover, the average duration of the overhang episodes is 23 years. Of course, there are many other factors that determine longer-term GDP growth, including especially the rate of productivity growth. But given that official public debt is only one piece of the larger debt overhang issue, it is clear that the governments should be careful in their assumption that growth alone will be able to end the crisis. Instead, today's advanced economy governments may have to look increasingly to the approaches that have long been associated with emerging markets, and that advanced economies themselves once practiced not so long ago.

REFERENCES

Bailey, Thomas A., 1950, *A Diplomatic History of the American People* (New York: Appleton-Century-Crofts, Inc).

Barro, Robert, and Jose Ursua, 2009, "Stock-Market Crashes and Depressions," NBER Working Paper No. 14760 (Cambridge, Massachusetts: National Bureau of Economic Research).

Brunnermeier, Markus K., and Yuliy Sannikov, 2012, "Redistributive Monetary Policy," Paper prepared for the Federal Reserve Bank of Kansas City's Economic Policy Symposium, Jackson Hole, Wyoming, August 30–September 1.

Diaz-Alejandro, Carlos, 1985, "Good-bye Financial Repression, Hello Financial Crash," *Journal of Development Economics*, Vol. 19, No. 1-2, pp. 1–24.

Dornbusch, Rudiger, and Mario Draghi, 1990, *Public Debt Management: Theory and History*, (Cambridge, United Kingdom: Cambridge University Press).

International Monetary Fund, 2013, "Hopes, Realities, Risks," *World Economic Outlook*, April (Washington).

Kaminsky, Graciela L., and Carmen M. Reinhart, 1999, "The Twin Crises: The Causes of Banking and Balance of Payments Problems," *American Economic Review*, Vol. 89, June, pp. 473–500.

Laeven, Luc, and Fabian Valencia, 2010, "Resolution of Banking Crises: The Good, the Bad, and the Ugly," IMF Working Paper 10/146 (Washington: International Monetary Fund).

Lane, Philip, and Gian Maria Milesi-Ferretti, 2007, "The External Wealth of Nations Mark II: Revised and Extended Estimates of Foreign Assets and Liabilities, 1970–2004," *Journal of International Economics*, Vol. 73, pp. 223–50.

League of Nations, various years, *World Economic Survey: 1926–1944*. All issues. (Geneva: League of Nations).

Lindert, Peter H., and Peter J. Morton, 1989, "How Sovereign Debt Has Worked," in Jeffrey Sachs, ed., *Developing Country Debt and Economic Performance, Vol. 1* (Chicago: University of Chicago Press), pp. 39–106.

Lloyd Prichard, Muriel, 1970, *An economic history of New Zealand to 1939* (Auckland & London: Collins).

New York Times, 1934, "All Debtors to US Excepting Finland Default Today, June 15.

Pick, Franz, and René Sédillot, 1971, *All the Monies of the World: A Chronicle of Currency Values* (New York: Pick Publishing Corporation).

Redell, Michael, 2012, "The New Zealand Debt Conversion Act 1933: a case study in coercive domestic public debt restructuring," *Reserve Bank of New Zealand Bulletin*, 2012, Vol. 75, pp. 38–45.

Reinhart, Carmen M., 2010, "This Time Is Different Chartbook: Country Histories on Debt, Default, and Financial Crises," NBER Working Paper No. 15815 (Cambridge, Massachusetts: National Bureau of Economic Research).

Reinhart, Carmen M., 2012, "The Return of Financial Repression," CEPR Discussion Paper No. 8947 (London: Centre for Economic Policy Research).

Reinhart, Carmen M., Kenneth S. Rogoff, and Miguel A. Savastano, 2003, "Debt Intolerance," *Brookings Papers on Economic Activity*, Vol. 1, Spring, pp. 1–74.

Reinhart, Carmen M., Vincent R. Reinhart, and Kenneth S. Rogoff, 2012, "Public Debt Overhangs: Advanced-Economy Episodes since 1800," *Journal of Economic Perspectives*, Vol. 26, No. 3, pp. 69–86.

Reinhart, Carmen M., and Kenneth S. Rogoff, 2008, "Banking Crises: An Equal Opportunity Menace," NBER Working Paper No. 14587 (Cambridge, Massachusetts: National Bureau of Economic Research).

———, 2009, *This Time is Different: Eight Centuries of Financial Folly* (Princeton, New Jersey: Princeton University Press).

———, "Growth in a Time of Debt," 2010, *American Economic Review*, Vol. 100, No. 2, pp. 573–78.

———, "From Financial Crash to Debt Crisis," 2011, *American Economic Review,* Vol. 101, No. 5, pp. 1676–706.

Reinhart, Carmen M., and M. Belen Sbrancia, 2011, "The Liquidation of Government Debt," NBER Working Paper No. 16893 (Cambridge, Massachusetts: National Bureau of Economic Research).

Schedvin, C. B., 1970, *Australia and the great depression*, (Sydney: Sydney University Press).

Sturzenegger, Federico, and Jeromin Zettlemeyer, 2006, *Debt Defaults and Lessons from a Decade of Crises* (Cambridge, Massachusetts: MIT Press).

United Nations, 1948, Department of Economic Affairs, *Public Debt, 1914–1946* (New York: United Nations).

CHAPTER 4

Procyclicality and the Search for Early Warning Indicators

HYUN SONG SHIN

Finding a set of early warning indicators that can signal vulnerability to financial turmoil has emerged as a policy goal of paramount importance in the aftermath of the 2007–09 global financial crisis. There is a large literature on early warning indicators for crises, described well in Chamon and Crowe (2013). The crises in emerging market economies in the 1990s gave impetus to the work, which has been further developed in the aftermath of the 2007–09 global financial crisis that engulfed both advanced and emerging market economies.

The literature to date could be described as eclectic and pragmatic. It is eclectic in the sense that the exercise involves a wide variety of inputs, covering external, financial, real, and fiscal variables, as well as institutional and political factors and various measures of contagion. In their overview of the literature as of 1998, Kaminsky, Lizondo, and Reinhart (1998) catalogue 105 variables that had been used up to that point.

The literature has also been pragmatic in that it has focused on improving measures of goodness of fit rather than focusing on the underlying theoretical themes that could provide bridges between different crisis episodes.[1] For instance, crises in emerging market economies have typically been distinguished from those in advanced economies. Different sets of variables enter into the exercise for each category. Emerging market economy crises focus on capital flow reversals associated with "sudden stops," for which variables such as external borrowing denominated in foreign currency take center stage; for advanced economies, housing booms and household leverage take on importance. Claessens and others (2010) examine the evidence of the 2007–09 financial crisis on both categories.

The distinction between emerging market and advanced economies is also reflected in the work of the official sector. The IMF has added a new

---

Presented at the IMF conference on "Financial Crises: Causes, Consequences, and Policy Response," Washington, DC, September 14, 2012. The author thanks Stijn Claessens, Ayhan Kose, Luc Laeven, and Fabian Valencia for comments on an earlier draft, and Laura Yi Zhao for research support.
[1] The pragmatic focus has also meant that traditional regression techniques, such as the probit model used in Berg and Pattillo (1999), have increasingly given way to nonparametric techniques that minimize the signal-to-noise ratio as in Kaminsky, Lizondo, and Reinhart (1998). Nonparametric techniques fare better when there are a large number of explanatory variables.

Vulnerability Exercise for Advanced Economies to an existing Vulnerability Exercise for Emerging Market Economies, which both feed into a joint early warning exercise with the Financial Stability Board (IMF, 2010; Chamon and Crowe, 2013).

Although the compartmentalization into emerging market and advanced economies helps improve the goodness of fit, it tends to obscure the common threads that tie together emerging market and advanced economy crises. The capital flow reversals in Spain and Ireland in the European crisis have many of the features of a "sudden stop," except that the outflow of private sector funds has been compensated for by an inflow of official funds (Merler and Pisani-Ferry, 2012). However, because the euro area crisis is taking place within a common currency area, the traditional classification of emerging market "currency crises," in which currency movements play a key role, does not fit easily in the empirical exercise.

Given the common threads that run through apparently disparate crises, it can be useful to take a step back from the practical imperative of maximizing goodness of fit and instead consider the conceptual underpinnings of early warning models, which is the purpose of this chapter.

What follows suggests that the procyclicality of the financial system provides an organizing framework for selecting indicators of vulnerability to crises, especially those indicators that are associated with banks and financial intermediaries more generally. More specifically, the chapter examines three broad sets of indicators for early warning purposes, and assesses their relative likelihood of success. The three sets of indicators are

- indicators based on market prices, such as credit default swap (CDS) spreads, implied volatility, and other price-based measures of default or distress;
- gap measures of the credit-to-GDP ratio; and
- banking sector liability aggregates, including monetary aggregates.

To anticipate the conclusions, the first approach (based on market prices) seems most appropriate for obtaining indicators of concurrent market conditions but unlikely to be useful as early warning indicators that provide enough time for meaningful remedial action.

The credit-to-GDP gap measure is a distinct improvement over the first as an early warning indicator, with a good pedigree from the work of economists at the Bank for International Settlements. It has been explored extensively as part of the Basel III bank capital rules. Yet, there are doubts about its usefulness as a real time measure, or as a measure that yields a threshold that can be applied uniformly across countries.

That leaves the third approach, based on bank liability aggregates, including various components of the money stock. The chapter suggests that this third approach is the most promising because it preserves the advantages of the credit-to-GDP gap measure but also stands a good chance of yielding indicators that can be used in real time.

The downside, however, of the monetary approach is that any measure derived in this way will need to find meaning by reference to specific institutional features of the financial system rather than by being applied in an unthinking way.

In addition, the traditional thinking behind the definitions of monetary aggregates will have to be transcended to make the approach useful. Whereas traditional definitions of monetary aggregates exclude the liabilities between financial intermediaries, such liabilities turn out to be perhaps the most informative of them all.

PRICE-BASED EARLY WARNING INDICATORS

Figure 4.1 illustrates the credit default swap (CDS) spreads of Bear Stearns and Lehman Brothers. Panel b gives the longer perspective and shows how the spreads increased sharply with the onset of the crisis.

What is remarkable is how tranquil the CDS measure is before the crisis. There is barely a ripple in the series in the period 2004 to 2006 when vulnerability to the financial crisis was building up. Panel a, which plots the CDS series for the precrisis period of January 2004 to January 2007, shows that CDS spreads were actually falling, dipping below 20 basis points at the end of 2006. Other price-based measures, such as value-at-risk, implied volatility, and structural models of default based on equity prices, all painted the same picture.

The failure of price-based measures to succeed as early warning indicators can be traced to their implicit premise that market signals and the decisions guided by those signals always interact in a stabilizing virtuous circle. However, sometimes they go astray and act in concert in an amplifying vicious circle in which market signals and decisions guided by those signals reinforce an existing tendency toward procyclicality. Some of the forces toward procyclicality are described in the 2011 Mundell-Fleming lecture (Shin, 2012).

As an illustration of the outcome of the tendency toward procyclicality, the scatter chart in Figure 4.2 plots how much the change in the size of Barclays' balance sheet—representative of a typical global bank—is financed through equity and how much through debt. It also shows the change in risk-weighted assets as the balance sheet grows or shrinks.

The fact that risk-weighted assets barely increase in Figure 4.2 even as raw assets are increasing rapidly is indicative of the lowering of measured risks (such as spreads or value-at-risk) during lending booms. Lower measured risks and lending booms thus go together. The causation in the reverse direction will also have been operating: the compression of risk spreads is induced by the rapid increase in credit supply chasing available borrowers. Such two-way causation lays the groundwork for a feedback loop in which greater credit supply and the compression of spreads feed off each other.

The procyclicality evident in Figure 4.2 poses hard challenges for the traditional thinking that places faith in market discipline as an integral part of financial regulation, relying on prices to issue timely warning signals. Indeed, market discipline was one of the three pillars of the Basel II framework for international

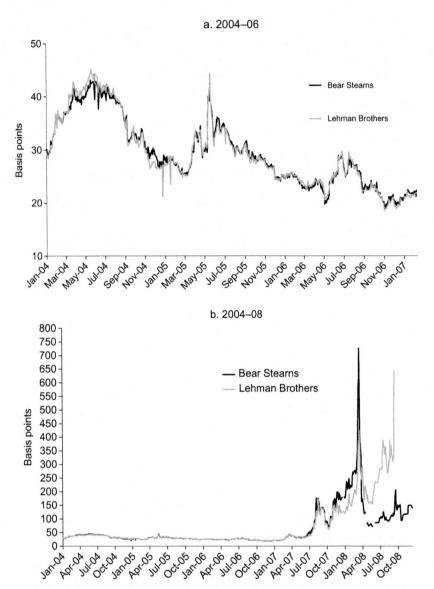

Figure 4.1 CDS Spreads for Bear Stearns and Lehman Brothers

Source: Thomson Reuters Datastream.
Note: CDS = credit default swap.

bank regulation. Economists associated with the Shadow Financial Regulatory Committee were influential in this regard. Calomiris (1999) argues for rules requiring banks to maintain a minimum amount of subordinated debt, the rationale being that banks that take on excessive risk will find it difficult to sell their subordinated debt, and will be forced to shrink their risky assets or to issue new

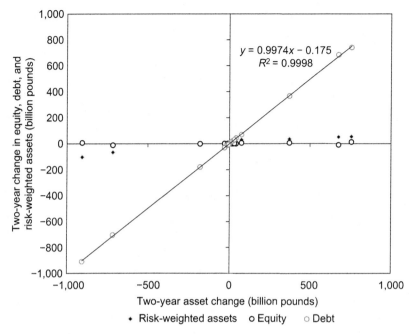

Figure 4.2 Two-Year Changes in Assets, Debt, Equity, and Risk-Weighted Assets of Barclays (1992–2010)

Source: Barclays' Annual Report.

equity to comply with the discipline imposed by private uninsured creditors. However, the experience in the run-up to the 2007–09 crisis showed how market risk premiums erode so as to nullify market discipline.

Larry Summers's quip that the achievement of finance researchers is to show that "two quart bottles of ketchup invariably sell for twice as much as one quart bottles of ketchup" (Summers, 1985, p. 634) is related to why price-based measures of early warning indicators are likely to fail. Absence of arbitrage means that prices at a point in time are consistent, but they are liable to flip to distress mode (again, fully consistent across assets) with the onset of the crisis. If the task is to give warning of the *onset* of the crisis, price-based measures have little to say about the transition.

Because the onset of a crisis is often accompanied by run-like events, the switch from a benign environment to a hostile one can be precipitous. The global games literature illustrates how the transition into financial distress—the "tipping point"—is associated with self-reinforcing effects between individual constraints and market outcomes, but how the onset of a crisis is triggered by apparently small changes in the underlying fundamentals. Outwardly, the switch has the flavor of a self-fulfilling crisis. Goldstein (2012) discusses how empirical research should take account of such tipping points, and shows how the global games framework (Morris and Shin, 1998, 2001, 2008) can be effectively invoked in the modeling exercise.

To the extent that market prices have been useful for early warning exercises at all, their usefulness comes precisely when the market price of risk is too low rather than too high. Thus, it is when asset prices are too high relative to some benchmark that warning signs are appropriate.

In their paper on the U.S. housing market, Himmelberg, Mayer, and Sinai (2005) argue that a high price-to-rent ratio or a high price-to-income ratio need not be indicators of a housing bubble because discount rates implied by low long-term interest rates had also fallen. But discount rates are prices, so the combination of low discount rates and high housing prices is arguably the kind of point-in-time consistency in prices that Summers (1985) had in mind.

CREDIT-TO-GDP GAP INDICATORS

Under the Basel III framework, the ratio of credit to GDP takes a central role as the basis for the countercyclical capital buffer. This ratio has been shown to be a practical indicator of the stage of the financial cycle, notably by Borio and Lowe (2002, 2004). To the extent that procyclicality drives financial vulnerability, detecting excessive credit growth is crucial. Normalizing credit to some underlying flow fundamental measure such as GDP and detecting deviations from trend would be one way to use the notion of excessive credit growth.

However, although the existence of a credit boom is clear in hindsight, there are several challenges to using the deviation of the credit-to-GDP ratio from trend as an early warning indicator in real time.

The first challenge is the difficulty of estimating the trend that serves as the benchmark for "excessive" growth. The difficulty is not unique to the credit-to-GDP ratio, but one shared by other macroeconomic time series. Edge and Meisenzahl (2011) find that ex post revisions to the credit-to-GDP ratio gap in real time are sizable for the United States and as large as the gap itself. The source of the ex post revisions is not the revision of the underlying data, but rather the revision of the estimated trend measured in real time.

The second difficulty is that credit growth and GDP dance to somewhat different tunes over the cycle, so the ratio of the two may sometimes issue misleading signals. Bank lending in particular may be influenced by preexisting contractual commitments, such as lines of credit, which are drawn down during the crisis. Ivashina and Scharfstein (2010) document the impact of such lines of credit on credit growth during the 2007–09 crisis. Therefore, lending may continue to increase for some time after the onset of a crisis.

Figure 4.3 is taken from Repullo and Saurina (2011) and shows the credit-to-GDP ratio for the United Kingdom and its Hodrick-Prescott (H-P)-filtered trend (panel a). The H-P filter parameter is set at $\lambda = 40,000$ as recommended by the Basel Committee, which effectively means a linear trend. Panel b shows the gap between the credit-to-GDP ratio and the trend.

From panel b of Figure 4.3, it can be noted the gap measure is large even as GDP growth is falling very sharply during the crisis. Thus, the ratio of the two gives a misleadingly large credit-to-GDP ratio during the crisis.

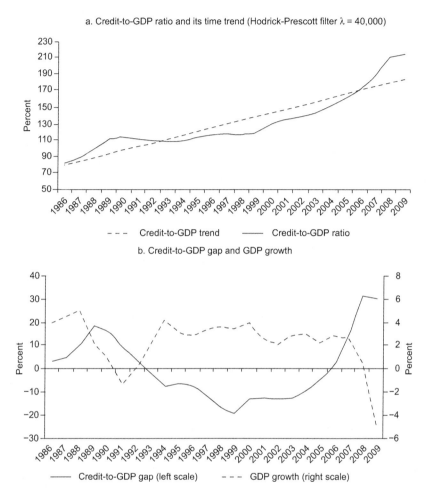

Figure 4.3   Credit-to-GDP Ratio and GDP Growth for the United Kingdom

Source: Repullo and Saurina (2011).

Basel III discussions have given a great deal of prominence to the credit-to-GDP gap measure (BCBS, 2009, 2010). To the extent that the Basel rules are expected to be applied uniformly (or at least in a consistent manner) to all Basel Committee member countries, finding common thresholds for the credit-to-GDP ratio would be a basic requirement.

BANK LIABILITY AGGREGATES, INCLUDING SOME MONETARY AGGREGATES

Rapid growth of bank lending is mirrored on the liabilities side of the balance sheet by shifts in the composition of bank funding. As intermediaries that borrow to lend, banks must raise funding to lend to their borrowers. When credit is growing faster than the available pool of funds that are usually drawn on by the bank (core liabilities), the bank will turn to other, noncore sources of funding to support its credit growth.

Thus, the ratio of noncore to core liabilities serves as a signal of the degree of risk taking by the bank and hence of the stage of the financial cycle. Hahm, Shin, and Shin (2012) conduct a cross-country panel probit study and find that the ratio of noncore to core liabilities (especially noncore liabilities to foreign creditors) consistently emerges to be the most robust predictor of a currency crisis or credit crisis.

The distinction between core and noncore bank liabilities has similarity to monetary aggregates. Traditionally, the importance of monetary analysis for the real economy rested on a stable money demand relationship that underpinned the link between money and macroeconomic variables. Money demand is seen to be the result of portfolio decisions of economic agents choosing between liquid and illiquid claims, regardless of whether based on an inventory holding of money for transactions purposes. For this reason, the traditional classifications of monetary aggregates focus on the transactions role of money as a medium of exchange.

However, unlike commodity money, monetary aggregates are the liabilities of banks and therefore have an asset-side counterpart. Recognition of the asset-side counterpart of money and of the determinants of bank lending focuses attention on the supply of money by banks. Indeed, rather than speaking of the *demand for money* by savers, the relationship could be turned on its head to speak of the *supply of funding* by savers. Similarly, by speaking of the supply of money as the *demand for funding*, the shift in language serves to focus attention on the banking sector and its balance sheet management over the cycle.

But monetary aggregates are traditionally measured by netting out claims between banks. For financial stability purposes, however, the claims between banks—especially when they are cross-border—take on great significance.

Figure 4.4 plots the four-quarter growth in cross-border assets and liabilities of euro area banks in euros. The destination of euro-denominated lending reached outside the euro area as euro area banks expanded into Central and Eastern Europe. However, the cross-border euro-denominated liabilities series in Figure 4.4 can be seen as noncore liabilities generated through capital inflows. From 1999:Q1 to 2008:Q3, cross-border liabilities rose almost 3.5-fold from 1.56 trillion euro to 5.4 trillion euro. This rapid spurt translates into a constant quarterly growth rate of 3.33 percent, which when annualized is close to 14 percent.

Core and Noncore Liabilities in China

However, what counts as core or noncore will depend on the financial system and the institutions. For economies with banks operating in developed, open capital markets, noncore funding will typically take the form of wholesale funding of the bank from capital markets, sometimes denominated in foreign currency. However, if the economy has a closed capital account, and if banks are prevented

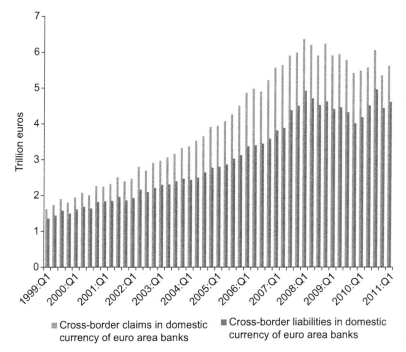

Figure 4.4   Cross-Border Euro-Denominated Assets and Liabilities of Euro Area Banks

Source: Bank for International Settlements, Locational Statistics, Table 5A.

from accessing capital market funding from abroad, what counts as noncore funding could be quite different.

Compare the Republic of Korea and China. Figure 4.5 plots the monthly growth rates of various banking sector liability aggregates for Korea (panel a) and for China (panel b). The growth rates have been filtered through an H-P filter at business cycle frequency. Note that the H-P filter is used here with hindsight to highlight differences in time series patterns, not the real-time, trend-finding exercise of Basel III.

In Korea, banks have access to capital markets, either directly or through the branches of foreign banks operating there. For this reason, the most procyclical components of the bank liability aggregates are those associated with wholesale funding, especially the series for the foreign exchange–denominated liabilities of the banking sector.[2] Before the 1997 Asian financial crisis and the 2007–09 global crisis, noncore liabilities grew rapidly, only to crash with the onset of the crises. In contrast, the growth of broad money (M2), reflecting household and corporate deposits, is much less variable over the cycle.

---

[2] The other noncore liabilities are bank debentures, repos, and other nondeposit items such as promissory notes (Shin and Shin, 2010).

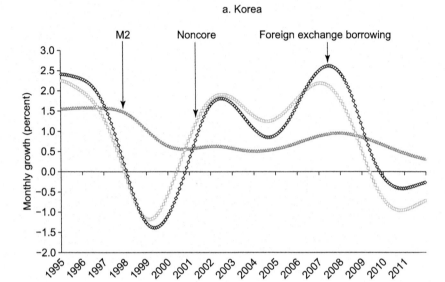

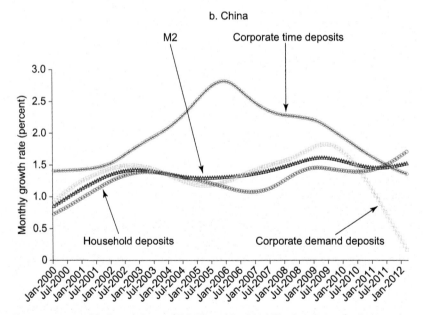

Figure 4.5 Monthly Growth Rates of H-P-Filtered Bank Liability Aggregates for Korea and China

Source: Author's compilation.
Note: H-P = Hodrick-Prescott; for this analysis, the H-P filter is set to 14,400.

However, panel b of Figure 4.5 demonstrates that in China, the subcomponents of M2 show considerable variation in their time series properties, with corporate deposits displaying the telltale procyclical patterns as compared with household deposits.

For an economy such as China, where banks are prevented from accessing international capital markets in the way that Korean banks do, applying the liability classifications from Korea of core and noncore would be inappropriate.

Instead, more thought is needed on how financial conditions are transmitted across the border into China. Just as water finds cracks to flow through, even a closed financial system is not entirely immune to global financial conditions, especially a highly trade-dependent economy such as China. If banks are prevented from accessing international capital markets, nonfinancial firms will be the conduit for the transmission of financial conditions.

Figure 4.6 depicts the activities of a Chinese nonfinancial firm with operations outside China, which borrows in U.S. dollars from an international bank in Hong Kong SAR, China, and posts renminbi deposits as collateral. The transaction would be akin to a currency swap, except that the settlement price is not chosen at the outset. The transactions instead resemble the operation of the old London Eurodollar market in the 1960s and 1970s. For the Chinese corporate, the purpose of having U.S. dollar liabilities and holding the proceeds in renminbi may be to hedge its export receivables, or simply to speculate on renminbi appreciation.

Figure 4.7 provides evidence for the transactions depicted in Figure 4.6. Figure 4.7 plots the claims and liabilities of Hong Kong banks in foreign currency to customers in China. Foreign currency, in this case, would be mainly U.S. dollars

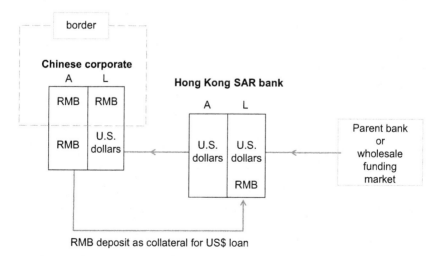

Figure 4.6   Structure of Borrowing Relationships for Nonfinancial Corporations in China

Source: Author's representation.
Note: RMB = renminbi.

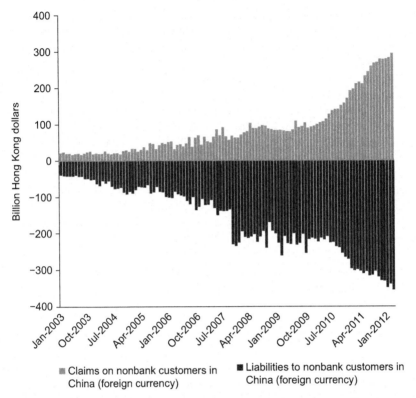

Figure 4.7 Hong Kong Banks' Claims and Liabilities to Nonbank Customers in China in Foreign Currency

Source: Hong Kong Monetary Authority.

for the assets and mainly renminbi for the liabilities. Both have risen dramatically in recent years, reflecting the rapidly increasing U.S. dollar funding of nonfinancial corporates.

The procyclical pattern in corporate deposits in panel b of Figure 4.5 may be caused by such activities of nonfinancial corporates.

In addition, such activities of nonfinancial corporates may explain why China experienced dollar shortages in 2011 with the deterioration of global funding markets caused by the crisis in Europe. During this period the renminbi came under pressure, depreciating against the U.S. dollar. Although China's banking system is largely closed, the global activities of its nonfinancial firms will be reflected in the corporate deposits within M2 when those firms hold the proceeds of dollar liabilities in their accounts in China.

Figure 4.8 illustrates the growth in the component of the money stock that is due to the deposits of corporates rather than households. Panel a shows the time trend in personal deposits and corporate deposits; panel b shows the ratio of corporate to personal deposits. The proportion of corporate deposits has increased

a. Components of China's monetary aggregates

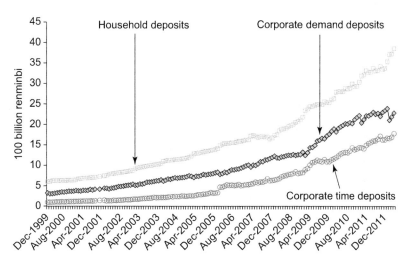

b. Ratio of corporate to personal deposits

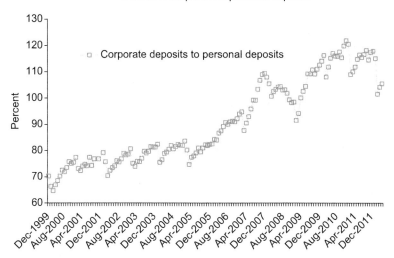

Figure 4.8 Components of China's Monetary Aggregates
Source: People's Bank of China.

in recent years, consistent with the operations of Chinese corporates as shown in Figure 4.6.

The excess liquidity generated by the activity of nonfinancial corporates in China is an important element of the lending boom in China, and is reminiscent of the lending boom in Japan in the 1980s following financial liberalization that allowed Japanese companies to access global capital markets. Both in Japan in the 1980s and in China more recently, monetary aggregates, especially corporate deposits, played the role of noncore liabilities in the way that foreign exchange borrowing by Korean banks plays the role of noncore liabilities in Korea.

The similarity between the foreign exchange liabilities in Korea and the corporate deposits in China is that both are liability components of banks. If the demarcation between core and noncore liabilities is correctly defined, the same method of tracking the ratio of noncore to core liabilities can serve as an early warning indicator of financial vulnerability.

REFERENCES

Basel Committee on Banking Supervision (BCBS), 2009, *Strengthening the Resilience of the Banking Sector* (Basel: Bank for International Settlements). http://www.bis.org/publ/bcbs164 .pdf.

———, 2010, "International Regulatory Framework for Banks (Basel III)" (Basel: Bank for International Settlements). http://www.bis.org/bcbs/basel3.htm.

Berg, Andrew, and Catherine Pattillo, 1999, "Are Currency Crises Predictable? A Test," *IMF Staff Papers*, Vol. 46, No. 2, pp. 107–38.

Borio, Claudio, and Philip Lowe, 2002, "Asset Prices, Financial and Monetary Stability: Exploring the Nexus," BIS Working Paper No. 114 (Basel: Bank for International Settlements).

———, 2004, "Securing Sustainable Price Stability: Should Credit Come Back from the Wilderness?" BIS Working Paper No. 157 (Basel: Bank for International Settlements).

Calomiris, Charles, 1999. "Building an Incentive-Compatible Safety Net," *Journal of Banking & Finance*, Vol. 23, No. 10, pp. 1499–519.

Chamon, Marcos, and Christopher Crowe, 2013, "'Predictive' Indicators of Financial Crises," in *Handbook in Financial Globalization: The Evidence and Impact of Financial Globalization*, ed. by Gerard Caprio (London: Elsevier), pp. 499–505.

Claessens, Stijn, Giovanni Dell'Ariccia, Deniz Igan, and Luc Laeven, 2010, "Cross-Country Experiences and Policy Implications from the Global Financial Crisis," *Economic Policy*, Vol. 62, pp. 267–93.

Edge, Rochelle M., and Ralf R. Meisenzahl, 2011, "The Unreliability of Credit-to-GDP Ratio Gaps in Real Time: Implications for Countercyclical Capital Buffers," *International Journal of Central Banking*, Vol. 7, No. 4, pp. 261–98.

Goldstein, Itay, 2012, "Empirical Literature on Financial Crises: Fundamentals vs. Panic," in *The Evidence and Impact of Financial Globalization*, ed. by G. Caprio (Waltham, Massachusetts: Academic Press), pp. 523–34.

Hahm, Joon-Ho, Hyun Song Shin, and Kwanho Shin, 2012, "Non-Core Bank Liabilities and Financial Vulnerability," NBER Working Paper No. 18428 (Cambridge, Massachusetts: National Bureau of Economic Research).

Himmelberg, Charles, Christopher Mayer, and Todd Sinai, 2005, "Assessing High House Prices: Bubbles, Fundamentals, and Misperceptions," NBER Working Paper No. 11643 (Cambridge, Massachusetts: National Bureau of Economic Research).

International Monetary Fund, 2010, "The IMF-FSB Early Warning Exercise: Design and Methodological Toolkit" (Washington: International Monetary Fund). www.imf.org/ external/np/pp/eng/2010/090110.pdf.

Ivashina, Victoria, and David Scharfstein, 2010, "Bank Lending during the Financial Crisis of 2008," *Journal of Financial Economics*, Vol. 97, No. 3, pp. 319–38.

Kaminsky, Graciela, Saul Lizondo, and Carmen Reinhart, 1998, "Leading Indicators of Currency Crisis," *IMF Staff Papers*, Vol. 45, No. 1, pp. 1–48.

Merler, Silvia, and Jean Pisani-Ferry, 2012, "Sudden Stops in the Euro Area," *Review of Economics and Institutions*, Vol. 3, No. 3.

Morris, Stephen, and Hyun Song Shin, 1998, "Unique Equilibrium in a Model of Self-Fulfilling Currency Attacks," *American Economic Review*, Vol. 88, No. 3, pp. 587–97.

————, 2001, "Rethinking Multiple Equilibria in Macroeconomic Modeling," *NBER Macroeconomics Annual 2000*, Vol. 15 (Cambridge, Massachusetts: MIT Press), pp. 139–61.

————, 2008, "Financial Regulation in a System Context," *Brookings Papers on Economic Activity*, Vol. 38, No. 2, pp. 229–74.

Repullo, Rafael, and Jesús Saurina, 2010, "The Countercyclical Capital Buffer of Basel III: A Critical Assessment," in *The Crisis Aftermath: New Regulatory Paradigms*, ed. by Mathias Dewatripont and Xavier Freixas (London: Centre for Economic Policy Research). http://www.voxeu.org/sites/default/files/file/Crisis_Aftermath.pdf.

Shin, Hyun Song, 2012, "Global Banking Glut and Loan Risk Premium," *IMF Economic Review*, Vol. 60, No. 2, pp. 155-192.

————, and Kwanho Shin, 2010, "Procyclicality and Monetary Aggregates," NBER Working Paper No. 16836 (Cambridge, Massachusetts: National Bureau of Economic Research).

Summers, Lawrence H., 1985, "On Economics and Finance," *Journal of Finance*, Vol. 40, No. 3, pp. 633–35.

CHAPTER 5

Resilience in Latin America: Lessons from Macroeconomic Management and Financial Policies

JOSÉ DE GREGORIO

Imagine a really big global crisis, second only to the Great Depression. What impact would it have on emerging market economies, particularly in Latin America? If this question had been asked 10 years ago, the unanimous answer would have been "disaster." Actually the crisis happened, but it was not a disaster in emerging markets. Emerging market economies around the world suffered the crisis, and some had sizable contractions, but overall the damage was limited and the recovery was very strong. Therefore, an appropriate answer today to the above question would be "bad, but not a disaster."

The purpose of this chapter is to examine the resilience of emerging market economies, with particular attention to Latin America. As argued below, this resistance to disaster is the reward for having implemented good macroeconomic and financial policies, which allowed a significant monetary and fiscal expansion to occur within a resilient financial system.

To tackle this issue, panel regressions could be performed on determinants of economic performance to gauge the main factors behind the recent economic success of emerging markets. Some interesting work, discussed below, has pursued this route. However, this kind of work has some limitations. For one, the sample period is still too short. Much better evidence will be gathered once a full business cycle has taken place. Now, the evidence that may be captured is the deepness of the contraction and the speed of a still-incomplete recovery. For another, dependent variables tend to be too blunt. The econometric work should be complemented with a more detailed analysis of particular cases, given that there are institutional nuances and differences among apparently similar policies that statistical work cannot capture. This is what this chapter will do in exploring the resilience of emerging market economies to the global financial crisis.

Although the focus is on Latin America, issues that go beyond the region are similar and relevant for the entire emerging market world. In several parts the

The author is very grateful to Stijn Claessens and Kevin Cowan for useful comments and discussions, and to José Tomás De Gregorio and Bastián Gallardo for valuable research assistance.

chapter will refer more generally to emerging market economies, and present evidence for a wider set of countries. This also allows the Latin American experience to be placed in a broader perspective.[1]

The chapter begins with a discussion of the main factors that explain the success of emerging market economies. In particular, it focuses on macroeconomic policies, exchange rate flexibility, and good luck. The next section is devoted in greater detail to the resilience of the financial system. Next is a discussion of international reserves, which are another factor that made emerging markets more resilient. The chapter concludes with some final remarks.

THE RESILIENCE OF EMERGING MARKET ECONOMIES

Emerging markets, in particular Latin American economies, were very resilient to the 2007–09 global financial crisis. Most suffered recessions, the others severe economic slowdowns. But the effects of the crisis were much milder than traditional adjustments following global recessionary shocks. The recovery, in turn, has been very strong. Now that economies have fully recovered and GDP has reached levels consistent with full capacity utilization, and even more in some cases, new challenges appear.

A number of factors help explain the performance of the emerging market economies; this section briefly discusses some of them, leaving the others for the next sections. The main factors behind this unprecedented performance were the following:

1. Good initial macroeconomic conditions allowed for strong monetary and fiscal stimulus in reaction to the crisis.

2. A cornerstone of the macroeconomic framework was exchange rate flexibility. As flight to safety took place, currencies of emerging market economies depreciated sharply, eliminating incentives for speculation against them. The fear of floating of many other previous experiences was over. Flexibility was not extreme—several countries used a combination of exchange rate intervention and capital controls to mitigate the appreciation of their currencies.

3. Good luck. Before the crisis, emerging market economies faced very good international conditions for expanding exports. Latin American countries, most of them exporters of primary commodities, enjoyed very good terms of trade as commodity prices skyrocketed during the second half of the first decade of the 2000s. After a sharp decline in commodity prices during the crisis, they bounced back to very high levels, which persist to this day.

4. Strong, well-regulated, and fairly simple financial systems provided suitable conditions. The exchange rate depreciation did not cause a financial collapse

---

[1] To limit the number of countries, the analysis includes Argentina, Brazil, Chile, Colombia, Mexico, Peru, Uruguay, and Venezuela. In some cases countries with no data available are excluded, which happens occasionally for Venezuela and Uruguay. For Asia, the analysis considers the Republic of Korea, India, Indonesia, Malaysia, the Philippines, and Thailand. For emerging Europe it considers the Czech Republic, Hungary, Latvia, Lithuania, Poland, and Romania.

and financial systems were able to resume lending as soon as circumstances improved.

5. High levels of international reserves were one of the few explanatory variables found to be relevant in potential explanations of why emerging market economies performed well during the crisis. Regardless of the reason for accumulating foreign assets, high levels of reserves played an important role as a deterrent to attacks on the currency and fear of foreign insolvency. They reduced the probability of a sudden stop. They also provided a cushion, although not used massively, against a potential lack of foreign financing.

This section focuses on the first three points, while the next section will be devoted to the financial sector, and the following to reserves accumulation.

The ability to conduct expansionary macroeconomic policies hinged on the sound initial macroeconomic conditions that emerging market economies enjoyed. Fiscal accounts were healthy as ever. Levels of public debt were relatively low. Countries that had windfall gains from high terms of trade saved before the crisis, accumulating resources to spend during the downturn. Other countries were able to borrow to finance their fiscal expansions.

On the monetary side, inflation control was key to allowing monetary loosening. Despite the sharp rise of commodity prices during the buildup to the crisis, which led to increases in inflation, the subsequent slowdown put enough downward pressure on inflation to leave room to cut interest rates. The response of inflation to exchange rate developments was much more muted than in previous episodes as a result of exchange rate flexibility that reduced the pass-through from exchange rates to inflation.[2]

Figure 5.1 shows the levels of public debt in Latin American economies; public debt was not only historically low, but declined in the years before the crisis. Argentina and Brazil had debt close to 60 percent of GDP, while the rest had levels below those of other emerging markets and of course, much below the levels of advanced economies.

The fiscal policy actions during the crisis were in sharp contrast with the traditional policy responses of Latin American countries to recessionary shocks coming from abroad. In the past, authorities relied on monetary and fiscal tightening. Fiscal policy usually had to be contractionary, not because of bad judgment, but because there was no space to expand fiscal policy. Creditworthiness would deteriorate during periods of bad external conditions and the ability to finance the budget would be severely impaired. Therefore, liquidity constraints became binding, forcing a fiscal adjustment. This gave origin to procyclical fiscal policies, which followed a simple rule that can be summarized as "spend as much as you can finance."[3]

---

[2] For further discussion on exchange rate flexibility and declining pass-throughs, see De Gregorio and Tokman (2007).

[3] Frankel, Végh, and Vuletin (2011) provide an empirical investigation of the procyclicality of fiscal policies in EMs. Their analysis takes decades as periods, so it cannot isolate the cyclicality of the budget during the crisis. However, they still find countries graduating from procyclicality in the period 2000–09.

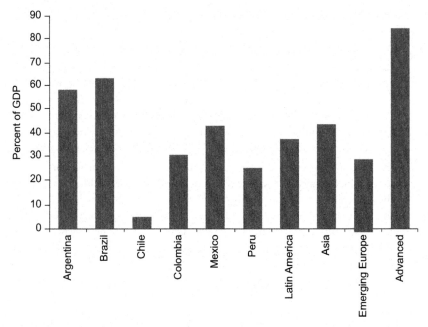

Figure 5.1 Gross Public Debt, 2008

Source: IMF, Fiscal Monitor database.
Note: Advanced = Canada, France, Germany, Italy, Japan, United Kingdom, and United States. Asia = India, Indonesia, Korea, Malaysia, Philippines, and Thailand. Emerging Europe = Czech Republic, Hungary, Latvia, Lithuania, Poland, and Romania. Latin America = Argentina, Brazil, Chile, Colombia, Mexico, Peru, Uruguay, and Venezuela.

In previous external crises monetary policy was usually tightened because of fear of depreciation. The potential inflationary and financial repercussions of the weakening of the currency were so pervasive that authorities were reluctant to allow a full exchange rate adjustment, and defended parity with high interest rates. To a large extent, this was the result of rigidities in the exchange rate regime that induced currency mismatches in the corporate sector and a high response of price setters to infrequent changes in the exchange rate.[4]

In contrast to previous responses, Brazil, Chile, Colombia, Mexico, and Peru cut rates to historical lows during the global financial crisis. Although in most cases they have since been raised, they still have not returned to precrisis levels (Figure 5.2). From a comparative perspective, the monetary and fiscal expansions of Latin American countries, as well as Asian countries, were sizable (Figure 5.3). In Latin America, the monetary stimulus was relatively large. Chile's fiscal stimulus was among the largest, owing to large fiscal resources available in the sovereign wealth funds built up during the copper price boom that preceded the crisis.

---

[4] There is some evidence that even in periods before the floating of exchange rates the corporate sector's assets and liabilities in foreign currency were fairly well matched. Therefore, the fear of a financial crisis after a depreciation may have been unfounded. For Chile, see Cowan, Hansen, and Herrera (2005).

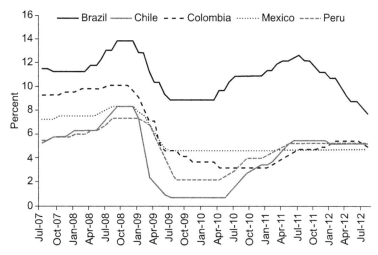

Figure 5.2   Monetary Policy Interest Rates

Source: Bloomberg, L.P.

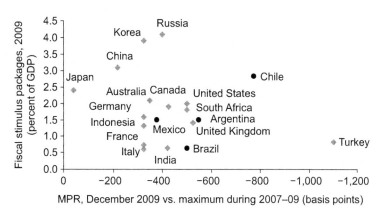

Figure 5.3   Monetary and Fiscal Stimulus

Sources: Bloomberg, L.P.; Central Bank of Chile; IMF, *Fiscal Monitor*, November 2009; and Ministries of Finance.
Note: MPR = monetary policy rate.

Most Latin American countries use flexible inflation targets to conduct monetary policy. Although this strategy has been questioned in many advanced economies for ignoring financial factors, it was essential to allowing for sharp, credible, and effective monetary expansions. Evidence has shown that since August 2008, inflation targeting regimes have had a positive effect on postcrisis economic performance (de Carvalho Filho, 2010). This should come as no surprise—monetary policy played a secondary role during the crisis because the crisis was mainly the result of severe financial dislocations. Therefore, countries with sound financial systems were able to engineer large expansionary policies.

Before the global financial crisis, the problem with monetary policy was precisely its deviation from the pursuit of price stability. In the United States, when the bubble burst, monetary policy was loosened to provide a safety net to the financial system. This strategy of letting the bubble grow and mopping up the mess after it burst was the so-called Greenspan put. This was a key ingredient to bubble formation. The collapse of the housing bubble was so large that the Greenspan put was ineffective. A parallel can be drawn with emerging markets' tradition of managing exchange rates. Permanent promises of exchange rate stability, which set bounds on asset prices on the way up when the currency appreciated and on the way down when the currency depreciated, induced currency mismatches in the private sector. The fear of floating provided implicit insurance against sharp currency fluctuations and reduced private sector incentives to hedge currency exposure. In contrast, the period of floating exchange rates has been characterized by the development of foreign exchange forward markets (De Gregorio and Tokman, 2007).[5]

Exchange rate flexibility played a crucial role in dampening the adjustment. At the height of the crisis, currencies in Latin America had depreciated sharply, and the financial systems were able to accommodate the depreciation without untenable stress. In a period of a few months, depreciations were about 60 percent, something never seen before (Figure 5.4). The figure shows that this depreciation happened not only in Latin America, but also in Asia. The depreciation responded to fundamentals, acknowledging the potential that emerging markets could be hit disproportionately by the crisis. When they were not, currencies strengthened. But the search for safe havens also resulted in depreciation of riskier and less-liquid emerging markets' assets. Exchange rates' abrupt adjustment reduced

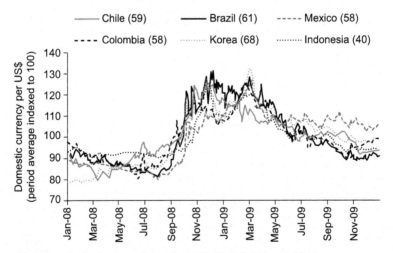

Figure 5.4 Exchange Rates during the 2008–09 Global Financial Crisis

Source: Bloomberg, L.P.

Note: Figure in parentheses indicates maximum depreciation. An increase indicates a depreciation of the currency.

---

[5] In the context of the Greenspan put, the issue of excessive risk taking and lack of proper risk management was raised more than 10 years ago by Miller, Weller, and Zhang (2002).

incentives to speculate against further weakening. The war chest that reserves provided also helped exchange rates to adjust without major disruptions.

Finally, emerging market economies also faced very good external conditions, the good luck component of the resilience. Rapid growth in developing economies, in particular China, generated strong demand for exports from developing countries. In Latin America, on top of greater market access, several countries that were primary commodity exporters enjoyed significant terms-of-trade gains. These gains did not happen in Asia because terms of trade were stable, owing primarily to the broad industrial production bases in Asia economies. Panel a of Figure 5.5

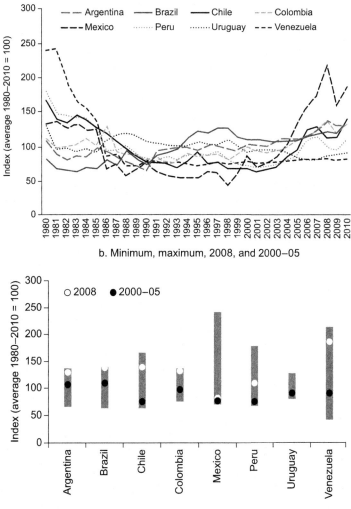

Figure 5.5 Terms of Trade

Source: World Bank, Net Barter Terms of Trade Index, http://data.worldbank.org/indicator/TT.PRI.MRCH.XD.WD.

shows the evolution of the terms of trade since 1980. In panel b, the bars corresponds to the range between the minimum and maximum levels for the period 1980–2010, and the figure shows the last data and the average for the period 2000–05. Every country, with the exception of Mexico and Uruguay, has enjoyed significant gains since 2005.

One of the main risks in Latin America is a decline in the terms of trade. IDB (2012) provides some simulations with a decline in terms of trade. They consider a risk scenario that involves a deepening of the euro area crisis and a slowdown in China, which would result in a decline of 30 percent in commodity prices. The simulation exercise, which yields a worldwide recession, with Chinese growth falling 3 percentage points and recessions in the United States and Europe, would cause a decline in output in Latin America of 0.6 percent, somewhat smaller, but more persistent, than that of the 2007–09 global financial crisis. Overall, this simulation confirms the vulnerability of the region to a global slowdown and a decline in the price of commodities. But, as during the 2007–09 crisis, Latin America would not suffer a major collapse, as it typically would have in the past. Although the simulation does not account for differences across countries, the impact should be differentiated as long as the resilience to terms-of-trade shocks relies on the government budget's dependence on terms of trade. Not all countries are in the same position, particularly since the crisis, because governments used a significant portion of their fiscal space.

THE RESILIENCE OF FINANCIAL SYSTEMS

The purpose of regulation of the financial system is to ensure that institutions are solvent and liquid. Since the 2007–09 financial crisis, much discussion has focused on financial regulation to limit the risk of spillovers from the financial system and particular institutions to the whole economy. Thus, in addition to traditional microprudential tools, the use of macroprudential rules that limit systemic financial risks is a necessary complement.

Systemic financial risk may arise from the behavior of the financial system through the cycle—the time series dimension—or from the interaction of particular institutions with the rest of the financial system—the cross-section dimension. The most important concern with regard to the business cycle is the excess procyclicality of financial activities. With regard to contemporaneous spillovers, the concern is mostly with systemically important financial institutions whose risks can contaminate the entire financial system.

Whether a particular policy is macro- or microprudential is not always obvious. For example, limiting currency mismatches has both a micro component to limit foreign exposure of particular financial intermediaries, and a macro component to minimize the risk of a financial crisis caused by significant aggregate mismatches. A rule that reduces the risk of insolvency of single institutions caused by macroeconomic shocks by definition will also be protecting the integrity of the whole system.

Latin American countries have been applying macroprudential rules for a long time, even if they did not call it that. The remainder of this section discusses some

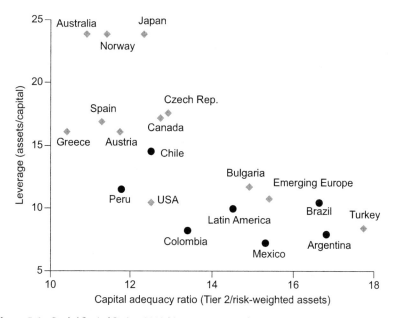

Figure 5.6 Banks' Capital Ratios, 2008 (times, percentage)

Source: Central Bank of Chile, *Financial Stability Report*, 2009:QI.

Note: The figure considers only commercial banks. Investment banks are excluded; they had leverage ratios in 2008 of about 26.

features of Latin American banking systems that help explain their resilience to the global financial crisis.[6]

A first characteristic of Latin American banking systems is their relatively high levels of capital and low levels of leverage (Figure 5.6). All countries had regulatory capital greater than the 8 percent required by Basel II.[7] This is the result of higher regulatory capital requirements and limits on leverage, as well as the internal strategies of local banks that are willing to hold larger levels of capital.

Of course, the crisis revealed that leverage could have been larger through off-balance-sheet investment operations that artificially reduced leverage. This possibility is at the center of the issue of leverage in the trading book. Proposals along the lines of the Volcker rule, which prohibits commercial banks from engaging in proprietary trading, go in the direction of reducing financial risks. The route followed in emerging markets, which avoids complicated regulation, is to set limits on the instruments that can be held by banks. For example, in Chile, banks can

---

[6] For recent examinations of the use of macroprudential tools and the institutional arrangements of financial regulation in Latin America, see Céspedes and Rebucci (2011), Cifuentes and others (2011), Jácome, Nier, and Imam (2012), and Tovar, Garcia-Escribano, and Martin (2012). Given the complexities of a full comparative analysis, the reviews in general are partial and focused on specific country experiences, as is this section: most of the examples and details come from the Chilean experience.

[7] Chile appears to have the largest leverage ratio in the region. However, it is among the countries that had the lowest volatility of output, and the evidence shows that the lower the volatility, the higher the leverage. See Central Bank of Chile (2009) for further evidence.

only hold corporate and Chilean bonds. Only interest rate and exchange rate derivatives are allowed. All other operations must be conducted through other financial institutions, which are also subject to financial regulation and can be subsidiaries of banks. Brazil and Mexico have also been limiting the use of derivatives in their banking systems.

The region's strong financial systems did not prevent a sharp contraction of credit during the peak of the crisis. However, credit expansion resumed as the economies recovered. It is difficult to disentangle how much of the contraction was due to a decline in the demand for credit and how much to restrictions from the supply side. Both factors may have played a role because the increase in uncertainty tightened financial conditions and reduced demand, as surveys on financial conditions showed.

The degree of financial depth of the banking system is usually measured by the ratio of private banking credit to GDP. Latin America ranks relatively low, as do many other emerging markets. Therefore, periods of financial deepening may be associated with credit booms, not only because average household debt is increasing, but also because of the entrance of new households into the banking system.

Figure 5.7 shows the depth of the banking system for Latin America and other regions. The depth is indeed quite low, except for Chile, but in most countries of the region it increased during the 2000s. However, this increase was much milder than those in emerging Europe and in the advanced economies. In the latter regions, it is more appropriate to talk about credit booms. The recent evidence is in sharp contrast to the Latin American experience with liberalization

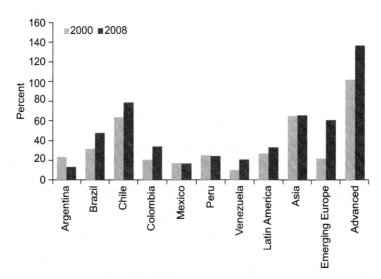

Figure 5.7 Private Credit as a Share of GDP

Source: IMF, *International Financial Statistics.*
Note: Advanced = Canada, France, Germany, Italy, Japan, United Kingdom, and United States. Asia = India, Indonesia, Korea, Malaysia, Philippines, and Thailand. Emerging Europe = Czech Republic, Hungary, Latvia, Lithuania, Poland, and Romania. Latin America = Argentina, Brazil, Chile, Colombia, Mexico, Peru, Uruguay, and Venezuela.

in the 1980s, which featured significant credit booms that were followed by the debt crisis and the so-called lost decade. During that period domestic credit increased rapidly, fueled largely by capital inflows in the form of external debt. Countries that had larger expansions also had greater output losses from the crisis (De Gregorio and Guidotti, 1995). Prudential regulation together with macroeconomic policies that did not pursue unsustainable expansions may have been behind the avoidance of a credit boom in Latin America in the first decade of the 2000s, although more empirical research is needed to contrast the two experiences.

Another myth that the Latin American debt crisis of the 1980s put to rest was the idea that when external imbalances originate privately they are not a problem (the Lawson doctrine). The Chilean case during the debt crisis was a prime example of a large private imbalance that caused a very severe crisis. In the aftermath of the 2007–09 global crisis, privately originated imbalances caused crises throughout Europe.

The instrument used most frequently to reduce credit expansion has been reserve requirements, by which banks are required to hold some fraction of their deposits as liquid reserves. Raising reserve requirements increases the costs of borrowing, but to be used as a macroprudential rule the requirements must change in response to the business cycle. Brazil, Colombia, and Peru have used changes in reserve requirements to stem credit booms. According to Tovar, Garcia-Escribano, and Martin (2012), the effects of this policy are moderate and transitory. Although reserve requirements may be effective, they also have some side effects—banks will look for new forms of funding to counteract higher requirements, which may end up generating vulnerabilities. Reserve requirements may also shift credit to unregulated credit providers, providing incentives to the shadow banking system.

The Achilles heel of financial systems in emerging markets has been currency mismatches. The problem has not been in banks' balance sheets, but in the exposure of corporations that borrowed in foreign currency and have most of their activities in the nontraded goods sector. In emerging Europe even mortgages were denominated in foreign currency. These activities expose the financial system to weaknesses stemming from the currency mismatches of the borrowers. All Latin American countries surveyed in IDB (2005) have regulations on currency mismatches in the banking system. These requirements range from quantitative limits on currency exposure to including exchange rate exposure in quantifications of credit risk, with its consequences for capital requirements. At the corporate level, regulation also requires that the risk of currency exposure of borrowers be internalized. For example, in Chile, provisioning requirements are higher for foreign currency lending when the borrowers have most of their income in domestic currency. Of course, this requires more forward-looking provisioning, which is currently being implemented in several Latin American countries (Cifuentes and others, 2011). In Peru (a dollarized economy) and in Uruguay, additional capital requirements are applied to foreign currency lending to unhedged borrowers.

As shown in the previous section, the balance sheets of banks were resilient to the unprecedented fluctuations in the exchange rate that accompanied the global financial crisis. Only in Brazil and Mexico in Latin America, and in the Republic of Korea in Asia, were some large corporations exposed to exchange rate derivatives. These derivatives were highly complex, which raised financial stability concerns. The lesson is that markets need more disclosure about effective currency exposures in corporations' financial statements, especially when dealing with complex instruments. Banks should take this into account when making provisions and extending credit.

Another important source of financial risk is the exposure of the domestic banking system to foreign banks. Cross-border flows are highly volatile. Figure 5.8 shows the evolution of cross-border claims of foreign banks in Latin America and Asia. The cycle was more pronounced in Asia. In Korea and Malaysia, the declines in the fourth quarter of 2008 were 6.7 percent and 5.0 percent of GDP, respectively, whereas the maximum decline in Latin America was in Chile, with a fall of 3 percent of GDP in the same quarter.

The composition of foreign claims according to source country is presented in Figure 5.9 for emerging Europe, Asia, and Latin America. Emerging Europe is more exposed to European banks, Asia is relatively equally exposed across regions, and Latin America is exposed primarily to Spanish banks, mainly Santander and BBVA. Spanish banks have followed an arm's-length strategy, letting their subsidiaries operate as independent units. But the main feature that could have made Latin American countries less affected by exposure to foreign banks is that most foreign banks operating as commercial banks have their domestic affiliates constituted as subsidiaries rather than branches. Thus, the subsidiary operates just as a domestic bank would, with its own capital, its own

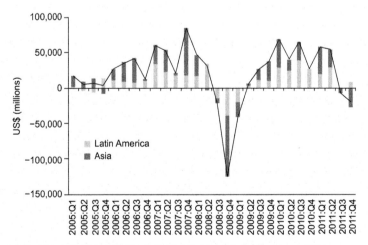

Figure 5.8 Quarterly Change in Cross-Border Claims on Latin America and Asia.
Source: Consolidated Banking Statistics (immediate borrower basis), Bank for International Settlements.

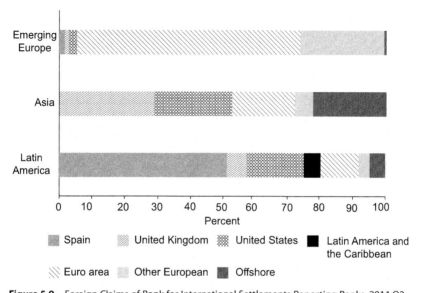

Figure 5.9 Foreign Claims of Bank for International Settlements Reporting Banks, 2011:Q2

Source: Consolidated Banking Statistics (immediate borrower basis), Bank for International Settlements.

Note: Asia = India, Indonesia, Korea, Malaysia, Philippines, and Thailand. Emerging Europe = Czech Republic, Hungary, Latvia, Lithuania, Poland, and Romania. Latin America = Argentina, Brazil, Chile, Colombia, Mexico, Peru, Uruguay, and Venezuela.

board of directors, and strict rules for deposits of the subsidiary in the parent bank.[8]

Subsidiarization does not necessarily produce full ring-fencing, as the cases of several Central and Eastern European countries show, where foreign banks also operated as subsidiaries. But subsidiarization induces more local funding. Figure 5.10 shows that among the three regions, funding comes more from local sources in Latin America.[9] Kamil and Rai (2010) examine why Latin American financial systems were resilient to the global financial crisis. Their analysis indicates that the resilience stemmed from the fact that global banks' credit was mostly channeled in domestic currency and foreign banks operated as local subsidiaries, funded mostly with domestic deposits. Therefore, subsidiarization, strong regulation of currency mismatches, a broad base of deposit funding, low reliance on short-term wholesale funding, and a simple trading book may help explain the strength and resilience of the banking system in the region.

---

[8] Many countries regulate branches and subsidiaries identically. The most relevant difference is that branches do not have local boards of directors, whereas subsidiaries do. With branches, the foreign bank is responsible for any problem in its affiliate, thus, a subsidiary limits contagion. In addition, subsidiaries can have local or other partners. These are strong incentives for banks to use the subsidiary model to expand across regions.

[9] For further discussion on cross-border banking, see CIEPR (2012), and for an analysis of vulnerabilities of Latin American economies to exposure to Spanish banks, see Chapter 8 of IDB (2012).

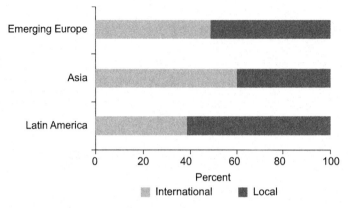

Figure 5.10 Composition of Foreign Claims, 2011:Q2.

Source: Consolidated Banking Statistics (immediate borrower basis), Bank for International Settlements.

Note: Advanced = Canada, France, Germany, Italy, Japan, United Kingdom, and United States. Asia = India, Indonesia, Korea, Malaysia, Philippines, and Thailand. Emerging Europe = Czech Republic, Hungary, Latvia, Lithuania, Poland, and Romania. Latin America = Argentina, Brazil, Chile, Colombia, Mexico, Peru, Uruguay, and Venezuela.

Finally, another macroprudential tool under discussion for use in emerging markets is capital controls. Similar to reserves accumulation (discussed in the next section), capital controls are instruments with two purposes: to limit exchange rate appreciation and to foster financial stability. However, concerns with exchange rate appreciation and financial stability arise from two different sources within financial accounts. Pressures on the exchange rate depend on net capital flows, whereas financial stability considerations depend on gross flows.

Net inflows are the counterpart of the current account deficit, and the exchange rate depends on the saving-investment balance of the economy. Since the mid-2000s, and contrary to the surge of capital inflows of the early 1990s, current account deficits in emerging markets have been limited, and even many commodity-exporting countries have built current account surpluses. Therefore, they are net exporters of capital. Of course, the data may reveal large net inflows, but these inflows have mostly been associated with the accumulation of reserves primarily to protect competitiveness.

Gross flows have significantly increased as a result of greater financial integration. These flows can have important effects on financial stability, and the use of macroprudential instruments may be called for, as in Korea, where large inflows to the banking system have been considered a source of potential financial risk. Korea has very large foreign funding. The country implemented a capital levy on noncore liabilities in August 2011. Banks pay a levy of 20 basis points for foreign-currency-denominated liabilities of less than 12-month maturity (CIEPR, 2012). Although this levy may reduce foreign borrowing by banks, it does not necessarily reduce net inflows because portfolio shifts may change the source of external funding. In Latin America, Peru has used a similar levy on foreign borrowing and has also applied fees for the sale of Central Bank of Peru bonds. Brazil has experimented with broader capital controls, such as reserve requirements on foreign borrowing and a tax on transactions of fixed-income instruments and equity. Colombia applied an unremunerated reserve requirement, similar to Chile's in the 1990s, during 2007–08.

The evidence of the effects of capital controls on financial stability and on exchange rates is inconclusive. Financial stability has been preserved in countries that have and that have not applied capital controls, and exchange rates have behaved in similar patterns regardless of the use of capital controls. The jury is still out, but two final comments are in order. First, capital controls may be a disguise for fighting other distortions that encourage capital inflows, such as very high interest rates. This may have been the case in Brazil before the global financial crisis. Second, Chile, the poster child for capital controls during the 1990s, was able to weather the big financial storm of 2008–09 without the use of controls. Perhaps Chile's experience of the 1990s was predictive of the more recent occurrences in Brazil, where very large interest rate differentials encouraged capital inflows.[10]

THE ACCUMULATION OF INTERNATIONAL RESERVES

As discussed before, emerging markets have accumulated large amounts of reserves since 2000 (Figure 5.11).[11] The holding of international reserves is one

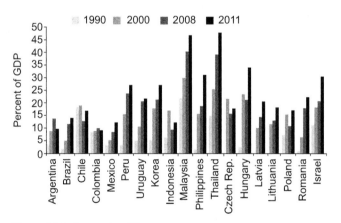

Figure 5.11 International Reserves

Sources: IMF, *International Financial Statistics* and World Economic Outlook database.

---

[10] For a review of the Chilean experience with capital controls, see Cowan and De Gregorio (2007), and for a large set of countries, see Magud, Reinhart, and Rogoff (2011).

[11] The data in Figure 5.11 are expressed as percentages of GDP. In some cases this ratio declined simply because reserves have grown less than GDP valued in dollars, as in Chile and Indonesia, although their levels in dollars have increased over time. The fact that in 2011 most countries had more reserves as a fraction of GDP does not imply that the reserves were never used; some countries actually used a small fraction of their reserves during the 2007–09 crisis, although they resumed accumulating reserves thereafter.

of the most common macroprudential policies in emerging markets for reducing the risk of a balance of payments crisis, but reserves accumulation also serves for exchange rate purposes.[12]

International reserves play a dual role (Aizenman and Lee, 2005). On the one hand, they provide a buffer against sudden stops of capital inflows. This is the self-insurance, or precautionary, motive for accumulating reserves. International reserves reduce the risk of balance of payments crises. On the other hand, the accumulation of reserves entails intervention in the foreign exchange market, ameliorating the pressures for appreciation. This is the mercantilist motive for reserves accumulation. Although the impact of sterilized intervention is not entirely clear, it may transitorily prevent an appreciation of the currency.

The high level of reserves during the global financial crisis played an important role in the resilience displayed by emerging economies. The level of international reserves has been one of the few variables shown to be relevant in mitigating the output costs of the crisis (Frankel and Saravelos, 2010; Gourinchas and Obstfeld, 2012). During the peak of the crisis, countries that had larger volumes of reserves experienced smaller increases in their credit default swap spreads. This reduced the impact of the crisis on financing costs.

International reserves may have rendered credible the provision of liquidity in some cases and protected the exchange rate in others. In particular, Brazil, Korea, and Mexico intervened in complicated moments during the financial crisis because of difficulties in their corporate sectors and may have seen the credibility of these measures enhanced by their massive reserves holdings. Thus, the level of reserves and the significant depreciation of their currencies may have helped mitigate the effects of the global financial crisis. Most countries did not deplete reserves massively, which could be interpreted as reserves having little impact as insurance. However, the financial resilience of emerging market economies strongly suggests that having a high level of reserves, even if unused, can be a strong deterrent to speculation when facing sharp changes in global financial conditions. The majority of models seeking to determine the adequate level of reserves assume that they are used. Still, their deterrent effect is substantial, whether used or unused.

The dual role of reserves accumulation explains why self-insurance is so prevalent in emerging markets, and the current level of reserves could indicate that emerging market economies are over-insured. But over-insurance is related to the other component of demand for reserves: to affect the exchange rate.

Other forms of insurance exist that are less costly than reserves, but with no incidence on the exchange rate. These forms of insurance could also generate pressure to appreciate the currency by signaling less vulnerability to external financial turbulence. Commodity-exporting countries can use commodity hedges instead of hoarding reserves, and hedging could be a better instrument from a financial standpoint. Multilateral contingent credit lines, such as the IMF's

---

[12] The issues discussed in the remainder of this section are developed in greater detail in De Gregorio (2011).

Flexible Credit Line, can be used. Bilateral agreements on currency swap lines can also be signed, which, although common in relatively large economies, are not available for smaller ones.

This dual effect of reserves accumulation could explain why many countries seem to have invested more than necessary in this self insurance. In fact, interventions in foreign exchange markets originate from fear of having a misaligned exchange rate. The dual role of reserves may also explain why so few countries have made use of the IMF's Flexible Credit Line.

The Flexible Credit Line is a good idea as insurance. However, what would happen if a country decided to take a contingent credit facility instead of hoarding reserves? First, its economy would be safer, encouraging more capital inflows. Second, it would have less reason to intervene in the foreign exchange market because it would already be overinsured and would have other ways to obtain external funding if there were to be a sudden stop of private sources. But the difficulty that countries face when looking for cheaper insurance mechanisms is that reserves decisions also affect the exchange rate.

In sum, reserves held as an insurance mechanism are security against sudden stops of capital inflows and a deterrent to destabilizing speculation against the currency. But reserves accumulation has also been a tool for exchange rate management. Certainly the holding of reserves has a relevant carry cost that must be appropriately weighed when deciding to intervene in the foreign exchange market.

The optimal level of reserves is an issue that has produced significant amounts of research, but is still not clear. However, the evidence from the crisis shows that emerging market economies were well protected with their actual levels of reserves, so at least they were not underinsured. However, keeping these levels of reserves is costly, which limits the space for further accumulation, especially when the costs of holding reserves are appropriately taken into account.

FINAL REMARKS

Big financial crises have been common in emerging market economies. The debt crisis in the early 1980s in Latin America generated many lessons for financial regulation. A first and major lesson was that more was no better than less financial deepening. The development of financial markets is good, but leaving them to grow unfettered is extremely risky and is an almost sure route to crisis. De Gregorio and Guidotti (1995), come to the conclusion that in Latin America, growth during the 1980s was lower in countries with more highly developed financial systems because the collapse of their economies during the debt crisis was larger. Carlos Diaz-Alejandro (1985) eloquently wrote "Good-bye Financial Repression, Hello Financial Crash." Recent research also points in the same direction—beyond a certain level, the contribution of financial depth to growth is marginal (Arcand, Berkes, and Panizza, 2012; Cecchetti and Kharroubi, 2012).

Today, serious international efforts are being made to establish guidelines to strengthen financial markets. However, "if it ain't broke, don't fix it" is a reasonable starting point for reform in emerging markets. Current regulatory proposals are particularly geared to regulating complex financial institutions, which are not the typical banks in emerging markets. Banks in emerging markets are simpler, which is a strong reason for their resilience. Regulation must follow the complexity of institutions, and a first rule in emerging markets is to examine whether to allow financial innovation. Does its potential benefits outweigh its risks? Once that question is answered, appropriate regulation must then be discussed. A wholesale overhaul of existing regulation is not the best starting point.

Many countries have been creating financial stability boards to coordinate all relevant agencies dealing with financial stability. Those boards have to be given clear mandates and assigned responsibilities to avoid overlap and conflicts among agencies. New layers of financial regulation must be consistent with the existing duties of current regulatory agencies. Central banks have to play a critical role in this area, not only because they should lead the design of macroprudential tools and preserve financial stability, but also because they have the independence, or should be granted it where they do not have it, to perform this task effectively. However, independent central banks with a clear mandate for financial stability and the creation of financial stability boards will not prevent future crises, but it should minimize the probability of their happening, and should facilitate resolution. Several relevant steps have been taken in Latin America in this regard.

Efficient and strict regulation of the banking system is essential for promoting financial stability. However, this endeavor also has its risks. As the banking system becomes better capitalized and more regulated, incentives to move financial intermediation to unregulated institutions increase. Thus, the shadow banking system may become larger and riskier. There will always be tension between the extent and the perimeter of regulation, which must be permanently addressed. This has been a persistent problem with the application of capital controls.

Banking systems in Latin America are small and concentrated. Efforts to increase competition are always welcome, but new tensions will appear because competition also encourages search for yield. Indeed, the search for yield in advanced economies was also responsible for excessive risk taking. Coordination between competition authorities and financial regulators is important. Competition cannot be promoted at the cost of increased vulnerability.

As argued by Haldane and Madouros (2012), rules that become too complex are not necessarily robust.[13] Preserving simplicity in a complex financial system is not always possible, but avoiding complexity to accommodate the demands of different segments of the market may lead to inefficient regulation. The potential capture by vested interests may endanger financial stability.

One important attribute of regulators in emerging market economies, after having survived many crises, is a reasonable degree of prudence. In general, regulators allow activities that can be handled appropriately by financial intermediar-

---

[13] See also comments by De Gregorio (2012).

ies, but above all that can be understood and monitored adequately by market participants and financial regulators. The same prudent behavior is followed by a significant part of the private sector, who know firsthand the perils of financial innovation. Indeed, once the private sector has paid the costs of its own mistakes it should become more aware of the risks. Bailing out those responsible for causing a crisis creates moral hazard and does not induce prudence and discipline. However, the experience of some nonfinancial corporations dealing with complex derivatives before the crisis demonstrates that financial policies cannot rely on the good judgment of the private sector. Regulation, as well as appropriate risk management within firms, is central to preserving financial stability and minimizing the cost of disruptions.

Good macroeconomic policies and a strong financial system, enhanced by a little bit of luck, allowed emerging market economies to perform reasonably well during the 2007–09 crisis in the world economy. Persevering in fiscal responsibility, inflation control, flexible exchange rates, and robust prudential regulation of the financial system are essential for proceeding from recovery to sustained economic progress.

REFERENCES

Aizenman, J., and J. Lee, 2005, "International Reserves: Precautionary vs. Mercantilist Views, Theory and Evidence," IMF Working Paper 05/198 (Washington: International Monetary Fund).

Arcand, Jean-Louis, Enrico Berkes, and Ugo Panizza, 2012, "Too Much Finance?" IMF Working Paper 12/161 (Washington: International Monetary Fund).

Cecchetti, Stephen, and Enisse Kharroubi, 2012, "Reassessing the Impact of Finance on Growth," BIS Working Paper No. 381 (Basel: Bank for International Settlements).

Central Bank of Chile, 2009, *Financial Stability Report*, first half (Santiago).

Céspedes, Luis Felipe, and Alessandro Rebucci, 2011, "Macro-prudential Policies in Latin America: A Survey" (unpublished; Washington: Inter-American Development Bank).

Cifuentes, Rodrigo, Rodrigo Alfaro, Eduardo Olaberría, and Rubén Poblete, 2011, "The Chilean Financial System and Macroprudential Policies," *Financial Stability Report*, first half (Santiago: Central Bank of Chile).

Committee on International Economic Policy Reform (CIEPR), 2012, "Banks and Cross-Border Capital Flows: Policy Challenges and Regulatory Responses" (Washington: Brookings Institution).

Cowan, Kevin, and José De Gregorio, 2007, "International Borrowing, Capital Controls and the Exchange Rate: Lessons from Chile," in *Capital Controls and Capital Flows in Emerging Economies: Policies, Practices and Consequences*, ed. by S. Edwards (Chicago: National Bureau of Economic Research and the University of Chicago Press).

Cowan, Kevin, Erwin Hansen, and Luis Oscar Herrera, 2005, "Currency Mismatches, Balance Sheet Effects and Hedging in Chilean Non-financial Corporations," in *External Vulnerability and Preventive Policies*, ed. by R. Caballero, C. Calderón, and L.F. Céspedes (Santiago: Central Bank of Chile).

de Carvalho Filho, Irineu, 2010, "Inflation Targeting and the Crisis: An Empirical Assessment," IMF Working Paper 10/45 (Washington: International Monetary Fund).

De Gregorio, José, 2011, "International Reserves Hoarding in Emerging Markets," Economic Policy Paper No. 40 (Santiago: Central Bank of Chile).

————, 2012, "Comments on Haldane and Madouros," Presentation at the Federal Reserve Bank of Kansas City's economic policy symposium, "The Changing Policy Landscape," Jackson Hole, Wyoming, August 30–September 1.

————, and Pablo Guidotti, 1995, "Financial Development and Economic Growth," *World Development*, Vol. 23, No. 3, pp. 433–48.

De Gregorio, José, and Andrea Tokman, 2007, "Overcoming Fear of Floating: Exchange Rate Policies in Chile," in *Monetary Policy in Emerging Markets and Other Developing Countries*, ed. by N. Batini (New York: Nova Science Publishers Inc.).

Diaz-Alejandro, Carlos, 1985, "Good-bye Financial Repression, Hello Financial Crash," *Journal of Development Economics*, Vol. 19, No. 1–2, pp. 1–24.

Frankel, Jeffrey, and George Saravelos, 2010, "Are Leading Indicators of Financial Crises Useful for Assessing Country Vulnerability? Evidence from the 2008–09 Global Crisis," NBER Working Paper No. 16047 (Cambridge, Massachusetts: National Bureau of Economic Research).

Frankel, Jeffrey, Carlos Végh, and Guillermo Vuletin, 2011, "On Graduation from Procyclicality," NBER Working Paper No. 17619 (Cambridge, Massachusetts: National Bureau of Economic Research).

Gourinchas, Pierre-Olivier, and Maurice Obstfeld, 2012, "Stories of the Twentieth Century for the Twenty-First," *American Economic Journal: Macroeconomics*, Vol. 4, No. 1, pp. 226–65.

Haldane, Andrew G., and Vasileios Madouros, 2012, "The Dog and the Frisbee," Presented at the Federal Reserve Bank of Kansas City's 36th economic policy symposium, "The Changing Policy Landscape," Jackson Hole, Wyoming, August 30–September 1.

Inter-American Development Bank (IDB), 2005, *Unlocking Credit: The Quest for Deep and Stable Bank Lending*, Economic and Social Progress in Latin America: 2005 Report (Washington: Inter-American Development Bank).

————, 2012, *The World of Forking Paths: Latin America and the Caribbean Facing Global Economic Risks*, The Latin American and Caribbean Macro Report 2012 (Washington: Inter-American Development Bank).

Jácome, Luis I., Erlend W. Nier, and Patrick Imam, 2012, "Building Blocks for Effective Macroprudential Policies in Latin America: Institutional Considerations," IMF Working Paper 12/183 (Washington: International Monetary Fund).

Kamil, Herman, and Kulwant Rai, 2010, "The Global Credit Crunch and Foreign Banks' Lending to Emerging Markets: Why Did Latin America Fare Better?" IMF Working Paper 10/102 (Washington: International Monetary Fund).

Magud, N., C. Reinhart, and K. Rogoff, 2011, "Capital Controls: Myth and Reality—A Portfolio Balance Approach," NBER Working Paper No. 16805 (Cambridge, Massachusetts: National Bureau of Economic Research).

Miller, Marcus, Paul Weller, and Lei Zhang, 2002, "Moral Hazard and the U.S. Stock Market: Analyzing the Greenspan Put," *Economic Journal*, Vol. 112, No. 478, pp. C171–86.

Tovar, Camilo E., Mercedes Garcia-Escribano, and Mercedes Vera Martin, 2012, "Credit Growth and the Effectiveness of Reserve Requirements and Other Macroprudential Instruments in Latin America," IMF Working Paper 12/142 (Washington: International Monetary Fund).

CHAPTER 6

External Imbalances and Financial Crises

ALAN M. TAYLOR

EXTERNAL IMBALANCES VERSUS CREDIT BOOMS

Is it true that "global imbalances helped to fuel the financial crisis" (King, 2011, p. 1)? In the years since the 2007–09 global crisis, current account imbalances have narrowed, but endogenously, because trade collapsed, and because emerging market economies outgrew the United States and other advanced economies. But before 2008 these global capital flows were much larger. Many prominent policymakers, commentators, and economists had focused on large current account imbalances in the United States, but also in other countries with pronounced booms, and had warned about the potential for a jarring shock should those flows be subject to adjustments caused by incipient changes in portfolio allocation, and concomitant shifts in interest rates, growth rates, and perceived country or currency risks. Harsh adjustments, sudden stops, or reversals, it was thought, could wreak serious havoc. Much attention was given to the role of the large lenders and creditors in emerging Asia (especially China) causing a "saving glut" while others focused on saving shortfalls in large borrowers and debtors like the United States.[1]

In these arguments, the public or official sectors tended to attract the most scrutiny, be it the official reserves accumulation trends in developing countries, or the path of government deficits and debt in the United States. However, those focusing on the public sector dimensions of the flows ended up missing the main story. Without minimizing fiscal challenges (many of them a result of the crisis), the kind of crises the world ended up having were in almost all cases not fiscal crises at all. In the United States, where large-scale financial pressure was first seen, the dollar has rallied on the flight to safety, as have treasuries, notwithstanding what credit rating agencies have said. In Europe, intraregional imbalances are now seen to have been a source of instability, but before the crisis these cross-border flows (with the exception of Greece) were largely private sector debt flows, much of them flowing through bank channels from savers in the "North" to finance real estate or consumption booms in the "South"; public debts and

---

[1] The term "saving glut" is credited to the chairman of the Federal Reserve Board (Bernanke, 2005).

deficits in places like Ireland and Spain only exploded later, as harsh recessions and banking rescues ate resources.

Thanks to scholars taking a more granular view of the data, more revealing trends are now visible. It is clear, for example, that China and other emerging market purchasers of U.S. assets focused on truly safe AAA assets like treasuries, or government-sponsored-enterprise issues; in contrast, it was advanced country investors, notably in Europe, that crowded into the securitized products channeling funds to the real estate bubble. Within Europe, the growing debt exposure between countries is now seen to have been a two-way street, with gross flows much larger than net flows. The cross-sectional experience of the euro area economies, as well as U.S. states and counties, also strongly suggests that even in a currency union, where balance of payments problems and currency risk are, in theory, absent, or defined away, the threat of a macrofinancial crisis via private debt dynamics is still very much present. In light of these experiences, the answer to "does the current account matter?" is probably still yes; but in a world in which bank-driven expansions in private sector leverage have reached historically unprecedented levels in advanced economies, it is no longer the only, or even necessarily the most important, question one might ask when evaluating macroeconomic and financial risks.[2]

HISTORICAL PERSPECTIVE: EBB AND FLOW OF FINANCE ACROSS AND WITHIN BORDERS

Historically, there has been a broad correlation between the prevalence of external imbalances and the frequency of financial crises. This correlation is all too apparent in the data, but needs to be subject to careful causal interpretation.

It is a stylized fact that international capital mobility has followed a U-shape over the course of recent history (Obstfeld and Taylor, 2004). Under the classical gold standard, until 1913 there were virtually no policy barriers to cross-border financial flows, and the last serious technological impediments were broken down by the arrival of the cable. The interwar period, especially the 1930s, saw policies veer toward autarky; this configuration persisted until the 1970s, as governments reconfigured their responses to the trilemma when confronted by shocks like wars and depressions. Only since the 1980s has consensus moved back toward freer capital movements as tolerance for floating exchange rates accommodated ongoing monetary policy autonomy. This trend has gone furthest in the advanced economies. Documenting these trends, Figure 6.1 shows both policy-based and outcome-based indicators of capital mobility over the past century and a half.

Coincidentally or not, a similar historical pattern characterizes financial crisis events (Reinhart and Rogoff, 2009). Financial instability was a normal feature of

---

[2] See, among others, Schularick and Wachtel (2012) on private versus public financing of the U.S. lending boom; Shin (2012) on the "global banking glut"; and Lane (2012) and Obstfeld (2012) on the importance of gross versus net positions.

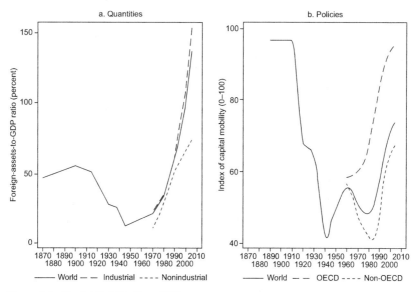

Figure 6.1   Capital Mobility Since 1870

Sources: Foreign-assets-to-GDP-ratio from Obstfeld and Taylor (2004) up to 1970 and from Lane and Milesi-Ferretti (2007) thereafter. Capital account openness from index used by Quinn and Voth (2008).

Note: OECD = Organization for Economic Co-operation and Development.

all advanced economies in the late nineteenth century, a feature that continued into the 1930s when the intensity of crises reached an all-time high during the Great Depression. But from the 1940s until the early 1970s, the world was virtually free of financial crises, with a few crises witnessed in emerging markets, but none seen at all in advanced economies. This unusually prolonged period of financial calm stands out from what went before and what has happened since (Bordo and others, 2001). In the 1980s and 1990s, emerging markets experienced many financial crises; a few also occurred in advanced economies, followed by one of history's worst globally synchronized financial crises, in 2008, across a large swaths of so-called advanced economies. To illustrate these patterns, Figure 6.2 shows financial crisis indicators for the past two centuries.

Looking at the only available economic laboratory—that is, history—these two summary figures would appear on the surface to support the notion that, at least empirically, international financial integration (the scope for external imbalances) go hand in hand with financial instability (the prevalence of banking crises). But correlation is not causation, and such inferences may not be justified for various reasons. For example, no statistical controls have been performed here, nor have concerns been addressed about possible simultaneity and the role of omitted common factors potentially driving both patterns.

One obvious area for concern with respect to proper statistical control would be changes in other aspects of the macroeconomic and financial policy regime over time and across countries. For example, the period of unusual calm in the 1940–70 period is known to have coincided with what was historically the most

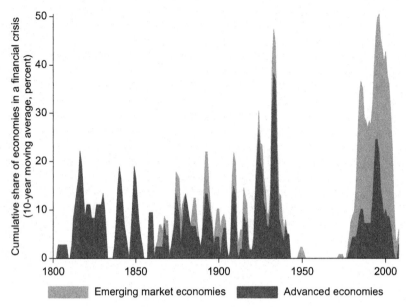

Figure 6.2 Banking Crises in the Past Two Centuries

Source: Data from Qian, Reinhart, and Rogoff (2010).

Note: The figure shows the cumulative percent of economies in a banking crisis in each year from 1800 to 2008, 10-year moving average.

stringent era of capital controls (imposed under IMF auspices as the very basis of the Bretton Woods fixed exchange rate regime), and thus the era in which global imbalances were at their all-time nadir. However, it also coincided with a very stringent era of domestic financial regulation in most countries around the world. Policymakers reacted strongly to the bank panics and financial distress of the 1930s with a combination of rules and supervision, plus backstops and insurance (in the U.S. case, for example, Glass-Steagall ring-fencing, supervisory agencies, reserve requirements, the Federal Deposit Insurance Corporation, and Federal Reserve lender-of-last-resort actions).

Even absent the move toward financial autarky in this period, changes in the domestic financial landscape also pushed economies toward a less risky, less leveraged macroeconomic and financial regime. It would be a mistake, without further careful analysis, to claim that one or the other set of policies played a primary role in creating that stable environment. If we are to learn from the past, such work is needed as we sit at another historical turning point when the policy architecture is again under heated discussion and under pressure to be redesigned.

EVENT STUDIES: CORRELATES OF CRISES

One clear and simple way to begin to explore at least the proximate causes of financial crises is to use event study techniques. This approach looks systematically at the behavior of key variables in the run-up to, and in the aftermath of, financial crisis events, with the goal of identifying systematic differences between tranquil periods or "normal" "times" outside the crisis window, and what happens in periods close to a financial crisis. Such analysis serves several purposes: overall patterns impose theoretical discipline on economic models designed to account for crises; precrisis patterns may lead to early warning signals of use to policymakers and others wishing to avert or anticipate problems; and postcrisis patterns should set appropriate historical benchmarks for the evaluation of conditional economic performance (e.g., disputes over whether a recovery is sluggish).

A number of works in the economic literature have followed this approach successfully, such as Cerra and Saxena (2008), Reinhart and Rogoff (2009), Claessens and others (2010), Gourinchas and Obstfeld (2011), Reinhart and Reinhart (2011), Schularick and Taylor (2012), and Reinhart, Reinhart, and Rogoff (2012), among many others. The technique is also widely used in the policy world, for example, in IMF analyses for the *World Economic Outlook* and other publications since the 2008 crisis. Other related works in this vein include Chamon and Crowe (2012) focusing on a range of indicators; Goldstein (2012) on the link between fundamentals and panics; Dell'Ariccia and others (2012) looking at credit boom warning signals; and Claessens, Kose, and Terrones (2012) who look at the coherence of business and financial cycles.

Most of this literature is in broad agreement. For representative evidence from a recent sample that includes both advanced and emerging market economies using annual data from 1973 to 2010, Figure 6.3 shows empirical regularities for nine key macroeconomic and financial variables in five-year windows on each side of banking crisis events drawn from Gourinchas and Obstfeld (2011).

The results can be summed up as follows, with some tentative hypotheses that can be carried forward:

- Output is slightly above normal just before a crisis, but collapses dramatically afterward. The boom may be slightly larger in emerging economies. Advanced economies fare no better than emerging in the aftermath. *A long recession is typical.*

- Inflation is close to normal just before a crisis, but collapses afterward. Real interest rates are not atypical before a crisis, but can rise afterward, with the effect seemingly stronger in emerging economies. *Deflationary pressures are strong.*

- Public debt levels are normal just before a crisis, but increase dramatically afterward, with a wide range. *Crises have adverse fiscal consequences.*

- Domestic credit expansion is typically much higher than normal before a banking crisis event. The shift is very strong in advanced economies and highly statistically significant. *Credit booms tend to precede banking crises.*

Looking at external indicators, external leverage (gross positions) and the current account do not seem out of line in the window, although in advanced economies these variables get close to borderline significance. Real exchange rates

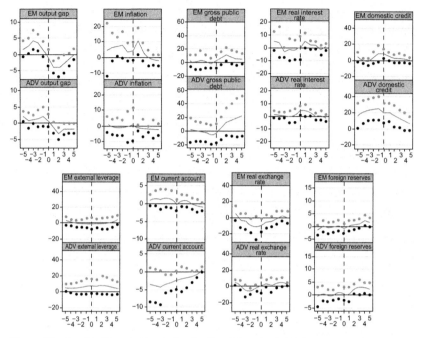

Figure 6.3   Empirical Regularities during Banking Crises, 1973–2010

Source: Gourinchas and Obstfeld, 2011.

Note: ADV = advanced economies; EM = emerging market economies. Units are percent per year (inflation and real interest rate); percent deviation from log trend (output gap and real exchange rate); and percent of GDP (all other variables). The estimates of conditional means of each variable, relative to "tranquil times" are reported on the vertical axes. The horizontal axes represent the number of years before (negative sign) and after a crisis (in the different columns). Estimates in the top row are for emerging market economies; in the bottom row for advanced economies. The dots denote a 95 percent confidence interval for each conditional mean.

tend to be strong before a crisis, and weaken a lot afterward, compared with normal times. Foreign reserves show no unusual precrisis trend but tend to accumulate afterward as the currency weakens and the external accounts move more to surplus. Thus, external imbalances and currency appreciation may also be indicative of added crisis risk.

CREDIT AND THE CURRENT ACCOUNT: TWO SIDES OF THE SAME COIN?

The main argument in this chapter is that unusually high rates of credit growth tend to be the primary warning signal of incipient financial crises. However, as the preceding discussion indicates, other indicators could also be relevant, and one goal of the chapter is to relate these perspectives to external imbalances, which have been a focus of debate since 2000.

From a simple accounting perspective, and thinking in conventional theoretical terms, simultaneous correlation between higher credit growth and external

```

deficits in open economies might be expected. Countries experiencing booms tend to have higher investment, and may also have lower savings, if consumption-smoothing motives are at work. The investment may, to some degree, be financed through bank lending channels, suggesting that loan growth and current accounts might be negatively correlated.

However, in the data, this correlation is far from perfect. Consider the long-term advanced economy data set of Schularick and Taylor (2012). If the change in credit-to-GDP ratios were to be regressed on the change in current-account-to-GDP ratios in every year, then this bivariate relationship has significance (an $F$-statistic greater than 5) in about one out of every six years over the course of history since 1870. Some panel tests over multiyear samples are shown in Table 6.1.

Over the entire sample, in column (1), the coefficient on the external imbalance is only –0.12, reflecting the fact that capital inflows can come in a variety of forms, including foreign direct investment or private portfolio securities, or sovereign loans, which have nothing to do with the destination-country banking sector. Indeed, this "pass-through" coefficient suggests that about 90 percent of the time, such flows have bypassed banks. This coefficient rises to –0.31 in the post-1980 era of financial globalization, suggesting that the conduits of external imbalances in recent decades have shifted more toward banking channels; but even then 70 percent of flows appear to be moving outside bank channels.

These results caution that the nexus of financial crises—the domestic banking sector—is only partially coupled to the external balance of payments imbalances of any country, an obvious point. Countries can experience capital inflows that take nonbank forms, so the causation from external to internal is not a given; and they can have credit booms driven by expansion of leverage in domestic banks that need not be related to any new financing flows from abroad, so the causation from internal to external is not a given either.

The historical data back up this idea that the two measures are for the most part distinct, and should therefore not necessarily be expected to play the same role with respect to crisis risk, a point the chapter now examines in greater detail.

**TABLE 6.1**

Credit Booms and External Imbalances: Only Weakly Correlated since 1870

Dependent variable: Change in credit-to-GDP ratio

|  | (1)<br>All years | (2)<br>Post-1980 | (3)<br>Pre-1914 | (4)<br>1914–80 |
|---|---|---|---|---|
| Change in current-account-to-GDP ratio | −0.122** | −0.311* | −0.184** | −0.0731 |
|  | (−2.83) | (−2.31) | (−2.80) | (−1.38) |
| Number of observations | 1,531 | 392 | 412 | 727 |

Source: Data from Jordà, Schularick, and Taylor (2011a).
Note: $t$-statistics are in parentheses. *, **, and *** indicate that the results are significant at the 10 percent, 5 percent, and 1 percent levels, respectively.
```

LET THE DATA SPEAK 1: PREDICTIVE ABILITY TESTS

Up to now the chapter has documented some basic empirical regularities, but in that framework only so much can be achieved. The comparisons are just one variable at a time and ultimately a more formal analysis is needed to evaluate which variables really do seem to have distinct dynamics in crisis times as compared with their normal behavior. Given the focus of this chapter, and the results of the last section, the analysis now concentrates on the competing hypotheses relating to whether it is external imbalances or credit booms that are the main feature of crisis events.

Research has turned to the question of predictive modeling, that is, attempting to establish whether certain past variables may contain ex ante early warning information about the likelihood of a financial crisis today. In the wake of the 2007–09 crisis, which caught most economists and policymakers by surprise, the need for careful, robust, and replicable work in this area is urgent, but this is not to say important previous work did not exist. Work on the determinants of emerging market financial crises certainly existed (among others, Kaminsky and Reinhart, 1999). Work on financial crises in samples including advanced economies had also been undertaken (e.g., Bank for International Settlements studies, including, famously, Borio and White, 2004; and Eichengreen and Mitchener, 2004), although it was not heeded by many. This literature tended to find that credit booms, meaning faster growth in bank lending relative to "normal times" were indicative of elevated crisis risk. There was also evidence that higher levels of foreign reserves in emerging markets could perhaps mitigate risks, all else equal.

These findings have been echoed in more recent work, for example, in the logit predictive models presented by Gourinchas and Obstfeld (2011) and Schularick and Taylor (2012). The former employs a short-wide annual panel of both advanced and emerging economies since the 1970s; the latter constructs a long-narrow annual panel from a historical data set for the advanced economies going back to 1870.

In the context of this chapter, however, it is important to ask whether in these and other works one can find any role, much less an independent role, for external imbalances as crisis determinants. The answer, so far at least, seems to be no. In the Gourinchas and Obstfeld (2011) study, the current account is unrelated to banking crisis risk in both the advanced country sample and the emerging market sample, once other controls are included, the most important of which is the credit variable.

Similar results were found by Jordà, Schularick, and Taylor (2011a), using the long-wide panel of advanced economies; a concise exposition of their tests is shown in Figure 6.4 using a tool referred to as the Correct Classification Frontier, or CCF.[3] Using any one of a family of competing logit models, such as those described above, the CCF curve plots the frontier of true positives (TP) and true negatives (TN) that each model delivers depending on how its trigger threshold is set. In a given set of data, with any model, a low enough threshold gets 100

---

[3] The CCF is a variant of the receiver operating characteristic curve.

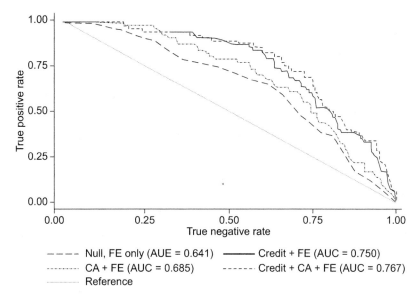

Figure 6.4 Using Lagged Credit Growth Plus Current Accounts or Public Debts as a Classifier to Forecast Financial Crises: The Correct Classification Frontier

Sources: Jordà, Schularick, and Taylor (2011a); and Taylor (2012).

Note: AUC = area under curve; CA = current account; FE = fixed effects. "CA" uses a five-year lagged moving average of change in the current-account-to-GDP ratio. In this figure, for all models, the predictions of separate prewar and postwar country-fixed-effects logit models are combined. Relative to either the "Null" or the "Credit" model, the addition of "CA" does not significantly improve the classifier.

percent TP but 0 percent TN; a high enough threshold scores the opposite. An uninformative model (a random signal) will achieve a CCF curve of TP and TN scores on the diagonal simplex between these points. Statistical tests are needed to evaluate whether a model can be judged to be informative, which amounts to having a CCF curve that lies above the diagonal.

A straightforward test, which requires no modeling of preferences, would be to look at the "area under the curve" or AUC as a test statistic. Under the uninformative null, AUC equals 0.5 and hypothesis tests are simplified by the asymptotically normal distribution of this statistic. Among other results, Jordà, Schularick, and Taylor (2011a) present tests based on the AUC for four models using the long panel:[4]

- A model with country fixed effects only (CFE, a better-than-random null);
- A model with the lagged credit variable (five-year moving-average change) plus CFE;
- A model with the lagged current account variable (five-year moving-average change) plus CFE;
- A model with both the lagged credit and current account variables plus CFE.

---

[4] The discussion draws on Taylor (2012).

As Figure 6.4 shows, adding the current account variable to the model slightly improves predictive ability relative to the country-fixed-effects null (AUC rises from 0.641 to 0.685; $p = 0.0165$), but adding the credit variable improves predictive ability much more (AUC rises to 0.745; $p = 0.0010$). Once credit is in the model, adding the current account on top achieves little. Why? As history has shown, over the long term economies can have credit booms fueled by external imbalances, but they can also have homegrown credit booms that are unrelated to shifts in the current account. Either type can potentially increase banking crisis risk, so changes in the balance of payments may not be all that informative.

LET THE DATA SPEAK 2: BEYOND BINARY CLASSIFICATION

Finally, it is worth noting the relevance of the credit cycle, not just for the rare events called financial crises but for all recessions (Jordà, Schularick, and Taylor, 2011b). To underscore this point, all recession events in all countries can be classified as normal recessions or financial recessions based on coincidence (±2 years) with a crisis event. In about 140 years for 14 countries from 1870 to 2008, 50 financial recessions, 173 normal recessions, and 223 recessions in total are observed. The corresponding event frequencies are 3.3 percent for financial recessions and 11.4 percent for normal recessions (approximately 1 in 30 years versus 1 in 9).[5]

Figure 6.5 shows that there is a more generalized echo of a credit boom in all recessions. A larger run-up in credit each year during the previous expansion years (in percentage of GDP per year) can be traced to weaker performance (lower levels of real GDP per capita) in the subsequent recession and recovery phase out to a horizon of five years beyond the cyclical peak. Thus, unusually rapid credit growth poses extra dangers. Not only does it raise the likelihood of a once-in-a-generation financial crisis event, as the binary prediction analysis shows, it is also systematically related to weaker recession paths in all peak-trough episodes, whether the country falls prey to a financial recession or a normal recession.

To put the "marginal effects" of the excess credit treatment in Figure 6.5 into perspective, the slope is 0.5 for normal recessions and 0.75 for financial recessions. Excess credit, measured in percent of GDP per year, has a historical mean of about 1¼ in expansions prior to financial recessions (standard deviation = 2½) and a mean of ¼ in expansions prior to normal recessions (standard deviation = 2). This implies that a 1 standard deviation increase in the credit variable during a "high leverage" expansion is associated with a five-year drag of −1 percent of the level of real GDP per capita after the peak in a normal recession, or −2 percent in the event of financial recession.

---

[5] To cleanse the effects of the two world wars from the analysis, the war windows 1914–18 and 1939–45 are excluded, as are data corresponding to peaks that are within five years of the wars looking forward, or two years looking backward (because these leads and lags are used in the analysis below).

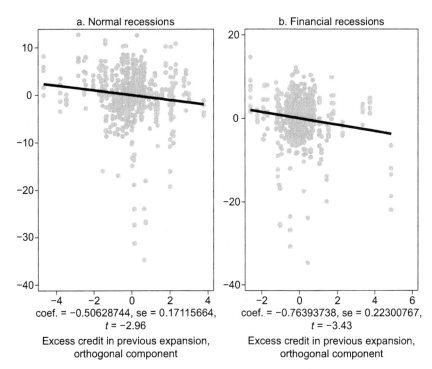

Figure 6.5   Credit Bites Back: "Excess" Credit Growth in the Expansion Phase and the Deviation of Real GDP per Capita in the Five-Year Next Recession and Recovery Phase

Source: Based on the data in Jordà, Schularick, and Taylor (2011b).

Note: coef. = coefficient; se = standard error; t = t-statistic. The figures show simple added-variable plots (partial scatters) between the deviation of the level of log real GDP per capita in recession or recovery years one through five after a normal or financial peak, and the annual rate of change of credit to GDP in the previous expansion. Panel a shows financial crisis recessions only, panel b normal recessions only. In the underlying regression, additional control variables include five-year time fixed effects interacted with normal and financial recession dummies. Both partial correlations are statistically significant at the 1 percent level.

These are nontrivial differences and deserve further scrutiny and causal investigation: credit booms sow the seeds of future deleveraging pain in all cycles. Monitoring credit is, therefore, a legitimate issue for policymakers concerned with overall macroeconomic stability at business-cycle frequencies, that is, even in more typical cycles when crises are averted and the economy suffers only a "normal" recession (see, e.g., Drehmann, Borio, and Tsatsaronis, 2011; and Turner, 2011).

CONCLUSIONS

The history of advanced economies shows that credit booms and busts can be driven just as easily by domestic saving as foreign saving. Gross stocks and flows can often be delinked from net flows across borders, so balance sheets can expand even if no cross-border flows are recorded. At a disaggregated level, current account flows can be composed of a widely varying mix of bank instruments, debt, equity, foreign direct investment, and other claims, and each type has very different risk characteristics, with bank and debt flows being the ones with roll-over risk (stops, flight).

Thus, there is absolutely no preordained reason why any dollar of gross or net capital flows should make a difference to the risk of a financial crisis in the home country. It is highly likely instead that the nature of the flow, and its route into the local economy, will matter far more. It is when financial flows *of local or foreign origin* build up into large credit exposures in the domestic financial system that the risks of a financial crisis are elevated and the likelihood of future deleveraging costs is increased.

Analysts need to move beyond monocausal stories in which the current account is relied upon as a unique, special indicator. Evidence shows that domestic credit conditions are a more salient feature of crisis dynamics, and even of the dynamics of normal business cycles.

A natural dichotomy is emerging. An "external variable" like current accounts may make sense as a key indicator in the analysis of proximate causes of "external crisis"—meaning capital market access, bad spreads, default, or recourse to IMF programs (Catão and Milesi-Ferretti, 2012). But an "internal variable" like credit might make much more sense as a key indicator in the analysis of proximate causes of "internal crisis," meaning distress in the domestic financial system, bank panics, failures, and so forth.

Future economic and policy analysis may benefit greatly if we can move beyond the narrow and simplistic "global imbalance" framework that all too often dominated discussions in the past decade.[6]

REFERENCES

Bernanke, Ben S., 2005, "The Global Saving Glut and the U.S. Current Account Deficit," Remarks at the Sandridge Lecture, Virginia Association of Economists, Richmond, Virginia, March 10.

Bordo, Michael, Barry Eichengreen, Daniela Klingebiel, and María Soledad Martínez-Pería, 2001, "Is the Crisis Problem Growing More Severe?" *Economic Policy*, Vol. 16, No. 32, pp. 51–82.

Borio, Claudio, and William R. White, 2004, "Whither Monetary and Financial Stability? The Implications of Evolving Policy Regimes," in *Monetary Policy and Uncertainty: Adapting to a Changing Economy*, Proceedings of a symposium sponsored by the Federal Reserve Bank of Kansas City, Jackson Hole, Wyoming, August 28–30, 2003, pp. 131–211.

Catão, Luis A.V., and Gian Maria Milesi-Ferretti, 2012, "External Liabilities and Crisis Risk" (unpublished; Washington: International Monetary Fund).

---

[6] See, for example, Lane (2012) and Obstfeld (2012) for suggestions as to the way ahead. See also the IEO (2011) post mortem of the global financial crisis, for example: "For much of the period [2004–07] the IMF was drawing the membership's attention to the risk that a disorderly unwinding of global imbalances could trigger a rapid and sharp depreciation of the dollar, and later on the risks of inflation from rising commodity prices. The IMF gave too little consideration to deteriorating financial sector balance sheets, financial regulatory issues, to the possible links between monetary policy and the global imbalances, and to the credit boom and emerging asset bubbles. It did not discuss macro-prudential approaches that might have helped address the evolving risks" (IEO, 2011, p. 7).

Cerra, Valerie, and Sweta Chaman Saxena, 2008, "Growth Dynamics: The Myth of Economic Recovery," *American Economic Review*, Vol. 98, No. 1, pp. 439–57.

Chamon, Marcos, and Christopher Crowe, 2012, "Evidence on Financial Globalization and Crisis: 'Predictive' Indicators of Crises–Macroprudential Indicators, Institutional Environment, Micro" (unpublished; Washington: International Monetary Fund).

Claessens, Stijn, Giovanni Dell'Ariccia, Deniz Igan, and Luc Laeven, 2010, "Cross-Country Experiences and Policy Implications from the Global Financial Crisis," *Economic Policy*, Vol. 25, pp. 267–93.

Claessens, Stijn, M. Ayhan Kose, and Marco E. Terrones, 2012, "How Do Business and Financial Cycles Interact?" *Journal of International Economics*, Vol. 87, No. 1, pp. 178–90.

Dell'Ariccia, Giovanni, Deniz Igan, Luc Laeven, and Hui Tong, 2012, "Policies for Macrofinancial Stability: Options to Deal with Credit Booms," IMF Staff Discussion Note 12/06 (Washington: International Monetary Fund).

Drehmann, Mathias, Claudio Borio, and Kostas Tsatsaronis, 2011, "Anchoring Countercyclical Capital Buffers: The Role of Credit Aggregates," *International Journal Of Central Banking*, Vol. 7, No. 4, pp. 189–240.

Eichengreen, Barry, and Kris James Mitchener, 2004, "The Great Depression as a Credit Boom Gone Wrong," *Research in Economic History*, Vol. 22, pp. 183–237.

Goldstein, Itay, 2012, "Empirical Literature on Financial Crises: Fundamentals vs. Panic," in *The Evidence and Impact of Financial Globalization*, ed. by Gerard Caprio (Amsterdam: Elsevier), pp. 523–34.

Gourinchas, Pierre-Olivier, and Maurice Obstfeld, 2012, "Stories of the Twentieth Century for the Twenty-First," *American Economic Journal: Macroeconomics*, Vol. 4, No. 1, pp. 226–65.

Independent Evaluation Office (IEO) of the International Monetary Fund, 2011, *IMF Performance in the Run-Up to the Financial and Economic Crisis: IMF Surveillance in 2004–07* (Washington: International Monetary Fund).

Jordà, Òscar, Moritz Schularick, and Alan M. Taylor, 2011a, "Financial Crises, Credit Booms, and External Imbalances: 140 Years of Lessons," *IMF Economic Review*, Vol. 59, No. 2, pp. 340–78.

———, 2011b, "When Credit Bites Back: Leverage, Business Cycles, and Crises," NBER Working Paper No. 17621 (Cambridge, Massachusetts: National Bureau of Economic Research).

Kaminsky, Graciela L., and Carmen M. Reinhart, 1999, "The Twin Crises: The Causes of Banking and Balance-of-Payments Problems," *American Economic Review*, Vol. 89, No. 3, pp. 473–500.

King, M., 2011, "Global Imbalances: The Perspective of the Bank of England," *Financial Stability Review*, No. 15, pp. 73–80.

Lane, Philip R., and Gian Maria Milesi-Ferretti, 2007, "The External Wealth of Nations Mark II: Revised and Extended Estimates of Foreign Assets and Liabilities, 1970–2004," *Journal of International Economics*, Vol. 73, No. 2, pp. 223–50.

Lane, Philip R., 2012, "Financial Globalisation and the Crisis," BIS Working Paper No. 397 (Basel: Bank for International Settlements).

Obstfeld, Maurice, 2012, "Does the Current Account Still Matter?" *American Economic Review*, Vol. 102, No. 3, pp. 1–23.

———, and Alan M. Taylor, 2004, *Global Capital Markets: Integration, Crisis, and Growth*. Japan–U.S. Center Sanwa Monographs on International Financial Markets (Cambridge, United Kingdom: Cambridge University Press).

Quinn, Dennis P., and Hans-Joachim Voth, 2008, "A Century of Global Equity Market Correlations," *American Economic Review*, Vol. 98, No. 2, pp. 535–40.

Reinhart, Carmen M., and Vincent R. Reinhart, 2011, "After the Fall," in *Macroeconomic Challenges: The Decade Ahead*, Proceedings of a symposium sponsored by the Federal Reserve Bank of Kansas City, Jackson Hole, Wyoming, August 26–28, 2010, pp. 17–60.

———, and Kenneth S. Rogoff, 2012, "Debt Overhangs: Past and Present," NBER Working Paper No. 18015 (Cambridge, Massachusetts: National Bureau of Economic Research).

Reinhart, Carmen M., and Kenneth S. Rogoff, 2009, *This Time is Different: Eight Centuries of Financial Folly* (Princeton, New Jersey: Princeton University Press).

Schularick, Moritz, and Alan M. Taylor, 2012, "Credit Booms Gone Bust: Monetary Policy, Leverage Cycles, and Financial Crises, 1870–2008," *American Economic Review*, Vol. 102, No. 2, pp. 1029–61.

Schularick, Moritz, and Paul Wachtel, 2012, "The Making of America's Imbalances," Discussion Paper Economics 2012/16 (Berlin: Free University of Berlin, School of Business and Economics).

Shin, Hyun Song, 2012, "Global Banking Glut and Loan Risk Premium," *IMF Economic Review*, Vol. 60, pp. 155–92.

Taylor, Alan M., 2012, "The Great Leveraging," NBER Working Paper No. 18290 (Cambridge, Massachusetts: National Bureau of Economic Research).

Turner, Adair, 2011, "Debt and Deleveraging: Long Term and Short Term Challenges," Presidential Lecture: Centre for Financial Studies, Frankfurt, November 21. http://www.fsa .gov.uk/library/communication/speeches/2011/1121_at.shtml.

PART III

Short-Term Effects: Crises, Recessions, and Recoveries

CHAPTER 7

The Global Financial Crisis: How Similar? How Different? How Costly?

STIJN CLAESSENS, M. AYHAN KOSE, AND MARCO E. TERRONES

The global economy is recovering from the deepest recession in the post–World War II era. The recession was triggered, albeit slowly, by the severe 2007–09 financial crisis in key advanced economies that coincided with the freezing of global financial markets and a collapse in global trade flows. The crisis quickly resulted in deep recessions in a number of advanced economies; the emerging market and developing economies were also seriously affected, but the impact varied across regions and countries.

Although the economic recovery is under way, the nature and implications of the crisis are still at the center of academic and policy discussions.[1] For example, there has been an intensive discussion about the similarities and differences between the latest crisis and past episodes. Some commentators, especially in the media, argue that the latest crisis was different. Its root causes are thought to lie in excessive global savings (a "saving glut"), flowing through a poorly regulated shadow banking system in the United States to its housing market (Krugman, 2009). Others claim that the idea of this crisis being different is misleading because an analysis of earlier crises presents remarkable similarities to the latest episode. In particular, the excessive accumulation of debt that took place in various forms ahead of the 2007–09 crisis was also a feature of previous crises (Reinhart and Rogoff, 2008).

Another dimension of the ongoing discussions about the crisis focuses on its global spread and cost. The crisis originated in the United States, but it took place in a highly integrated global economy in which the widespread use of sophisticated financial instruments, along with massive international financial flows, facilitated its rapid spread across markets and borders. Although it was not surprising that a global crisis led to a significant decline in global activity, explaining the extent and duration of this decline has been a major area of research.

This chapter was originally published in the *Journal of Asian Economics*, Vol. 21, No. 3, pp. 247–64. The authors would like to thank David Fritz and Ezgi Ozturk for providing outstanding research assistance.

[1] A number of papers provide detailed discussions about the evolution of the crisis (Borio, 2008; Brunnermeier, 2009; Calomiris, 2009; Gorton, 2009; and Shin, 2009).

Recessions associated with the global financial crisis, while displaying patterns similar to those of previous recession episodes, reflect an unlikely confluence of factors. Specifically, these recessions are associated with serious financial disruptions, including credit crunches, house price busts, equity price busts, and outright banking crises in some countries.

This chapter provides a brief analysis of the nature and cost of the crisis to shed light on these issues. In particular, it addresses three major questions. First, how similar is the latest crisis to previous episodes? Second, how different is the crisis from earlier ones? Third, how costly are recessions coinciding with serious disruptions in financial markets? The first two questions are studied in the first two sections. The basic conclusion is that the massive financial crisis that gripped the global economy beginning in 2008 was the result of a multitude of factors. Some of these factors are similar to those observed during the buildup to past financial crises, but some others are distinctly new. Although ranking the relative contributions of these various factors is difficult, together they help explain the latest episode's considerable scale and scope. Irrespective of any similarities or differences though, the crisis has been a very costly one for both the real and the financial sectors, as discussed in the third and fourth sections.

How similar was the 2007–09 crisis to previous episodes? The first section examines four primary similarities in the buildup to the crisis and other similarities in the postcrisis busts. How different was the latest crisis from previous crisis episodes? As presented in the second section, at least four new dimensions played important roles in the severity and global scale of the crisis that included surprising disruptions and breakdowns of several markets in the fall of 2008. How costly was the 2007–09 episode? The global financial crisis resulted in recessions in almost all advanced economies. Most of these recessions were accompanied by credit crunches, house price busts, and outright financial crises. The third section provides an analysis of how recessions associated with credit crunches, house price busts, and financial crises differ from other recessions. The results suggest that recessions with credit crunches or house price busts result in more costly macroeconomic outcomes than do those without such disruptions. When recessions are accompanied by financial crises, the costs are larger and much more pronounced for consumption and investment.

The fourth section presents the dynamics of the lingering recession in the United States, the epicenter of the current crisis, and compares them with those of past recessions in advanced economies. It also provides a short discussion of the speed and extent of deterioration of activity in the United States. The findings suggest that the U.S. recession in the wake of the global crisis was clearly an outlier in many respects. The financial crisis has taken a heavy toll on the real economy as evidenced by deep and long recessions in a number of advanced economies in addition to the United States. The cost of a recession is, of course, affected by a number of factors. The final section presents a brief discussion of these factors, discusses policy implications, and concludes.

THE CRISIS: HOW SIMILAR?[2]

The buildup to the ongoing financial crisis has four features similar to earlier episodes: First, asset prices rapidly increased in a number of countries before the crisis. Second, a number of key economies experienced episodes of credit booms ahead of the crisis. Third, a variety of marginal loans, particularly in the mortgage markets of several advanced economies expanded dramatically, which led to a sharp increase in systemic risk. Fourth, the regulation and supervision of financial institutions failed to keep up with developments.

Asset Price Booms

The exuberant pattern of asset prices in the United States and other advanced economies before the 2007–09 crisis is reminiscent of those observed in earlier major financial crisis episodes in the post-World War II period. The overall size of the U.S. housing boom and its dynamics—including house prices rising in excess of 30 percent in the five years preceding the crisis and peaking six quarters before the beginning of the crisis—was remarkably similar to house price developments in the so-called Big Five banking crisis episodes (Finland, 1990–93; Japan, 1993; Norway, 1988; Spain, 1978–79; and Sweden, 1990–93).[3]

The house price boom in the United States ahead of the 2007–09 crisis was, however, unusual both in its strength and duration. Sharp increases in house prices were also a common feature in other countries hit hard by the crisis, including the United Kingdom, Iceland, and many Eastern European countries. This synchronicity of house price increases across countries before the crisis may be surprising considering that housing is the quintessential nontradable asset. However, other analysis shows that such highly synchronized episodes were not uncommon in the past (Claessens, Kose, and Terrones, 2009). During the latest period, however, house price booms were partly fueled by low (short- and long-term) interest rates resulting from abundant global liquidity and high demand for safe assets (Caballero, 2010).

Credit Booms

The prolonged credit expansion in the run-up to the crisis was also similar to other episodes. Mendoza and Terrones (2008) document the main features of episodes of unusually sharp expansions in real credit that often ended in crisis. Credit booms generally coincide with large cyclical fluctuations in economic activity—with real output, consumption, and investment rising above trend

---

[2] A number of papers examine the differences and similarities between the latest episode and past crises (Furceri and Mourougane, 2009). Some parts of the first and second sections extend Claessens (2009) and Claessens and others (2010).

[3] Reinhart and Rogoff (2008) examine the run-up in house prices in the United States before 2007 and the Big Five crises in advanced economies and confirm significant increases in house prices before financial crises, and marked declines in the crisis year and in subsequent years. However, they note that the run-up in house prices before the U.S. crisis exceeded the run-ups in house prices before the Big Five.

during the buildup phase of credit booms and falling below trend in the unwinding phase (see Figure 7.1). In the upswing, the current account tends to deteriorate, often accompanied by a surge in private capital inflows. Increases in house prices and the real exchange rate often accompany such credit booms. At least for advanced economies, however, credit booms are not always associated with surges in inflation. Credit booms in these countries are also more likely when preceded by a period of gains in total factor productivity or financial sector reforms.[4]

Most of these movements were also features of the credit booms that took place in Iceland, Spain, the United Kingdom, the United States, and some other advanced economies ahead of the 2007–09 crisis. However, unlike this crisis, credit booms in the advanced economies were only occasionally associated with currency and banking crises. In the past, advanced economies experiencing credit booms were more likely to have currency crises than banking crises. The credit boom that preceded the 2007–09 crisis was also not limited to advanced economies, but extended to varying degrees to several emerging market countries caught in the storm. In the run-up to the crisis, credit aggregates grew very fast in several Eastern European countries and often fueled real estate booms.

As in past episodes, international financial integration helped facilitate some of these trends (Cardarelli, Kose, and Elekdag, 2010). Specifically, large capital inflows were associated with accelerating GDP growth and, for many countries, with credit expansion. In addition, output growth was accompanied by large swings in aggregate demand and in the current account balance, with strong deterioration of the current account during the inflow period (see Figure 7.2).

Marginal Loans and Systemic Risk

The rapid growth of credit was often directed toward households and resulted in sharply increased household leverage. The boom in household credit was associated with the creation of marginal assets whose viability relied on continued favorable conditions. In the United States (and to some extent the United Kingdom), a large portion of the mortgage expansion consisted of loans extended to subprime borrowers—households with limited credit and short employment histories. Therefore, debt servicing and repayment were vulnerable to economic downturns and changes in credit and monetary conditions. This situation maximized default correlations across loans, generating portfolios highly exposed to declines in house prices, confirmed ex post through the large nonperforming loans when house prices declined.[5]

---

[4] Some 40 percent of the credit booms in these countries followed large gains in total factor productivity, 33 percent followed significant financial sector reform, and 27 percent followed large capital inflows.

[5] Mayer, Pence, and Sherlund (2009) document that mortgage defaults and delinquencies were particularly concentrated among borrowers whose mortgages were classified as subprime or near prime. They report that many such borrowers put down small or no down payments when they purchased their homes, and were likely to have negative equity in their homes when house prices fell. This implies that they often were unable to sell before the bank could foreclose.

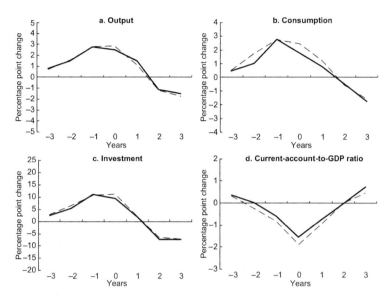

Figure 7.1 Credit Booms and Macroeconomic Variables (cross-country means and medians of cyclical components)

Source: Authors' calculations.

Note: The solid (dashed) line represents the median (mean) of each variable around the time of a credit boom. Peak in the cyclical component of per capita real credit at year 0.

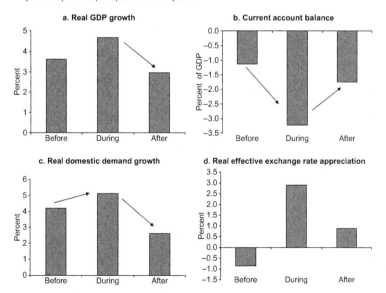

Figure 7.2   Selected Macroeconomic Variables in Periods Surrounding Large Capital Inflows

Source: Authors' calculations.

Note: Median across all completed episodes. "Before" denotes averages of the macro variables in the two years before the episodes. "After" denotes averages of the macro variables in the two years after the episodes. The arrows indicate that the difference between medians is significant at a 10 percent level or better. For example, in panel a, the average real GDP growth in the two years after the episode is statistically significantly different from the average real GDP growth during the episodes. Real effective exchange rate appreciation is the cumulative change within periods.

A similar pattern led to large portions of domestic credit denominated in foreign currency, particularly in emerging Europe. Large foreign currency exposures in the corporate and financial sectors had been a common feature in the Asian crisis of the late 1990s. In the 2007–09 crisis, in several Eastern European economies large portions of domestic credit (including to households) were denominated in foreign currency (euros, Swiss francs, and yen—Árvai, Driessen, and Ötker-Robe, 2009). Although lower interest rates relative to local currency increased affordability, borrowers' ability to service loans and their creditworthiness depended on continued exchange rate stability. As with U.S. subprime loans, this meant high default risk correlations across loans and systemic exposure to macroeconomic shocks.

As a result of buoyant housing and corporate financing markets, derivative markets in many forms expanded greatly. In particular, favorable conditions spurred the emergence of large-scale derivative markets, such as mortgage-backed securities and collateralized debt obligations with payoffs that depended in complex ways on underlying asset prices. The pricing of these instruments was often based on a continuation of increasing house prices that facilitated the refinancing of underlying mortgages. The corporate credit default swap market also expanded dramatically based on favorable spreads and low volatility.

Regulation and Supervision

Episodes of large credit expansion have reflected not only macroeconomic conditions, but also various structural deficiencies, such as explicit or implicit government guarantees, herding behavior by investors, reduced lending standards, excessive competition, and information asymmetries. These episodes have also been associated with rapid financial liberalization and poorly supervised and unregulated financial innovation.

Evidence shows that past crises often followed credit expansions triggered by financial liberalization not accompanied by necessary regulatory and prudential reforms (Demirgüç-Kunt and Detragiache, 1998). Moreover, imbalances often resulted from poorly sequenced regulatory reforms. Underdeveloped domestic financial systems were often unable to intermediate large capital inflows in the wake of capital account liberalization. Poorly designed financial reforms and deficient supervision often led to currency and maturity mismatches and to large and concentrated credit risks.

In the run-up to the 2007–09 crisis, regulatory approaches to and supervisory oversight of financial innovation were insufficient, although perhaps in more subtle forms. As in previous crises, but this time in advanced economies, financial companies, merchant banks, investment banks, and off-balance-sheet vehicles of commercial banks operated—to varying degrees—outside banking regulations. However, while this shadow banking system provided increasingly important avenues for intermediation, it grew without adequate oversight and led to systemic risks. Unhealthy turf competition between various supervisory agencies in some countries and conflict of interest issues at rating agencies exacerbated

problems. Regulators also underestimated the conflicts of interest and information problems associated with the originate-to-distribute model.[6] Not only did
this harm consumers of financial services, but it also created the potential for a
chain reaction leading to systemic risk.

Dynamics of the Bust

As in earlier crises, the increase in asset prices, the rapid growth of credit combined with poor lending practices, the increase in systemic risk, and failures in
regulation and supervision created many vulnerabilities. Although only a small
number of credit booms end in banking crises—about one-quarter of all asset
price booms end in busts (Helbling and Terrones, 2003)—the probability of a
crisis increases with a boom (Dell'Ariccia, Barajas, and Levchenko, 2008). More
generally, research documenting the main features of these types of credit booms
highlights the strong association with subsequent busts (Mendoza and Terrones,
2008). Furthermore, the larger the size and duration of a boom, the greater the
likelihood it will result in a crisis. The mechanisms linking credit booms to crises
include increases in leverage of borrowers (and lenders) and a decline in lending
standards. In the U.S. episode, both channels were at work (Dell'Ariccia, Igan,
and Laeven, 2008).

When asset booms turn into busts, significant output losses often result. The
outcome depends on the nature of the asset booms, with important differences
between house price busts and equity busts (Claessens, Kose, and Terrones,
2008). First, the magnitude of the asset price fall during a bust depends on the
size of the run-up in prices before the bust. But price corrections during house
price busts are smaller than those during equity price busts. This reflects, in part,
the lower volatility and liquidity of housing markets. Second, the association
between booms and busts is stronger for housing than for equity prices. The
implied probability of a house price boom being followed by a bust is about 40
percent. Third, house price busts last longer than equity price busts do. Moreover,
the output loss associated with a typical house price bust is twice as large as that
associated with an equity price bust.

Fourth, bank-based financial systems suffer larger output losses than market-
based financial systems during house price busts, while market-based systems
tend to suffer larger output losses than bank-based systems during equity price
busts (Helbling and Terrones, 2003). This outcome is consistent with the high
exposure of banks to real estate lending, and the larger importance of equities in
households' assets in market-based systems. Last, both equity and house price
busts are often synchronized across countries, but the degree of synchronization
in equity price busts is particularly high. This time, however, the downturn in

---

[6] Gorton (2009) describes the trend toward the originate-to-distribute model and explains how it
led to a decline in lending standards. He claims that banks increasingly financed their asset holdings
with shorter maturity instruments, which left them particularly exposed to the drying up of funding
liquidity.

house prices was highly synchronized across countries, with implications for global economic activity. Indeed, as of 2010, most advanced economies had experienced a recession for at least a year (Kose, Loungani, and Terrones, 2010).

The degree of international financial integration before the crisis also affects the bust. Cardarelli, Kose, and Elekdag (2010) examine developments subsequent to surges in private capital inflows for a group of emerging market and open advanced economies since 2000. After a period of capital inflows, growth can drop significantly. In fact, average GDP growth in the two years after episodes that end abruptly tends to be about 3 percentage points lower than during the episode, and about 1 percentage point lower than during the two years before the episode (see Figure 7.2). Past episodes characterized by sharper post-inflow declines in GDP growth tend to be those with faster acceleration in domestic demand, sharper increases in inflation, and larger real appreciation during the inflow period (see Figure 7.3).

The surge in capital inflows also appears to be associated with a real effective exchange rate appreciation. Hence, the sharper post-inflow decline in GDP growth seems to be associated with persistent, expansionary capital inflows, which compound external imbalances and sow the seeds of the eventual sharp reversal. Then, a sharp reversal also often occurs in the current account. The end of the inflow episodes typically entailed a sharp reversal of non-foreign direct investment flows, while foreign direct investment proved much more resilient. This was the pattern in several Eastern European countries during the 2007–09 crisis.

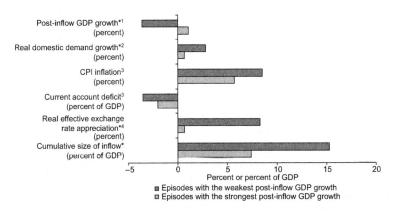

Figure 7.3 Large Capital Inflows: Post-Inflow GDP Growth and Selected Macroeconomic Variables

Source: Authors' estimates.

Note: Values reported are medians for the two groups of episodes. Episodes with the weakest (strongest) post-inflow GDP growth are those with above (below) median differences between average GDP growth in the two years after the episode and the average during the episodes.

* indicates that the difference between medians is significant at a 10 percent level or better.

[1] Average real GDP growth in the two years after the episodes less average during episodes.

[2] Average during episodes minus average in the two years before the episode.

[3] Average during episodes. CPI = consumer price index.

[4] Cumulative change during episodes.

As often before, poor crisis management played an important role in aggravating the financial crisis. For instance, similar to past episodes, it was difficult to get ahead of a quickly evolving situation to contain the financial turmoil and reduce its impact on the real economy (Cecchetti, 2009). The chronology of the crisis (Calomiris, 2009; and Gorton, 2009) shows how events and market developments triggered and conditioned specific subsequent developments and policy responses, that, in retrospect at least, probably made the crisis more severe (Taylor, 2009). The focus of authorities typically remained primarily on the liquidity and insolvency of individual institutions, rather than on the resilience of the whole financial system. Incomplete information and partial assessments of the serious financial problems led to ad hoc and piecemeal interventions, which at times created further disruptions and loss of confidence among creditors and investors. These shortcomings meant an underestimation of the probability and costs of systemic risk in many countries.

At the international level, insufficient coordination among regulators and supervisors and the absence of clear procedures for the resolution of global financial institutions has been a long-standing problem. In the 2007–09 crisis especially, these issues hindered efforts to prevent and contain the impact and transmission of the crisis (Claessens, 2009). As clearly demonstrated by the failures of Lehman Brothers and some Icelandic banks (among many other financial institutions), countries could not deal with large, complex, globally active financial institutions on their own because these institutions affect many markets and countries. Various government interventions, although necessary and often unavoidable, led to unintended effects on other countries, creating large distortions in international capital flows and financial intermediation. Overall, the lack of global agreements on tools for intervention made the crisis worse.

THE CRISIS: HOW DIFFERENT?

New dimensions played important roles in the severity and global scale of the 2007–09 crisis—particularly with respect to its transmission and amplification—including surprising disruptions and breakdowns of several markets in the fall of 2008. The crisis was different from previous ones in at least four respects. First, there was widespread use of complex and opaque financial instruments. Second, the interconnectedness among financial markets, nationally and internationally, with the United States at the core, had increased in a short period. Third, the degree of leverage of financial institutions had accelerated sharply. Fourth, the household sector played a central role. These new elements combined to create unprecedented sell-offs in the fall of 2008 that resulted in the global financial crisis.

Increased Opaqueness

Securitization spurred by the use of innovative (but complex) financial instruments was a critical element of the credit expansion, particularly mortgage credit, in the United States. Securitization—a long-standing practice for prime loans conforming to the underwriting standards of government sponsored entities—changed in scope beginning in the mid-1990s, with more than 70 percent of nonconforming mortgages in the United States being securitized by 2007, up from less than 35 percent in 2000 (Ashcraft and Schuermann, 2007). Other assets were increasingly packaged as well, and cash-flow streams from securities were further separated and tranched into other securities such as collateralized debt obligations (Blanchard, 2009).

The increased recourse to securitization and the expansion of the originate-and-distribute model exacerbated agency problems (Furceri and Morurougane, 2009). The progressive expansion of more-opaque and complex securities and the increasing delinking of borrowers from lenders further worsened agency problems. Risk assignments became increasingly unclear and incentives for due diligence decreased, leading to insufficient monitoring of loan originators and an emphasis on boosting volumes to generate fees. The distribution model led to widespread reliance on ratings for the pricing of credit risks, with investors often unable or unwilling to fully assess underlying values and risks themselves.

As discussed in Mishkin (2009), the quality of balance sheets of households and firms is a key element of the financial accelerator mechanism, because some of the assets of each borrower may serve as collateral for its liabilities, which helps mitigate the problem of asymmetric information. In case of default, the lender can take title to the borrower's collateral and recover some or all of the value of the loan. In a macroeconomic downturn, however, the value of many forms of collateral decreases. This, in turn, exacerbates the impact of frictions in credit markets and reinforces the propagation of adverse feedback loops.

Financial Integration and Interconnectedness

Financial integration has increased dramatically since 1990. Capital account openness and financial market reform have led to massive increases in cross-border gross positions, especially among member countries of the Organization for Economic Cooperation and Development (OECD). The presence of foreign intermediaries has also increased in several banking systems, including in many emerging markets (Goldberg, 2009). As a result, international risk sharing and competition and efficiency have increased, but so has the risk of rapid spread of financial shocks across borders. Several emerging markets have experienced sudden stops in this period.

Financial integration can result in indirect and catalytic growth benefits (Kose and others, 2009). Far more important than the direct growth effects of access to more capital is the potential for capital flows to generate collateral benefits (so called because they may not be countries' primary motivations for undertaking financial integration). In particular, as reviewed by Kose and others (2009), growing evidence shows that financial openness can promote development of the domestic financial sector, impose discipline on macroeconomic policies, generate efficiency gains among domestic firms by exposing them to competition from foreign entrants, and unleash forces that result in better government and corporate governance. These collateral benefits could enhance efficiency and, by extension, total factor productivity growth (see Kose and others, 2010).

However, the 2007–09 financial crisis serves as a reminder of the risks of financial integration for both advanced and emerging market economies (Obstfeld, 2009). Specifically, increasing interconnectedness of financial institutions and markets, and more highly correlated financial risks, intensified cross-border spillovers early on through many channels—including liquidity pressures, a global sell-off in equities (particularly financial stocks), and depletion of bank capital. The sheer size of the U.S. financial market and its central role as an investment destination contributed to the spread of the crisis. Any shock to the U.S. financial markets is bound to have global effects. Before the crisis, U.S. financial assets represented about 31 percent of global financial assets, and the U.S. dollar share in reserve currency assets was about 62 percent. In the years before the crisis especially, U.S. financial assets were perceived to offer the combination of safety and liquidity attractive to private and public investors alike.

The crisis also triggered an unwinding of imbalances in other countries. In part because of closer international financial integration, benign financial and macroeconomic conditions—notably, low interest rates and narrower risk spreads—were in place on a global basis and asset price booms developed in many economies. However, for similar reasons, the busts came in a highly synchronized manner as well, in more intense and different ways compared with previous crises.

The Role of Leverage

The buildup of an unusually high degree of leverage of financial institutions and borrowers contributed to the propagation of shocks (Brunnermeier, 2009). Leverage increased sharply in the financial sector, directly at commercial banks in Europe, and through the shadow banking system and the rising share of investment banks and non-deposit-taking institutions in the United States. The leverage buildup among households especially differed from previous crises. In the run-up to Japan's real estate crisis in the 1990s, for example, although the household debt-to-income ratio increased sharply, measures of household leverage (the household debt-to-assets ratio) declined, suggesting that Japanese homeowners built equity in their properties as real estate prices soared.

The high leverage preceding the 2007–09 crisis limited the system's ability to absorb even small losses and contributed to the rapid decline in confidence and increase in counterparty risk early on. Loan-to-income values larger than in the past left households highly exposed to shocks, while at the same time high loan-to-value mortgages caused even moderate declines in house prices to push many households into negative equity. In the financial sector, high leverage meant that initial liquidity concerns quickly gave way to solvency worries. The buildup in leverage (including rising household indebtedness) was not restricted to advanced economies.

The Role of Households

Problems in the household sector played a more prominent role in the 2007–09 crisis than in previous crises. Most previous episodes of financial distress stemmed from problems in the official sector (e.g., Latin America's debt crises of the 1980s) or the corporate sector (e.g., the Asian crises of the late 1990s). The 2007–09 crisis, however, largely originated from overextended households, in particular with respect to subprime mortgage loans. Although aggregate credit growth in the United States was less pronounced than in previous episodes, reflecting slower corporate credit expansion and the securitization of mortgages, the growth of household debt was excessive. Credit to households rose rapidly after 2000, driven largely by mortgages outstanding, with interest rates below historical averages and financial innovation contributing to an increase in outstanding household debt. Despite low interest rates, debt service relative to disposable income reached a historical high. The increased leverage left households vulnerable to a decline in house prices, a tightening in credit conditions, and a slowdown in economic activity. Similar patterns existed in several crisis countries.

Household balance sheet vulnerabilities also built up in other advanced economies and several emerging markets. Household debt-to-income ratios also rose sharply in several Western European countries (most notable in Ireland, Spain, and the United Kingdom). In several emerging markets, household credit expanded rapidly as well, leading to sharp increases in leverage and vulnerabilities. The decline in real estate prices adversely affected the quality of loan portfolios and put financial intermediaries at risk, especially in markets in which values had grown rapidly. This rapid growth of household debt had major implications for the transmission of the crisis from the financial to the real sector and complicated the resolution mechanisms and policy responses.

Old and New Elements Combined in Causing the Crisis

The various new elements combined with those factors observed in more "traditional" boom and bust cycles resulted in an unprecedented financial crisis. In the United States, a vicious cycle of rising foreclosures, falling home values, and disappearing securitization markets quickly developed. Vulnerable cohorts of borrowers became increasingly susceptible to rising interest rates and falling home values, and could no longer refinance their mortgages, leading to higher monthly payments and rising delinquency and default rates.

A wave of failures in financial companies—suddenly no longer able to securitize subprime mortgages—led to a virtual breakdown in mortgage origination and more abrupt adjustments in prices. Adverse feedback loops—of rising foreclosures placing additional downward pressures on house prices—started. With U.S. house prices declining on a national basis for the first time since the Great Depression, many heavily indebted borrowers confronted with substantial negative home equity faced incentives to "walk away" from their mortgages.

Tighter standards for new mortgages and consumer credit led to a sharp compression in consumer spending that compounded already difficult situations in the real sector. With households' savings and net assets already at historical lows, financial constraints imposed by financial institutions under stress directly translated into reduced consumer spending, leading to initially localized but gradually spreading cycles of declines in corporate sector profitability, increases in layoffs and unemployment, and slowing economies—resulting in more foreclosures (Furceri and Morurougane, 2009).

Although initial recapitalizations were relatively large and rapid (including through the participation of sovereign wealth funds), they were limited to only a few banks and increasingly fell short of losses. As financial institutions incurred large losses and wrote down illiquid securities, solvency concerns across markets fueled a process of rapid deleveraging and forced asset sales. Mark-to-market rules forced further deleveraging and fire sales. Hedge funds—facing financing constraints and redemption pressures—further fueled this rapid unwinding process. This flurry of deleveraging led to further asset price declines, prompting distressed asset sales and rising recapitalization needs, resulting in further loss of confidence, causing a near meltdown in October 2008.

During fall 2008, increased balance sheet opaqueness and reliance on wholesale funding increased systemic fragility (Gorton and Metrick, 2009). Once U.S. house prices began to decline and defaults began to rise (affecting the expected value of the assets underlying mortgage-backed securities and collateralized debt obligations), the complexity of instruments undermined price discovery and led to market illiquidity and a freeze in securitization activity. The increased opaqueness of balance sheets (including that caused by the widespread recourse to off-balance-sheet instruments) made it difficult to distinguish healthy from unhealthy institutions. The resulting adverse selection problems contributed to the freezing of interbank markets and forced further sales of securities to raise funds. The increased centrality and systemic importance in many countries of highly leveraged, underregulated intermediaries relying on wholesale and short-term funding exacerbated problems.

Housing market vulnerabilities also came home to roost in several countries, notably in Europe. In the United Kingdom, mortgage lenders came under intense pressure, beginning in the fall of 2007 with a bank run on Northern Rock, which had been heavily reliant on interbank markets rather than deposits for funding. Large pressures also hit Hungary, Iceland, and the Baltic countries, where imbalances were more pronounced. The increased connections and simultaneous buildup of systemic risks across multiple countries made the management of shocks more complex, especially in light of institutional deficiencies in many countries—including the inability to quickly resolve large, cross-border financial institutions—and led to the rapid global spreading of turmoil.

Mortgage-backed securities and other U.S.-originated instruments were widely held by institutions in other advanced economies and the official sector in several emerging markets. Through these direct exposures and associated funding problems, spillovers quickly surfaced among European banks, including in

Germany (IKB, July 2007) and France (BNP Paribas' money market fund, August 2007). Because troubled intermediaries hit by losses and scrambling for liquidity were forced to sell other assets and cut lending, the crisis gradually spread to other markets and institutions through common lender effects.

Emerging markets—especially those that had relied heavily on external financing, and paradoxically those with more liquid markets—were affected through capital account and bank funding pressures. Amid global deleveraging, heightened investor risk aversion, and repatriation of funds, many emerging market economies suddenly found foreign funding sources increasingly scarce and were confronted with sudden stops or reversals of capital flows. In addition, emerging market corporations faced much higher borrowing costs, limited opportunity to issue equity, and few alternative sources of financing. Although official financing filled some of the gaps, a number of emerging markets had to make rapid adjustments, leading to real economic dislocations.

With the crisis still ongoing in many parts of the world, it is premature to opine on its implications for the broader debate on the costs and benefits of international financial integration. Nevertheless, there are two preliminary observations that are pertinent. First, the differential effects of the crisis across countries confirm that it is not just financial openness, but a country's structural features and its precrisis policy choices that determined the overall impact of the crisis on a country. Second, outflows of capital triggered by the crisis did not lead to a resurgence of capital controls in emerging market economies.

RECESSIONS AND FINANCIAL MARKET TURMOIL: HOW COSTLY?

The global financial crisis resulted in recessions in almost all advanced economies. As discussed in the previous sections, most of these recessions were accompanied by credit crunches or house price busts. This raises two specific questions about recessions associated with disruptions in credit and housing markets: How do recessions associated with credit crunches or house price busts differ from other recessions? And are recessions that coincide with financial crises more costly and longer than other recessions?

Building on earlier research (Claessens, Kose, and Terrones, 2009; 2010), this section analyzes the features of recession episodes that coincide with disruptions in credit or housing markets. To complement and expand on other studies focusing on the parallels between the 2007–09 financial crisis and past crises (Reinhart and Rogoff, 2008; 2009), it also examines the implications of recessions associated with financial crisis episodes.[7]

---

[7] Reinhart and Rogoff (2008) focus on the so-called Big Five financial crisis episodes, which include Finland (1990–93), Japan (1993), Norway (1988), Spain (1978–79), and Sweden (1990–93). These crises took a long time to resolve and all led to substantial fiscal costs.

This section first briefly describes the database and methodology. Next, it discusses the characteristics of recessions associated with credit crunches or house price busts compared with other types of recessions. Finally, an analysis is made of recession episodes coinciding with financial crises, and the implications of such episodes are compared with those from recessions without a crisis.

Database and Methodology

A comprehensive database of key macroeconomic and financial variables for 21 OECD countries over the period 1960–2007 is used. The data are quarterly series mostly from the OECD Analytical Database and the IMF International Financial Statistics Database. The advantages of using OECD countries are the frequency and good quality of the data. Analyzing a large sample of emerging markets and developing countries would mean using annual data, a frequency at which detecting business cycles is much more challenging.[8] The quarterly time series of macroeconomic variables are seasonally adjusted whenever necessary and are in constant prices. The financial variables considered are credit, house prices, and equity prices. All financial variables are converted into real terms by deflating them by the respective country's consumer price index.

Before analyzing recessions and their interactions with financial crises, it is necessary to determine the dates of these events. The methodology focuses on changes in the levels of variables to identify cycles. This is consistent with the guiding principles of the National Bureau of Economic Research (NBER), which is the unofficial arbiter of U.S. business cycles. This methodology assumes that a recession begins just after the economy reaches a peak and ends as the economy reaches a trough. The methodology determines the peaks and troughs of any given series by first searching for maximums and minimums during a given period. It then selects pairs of adjacent, locally absolute maximums and minimums that meet censoring rules requiring a certain minimum duration of cycles and phases.

In particular, the analysis uses the algorithm introduced by Harding and Pagan (2002), which extends the so-called BB algorithm developed by Bry and Boschan (1971), to identify the cyclical turning points in the log-level of a series. A complete cycle goes from one peak to the next peak with its two phases, the contraction (recession) phase (from peak to trough) and the expansion phase (from trough to peak). The algorithm requires the minimum duration of the complete cycle to be at least five quarters and each phase to be at least two quarters. This methodology closely replicates the dates of U.S. business cycles as determined by the NBER.

---

[8] Hong, Lee, and Tang (2009) examine the impact of shocks in 21 industrial, mostly OECD, countries on 21 developing Asian economies using annual data. They show that developing Asian (OECD) countries on average are in recession about 13.0 (8.5) percent of the time, and each recession lasted about 1.6 (1.3) years, with a cumulative loss of about 12.0 (2.6) percent.

With this methodology, cycles in output (GDP) are identified to provide a broad measure of economic activity for the 21 OECD countries. The exercise identifies 122 recessions, implying that a typical OECD country experienced about six recessions during 1960–2007. A recession on average lasts about four quarters (one year) with substantial variation across episodes—the shortest recession is 2 quarters and the longest 13 quarters. The typical decline in output from peak to trough, the recession's amplitude, tends to be about 2 percent. A measure of cumulative loss is also computed, combining information about both duration and amplitude to proxy the overall cost of a recession. The cumulative loss of a recession is typically about 3 percent of GDP, but this number varies quite a bit across episodes.

Using the same methodology, the periods of decline in real credit and house prices are determined. The main focus is on those disruptions in credit or housing markets characterized by a peak-to-trough decline that falls into the top quartile of all credit or house price declines. These episodes are called credit crunches and house price busts, respectively. This method identifies 113 contractions and 28 crunches in credit, and 114 declines and 28 busts in house prices.

The episodes of credit crunches and house price busts tend to be long and deep. While a credit contraction episode typically lasts about six quarters, a credit crunch lasts a year longer. Credit contractions typically mean a 4 percent decrease in credit from peak to trough, but for crunches, the decrease is more than three times larger. House price busts tend to last even longer than credit crunches do. The typical episode of a decline in house prices is about nine quarters, whereas a house price bust usually persists twice as long. A typical house price decline is only 6 percent, but house prices tend to fall by five times as much during a house price bust.

Next, a simple episode-dating rule is used to determine whether a specific recession is associated with a credit crunch or house price bust period. If a recession episode starts at the same time as or after the beginning of an ongoing credit crunch or house price bust, the recession is considered to be associated with the credit crunch or house price bust. This rule, by definition, basically describes a timing association (a coincidence) between the two events but does not imply a causal link. With this rule, 48 recession episodes are identified to be associated with at least a credit crunch or house price bust. Out of these 48 episodes, 33 episodes are associated with house price busts and 21 with credit crunches.

Because the features of recessions associated with financial crises are also of interest, the relevant crisis episodes in the sample of advanced economies need to be identified. Following the same logic used above, Terrones, Scott, and Kannan (2009) identify whether a specific recession is associated with a financial crisis. They define financial crises as episodes during which there is widespread disruption to financial institutions and the functioning of financial markets. If a recession episode starts at the same time or after the beginning of an ongoing financial crisis, they classify that recession as being associated with the respective crisis.

They report that using this rule, 15 recession episodes are associated with financial crises for the sample of countries used in this analysis.[9]

Recessions Associated with Disruptions in Credit or Housing Markets

Recessions associated with disruptions in credit or housing markets are simply different from other recessions without such disruptions. The analysis of these differences first focuses on the main characteristics of recessions: their duration and amplitude (Harding and Pagan, 2002). The duration of a recession, D, is the number of quarters, k, between a peak and the next trough. The amplitude of a recession, A, measures the change in output from a peak (y_0) to the next trough (y_k)—that is, $A = y_k - y_0$.

Another widely used measure, the cumulative loss, is also used to analyze the adverse impact of recessions on output. This measure combines information about the duration and amplitude of a phase to proxy the overall cost of a recession. To provide a sense of the variation in the recessions, the features of recessions coinciding with severe credit crunches or house price busts are also examined. These severe crunch or bust episodes consist of the top 12.5 percent of all credit contractions or house price declines (or the top half of all credit crunches or house price busts). Six recessions are accompanied by both a house price bust and a credit crunch. Some 26 recessions coincide with either a severe credit crunch or a severe house price bust.[10]

There are a number of statistically significant differences between recessions coinciding with credit crunches or house price busts and those not coinciding (Table 7.1). In particular, recessions associated with such episodes are on average more than a quarter longer than those without busts (4.3 versus 3.2 quarters). Moreover, output declines (and corresponding cumulative losses) are typically much larger in recessions with crunches or busts: 2.5 (4.8) percent versus 1.6 (2.3) percent in those without crunches or busts.

These sizable differences also extend to the other macroeconomic variables, including consumption, investment, and the unemployment rate. For example, although consumption typically does not contract much in recessions, there is a statistically significant decline in consumption in recessions associated with credit

---

[9] The recession episodes associated with financial crises are the following: Australia, 1990:Q2–1991:Q2; Denmark, 1987:Q1–1988:Q2; Finland, 1990:Q2–1993:Q2*; France, 1992:Q2–1993:Q3; Germany, 1980:Q2–1980:Q4; Greece, 1992:Q2–1993:Q1; Italy, 1992:Q2–1993:Q3; Japan, 1993:Q2–1993:Q4*; Japan, 1997:Q2–1999:Q1; New Zealand, 1986:Q4–1987:Q4; Norway, 1988:Q2–1988:Q4*; Spain, 1978:Q3–1979:Q1*; Sweden, 1990:Q2–1993:Q1*; United Kingdom, 1973:Q3–1974:Q1; United Kingdom, 1990:Q3–1991:Q3. * Denotes the Big Five financial crises in Reinhart and Rogoff (2008, 2009), who provide a detailed history of these and other crisis episodes.

[10] The sample includes 20 recessions associated with severe house price busts and 11 recessions associated with severe credit crunches.

TABLE 7.1

Recessions Associated with House Price Busts or Credit Crunches *(percent change unless indicated otherwise)*

	Median values			Mean values		
	Without busts and crunches	With busts or crunches	With severe busts or crunches	Without busts and crunches	With busts or crunches	With severe busts or crunches
Output						
Duration[1]	3.00	3.00**	3.00**	3.20	4.31***	4.50**
Amplitude	-1.56	-2.54***	-2.64**	-1.98	-3.64***	-4.13**
Cumulative loss	-2.30	-4.8**	-5.23**	-3.67	-10.60***	-14.17***
Components of output						
Consumption	0.27	-0.64**	-0.88	0.41	-1.05***	-1.16***
Total investment	-3.45	-6.07**	-6.07	-4.33	-8.40**	-8.46*
Residential investment	-1.96	-6.85**	-7.52*	-4.13	-10.63***	-12.50***
Nonresidential investment	-2.85	-4.31	-4.44	-3.95	-6.87	-6.51
Exports	-0.77	0.50	0.67	-0.85	-0.57	0.25
Imports	-2.87	-5.27	-5.30	-2.98	-6.08*	-6.49*
Net exports (% of GDP)[2]	0.39	1.20***	1.29**	0.24	1.57***	1.58**
Current account (% of GDP)[2]	0.17	0.92**	0.63*	0.17	1.15**	1.20*
Other macroeconomic variables						
Industrial production	-3.97	-4.79	-5.31	-3.80	-4.29	-4.78
Unemployment rate[2]	0.47	1.18**	1.16	0.80	1.74***	1.77***
Inflation rate[2]	-0.10	-0.63	-0.33	-0.16	-0.44	-0.12
Financial variables						
House prices	-0.24	-5.96***	-6.30***	-0.02	-8.44***	-10.13***
Equity prices	-8.85	-0.58*	-2.63	-6.79	-0.48*	-0.40
Credit	2.24	-1.64***	-2.06***	3.44	-2.50***	-3.17***

Source: Authors' estimates.

Note: A severe house price bust or credit crunch is a bust or crunch in the top half of all busts or crunches. In each cell, the mean (median) change in the respective variable from peak to trough of recessions associated with house price busts or credit crunches is reported, unless indicated otherwise. The symbols *, **, and *** indicate that the difference between means (medians) of recessions with house price busts or credit crunches and recessions without house price busts or credit crunches is significant at the 10 percent, 5 percent, and 1 percent levels, respectively.

[1] Number of quarters.

[2] Change in the levels.

crunches or house price busts, and for severe crunches and busts a 1 percentage point greater decline. The large decline likely reflects the substantial adverse effects of the lack of credit and erosion of housing wealth on consumption during these episodes. These findings indicate that recessions with credit crunches or house price busts result in more costly macroeconomic outcomes than do those without such disruptions. This is consistent with a large body of literature suggesting that credit and housing market developments play an important role in driving business cycles (Leamer, 2007; Mendoza and Terrones, 2008).

Trade variables also exhibit substantial differences between the recessions coinciding with crunches or busts and other types of recessions. In part reflecting the substantial decline in domestic demand, imports fall more in recessions with credit crunches or with house price busts. Along with an increase in exports, both net exports and the current account balance improve significantly more in recessions with such financial shocks.

With respect to financial outcomes, credit, house, and equity prices fall much more in recessions with credit crunches or house price busts. In particular, although credit continues to grow, albeit at a slower rate, during recessions without severe credit market problems, it contracts by about 1.6 percent during recessions coinciding with crunches or busts. House prices tend to register a decline of roughly 6 percent during these episodes. Equity prices also drop during these types of recessions.

The lag between the start of a credit crunch and the beginning of the corresponding recession is also examined. If a recession is associated with a credit crunch, it typically starts three quarters after the onset of the crunch. Because credit crunches last longer than recessions do, the latter tend to end two quarters before their corresponding credit crunch episodes. These findings suggest that the phenomenon of creditless recoveries is not specific to sudden stop episodes observed in emerging markets (Calvo, Izquierdo, and Talvi, 2006) but is also a feature of business cycles in advanced economies.

Similar to those recessions associated with credit crunches, recessions associated with house price busts tend to begin three quarters after the start of their respective house price busts. However, they end nine quarters ahead of the corresponding house price busts because house price busts typically last three times longer than recessions do. Moreover, when a recession is associated with a house price bust, residential investment stays depressed for a prolonged period and typically recovers only three to five quarters after the end of that recession.

These observations imply that recessions can end, and recoveries start, without a revival in credit growth and improvement in asset prices. This raises a natural question: What drives recoveries after recessions associated with credit crunches and house price busts? There could be several explanations. First, not all forms of demand depend on the availability of credit. In particular, consumption is typically the most important contributor to output growth during recoveries. Investment (especially nonresidential) recovers only with a lag, with the contribution of fixed investment growth to recovery often relatively small. Because consumption can be less credit intensive, a recovery could start without the stress in financial markets having been overcome. Second, firms and households may be able to get external financing from sources other than commercial banks. These sources are not captured in the aggregate credit series focused on by this analysis. Third, there can be a switch from more to less credit-intensive sectors in such a way that overall credit does not expand, yet, because of productivity gains, output increases. The aggregate data used in this analysis hide such reallocations of credit across sectors, including between corporations and households that vary in their credit intensity.

Recessions Associated with Financial Crises

The analysis now turns to the characteristics of recessions associated with financial crises. Some of these episodes also coincide with house price busts or credit crunches. Table 7.2 presents the findings, and compares the changes in the main macroeconomic and financial variables during recessions associated with crisis episodes and other recessions. Following Reinhart and Rogoff (2008), the implications of the Big Five financial crises are studied separately. The statistics associated with those recessions are reported under the column "with severe crises."

TABLE 7.2

Recessions Associated with Financial Crises *(percent change unless indicated otherwise)*

	Median values			Mean values		
	Without crises	With crises	With severe crises	Without crises	With crises	With severe crises
Output						
Duration[1]	3.00	5.00***	3.00*	3.36	5.67**	6.80
Amplitude	−1.80	−2.52	−2.76	−2.54	−3.28	−4.64
Cumulative loss	−2.64	−4.9***	−4.90	−5.24	−14.68	−27.20
Components of output						
Consumption	0.14	−2.03***	−3.09	0.14	−2.33**	−3.61
Total investment	−3.82	−10.44*	−11.09	−5.12	−11.56	−18.65
Residential investment	−3.67	−10.98***	−12.27	−5.69	−13.24*	−17.27
Nonresidential investment	−3.52	−9.78	−17.44	−4.34	−10.27	−19.78
Exports	−0.80	2.74**	3.68	−1.34	3.50**	4.09
Imports	−3.75	−6.50	−3.52	−4.25	−3.84	−4.06
Net exports (% of GDP)[2]	0.56	1.14	0.18	0.70	1.17	1.32
Current account (% of GDP)[2]	0.46	0.79	0.41	0.53	0.72	0.32
Other macroeconomic variables						
Industrial production	−3.92	−5.66	−2.79	−3.92	−4.47	−3.07
Unemployment rate[2]	0.56	1.38**	4.66**	0.94	2.54	5.83
Inflation rate[2]	−0.20	−1.06***	−4.13**	−0.04	−1.97**	−3.15*
Financial variables						
House prices	−1.84	−4.97**	−6.21**	−2.68	−8.68	−16.60
Equity prices	−5.28	−9.78	−17.16	−3.81	−8.74	−8.26
Credit	0.78	−0.16	−2.29**	1.03	1.31	−5.76

Source: Authors' calculations.

Note: A severe crisis refers to one of the Big Five crises. In each cell, the mean (median) change in the respective variable from peak to trough of recessions associated with financial crises is reported, unless indicated otherwise. The symbols *, **, and *** indicate that the difference between means (medians) of recessions with financial crises and reessions without financial crises is significant at the 10 percent, 5 percent, and 1 percent levels, respectively.

[1] Number of quarters.
[2] Change in level.

The average duration of a recession associated with a (severe) financial crisis exceeds that without a crisis by two (three) quarters. There is typically a larger output decline in recessions associated with crises compared with other recessions, –2.5 percent versus –1.8 percent, or a 0.7 percentage point difference (although not statistically significant). For recessions with severe crises, the difference in output decline is even larger, 0.9 percentage point, but is also statistically insignificant.

The cumulative output loss of recessions associated with a (severe) crisis is typically significantly larger than those without. In particular, the median cumulative loss of a recession associated with a crisis is roughly two times that of a recession without a crisis. Recessions with a crisis are generally associated with greater contractions in consumption, investment, industrial production, employment, exports, and imports, compared with those recessions without a crisis. These differences are significant for most variables. Recessions associated with financial crises often coincide with a rapid acceleration of the rate of unemployment. In particular, the increase in unemployment during recessions associated with severe financial crises is almost eight times larger than those recessions without crises. This suggests that the welfare costs of recessions with financial crises are much larger.

Credit, almost by construction, registers much larger (and statistically significant) declines in recessions with severe financial crises than those without. House prices also fall statistically significantly more in recessions with crises than those without. This might stem from the high sensitivity of housing activity to credit conditions. Equity prices also decrease much more in recessions with crises.

Dynamics of Recessions Associated with Financial Crises

Next, this chapter examines how the various macroeconomic and financial variables behave around recessions associated with crises compared with recessions that do not coincide with crises episodes (Figure 7.4). It focuses on patterns in the year-over-year growth in each variable over a six-year window—12 quarters before and 12 quarters after a peak. All panels include the median growth rate, that is, the typical behavior of events under consideration. As noted earlier, the sample includes 15 recessions associated with financial crises and 107 other recession episodes.

The pattern of output growth around these recessions is as expected. Output registers a larger decline and takes a longer time to recover during recessions associated with financial crises than for other recessions. Consumption, investment, and industrial production also follow similar patterns. It is interesting that in recessions without crises, the growth rate of consumption slows down but does not fall below zero. In contrast, consumption contracts during recessions associated with financial crises. In recessions without a crisis, investment tends to take five to six quarters to expand again on an annual basis, but it often takes up to 10 quarters to do so during a recession accompanied by a crisis. Industrial production also exhibits a protracted period of contraction during recessions with crises.

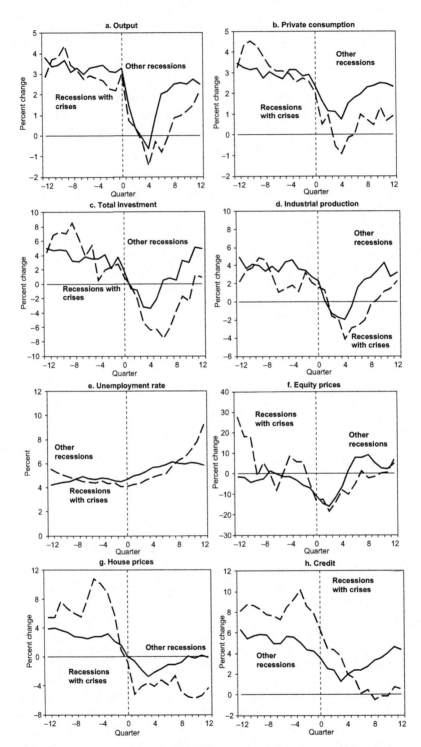

Figure 7.4 Recessions and Financial Crises *(percent change from a year earlier)*

Source: Authors' calculations.

Note: The solid line denotes recessions not associated with financial crises, while the dotted line represents those recessions associated with financial crises. Zero on the x-axes is the quarter after which a recession begins (peak in the level of output).

The rate of unemployment continues to rise up to three years after the recession starts when it is combined with a financial crisis.

With regard to financial variables, the growth rate of credit slows down in a typical recession whereas credit contracts somewhat during recessions associated with crises. House prices also decline more sharply during recessions with crises. Ahead of recessions associated with crises, both credit and house prices tend to grow at much higher rates than they do before other recessions, confirming the boom-bust cycles in these variables discussed in the previous section. Equity prices take a longer time to recover during recessions accompanied by crises.

AN ANATOMY OF RECESSIONS AFTER THE FINANCIAL CRISIS

As noted previously, the majority of advanced economies in the sample entered into recession in late 2007 or early 2008. How similar to or different from earlier recessions are these recessions associated with the 2007–09 crisis? This section addresses this question using the data up to mid-2009, paying particular attention to the recession dynamics in the United States, the epicenter of the crisis.

As in the earlier section, this section studies the behavior of key macroeconomic and financial variables. It focuses on patterns in the year-over-year growth in each variable over a six-year window—12 quarters before and 12 quarters after a peak (Figure 7.5).[11] All panels include the median year-over-year growth rate of these variables for all 122 recessions in 21 OECD countries in the sample, along with their upper and lower quartile bands. These bands allow the likelihood of various outcomes to be gauged, with the lower band representing worse than typical outcomes. Overlaid on each chart is information for the United States as of end 2009.

The U.S. recession was clearly an outlier in many respects. First, confirming its severity, output registered a rate of growth below the median of the lower quartile of previous recession episodes five quarters after the beginning of the recession. Second, private sector demand also exhibited lower than typical growth. In particular, private consumption growth in the United States fell below the lower quartile band as households tried to cope with the sharp losses in their wealth and rebuilt their balance sheets. Investment growth declined more sharply than typical, reflecting the collapse in residential investment. The collapse in U.S. residential investment growth was exceptional, reflecting the bust in house prices and disruptions in credit markets.

Third, industrial production registered a much sharper decline than that of the lower quartile of all recessions. This suggests that the manufacturing cycle was more severe than in the past owing in part to the sharp decline in durables con-

---

[11] At the quarterly frequency, year-over-year changes in the growth rates are used because quarter-over-quarter changes can be quite volatile and provide a noisy presentation of recession dynamics. For the unemployment rate the level rate is used.

sumption. Moreover, unemployment climbed above the upper quartile of earlier episodes. The steep increase in unemployment reflects the sharp downsizing in many sectors of the U.S. economy, particularly in the financial sector.

With respect to asset prices, the U.S. recession was also quite different from previous ones. Although the decline in U.S. house prices was as steep as those observed during the Big Five episodes discussed previously, there was a much sharper decline in the growth rate of house prices than is typical in the OECD recessions. This is related, of course, to the sharp drop in residential investment. Although equity prices had increased until a few quarters before the recession began, a pattern not usually seen in the run-up to a recession, this quickly reversed and equity prices registered sharper than typical declines. Although house and equity prices rebounded in late 2009, they were still well below their precrisis highs.

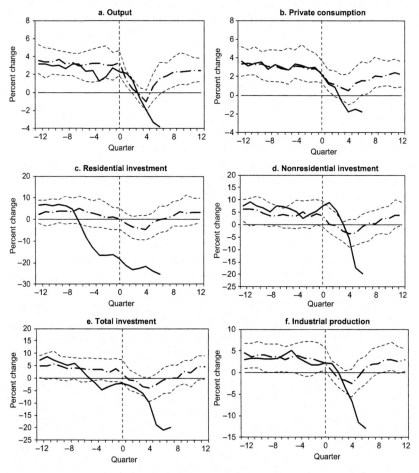

Figure 7.5 Recessions in Organization for Economic Cooperation and Development Countries and Recent United States Recession (percent change from a year earlier)

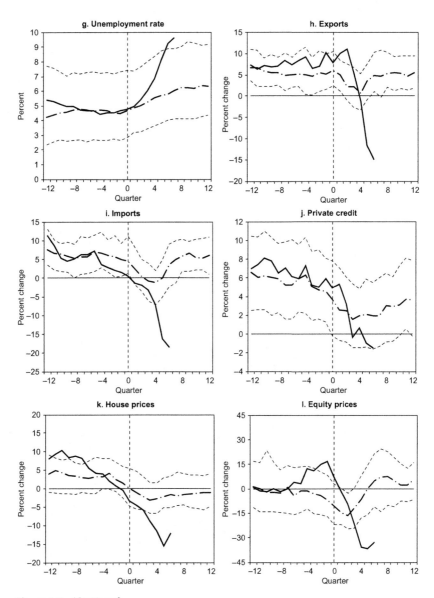

Figure 7.5 (*Continued*)

Source: Authors' calculations.

Note: The solid line denotes the recent U.S. recession with 2007:Q4 as $t = 0$. The thick dotted line denotes the median of all observations while the thin dotted lines correspond to upper and lower quartiles. Zero on the *x*-axis is the quarter after which a recession begins (peak in the level of output). Unemployment rate is the level in percent. The date of the latest observation for the United States is 2009:Q2. (For total investment and unemployment it is 2009:Q3.)

Credit growth also started to slow down before the onset of the recession as the signs of financial stress began to emerge. This is more evidence of the negative feedback between asset prices, credit, and domestic demand, which, as discussed in the previous section, is common in severe recessions associated with financial crises. The growth rates of exports and imports both collapsed as the forces of recession became more intense over 2009. This observation is related to the highly synchronized nature of national recessions.

Another important feature of the 2007–09 recession is its global reach. Kose, Loungani, and Terrones (2010) analyze the implications of three previous global recessions (1975, 1982, and 1991) and compare these with the one in 2007–09. They define a global recession as a contraction in world real per capita GDP accompanied by a broad decline in various other measures of global economic activity. They reported at that time that the 2007–09 global recession easily qualifies as the most severe of the four global recessions: output—depending on the measure—was projected to fall between four and six times as much as it did on average in the three other global recessions, and unemployment was likely to increase twice as much. The collapse in world trade in 2009 dwarfs that in past global recessions. Moreover, no previous global recession has had so many countries in a state of recession simultaneously, both in advanced and developing economies.

CONCLUSION

This chapter provides a brief analysis of the three central questions about the global financial crisis. First, how similar is the most recent crisis to previous episodes? The latest crisis featured some close similarities to earlier ones, including the presence of credit and asset price booms fueled by rapid debt accumulation in a number of advanced economies. Second, how different is the most recent crisis from earlier episodes? As much similarity as the latest crisis had with the earlier episodes, it also featured some significant differences, such as in the explosion of opaque and complex financial instruments and in highly integrated global financial markets. Third, how costly were the recessions that followed the crisis? To answer this question, the chapter first examined whether recessions associated with financial market disruptions or outright financial crises are more damaging than other "normal" recessions. The findings indicate that the recessions in the former group result in much larger declines in economic activity and tend to last much longer. The analysis also considered the depth of the recession in the United States following the 2007–09 financial crisis and examined its severity in light of earlier recession episodes in a large sample of OECD countries. The latest recession is indeed an outlier in a number of respects.

In addition to the issues discussed in this chapter, the global financial crisis and associated recessions have led to an extensive discussion about the ability of macroeconomic and financial sector policies to mitigate the costs stemming from such episodes. The cost of a recession is, of course, affected by a number of factors. First, changes in credit and asset prices can have important implications for the severity of the recession. Second, prevailing economic conditions at the onset of a recession, such as global economic conditions and oil prices, can also be associated with different recession outcomes. Third, countercyclical macroeconomic and financial sector policies might mitigate the cost of a recession.

Although some observers argue that these macroeconomic and financial sector policies can help moderate recessions, others claim that they can worsen recession outcomes. Recent work, however, suggests that discretionary monetary and fiscal policies could help reduce the duration of recessions in the advanced economies (Terrones, Scott, and Kannan, 2009). In particular, evidence indicates that discretionary monetary policy is associated with shorter recessions, although fiscal policy does not have a significant impact on duration. By contrast, expansionary discretionary fiscal policies tend to shorten the duration of recessions associated with financial crises. This finding is consistent with evidence that fiscal policy is particularly effective when agents face tighter liquidity constraints.

The evidence on the effects of policies on the amplitude of a recession is, however, less robust. Claessens, Kose, and Terrones (2009) report that fiscal and monetary policies do not seem to have a significant impact on the depth of recessions. This finding could reflect several potential factors, including the coarse nature of the fiscal and monetary policy proxies they employ; lags on the policy effects, particularly with regard to fiscal policy; and several instances in which procyclical policies were in place to fight inflation. In summary, the evidence on the effectiveness of countercyclical policies during recessions is at best mixed, indicating fertile ground for future research.

The crisis has also provided important lessons about financial sector policies. In particular, it has exposed flaws in the precrisis regulatory framework and has shown the limits of policy measures in dealing with financial meltdowns. Although many elements of existing regulatory frameworks remain valid, the crisis has forced the relevant actors to think about the future architecture of regulatory policies. Although improvements in microprudential regulations are needed to reduce financial market procyclicality, rules calling for well-capitalized and transparent banks adhering to sound accounting standards are still critical. The crisis has made clear, however, that greater coordination between macroeconomic and financial policy is needed. Prudential regulation has to acquire a more macro, systemwide, dimension. The global nature of the financial crisis has also shown that although financially integrated markets have benefits, they also have risks, with large real economic consequences. It has shown that the international financial architecture is still far from institutionally matching the closely integrated financial systems.

The crisis has also had major financial and economic repercussions for emerging markets and developing economies, even though many of them were innocent bystanders. Some of these countries benefited from their improved fundamentals and were better able to tackle the adverse effects of the crisis on their economies. Short-term policy responses, involving more accommodative fiscal and monetary policies and better, restructured frameworks, were more effective than they were in earlier periods. However, the crisis also highlighted some specific financial sector reform challenges for emerging markets and developing economies.

Although there are a number of lessons for macroeconomic policy and regulation of the financial sector, many areas remain for which further policy research would be useful. These include competition policy for a more stable financial system, integration of macroeconomic and financial policy choices, approaches to consumer protection in financial services, and resolution of the political economy pressures regarding financial deregulation, financial openness, and financial crises.

REFERENCES

Árvai, Zsófia, Karl Driessen, and Inci Ötker-Robe, 2009, "Regional Financial Interlinkages and Financial Contagion Within Europe," IMF Working Paper 09/6 (Washington: International Monetary Fund).

Ashcraft, Adam, and Til Schuermann, 2007, "Understanding the Securitization of Subprime Mortgage Credit," Staff Report No. 318 (New York: Federal Reserve Bank of New York).

Blanchard, Olivier, 2009, "The Crisis: Basic Mechanisms, and Appropriate Policies," IMF Working Paper 09/80 (Washington: International Monetary Fund).

Borio, Claudio, 2008, "The Financial Turmoil of 2007–?: A Preliminary Assessment and Some Policy Considerations," BIS Working Paper No. 251 (Basel: Bank for International Settlements).

Brunnermeier, Markus K., 2009, "Deciphering the 2007–08 Liquidity and Credit Crunch," *Journal of Economic Perspectives*, Vol. 23, No. 1, pp. 77–100.

Bry, Gerhard, and Charlotte Boschan, 1971, "Cyclical Analysis of Economic Time Series: Selected Procedures and Computer Programs," NBER Technical Working Paper No. 20 (Cambridge, Massachusetts: National Bureau of Economic Research).

Caballero, Ricardo, 2010, "The 'Other' Imbalance and the Financial Crisis," NBER Working Paper No. 15636 (Cambridge, Massachusetts: National Bureau of Economic Research).

Calomiris, Charles W., 2009, "The Subprime Turmoil: What's Old, What's New, and What's Next," *Journal of Structured Finance*, Vol. 15, No. 1, pp. 6–52.

Calvo, Guillermo A., Alejandro Izquierdo, and Ernesto Talvi, 2006, "Phoenix Miracles in Emerging Markets: Recovering without Credit from Systemic Financial Crises," NBER Working Paper No. 12101 (Cambridge, Massachusetts: National Bureau of Economic Research).

Cardarelli, Roberto, M. Ayhan Kose, and Selim Elekdag, 2010, "Capital Inflows: Macroeconomic Implications and Policy Responses," *Economic Systems*, Vol. 34, No. 4, pp. 333–56.

Cecchetti, Stephen G., 2009, "Crisis and Responses: The Federal Reserve in the Early Stages of the Financial Crisis," *Journal of Economic Perspectives*, Vol. 23, No. 1, pp. 51–75.

Claessens, Stijn, 2009, "Lessons from the Recent Financial Crisis for Reforming National and International Financial Systems," Paper prepared for the Annual Bank Conference on Development Economics, "The Road Ahead to a Sustainable Global Economic System," Seoul, June 22–24.

———, Giovanni Dell'Ariccia, Deniz Igan, and Luc Laeven, 2010, "Cross-Country Experience and Policy Implications from the Global Financial Crisis," *Economic Policy*, Vol. 25, No. 2, pp. 267–93.

Claessens, Stijn, M. Ayhan Kose, and Marco E. Terrones, 2009, "What Happens during Recessions, Crunches and Busts?" *Economic Policy*, Vol. 60, pp. 653–700.

———, 2010, "Recessions and Financial Disruptions in Emerging Markets," *Economía Chilena*, Vol. 13, No. 2, pp. 55–84.

Dell'Ariccia, Giovanni, Adolfo Barajas, and Andrei Levchenko, 2008, "Credit Booms: The Good, the Bad, and the Ugly" (unpublished; Washington: International Monetary Fund).

Dell'Ariccia, Giovanni, Deniz Igan, and Luc Laeven, 2008, "Credit Booms and Lending Standards: Evidence from the U.S. Subprime Mortgage Market," IMF Working Paper 08/106 (Washington: International Monetary Fund).

Demirgüç-Kunt, Asli, and Enrica Detragiache, 1998, "Financial Liberalization and Financial Fragility," IMF Working Paper 98/93 (Washington: International Monetary Fund).

Furceri, Davide, and Annabelle Mourougane, 2009, "Financial Crises: Past Lessons and Policy Implications" (Paris: Organization for Economic Cooperation and Development).

Goldberg, Linda S., 2009, "Understanding Banking Sector Globalization," *IMF Staff Papers*, Vol. 56, No. 1, pp. 171–97.

Gorton, Gary, 2009, "Slapped in the Face by the Invisible Hand: Banking and the Panic of 2007," Paper prepared for the Federal Reserve Bank of Atlanta's 2009 Financial Markets Conference "Financial Innovation and Crisis," May 11–13.

———, and Andrew Metrick, 2009, "Haircuts," NBER Working Paper No. 15273 (Cambridge, Massachusetts: National Bureau of Economic Research).

Harding, Don, and Adrian Pagan, 2002, "Dissecting the Cycle: A Methodological Investigation," *Journal of Monetary Economics*, Vol. 49, pp. 365–81.

Helbling, Thomas, and Marco Terrones, 2003, "Real and Financial Effects of Bursting Asset Price Bubbles," *World Economic Outlook*, April (Washington: International Monetary Fund).

Hong, Kiseok, John-Wha Lee, and Hsia Chink Tang, 2009, "Crises in Asia: Historical Perspectives and Implications," *Journal of Asian Economics*, Vol. 21, No. 3, pp. 265–79.

Kose, M. Ayhan, Prakash Loungani, and Marco Terrones, 2010, "Global Recessions and Recoveries" (unpublished; Washington: International Monetary Fund).

Kose, M. Ayhan, Eswar Prasad, Kenneth Rogoff, and Shang-Jin Wei, 2009, "Financial Globalization: A Reappraisal," *IMF Staff Papers*, Vol. 56, No. 1, pp. 8–62.

———, 2010, "Financial Globalization and Economic Policies," in *Handbook of Development Economics,* Vol. 5, ed. by Dani Rodrik and Mark Rosenzweig (Amsterdam: Elsevier), pp. 4283–362.

Krugman, Paul, 2009, "Revenge of the Glut," *New York Times*, March 1.

Leamer, Edward E., 2007, "Housing IS the Business Cycle," NBER Working Paper No. 13428 (Cambridge, Massachusetts: National Bureau of Economic Research).

Mayer, Christopher, Karen Pence, and Shane M. Sherlund, 2009, "The Rise in Mortgage Defaults," *Journal of Economic Perspectives*, Vol. 23, No. 1, pp. 27–50.

Mendoza, E., and M.E. Terrones, 2008, "An Anatomy of Credit Booms: Evidence from Macro Aggregates and Micro Data," NBER Working Paper No. 14049 (Cambridge, Massachusetts: National Bureau of Economic Research).

Mishkin, Frederic S., 2009, "Is Monetary Policy Effective during Financial Crises?" NBER Working Paper No. 14678 (Cambridge, Massachusetts: National Bureau of Economic Research).

Obstfeld, Maurice, 2009, "International Finance and Growth in Developing Countries: What Have We Learned?" *IMF Staff Papers*, Vol. 56, pp. 63–111.

Reinhart, Carmen M., and Kenneth S. Rogoff, 2008, "Is the 2007 U.S. Subprime Crisis So Different? An International Historical Comparison," *American Economic Review*, Vol. 98, No. 2, pp. 339–44.

———, 2009, *This Time Is Different: Eight Centuries of Financial Folly* (Princeton, New Jersey: Princeton University Press).

Shin, Hyun Song, 2009, "Reflections on Northern Rock: The Bank Run that Heralded the Global Financial Crisis," *Journal of Economic Perspectives*, Vol. 23, No. 1, pp. 101–19.

Taylor, John B., 2009, "The Financial Crisis and the Policy Responses: An Empirical Analysis of What Went Wrong," NBER Working Paper No. 14631 (Cambridge, Massachusetts: National Bureau of Economic Research).

Terrones, Marco E., Alasdair Scott, and Prakash Kannan, 2009, "From Recession to Recovery: How Soon and How Strong?" *World Economic Outlook*, April (Washington: International Monetary Fund).

CHAPTER 8

From Recession to Recovery: How Soon and How Strong?

Prakash Kannan, Alasdair Scott, and Marco E. Terrones

This chapter was initially published in the April 2009 IMF *World Economic Outlook* when the world economy was experiencing one of the most severe recessions in modern times. The main text of the chapter is reproduced virtually unaltered as a test of its originality and the durability of its main findings.

At the time it was written, many felt that the recovery from the recession associated with the 2007–09 global financial crisis would be quick and robust. To test this belief, previous experiences of recessions and recoveries in advanced economies were examined. Crucially, the chapter made two distinctions. The first was to divide recessions into those following financial crises from those arising from other shocks (e.g., energy prices or monetary policy). The second was to look at globally synchronized recessions. The findings were stark: First, recessions associated with financial crises are typically severe and protracted and their recoveries slow and weak. Second, globally synchronized recessions are often long and deep, and recoveries from these recessions are generally weak and protracted. The implications of these findings for the global economy were that the ongoing recession was likely to be unusually long and severe and that the recovery would be weak and sluggish.

For policies, the message was that early intervention could make a material difference to the duration and severity of the recession and to the strength of the recovery. But that came with caveats: the bang per buck of monetary policy was found to be lower in the aftermath of a financial crisis, and fiscal policy was likely to be less effective when public debt was high.

In retrospect, the chapter was, if anything, not pessimistic enough. Even on the basis of the evidence presented, it would have seemed incredible that a crisis that began in 2007 would linger for at least five years. There are developments that at the time this chapter was written could not have been anticipated. The zero nominal bound on interest rates would prove more quickly binding than

The authors are grateful to Olivier Blanchard, Charles Collyns, Jorg Decressin, Francis Diebold, Don Harding, and David Romer for their comments and suggestions. Gavin Asdorian and Emory Oakes provided outstanding research assistance.

anticipated, and the deterioration of public finances in several advanced economies as a result of the downturn was substantial. The financial crisis and ensuing recession exposed fundamental weaknesses in the design of the euro area, which experienced its own distinct crisis.

Nonetheless, the chapter's main findings, made early in 2009, hold up well at the end of 2012.

INTRODUCTION

The global economy experienced its deepest downturn in the post-World War II period as the 2007–09 financial crisis rapidly spread around the world. A large number of advanced economies fell into recession, and economies in the rest of the world slowed abruptly. Global trade and financial flows shrank, while output and employment losses mounted. Credit markets remained frozen as borrowers engaged in a drawn-out deleveraging process and banks struggled to improve their financial health.

Many aspects of the current crisis were new and unanticipated.[1] Uniquely, the disruption combined a financial crisis at the heart of the world's largest economy with a global downturn. But financial crises—episodes during which there is widespread disruption to financial institutions and the functioning of financial markets—are not new.[2] Nor are globally synchronized downturns. Therefore, history can be a useful guide to understanding the present.

To put the recession caused by the 2007–09 global crisis in historical perspective, some broad questions about the nature of recessions and recoveries and the role of countercyclical policies are addressed in this chapter. In particular,

- Are recessions and recoveries associated with financial crises different from other types of recessions and recoveries?
- Are globally synchronized recessions different?
- What role do policies play in determining the shape of recessions and recoveries?

To shed light on these questions, this chapter examines the dynamics of business cycles that occurred during the past half century. It complements existing literature on the business cycle along several dimensions.[3] These dimensions include a comprehensive study of recessions and recoveries in 21 advanced economies,[4] a classification of recessions based on their underlying sources, and

---

[1] For detailed accounts of the financial aspects of this crisis, see IMF (2008), Greenlaw and others (2008), and Brunnermeier (2009).

[2] A classic analysis of financial crises is Kindleberger (1978). Reinhart and Rogoff (2008a) show that financial crises have occurred with "equal opportunity" in advanced and less advanced economies.

[3] In particular, this work builds on IMF (2002, 2008b) and Claessens, Kose, and Terrones (2008).

[4] The sample includes the following countries: Australia, Austria, Belgium, Canada, Denmark, Finland, France, Germany, Greece, Ireland, Italy, Japan, the Netherlands, New Zealand, Norway, Portugal, Spain, Sweden, Switzerland, the United Kingdom, and the United States.

an assessment of the impact of fiscal and monetary policies in recessions and recoveries. Similar to most other studies in this area, this chapter makes extensive use of event analysis and statistical associations.

The main findings related to common elements across business cycles are as follows:

- Recessions in the advanced economies since 1990 have become less frequent and milder, whereas expansions have become longer, reflecting in part the "Great Moderation" of advanced economies' business cycles.

- Recessions associated with financial crises have been more severe and longer lasting than recessions associated with other shocks. Recoveries from such recessions have typically been slower, associated with weak domestic demand and tight credit conditions.

- Recessions that are highly synchronized across countries have been longer and deeper than those confined to one region. Recoveries from these recessions have typically been weak, with exports playing a much more limited role than in less synchronized recessions.

The implications of these findings for the global financial crisis situation were sobering at the time. The downturn was highly synchronized and was associated with a deep financial crisis, a rare combination in the postwar period. Accordingly, the downturn was likely to be unusually severe, and the recovery was expected to be sluggish. It is not surprising, therefore, that many commentators looking for historical parallels for the 2007–09 crisis episode focused on the Great Depression of the 1930s, by far the deepest and longest recession in the history of most advanced economies.

Regarding policies, these are the main findings:

- Monetary policy seems to have played an important role in ending recessions and strengthening recoveries. Its effectiveness, however, is weakened in the aftermath of a financial crisis.

- Fiscal stimulus appears to be particularly helpful during recessions associated with financial crises. Stimulus is also associated with stronger recoveries; however, the impact of fiscal policy on the strength of the recovery is found to be smaller for economies that have higher levels of public debt.

These results suggested that to mitigate the severity of the recession following the global crisis and to strengthen the recovery, aggressive monetary and particularly fiscal measures were needed to support aggregate demand in the short term, but care needed to be taken to preserve public debt sustainability in the medium term. Even with such measures, a return to steady economic growth would depend on restoring the health of the financial sector. One of the most important lessons from the Great Depression, and from more recent episodes of financial crisis, is that restoring confidence in the financial sector is crucial for recovery to take hold.

The rest of the chapter is structured as follows. The next section presents key stylized facts on recessions and recoveries for the advanced economies during the past 50 years. The second section reviews the major differences across recessions and recoveries resulting from different types of shocks and different degrees of synchronization. Particular attention is paid to the influence of financial crises. The third section analyzes the effects of discretionary monetary and fiscal policies on the severity of recessions and on the strength of recoveries. It also examines how the level of public debt conditions the effectiveness of fiscal policy. The last section places the downturn associated with the 2007–09 crisis in historical perspective and discusses its policy implications.

BUSINESS CYCLES IN THE ADVANCED ECONOMIES

To put the recession caused by the 2007–09 crisis in historical perspective, the features of previous cycles are first identified. Each cycle is divided into two main phases: a recession phase, characterized by a decline in economic activity, and an expansion phase. Following the long-standing tradition of Burns and Mitchell (1946), this chapter employs a "classical" approach to dating turning points in a large sample of advanced economies from 1960 to 2007. It focuses on quarterly changes in real GDP to determine cyclical peaks and troughs (Figure 8.1).[5]

The two main properties of the cycle are considered:

- Duration: the number of quarters from peak to trough in a recession, or from trough to the next peak in an expansion.

- Amplitude: the percentage change in real GDP, from peak to trough in a recession, or from trough to the next peak in an expansion.

The analysis also examines the slope of a recession (or expansion), that is, the ratio of amplitude to duration, which indicates the steepness of each cyclical phase.

Recessions and Expansions: Basic Facts

On average, advanced economies have experienced six complete cycles of recession and expansion since 1960.[6] The number of recessions, however, varies significantly across countries, with some (Canada, Ireland, Japan, Norway, and Sweden) experiencing only three recessions and others (Italy, New Zealand, and Switzerland) experiencing nine or more.

---

[5] The procedure used to date business cycles in this chapter has been referred to as BBQ (Bry-Boschen procedure for quarterly data; see Harding and Pagan, 2002). It identifies local maximums and minimums of a given series, here the logarithm of real GDP, that meet the conditions for a minimum duration of a cycle and of each phase (in this chapter, these are set at five and two quarters, respectively). Alternative dating algorithms, such as those developed by Chauvet and Hamilton (2005) and Leamer (2008), are more difficult to implement for a large sample of countries. The National Bureau of Economic Research (NBER), which dates business cycles in the United States, uses several measures of economic activity to determine peaks and troughs. These measures include—in addition to real GDP—employment, real income, industrial production, and sales. NBER dating is, however, subjective and not replicable internationally.

[6] In the sample period, there were 122 completed and 13 ongoing recessions at the time of the writing of this chapter in 2009.

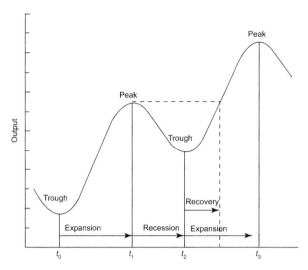

Figure 8.1 Business Cycle Peaks and Troughs
Source: Authors' calculations.

Recessions are distinctly shallower, briefer, and less frequent than expansions. In a typical recession, GDP falls by about 2¾ percent (Table 8.1).[7] In contrast, during an expansion, GDP tends to rise by almost 20 percent. This illustrates mainly the importance of trend growth; the higher the long-term growth rate of an economy, the shallower the recession and the greater the amplitude of expansions. Some recessions, however, are severe, with peak-to-trough declines in output exceeding 10 percent. These episodes are often called depressions (IMF, 2002). Since 1960, there have been six depression episodes in the advanced economies; the latest was observed in Finland in the early 1990s. In contrast, some expansions witness trough-to-peak output increases larger than 50 percent—the "Irish Miracle" during the first decade of the 2000s being a recent example.

A typical recession persists for about a year, whereas an expansion often lasts more than five years. As a result, advanced economies are in a recession phase of the cycle only 10 percent of the time. The longest episodes of recessions and expansions in these countries lasted more than 3 years and 15 years, respectively. Finland and Sweden experienced two of the longest recessions and Ireland and Sweden experienced two of the longest expansions.

Since the mid-1980s, recessions in advanced economies have become less frequent and milder, and expansions have become longer lasting, a development associated with the Great Moderation (Figure 8.2).[8] A host of factors may explain

---

[7] Related findings are reported in the April 2002 *World Economic Outlook*.
[8] This phenomenon has been documented in several papers, including McConnell and Perez-Quiros (2000) and Blanchard and Simon (2001). During this period the average slope of a recession—a proxy for how steep or abruptly output contracts—is about –0.6 percent, which is lower in absolute value than the average –1.0 percent for other recession periods.

TABLE 8.1

Business Cycles in Advanced Economies: Summary Statistics						
	Duration (quarters)			Amplitude (percent change in real GDP)		
	Recession	Recovery[1]	Expansion	Recession	Recovery[2]	Expansion
All						
1. Mean	3.64	3.22	21.75	−2.71	4.05	19.56
2. Standard deviation	2.07	2.72	17.89	2.93	3.12	17.50
3. Coefficient of variation (line 2 ÷ line 1)	0.57	0.84	0.82	1.08	0.77	0.89
4. Number of events	122	109	122	122	112	122
By driver of recession						
Financial crises						
5. Mean	5.67**	5.64**	26.40**	−3.39	2.21***	19.47
6. Standard deviation	3.15	3.32	24.74	3.25	1.18	20.46
7. Coefficient of variation (line 6 ÷ line 5)	0.56	0.59	0.94	0.96	0.53	1.05
8. Number of events	15	11	15	15	13	15
Other[3]						
9. Mean	3.36**	2.95**	21.09**	−2.61	4.29***	19.58
10. Standard deviation	1.71	2.52	16.77	2.89	3.22	17.15
11. Coefficient of variation (line 10 ÷ line 9)	0.51	0.85	0.79	1.11	0.75	0.88
12. Number of events	107	98	107	107	99	107
By extent of synchronization						
Highly synchronized						
13. Mean	4.54***	4.19*	19.97***	−3.45*	3.66**	16.24*
14. Standard deviation	2.50	3.59	15.32	2.96	1.72	11.85
15. Coefficient of variation (line 14 ÷ line 13)	0.55	0.86	0.77	0.86	0.47	0.73
16. Number of events	37	32	37	37	34	37
Other[4]						
17. Mean	3.25***	2.82*	22.52***	−2.39*	4.21**	21.01*
18. Standard deviation	1.73	2.16	18.94	2.88	3.56	19.33
19. Coefficient of variation (line 18 ÷ line 17)	0.53	0.77	0.84	1.21	0.85	0.92
20. Number of events	85	77	85	85	78	85

Memo item:

Recessions associated with financial crises that are highly synchronized

Mean	7.33	6.75	24.33	−4.82	2.82	18.83

Source: Authors' calculations.
Note: The symbols *, **, and *** indicate statistical significance at the 10, 5, and 1 percent levels, respectively. Statistical significance for recessions associated with financial crises (highly synchronized recessions) calculated versus other recessions.
[1]Number of quarters after trough and before real GDP recovers its level achieved in the previous peak.
[2]Percent increase in real GDP one year after the trough.
[3]Recessions not associated with a financial crisis.
[4]Recessions that are not highly synchronized.

this, including global integration, improvements in financial markets, changes in the composition of aggregate output toward the service sector and away from manufacturing, and better macroeconomic policies (Blanchard and Simon, 2001; Romer, 1999). Another possibility is that the Great Moderation was the result of good luck, primarily reflecting the absence of large shocks to the world economy.

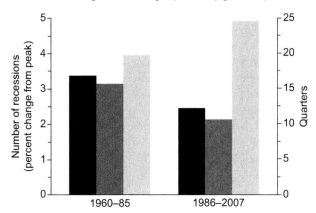

■ Number of recessions in a country (left scale)
■ Output loss during recession (left scale)
▨ Length of following expansion (right scale)

Figure 8.2   Business Cycles Have Moderated over Time
Source: Authors' calculations.

The recovery phase of the cycle has been an object of constant interest in policy circles.[9] An economy typically recovers to its previous peak output in less than a year (see Table 8.1). Perhaps more important, recoveries are typically steeper than recessions—the average growth per quarter during a recovery exceeds the rate of contraction during a recession by more than 25 percent. In fact, there is evidence of a bounce-back effect: output growth during the first year of recovery is significantly and positively related to the severity of the preceding recession. A number of factors can drive an economy to bounce back, including fiscal and monetary policies (this possibility is explored later in the chapter), technological progress, and population growth.[10]

DOES THE CAUSE OF A DOWNTURN AFFECT THE SHAPE OF THE CYCLE?

This section associates recessions and their recoveries with different types of shocks: financial, external, fiscal policy, monetary policy, and oil price shocks.[11]

---

[9] There is no common definition of recovery. Some define it as the time it takes for the economy to return to the peak level before the recession; others measure it by the cumulative growth achieved after a certain period, say a year, following the trough. In this chapter, both definitions are used. These two definitions are complementary and display a sort of duality—the first one determines the time it takes to achieve a given amplitude, and the second one determines the amplitude observed after a given time.

[10] Wynne and Balke (1993) and Sichel (1994) provide evidence of a bounce-back effect in U.S. business cycles. Romer and Romer (1994) report that monetary policy has been instrumental in ending U.S. recessions and helping recoveries during the postwar period.

[11] Term spreads, which have often been used as an indicator of monetary policy stance and as a predictor of short-term output growth—see, for example, Estrella and Mishkin (1996)—were also analyzed and found to give results very similar to those for monetary policy shocks.

The objective of this exercise is to determine whether there have been important differences between the recessions associated with financial crises and those associated with other shocks. In addition, this section examines whether there is a difference between highly synchronized and nonsynchronized recessions.

Different shocks are found to be associated with different patterns of macroeconomic and financial variables during recessions and recoveries. In particular, recessions associated with financial crises have typically been severe and protracted, whereas recoveries from recessions associated with financial crises have typically been slower, held back by weak private demand and credit. In addition, highly synchronized recession episodes are longer and deeper than other recessions, and recoveries from these recessions are typically weak. Moreover, developments in the United States play a pivotal role both in the severity and duration of these highly synchronized recessions.

Categorizing Recessions and Recoveries

The analysis begins categorizing recessions and recoveries by first defining financial crises as episodes during which there is widespread disruption to financial institutions and the functioning of financial markets. Financial crises are identified using the narrative analysis of Reinhart and Rogoff (2008a, 2008b, 2009),[12] which in turn draws on the work of Kaminsky and Reinhart (1999).[13] Next, a recession is said to be associated with a financial crisis if the recession episode starts at the same time as or after the beginning of the financial crisis.[14] Of the 122 recessions in the sample, 15 are associated with financial crises (Table 8.2).[15] The other disturbances are identified using simple statistical rules of thumb (see Appendix 8A).[16] More than half of the 122 recessions in the sample are associated with one or more of these shocks.[17] Oil shocks are the most widespread type,

---

[12] An alternative method of defining financial crises is to use a time series or some combination of series as an indicator, based on some threshold (the method used for the other shocks). An advantage of using a narrative-based method is that it avoids having to define episodes according to characteristics in the very factors one is interested in—for example, a financial crisis could be defined as an episode in which there is a large reduction in credit, but that would preclude assessing the behavior of credit during and following financial crises.

[13] Banking crises, which are defined by Kaminsky and Reinhart (1999, p. 476) as episodes leading to bank runs or large-scale government assistance to financial institutions, are of particular interest.

[14] On these grounds, Reinhart-Rogoff episodes not immediately associated with recessions—for example, the savings and loan crisis of the early 1980s in the United States—are omitted.

[15] In principle, there is a potential endogeneity problem here, because the financial crisis could lead to a recession and vice versa. To address this issue, the dating of crises and cyclical turning points is done using two different methods, as explained in the chapter.

[16] These rules have the advantage of being transparent and of being easily and consistently applied to the GDP series for the 21 countries in the sample. There will always be cases that are not well identified by simple rules. However, a more thorough analysis of the nonfinancial shocks for each country is outside the scope of this chapter.

[17] The scores often coincide, with 105 scores for the 65 recessions that are associated with these shocks, which indicates how misleading it can be to talk about a recession as a result of a single "cause."

TABLE 8.2

Financial Crises and Associated Recessions	
Australia	1990:Q2–1991:Q2
Denmark	1987:Q1–1988:Q2
Finland	1990:Q2–1993:Q2*
France	1992:Q2–1993:Q3
Germany	1980:Q2–1980:Q4
Greece	1992:Q2–1993:Q1
Italy	1992:Q2–1993:Q3
Japan	1993:Q2–1993:Q4*
Japan	1997:Q2–1999:Q1
New Zealand	1986:Q4–1987:Q4
Norway	1988:Q2–1988:Q4*
Spain	1978:Q3–1979:Q1*
Sweden	1990:Q2–1993:Q1*
United Kingdom	1973:Q3–1974:Q1
United Kingdom	1990:Q3–1991:Q3

Source: Authors' calculations.
* The Big Five financial crises (Reinhart and Rogoff, 2008a).

affecting 17 economies in the sample. Monetary and fiscal policy shocks are less common, and external demand shocks are the least common of all, affecting only a handful of the smaller and more open economies (see Table 8A.2 in the appendix to this chapter). Although recessions have become less common overall during the Great Moderation, those associated with financial crises have become more common (Figure 8.3).

Summaries of the stylized facts of these different categories of recessions and recoveries are presented in Table 8.1 and Figure 8.4. With the notable exception of oil shocks, the amplitude of a recession is closely related to its duration.[18] Recessions associated with financial crises are longer and generally more costly than others; those associated with the Big Five financial crises identified by Reinhart and Rogoff (2008a) were particularly costly (Figure 8.4, panel a).[19] Financial crises are also followed by weak recoveries: the time taken to recover to the level of activity reached in the previous peak is as long as the recession itself, whereas cumulative GDP growth in the four quarters after the trough is typically lower than following other types of recessions (Figure 8.4, panel b).[20] Note that the cumulative growth one year after the trough for a financial crisis is up to 2½ percentage points lower than in other cases, after controlling for the severity and duration of the previous recession.

---

[18] Overall, oil shocks typically lead to recessions that are very costly but relatively short lived. This is particularly true of the 1973–74 oil shocks, after which GDP growth bounced back relatively quickly.
[19] The Big Five financial crises episodes include Finland (1990–93), Japan (1993), Norway (1988), Spain (1978–79), and Sweden (1990–93).
[20] Recessions and recoveries are clearly different in their severity depending on the type of shock they are associated with. But, for the same shock, they are also roughly symmetric—the slope of the recession phase is closely matched by the slope of the recovery phase.

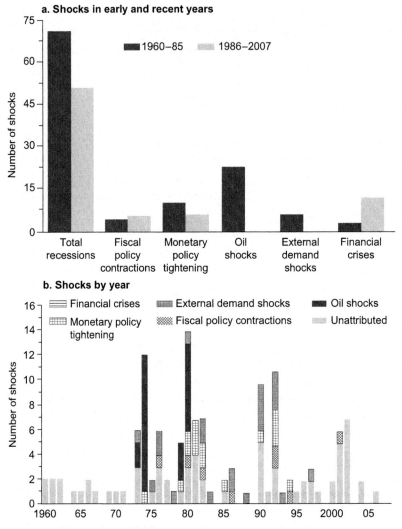

Figure 8.3 Temporal Evolution of Recessions by Type of Shock

Source: Authors' calculations.

Why Are Financial Crises Different?

What are the mechanisms that differentiate recessions and recoveries associated with financial crises? An answer to this question needs to take into account the nature of the expansions that preceded these recessions. Narrative evidence indicates that financial crisis episodes have often been associated with credit booms involving overheated goods and labor markets, house price booms, and frequently, a loss of external competitiveness.[21] This can be seen in Figure 8.5, which shows

---

[21] For a comprehensive analysis of credit booms in the advanced and emerging market economies, see, for instance, Mendoza and Terrones (2008).

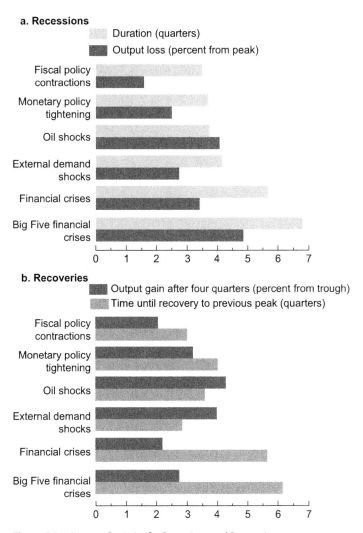

Figure 8.4 Average Statistics for Recessions and Recoveries

Source: Authors' calculations.
Note: The Big Five financial crises are Finland (1990–93), Japan (1993), Norway (1988), Spain (1978–79), and Sweden (1990–93—Reinhart and Rogoff, 2008a).

median values of macroeconomic variables during the eight quarters before the peak in GDP. Credit growth during the expansions preceding financial crises is higher than during other expansions, and this is associated with higher-than-usual consumption as a share of GDP leading up to the peak. Relative to other expansions, labor market participation is high, nominal wage growth is high, and unemployment is low. Price increases—for example, the GDP deflator, house prices, and equity prices—are all noticeably higher than usual. Credit booms have

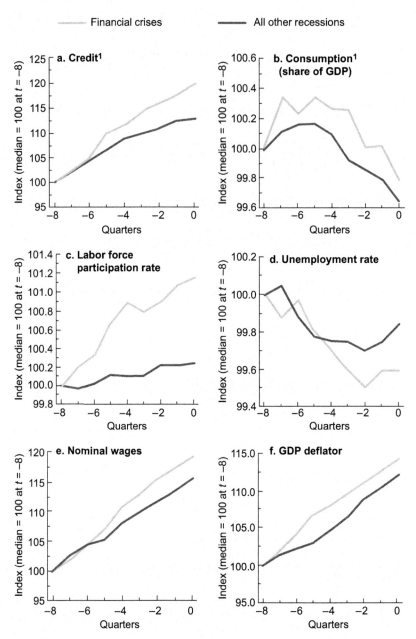

Figure 8.5 Expansions in the Run-Up to Recessions Associated with Financial Crises and Other Shocks

Source: Authors' calculations.
[1]Data in real terms.

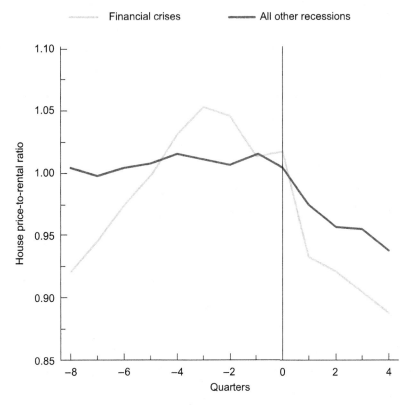

Figure 8.6   House Price-to-Rental Ratios for Recessions Associated with Financial Crises and Other Shocks

Source: Authors' calculations.
Note: Peak in output at $t = 0$.

frequently followed financial deregulation.[22] There is some evidence of asset price bubbles: in the period leading up to financial crisis episodes, the ratio of house prices to housing rental rates rises above that during other recession episodes, starting from levels well below (Figure 8.6).

Rapid credit growth has typically been associated with shifts in household saving rates and a deterioration of the quality of balance sheets.[23] Panel a of Figure 8.7 shows that household saving rates out of disposable income are noticeably lower in expansions before financial crises. However, after a financial crisis strikes, saving rates increase substantially, especially during recessions. In

[22] For example, Table 8A.3 in the appendix shows that almost all of the 15 financial crises considered here followed deregulation in the mortgage market.

[23] Unfortunately, comprehensive balance sheet data are not available for most of the financial crisis episodes. But, as an example, analysis of data for the United Kingdom shows a pronounced deterioration in the ratio of total household liabilities to liquid assets in the years before the recession of 1990–91, with a gradual recovery in the quality of household balance sheets during and after the recession.

the Big Five episodes, the turnaround in household saving rates was larger still. Data for net lending paint a complementary picture (Figure 8.7, panel b). Although these data cover only a few of the financial crisis episodes under consideration here, patterns from some of the most relevant episodes—Denmark (1985–89), Finland (1988–92), Norway (1986-90), and the United Kingdom (1988–92)—show that households' net lending balances increased substantially during recessions.

Taken together, the behavior of these variables suggests that expansions associated with financial crises may be driven by overly optimistic expectations for

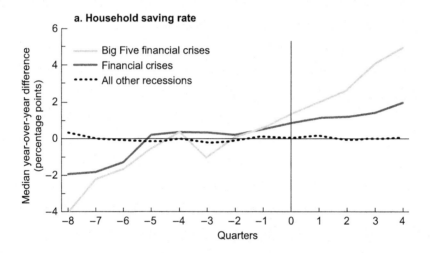

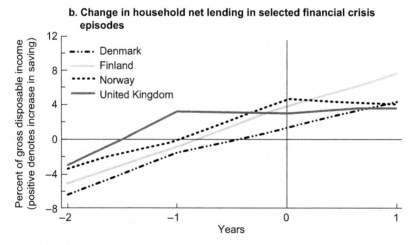

Figure 8.7 Household Saving Rate and Net Lending before and after Business Cycle Peaks

Source: Authors' calculations.

Note: Peak in output at $t = 0$. The Big Five financial crises are Finland (1990–93), Japan (1993), Norway (1988), Spain (1978–79), and Sweden (1990–93—Reinhart and Rogoff, 2008a).

growth in income and wealth.[24] The result is overvalued goods, services, and in particular, asset prices. For a period, this overheating appears to confirm the optimistic expectations, but when expectations are eventually disappointed, restoring household balance sheets and adjusting prices downward toward something approaching fair value require sharp adjustments in private behavior. Not surprisingly, a key reason recessions associated with financial crises are so much worse is the decline in private consumption.

Turning to the recovery phase, the weakness in private demand tends to persist in upswings that follow recessions associated with financial crises (Figure 8.8).

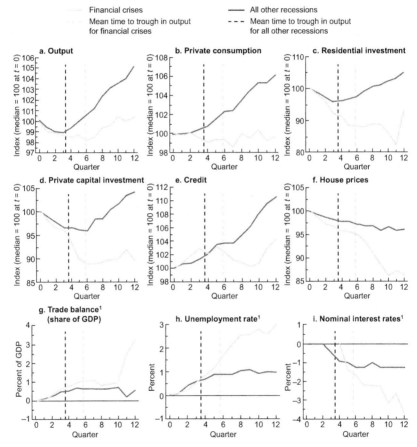

Figure 8.8 Recessions and Recoveries Associated with Financial Crises and Other Shocks

Source: Authors' calculations.
Note: Data in real terms unless noted otherwise. Peak in output at $t = 0$.
[1]Difference for level at $t = 0$, in percentage points.

---

[24] In fact, real GDP growth rates before recessions associated with financial crises have not been exceptionally high compared with those before other recessions. Similarly, the relationship between the average level of the output gap in the four quarters before the peak and the output loss in the ensuing recession is positive, but financial crises do not stand out.

Private consumption typically grows more slowly than during other recoveries. Private investment continues to decline after the recession trough; in particular, residential investment typically takes two years merely to stop declining. Thus, output growth is sluggish, and the unemployment rate continues to rise by more than usual. Credit growth falters, whereas in other recoveries it is steady and strong. Asset prices are generally weaker; house prices in particular follow a prolonged decline. However, although the recovery of domestic private demand from financial crises is weaker than usual, economies hit by financial crises have typically benefited from relatively strong demand in the rest of the world, which has helped them export their way out of recession.

What do these observations reveal about the dynamics of recovery after a financial crisis? First, households and firms either perceive a stronger need to restore their balance sheets after a period of overleveraging or are constrained to do so by sharp reductions in credit supply. Private consumption growth is likely to be weak until households are comfortable that they are more financially secure. It would be a mistake to think of recovery from such episodes as a process in which an economy simply reverts to its previous state.

Second, expenditures with long planning horizons—notably real estate and capital investment—suffer particularly from the aftereffects of financial crises. This appears to be strongly associated with weak credit growth. The nature of these financial crises and the lack of credit growth during recovery indicate that this is a supply issue. Furthermore, industries that conventionally rely heavily on external credit recover much more slowly after these recessions.

Third, given the below-average trajectory of private demand, an important issue is the extent to which public and external demand can contribute to growth. In many of the recoveries following financial crises examined in this section, an important condition was robust world growth. This raises the question of what happens when world growth is weak or nonexistent.

Are Highly Synchronized Recessions and Their Recoveries Different?

The 2007–09 downturn was global, implying that the recovery could not in the aggregate be driven by a turnaround in net exports (although this could be true for individual economies). Therefore, an examination of the features of synchronized recessions may help in gauging the evolution of the recession and prospective recovery.

To address this issue, highly synchronized recessions are defined as those during which 10 or more of the 21 advanced economies in the sample were in recession at the same time.[25] In addition to the cycle kicked off by the 2007–09 crisis,

---

[25] Alternatively, synchronized recessions could be defined as recession events whose peaks coincide within a given time window, say a year. The results reported in the text are robust to this definition.

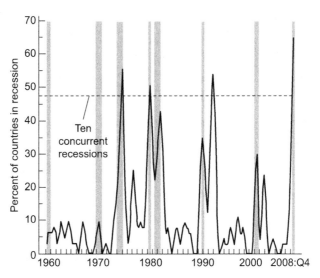

Figure 8.9 Highly Synchronized Recessions

Source: Authors' calculations.
Note: Shaded areas denote U.S. recession.

there were three other episodes of highly synchronized recessions: 1975, 1980, and 1992 (Figure 8.9).[26] As seen in Table 8.1, highly synchronized recessions are longer and deeper than others: the average duration of a synchronous recession is 40 percent greater than that of other recessions, and the amplitude is 45 percent greater.

What are the distinctive features of highly synchronized recessions? The most obvious is that they are severe, as seen in Figure 8.10. Moreover, recoveries from synchronous recessions are, on average, very slow, with output taking 50 percent longer on average to recover its previous peak than after other recessions. Credit growth is also weak, in contrast to recoveries from nonsynchronous recessions, during which credit and investment recover rapidly. As with financial crises, investment and asset prices continue to decline after the trough in GDP. However, a key difference from the recoveries following localized financial crises is that net trade is much weaker. When compared with nonsynchronous recessions, exports are typically more sluggish in synchronous recessions.

The United States has typically been at the center of synchronous recessions. Three of the four synchronous recessions (including the one associated with the 2007–09 crisis) were preceded by, or coincided with, a recession in the United States. During both the 1975 and 1980 recessions, sharp drops in U.S. imports

---

[26] Note that the global crisis recessions were excluded from this analysis. Almost one-third of all recessions were highly synchronized.

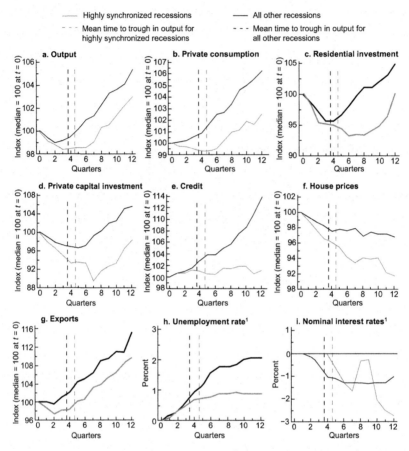

Figure 8.10 Are Highly Synchronized Recessions Different?

Source: Authors' calculations.

Note: Data in real terms unless noted otherwise. Peak in output at $t = 0$.

[1]Difference from level at $t = 0$, percentage points.

caused significant contractions in world trade.[27] In addition to strong trade linkages, downward movements in U.S. credit and equity prices are likely to be transmitted to other economies.

Does Bad Plus Bad Equal Worse?

Recessions that are associated with both financial crises and global downturns have been unusually severe and long lasting. Since 1960, there have been only 6

---

[27] In these two recessions, U.S. imports fell by 11 percent and 14 percent, respectively. In the other five U.S. recessions, imports contracted by 3 percent, on average. These cases are picked up as recessions associated with external demand shocks for some countries, but not all, owing to the threshold that the identification imposes (see Appendix 8A).

recessions out of the 122 in the sample that fit this description: Finland (1990), France (1992), Germany (1980), Greece (1992), Italy (1992), and Sweden (1990). On average, these recessions lasted almost two years (Table 8.1, final row). Moreover, during these recessions GDP fell by more than 4¾ percent. Reflecting in part the severity of these recessions, recoveries from synchronized recessions are weak.

CAN POLICIES PLAY A USEFUL COUNTERCYCLICAL ROLE?

Up to this point, this chapter has examined the dynamics of recessions and recoveries without accounting for economic policy responses. Policymakers, however, generally try to reduce fluctuations in output. Narrative studies of the policy decision-making process, such as Romer and Romer (1989, 2007), show that concerns about the state of the economy are a key input to the formulation of policy.

This section examines how monetary and fiscal policies have been used as countercyclical tools during business cycle downturns. The effectiveness of policy interventions in smoothing the business cycle is a topic of long debate in the academic literature. Much of the debate centers on the impact of active, or discretionary, policies rather than on the component of policies that automatically responds to the business cycle. The debate about the role of fiscal policy has been particularly intense, and estimates of how output responds to discretionary changes in policy vary dramatically depending on the methodology used, the sample of countries, and the period examined. Indeed, there is evidence that the multipliers can at times be negative. The consensus, however, is that discretionary fiscal policy does have a positive impact on growth, though the magnitude is fairly small.[28]

The effectiveness of policy interventions in smoothing the business cycle is a topic of long debate in the academic literature. Much of the debate centers on the impact of active, or discretionary, policies rather than the component of policies that automatically responds to the business cycle. The debate over the role of fiscal policy has been particularly intense, and estimates of how output responds to discretionary changes in policy vary dramatically depending on the methodology employed, the sample of countries, and the time period examined. Indeed, there is evidence that the multipliers can at times be negative. The consensus, however, is that discretionary fiscal policy does have a positive impact on growth, though the magnitude is fairly small.

A common challenge faced in empirical research on macroeconomic policies is the appropriate measurement of discretionary policy. In general, any measure

---

[28] See Chapter 5 of IMF (2008) for a summary. See also Blanchard and Perotti (2002), Romer and Romer (2007), and Ramey (2009) for recent attempts at identifying the impact of discretionary fiscal policy.

of macroeconomic policy is interrelated with output, making causal inference difficult. To address this problem, this section distinguishes the automatic response of policy (which depends on economic activity) from the discretionary one by using a simple regression framework. The discretionary component of fiscal policy is proxied by the cyclically adjusted primary fiscal balance as well as by cyclically adjusted real government consumption.[29] Similarly, the discretionary component of monetary policy is proxied by the nominal interest rate and real interest rate deviations from a Taylor rule, which attempts to capture how the central bank responds to fluctuations in the output gap and to deviations from an explicit, or implicit, inflation target. For each recession phase, the baseline measure of policy response is the peak-to-trough change, a cumulative measure of the degree of loosening or tightening of policy over the whole recession.[30]

Discretionary fiscal and monetary policies have typically been expansionary during recessions (Figure 8.11).[31] The mean increase in the discretionary component of government consumption during a recession is about 1.1 percent a quarter, whereas the average decline in real interest rates, beyond that implied by a Taylor rule, is about 0.2 percentage point a quarter.[32] The advanced economies have historically responded more aggressively using monetary policy than other countries.[33] However, some European economies are unable to lower interest rates independently during recessions because of their commitment to the European Exchange Rate Mechanism and membership in the euro area.

Do Policies Help Mitigate the Duration of Recessions?

The impact of discretionary monetary and fiscal policies on the duration of recessions is examined by looking at the cross-country experience across various

---

[29] To check for the robustness of these results, an alternative measure of fiscal policy is also used. This measure—the percentage change in non–cyclically adjusted real government consumption—is based on the premise that changes in real government expenditures are largely independent of the cyclical fluctuations in output. As discussed in Appendix 8A, most of the results are preserved. Public investment spending would have been another option. However, its size is much smaller than that of government consumption, and its association with economic recovery is often limited, owing to significant implementation lags (Spilimbergo and others, 2008).

[30] Details are presented in Appendix 8A. For the measures of monetary policy, the policy stimulus is computed as the sum of the deviations in each quarter that the economy is in recession. Most empirical studies, including those cited previously, do not discriminate among the various phases of the business cycle. Exceptions include Peersman and Smets (2001) and Tagkalakis (2008), who show, respectively, that monetary policy and fiscal policy tend to have larger effects during recessions than during expansions

[31] Lane (2003) finds that current government spending, excluding interest payments, is countercyclical for a sample of Organization for Economic Cooperation and Development (OECD) countries, though he claims that automatic stabilizers are the main driving force behind the countercyclicality.

[32] Note that these figures show the measures of the discretionary component of policy. Direct measures of policy, such as changes in interest rates or the primary balance, show more marked reductions during recessions.

[33] The advanced economies comprise Canada, France, Germany, Italy, Japan, the United Kingdom, and the United States.

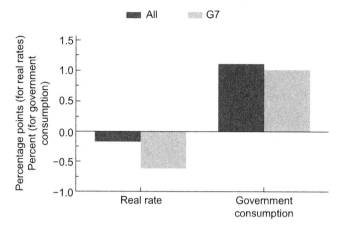

Figure 8.11 Average Policy Response during a Recession

Source: Authors' calculations.
Note: G7 economies include Canada, France, Germany, Italy, Japan, the United Kingdom, and the United States.

recession episodes using duration analysis. Duration analysis models the probability that an event, such as the end of a recession, will occur. Previous studies have used these models to address the question of whether recessions are more likely or less likely to end as they continue.[34] This chapter adds to this analysis by looking at the impact of policies on the likelihood that an economy exits a recession.

Across all types of recessions, there is evidence that expansionary monetary policy is typically associated with shorter recessions, whereas expansionary fiscal policy is not. A 1 percent reduction in the real interest rate beyond that implied by the Taylor rule increases the probability of exiting a recession in a given quarter by about 6 percent. However, fiscal policy, measured either by changes in the primary balance or in government consumption, is not found to have a significant impact on the duration of recessions when examined across all recessions.

However, both expansionary fiscal and monetary policies tend to shorten the duration of recessions associated with financial crises, although the effect of monetary policy is not statistically significant (Table 8.3). During these episodes, a 1 percent increase in government consumption is associated with an increase in the probability of exiting a recession of about 16 percent. The stronger impact of fiscal policy in these events is consistent with evidence that fiscal policy is more effective when economic agents face tighter liquidity constraints (Tagkalakis, 2008).[35] The lack of a statistically significant effect from monetary policy could be a result of the stress experienced by the financial sector during financial crises,

---

[34] Previous studies find that postwar recessions in the United States are more likely to end the longer they progress (Diebold and Rudebusch, 1990; and Diebold, Rudebusch, and Sichel, 1993).
[35] Bernanke and Gertler (1989) suggest that liquidity constraints are more prevalent in recessions than expansions.

TABLE 8.3

Impact of Policies on the Probability of Exiting a Recession				
	(1)	(2)	(3)	(4)
Recession associated with	−1.275***	−2.238***	−0.454	−1.391**
financial crisis[1]	(0.381)	(0.602)	(0.612)	(0.763)
Government consumption[2]		−0.110***		−0.131***
		(0.027)		(0.029)
Government consumption ×		0.278**		0.284**
financial crisis		(0.143)		(0.139)
Real rate[3]			−0.024***	−0.033***
			(0.008)	(0.009)
Real rate × financial crisis			−0.028	−0.024
			(0.031)	(0.031)
Constant	−3.224***	−3.269***	−3.571***	−3.742***
	(0.449)	(0.459)	(0.499)	(0.514)
Ln p[4]	0.900***	0.983***	0.960***	1.070***
	(0.069)	(0.069)	(0.072)	(0.072)
Fixed effects	Yes	Yes	Yes	Yes
Number of observations	121	120	117	117

Source: Authors' calculations.

Note: The baseline hazard function is assumed to follow a Weibull distribution. Coefficient values of the individual covariates in the hazard function are reported. Standard errors are reported in parentheses. The symbols ***, **, and * indicate significance at the 1, 5, and 10 percent levels, respectively.

[1] Recession associated with financial crisis is an indicator variable that takes on a value of 1 when the recession is identified as being related to a financial crisis as described in the text.

[2] Government consumption refers to the change in discretionary government consumption during a recession.

[3] Real rate refers to the cumulative deviations of real interest rates from a Taylor rule during a recession.

[4] Ln p reports the value of the (logged) Weibull parameter that governs the shape of the hazard function.

which hampers the effectiveness of the interest-rate and bank-lending channels of the monetary policy transmission mechanism.[36]

A useful way of visualizing the impact of monetary and fiscal policies on the duration of recessions is to look at estimates of the probability that an economy will stay in a recession beyond a certain number of quarters (Figure 8.12, panel a). The estimated probabilities are significantly higher for recessions associated with financial crises relative to the average recession, indicating that the former type lasts longer than the latter. The implementation of expansionary policies clearly helps reduce the median duration of the recession (Figure 8.12, panel b). For instance, a one-standard-deviation increase in government consumption reduces the median duration of a recession associated with financial crisis from 5.1 quarters to 4.1 quarters. In contrast, the effect of monetary policy, although still helping to reduce the duration of a recession associated with financial crisis, is insignificant.

Do Policies Help Boost Recoveries?

As noted previously, recessions are typically followed by swift recoveries. Although, as discussed earlier, factors such as technological progress and popula-

---

[36] See Bernanke and Gertler (1995) for a detailed discussion of the credit channel of the monetary policy transmission mechanism.

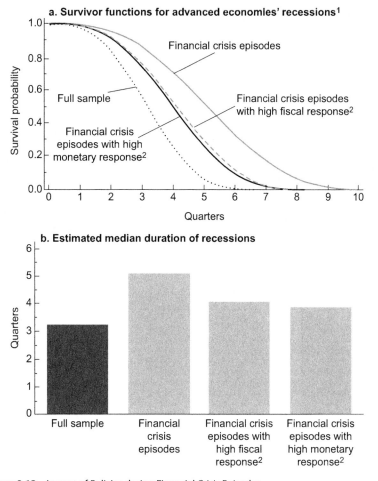

Figure 8.12   Impact of Policies during Financial Crisis Episodes

Source: Authors' calculations.

Note: Recessions associated with financial crises, as described in the text.

[1]Survivor functions show the probability of remaining in a recession beyond a certain number of quarters.

[2]Refers to a one-standard-deviation increase in government consumption or decrease in real interest rates, respectively.

tion growth help the economy eventually recover, this section investigates whether fiscal and monetary policies undertaken during the recession also contribute to the strength of the economic recovery, using an event study to exploit the cross-country variation in the data. The variable of interest in this case is the cumulative output growth one year after the cyclical trough, which is used as a proxy for the strength of the recovery. An economy emerging from recession has typically surpassed its previous peak output by this time. The measures of policy used are the same as in the duration analysis, which were measured as cumulative changes during the recession phase. In addition to the policy variables, both the duration and amplitude of the preceding recession are included as controls.

TABLE 8.4

Impact of Policies on the Strength of Recoveries

	(1)	(2)	(3)	(4)	(5)	(6)	(7)	(8)
Recession duration	−0.044	0.111	−0.248	−0.208	−0.201*	−0.056	−0.406	−0.342
	(0.121)	(0.126)	(0.156)	(0.211)	(0.110)	(0.144)	(0.251)	(0.286)
Recession amplitude	0.155	0.092	0.446***	0.426***	0.415***	0.353***	0.358***	0.323**
	(0.116)	(0.102)	(0.082)	(0.103)	(0.069)	(0.082)	(0.117)	(0.137)
Government consumption[1]	0.201**	0.173**	0.252**	0.236*				
	(0.080)	(0.082)	(0.119)	(0.131)				
Government consumption × debt			−0.437**	−0.415*				
			(0.186)	(0.209)				
Primary balance[2]					−0.040	−0.041	−0.567**	−0.575**
					(0.070)	(0.071)	(0.247)	(0.236)
Primary balance × debt							1.029***	1.056***
							(0.354)	(0.340)
Real rate[3]		−0.035***		−0.010		−0.028*		−0.015
		(0.011)		(0.025)		(0.016)		(0.025)
Public debt[4]			−1.505**	−1.468**			−3.890***	−3.755***
			(0.647)	(0.670)			(0.797)	(0.885)
Fixed effects	Yes	Yes	Yes	Yes	Yes	Yes	Yes	Yes
Number of observations	112	109	75	75	96	93	72	72
R^2	0.10	0.13	0.34	0.34	0.12	0.16	0.46	0.46

Source: Authors' calculations.
Notes: Dependent variable is the cumulative growth one year into the recovery phase. Robust standard errors clustered by country are reported in parentheses. The symbols ***, **, and * indicate significance at the 1, 5, and 10 percent levels, respectively.
[1]Government consumption refers to the change in discretionary government consumption during the preceding recession.
[2]Primary balance refers to the change in the cyclically adjusted primary balance during the preceding recession.
[3]Real rate refers to the cumulative deviations of real interest rates from a Taylor rule during a recession.
[4]Public debt refers to the ratio of public debt to GDP at the start of the recession.

The results suggest that both fiscal and monetary expansions undertaken during a recession are associated with stronger recoveries (Table 8.4). In particular, increases in government consumption and reductions in both nominal and real interest rates, beyond that implied by the Taylor rule, have a positive effect on the strength of economic recovery (Figure 8.13).[37] Table 8.4 shows the quantitative impact of each policy measure separately and in combination. The coefficient on the government consumption variable, which is about 0.2, implies that a one-standard-deviation increase in government consumption during a recession is associated with an increase in the cumulative growth rate during the recovery phase of about 0.7 percent. The response to a one-standard-deviation reduction in real interest rates, beyond that implied by the Taylor rule, is about 0.4 percent. However, changes in the cyclically adjusted primary balance during a recession are not significantly associated with output growth during recovery.[38]

---

[37] This positive impact of policy continues to remain statistically significant even after policies that were undertaken in the early stages of recovery are included.

[38] It should be noted that no systematic relationship was found linking monetary or fiscal policy with the strength of recoveries associated with financial crises.

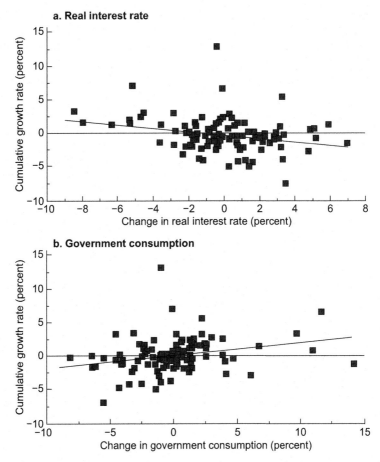

Figure 8.13   Effect of Policy Variables on the Strength of Recovery

Source: Authors' calculations.

Note: Scatter plots shown here are conditional plots that take into account the effect of several other controlling variables, as noted in Appendix 8A.

The aggressive use of discretionary fiscal policy raises concerns about the sustainability of public finances. For instance, Perotti (1999), using a sample of 19 OECD countries, finds that a fiscal stimulus reduces private consumption in periods during which the level of government debt is particularly high.[39] Do concerns about fiscal sustainability detract from the effectiveness of fiscal stimulus during recoveries? To address this question, the levels of public debt relative to GDP that were prevalent at the beginning of the recession are introduced into the

---

[39] The procyclicality of fiscal policy in emerging markets is also largely attributable to the fact that constraints on the financing of government debt are usually tighter during recessions (see Gavin and Perotti, 1997, for a discussion on Latin America).

benchmark regression framework interacted with the proxy of fiscal policy. The results, shown in Table 8.4, suggest that the degree of public indebtedness reduces the effectiveness of fiscal policy. Thus, fiscal stimulus in economies that have low levels of public debt has a higher impact on the strength of the recovery relative to economies that have higher levels of public debt. For public debt levels in excess of 60 percent of GDP, the fiscal stimulus becomes ineffective and even detrimental; however, there is high uncertainty in the estimation of this threshold debt level.

These findings point to the need for a commitment to medium-term fiscal sustainability to accompany any short-term fiscal stimulus. Doubts about debt sustainability can slow the recovery process through lower consumer spending and higher long-term real interest rates. To ensure policy effectiveness, it is crucial that the implementation of temporary stimulus measures occur in a framework that guarantees fiscal sustainability.[40]

This section has focused on fiscal and monetary policy; however, previous experiences of recessions associated with financial crises strongly suggest that the effectiveness of monetary and fiscal policies is substantially reduced without the implementation of prompt and well-targeted financial policies. Many observers consider the policies undertaken by Sweden in the early 1990s to have been highly effective in restoring the health of the financial sector, paving the way for strong recovery (Jackson, 2008, and references therein). A key component of those measures was the establishment of independent asset management companies, which removed bad assets from the balance sheets of banks so that the banks could resume normal lending activities. In Japan, slow recognition of the extent of the bad-loan problem contributed to the slow recovery from the financial crises of the 1990s (see, for instance, Hoshi and Kashyap, 2008).

Financial sector support typically has fiscal costs. However, a substantial part of the up-front gross cost is usually recovered, through asset sales, in the medium term. For example, in the Scandinavian countries and in Japan, the gross cost of recapitalization averaged some 5 percent of GDP, whereas the average recovery rate in the first five years was about 30 percent.[41] The speed of the economic recovery and associated improvement in financial conditions are important factors in determining the recovery rate. In Sweden, for example, more than 90 percent of the initial outlay was recovered within the first five years. The

---

[40] See Spilimbergo and others (2008) for further details on the design of appropriate policies that address sustainability concerns. Reinhart and Rogoff (2008a) find that financial crisis episodes are often associated with sharp increases in the level of public debt, potentially raising concerns about medium-term debt sustainability. However, they do not examine the behavior of long-term interest rates following such crises.

[41] This rate is relatively low compared with the 55 percent recovery rate that advanced economies typically experience from the sale of assets acquired through interventions. Detailed data on financial policy responses for several of the financial crisis episodes studied in this chapter are available in Laeven and Valencia (2008a, 2008b).

equivalent rate for the Japanese recession in the late 1990s, however, was just about 10 percent; it reached almost 90 percent by 2008.

LESSONS FOR THE RECESSION FOLLOWING THE 2007–09 CRISIS AND PROSPECTS FOR RECOVERY

Data through the fourth quarter of 2008 indicated that 15 of the 21 advanced economies considered in this chapter were in recession. Based on output turning points, Ireland was in decline for seven quarters; Denmark for five; Finland, New Zealand, and Sweden for four; Austria, Germany, Italy, Japan, the Netherlands, and the United Kingdom for three; and Portugal, Spain, Switzerland, and the United States for two (although the U.S. recession was already four quarters old at the end of 2008 using NBER dating).[42] This section looks at the prospects for recovery from these recessions in light of the findings of this chapter.

Many of the economies in recession after the global crisis saw expansions that closely resembled those preceding previous episodes of financial stress, as discussed in the chapter, exhibiting similarly overheated asset prices and rapid expansions in credit.[43] At end-2008, there were clear signs that, consistent with previous experiences of financial stress (IMF, 2008b), these recessions were already more severe and longer than usual. Figure 8.14 plots median growth rates of key macroeconomic variables for all 122 previous recessions, along with upper and lower quartile bands. Overlaid on each are data for the latest U.S. recession and the median for all other concurrent recessions.[44] GDP data indicate that these economies had been deteriorating at a relatively rapid pace. In particular, declines in goods, labor, and asset markets in the United States were steep. Three aspects of these developments are especially notable.

First, there was evidence of negative feedback between asset prices, credit, and investment, which, as seen in the previous sections, is common in severe recessions associated with financial crises. The evidence showed exceptional reductions in credit. The deterioration in financial wealth, as represented by equity prices, was sharp. The decline in U.S. house prices was as steep as those in the Big Five episodes discussed previously. Residential investment clearly showed exceptional declines compared with previous recessions.

Second, the evidence indicated that the sharp falls in household wealth seen in several economies and the need to rebuild household balance sheets would result in larger-than-usual declines in private consumption. The reduction in U.S. consumption in the most recent quarters was clearly atypical. Consumer

---

[42] The NBER has declared that the peak in U.S. output before the 2007–09 crisis was in December 2007.

[43] Notable exceptions include Germany and Japan, although their economies were also experiencing financial stress.

[44] The calculation of the median is limited to at least four observations, which is why the series for recent recessions did not extend to six quarters at the time the analysis was undertaken.

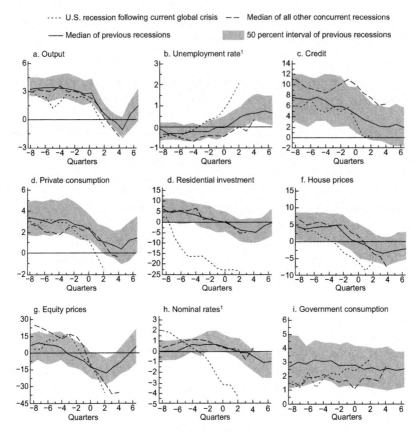

Figure 8.14 Economic Indicators around Peaks of Current and Previous Recessions

Source: Authors' calculations.
Note: Median log differences from one year earlier unless noted otherwise. Peak in output at $t = 0$. Data in real terms unless noted otherwise.
[1]Median percentage point difference from one year earlier.

confidence in all economies had been steadily weakening, suggesting that declines in private demand and confidence would make for a protracted recovery.

Finally, the recessions following the global crisis were also highly synchronized, further dampening prospects of a normal recovery. In particular, the rapid drop in consumption in the United States represented a large decline in external demand for many other economies.

Hence, it seemed unlikely that overleveraged economies would be able to bounce back quickly via strong growth in domestic private demand—fundamentally, a prolonged period of above-average saving would have been required. In many previous cases of banking system stress, net exports led the recovery, facilitated by robust demand from the United States and by exchange rate depreciations or devaluations. But that option would not be available in this episode, given the unique stress at the heart of the world's largest economy.

Given the likely shortfalls in both domestic private demand and external demand, policy needed to be used to arrest the cycle of falling demand, asset prices, and credit. Monetary policy had been loosened quickly in most advanced economies, much more so than in previous recessions, and extraordinary measures had been taken to provide liquidity to markets. Further effective easing was possible, even as nominal interest rates approached zero. However, evidence from the analysis indicates that interest rate cuts would likely have less of an impact during a financial crisis. In view of the continued distress in the financial sector, authorities would have been wise not to rely solely on standard policy measures.

The evidence in this chapter shows that fiscal policy can make a significant contribution to reducing the duration of recessions associated with financial crises. In effect, governments can break the negative feedback between the real economy and financial conditions by acting as "spender of last resort." But this presupposes that public stimulus can be delivered quickly. Moreover, as the chapter shows, the sustainability of the eventual debt burden constrains the scope of expansionary fiscal policy, and it will not be possible to support demand for an extended period in economies that have entered recession with weak fiscal balances and large levels of public debt. In the event of severe and prolonged recessions during which deflation is an important risk, fiscal and monetary policies should be tightly coordinated to contain downward demand pressures. Furthermore, given the globally synchronized nature of the recession following the 2007–09 crisis, fiscal stimulus should be provided by a broad range of countries with fiscal room to do so, so as to maximize the short-term impact on global economic activity.

Restoring the health of the financial sector is an essential component of any policy package.[45] Experiences with previous financial crises—especially those involving deleveraging, such as in Japan in the 1990s—strongly signal that coherent and comprehensive action to restore financial institutions' balance sheets, and to remove uncertainty about funding, is required before a recovery will be feasible. Even then, recovery is likely to be slow and relatively weak.

APPENDIX 8A. DATA SOURCES AND METHODOLOGIES

This appendix provides details on the data and briefly reviews the methodologies used to identify "large shocks" and discretionary fiscal and monetary policies. The appendix also reports robustness exercises on the measure of fiscal policy.

Data Sources

The main data source for this chapter is Claessens, Kose, and Terrones (2008), from here on denoted as CKT. Other sources are listed in Table 8A.1.

---

[45] See, for instance, Decressin and Laxton (2009) for a discussion of unconventional monetary policy options, fiscal policy, synergies with financial sector policy, and lessons from the experience of Japan.

TABLE 8A.1

Data Sources	
Variable	**Source**
Output	CKT, Haver Analytics
Real private consumption	CKT, Haver Analytics
Real government consumption	CKT, Haver Analytics
Real private capital investment	CKT
Real residential investment	CKT, Haver Analytics
Real exports	CKT
Real net exports	Organization for Economic Cooperation and Development (OECD) Analytical Database
GDP deflator	OECD Analytical Database
Consumer price index	CKT, IMF International Financial Statistics (IFS) database
Oil prices	IMF Primary Commodity Prices database
Real house prices	CKT, Bank for International Settlements (BIS), OECD
Stock prices	CKT, IFS database
Credit	CKT, IFS database
Nominal interest rate	CKT, IFS database, Thomson Datastream
Unemployment rate	CKT, Haver Analytics
Labor force participation rate	OECD Analytical Database
Nominal wages	IFS database, OECD Analytical Database
House-price-to-rental ratio	OECD
Household saving rate	OECD Analytical Database
Household net lending	OECD Analytical Database
Public debt	International Monetary Fund

Note: House prices; stock prices, credit, and interest rates are deflated using consumer price indices.

Methodology Used to Categorize Recessions and Recoveries

The statistical rules for the nonfinancial shocks identify large changes in macro-economic variables, as follows:

- *Oil shocks.* An indicator of oil price movements records, at a given date and for each country, the maximum change in nominal local oil prices in the preceding 12 quarters.[46] Oil shocks are defined as those in which the indicator is greater than the mean plus 1.75 standard deviations of this index.

- *External demand shocks.* The indicator of external demand is constructed as percentage deviations from trend of the trade-weighted GDP for each economy.[47] External demand shocks are defined as those in which the

---

[46] This is a version of Hamilton's (2003) proposed filter for identifying oil shocks in the United States. The local price is defined as the world average spot price in U.S. dollars times the nominal exchange rate for the country in question. In addition, results using year-over-year changes in real and nominal local-currency oil prices and vector-autoregression-based identifications of oil supply shocks were also examined (Kilian, 2006).

[47] The trend is implemented using the Hodrick-Prescott (H-P) filter with λ set to 1,600. Two key assumptions are, first, that domestic absorption is well approximated by GDP, and second, that the trade weights are of the other advanced economies alone. Some economies have significant trade relationships with nonadvanced economies that have suffered sharp declines in demand (e.g., New Zealand exports to east Asia during 1997–98). Robustness to using terms of trade and world GDP has been explored.

indicator is less than the mean minus 1.75 standard deviations of the indicator.

- *Fiscal policy shocks.* For the indicator of discretionary fiscal policy, a measure of the cyclically adjusted primary balance is constructed.[48] Fiscal contractions are those in which the year-over-year difference of the cyclically adjusted primary balance is greater than the mean plus 1.75 standard deviations of the cyclically adjusted primary balance.[49]

- *Monetary policy shocks.* For the indicator of discretionary monetary policy, the residuals from estimated Taylor rules are employed. Monetary policy contractions are those in which the residual is greater than 1.75 standard deviations. The analysis also examines term spreads (the difference between yields on 3-month government bills and 10-year government bonds), recording as contractionary those instances in which the spread is greater than 1.75 standard deviations above trend.

- The next step is to associate recessions with these shocks. A shock in the four quarters preceding a peak in GDP is attributed one point for correctly calling the downturn ahead. This leads to the results in Table 8A.2. Finally, Table 8A.3 provides some evidence on the association between financial crises and the deregulation of mortgage markets.

Methodology Used to Identify Fiscal and Monetary Policies

Two measures of fiscal policy are used: cyclically adjusted government consumption and cyclically adjusted primary balances. In instances in which only one measure is discussed or presented, it is cyclically adjusted government consumption. In all cases, changes in policy are measured as changes in the respective variable from the peak of a particular cycle to the trough.

The cyclically adjusted primary balance is computed using OECD elasticities on the different tax and expenditure components. For government consumption, however, such elasticities are not readily available and thus have to be estimated. The elasticity of government consumption with respect to the business cycle is computed as follows:

$$\ln gc_t = \beta_0 + \beta_1 \times gap_t + \beta_2 \times trend + \varepsilon_t,$$

---

[48] This follows standard IMF methodology (Heller, Haas, and Mansur, 1986). The H-P (1,600) filter is used to estimate potential. OECD estimates of income elasticities for revenues and expenditures are used to construct measures of discretionary changes in the fiscal stance and to filter out passive changes from preset targets and automatic stabilizers. There are a number of important assumptions, notably that the H-P filter estimates potential output well; that the income elasticities of expenditures and revenues are constant; that revenue shares (used to construct aggregate income elasticity of revenues) are constant; and that the GDP deflator (used to deflate nominal government expenditures) is a good proxy for the true government expenditures deflator.

[49] A positive value corresponds to fiscal tightening because the primary balance is defined as tax revenues minus expenditures.

TABLE 8A.2

Results from Categorizing Recessions

	Number	Percent
Episodes with positive overall "pre-peak" scores (total of all indicators; at least one indicator is > 0 during pre-peak period)	56	46
Episodes with scores greater than zero (by indicator)		
Oil	23	19
External demand	6	5
Fiscal policy	8	7
Monetary policy	15	12
Financial crisis	15	12

		Number of recessions with positive "pre-peak" score by country and type of shock				
	Number of recessions	Oil	External demand	Fiscal policy	Monetary policy	Financial crisis
Australia	6	0	1	0	1	1
Austria	6	1	1	0	1	0
Belgium	7	1	0	1	2	0
Canada	3	1	0	0	1	0
Denmark	7	1	0	1	1	1
Finland	5	0	0	2	0	1
France	4	2	0	1	0	1
Germany	8	2	0	0	2	1
Greece	8	2	0	2	1	1
Ireland	3	0	0	0	0	0
Italy	9	1	0	0	0	1
Japan	3	0	0	0	0	2
Netherlands	5	2	1	0	2	0
New Zealand	12	1	1	0	1	1
Norway	3	1	0	0	1	1
Portugal	4	1	1	1	1	0
Spain	4	1	0	0	0	1
Sweden	3	1	1	0	0	1
Switzerland	9	1	0	0	0	0
United Kingdom	5	2	0	0	0	2
United States	6	2	0	0	1	0

Source: Authors' calculations.

in which gc_t is government consumption at time t, gap_t is a measure of the output gap at time t ("potential output" is measured using the Hodrick-Prescott [H-P] filter) and *trend* is a time trend. In estimating the equation above, the lagged value of the output gap is used as an instrument. Cyclically adjusted government consumption ($cagc_t$) is then computed as

$$cagc_t = gc_t \left(1 - \beta_1 \times gap_t\right).$$

Two measures of monetary policy are used: nominal and real interest rates. Both of these variables are measured as deviations from a "policy rule." When only one measure is used, it is the real rate. The policy response over the course of a

TABLE 8A.3

Financial Crises and Deregulation in the Mortgage Market		
Country	Year	Measure
Australia	1986	Removal of ceiling on mortgage interest rates
Denmark	1982	Liberalization of mortgage contract terms; deregulation of interest rates
Finland	1986–87	Deregulation of interest rates; removal of guidelines on mortgage lending
France	1987	Elimination of credit controls
Germany	1967	Deregulation of interest rates
Italy	1983–87	Deregulation of interest rates; elimination of credit ceilings
Japan	1993–94	Reduction of bank specialization requirements; deregulation of interest rates
New Zealand	1984	Removal of credit allocation guidelines; deregulation of interest rates
Norway	1984–85	Abolition of lending controls; deregulation of interest rates
Sweden	1985	Abolition of lending controls for banks; deregulation of interest rates
United Kingdom	1980–86	Credit controls eliminated; banks allowed to compete with building societies for housing finance; building societies allowed to expand lending activities; guidelines on mortgage lending removed

Source: Debelle (2004).

recession is measured as the sum of the impulse relative to the policy rule for each quarter of the recession period. A policy rule of the following form is estimated:

$$i_t = \beta_2 + \beta_3 \times dummy\_85 + \beta_4 \times \pi_t + \beta_5 \times gap_t + \upsilon_t,$$

in which i_t is the nominal interest rate, $dummy\_85$ is a dummy for periods after 1985 (to allow for a shift in the equilibrium real rate), π_t is the inflation rate, and gap_t is a measure of the output gap ("potential GDP" is measured using the H-P filter). The measure of monetary policy that is used in the analysis is

$$i^{MP} = i - \hat{i},$$

in which $\hat{i}$ is the fitted value of the regression.

Real rates are simply measured as $i_t - \pi_t$, and the steps taken to get the measure of monetary policy are the same as above.

ROBUSTNESS TEST USING GOVERNMENT CONSUMPTION AS A PROXY FOR FISCAL POLICY

Apart from the two measures of fiscal policy presented in the chapter, the same set of regressions were also run using changes in real government consumption during preceding recessions, without any cyclical adjustment. Table 8A.4 contains the results of regressions using the alternative measure of fiscal policy. Although most of the main results in the chapter are preserved, the interaction term with public debt is statistically significant only at the two- and three-quarter horizon during the recovery phase. The limitations of the data may be one possible cause.

TABLE 8A.4

Impact of Policies on the Strength of Recoveries Using an Alternative Measure of Fiscal Policy

	Dependent variable							
	Cumulative growth four quarters into recovery phase				Cumulative growth three quarters into recovery phase			
	(1)	(2)	(3)	(4)	(5)	(6)	(7)	(8)
Recession dura-tion	−0.027	−0.209	−0.179	0.090	−0.076	−0.040	0.015	0.009
	(0.110)	(0.194)	(0.217)	(0.123)	(0.092)	(0.145)	(0.174)	(0.107)
Recession amplitude	0.203**	0.439***	0.421***	0.154*	0.217*	0.283***	0.254**	0.176**
	(0.083)	(0.080)	(0.096)	(0.086)	(0.085)	(0.093)	(0.103)	(0.077)
Government consumption[1]	0.289***	0.203	0.177	0.269**	0.261***	0.489***	0.414***	0.229***
	(0.088)	(0.157)	(0.178)	(0.098)	(0.042)	(0.129)	(0.117)	(0.050)
Public debt[2]		−2.066**	−2.047**			−0.801	−0.807	
		(0.829)	(0.851)			(0.672)	(0.694)	
Government consumption × debt		−0.224	−0.200			−0.714***	−0.638***	
		(0.285)	(0.302)			(0.180)	(0.175)	
Real rate[3]			−0.009	−0.026*			−0.022	−0.022*
			(0.026)	(0.013)			(0.018)	(0.012)
Fixed effects	Yes	Yes	Yes	Yes	Yes	Yes	Yes	Yes
Number of observations	112	75	75	109	117	80	80	114
R^2	0.12	0.33	0.33	0.14	0.14	0.40	0.42	0.15

Source: Authors' calculations.
Note: Robust standard errors clustered by country are reported in parentheses. The symbols ***, **, and * indicate signifi-cance at the 1, 5, and 10 percent levels, respectively.
[1]Government consumption refers to the change in government consumption during preceding recessions.
[2]Public debt refers to the ratio of public debt to GDP at the start of the recession.
[3]Real rate refers to the cumulative deviations of real interest rates from a Taylor rule during a recession.

REFERENCES

Bernanke, Ben S., and Mark Gertler, 1989, "Agency Costs, Net Worth, and Business Fluctuations," *American Economic Review*, Vol. 79 (March), pp. 14–31.

———, 1995, "Inside the Black Box: The Credit Channel of Monetary Policy Transmission," *Journal of Economic Perspectives*, Vol. 9 (Autumn), pp. 27–48.

Blanchard, Olivier, and Roberto Perotti, 2002, "An Empirical Characterization of the Dynamic Effects of Changes in Government Spending and Taxes on Output," *Quarterly Journal of Economics*, Vol. 107 (November), pp. 1329–68.

Blanchard, Olivier, and John Simon, 2001, "The Long and Large Decline in U.S. Output Volatility," *Brookings Papers on Economic Activity*, Vol. 32, No. 1, pp. 135–74.

Brunnermeier, Marcus, 2009, "Deciphering the 2007–08 Liquidity and Credit Crunch," *Journal of Economic Perspectives*, Vol. 23, No. 1, pp. 77–100.

Burns, Arthur F., and Wesley C. Mitchell, 1946, *Measuring Business Cycles* (New York: National Bureau of Economic Research).

Chauvet, Marcelle, and James D. Hamilton, 2005, "Dating Business Cycle Turning Points," NBER Working Paper No. 11422 (Cambridge, Massachusetts: National Bureau of Economic Research).

Claessens, Stijn, M. Ayhan Kose, and Marco E. Terrones, 2008, "What Happens during Recessions, Crunches, and Busts?" IMF Working Paper 08/274 (Washington: International Monetary Fund).

Debelle, Guy, 2004, "Macroeconomic Implications of Rising Household Debt," BIS Working Paper No. 153 (Basel: Bank for International Settlements).

Decressin, Jörg, and Douglas Laxton, 2009, "Gauging Risks for Deflation," IMF Staff Position Note 09/01 (Washington: International Monetary Fund).

Diebold, Francis, and Glenn Rudebusch, 1990, "A Nonparametric Investigation of Duration Dependence in the American Business Cycle," *Journal of Political Economy*, Vol. 98, pp. 596–616.

———, and Daniel Sichel, 1993, "Further Evidence on Business Cycle Duration Dependence," in *Business Cycles, Indicators and Forecasting*, ed. by James H. Stock and Mark W. Watson (Chicago: University of Chicago Press).

Estrella, Arturo, and Frederic S. Mishkin, 1996, "The Yield Curve as a Predictor of U.S. Recessions," *Current Issues in Economics and Finance*, Vol. 2, No. 7, pp. 1–6.

Gavin, Michael, and Roberto Perotti, 1997, "Fiscal Policy in Latin America," *NBER Macroeconomics Annual*, Vol. 12, pp. 11–72.

Greenlaw, David, Jan Hatzius, Anil Kashyap, and Hyun Song Shin, 2008, "Leveraged Losses: Lessons from the Mortgage Market Meltdown," Proceedings of the 2008 Monetary Policy Forum, Feb. 29, New York.

Hamilton, James D., 2003, "What Is an Oil Shock?" *Journal of Econometrics*, Vol. 113 (April), pp. 363–98.

Harding, Don, and Adrian Pagan, 2002, "Dissecting the Cycle: A Methodological Investigation," *Journal of Monetary Economics*, Vol. 49, No. 2, pp. 365–81.

Heller, Peter S., Richard D. Haas, and Ahsan S. Mansur, 1986, *A Review of the Fiscal Impulse Measure*, IMF Occasional Paper No. 44 (Washington: International Monetary Fund).

Hoshi, Takeo, and Anil K. Kashyap, 2008, "Will the U.S. Bank Recapitalization Succeed? Lessons from Japan," NBER Working Paper No. 14401 (Cambridge, Massachusetts: National Bureau of Economic Research).

International Monetary Fund (IMF), 2002, *World Economic Outlook*, April (Washington).

———, 2008a, *Global Financial Stability Report: Financial Stress and Deleveraging—Macro-Financial Implications and Policy*, October (Washington).

———, 2008b, *World Economic Outlook*, October (Washington).

Jackson, James, 2008, "The U.S. Financial Crisis: Lessons from Sweden," CRS Report for Congress (Washington: Congressional Research Service).

Kaminsky, Graciela L., and Carmen M. Reinhart, 1999, "The Twin Crises: The Causes of Banking and Balance of Payments Problems," *American Economic Review*, Vol. 89, No. 4, pp. 473–500.

Kilian, Lutz, 2006, "Not All Oil Price Shocks Are Alike: Disentangling Demand and Supply Shocks in the Crude Oil Market," CEPR Discussion Paper No. 5994 (London: Centre for Economic Policy Research).

Kindleberger, Charles, 1978, *Manias, Panics, and Crashes: A History of Financial Crises* (Hoboken, New Jersey: John Wiley & Sons).

Laeven, Luc, and Fabian Valencia, 2008a, "Systemic Banking Crises: A New Database," IMF Working Paper 08/224 (Washington: International Monetary Fund).

———, 2008b, "The Use of Blanket Guarantees in Banking Crises," IMF Working Paper 08/250 (Washington: International Monetary Fund).

Lane, Phillip, 2003, "The Cyclical Behaviour of Fiscal Policy: Evidence from the OECD," *Journal of Public Economics*, Vol. 87 (December), pp. 2661–75.

Leamer, Edward, 2008, "What's a Recession, Anyway?" NBER Working Paper No. 14221 (Cambridge, Massachusetts: National Bureau of Economic Research).

McConnell, Margaret, and Gabriel Perez-Quiros, 2000, "Output Fluctuations in the United States: What Has Changed Since the Early 1980s?" *American Economic Review*, Vol. 90, No. 5, pp. 1464–76.

Mendoza, Enrique, and Marco E. Terrones, 2008, "An Anatomy of Credit Booms: Evidence from Macro Aggregates and Micro Data," NBER Working Paper No. 14049, (Cambridge, Massachusetts: National Bureau of Economic Research).

Peersman, Gert, and Frank Smets, 2001, "Are the Effects of Monetary Policy Greater in Recessions than in Booms?" ECB Working Paper No. 52 (Frankfurt: European Central Bank).

Perotti, Roberto, 1999, "Fiscal Policy in Good Times and Bad," *Quarterly Journal of Economics*, Vol. 114 (November), pp. 1399–436.

Ramey, Valerie A., 2009, "Identifying Government Spending Shocks: It's All in the Timing," NBER Working Paper No. 15464 (Cambridge, Massachusetts: National Bureau of Economic Research).

Reinhart, Carmen, and Kenneth Rogoff, 2008a, "Banking Crises: An Equal Opportunity Menace," NBER Working Paper No. 14587 (Cambridge, Massachusetts: National Bureau of Economic Research).

———, 2008b, "Is the 2007 U.S. Sub-Prime Crisis So Different? An International Historical Comparison," NBER Working Paper No. 13761 (Cambridge, Massachusetts: National Bureau of Economic Research).

———, 2009, "The Aftermath of Financial Crises," NBER Working Paper No. 14656 (Cambridge, Massachusetts: National Bureau of Economic Research).

Romer, Christina, 1999, "Changes in Business Cycles: Evidence and Explanations," *Journal of Economic Perspectives*, Vol. 13, No. 2, pp. 23–44.

———, and David Romer, 1989, "Does Monetary Policy Matter? A New Test in the Spirit of Friedman and Schwartz," in *NBER Macroeconomics Annual,* Vol. 4, ed. by Olivier Jean Blanchard and Stanley Fischer (Cambridge, Massachusetts: National Bureau of Economic Research).

———, 1994, "What Ends Recessions?" in *NBER Macroeconomics Annual 1994*, ed. by Stanley Fischer and Julio Rotemberg (Cambridge, Massachusetts: MIT Press).

———, 2007, "The Macroeconomic Effects of Tax Changes: Estimates Based on a New Measure of Fiscal Shocks," NBER Working Paper No. 13264 (Cambridge, Massachusetts: National Bureau of Economic Research).

Sichel, Daniel, 1994, "Inventories and the Three Phases of the Business Cycle," *Journal of Business and Economic Statistics*, Vol. 12 (July), pp. 269–77.

Spilimbergo, Antonio, Steve Symansky, Olivier Blanchard, and Carlo Cottarelli, 2008, "Fiscal Policy for the Crisis," IMF Staff Position Note 08/01 (Washington: International Monetary Fund).

Tagkalakis, Athanasios, 2008, "The Effects of Fiscal Policy on Consumption in Recessions and Expansions," *Journal of Public Economics*, Vol. 92 (June), pp. 1486–508.

Wynne, Mark A., and Nathan S. Balke, 1993, "Recessions and Recoveries," *Economic Review*, Federal Reserve Bank of Dallas (First Quarter).

PART IV

Medium-Term Effects: Economic Growth

CHAPTER 9

What's the Damage? Medium-Term Output Dynamics after Financial Crises

ABDUL ABIAD, RAVI BALAKRISHNAN, PETYA KOEVA BROOKS, DANIEL LEIGH, AND IRINA TYTELL

The recovery from the global financial crisis has been slow and bumpy, with unemployment remaining at high levels, and there are concerns about the prospect of long-term damage to economic activity. In this context, the aftermath of past financial crises may provide useful insights into the medium-term prospects for economies that recently experienced a crisis. To shed light on the medium-term outlook for such economies, this chapter examines the aftermath of banking crises in advanced, emerging, and developing economies over the past 40 years.

A first glance at several previous episodes suggests that although banking crises typically lead to large output losses in the short term, what happens to output in the medium term has varied widely (Figure 9.1). Some countries persistently grow at a slower rate than before, moving farther away from their precrisis trends, as in Japan and Thailand in the late 1990s. Some return to the precrisis growth rate, but fail to recover the initial output loss, as in Sweden (1991) and the Republic of Korea (1997). Some eventually return to their precrisis trend (Turkey, 2000), and some recover quickly and outperform the previous trend (Mexico, 1994).

A great deal of work exists on the output effects of financial crises in the short term, but until recently, the emphasis on the medium term following banking crises has been much more limited, with the notable exceptions of Boyd, Kwak, and Smith (2005), Cerra and Saxena (2008), and Reinhart and Rogoff (2009a).[1] Given the banking crises in a number of economies, including the United States, in the aftermath of the 2007–09 global economic and financial crisis, interest in

The authors would like to especially thank David Romer for his many insights and suggestions. They are grateful also to Olivier Blanchard, Charles Collyns, Jorg Decressin, and to participants at an IMF Research Department seminar. Chris Papageorgiou kindly provided the authors with computer code to implement the Bayesian model averaging analysis. Stephanie Denis, Murad Omoev, and Min Song provided excellent research assistance. This chapter expands on ideas presented in Chapter 4 of the October 2009 *World Economic Outlook* (IMF, 2009b).

[1] Studies that examine the short-term effects of financial crises include, for example, Hutchison and Noy (2002), Borda (2006), Gupta, Mishra, and Sahay (2007), Haugh, Ollivaud, and Turner (2009), and IMF (2009a).

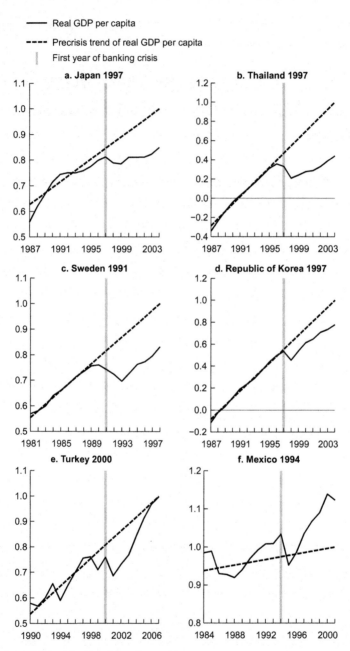

Figure 9.1 Selected Banking Crises (*Log scale*)

Sources: World Bank, *World Development Indicators;* Laeven and Valencia (2008) for banking crisis dates; and IMF staff calculations.
Note: See text for definition of precrisis trend.

the topic has risen. For instance, Furceri and Mourougane (2009) apply the Cerra-Saxena approach, which involves using an autoregressive model of output growth rates augmented by crisis dummies, to growth rates of potential output for Organization for Economic Cooperation and Development countries. Pisani-Ferry and van Pottelsberghe (2009) also discuss the persistent impact on output of banking crises using several case studies. In another study, Haugh, Ollivaud, and Turner (2009) analyze the impact of banking crises on potential growth in Finland, Japan, Norway, and Sweden.

This chapter extends those studies in six main ways. First, it examines the medium-term dynamics of output in a particularly broad sample that includes 88 banking crises over the past four decades and across countries with high, middle, and low income levels. Second, it explores not only how the postcrisis level of output compares to the precrisis trend (output loss), but also how the postcrisis growth rate of output compares with its precrisis trend growth rate (growth loss). Third, with regard to methodology, the estimation of the precrisis trend ends several years before the crisis so that it is not contaminated by the possibility of an unsustainable boom in the run-up to the crisis or a precrisis slowdown. Fourth, the analysis decomposes the medium-term dynamics of output into both factor components (capital, employment, labor force participation, and total factor productivity) and demand-side factors (consumption, investment, exports, and imports). Fifth, given the wide range of postcrisis outcomes, the analysis assesses the correlation between postcrisis output and growth losses and variables measuring initial conditions and policy responses. Finally, with five years of data since the start of the global financial crisis, some initial evidence is provided on the medium-term implications of the most recent banking crisis episodes.

The first main finding is that the path of output tends to be depressed substantially and persistently following banking crises, with no rebound on average to the precrisis trend in the medium term. Seven years after a crisis, the level of output has typically declined by about 10 percent relative to the precrisis trend. Growth does, however, tend to eventually return to its precrisis rate.

Second, the depressed path of output tends to result from long-lasting reductions of roughly equal proportions in the employment rate, the capital-to-labor ratio, and total factor productivity. In the short term, the output loss is mainly accounted for by total factor productivity, but unlike the employment rate and capital-to-labor ratio, the level of total factor productivity recovers somewhat to its precrisis trend in the medium term. In contrast, capital and employment suffer enduring losses relative to trend.

Third, initial conditions appear to have a strong association with the size of the output loss. What happens to short-term output is also a good predictor of the medium-term outcome, as is the joint occurrence of a currency crisis and a banking crisis. This is consistent with the notion that the output drop is especially persistent following large shocks, carrying over into the medium term. A high precrisis investment share is a reliable predictor of high medium-term output losses, through its correlation with the dynamics of capital after the crisis.

Evidence also suggests that limited precrisis policy space tends to be associated with more muted medium-term recoveries. An interesting finding is that postcrisis output losses are not significantly correlated with the level of income.

Fourth, the medium-term output loss is not inevitable. Some countries succeed in avoiding it, ultimately exceeding the precrisis trajectory. Although postcrisis output dynamics are hard to predict, the evidence suggests that economies that apply countercyclical fiscal and monetary stimulus in the short term after the crisis tend to have smaller output losses in the medium term. There is also some mixed evidence that structural reform efforts are associated with better medium-term outcomes. In addition, a favorable external environment is generally associated with smaller medium-term output losses.

Finally, the performance of economies that experienced banking crises during 2007–09 bears a sobering resemblance to performance in previous banking crises. These economies have experienced even deeper output losses, averaging 17 percent relative to the precrisis trend as of 2012. Moreover, little evidence indicates that output is returning to the precrisis trend.

How do these findings relate to shifts in potential output following financial crises? The term "potential output" typically refers to the level of output consistent with stable inflation and is a function of structural and institutional factors. A medium-term decline in output relative to the previous trend could reflect a decline in potential output, but it could also partly reflect a persistent fall in aggregate demand. The experiences of a number of economies, including Japan, suggest that if output remains below its precrisis trend in the medium term, a substantial part of the shortfall reflects lower potential. Therefore, to the extent that this chapter identifies output losses seven years after a financial crisis, it is likely that lower potential explains a substantial part of those losses. However, attempting to identify precise shifts in potential output is beyond the scope of this chapter.

The chapter is organized as follows. The first section describes key features of medium-term output dynamics following banking crises based on international experience during the past 40 years. The second section decomposes medium-term output losses into their factor components (capital, labor, and productivity), as well as their demand-side drivers (consumption, investment, exports, and imports). The third section analyzes the way in which medium-term output losses relate to country characteristics and macroeconomic conditions prevailing before the crisis. It also examines the role of domestic policies and the external environment after the onset of the crisis. The fourth section compares the experience through late 2012 of economies that entered banking crises during 2007–09 with the historical pattern. The last section concludes the chapter.

DOES OUTPUT RECOVER IN THE MEDIUM TERM?

This section presents key stylized facts on the output losses associated with banking crises. It starts with methodological issues and then reports stylized facts on the estimated output losses at both the country level and the global level.

The analysis focuses on banking crises, and uses a comprehensive set of banking crisis events from Laeven and Valencia (2008) from the early 1970s through 2002. The Laeven-Valencia data set is constructed by combining quantitative indicators measuring banking sector distress, such as a sharp increase in nonperforming loans and bank runs, with a subjective assessment of the situation. Currency crises are also considered for purposes of comparison; currency crisis dates are identified based on the methodology of Milesi-Ferretti and Razin (1998). This definition requires (1) a 15 percent minimum rate of nominal depreciation with respect to the U.S. dollar; (2) a minimum 10 percent increase in the rate of depreciation with respect to the previous year; and (3) a rate of depreciation of less than 10 percent in the previous year. The sample includes 88 banking crises and 222 currency crises, distributed across countries with high, middle, and low incomes. The sample excludes transition countries because the output developments observed in these economies were strongly related to the shift away from central planning rather than to financial crises.[2] Countries with populations of less than 1 million are also dropped.

The medium-term output loss for each episode is computed as illustrated in Figure 9.2. The idea behind the exercise is to measure the output loss associated with a crisis as the difference between the actual level of output and the level that would have been expected based on the prevailing precrisis trend. In line with the focus on the medium term, the analysis uses a postcrisis window of seven years, looking beyond the effects of short-term fluctuations of the economy. In addition, because it is possible that the slope of the trend may be affected by the crisis, growth losses are computed as the difference between the growth rate after the crisis and the precrisis trend growth rate. The precrisis trend growth rate is defined as the slope of the precrisis trend depicted in Figure 9.2.

Estimating the precrisis trend is challenging because the analysis needs to be insulated from the impact of any immediate precrisis boom or slump, and there is no well-established method for doing this.[3] In this work, a linear trend is estimated through the actual output series during a seven-year precrisis period that ends three years before the onset of the crisis. In a number of cases, however, this procedure yielded negative trend growth rates, implying that output per capita would decline indefinitely even in the absence of a crisis. In these cases, the precrisis window was extended to 20 years before the crisis and this period was used instead.

One appeal of this approach is that it is simple, transparent, and easy to implement for a large set of countries. It is important that its linearity also facilitates the decomposition of output losses into the factors of production, namely losses in capital, labor, and total factor productivity. The use of a seven-year horizon allows the analysis to abstract from the immediate postcrisis fluctuations in out-

---

[2] "Transition countries" are defined based on the classification in the IMF *World Economic Outlook* of May 1993.
[3] See Angkinand (2008) for a review of alternative methods for estimating output losses associated with a crisis.

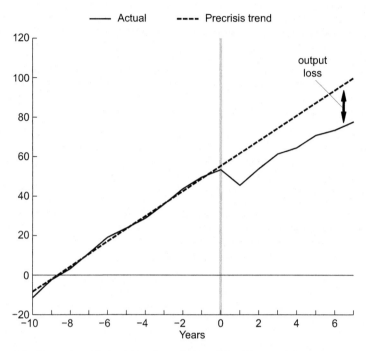

Figure 9.2 Output Loss Methodology Example (Republic of Korea 1997)

Sources: World Bank, *World Development Indicators*; and IMF staff calculations.
Note: First year of crises at $t = 0$. The precrisis trend is estimated up to year $t = -3$, and is extrapolated linearly thereafter. Trend equals 100 in year $t = 7$.

put and focus on medium-term effects. An even longer horizon, such as a 10-year horizon, would have been preferable, but such a horizon would have limited the ability to study a number of crises that occurred in the late 1990s and early 2000s.

The key stylized facts that emerge from the analysis are sobering: output typically does not recover to its precrisis trend. On average, output falls steadily below its precrisis trend until the third year after the crisis, and does not rebound thereafter (Figure 9.3, panel a). The medium-term output losses following banking crises are substantial: seven years after the crisis, output has declined relative to trend by close to 10 percent on average. As the shaded area measuring the 90 percent confidence band indicates, the average decline relative to trend is statistically significant. To put the losses associated with banking crises in perspective, Figure 9.3 also reports the evolution of output relative to trend following currency crises in panel b. Estimated losses following currency crises are much smaller, about one-third of the average loss associated with banking crises.

At the same time, however, the slope of the trend itself does not appear to be affected by the crisis. Although annual growth tends to fall substantially below the precrisis trend during the first two years of the crisis, it is statistically indistin-

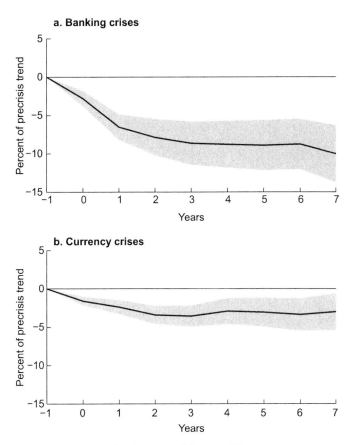

Figure 9.3 Output Evolution after Banking and Currency Crises

Sources: World Bank, *World Development Indicators*; and IMF staff calculations.
Note: Figure reports mean difference form year $t = -1$; 90 percent confidence interval for estimated mean (shaded area);
first year of crisis at $t = 0$.

guishable from the precrisis trend thereafter (Figure 9.4, panel a). The above-normal growth required to return output to the previous trend does not tend to materialize. The four-year average of growth ending in the seventh year after the crisis has a mean difference with respect to the precrisis trend growth rate of only –0.2 percentage point per year, with a standard error of 0.5 percentage point.

In addition, the variation in outcomes is substantial. For example, although the change in output relative to trend following banking crises has a mean of –10 percent, the middle 50 percent of cases had a range of –26 percent to +6 percent. On average there is no rebound to the precrisis trend, but more than a quarter of cases ultimately exceeded the precrisis trend. Similarly, whereas growth tends to return to the precrisis trend rate, the middle 50 percent of cases had a deviation relative to the precrisis growth trend ranging from of –2.8 percentage points to +1.7 percentage points.

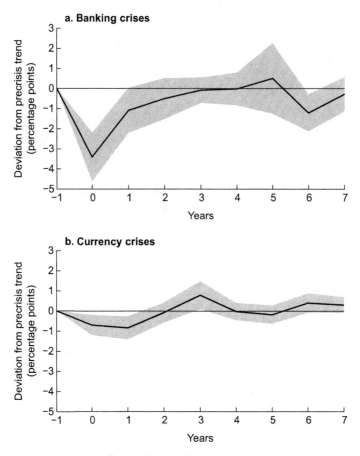

Figure 9.4 Growth Evolution after Banking and Currency Crises

Sources: World Bank, *World Development Indicators*; and IMF staff calculations.
Note: First year of crisis at $t = 0$; 90 percent confidence interval for estimated mean (shaded area).

To set these findings against a significant historical benchmark, the same methodology was applied to a measure of global output in the aftermath of the Great Depression.[4] Following a stock market crash in the United States in 1929, numerous economies experienced banking crises. Consistent with the cross-country results discussed previously, the level of global output did not return to its precrisis trend in the medium term, and was 27 percent below the precrisis trend by 1936, with the bulk of the decline occurring during 1929–32. At the same time, the global growth rate eventually returned to the precrisis trend (by 1934), in line with the more recent crisis episodes.

---

[4] For this exercise, an aggregate purchasing-power-parity-weighted real GDP was constructed of a broad sample of countries going back more than 100 years, with the help of the Maddison (2003) Historical Statistics database.

The robustness of the results was checked by considering alternative approaches to estimating the precrisis trend. First, the calculations were repeated with the precrisis window ending one year rather than three years before the crisis. Second, the precrisis trend was computed based on a longer precrisis window (from $t - 20$ to $t - 3$). Third, the precrisis trend was computed using the real-time growth projections of IMF staff prepared for the spring *World Economic Outlook* in the year before the crisis. Overall, as reported in Appendix 9A, the output losses obtained using the different approaches were statistically indistinguishable from the baseline. Similarly, the result that the growth rate eventually returns to the precrisis trend is robust to using these alternative precrisis trend measures. To understand better which components of output are adversely affected during banking crises, the chapter now turns to analyzing the underlying factors behind the postcrisis medium-term output dynamics.

DECOMPOSITIONS: WHY DOES OUTPUT NOT RECOVER?

This section decomposes medium-term output losses into factor inputs and demand components to help understand which factors drive them. Learning about the underlying forces could provide insights into the likely evolution of output after the banking crises associated with the 2007–09 global crisis, and what type of policies may be relevant to reduce the ultimate losses. Before presenting the results, the main channels through which banking crises may affect output in the medium term are reviewed.

What Are Possible Effects on the Key Sources of Output?

A useful way to examine why output per capita often does not recover to its pre-crisis trend is to analyze what happens to the key elements of an economy's production process—labor inputs (which can be thought of as depending on the employment rate and labor force participation), capital inputs, and total factor productivity. Of course, changes in output components following banking crises could reflect a decline in the productive potential of the economy, but they could also reflect a persistent fall in aggregate demand, although the latter is likely to explain only a small part of the *medium*-term losses. From a theoretical perspective, banking crises may affect these production components in several ways.

First, the medium-term effect of a crisis on labor force participation is uncertain because there are two opposing forces. On the one hand, grim employment prospects may discourage job seekers and prompt them to leave the labor force, especially if there are incentives to retire early. On the other hand, in times of economic hardship, second-income earners may enter the labor force to help compensate for the loss of family income or wealth.[5]

---

[5] There is some evidence suggesting that the additional-worker effect may have played a role in the 2007–09 crisis, because the female participation rate rose as the male participation rate fell in the United States (Daly, Hobijn, and Kwok, 2009).

Second, the medium-term employment rate would be affected adversely if banking crises lead to an increase in the underlying (so-called structural) unemployment rate. For example, the crisis may imply a need for a substantial reallocation of labor across sectors, which can take time and increase medium-term frictional unemployment. Perhaps more important, the large initial increase in the actual unemployment rate induced by the crisis could persist if rigid labor market institutions (strict employment protection laws, generous unemployment benefits, and the like) complicate the task of finding a new job. Long spells without employment may also impair professional and on-the-job skills, making it even more difficult for the long-term unemployed to find jobs, resulting in so-called hysteresis effects (Blanchard and Wolfers, 2000; Nickell, Nunziata, and Ochel, 2005; and Bassanini and Duval, 2006; among others).

Third, a banking crisis may slow capital accumulation by depressing investment over a protracted period. As the supply of credit becomes more limited, firms face tougher financing conditions in the form of tighter lending standards and higher effective costs of borrowing, and profit rates are likely to suffer (Bernanke and Blinder, 1988; and Bernanke and Gertler, 1989). The ability of firms to borrow and invest may be hampered further if the crisis leads to lower asset prices that weaken corporate balance sheets and erode collateral values (Kiyotaki and Moore, 1997). Investment may also suffer if the crisis leads to a sustained increase in uncertainty and risk premiums.

Finally, the effect on total factor productivity is ambiguous based on theoretical considerations, but likely to be negative. On the negative side, as it recovers from the crisis, the financial system may not be able to allocate loanable funds as productively as before the crisis, particularly if high-risk but high-return projects are discouraged by more cautious lending attitudes. In addition, productivity may also suffer as a result of less innovation, given that research and development spending tends to be cut back in bad times (Guellec and van Pottelsberghe, 2001). Also, high-productivity firms may fail because of lack of financing. On the positive side, however, banking crises may have a cleansing effect on the economy by removing inefficient firms and activities and creating incentives to restructure and improve efficiency (Caballero and Hammour, 1994; and Aghion and Saint-Paul, 1998).[6]

What Do the Data Show?

Medium-term output losses following banking crises are decomposed into underlying components using the following approach: The starting point is the observation that the logarithm of output per capita is equal to the weighted sum of the logarithms of labor force participation, the employment rate, the capital-to-labor ratio, and total factor productivity. Note that, because of data limitations, the decompositions into factor components are based on a smaller sample of 27 observations.

---

[6] The underlying concept of "creative destruction" was first introduced by Schumpeter (1942).

Applying the same procedure for estimating precrisis trends and attributing output losses to their underlying components allows output losses to be decomposed into losses attributable to changes in the employment rate, labor force participation, the capital-to-labor ratio, or total factor productivity. Specifically, for each output component, the precrisis trend is estimated for the same precrisis period as the output trend. This approach ensures that, based on the assumed Cobb-Douglas production function, the factor input contributions add up exactly to the total output loss.

The decompositions are based on a Cobb-Douglas production function of the form $Y = AE^{\alpha} K^{1-\alpha}$, where A denotes total factor productivity, E denotes employment, and K denotes the capital stock. The employment share α is assumed to be 0.65. Given the assumption of constant returns to scale, the production function can be expressed in per capita terms by dividing by population, P, yielding

$$\frac{Y}{P} = A \left(\frac{E}{P} \right)^{\alpha} \left(\frac{K}{P} \right)^{1-\alpha}.$$

Finally, taking logs, and noting that

$$\frac{E}{P} = \left(\frac{E}{LF} \times \frac{LF}{P} \right) \text{ and } \frac{K}{P} = \left(\frac{K}{E} \times \frac{E}{LF} \times \frac{LF}{P} \right),$$

in which LF denotes the labor force, yields the decomposition used in the analysis:

$$\log \left(\frac{Y}{P} \right) = (1 - \alpha) \log \left(\frac{K}{E} \right) + \log \left(\frac{E}{LF} \right) + \log \left(\frac{LF}{P} \right) + \log(A),$$

in which $\frac{K}{E}$ represents the capital-to-labor ratio, $\frac{E}{LF}$ is the employment rate, and $\frac{LF}{P}$ is the labor force participation rate. Note that because total factor productivity, A, is obtained as the residual from the decomposition, it may reflect errors in the measurement of the factor inputs.

To complement the analysis, an analogous decomposition is performed for the demand-side components of output: investment, consumption, exports, and imports. Note, however, that because the demand components are additive, the losses of the aggregate demand components do not sum exactly to the total output loss. The results for the two types of output loss decompositions are presented in Figure 9.5 and Figure 9.6. For each component of output, the 90 percent confidence bands are reported to indicate the statistical significance of the estimates.

The decomposition shows that the measured medium-term losses in GDP per capita can be attributed to roughly equal losses in three of the four components of output—the employment rate, the capital-to-labor ratio, and total factor

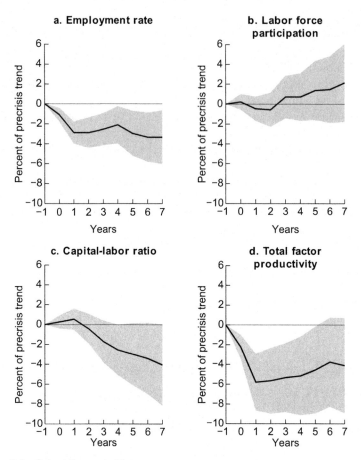

Figure 9.5 Output Decomposition

Sources: World Bank, *World Development Indicators*; and IMF staff calculations.
Note: Figure reports mean difference form year $t = -1$; 90 percent confidence interval for estimated mean (shaded area); first year of crisis at $t = 0$.

productivity (Figure 9.5).[7] Regarding total factor productivity, after a significant initial decline, the level gradually moves closer to the precrisis trend toward the end of the seven-year horizon. This is consistent with the notion of labor hoarding that decreases over time. Nevertheless, the medium-term loss in total factor productivity still accounts for about one-third of the total output loss. Its magnitude, however, is not statistically significant seven years after the crisis, although it is significant in the short term. Regarding the other two key components, the initial loss in the employment rate persists into the medium term, while capital losses worsen steadily. The finding of an adverse impact on the capital-to-labor

---

[7] The contribution of labor force participation is positive, albeit small and statistically insignificant.

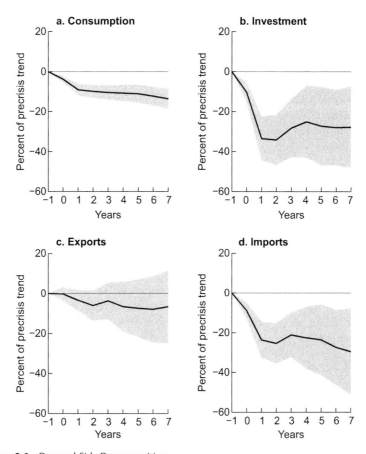

Figure 9.6 Demand-Side Decomposition

Sources: World Bank, *World Development Indicators*; and IMF staff calculations.
Note: Figure reports mean difference form year $t = -1$; 90 percent confidence interval for estimated mean (shaded area);
first year of crisis at $t = 0$.

ratio is consistent with the demand-side decompositions that show a large and significant decline in investment of about 30 percent relative to its precrisis trend (Figure 9.6). The consumption loss is also notable and significant, at about 15 percent.

Overall, the decompositions suggest that higher unemployment rates, slower capital accumulation, and lower productivity growth play an important role in explaining medium-term output losses following banking crises. In other words, output per capita does not recover to its precrisis trend because capital per worker, the unemployment rate, and productivity do not typically return to their precrisis trends within seven years of the crisis. This finding suggests that pre- and postcrisis macroeconomic conditions and policies could play a role in shaping medium-term output dynamics—an issue examined in the next section.

WHAT FACTORS ARE ASSOCIATED WITH MEDIUM-TERM OUTPUT LOSSES?

As illustrated in the previous sections, there is substantial variation in medium-term output losses across banking crises. To explain these variations, this section explores how output losses are related to various factors—such as macroeconomic, structural, and policy conditions—both before and after the crisis. The subsequent section explores the relationship between these factors and postcrisis growth losses.

The analysis of pre- and postcrisis factors proceeds in two steps. First, the results of small-scale ordinary least squares (OLS) regressions that consider several factors at a time are presented. These small-scale regressions typically include one or two variables of interest in addition to key control variables. The robustness of the results is then explored using a large-scale OLS regression that considers all of the factors simultaneously.

In addition to the OLS regressions, Bayesian model averaging (BMA) is also used, which allows an examination of whether the associations found for each variable are robust to including additional controls in *all* the possible ways that those additional controls can be added. The procedure summarizes the results obtained across all possible specifications using two key statistics: the average coefficient value obtained for each variable, and the probability that each variable is statistically "effective" and should be used to predict output losses. A conventional approach in the BMA literature is to refer to a variable as "effective" if its estimated inclusion probability is greater than 50 percent.[8] BMA is particularly useful in this investigation because theory is not sufficiently explicit about which variables should be included in the "true" regression. At the same time, however, BMA has substantial data requirements that reduce by half the number of available observations for this analysis. Thus, both the small-scale results (based on a broad sample) and the larger-scale models (based on a restricted sample) are used.

Do Initial Conditions Help Predict Medium-Term Output Losses?

What are the precrisis factors that might explain the magnitude of the eventual output losses? The analysis examines the importance of a range of macroeconomic, structural, and policy environment variables. The sources of the data are reported in Appendix 9A.

The precrisis output position (which identifies the starting position of output relative to trend) and the initial change in output during the first year of the crisis (which indicates the severity of the crisis in the short term) are potentially important control variables. Both the small-scale OLS results and the BMA analysis indicate that the severity of the crisis, measured by the first-year change

---

[8] For additional details on BMA, see, for example, Hoeting and others (1999), and Masanjala and Papageorgiou (2008).

in output, has strong predictive power for medium-term output losses (Table 9.1, row 20). A 1 percentage point fall in output relative to trend in the first year of the crisis is associated with a 1.1 to 1.8 percentage point gap between output and the precrisis trend by year $t + 7$. This result underscores the notion that banking crises have long-lasting effects on output. At the same time, a depressed level of output relative to trend before the crisis appears to carry over, and is associated with a significantly larger medium-term output loss (Table 9.1, row 19).[9] Based on these results, the two initial output variables are included as controls in all the remaining regressions.

The prominent role of investment and capital losses would suggest that the level and evolution of precrisis investment would be good predictors of the eventual output losses. Regression results provide strong evidence that countries with high precrisis investment-to-GDP ratios, measured as the average investment-to-GDP ratio during the three years before the crisis, tend to have large output losses (Table 9.1, row 1; Figure 9.7). In contrast, the investment gap, defined as the deviation of the investment-to-GDP ratio during the last three years from its historical average, is not statistically significant (Table 9.1, row 2).[10] Potential interpretations of these results are returned to later in the section. Nevertheless, the precrisis investment share result is particularly robust and holds even after controlling for the level of the current account balance. This outcome suggests that countries with high investment rates tend to experience larger output declines following banking crises, irrespective of whether the investment is financed by foreign or domestic savings.

By limiting the room for policy maneuvering, the buildup of macroeconomic imbalances may also imply higher medium-term output losses after a crisis. The analysis considers the precrisis levels and dynamics of several variables—such as inflation, the current account balance, the fiscal balance, the real exchange rate, the real interest rate—that may capture the notion of macroeconomic imbalances.[11] The evidence is mixed that rising imbalances, and by implication, more limited policy space that would constrain the ability of countries to run countercyclical macroeconomic policies, are associated with larger output losses. In particular, the results based on the small-scale regressions suggest that countries with

---

[9] Note that, in the three years before a banking crisis episode, the level of output is, on average, below its trend, suggesting that banking crises are not typically preceded by a precrisis boom. In the sample of 88 banking crises, the average deviation is about –3 percent.

[10] The precrisis historical average level is based on the seven-year period ending three years before the crisis.

[11] The dynamics are captured by considering the deviations of these variables from their country-specific historical averages during the precrisis period (the gaps). Using country-specific averages allows for the possibility that different countries may have different explicit or implicit inflation targets or fiscal rules. For example, a 3 percent inflation rate may provide less space for monetary easing in a country with inflation normally at 1 percent than in a country with an inflation norm of 5 percent. For each variable, the gap value is constructed as a deviation of the average precrisis value (from $t - 3$ to $t - 1$) from the country-specific average value (from $t - 10$ to $t - 3$). Using government debt to measure fiscal space was not possible for the sample of countries considered here because of limited data availability.

TABLE 9.1.

Output Losses versus Initial Conditions
(Dependent variable: output at t + 7 in percent of precrisis trend)

	(1)	(2)	(3)	(4)	(5)	(6)	(7)	(8)	(9)	(10)	(11)	(12)	(13)
(1) Investment/GDP	-0.989*** [-3.120]											-1.211*** [-2.825]	-1.602 (1.000)
(2) Investment/GDP gap		0.335 [0.889]										-1.049 [-1.671]	-0.388 (0.381)
(3) Current account/GDP			0.765** [2.016]									0.0632 [0.167]	0.000 (0.000)
(4) Current account/GDP gap			0.964 [1.593]									0.525 [0.571]	0.189 (0.196)
(5) Inflation				0.116 [1.500]								0.00535 [0.0632]	-0.002 (0.042)
(6) Inflation gap				-0.196** [-2.243]								-0.0627 [-0.475]	-0.032 (0.258)
(7) Fiscal balance					0.501 [1.205]							-0.541 [-1.102]	0.000 (0.000)
(8) Fiscal balance gap					1.256** [2.042]							0.480 [0.796]	0.013 (0.022)
(9) Real exchange rate gap						-0.176 [-1.274]						⋮	⋮
(10) Real interest rate gap						-0.127 [-0.166]						⋮	⋮
(11) Log (PPP GDP per capita)							0.0175 [0.736]					⋮	⋮
(12) Credit/GDP								-0.152 [-1.616]				0.0283 [0.635]	0.000 (0.000)
(13) Credit/GDP gap								0.204 [0.503]				-0.0316 [-0.299]	0.005 (0.073)
												0.438 [0.993]	0.027 (0.109)

	(1)	(2)	(3)	(4)	(5)	(6)	(7)	(8)	(9)	(10)	(11)	(12)	(13)
(14) Currency crisis									-0.141* [-1.878]	-0.155 [-1.483]			-0.082 (0.558)
(15) U.S. Treasury bill rate									0.543 [0.528]	1.011 [0.999]			0.026 (0.038)
(16) External demand shock									-0.100 [-1.200]	-0.113* [-1.960]			-0.012 (0.089)
(17) Financial openness/GDP									0.059*** [3.031]	0.00750 [0.499]			0.002 (0.094)
(18) Trade openness/GDP									-0.133 [-1.549]	-0.0297 [-0.421]			0.000 (0.000)
(19) Precrisis output	1.601*** [3.844]	1.328*** [3.875]	1.598*** [4.855]	1.027*** [2.691]	0.950*** [3.174]	1.425** [2.435]	1.538*** [3.639]	0.900*** [2.700]	1.685*** [3.931]	1.632*** [3.807]	0.751** [2.175]	0.901 [1.437]	0.916 (0.871)
(20) First-year output change	1.681*** [3.051]	1.583*** [3.551]	1.573*** [3.608]	1.781*** [3.406]	1.841*** [3.547]	1.069 [0.992]	1.752*** [3.039]	1.665*** [3.280]	1.552*** [2.694]	1.799*** [3.046]	1.289*** [3.379]		1.175 (1.000)
(21) Constant term	-0.0558** [-2.652]	0.162** [2.156]	-0.0181 [-0.726]	-0.0929** [-2.759]	-0.0511* [-1.970]	-0.0662 [-1.182]	-0.0771* [-2.036]	-0.0214 [-0.806]	0.0451* [-2.003]	-0.0863 [-1.271]	-0.0486 [-1.159]	0.125 [0.791]	0.337 (1.000)
Number of observations	88	85	80	87	81	26	88	77	88	88	52	44	44
R-squared	0.334	0.408	0.409	0.334	0.369	0.256	0.338	0.295	0.353	0.339	0.314	0.763	...

Source: IMF staff calculations.

Note: PPP = purchasing power parity. Columns 1–12 report estimation results based on ordinary least squares with robust t-statistics in square brackets. The symbols ***, **, and * indicate significance at the 1, 5, and 10 percent levels, respectively. Column 13 reports estimation results based on Bayesian model averaging with the estimated probability of inclusion of each variable in parentheses. The term "gap" denotes the deviation of the variable from its precrisis historical average (years t–10 to t–17, where t denotes the crisis year) during the last three years preceding the crisis.

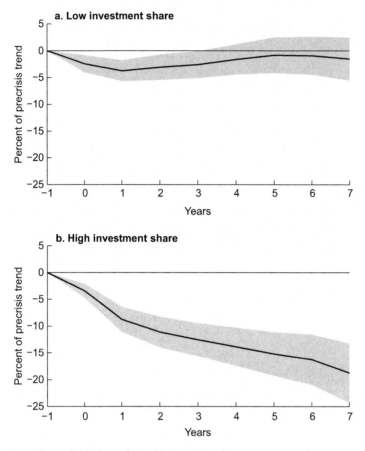

Figure 9.7   Output Evolution and Precrisis Investment Share

Sources: World Bank, *World Development Indicators*; and IMF staff calculations.

Note: Figure reports mean difference from year $t = -1$ for countries with precrisis investment share below median (panel a) and above median (panel b); 90 percent confidence interval for estimated mean (shaded area); first year of crisis at $t = 0$.

larger current account deficits, rising inflation, and a deteriorating fiscal balance before the crisis experienced significantly larger output losses (Table 9.1, rows 3, 6, 8). But the BMA analysis (Table 9.1, column 13) suggests that the evidence is strong only for rising inflation before the crisis. It is important to bear in mind that more policy space does not necessarily mean that it was used—an issue returned to later.[12]

An interesting finding is that postcrisis output losses are not significantly correlated with the level of income (Table 9.1, row 11). In fact, the evolution of

---

[12]Two other domestic policy variables—the real exchange rate and the real interest rate before the crisis, measured relative to their historic averages—do not appear to have predictive power for medium-term output losses (Table 9.1, row 9 and row 10).

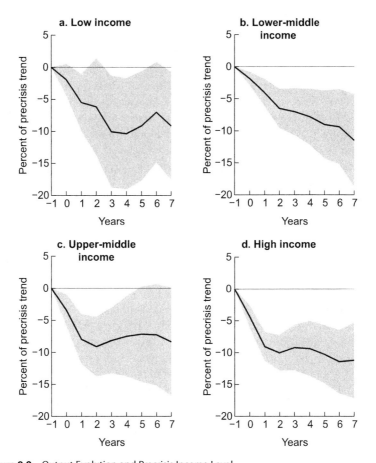

Figure 9.8 Output Evolution and Precrisis Income Level

Sources: World Bank, *World Development Indicators*; and IMF staff calculations.

Note: Figure reports mean difference from year $t = -1$ by quartile of real purchasing-power-parity GDP per capita; 90 percent confidence interval for estimated mean (shaded area); first year of crisis at $t = 0$.

output after banking crises for high-income, middle-income, and low-income countries is similar (Figure 9.8). This finding is consistent with the notion that banking crises represent an "equal opportunity menace" (Reinhart and Rogoff, 2009b) for countries across the income distribution. At the same time, there is mixed evidence that a higher precrisis level of financial development is associated with larger output losses (Table 9.1, row 12).[13]

Currency crises that coincide with banking crises, so-called twin crises, are robustly associated with larger output losses (Table 9.1, row 14). The results for

---

[13] The analysis also considers whether an increase in the credit-to-GDP ratio relative to each country's own historical average level (the credit-to-GDP gap) plays a role, finding it to be statistically insignificant. The question of whether there is a nonlinear link between the level of financial deepening and output losses is left for further research.

the openness indicators, however, are mixed (Table 9.1, row 17 and row 18). The small-scale regression approach suggests that financial openness is associated with smaller losses, and is consistent with work that finds that deeper financial integration reduces the risk of a sudden stop in capital flows, and enhances the ability to smooth spending (Calvo, Izquierdo, and Mejia, 2008; and Abiad, Leigh, and Mody, 2009). However, the evidence is weaker based on the broader specification. Evidence for trade is even weaker. Turning to external conditions, the level of the U.S. Treasury bill rate before the crisis is not found to be a significant predictor of output losses (Table 9.1, row 15). The evidence that an adverse external demand shock occurring at the time of the banking crisis is correlated with larger output losses is mixed (Table 9.1, row 16).[14]

Finally, the precrisis levels of various structural policy reform indicators are not significantly correlated with medium-term output losses, and are not presented in Table 9.1. The discussion returns to the possible role of structural policies in the next section, which considers whether countries that undertook structural reforms following the crisis experienced smaller output losses.[15]

What key points should be taken away from these regression results? The empirical analysis suggests that the first-year loss is important in predicting the eventual output losses following a banking crisis. This outcome is consistent with the notion that output dynamics are especially persistent following large shocks. What could explain this? A possible explanation is that bankruptcies lead to fire sales of capital assets that have significant sunk costs and take time to rebuild. Also, an impaired financial system may need time to heal and intermediate financial capital effectively, and labor and product market rigidities could impede the necessary reallocation of labor and capital following a crisis. These interpretations are consistent with the finding that all factors of production contribute to medium-term output losses.

Related to the dynamics of capital accumulation, the finding that the precrisis investment rate is a robust predictor of the postcrisis output loss is particularly striking. This finding, together with the earlier result that investment and capital deepening decline in the medium term following banking crises, is consistent

---

[14] The external demand shock is measured as a dummy variable that equals 1 in year t whenever partner-country growth from year t through $t + 4$ is in the lowest 5 percent of the entire sample. Partner-country growth is defined as the per capita output growth of a country's trading partners weighted by their shares in the country's total exports.

[15] The analysis draws on the database of structural reforms prepared by the Research Department of the IMF. The database covers 150 advanced and developing countries and eight sectors. This chapter uses the domestic financial sector reform index (which includes measures of securities markets and banking sector reforms) and the capital account liberalization index (which summarizes a broad set of restrictions), the trade liberalization index (based on average tariffs), and the fiscal sector reform index (based on tax rates and the efficiency of revenue collection and public spending). It also uses various measures of labor market flexibility, including on employment protection, unemployment benefit replacement ratios, and tax wedges. See IMF (2008) and Giuliano, Mishra, and Spilimbergo (2009) for more details. The indices for product market reforms were not used in the analysis because of insufficient data coverage.

with a number of potential interpretations.[16] In some cases, it may be that the output loss reflects the unwinding of excessive investment built up over a protracted period. To the extent that some investment during the precrisis period was wasteful, output losses may have taken place even without a crisis, but gradually. However, a full investigation into the underlying reasons for the remarkably strong correlation between the precrisis investment level and medium-term output losses is an issue that merits further investigation but is beyond the scope of this chapter.

After the Crisis: What Is Associated with Smaller Output Losses?

What role do policies have in mitigating the ultimate output loss after the crisis has hit? It is important to acknowledge that the following discussion seeks to identify patterns rather than establish causality between postcrisis output evolution and policies. As discussed in the literature, the two-way relationship between postcrisis policies and outcomes complicates any causal inference. For example, is it that financial reform during or after a banking crisis leads to increased financial intermediation and a lower output loss? Or, that a lower output loss leads to higher demand and thus higher financial intermediation and also gives the authorities the policy space to implement important financial sector reforms? These difficult questions cannot be answered within this chapter's regression framework.

The discussion focuses on domestic macroeconomic policies and structural reforms, and on external conditions and policies abroad. As in the analysis of precrisis factors, this section present the regression results (Table 9.2) based on both full-sample OLS and restricted-sample BMA analysis. As before, all regressions control for key initial output variables.

Short-term demand management policies (fiscal and monetary) implemented after the crisis has hit may play a role both in reducing the size of the initial output loss and in aiding the recovery. To measure changes in discretionary fiscal policy, the analysis follows the approach of IMF (2009a) and uses the growth in real government consumption. Given data availability, the monetary policy stance is measured as the change in real lending rates. In both cases, to capture the short-term response of macroeconomic policies, the variables are computed for the crisis year and the subsequent three years. The variables are designed to measure a notion of stimulus (rather than policy space), and thus differ from those used in the precrisis analysis. The findings are that a stronger short-term fiscal policy response (a larger increase in government consumption) is significantly associated

---

[16] Note that the correlation between the precrisis investment share and the medium-term output loss is largely a reflection of large postcrisis investment losses. In particular, additional regression results not reported here reveal that although a large precrisis investment share is strongly correlated with medium-term investment losses, it is only weakly correlated with medium-term consumption and export losses.

TABLE 9.2.

Output Losses versus Postcrisis Conditions and Policies
(Dependent variable: output at $t + 7$ in percent of precrisis trend)

	(1)	(2)	(3)	(4)	(5)	(6)	(7)	(8)	(9)	(10)	(11)	(12)	(13)
(1) Real government consumption growth	0.202** [2.520]									0.244* [1.843]		0.405** [2.264]	0.263 (0.648)
(2) Change in real interest rate		−0.0850 [−0.404]								−0.493** [−2.280]		−0.580 [−1.577]	−0.530 (0.708)
(3) Real exchange rate appreciation			0.135* [1.785]							−0.0105 [−0.0753]		−0.418* [−2.047]	−0.038 (0.166)
(4) Change in capital account liberalization				0.166*** [4.627]							0.147** [2.290]	0.0297 [0.433]	0.007 (0.085)
(5) Change in financial liberalization index					0.108*** [2.583]						0.0170 [0.302]	0.149* [1.769]	0.002 (0.044)
(6) Change in trade liberalization index						−0.0456 [−0.950]					−0.0632 [−1.123]	−0.122 [−1.506]	−0.013 (0.149)
(7) Change in government efficiency index							−0.00500 −0.0774				0.0132 [0.213]	0.129* [2.044]	0.078 (0.608)
(8) U.S. Treasury bill rate								−1.404 [−1.012]		0.490 [0.178]		−4.459 [−1.524]	−2.820 (0.400)
(9) External demand shock									−0.960*** [−3.156]	−1.161 [−1.611]		−1.073 [−1.668]	−0.415 (0.411)
(10) Precrisis output	1.213*** [4.666]	1.038*** [2.791]	1.371*** [4.292]	1.079*** [3.537]	0.997*** [4.358]	1.384*** [4.456]	1.162*** [2.398]	1.601*** [3.783]	1.753*** [4.427]	1.137*** [3.453]	1.124*** [3.061]	0.907 [1.687]	0.143 (0.184)
(11) First-year output change	2.032*** [3.396]	2.107*** [2.941]	1.750*** [2.884]	2.191*** [3.560]	2.262*** [3.529]	2.145*** [3.526]	1.749*** [2.591]	1.714*** [3.158]	1.875*** [3.558]	2.365*** [2.667]	2.220*** [3.330]	3.136*** [2.889]	2.693 (1.000)
(12) Constant term	0.0560* [−2.065]	0.0470* [−2.059]	−0.0341 [−1.471]	0.0929*** [−4.010]	0.0882** [−3.510]	−0.0198 [−0.869]	−0.0535 [−1.485]	0.0227 [0.284]	−0.00409 [−0.177]	−0.0366 [−0.260]	−0.0789* [−1.964]	0.0639 [0.385]	0.052 (1.000)
Number of observations	77	59	74	65	65	78	53	88	88	50	49	30	30
R-squared	0.398	0.283	0.342	0.459	0.397	0.388	0.281	0.344	0.396	0.506	0.450	0.709	⋯

Source: IMF staff calculations.

Note: Columns 1–12 report estimation results based on ordinary least squares with robust t-statistics in square brackets. The symbols ***, **, and * indicate significance at the 1, 5, and 10 percent levels, respectively. Column 13 reports estimation results based on Bayesian model averaging with the estimated probability of inclusion of each variable in parentheses. Structural reform variables (trade, financial capital account, and government efficiency) measure change in index from t to $t + 7$.

with smaller medium-term output losses (Table 9.2, row 1).[17] The evidence on the monetary policy stance is mixed, possibly reflecting a weaker monetary policy transmission mechanism after banking crises. A decline in real interest rates is associated with smaller output losses, but only in some specifications (Table 9.2, row 2). There is also mixed evidence that real exchange rate depreciations are associated with smaller output losses (Table 9.2, row 3).

Advancing structural reforms may also play a role in boosting output during the postcrisis period. The exercise considers reform efforts in several areas, such as domestic financial reform, capital account and trade liberalization, and structural fiscal reforms. In each case, the reform effort is measured as the change in various indices mentioned earlier during the postcrisis period (rather than the levels that were used in the precrisis analysis).[18] Overall, the evidence that structural reform efforts are significantly associated with smaller output losses is mixed. Liberalization of the capital account is highly correlated with smaller output losses in small-scale regressions, although its statistical significance declines when considered in larger-scale frameworks (Table 9.2, row 4). Domestic financial reforms are also significantly positively associated with output losses in small-scale regressions, but less so in larger-scale frameworks (Table 9.2, row 5). Trade liberalization is not significantly related to output losses (Table 9.2, row 6). Finally, there is some positive evidence on the link between improvements in government efficiency and output losses, although the increased significance of this structural variable in the broader specifications appears to be partly due to the change in the sample composition (the number of observations drops to 30).

Finally, policies and conditions abroad may also be important in reducing output losses by improving the external environment during the postcrisis period. The results indicate that larger domestic output losses are significantly related to the occurrence of adverse external demand shocks during the postcrisis period (Table 9.2, row 9). In addition, there is some evidence that larger output losses are significantly associated with higher global short-term interest rates (Table 9.2, row 8).[19]

How should these empirical findings be interpreted? Overall, the findings suggest that expansionary short-term macroeconomic policies are associated with

---

[17] The results imply that raising government consumption by 1 percent of GDP is associated with a reduction in the medium-term output loss of about 1.5 percentage points. The change in government consumption, rather than the change in tax revenue or the fiscal balance, is used as a measure of fiscal stimulus because it lessens reverse-causality concerns. Measuring fiscal stimulus based on the change in tax revenue or the change in the fiscal balance would cause difficulties. A larger deterioration in output implies a greater deterioration in tax revenue and the fiscal balance, complicating the interpretation of the regression coefficients. As expected, repeating the analysis using the change in the fiscal balance yielded a regression coefficient that was statistically indistinguishable from zero.

[18] Regarding labor market liberalization indicators, data availability is limited for the sample of banking crisis countries. Moreover, when data are available, there is often little change post crisis. For these reasons, results for postcrisis labor market indicators are not reported.

[19] Unlike in the small-scale regressions, the global interest rate is significantly related to output losses in the large-scale OLS regression and has a relatively high probability of inclusion (0.63) in the BMA framework.

smaller medium-term output losses. This is consistent with the notion that countercyclical fiscal and monetary policies may help dampen path-dependence effects by cushioning the downturn after the crisis, which carry over into smaller measured output losses in the medium term.

The relationship between postcrisis structural policy reforms and output losses is somewhat weaker. However, this could be due to well-known difficulties in measuring the timing, magnitude, and sequencing of structural reforms,[20] as well as the possibility that structural reforms and capacity building may take a longer time to bear fruit by increasing output. At the same time, the spillover effects of global conditions may be important, given the strong association between the external environment and the eventual output losses.

Overall, the regression analysis provides suggestive evidence that domestic fiscal and monetary stimulus and favorable global conditions may mitigate medium-term output losses. There is also some mixed evidence on the beneficial role of structural policy reform. However, much can still be learned about the processes and interactions associated with output losses following banking crises.

IS THIS TIME DIFFERENT?

So far, this chapter has assessed macroeconomic performance after previous banking crises—those before the 2007–09 global financial crisis. A natural question is whether, in economies that suffered banking crises during 2007–09, output has evolved in line with the historical pattern found for earlier crises.

The analysis now estimates medium-term output losses for the 25 economies that entered banking crises during 2007–09 and compares them with those of previous banking crises.[21] Exactly the same approach as described above is used here.

The results suggest that the most recent banking crisis economies have experienced output losses that are larger than the historical average. As of 2012, output is, on average, about 17 percent below the precrisis trend (Figure 9.9), which compares with an average output loss for previous crises after five years of 9 percent. In addition, some evidence suggests that the output losses may be longer lasting. About one-third of previous banking crises saw output return to or exceed the precrisis trend within five years. In contrast, as of 2012, none of the 25 recent banking crisis economies (except Mongolia) have seen output return to or exceed

---

[20] Note that measurement error in the structural reform indicators will bias the regression coefficients toward zero, making it more difficult to find that the results are statistically significant. Also, the size of the bias depends directly on the magnitude of the measurement error, which is likely to be much larger for unobserved structural reform indicators (such as labor market flexibility or financial sector reform) than for macroeconomic variables (such as government consumption or interest rates).

[21] The 25 systemic banking crises are those that Laeven and Valencia (2012) identify as having begun during 2007–09: Austria, Belgium, Denmark, France, Germany, Greece, Hungary, Iceland, Ireland, Italy, Kazakhstan, Latvia, Luxembourg, Mongolia, the Netherlands, Nigeria, Portugal, the Russian Federation, Slovenia, Spain, Sweden, Switzerland, Ukraine, the United Kingdom, and the United States.

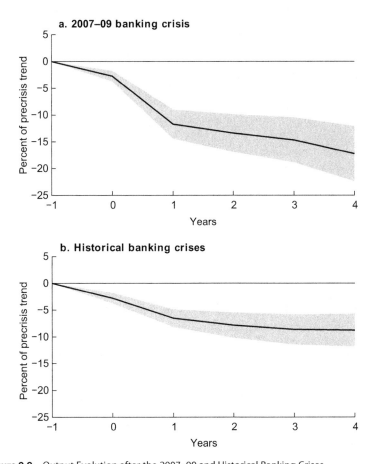

Figure 9.9   Output Evolution after the 2007–09 and Historical Banking Crises

Sources: World Bank, *World Development Indicators*; and IMF staff calculations.
Note: Figure reports mean difference from year $t = -1$; 90 percent confidence interval for estimated mean (shaded area); first year of crisis at $t = 0$.

the precrisis trend. Overall, therefore, the output losses appear to be larger than in the past, and may be more persistent.

CONCLUSIONS

Based on an investigation of 88 historical banking crises in a wide range of economies, this chapter finds that economic activity tends to contract sharply following such crises, with no rebound to the precrisis trend in the medium term. On average, seven years after the crisis, output has declined by about 10 percent relative to the precrisis trend. The above-average growth needed to return output to the previous trend does not tend to materialize, although growth does eventually return to its precrisis rate. Also, the depressed path of output tends to result from reductions of roughly equal proportions in the employment rate, the capital-to-labor ratio, and total factor productivity.

A large variation in outcomes across countries is also found, with output eventually returning to or even exceeding the precrisis trend in one-third of cases. An exploration of this variation in outcomes finds that medium-term output losses are strongly correlated with conditions at the onset of the crisis, including the severity of the initial contraction in activity, the occurrence of twin banking and currency crises, and a high precrisis level of investment. Short-term fiscal and monetary stimulus is also associated with smaller medium-term output losses. There is also some evidence that structural policy reforms implemented after the onset of the crisis can play a supportive role. Although the contemporaneous nature of these variables complicates a causal interpretation, the results are consistent with the notion that policies implemented in the aftermath of a crisis can help to limit the medium-term damage.

Finally, the performance of economies that experienced banking crises during 2007–09 bears a strong resemblance to previous banking crises. These economies have suffered even deeper output losses, as of 2012 averaging 17 percent relative to the precrisis trend. Moreover, there is little evidence of output returning to the precrisis trend. The greater output losses may reflect the highly synchronized nature of the recent episodes, as part of the global financial crisis, and in some cases, the additional role of sovereign debt problems. We leave a further investigation of the recent crises to future research.

APPENDIX 9A. DATA AND ROBUSTNESS RESULTS

This appendix provides details on the data used in the analysis, a list of the 88 banking crisis episodes considered in the analysis (Table 9A.1), and the results of robustness exercises on measuring output losses.

Data Sources

The main data sources for this chapter are the IMF's World Economic Outlook (WEO) and International Financial Statistics (IFS) databases, and the World Bank's *World Development Indicators* (WDI). Additional data sources are listed below.

Data on real GDP and its demand components are from the WDI, and are spliced with WEO data for observations after 2007 for which WDI data are unavailable. The current account balance, the GDP deflator, and the fiscal balance are also taken from the WEO, while the exchange rate series are taken from the IFS. The domestic real interest rate is defined as the difference between the nominal lending rate, taken from the IFS, and GDP-deflator inflation.

For the growth accounting exercises, the capital stock data are taken from Bosworth and Collins (2003). For observations not included in the Bosworth and Collins data set, the capital stock is constructed using the perpetual inventory method, with a depreciation rate of 5 percent, and using real investment data. The employment and labor force data come from the WEO.

TABLE 9A.1

List of Historical Banking Crisis Episodes

Country	Year	Output loss	Country	Year	Output loss
Algeria	1990	−14	Jordan	1989	−29
Argentina	1980	−15	Kenya	1985	−8
Argentina	1989	19	Kenya	1992	−16
Argentina	1995	−12	Korea	1997	−23
Argentina	2001	3	Kuwait	1982	23
Bangladesh	1987	13	Liberia	1991	−10
Benin	1988	−11	Madagascar	1988	5
Bolivia	1986	1	Malaysia	1997	−38
Bolivia	1994	5	Mali	1987	−8
Brazil	1990	−12	Mauritania	1984	−10
Brazil	1994	3	Mexico	1981	−28
Burkina Faso	1990	1	Mexico	1994	9
Burundi	1994	−36	Morocco	1980	−26
Cameroon	1987	−86	Nepal	1988	13
Cameroon	1995	9	Nicaragua	1990	18
Central African Rep.	1976	−18	Nicaragua	2000	7
Central African Rep.	1995	18	Niger	1983	−44
Chad	1983	40	Nigeria	1991	3
Chad	1992	−35	Norway	1991	0
Chile	1976	6	Panama	1988	0
Chile	1981	7	Paraguay	1995	−26
Colombia	1982	−13	Peru	1983	−42
Colombia	1998	−15	Philippines	1983	−33
Congo, Dem. Rep. of	1983	−8	Philippines	1997	17
Congo, Dem. Rep. of	1991	−69	Senegal	1988	−7
Congo, Dem. Rep. of	1994	−32	Sierra Leone	1990	−54
Congo, Republic of	1992	−37	Spain	1977	−37
Costa Rica	1987	11	Sri Lanka	1989	2
Costa Rica	1994	3	Swaziland	1995	−23
Côte d'Ivoire	1988	−19	Sweden	1991	−14
Ecuador	1982	−32	Thailand	1983	8
Ecuador	1998	8	Thailand	1997	−52
Egypt	1980	−12	Togo	1993	8
El Salvador	1989	38	Tunisia	1991	16
Finland	1991	−15	Turkey	1982	1
Ghana	1982	−2	Turkey	2000	7
Guinea	1993	6	Uganda	1994	18
Guinea-Bissau	1995	−39	United States	1988	0
Haiti	1994	−11	Uruguay	1981	−31
India	1993	3	Uruguay	2002	11
Indonesia	1997	−47	Venezuela	1994	−7
Israel	1977	−34	Vietnam	1997	3
Jamaica	1996	−32	Zambia	1995	17
Japan	1997	−12	Zimbabwe	1995	−21

Note: Table reports first year of banking crisis, and output loss in percent of precrisis trend seven years after the crisis (log points).

Financial development is measured using the ratio of bank credit to GDP, following Abiad, Dell'Ariccia, and Li (2011). Bank credit to the private nonfinancial sector is taken from the IFS. Breaks in these data are identified using the IFS *Country Notes* publication, and data are growth-spliced at these points.

Financial openness is calculated as the sum of foreign assets and foreign liabilities divided by GDP, using the External Wealth of Nations Mark II database of Lane and Milesi-Ferretti (2006). Trade openness is defined as the sum of exports and imports divided by GDP. Partner-country growth, used to compute the external demand shocks, is taken from the WEO, and the three-month U.S. Treasury bill rate is obtained from Thomson Reuters Datastream.

The structural reform indicators measuring trade liberalization, capital account liberalization, financial liberalization, and government efficiency come

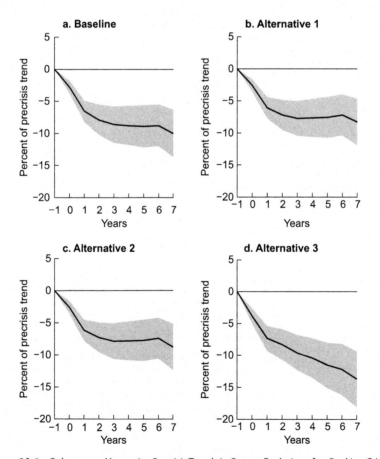

Figure 9A.1 Robustness: Alternative Precrisis Trends in Output Evolution after Banking Crises

Sources: World Bank, *World Development Indicators*; and IMF staff calculations.
Note: Figure reports the estimated mean difference from year *t* = –1; 90 percent confidence interval for estimated mean (shaded area); first year of crisis at *t* = 0.

from the IMF, and are described in greater detail in Giuliano, Mishra, and Spilimbergo (2009) and IMF (2008).

Robustness: Alternative Measures of Output Losses

The baseline measure of the output loss is compared with three alternative measures based on the following different versions of the precrisis trend.

- *Alternative 1. Precrisis window ending one year before crisis.* The precrisis trend is computed as in the baseline, except that the estimation window for the precrisis trend ends one year before the crisis, rather than three years before the crisis as it does in the baseline.

- *Alternative 2. Longer estimation window.* The estimate of the precrisis trend is obtained based on a longer precrisis window going back 20 years before the crisis and ending 3 years before the crisis.

- *Alternative 3. Precrisis trend based on real-time IMF staff forecasts.* The output losses were recomputed using the real-time medium-term growth projections of IMF staff prepared for the spring *World Economic Outlook* in the year before the crisis. In particular, the precrisis trend growth rate is defined as the IMF country desk forecast for real GDP growth in year $t = 4$ made in year $t = -1$, where $t = 0$ is the year of the crisis. Note that these real-time forecasts were only available for the post-1989 period.

Overall, as Figure 9A.1 reports, the losses obtained using the different approaches were highly correlated, and all confirm the finding of large and statistically significant output losses after banking crises. The 90 percent confidence bands for each measure overlap with the baseline measure.

REFERENCES

Abiad, A., G. Dell'Ariccia, and B. Li, 2011, "Creditless Recoveries," IMF Working Paper 11/58 (Washington: International Monetary Fund).

Abiad, Abdul, Daniel Leigh, and Ashoka Mody, 2009, "Financial Integration, Capital Mobility, and Income Convergence," *Economic Policy*, Vol. 24, No. 58, pp. 241–305.

Aghion, Philippe, and Gilles Saint-Paul, 1998, "On the Virtue of Bad Times: An Analysis of the Interaction between Economic Fluctuations and Productivity Growth," *Macroeconomic Dynamics*, Vol. 2, No. 3, pp. 322–44.

Angkinand, Apanard P., 2008, "Output Loss and Recovery from Banking and Currency Crises: Estimation Issues" (Springfield, Illinois: University of Illinois).

Bassanini, Andrea, and Romain Duval, 2006, "The Determinants of Unemployment across OECD Countries: Reassessing the Role of Policies and Institutions," *OECD Economic Studies*, Vol. 2006, No. 1, pp. 7–86.

———, and Alan S. Blinder, 1988, "Credit, Money, and Aggregate Demand," *American Economic Review*, Vol. 78, No. 2 (May), pp. 435–39.

Bernanke, Ben S., and Mark Gertler, 1989, "Agency Costs, Net Worth, and Business Fluctuations," *American Economic Review*, Vol. 79, No. 1 (March), pp. 14–31.

———, 1995, "Inside the Black Box: The Credit Channel of Monetary Policy Transmission," *Journal of Economic Perspectives*, Vol. 9, No. 4 (Autumn), pp. 27–48.

Blanchard, Olivier, and Justin Wolfers, 2000, "The Role of Shocks and Institutions in the Rise of European Unemployment: The Aggregate Evidence," *Economic Journal*, Vol. 110, No. 462 (March), pp. 1–33.

Bordo, Michael, 2006, "Sudden Stops, Financial Crises, and Original Sin in Emerging Countries: Déjà vu?" NBER Working Paper No. 12393 (Cambridge, Massachusetts: National Bureau of Economic Research).

Bosworth, Barry P., and Susan M. Collins, 2003, "The Empirics of Growth: An Update," *Brookings Papers on Economic Activity*, Vol. 2 (2003), pp. 113–206.

Boyd, John H., Sungkyu Kwak, and Bruce Smith, 2005, "The Real Output Losses Associated with Modern Banking Crises," *Journal of Money, Credit, and Banking*, Vol. 37, No. 6, pp. 977–99.

Caballero, Ricardo, and Mohammed Hammour, 1994, "The Cleansing Effect of Recessions," *American Economic Review*, Vol. 84, No. 5, pp. 1350–68.

Calvo, Guillermo A., Alejandro Izquierdo, and Luis-Fernando Mejía, 2008, "Systemic Sudden Stops: The Relevance of Balance-Sheet Effects and Financial Integration," NBER Working Paper No. 14026 (Cambridge, Massachusetts: National Bureau of Economic Research).

Cerra, Valerie, and Sweta Saxena, 2008, "Growth Dynamics: The Myth of Economic Recovery," *American Economic Review*, Vol. 98, No. 1, pp. 439–57.

Daly, Mary, Bart Hobijn, and Joyce Kwok, 2009, "Labor Supply Response to Changes in Wealth and Credit," *FRBSF Economic Letter*, January 30.

Furceri, Davide, and Annabelle Mourougane, 2009, "The Effect of Financial Crises on Potential Output: New Empirical Evidence from OECD countries," OECD Economics Department Working Paper No. 699 (Paris: Organization for Economic Cooperation and Development).

Giuliano, Paola, Prachi Mishra, and Antonio Spilimbergo, 2009, "Democracy and Reforms," IZA Discussion Paper No. 4032 (Bonn: Institute for the Study of Labor).

Guellec, Dominique, and Bruno van Pottelsberghe de la Potterie, 2008, "R&D and Productivity Growth: Panel Data Analysis for 16 OECD Countries," *OECD Economic Studies*, Vol. 2001, No. 2, pp. 103–25.

Gupta, Poonam, Deepak Mishra, and Ratna Sahay, 2007, "Behavior of Output during Currency Crises," *Journal of International Economics*, Vol. 72, No. 2, pp. 428–50.

Haugh, David, Patrice Ollivaud, and David Turner, 2009, "The Macroeconomic Consequences of Banking Crises in OECD Countries," OECD Economics Department Working Paper No. 683 (Paris: Organization for Economic Cooperation and Development).

Hoeting, Jennifer A., David Madigan, Adrian E. Raftery, and Chris T. Volinsky, 1999, "Bayesian Model Averaging: A Tutorial," *Statistical Science*, Vol. 14, No. 4, pp. 382–401.

Hutchison, Michael, and Ilan Noy, 2002, "How Bad Are Twins? Output Costs of Currency and Banking Crises," *Journal of Money, Credit, and Banking*, Vol. 37, No. 4, pp. 725–52.

International Monetary Fund (IMF), 2008, "Structural Reforms and Economic Performance in Advanced and Developing Countries" (Washington: International Monetary Fund). http://www.imf.org/external/np/res/docs/2008/0608.htm.

———, 2009a, "From Recession to Recovery: How Soon and How Strong?" in *World Economic Outlook*, April (Washington: International Monetary Fund).

———, 2009b, "What's the Damage? Medium-Term Output Dynamics after Financial Crisis," in *World Economic Outlook*, October (Washington: International Monetary Fund).

Kiyotaki, Nobuhiro, and John Moore, 1997, "Credit Cycles," *Journal of Political Economy*, Vol. 105, No. 2 (April), pp. 211–48.

Laeven, Luc, and Fabian Valencia, 2008, "Systemic Banking Crises: A New Database," IMF Working Paper 08/224 (Washington: International Monetary Fund).

———, 2012, "Systemic Banking Crises Database: An Update," IMF Working Paper 12/163 (Washington: International Monetary Fund).

Lane, Philip R., and Gian Maria Milesi-Ferretti, 2006, "External Wealth of Nations Mark II: Revised and Extended Estimates of Foreign Assets and Liabilities, 1970–2004," *Journal of International Economics*, Vol. 73, No. 2, pp. 223–50.

Masanjala, Winford H., and Chris Papageorgiou, 2008, "Rough and Lonely Road to Prosperity: A Reexamination of the Sources of Growth in Africa Using Bayesian Model Averaging," *Journal of Applied Econometrics*, Vol. 23, No. 5, pp. 671–82.

Milesi-Ferretti, Gian Maria, and Assaf Razin, 1998, "Current Account Reversals and Currency Crises: Empirical Regularities," NBER Working Paper No. 6620 (Cambridge, Massachusetts: National Bureau of Economic Research).

Nickell, Stephen, Luca Nunziata, and Wolfgang Ochel, 2005, "Unemployment in the OECD since the 1960s: What Do We Know?" *Economic Journal*, Vol. 115, No. 500, pp. 1–27.

Pisani-Ferry, Jean, and Bruno van Pottelsberghe, 2009, "Handle with Care! Post-Crisis Growth in the EU," Bruegel Policy Brief No. 2009/02 (Brussels: Bruegel).

Reinhart, Carmen, and Kenneth Rogoff, 2009a, "The Aftermath of Financial Crises," *American Economic Review*, Vol. 99, No. 2, pp. 466–72.

———, 2009b, "Banking Crises: An Equal Opportunity Menace," NBER Working Paper No. 14587 (Cambridge, Massachusetts: National Bureau of Economic Research).

Schumpeter, Joseph, 1942, *Capitalism, Socialism and Democracy* (New York: Harper, 1975; originally published in 1942).

CHAPTER 10

What Have We Learned about Creditless Recoveries?

ABDUL ABIAD, GIOVANNI DELL'ARICCIA, AND BIN LI

Bank credit is considered to be a critical factor in facilitating economic activity. However, creditless recoveries, that is, economic growth without credit growth, can be observed after some recessions. This phenomenon was first documented by Calvo, Izquierdo, and Talvi (2006), who study what happens to output and credit after global or systemic sudden stop episodes. They find that, on average, output returns quickly to precrisis levels, but with weak investment and virtually no recovery in domestic or external credit (so-called Phoenix miracles).

Abiad, Dell'Ariccia, and Li (2011) address a broad set of questions regarding creditless recoveries. How common are they, and under what conditions do they tend to occur? How do they differ from "normal" recoveries? Do they reflect impaired financial intermediation? And finally, can and should policymakers respond to them? This chapter provides a nontechnical summary of the findings in Abiad, Dell'Ariccia, and Li (2011) and discusses some of the policy-related issues.

The study proceeds in two steps. First, macroeconomic data are used to identify and examine creditless recoveries in a broad set of countries. This analysis focuses on correlations and studies the frequency, duration, shape, and composition of the recoveries. It investigates which types of downturns are more prone to being followed by creditless recoveries. And it asks whether creditless recoveries are associated with worse growth performance and, if so, which components of growth are most affected. Second, the study turns to sectoral data to investigate the mechanism behind creditless recoveries. In particular, it uses a difference-in-difference approach to identify causal links between credit growth and output performance. If disruptions of financial intermediation are at the root of creditless recoveries, their effect should be felt disproportionately more by those sectors that rely more heavily on external finance.

The authors thank Olivier Blanchard, Stijn Claessens, Gianni De Nicolò, Prakash Kannan, Angela Maddaloni, David Romer, and participants in seminars at the IMF, the Bank for International Settlements, the European Central Bank, the 2012 American Economic Association meeting, the 2012 Midwest Macro Meeting, the 2012 International Conference on Economic and Financial Challenges in Asia-Pacific, the 2010 Econometric Society World Congress, and the 2010 Financial Intermediation Research Society Conference (Fiesole) for helpful comments. Zeynep Elif Aksoy provided excellent research assistance.

The findings indicate that creditless recoveries—defined as episodes in which real credit growth is negative in the first three years following a recession—are not rare. They follow about one in five recessions in a wide set of countries. And although they seem to be more common in developing economies and emerging markets, they also occur in advanced economies.

Creditless recoveries are incomplete "miracles." On average, activity recovers substantially less than in recoveries with credit: output growth is on average a third lower. Put differently, creditless recoveries tend to be weaker and more protracted (i.e., it takes longer for output to return to trend). This result remains when controlling for the characteristics of the preceding recession. However, these averages mask wide variations—many creditless "recoveries" are followed by stagnant growth.

Considering the preconditions that tend to precede creditless recoveries, the frequency of creditless recoveries doubles when the downturns follow credit booms, and more than doubles when the downturns follow or coincide with a banking crisis. If the downturn is preceded by both a banking crisis *and* a credit boom, the subsequent recovery is almost certain to be creditless. Currency and sovereign debt crises have smaller effects, and in the presence of a banking crisis they do not significantly increase the likelihood of a creditless recovery. These findings suggest that the relatively weak macroeconomic performance during creditless recoveries is the result of constrained growth caused by impaired financial intermediation. This is consistent with Calvo, Izquierdo, and Talvi (2006), who argue that the lack of credit growth during these recoveries can be rationalized by financial frictions preventing firms from obtaining funding for new investment.

Output decompositions buttress this perspective. Investment, which is likely to depend more on credit than does consumption, has a disproportionately smaller contribution to growth in creditless recoveries relative to other recoveries, although consumption takes a hit as well. An interesting finding is that creditless recoveries are not jobless recoveries—employment dynamics are no different on average from those in normal recoveries. Instead, productivity and capital deepening are adversely affected.

Using sectoral data, the analysis more formally tests the hypothesis that the weaker macroeconomic performance during creditless recoveries stems from disruptions of financial intermediation. Industry-level data are used covering 28 manufacturing industries in 48 countries, from 1964 through 2004. The analysis follows Braun and Larrain (2005), who focus on recessions rather than recoveries and analyze an industry's performance using the growth rate of industrial production. This measure is then regressed on an array of controls, including multiple sets of fixed effects (to take care of industry-year- and industry-country-specific omitted factors), and the variable of interest, which is the interaction of a measure of the industry's financial dependence and the creditless recovery dummy.

Braun and Larrain (2005) find that more financially dependent industries perform relatively worse during recessions. Consistent with their result, Abiad,

Dell'Ariccia, and Li (2011) finds that these industries perform relatively better than less financially dependent industries during all typical recoveries (although, similar to Braun and Larrain's analysis of "booms," the result is generally weak and not always significant). During creditless recoveries, however, industries that are more dependent on external finance tend to grow disproportionately less than those that are more self-financed. This result appears economically meaningful. During creditless recoveries, the growth rate of industries that are highly dependent on external finance (at the 85th percentile of the index distribution) is more than 1.5 percentage points lower than in normal recoveries. The same difference drops to 0.4 percentage point for low-dependence industries (those at the 15th percentile). This differential effect appears robust. It is present in both advanced economies and emerging markets. It survives when controlling for capital inflows. And it does not seem to depend on measurement issues that may stem from large fluctuations in credit aggregates caused by exchange rate movements (in the presence of foreign-currency-denominated loans).

The finding that creditless recoveries are suboptimal outcomes associated with impaired financial intermediation is relevant from a policy standpoint. Had causality gone the other way—that is, had creditless recoveries resulted instead from an exogenous decline in the demand for credit caused, for example, by weak growth prospects—there would be little room for policy action beyond counter-cyclical macro measures typically adopted in normal recoveries. Given the evidence, however, policies aimed at restoring credit supply should lead to fewer credit constraints and higher growth. The findings are also relevant for the 2007–09 global financial crisis. Given the widespread financial sector distress, the retrenchment in cross-border capital flows, and the occurrence of credit and property booms in several countries, the recovery from the crisis is likely to be creditless in a number of economies, and thus slower than average. To contain this effect, continued policy action is required to restore the supply of credit, cushion the effects of deleveraging, and address the undercapitalization of several financial institutions.

The rest of the chapter is organized as follows: the first section examines creditless recoveries from a macro perspective. The second section presents the sectoral analysis. The final section concludes.

MACRO PERSPECTIVE

This section studies creditless recoveries from a macro perspective. It examines how creditless recoveries differ from normal recoveries, and analyzes and compares the duration, shape, and frequency of these recoveries. It also examines whether creditless recoveries are peculiar to certain sets of countries or follow particular events such as banking crises, currency crises, debt crises, sudden stops, or credit booms. For now, the analysis focuses on associations and does not attempt to establish causal links between the variables, leaving that for the sectoral analysis in the next section.

What has been learned about creditless recoveries?

1. How are they defined?

2. How common are they?

3. How are they different from other recoveries?

4. How can they be decomposed?

Before creditless recoveries can be defined a definition of what countries are recovering from is needed. Economic downturns are identified following the methodology in Braun and Larrain (2005). Recessions are identified based on fluctuations of real annual GDP.[1] Specifically, a Hodrick-Prescott filter is used to extract the trend in the logarithm of real GDP. The smoothing parameter is set at 6.25 as recommended for annual data by Ravn and Uhlig (2002). Recessions are identified whenever the cyclical component of GDP (detrended real output) exceeds one country-specific standard deviation below zero. The recession is then dated as starting the year following the previous peak in detrended real output, and continuing until the year of the trough (when the cyclical component is at its lowest point). The recovery period is then defined as the first three years following the trough of a recession. This simplifies the distinction between creditless and normal recoveries and limits problems associated with "double-dip" recessions. This methodology identifies 388 recoveries, roughly equally divided between advanced Organization for Economic Cooperation and Development countries, emerging markets, and low-income countries.[2]

The focus is bank credit to the private sector, as measured in line 22d of the IMF's *International Financial Statistics*. This is a choice of necessity. This series is the only one available with broad cross-country and time series coverage. One shortcoming is that it does not include credit extended by nonbank financial intermediaries. For most countries this is not a major issue. But for a couple of cases, such as the United States, a critical portion of the financial sector is not covered by the data. A creditless recovery is then defined as one in which the growth rate of real bank credit (deflated by the GDP deflator) is zero or negative in the first three years of recovery.

Creditless recoveries are not rare. They represent about one-fifth of all recoveries. However, the differences in their distribution across country groups are not trivial. In particular, creditless recoveries are more common in low-income countries and emerging markets than in advanced economies, where they represent only about 10 percent of all recoveries. A Pearson chi-square test rejects at the 10

---

[1] Real GDP data from the World Bank's *World Development Indicators* are used, extended to 2007–09 using the IMF's *World Economic Outlook* data where available. These data cover 172 countries, 1960–2009 (unbalanced).

[2] The country groups are defined in the Data Appendix of Abiad, Dell'Ariccia, and Li (2011). Emerging markets are the 26 countries covered in the MSCI Emerging Markets Index, advanced OECD refers to the 23 members of the Organization for Economic Cooperation and Development not in the emerging markets group, and LIC refers to low-income countries according to the World Bank's income classification.

percent level the null hypothesis that the relative frequency of creditless recoveries is the same across country groups. This outcome suggests that these events tend to be more common in countries with less-developed financial markets. The cross-country correlation between financial development (measured by the average credit-to-GDP ratio during the sample period) and the frequency of creditless recoveries is about –0.2.

There is also substantial time series variation in the relative frequency of creditless recoveries. In particular, creditless recoveries tend to be clustered geographically and around three peak periods (Figure 10.1). These clusters follow the Latin American debt crisis of the early 1980s, the European Exchange Rate Mechanism crisis and Scandinavian banking crisis of the early 1990s, and the Asian crises of the late 1990s.

The questions then arise: To what extent are creditless recoveries associated with the nature of the preceding recession? In particular, what is the predictive power of specific events such as credit booms, banking and currency crises, and real estate booms and busts? If creditless recoveries are the result of impaired financial intermediation, they should be more likely to occur in the aftermath of events associated with disruptions in the credit supply.

The analysis first focuses on downturns associated with systemic banking crises, as defined by Laeven and Valencia (2008). The frequency of creditless recoveries is three times as high if a systemic banking crisis occurs in the two years

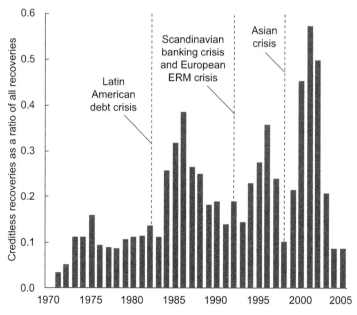

Figure 10.1 Creditless Recoveries over Time

Source: Authors' calculations.
Note: ERM = Exchange Rate Mechanism.

before or the year coinciding with a downturn than when there is no banking crisis. Nevertheless, only about half of banking crises are followed by creditless recoveries.

Both currency and sovereign debt crises seem to have some influence independent of the effect of banking crises. In the absence of a banking crisis, a currency crisis preceding a recession doubles the frequency of creditless recoveries, and a sovereign debt crisis more than doubles it. But if there is a banking crisis, the occurrence of either a currency crisis or a sovereign debt crisis does not seem to be associated with a significantly higher frequency of creditless recoveries.

Finally, the analysis looks at downturns preceded by credit booms, using the methodology developed in Mendoza and Terrones (2008). The occurrence of credit booms before downturns doubles the relative frequency of creditless recoveries. However, the effects of a credit boom are weak if there is no banking crisis; instead, creditless recoveries become most likely when downturns are preceded by both credit booms *and* banking crises.

If creditless recoveries tend to follow a credit boom-bust cycle, do they also tend to follow boom-bust cycles in the property market? In the absence of reliable cross-country house price data, construction investment data are used as a proxy, and the findings indicate that creditless recoveries are associated with construction boom-bust cycles. In particular, on average, creditless recoveries are preceded by collapses in construction investment (with an average decline of about 17 percent). In contrast, construction investment growth is essentially zero before recoveries with credit. To the extent that a collapse in construction investment signals a house price bust, this result is interpreted as evidence that creditless recoveries are associated with the destruction of collateral value (and the consequent increase in agency problems) stemming from sharp declines in real estate prices.

Creditless recoveries are less desirable than normal ones from a growth performance standpoint. For the broader sample of recessions, average output growth in creditless recoveries is 4.5 percent per year, compared with about 6.3 percent in recoveries with credit. As a consequence, output is also slower to return to trend. Output returns to trend within three years of the end of the recession in fewer than half of creditless recoveries, compared with more than two-thirds of recoveries with credit. In part, this difference reflects the fact that creditless recoveries tend to be preceded by deeper recessions, but it is also the result of the differential in growth rates. This is consistent with financial accelerator models. Greater destruction of collateral value associated with a deeper recession will translate into more sluggish credit and weaker growth in the recovery, as shown in Figure 10.2.

Calvo, Izquierdo, and Talvi (2006) document the characteristics of recoveries after systemic sudden stop (3S) episodes. They find that after these episodes, economies on average experience a quick, but creditless, recovery; they dubbed the phenomenon a "Phoenix miracle." Abiad, Dell'Ariccia, and Li (2011) find that more than half of 3S episodes are creditless, and average growth during 3S creditless recoveries is quite high—3.9 percent, compared with 4.3 percent during

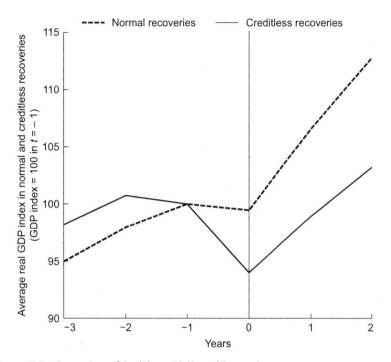

Figure 10.2 Comparison of Creditless with Normal Recoveries
Source: Authors' calculations.

3S recoveries with credit—which is consistent with Calvo, Izquierdo, and Talvi's (2006) findings.

A closer inspection, however, reveals a bimodal distribution, similar to that described by Huntley (2008). But going beyond Huntley (2008), this analysis identifies the cause of the bimodality: what matters is whether the 3S episode is associated with a banking crisis. For 3S episodes that do not result in banking crises, the recovery has always exhibited positive real credit growth, and output returns to trend within three years in most (five out of six) cases. In contrast, 80 percent of the recoveries following 3S episodes are creditless, and in two-thirds of these episodes, output does not return to trend within three years.

However, a few "true miracles"—exceptional cases in which output recovers sharply in the absence of credit growth—are found. In the sample, Chile and Uruguay in 1984–86, Mexico in 1995–98, and Argentina in 2003–05 fit this description. Figure 10.3 shows an example of a true Phoenix miracle, observed in Mexico in the 1995 episode. Phoenix miracles follow exceptionally deep recessions. Mexico, the possible exception, experienced a drop in output in excess of 6 percent in 1996, and the other three countries all witnessed double-digit falls during their recessions. Thus, it is possible that these "miracles" are in part due to rebound effects.

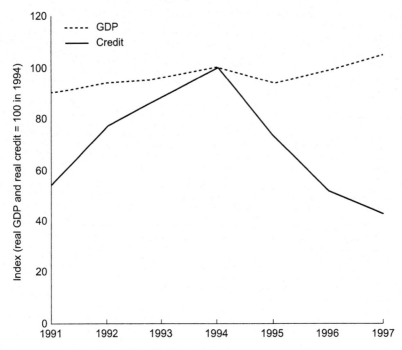

Figure 10.3 A True Phoenix Miracle: Mexico, 1995

Sources: IMF, *International Financial Statistics* and *World Economic Outlook* databases; World Bank, *World Development Indicators* database; and authors' calculations.

To shed light on the difference in macroeconomic performance between creditless and normal recoveries, aggregate growth is decomposed into its demand components. During creditless recoveries, the contributions of consumption and investment to output growth are roughly 1 percentage point lower than during normal recoveries, fully accounting for the 2 percentage point difference in output growth between creditless and normal recoveries. In relative terms, however, the contribution of investment falls by roughly half as compared with a fall of a third in consumption's contribution. This suggests that the components of aggregate demand that are more dependent on credit contribute the most to the difference in growth rates relative to normal recoveries. Net exports do not, on average, contribute to output growth during recoveries, regardless of credit dynamics. To be clear, the external sector does contribute positively to growth during the recession as the current account improves (often swinging from negative to positive); but during the recovery, both exports and imports increase, resulting on average in a roughly null contribution to growth.

Growth accounting points in the same direction. Lower growth during creditless recoveries can be ascribed to lower capital accumulation and lower total factor productivity growth. These results are consistent with what Calvo, Izquierdo, and Talvi (2006) find for 3S episodes. Lower capital accumulation is consistent with the results for demand decomposition. Lower total factor productivity growth may indicate that younger and start-up firms, which typically have higher productivity growth, find it more difficult than others to obtain credit during these episodes. It is also consistent with the notion that an impaired financial system is less efficient in reallocating capital across sectors as needed to absorb asymmetric shocks.

In contrast, employment growth (or alternatively, the decline in the unemployment rate) seems to be independent of the evolution of credit during the recovery. These results are interpreted as suggesting that it is, again, the more credit-dependent components that suffer during creditless recoveries. As pointed out by Calvo, Izquierdo, and Talvi (2006), these results are consistent with a situation in which, because of financial frictions, firms can obtain short-term credit for working capital but cannot obtain long-term financing for physical capital.

SECTORAL ANALYSIS

This section empirically tests the hypothesis that creditless recoveries (and the associated lower output performance) result from impaired financial intermediation. The identification strategy relies on the notion that, in the presence of market imperfections, different sources of funds (bank credit, the issuance of tradable bonds, and equity) are not perfect substitutes. Then, if creditless recoveries stem from disruptions in the supply of bank credit, firms and industries that are more reliant on credit should perform relatively worse. By contrast, if the creditless nature of the recovery were demand driven, sectors' performances should not differ in a systematic way.

The analysis follows the difference-in-difference approach used by several studies focusing on the real effects of banking crises and financial development. The exercise uses industry-level data from manufacturing sectors in both advanced and emerging market economies for 1970–2004. Industries are ranked according to the Rajan and Zingales (1998) index of external financial dependence, defined as capital expenditures minus cash flow from operations divided by capital expenditures. The differential performance of growth in real value added and industrial production during recoveries across these industries within a particular country is the main channel through which the real impact of credit is identified.

The study adopts the same working assumptions as in Rajan and Zingales (1998), later used by, among others, Braun and Larrain (2005); Krozner, Laeven, and Klingebiel (2007); and Dell'Ariccia, Detragiache, and Rajan (2008): external dependence is determined by technological factors, such as production time, capital intensity, and the importance of investment in research and development. Although the absolute value of the index may vary across countries and time, for the methodology to work it is sufficient that the industry ranking remains broadly the same. Rajan and Zingales (1998) support this assumption with data from Canada.

The starting point is the relative performance of credit-dependent sectors during all recoveries (irrespective of credit conditions). Braun and Larrain (2005) find that more-credit-dependent sectors suffer disproportionately during recessions (when agency problems become more severe). Hence, one would expect them to perform relatively better during recoveries as agency problems diminish.

The following regression is run on recoveries as the baseline specification:

$$Growth_{i,c,t} = \alpha_1 Share_{i,c,t-1} + \alpha_2 Recovery_{c,t} + \alpha_3 CreditlessRecovery_{c,t}$$

$$+ \alpha_4(Recovery_{c,t} \times Dependence_i) + \alpha_5(CreditlessRecovery_{c,t}$$

$$\times Dependence_i) + \sum_{i,c}\beta_{i,c} \times d_{i,c} + \sum_{i,t}\beta_{i,t} \times d_{i,t} + \varepsilon_{i,c,t}$$

The dependent variable is the growth rate of industrial production in industry i at time t in country c. Regressors include two sets of fixed effects (industry-year and industry-country) and the variable of interest, an interaction term equal to the product of the financial dependence measure for industry i and the recovery dummy for year t and country c. Following Rajan and Zingales (1998), the regression also includes the lagged share of industry i in country c to account for convergence effects, that is, the tendency of larger industries to experience slower growth.

The variable $d_{i,t}$ denotes the industry-year dummy, and $d_{i,c}$ is the industry-country dummy. $Share_{i,c,t-1}$ is the size of the industry in the country at the time $t-1$. $Dependence_i$ is the industry-level financial dependence, which follows the Rajan and Zingales (1998) methodology, and is assumed to be constant across years. $Recovery_{c,t}$ is a dummy taking value 1 in the three years following the trough of a recession in country c at year t. $CreditlessRecovery_{c,t}$ is a dummy equal to 1 when real credit growth is negative during a recovery. The sum of α_2 and α_3, reflecting the level effect of creditless recoveries, is expected to be positive. However, based on the results from the macro section, α_3 is expected to be negative; macroeconomic performance during creditless recoveries is weaker than during normal ones. Furthermore, the coefficient α_5 allows a comparison to be made between sectoral growth and the type of recovery. In particular, a negative α_5 would indicate that sectors more reliant on external finance perform relatively worse during creditless recoveries. This would, in turn, lend support to the claim that creditless recoveries are the result of disruptions in the credit supply.

The evidence from sectoral data suggests that creditless recoveries are indeed the result of impaired financial intermediation. During these episodes, sectors more dependent on external finance perform relatively worse. These results are statistically and economically significant and survive several robustness tests.

The findings of the regression are shown in Table 10.1. The level coefficient for creditless recoveries is negative as expected, but is not significant, suggesting that the gap in performance between creditless and normal recoveries identified

TABLE 10.1

The Effect of Creditless Recoveries on Sectoral Growth			
Variables	OECD + EM	OECD	EM
Size (lagged)	−0.0064	0.0703*	−0.0654
	[−0.187]	[1.873]	[−1.249]
Recovery	0.0273***	0.0230***	0.0328***
	[17.645]	[14.366]	[11.473]
Creditless recovery	−0.004	−0.0048	−0.004
	[−1.147]	[−1.291]	[−0.639]
Recovery x dependence	0.0091**	0.0049	0.0147**
	[2.380]	[1.193]	[2.105]
Creditless recovery x dependence	−0.0190**	−0.0200**	−0.0265*
	[−2.169]	[−2.033]	[−1.730]
Observations	35,796	20,006	15,790
R-squared	0.207	0.347	0.186
Creditless recovery			
Change in growth rate for high dependence industry (percent)	−1.5	−1.6	−2.0
Change in growth rate for low dependence industry (percent)	−0.4	−0.4	−0.4
Implied differential effect (percent)	−1.1	−1.2	−1.5

Source: Authors' calculations.

Note: EM = emerging market; OECD = Organization for Economic Cooperation and Development. Robust t-statistic in brackets. The symbols *, **, and *** indicate significance at the 10, 5, and 1 percent levels, respectively. The dependent variable is the yearly growth rate in the production index of each ISIC-3 industry in each country computed from the UNIDO Indstat-3 (2006) data set. Lagged size is the share of a country's total manufacturing value added that corresponds to the industry in the previous year.

in the macro analysis depends in large part on sectoral effects. The coefficient of the interaction term of creditless recoveries and credit dependence is consistently negative across all specifications, indicating that industries more dependent on external finance perform relatively worse when the recovery is not accompanied by credit growth. The result loses some significance but remains stable when the sample is split between advanced economies and emerging markets. The difference in performance is economically meaningful. During creditless recoveries, the growth rate of industries that are highly dependent on external finance (at the 85th percentile of the index distribution) is more than 1.5 percentage points lower than in normal recoveries. The same difference drops to 0.4 percentage point for low-dependence industries (those at the 15th percentile). This across-industry difference in performance is even more pronounced in emerging markets (the cross-sector differential is 1.5 percentage points versus 1.2 percentage points for advanced economies), likely reflecting the scarcity of alternative sources of funding or more pervasive agency problems.

In addition to the baseline specification, a variety of robustness tests are performed. Details are provided in Abiad, Dell'Ariccia, and Li (2011). The results of the robustness tests support the baseline findings. First, all episodes with exchange rate depreciations in excess of 20 percent are excluded. The concern is that sharp exchange rate falls may lead to a misclassification of creditless recoveries as normal recoveries, through their effect on the stock of foreign credit measured in domestic currency. The main coefficient of interest maintains sign and significance. Furthermore, consistent with the concern that exchange rate depreciation might blur the line between creditless and normal recoveries, the coefficient is larger than in the baseline specification. Second, the effect of capital inflows is controlled for. Again, the coefficient of interest maintains sign and significance, and remains broadly stable in size. The coefficient of the capital-flows-to-GDP variable is positive and significant as expected. In addition, capital flows seem to favor sectors that are more heavily dependent on external finance.

In addition, to control for omitted country-time-specific variables, a third set of fixed effects is included in the regression. As discussed above, these will take care of any omitted variable that does not vary simultaneously across all three dimensions of the data. All coefficients maintain the same sign and significance as in the previous regressions. The differential effect between sectors at the 85th percentile and the 15th percentile of the distribution of the external dependence index continues to range between about 1 percentage point and 1.5 percentage points, which is roughly the same magnitude as in the other regressions.

CONCLUSION

This chapter summarizes the findings in Abiad, Dell'Ariccia, and Li (2011) regarding the puzzling phenomenon of creditless recoveries. In contrast to previous studies, the analysis finds the following: First, creditless recoveries, while not the norm, are far from rare. They follow about one in five recessions. Second, creditless recoveries are somewhat less desirable than normal recoveries. Output growth is on average a third lower. Third, they are preceded by events likely to disrupt the supply of credit, such as banking crises, credit booms, and real estate boom-bust cycles. Fourth, investment has a disproportionately lower contribution to growth than in normal recoveries, and productivity and capital deepening are adversely affected. Finally, industries more reliant on external finance seem to grow disproportionately less during creditless recoveries.

Overall, both the macro-level and sectoral evidence support the hypothesis that creditless recoveries are the result of impaired financial intermediation: the lower growth performance in creditless recoveries is likely the outcome of a constrained allocation of resources. The results are consistent with agents delaying or downsizing their more credit-dependent investment and expenditure decisions and firms more dependent on external finance being forced to curtail their activities.

This finding is relevant from a policy standpoint. During creditless recoveries, policy measures aimed at restoring financial intermediation are likely to lead to higher growth. Of course, the obstacles to efficient financial intermediation will vary from case to case, and policies should be adapted accordingly. For instance, the lack of credit growth may be caused by stress on banks' balance sheets that could be addressed by recapitalizing banks (possibly with public intervention). Alternatively, the lack of credit growth could result from an overindebted private nonfinancial sector. Even in the presence of relatively healthy banks, debt overhang would exacerbate agency problems and prevent the efficient allocation of capital. In this case, the response would be much more complex and would have to include policies to facilitate deleveraging or possibly debt restructuring. Finally, given the association of creditless recoveries with banking crises, credit booms, and real estate boom-bust cycles and their lower growth performance, supportive measures (including a more expansionary macroeconomic stance) could be taken in anticipation of a less buoyant recovery phase when a recession is associated with these events.

REFERENCES

Abiad, A., G. Dell'Ariccia, and B. Li, 2011, "Creditless Recoveries," IMF Working Paper 11/58 (Washington: International Monetary Fund).

Braun, M., and B. Larrain, 2005, "Finance and the Business Cycle: International, Inter-Industry Evidence," *Journal of Finance*, Vol. 15, No. 3, pp. 1097–128.

Calvo, G., A. Izquierdo, and E. Talvi, 2006, "Sudden Stops and Phoenix Miracles in Emerging Markets," *American Economic Review*, Vol. 96, No. 2, pp. 405–10.

Dell'Ariccia, G., E. Detragiache, and R. Rajan, 2008, "The Real Effect of Banking Crises," *Journal of Financial Intermediation*, Vol. 17, No. 1, pp. 89–112.

Huntley, J., 2008, "Phoenix Falling: Recovering from Sudden Stops in Emerging Markets" (unpublished; Evanston, Illinois: Northwestern University).

Krozner, R., L. Laeven, and D. Klingebiel, 2007, "Banking Crises, Financial Dependence and Growth," *Journal of Financial Economics*, Vol. 84, No. 1, pp. 187–228.

Laeven, L.A., and F.V. Valencia, 2008, "Systematic Banking Crises: A New Database," IMF Working Paper 08/224 (Washington: International Monetary Fund).

Mendoza, E., and M. Terrones, 2008, "An Anatomy of Credit Booms: Evidence from Macro Aggregates and Micro Data," NBER Working Paper No. 14049 (Cambridge, Massachusetts: National Bureau of Economic Research).

Rajan, R.G., and L. Zingales, 1998, "Financial Dependence and Growth," *American Economic Review*, Vol. 88, No. 3, pp. 559–86.

Ravn, M.O., and H. Uhlig, 2002, "On Adjusting the Hodrick-Prescott Filter for the Frequency of Observations," *Review of Economics and Statistics,* Vol. 84, No. 2, pp. 371–76.

PART V

Policy Measures to Prevent Booms, Mitigate Busts, and Avoid Financial Crises

CHAPTER 11

Policies for Macro-Financial Stability: Dealing with Credit Booms and Busts

Giovanni Dell'Ariccia, Deniz Igan, Luc Laeven, and Hui Tong

Credit booms—episodes of rapid credit growth—pose a policy dilemma. More credit means increased access to finance and greater support for investment and economic growth (Levine, 2005). But when expansion is too fast, booms may lead to vulnerabilities through looser lending standards, excessive leverage, and asset price bubbles. Credit booms are also associated with financial crises (Reinhart and Rogoff, 2009). Historically, only a minority of booms have ended in crashes, but some of these crashes have been spectacular, contributing to the notion that credit booms are at best dangerous and at worst a recipe for disaster (Gourinchas, Valdes, and Landerretche, 2001; Borio and Lowe, 2002; Enoch and Ötker-Robe, 2007).

These dangers notwithstanding, until the 2007–09 global financial crisis the policy debate paid limited heed to credit booms, especially in advanced economies.[1] This lack of attention may have reflected two issues. First, with the diffusion of inflation targeting, monetary policy had increasingly focused on interest rates and had come largely to disregard monetary aggregates.[2] And regulatory policy, with its focus on individual institutions, was ill equipped to deal with aggregate credit dynamics.[3] Second, with regard to asset price bubbles, the

---

The authors would like to thank Olivier Blanchard, Claudio Borio, Stijn Claessens, Luis Cubeddu, Laura Kodres, Srobona Mitra, José-Luis Peydró, Ratna Sahay, Marco Terrones, and Kostas Tsatsaronis for useful comments and discussions. Roxana Mihet and Jeanne Verrier provided excellent research assistance.

[1] In a few emerging markets, however, credit booms were an important part of the policy discussions, and warnings on possible risks were put out before the crisis. See, for instance, Backé, Égert, and Zumer (2006); Boissay, Calvo-Gonzales, and Kozluk (2006); Cottarelli, Dell'Ariccia, and Vladkova-Hollar (2003); Duenwald, Gueorguiev, and Schaechter (2005); Hilbers and others (2005); and Terrones (2004).

[2] Of course, there were exceptions, such as the "two-pillar" policy of the European Central Bank and the more credit-responsive approach of central banks in India and Poland.

[3] Again, there were exceptions, like the Bank of Spain's dynamic provisioning, the loan eligibility requirements of the Hong Kong Monetary Authority, and the multipronged approach of the Croatian National Bank.

long-standing view was that it was better to deal with the bust than to try to prevent the boom, because unhealthy booms were difficult to separate from healthy ones and, in any event, policy would be able to contain the effects of a bust.

The crisis, preceded by booms in many of the harder-hit countries, has challenged that view. In its aftermath, calls for more effective tools to monitor and control credit dynamics have come from several quarters (e.g., FSA, 2009). And the regulatory framework has already started to respond. For instance, Basel III introduced a capital buffer range that is adjusted "when there are signs that credit has grown to excessive levels" (Basel Committee on Banking Supervision, 2010).

Yet, although a consensus is emerging that credit booms are too dangerous to be left alone, little agreement is to be found on what the appropriate policy response should be. First is the issue of whether and when to intervene. After all, not all booms end up in crises, and the macro costs of curtailing credit can be substantial. Second, should intervention be deemed necessary, there are questions about what form such intervention should take. Is this a natural job for monetary policy, or are there concerns that favor other options? This chapter addresses both of these issues by exploring several questions about past credit booms and busts: What triggers credit booms? When do credit booms end up in busts, and when do they not? Can policymakers and other observers determine in advance those that will end up badly? What is the role of different policies in curbing credit growth or mitigating the associated risks?

The chapter proceeds as follows. The first section presents some stylized facts on the characteristics of credit booms. The second section discusses the triggers of credit booms. The third section analyzes the characteristics of booms that end up in busts or crises. The fourth section discusses the policy options and their effectiveness in dealing with credit booms. The final section concludes.

CREDIT BOOMS: DEFINITION AND CHARACTERISTICS

Two caveats: First, this chapter limits its attention to bank credit. Obviously, there are other sources of credit in the economy (bond markets, nonbank financial intermediaries, trade credit, informal finance, and so on). But data availability makes a cross-country analysis of these alternative sources difficult, and with a few exceptions (notably the United States), bank credit accounts for an overwhelming share of total credit. Hence, the vast majority of macro-relevant episodes are captured. Second, for similar reasons, attention is confined to countries with credit-to-GDP ratios above 10 percent. Unfortunately, this automatically excludes most low-income countries. However, given these countries' different institutional and structural characteristics, an analysis of their credit dynamics is better conducted in a separate effort.

This chapter focuses on episodes that can be characterized as "extraordinary" positive deviations in the relationship between credit and economic activity.

Admittedly, what constitutes an extraordinary deviation and how the "normal" level of credit growth should be computed are both open to interpretation (Gourinchas, Valdes, and Landerretche, 2001; Mendoza and Terrones, 2008; Barajas, Dell'Ariccia, and Levchenko, 2008; Jordà, Schularick, and Taylor, 2011; Claessens, Kose, and Terrones, 2012; Mitra and others, 2011). Most methodologies in the literature compare a country's credit-to-GDP ratio to its nonlinear trend (some focus on absolute growth thresholds). But the methodologies differ in several respects, such as whether the trend and the thresholds identifying the booms should be country specific, whether information unavailable at the time of the boom should be used for its identification, and whether the credit series and GDP series should be filtered separately or directly as a ratio. Luckily, the set of booms identified using different methods is rather robust.

The aim of this chapter is to provide a definition that can be applied using the standard information that is available and therefore can be used as a guide in policymaking. For that reason, feasibility is the primary focus and the cost of ignoring information that exists today but was not available to policymakers in real time is accepted. This approach contrasts with methodologies that use the entire time series to detect deviations from trend (e.g., Mendoza and Terrones, 2008). A mix of country-specific, path-dependent thresholds and absolute numerical thresholds is also applied because thresholds for the credit-to-GDP gap are often hard to determine or interpret (and have been shown to miss many of the episodes associated with financial crises; Mitra and others, 2011). In contrast, absolute thresholds for credit growth are easier to interpret, but abstract from country- and time-specific characteristics. Overall, this methodology allows differences across countries as well as changes over time within the same country to be accounted for, and it avoids the risk of missing episodes because of an overfitting trend. (More details on this approach, its pros and cons, and comparison to other methodologies are in Appendix 11A.)

Specifically, boom episodes are identified by comparing the credit-to-GDP ratio in each year t and country i to a backward-looking, rolling, country-specific, cubic trend estimated for the period between years $t - 10$ and t. An episode is classified as a boom if either of the following two conditions is satisfied: (1) the deviation from trend of the credit-to-GDP ratio is greater than 1.5 times its standard deviation and its annual growth rate exceeds 10 percent; or (2) the annual growth rate of the credit-to-GDP ratio exceeds 20 percent. The second condition is introduced to capture episodes in which aggregate credit accelerates very gradually but the credit growth rate reaches levels that are well above those previously observed in the country. Similar thresholds identify the beginning and end of each episode. Because only information on GDP and bank credit to the private sector available at time t is used, this definition can, in principle, be made operational.

This definition is applied to a sample of 170 countries with data starting as far back as the 1960s and extending to 2010. Some 175 credit boom episodes are

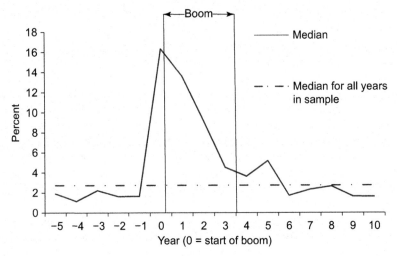

Figure 11.1 A Typical Credit Boom *(growth rate of credit-to-GDP ratio around boom episodes)*

Sources: IMF, *International Financial Statistics*; and IMF staff calculations

identified.[4] This translates into a 14 percent probability of a country experiencing a credit boom in a given year.[5] Based on this sample, the stylized facts that characterize credit booms are as follows:

- The median boom lasts three years, with the credit-to-GDP ratio growing at about 13 percent per year, or about five times its median growth in non-boom years (Figure 11.1).

- Credit booms are not a recent phenomenon. But the fraction of countries experiencing a credit boom in any given year has been on an upward trend since the financial liberalization and deregulation of the 1980s. It reached an all-time high (30 percent in 2006; see Figure 11.2) in the run-up to the global financial crisis when a combination of factors—such as the financial reform associated with European Union accession and the expansion of securitization in the United States—provided further support for credit growth.

- Most booms happen in middle-income countries, which is consistent with the view that, at least in part, credit booms are associated with catching-up

---

[4] Following similar practice in the literature, cases in which the credit-to-GDP ratio is less than 10 percent are dropped. The reason for this is twofold: First, financial deepening is more likely to be the main driver of rapid credit expansion episodes in such financially underdeveloped economies. Second, the data series tend to be less smooth, making it difficult to distinguish between trend-growth and abnormal growth episodes.

[5] This probability is calculated by dividing the number of country-year observations that correspond to a credit boom episode by the number of nonmissing observations in the data set.

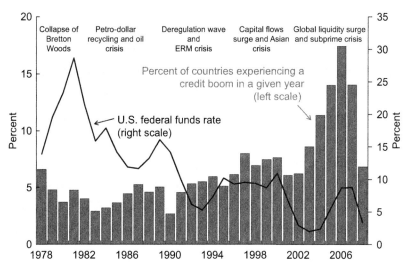

Figure 11.2 Concurrence of Credit Booms, 1978–2008

Sources: IMF, *International Financial Statistics*; and IMF staff calculations.
Note: ERM = Exchange Rate Mechanism.

effects. Yet high-income countries are not immune to booms, suggesting that other factors are also at play.

- More booms happen in relatively undeveloped financial systems. The median credit-to-GDP ratio at the start of a boom is 19 percent, compared with a median credit-to-GDP ratio of about 30 percent for the entire data set. This supports the notion that booms can play a role in financial deepening.

- Geographically, booms are more likely to be observed in sub-Saharan Africa and Latin America, which partially reflects these regions' country composition and historically volatile macroeconomic dynamics. Eastern Europe stands out in the later period, reflecting the expansion of the European Union and the associated integration and catching up that fueled booms in many of the new or prospective member states. Of course, this summarizes past experience, and inferences about the probability of future booms should be drawn with caution.

Macroeconomic Performance around Credit Booms

Real economic activity and aggregate credit fluctuations are closely linked through wealth effects and the financial accelerator mechanism (among others, Bernanke and Gertler, 1989; Kiyotaki and Moore, 1997; and Gilchrist and Zakrajsek, 2008). In an upturn, better growth prospects improve borrower creditworthiness and collateral values. Lenders respond by increasing the supply of credit and, sometimes, by loosening lending standards. More abundant credit

TABLE 11.1

Economic Performance *(average annual change, percent)*		
	Nonboom years	**Boom years**
Credit-to-GDP ratio	1.6	16.8
GDP	3.1	5.4
Consumption	4.0	5.4
Investment	4.2	10.3
Equity prices	3.8	11.0
House prices	1.8	9.5
Exchange rate	5.1	2.5
Consumer prices	10.7	9.3

Sources: IMF, *International Financial Statistics*; Organization for Economic Co-operation and Development; and IMF staff calculations.
Note: Average across all credit boom episodes. Average annual changes expressed in percent.

allows for greater investment and consumption and further increases collateral values. In a downturn, the process is reversed.

Not surprisingly, economic activity is significantly higher during booms compared with nonboom years (Table 11.1). Real GDP growth during booms exceeds the rate observed in nonboom years by roughly 2 percentage points, on average.[6] Private consumption expands faster during booms. But it is private investment that picks up markedly, with the average growth rate more than doubling compared with nonboom years. This is in line with the important role played by banks in financing real estate and corporate investment in many countries, but it also reflects, at least in part, the role played by capital inflows in the form of foreign direct investment.[7]

The increase in consumption and investment associated with credit booms is often more pronounced in the nontradables sector. Consistently, booms are typically associated with real exchange rate appreciations (Terrones, 2004). It is interesting that inflation remains subdued (more on this later). Taken together, these findings suggest that domestic imbalances that may be building up vent through the external sector. During a boom the current account balance deteriorates, on average, by slightly more than 1 percentage point of GDP per year. Most of the associated increase in net foreign liabilities comes from the "other flows" category, which includes banks' funding by foreign sources.

Because asset price cycles tend to comove with business and credit cycles (Igan and others, 2011; Claessens, Kose, and Terrones, 2012), the comparison between nonboom years and booms carries over to these indicators. Both equity

---

[6] Note that nonboom years include (asset price and credit busts and recessions. The comparative statistics, however, remain broadly the same when the bust and recession years are excluded.
[7] See Mendoza and Terrones (2008), Igan and Pinheiro (2011), and Mitra and others (2011) for more on the behavior of macroeconomic variables and some micro-level analysis around credit booms. At the macro level, there is evidence of a systematic relationship between credit booms and economic expansion, rising asset prices, leverage, foreign liabilities of the private sector, real exchange rate appreciation, widening external deficits, and managed exchange rates. At the micro level, there is a strong association between credit booms and firm-level measures of leverage, market value, and external financing, and bank-level indicators of banking fragility.

and real estate prices surge during credit booms and lose traction at the end of a boom. The difference from nonboom years is more striking than for GDP components: during booms, equity prices rise at almost triple the rate they rise during nonboom years in real terms. House prices, on average, grow at an annual rate of about 2 percent in nonboom years but accelerate sharply during booms to a growth rate of 10 percent. This synchronization with asset price booms may create balance sheet vulnerabilities for the financial and nonfinancial sectors, with repercussions for the broader economy.

Long-Run Consequences of Credit Booms

Credit booms can also be linked to macroeconomic performance over the long term. After all, financial development—typically measured by the credit-to-GDP ratio, the same variable used to detect credit booms—has a positive effect on growth (King and Levine, 1993; Rajan and Zingales, 1998; Levine, Loayza, and Beck, 1999; and Favara, 2003).[8] Moreover, the economic magnitude of this effect is substantial: increasing financial depth (measured by the broad-money (M2)-to-GDP ratio) from 20 percent to 60 percent would increase output growth by 1 percent a year (Terrones, 2004).

Obviously, whether episodes that sharply increase the credit-to-GDP ratio have long-term beneficial effects depends on two factors. The first is the extent to which credit booms contribute to permanent financial deepening. The second is the extent to which the "quality" of financial deepening acquired through a sharp increase in credit resembles the deepening achieved through gradual credit growth.

As for the first question, booms are sometimes followed by financial crises (see next section) that are typically associated with sharp drops in the credit-to-GDP ratio. However, in about 40 percent of the episodes, the credit-to-GDP ratio seems to shift permanently to a new, higher "equilibrium" level. In fact, there is a positive correlation between long-term financial deepening (measured as the change in the credit-to-GDP ratio over the period 1970–2010) and the cumulative credit growth that occurred during boom episodes (Figure 11.3).

The second question can be answered only indirectly, by looking at the relationship between credit booms and long-term growth. This task is complicated, because growth benefits gained from increased financial deepening attributable to a boom are likely to take time to be fully realized, making it hard to measure them at a given point in time. However, some evidence points to such benefits. There is a positive correlation between the number of years a country has undergone a credit boom and the cumulative real GDP per capita growth achieved since 1970 (Table 11.2). However, this relationship seems to flatten when credit

---

[8] This causal interpretation is supported by its differential impact across sectors: financial development affects economic growth more for sectors with external financing needs for investment (Rajan and Zingales, 1998).

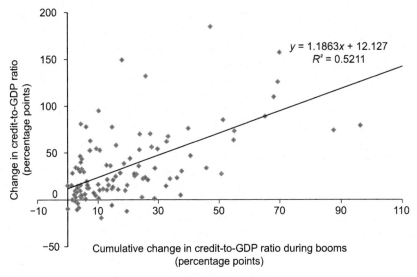

Figure 11.3 Credit Booms and Financial Deepening,1970–2010

Sources: IMF, *International Financial Statistics*; and IMF staff calculations.

TABLE 11.2

Long-Term Growth and Credit Booms		
	Change in Real per Capita Income (percent)	
Years spent in a boom	Mean	Median
None	40	38
Between 1 and 5	54	60
More than 5	61	59

Source: IMF staff calculations.

booms become too frequent, and because countries with more credit booms also experience more crises (on average), there seems to be a trade-off between macroeconomic performance and stability (Rancière, Tornell, and Westermann, 2008).

Credit Booms and Financial Crises

Balanced against the benefits just described is the notion that credit booms are dangerous because they lead to financial crises. This is not just an undeserved bad reputation caused by a small fraction of episodes that were particularly bad. Credit growth can be a powerful predictor of financial crises (Borio and Lowe, 2002; Mendoza and Terrones, 2008; Schularick and Taylor, 2009; and Mitra and others, 2011). In the sample, about one in three booms is followed by a banking

TABLE 11.3

Credit Booms Gone Wrong						

Followed by financial crisis?	Followed by economic underperformance?					
	No		Yes		Total	
	Number	Percent of total cases	Number	Percent of total cases	Number	Percent of total cases
No	54	31	64	37	118	67
Yes	16	9	41	23	57	33
Total	70	40	105	60	175	100

Source: IMF staff calculations.
Note: A boom is followed by a financial crisis if a banking crisis happened within the three-year period after the end of the boom and is followed by economic underperformance if real GDP growth was below its trend, calculated by applying a moving-average filter, within the six-year period after the end of the boom.

crisis (as defined in Caprio and others, 2005; and Laeven and Valencia, 2010) within three years of its end (Table 11.3).[9]

The 2007–09 global financial crisis has reinforced this notion. After all, the crisis had its roots in the rapid increase of mortgage loans in the United States. And it was exactly the regions that had experienced greater booms during the expansion that suffered greater increases in credit delinquency during the crisis (Figure 11.4; also Dell'Ariccia, Igan, and Laeven, 2008). In addition, across countries, many of the hardest-hit economies, such as Iceland, Ireland, Latvia, Spain, and Ukraine, had their own homegrown credit booms (Claessens and others, 2010).

Credit booms also preceded many of the largest banking crises of the past 30 years: Chile (1982); Denmark, Finland, Norway, and Sweden (1990–91); Mexico (1994); and the Republic of Korea, Malaysia, the Philippines, and Thailand (1997–98—Figure 11.5). And going farther back, the Great Depression was also cast as a credit boom gone wrong (Eichengreen and Mitchener, 2003).[10]

---

[9] This outcome is not very sensitive to the choice of methodology and thresholds used in identifying boom episodes. There is a slight tendency for methodologies based on a trend calculated over the whole sample to overestimate the probability of a credit boom ending badly, because the trend is then affected by the years that follow the boom. See Appendix 11A for a comparison of the good and bad booms identified here and those identified elsewhere in the literature. Actually, the baseline used here is the smallest when the percentage of booms followed by a banking crisis is compared across different methodologies used to identify booms.

[10] Credit booms are generally associated with banking crises rather than other types of crises. For comparison, 15 percent of the booms in the sample were followed by a currency crisis and 8 percent by a sovereign debt crisis. Although some of these same countries also had systemic banking crises, the positive association remains when these cases are excluded. And although some of these credit booms coincided with housing booms, the association is robust to excluding those cases (Crowe and others, 2011; and Leigh and others, 2012).

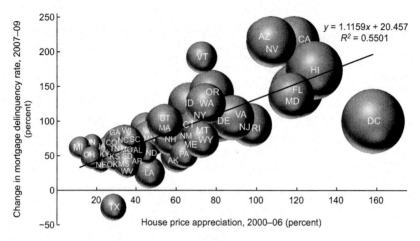

Figure 11.4 Leverage: Linking Booms to Defaults

Sources: Bureau of Economic Analysis; Federal Housing Finance Agency; Mortgage Bankers Association; U.S. Census Bureau; and IMF staff calculations.

Note: Each data point corresponds to a U.S. state, indicated by the two-letter abbreviations. Bubble size shows the percentage point change in the ratio of mortgage credit outstanding to household income from 2000 to 2006.

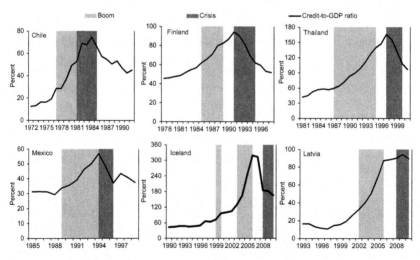

Figure 11.5 Credit Booms and Financial Crises: Examples of Bad Booms

Sources: IMF, *International Financial Statistics*; IMF staff calculations; and Laeven and Valencia (2010).

Several credit booms that did not end in full-blown crises were followed by extended periods of subpar economic performance, which adds further concern. In the sample, three out of five booms were characterized by below-trend growth during the six-year period following their end. During these below-trend periods, annual economic growth was on average 2.2 percentage points

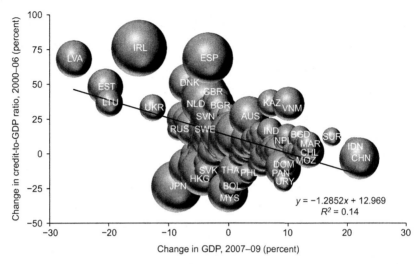

Figure 11.6 Credit Growth and Depth of Recession

Sources: IMF, *International Financial Statistics*; and IMF staff calculations.

Note: Each data point corresponds to a country, indicated by the three-letter abbreviations. Bubble size shows the level of credit-to-GDP ratio in 2006. AUS = Australia; BGD = Bangladesh; BRG = Bulgaria; BOL = Bolivia; CHE = Switzerland; CHN = China; DOM = Dominican Republic; DNK = Denmark; ESP = Spain; EST = Estonia; GBR = United Kingdom; HKG = Hong Kong SAR; IDN = Indonesia; IND = India; IRL = Ireland; JPN = Japan; KAZ = Kazakhstan; LTU = Lithuania; LVA = Latvia; MAR = Morocco; MOZ = Mozambique; MYS = Malaysia; NLD = Netherlands; NPL = Nepal; PAN = Panama; PHL = Philippines; RUS = Russia; SUR = Suriname; SWE = Sweden; THA = Thailand; UKR = Ukraine; URY = Uruguay; VMN = Vietnam.

lower than in normal times (excluding crises). Notably, the two types of events—financial crisis and weaker economic activity—often coincide but do not perfectly overlap. Overall, in the aftermath of credit booms something goes wrong about two times out of three (121 out of 175 cases). In line with this, in the 2007–09 global financial crisis, countries that had previously experienced bigger changes in their credit-to-GDP ratios were also the ones that had deeper recessions (Figure 11.6).[11] This is consistent with the view that credit booms leave large sectors of the economy overleveraged, leading to impaired financial intermediation in their aftermath, even when a full-blown crisis is avoided.

Indeed, credit booms are a good predictor of "creditless recoveries," that is, economic recoveries that happen in the absence of credit growth (typically in the aftermath of a crisis). Such recoveries are inferior, with average growth about a third lower than during normal recoveries (Abiad, Dell'Ariccia, and Li, 2011, and Chapter 10 in this volume). Industries that are dependent on external finance and financing-sensitive activities (e.g., investment) appear to suffer more during creditless recoveries, potentially indicating that resources may be allocated inefficiently across industries and activities.

---

[11] The extraordinary experience of the Baltic countries and Ireland may seem to be driving this finding. But this correlation holds for the rest of the episodes as well, albeit more weakly.

WHAT TRIGGERS CREDIT BOOMS?

So far, the chapter has summarized how credit booms are linked to short- and long-term economic performance and how often they coincide with financial crises. But macroeconomic and financial factors, including policies, may themselves contribute to the occurrence of credit booms. Hence, it is time to look at the other side of the coin: the triggers of credit booms. Identifying these triggers could help gauge a country's susceptibility to credit booms and devise policies to reduce this susceptibility.

Three often concurrently observed factors are frequently associated with the onset of credit booms (e.g., Mendoza and Terrones, 2008; Decressin and Terrones, 2011; Magud, Reinhart, and Vesperoni, 2012):

- The first factor is financial reform. Reforms usually aim to foster financial deepening and are linked to sharp increases in credit aggregates. Roughly a third of booms follow or coincide with financial liberalization. In contrast, only 2 percent follow or coincide with a reversal of such policies. Given that the sample contains more liberalization episodes than reversals, these percentages are less divergent when expressed in relative terms, but still point in the same direction: 18 percent of liberalizations are linked to credit booms, compared with 7 percent of reversals.

- The second factor is surges in capital inflows, often in the aftermath of capital account liberalization. Capital account liberalization generally leads to a significant increase in the funds available to banks, potentially relaxing credit constraints. In the sample, net capital inflows intensify during the three-year period before the start of a credit boom, increasing from 2.3 percent of GDP to 3.1 percent of GDP, on average.

- Third, credit booms generally start during or after buoyant economic growth.[12] More formally, lagged GDP growth is positively associated with the probability of a credit boom: in the three-year period preceding a boom, the average real GDP growth rate reaches 5.1 percent, compared with 3.4 percent in an average tranquil three-year period.

These triggers may occur across countries simultaneously. Financial liberalization happens in waves, affecting multiple countries more or less at the same time. In emerging markets, surges in capital flows often relate to changes in global liquidity conditions (as proxied by the U.S. federal funds rate;[13] see Figure 11.2) and, thus, are correlated across countries. The transmission of technological advances across borders synchronizes economic activity.

---

[12] From a longer-term perspective, technological groundbreakers and their diffusion are also likely to act as triggers. For instance, the ratio of bank loans to GDP on a "global" scale increased relatively quickly during the last third of the 19th century and then again starting in the early 1980s with the introduction of new financial products, thanks to the information technology revolution (Schularick and Taylor, 2009).

[13] See Borio, McCauley, and McGuire (2011) on the role of global conditions in the context of credit booms.

TABLE 11.4

Economic and Financial Policy Frameworks and Credit Booms, 1970–2009
(frequency distribution, percent)

	Exchange rate regime		Monetary policy		Fiscal policy		Banking supervision	
	Fixed	Floating	Loose	Tight	Loose	Tight	Low	High
1970–79	10.6	5.6	7.2	9.4	12.5	4.8	14.9	1.1
1980–89	11.3	9.4	16.5	2.2	19.2	7.7	22.3	0.6
1990–99	23.1	4.4	24.5	0.7	26.0	10.6	24.6	2.3
2000–09	27.5	8.1	33.8	5.8	13.5	5.8	18.9	15.4
All years	72.5	27.5	82.0	18.0	71.2	28.8	80.6	19.4

Sources: IMF staff calculations. Exchange rate regime categories are based on Reinhart and Rogoff (2004). Banking supervision quality measure is from Abiad, Detragiache, and Tressel (2008).
Note: Monetary policy is tight when the policy rate exceeds the predicted level based on a simple regression of policy rates on inflation and real GDP growth by more than 25 percent (the top quartile). Fiscal policy is tight when the change in the deficit/surplus exceeds its predicted level based on a simple regression of the deficit/surplus on real GDP growth by more than 1.7 percent of GDP (the top quartile).

Of course, domestic factors may also matter. The differential incidence of booms across countries suggests that local structural and institutional characteristics and policies are important. In particular, credit booms seem to occur more often in countries with fixed exchange rate regimes, expansionary macroeconomic policies, and low quality of banking supervision (Table 11.4). In economies with fixed exchange rate regimes, monetary policy is directed toward maintaining a fixed exchange rate and is therefore unable to respond effectively to the buildup of a credit boom. In such regimes, a lower global interest rate may translate into lower domestic interest rates, spurring domestic credit growth. By stimulating aggregate demand, expansionary macroeconomic policies risk building up asset price booms. Loose monetary policy, in particular, reduces the cost of borrowing and boosts asset price valuations, which in turn can trigger credit booms (however, see evidence in the section on "Monetary Policy" later in this chapter). Finally, the quality of banking supervision has a bearing on the enforcement of bank regulation and the effectiveness with which supervisory discretion is applied to deal with early signs of credit booms. For example, supervisors can use their discretion to take measures (such as higher capital requirements) to lower the pace of credit growth.

However, credit booms are still difficult to predict. Regression analysis suggests that the triggers and macroeconomic conditions described above have some bearing on assessing the susceptibility of a country to a credit boom. But the residual variability is substantial and identifying causality is difficult (see the discussion below on the results in Table 11.7 below).

CAN WE TELL BAD FROM GOOD CREDIT BOOMS?

The analysis in the previous sections implies that policymaking may face a trade-off between standing in the way of financial deepening (and thus in the way of present and perhaps future macroeconomic performance) and allowing dangerous imbalances to jeopardize financial stability. Can this trade-off be improved upon by distinguishing, ahead of time, bad booms from good ones?

This question is addressed by exploring whether a boom's characteristics, such as duration, size, and macroeconomic conditions, can help predict whether it will turn into a crisis or a prolonged period of subpar economic performance. Formally, a boom is classified as "bad" if it is (1) followed by a banking crisis within three years of its end date, or (2) associated with a recession or inferior (below-trend) medium-term growth performance.[14]

First, the summary statistics on the characteristics of bad booms are compared with those for good booms. Second, a regression analysis is conducted. As in similar exercises, there are limitations associated with cross-country regressions (see, e.g., Levine and Renelt, 1992). In particular, there is a trade-off between sample size and the homogeneity of the countries covered. This problem is mitigated by controlling for various country characteristics.

Given that a boom is in place, the probability of its turning bad is modeled as:

$$(Bad\ boom = 1)_{it} = \alpha + \beta X_{it} + \gamma P_{it} + \varepsilon_{it},$$

in which X is a vector of macroeconomic indicators and structural variables and P is a vector of measures of the policy stance during the boom. In summary,

- "Bad" credit booms tend to be larger and last longer (Figure 11.7), and
- Booms that start at a higher level of financial depth (measured as the level of the credit-to-GDP ratio) are more likely to end badly.

These findings are more or less in line with those reported elsewhere. For instance, the magnitude of a boom (manifested as a larger rise in the credit-to-GDP ratio from start to end or duration) has been identified as a predictor of whether the boom ends up in a banking crisis (Gourinchas, Valdes, and Landerretche, 2001; and Barajas, Dell'Ariccia, and Levchenko, 2008). Other macro variables, like larger current account deficits, higher inflation, lower-quality bank supervision, and faster growing asset prices, are sometimes associated with bad booms. But their coefficients are rarely significant and they are unstable across subsamples and model specifications. In addition, although there is a general tendency to think that credit booms in emerging markets are

---

[14] Subpar macroeconomic performance is defined in reference to the trend of log real GDP. Specifically, growth is deemed to be subpar if the current level of log real GDP is below its trend calculated using a moving-average filter for the past five years. This may be overstating how bad macroeconomic performance is because the trend calculations include the strong growth years during the boom, yet the findings are robust to using alternative definitions, for example, comparisons of the real GDP growth rate to its medium-term trend. In many cases, criteria (1) and (2) overlap: in 16 out of 57, or 28 percent, of the cases in which there is a crisis, growth stalls (see Table 11.3).

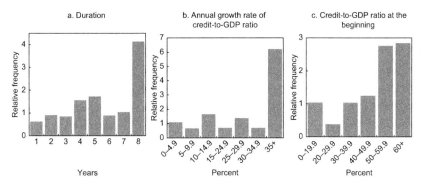

Figure 11.7   Bad versus Good Booms

Sources: IMF, *International Financial Statistics*; and IMF staff calculations.

Note: Relative frequency is the frequency of a given attribute in bad booms divided by the frequency in good booms. Credit booms are identified as episodes during which the growth rate of credit-to-GDP ratio exceeds the growth rate implied by this ratio's backward-looking, country-specific trend by a certain threshold. Bad booms are those that are followed by a banking crisis within three years of their end.

more likely than booms elsewhere to end up in crises, this is not observed in the sample.[15]

In general, the lack of statistically significant differences in key macroeconomic variables in bad versus good booms has been noted elsewhere (see, for instance, Gourinchas, Valdes, and Landerretche, 2001). Notably, indicators that have been identified as predictors of financial crises, such as sharp asset price increases, sustained worsening of the trade balance, and a marked increase in bank leverage (Mitra and others, 2011) lose significance once the presence of a credit boom (as defined in this chapter) is conditioned for. In the sample, although asset prices grow much faster during booms than in tranquil times (e.g., for equity prices about 11 percent versus 4 percent a year), they grow at about the same pace during both bad and good booms (again, for equity prices, about 11 percent a year for both).

Although statistical evidence for pinning down ahead of time whether a boom is a good or bad one is underwhelming, the results suggest that policy interventions to curb credit growth become increasingly justified as booms become larger and more persistent. In particular, close to half or more of the booms that either lasted longer than six years (4 out of 9), exceeded 25 percent of average annual growth (8 out of 18), or started at an initial credit-to-GDP ratio higher than 60 percent (15 out of 26) ended up in crises. These regularities (noted also by Mitra and others, 2011; and Borio, McCauley, and McGuire, 2011) can guide policymakers in weighing the benefits and costs of an ongoing boom and in setting thresholds that would trigger policy action.

---

[15] In absolute terms, many of the booms ending in banking crises occurred in emerging markets (27 out of 57). Yet in relative terms, 38 percent of the booms happening in emerging markets are followed by a crisis within three years of the end of the boom, while the ratio is 57 percent for advanced economies.

POLICY OPTIONS

The evidence presented so far shows that credit booms can stimulate economic activity and even promote long-term growth, but also that they are associated with disruptive financial crises. About one boom in three ends with a bust. More often, booms end without a full-blown crisis, but their associated leverage build-ups have a long-lasting impact on corporate and household behavior, leading to below-trend economic growth.

Theory has identified several channels through which financial frictions can lead to excessive risk taking during episodes of rapid credit growth. Contributing to looser lending standards and greater credit cyclicality may be managerial reputational concerns (Rajan, 1994), improved borrowers' income prospects (Ruckes, 2004), loss of institutional memory of previous crises (Berger and Udell, 2004), expectations of government bailouts (Rancière, Tornell, and Westermann, 2008), and a decline in adverse selection costs associated with improved information symmetry across banks (Dell'Ariccia and Marquez, 2006). In addition, externalities driven by strategic complementarities (such as cycles in collateral values) may lead banks to take excessive or correlated risks during the upswing of a financial cycle (De Nicolò, Favara, and Ratnovski, 2012). Such financial frictions can explain why, as the old banking maxim goes, "the worst loans are made at the best of times" and justify intervention to prevent excessive risk taking during the boom.

Some of these frictions and their associated risks were well known before the 2007–09 global financial crisis, yet policies paid limited attention to the problem (with notable exceptions in emerging markets). This limited attention reflected several factors.

First, with the adoption of inflation targeting regimes, monetary policy in most advanced economies and several emerging markets had increasingly focused on the policy rate and paid little attention to monetary aggregates. There were a few exceptions. Australia and Sweden adjusted their monetary policies in response to asset price and credit developments and communicated the reason explicitly in central bank statements. Other policies, such as the European Central Bank's "two-pillar" policy, were regarded as vestiges from the past and played a debatable role in actual policy setting.[16]

Second, bank regulation focused on individual institutions. It largely ignored the macroeconomic cycle and was ill equipped to respond to aggregate credit dynamics. As for asset price bubbles, by and large a notion of benign neglect prevailed, under the thinking that it was better to deal with the bust than try to

---

[16] The European Central Bank has rejected the notion that it followed a strict money-growth target from the start (ECB, 1999). In December 2002, the policy strategy was revised to reduce the prominence of "the monetary analysis" by placing it as the second rather than the first pillar and using it mainly as a "cross-check" for the results from the first pillar ("the economic analysis"). Even then, the two-pillar strategy was criticized by many (Svensson, 2003; and Woodford, 2008). And, in the eyes of several observers, the role played by monetary aggregates in the European Central Bank's policy has been debatable (Berger, de Haan, and Sturm, 2006).

prevent the boom. Again, there were exceptions. Spain introduced "dynamic provisioning." Bolivia, Colombia, Peru, and Uruguay adopted similar measures (Terrier and others, 2011). Other emerging markets experimented with applying prudential rules to counteract credit and asset price cycles (Table 11.5). But these exceptions formed a minority. Moreover, the measures taken were often small in scale and therefore did not always have their desired effect.

Third, financial liberalization and increased cross-border banking activities limited the effectiveness of policy action. In countries with de jure or de facto fixed-exchange-rate regimes, capital flows hindered the impact of monetary policy on credit aggregates. And prudential measures were subject to regulatory arbitrage, especially in countries with developed financial markets and widespread presence of foreign banks.

This section discusses the major policy options (monetary, fiscal, and macro-prudential tools) to deal with credit booms, with particular attention to their pros and cons, summarized in Table 11.6 in light of the experiences of various countries and econometric analysis. It examines what policies, if any, have successfully stopped or curbed episodes of fast credit growth. But it also investigates whether certain policies have been effective in reducing the dangers associated with booms, even if they did not succeed in stopping them. In that regard, the analysis looks at the coefficients of the policy variables obtained in the econometric analysis specification described in the previous section.

Monetary Policy

When it comes to containing credit growth, monetary policy seems the natural place to start. After all, M2, a common measure of the money supply, is highly correlated with aggregate credit. In principle, a tighter monetary policy stance increases the cost of borrowing throughout the economy, and lowers credit demand. Higher interest rates also reduce the ability to borrow through their impact on asset prices, and thus on collateral values, via the credit channel (Bernanke and Gertler, 1995). Finally, higher interest rates tend to reduce the growth of market-based financial intermediaries' balance sheets (Adrian and Shin, 2009) as well as leverage and bank risk taking (Borio and Zhu, 2008; and De Nicolò and others, 2010).

However, several factors may limit the effectiveness of monetary policy in preventing or stopping credit booms, or in ensuring good booms do not turn into bad ones. First, there may be a conflict of objectives. Of course, credit booms can be associated with general macro overheating. In that case, higher policy rates are the obvious answer. But booms can also occur under seemingly tranquil macroeconomic conditions, as was the case in several countries in the run-up to the 2007–09 global financial crisis (Figure 11.8). Under those conditions, the monetary stance necessary to contain the boom may differ substantially from that consistent with the inflation target (such conflicts are likely to be even stronger when the boom is concentrated in a single or a few sectors, for example, real estate loans). In addition, because tightening will buy lower

TABLE 11.5

Policy Responses to Credit Booms

Measure	Countries	Impact assessment
Macroeconomic policy		
Monetary tightening	Australia, Brazil, Chile, China, Colombia, Croatia, Hungary, Iceland, Latvia, Romania, Sweden	Higher interest rates did not prove to be effective in controlling domestic demand for loans. In some cases, increased capital inflows or shifts to foreign-exchange-denominated loans posed further challenges.
Fiscal tightening	Bulgaria, Hungary	Fiscal consolidation, in most cases, was not enough to offset the surge in domestic demand.
Removal of incentives for borrowing in the tax code	Estonia, Lithuania*, Netherlands, Poland, United Kingdom	Gradual phasing out of mortgage interest deductibility was somewhat successful in the United Kingdom but did not have much effect on household debt accumulation in the other cases.
Regulatory policy		
Reserve requirements	Albania, Bosnia, Brazil, Bulgaria, China, Colombia, Croatia, Estonia, Finland, India, Indonesia, Korea, Latvia, Malaysia, Mongolia*, Peru^*, Romania^, Russia^, Serbia, Ukraine, Uruguay^	Evidence remains mixed with success in taming the rate of growth reported in some cases (e.g., Bosnia) but not in others (e.g., Serbia).
Differentiated or time-varying capital requirements	Brazil, Bulgaria, Croatia, Greece, India, Nigeria, Poland^, Portugal^, Switzerland*	Sizable slowdown in credit growth rates was noted in several cases but reversal to higher pace was not uncommon. Some have argued that these tools, even when they failed to prevent or curb a credit boom, were effective in ensuring that the banking sector was better prepared for the bust because capital buffers were higher.
Higher risk weights	Albania, Bulgaria, Brazil*, Croatia, Estonia^, Iceland, India, Ireland, Italy, Malaysia, Norway^, Poland^, Serbia, Spain, Turkey, Uruguay^	
Liquidity requirements	Argentina^, Brazil^, Colombia, Croatia, France*, Iceland, New Zealand*, Turkey^, Uruguay^	Little impact on credit growth, but liquidity positions improved.
Dynamic/increased provisioning	Bolivia, Bulgaria, Colombia, Croatia, Greece, India, Mongolia*, Peru, Portugal, Russia, Spain, Uruguay	In many cases, there was some but not a large effect on the rate of credit growth. However, the buffer built during the boom appeared to have helped during the bust.

Limits on credit growth or new loans	Argentina^, Austria^, Bulgaria, Brazil^, China, Colombia, Croatia, Greece, Hong Kong SAR, Hungary^*, Korea^*, Malaysia, Romania^, Serbia, Singapore, Turkey^	There has been some effect, especially when the measures were applied only to narrowly defined categories of loans. Yet, overall effectiveness on aggregate credit was muted because lending shifted to foreign banks or less-regulated financial intermediaries.
Limits on loan-to-value ratio	Brazil^*, Canada*, Chile, China, Colombia, Hong Kong SAR, Hungary^*, India, Korea, Latvia, Malaysia, Norway*, Romania, Singapore, Slovak Republic, Sweden*, Thailand, Turkey*	Studies focusing on Asian countries report success for such loan eligibility criteria both in curtailing real estate price appreciation and in reducing defaults if and when a downturn starts. There tends to be, however, less support for these tools' ability to control household and bank leverage. Also, issues concerning the calibration of the policy response remain (see, e.g., Igan and Kang, 2011). Evidence for other countries is even more limited because the rules have only recently been enforced.
Limits on debt-to-income ratio	China, Colombia, France*, Greece, Hong Kong SAR, Hungary^*, Korea, Malaysia, Norway*, Poland*, Romania, Thailand	
Exposure or credit concentration limits	Colombia, France, Hong Kong SAR, Malaysia, Mexico, Mongolia*, New Zealand*, Nigeria, Peru*, Poland, Portugal, Romania, Serbia, South Africa, Thailand, Ukraine, Uruguay	Direct impact on aggregate credit growth rate is difficult to detect, but positive effect on the resilience of financial institutions seems to exist. Having said that, circumvention problems have been reported, especially in the case of exposure or credit concentration limits.
Net open position limits	Argentina, Colombia, Hungary, Indonesia, Israel^*, Korea^*, Malaysia, Mexico, Nigeria, Peru*, Romania, Russia, Serbia, South Africa, Thailand, Turkey, Uruguay	
Maturity mismatch regulations	Italy, Mexico, Mongolia*, New Zealand*, Singapore, South Africa, Uruguay	

Sources: IMF country reports; Enoch and Ötker-Robe (2007); Borio and Shim (2007); Crowe and others (2011); Lim and others (2011); Terrier and others (2011); Vandenbussche, Vogel, and Detragiache (2012).
Note: This is not intended to be an exhaustive list of all measures taken in all credit boom episodes identified in the sample but rather a simplified illustration of various tools used in various cases. Some measures can be classified under multiple categories, for example, application of higher risk weights or additional capital requirements based on whether the loan meets a loan-to-value limit criterion, and in most cases several policy tools are used in one package. Tools listed under regulatory policy have been used in a prudential rather than in a "macroprudential" sense in most cases, especially before the global financial crisis, and such usage may not necessarily fit within the definition of macroprudential policy used since the crisis (see BIS, 2011, and IMF, 2011a, for such definitions).
^ Denotes the cases in which the measure was applicable to a certain type of lending, most commonly, foreign-currency-denominated loans.
* Indicates that the measure was taken in 2010 or later, in several cases as a response to the global financial crisis rather than to an ongoing or looming credit boom.

TABLE 11.6

Policy Options to Deal with Credit Booms

	Potential impact	Side effects	Practical issues
Macroeconomic Policy			
Monetary measures			
Tightening of monetary policy (e.g., through a rise in key policy rates)	drain excess liquidity in the system, increase the cost of borrowing, and potentially reduce the deterioration in inflation and current account	inflict damage to economic activity and welfare; attract capital inflows; hurt fiscal position by raising the cost of borrowing	identifying "doomed" booms and reacting in time; weakness in monetary transmission mechanism; constraints imposed by monetary regime
Fiscal measures			
Tightening of fiscal policy	reduce potential overheating related to credit expansion and create room for stimulus in case of a bust	potential output costs that may come with significant tightening	considerable lag in fully mobilizing the measures and little room if the fiscal stance is already tight
Removal of incentives for borrowing (e.g., mortgage interest tax deductibility, subsidies and guarantees for mortgages, corporate tax shield provided by debt)	reduce distortions in the demand for bank loans and other types of debt	conflicts with socially motivated housing goals	only a one-off effect with little room for cyclical implementation
Financial sector taxation	reduce probability of crisis by dampening systemic excessive risk taking during the boom and cost of crisis by acting as a buffer in the bust phase	risk of imposing excessive costs on the financial sector and, thus, impairing financial intermediation	loopholes for tax arbitrage and tax havens in the absence of international coordination; design details still in infancy

Regulatory Policy

Macroprudential measures

Measure			
Reserve requirements Differentiated capital requirements Higher risk weights Liquidity requirements	increase cost of borrowing while building buffer to cope with the bust	costs associated with potential credit rationing	may get too complicated to enforce, especially in a cyclical context; effectiveness also limited when capital ratios are already high
Dynamic provisioning	increase cost of borrowing while building buffer to cope with the bust	earnings management	data requirements and calibration
Limits on credit growth	(could) limit rapid expansion and leverage	loss of benefits from financial deepening	move lending outside the regulatory periphery
Limits on loan-to-value ratio Limits on debt-to-income ratio	(could) limit rapid expansion and leverage while decreasing probability of default	costs associated with potential credit rationing	calibration is difficult, circumvention is easy
Credit concentration limits Net open position limits Maturity mismatch regulations	limit exposure to certain types or sources of risks	not directly aimed at aggregate credit growth; may shift risks to other types or sources of risk	window-dressing and circumvention may be an issue

Monitoring measures

Measure			
Intensified surveillance on vulnerable banks Stress testing Stronger disclosure requirements	improve resilience of the financial sector in the aftermath	reliance on hard information and less incentive to gather soft information; (potentially) increase rent-seeking	difficult to take action at good times, may still miss tail risks

Sources: Enoch and Ötker-Robe (2007); Borio and Shim (2007); Crowe and others (2011); and IMF country reports.

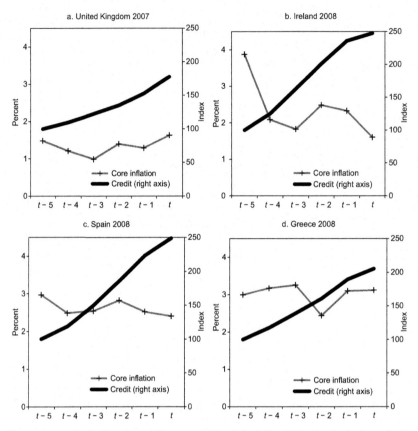

Figure 11.8 Credit Growth and Monetary Policy *(selected countries that had a boom in the run-up and a crisis in 2007–08)*

Sources: IMF, *International Financial Statistics*; IMF, *World Economic Outlook*; and IMF staff calculations.
Note: Credit is indexed with a base value of 100 five years before the crisis.

(unobservable) risk at the cost of a higher (observable) unemployment rate, it will likely run into strong social and political opposition, making the decision to raise policy rates harder.

A second tension may arise if crucial elements of the private sector (banks, corporates, and households) have weakened balance sheets. An increase in interest rates to tame credit growth with the objective of safeguarding future financial stability would have the side effect of increasing the present debt burden and lowering asset prices. If debt-service obligations are already at or near capacity, balance sheet stability would be threatened (similar to the threat discussed in the debate about whether central banks should be in charge of bank supervision).

Third, complications can arise when capital accounts are open and "the impossible trinity" comes into play. Countries with fixed exchange rate regimes simply do not have the option to use monetary policy. Others that float are seriously concerned about large exchange rate swings associated with carry trade when monetary policy is tightened. In addition, unless intervention can be fully steril-ized, capital inflows attracted as a result of higher interest rates can undo the effects of a tighter stance. Moreover, credit funded by capital inflows brings addi-tional dangers, including increased vulnerability to sudden stops.

Fourth, monetary tightening may fail to stop a boom and instead contribute to the risks associated with credit expansion. For instance, higher costs for loans denominated in domestic currency may encourage borrowers and lenders to sub-stitute foreign-currency loans. Alternatively, to make loans more affordable, shorter-term rates, teaser contracts, and interest-only loans may come to domi-nate new loan originations. This is especially relevant when there are explicit or implicit government guarantees that protect the banking system, or when there are widespread expectations of public bailouts should the currency depreciate sharply (Rancière, Tornell, and Westermann, 2008).

In line with these concerns, the empirical evidence that tighter monetary policy conditions (measured as deviations from a simple Taylor-rule-like equa-tion) are linked to a lower frequency of credit booms is mixed at best.[17] The coefficient on monetary tightening is unstable and rarely significant, suggesting that on average monetary policy is not very effective in dealing with booms, either by reducing their incidence (Table 11.7) or by reducing the probability that a boom already in place would end up badly (Table 11.8). A tighter stance may help slow down a boom, that is, it may be negatively linked to the speed of the boom, measured as the average annual rate of growth in the credit-to-GDP ratio (regression results available upon request). But it does not seem to slow the boom enough to contain the associated risks.[18] In contrast, a growing literature suggests that easy monetary policy conditions are conducive to lower lending standards, which in turn could lead to credit booms (see Maddaloni and Peydró, 2011, and references therein).

These regressions may underestimate the effectiveness of monetary policy because of an endogeneity problem. If central banks were to tighten the policy rate in reaction to credit booms, on average, higher rates would coincide with faster credit growth. Put differently, positive deviations from conditions consis-tent with a Taylor rule would stem from the credit booms themselves. This would tend to reduce the size and significance of the regression coefficients, that is, it would bias the results against monetary policy effectiveness.

Country cases lend very limited support to the notion that monetary policy can effectively deal with a credit boom. Since 2000, many Central and Eastern European countries tightened monetary policy to contain inflation pressures, but with little tangible effect on credit growth. In some cases, this misstep reflected

---

[17] Related evidence shows that credit booms happen more often in environments of high real lending rates. Moreover, such booms are more likely to be followed by problems in the banking sector.

[18] The lack of statistical evidence in support of monetary policy is in line with the findings in Mer-rouche and Nier (2010) for a sample of advanced economies ahead of the global financial crisis. By contrast, they find the strength of prudential policies was important in containing these booms.

TABLE 11.7

Regression Analysis: Incidence of Credit Booms

	Dependent variable: Dummy = 1 if there is a credit boom				
	(1)	(2)	(3)	(4)	(5)
GDP per capita	−0.0146	−0.0191	−0.0062	−0.0818**	−0.0643
	[0.0299]	[0.0299]	[0.0337]	[0.0379]	[0.0388]
GDP growth	0.0155	0.0125	0.0127	0.0260**	0.0270*
	[0.0133]	[0.0147]	[0.0152]	[0.0120]	[0.0161]
Capital inflow surge	0.0222	0.0124	0.0199	0.0185	0.0107
	[0.0147]	[0.0153]	[0.0204]	[0.0137]	[0.0204]
Financial reform	0.3142*	0.2126	0.1942	0.4379**	0.2199
	[0.1861]	[0.2074]	[0.1990]	[0.1889]	[0.2178]
Inflation	−0.0018	−0.0058	−0.0035	−0.0028	−0.0065
	[0.0054]	[0.0062]	[0.0057]	[0.0050]	[0.0063]
Current account balance	0.0079	0.0047	0.0006	0.0094	0.0024
	[0.0095]	[0.0112]	[0.0139]	[0.0081]	[0.0154]
Trade openness	−0.0020*	−0.0014	−0.0008	−0.0021**	−0.0006
	[0.0010]	[0.0011]	[0.0012]	[0.0010]	[0.0013]
Exchange rate regime	−0.0263**	−0.0182*	−0.013	−0.0173*	0.0007
	[0.0105]	[0.0103]	[0.0122]	[0.0104]	[0.0115]
Monetary policy stance		−0.0017**			−0.0011
		[0.0007]			[0.0009]
Fiscal policy stance			0.1233***		0.1190***
			[0.0339]		[0.0342]
Macroprudential controls				−0.0782***	−0.0724***
				[0.0189]	[0.0193]
Observations	150	147	134	150	131

Source: IMF staff calculations.

Note: All regressions are estimated using ordinary least squares. GDP per capita, in real terms, is in log. GDP growth is the annual growth rate of real GDP. Capital inflow surge is the sum of direct, other, and portfolio investment flows as percent of GDP. Financial reform is a normalized index, as calculated by Abiad, Detragiache, and Tressel (2008), with higher values indicating a more liberal and standardized regulatory framework. Inflation is the annual increase in consumer price index. Current account balance is expressed in percent of GDP. Trade openness is the sum of exports and imports divided by GDP. Exchange rate regime is the Reinhart-Rogoff fine classification, with higher values corresponding to more flexibility in exchange rate determination. Monetary policy stance is calculated as the error term by which the policy rate exceeds its predicted level based on a simple regression of policy rates on inflation and real GDP growth. Fiscal policy stance is computed as the error term by which the general government deficit or surplus in percent of GDP deviates from its predicted level based on a simple regression of the deficit or surplus on real GDP growth. Macroprudential controls variable is the count of macroprudential tools such as reserve and liquidity requirements, foreign exchange open position limits, or interest rate controls. All variables except the categorical ones are winsorized at the 5 percent level. All variables are lagged to reflect their average over the three-year period before the start of the boom. They are calculated as the average for the sample period if the country has undergone no booms. Robust standard errors are in brackets. The symbols ***, **, and * denote significance at the 1, 5, and 10 percent levels, respectively.

high euroization and ineffective monetary transmission channels. In others, increased capital inflows reversed the intended effects. Where the tightening seemed to have some short-lived impact on containing the boom (e.g., Hungary and Poland), shifts to foreign-currency-denominated lending were observed (Brzoza-Brzezina, Chmielewski, and Niedźwiedzińska, 2010).

Conversely, countries that allowed their exchange rates to appreciate more freely (e.g., the Czech Republic, Poland, and the Slovak Republic) experienced smaller credit booms. And in many advanced economies, the mortgage credit and house price booms recorded before the 2007–09 global financial crisis can be

TABLE 11.8

Regression Analysis: Policy Effectiveness in Preventing Credit Booms from Going Wrong

	DV: Dummy = 1 if bad				DV: Dummy = 1 if banking crisis				DV: Dummy = 1 if economic underperformance			
	(1)	(2)	(3)	(4)	(5)	(6)	(7)	(8)	(9)	(10)	(11)	(12)
Duration	0.0564**	0.0369	0.0530**	0.0392	0.0297	0.0425	0.0359*	0.0379	0.0461*	0.0077	0.0409*	0.0134
	[0.0234]	[0.0261]	[0.0210]	[0.0250]	[0.0234]	[0.0273]	[0.0213]	[0.0261]	[0.0244]	[0.0280]	[0.0229]	[0.0285]
Monetary policy	0.0482			0.056	-0.0512			-0.0656	0.0773			0.1876
	[0.1179]			[0.1502]	[0.1183]			[0.1580]	[0.1229]			[0.1503]
Fiscal policy		0.0160		0.1157		0.0735		0.0996		0.0757		0.1913
		[0.1137]		[0.1122]		[0.1193]		[0.1283]		[0.1218]		[0.1240]
Macroprudential policy			-0.2113***	-0.1342			-0.2372***	-0.2306**			-0.1015	-0.0248
			[0.0684]	[0.0994]			[0.0678]	[0.0906]			[0.0745]	[0.0989]
Observations	141	109	173	94	141	109	173	94	141	109	173	94

Source: IMF staff calculations.

Note: DV = dependent variable. All regressions are estimated using ordinary least squares. Duration, measured in years, shows how long the boom has lasted and is also a proxy for its size. Monetary or fiscal policy in a given year is measured by a dummy that is 1 if there was tightening. Monetary policy is deemed to have tightened when the policy rate exceeds the predicted level based on a simple regression of policy rates on inflation and real GDP growth by more than 25 percent (the top quartile). Fiscal policy is deemed to have tightened when the change in the deficit or surplus exceeds its predicted level based on a simple regression of the deficit or surplus on real GDP growth by more than 1.7 percent of GDP (the top quartile). Macroprudential policy is an indicator variable that takes on the value 1 if at least one macroprudential tool was introduced right before the start of the boom and 0 otherwise. For all policy variables except the indicator variable for macroprudential policy, which is the value in the year before the start of the boom, the average over the boom years is taken. Sample consists of boom episodes only. Standard errors are in brackets. The symbols ***, **, and * denote significance at the 1, 5, and 10 percent levels, respectively.

linked to lax monetary conditions (e.g., Crowe and others, 2011, and references therein). However, there is an emerging consensus that the degree of tightening that would have been necessary to have a meaningful impact on credit growth would have been substantial and would have entailed significant costs for GDP growth.

Summarizing, monetary policy is, in principle, the natural framework for intervention to contain a credit boom. In practice, however, there are constraints that limit its action. From the evidence above, monetary policy can be expected to be more effective in larger and more closed economies, where capital inflows and currency substitution are less of a concern. The benefits of monetary tightening will be more evident and its costs lower when credit booms occur in the context of general macro overheating. In contrast, the increase in interest rates necessary to stem booms associated with sectoral bubbles (such as those in real estate) may come with substantial costs—especially because, during these episodes, expected returns vastly overwhelm the effect of marginal changes in the policy rate.

Against this background, macroprudential measures and international policy coordination can improve the effectiveness of monetary policy. For instance, macroprudential policies targeted at net open foreign exchange positions may contain currency substitution, and cooperation with home supervisors of foreign banks may help reduce cross-border lending.

Fiscal Policy

Both cyclical and structural elements of the fiscal policy framework may play a role in curbing credit market developments. Most important, engaging in a prudent stance and conducting fiscal policy in a countercyclical fashion may help reduce overheating pressures associated with a credit boom. On the structural side, removing provisions in the tax code that create incentives for borrowing may reduce long-term leverage.

More critically, fiscal consolidation during the boom years can help create room for intervention to support the financial sector or stimulate the economy if and when the bust arrives. Based on the average gross fiscal cost of banking crises, estimates suggest that a buffer of 5 percent of GDP during the life of the boom would be actuarially fair (the number would drop to about 3 percent of GDP if based on net costs).[19]

From a practical point of view, however, traditional fiscal tools are unlikely to be effective in taming booms. As in the case of macroeconomic cycle management, the significant time lags associated with fiscal tools prevent a timely response. Political economy factors may also play an important role, with election

---

[19] The average gross fiscal cost of systemic banking crises is estimated to be about 15 percent of GDP (Laeven and Valencia, 2010). Multiplying this by the probability of a banking crisis following a credit boom (33 percent) gives 5 percent. This buffer comes on top of the margins one would normally associate with prudent fiscal policy over the cycle and may not be enough to leave room for fiscal stimulus if there were to be a recession.

cycles introducing additional oscillations. And in the long term, the removal of incentives for borrowing in the tax code is unlikely to have a cyclical effect on credit growth.

Empirical evidence supports these considerations. Fiscal tightening is not associated with a reduced incidence of credit booms (Table 11.7), nor a lower probability of a boom ending badly (Table 11.8).[20] A review of country experiences attests to the one-off effect from the removal of tax incentives to take on debt (e.g., the 2002 introduction of limits on mortgage interest deductibility in Estonia). And recent experience in Central and Eastern Europe suggests that fiscal policy contributed to credit growth.

New fiscal tools have been proposed in the aftermath of the global financial crisis. These could take the form of levies imposed on financial activities—measured by the sum of profits and remuneration (Claessens, Keen, and Pazarbasioglu, 2010)—or a countercyclical tax on debt aiming to reduce leverage and mitigate the credit cycle (Jeanne and Korinek, 2010). These measures would go directly to the heart of the problem: the externalities associated with leverage and risk taking. Such "financial activities taxes" or "taxes linked to credit growth" could put downward pressure on the speed of individual financial institutions' expansions, preventing them from becoming too systemically important to fail. The revenues could be used to create a public buffer rather than private buffers for individual institutions (as capital requirements do). Moreover, unlike prudential regulation that applies only to banks, the proposed tools could contain credit expansion by nonbank financial institutions as well.

However, the newly proposed fiscal tools have their own practical difficulties. Incentives to evade the new levies may lead to an increase in the resources devoted to "tax planning." These incentives may actually strengthen when systemic risk is elevated because, as the possibility of having to use the buffers increases, financial institutions may attempt to avoid transfers to others through the public buffer. A further complication may arise if there are provisions to protect access to finance by certain borrowers or access to certain types of loans: circumvention through piggy-back loans or by splitting liabilities among related entities may generate a worse situation for resolution if the bust comes. In addition, for these new measures to be effective, they would have to take into account how banks will react to their imposition. This would likely mean diversified treatment for different categories of banks (which opens up the risk of regulatory arbitrage) and progressive rates based on information similar to what is used for risk-weighted capital requirements (Keen and de Mooij, 2012).

In summary, although fiscal policy is important for taming the overheating in the economy and for creating room to provide stimulus and financial support if and when the bust comes, its effectiveness in directly dealing with credit booms

---

[20] Actually, the regression results suggest that fiscal tightening is positively related to the incidence of booms, perhaps reflecting the unexpectedly high tax revenues with buoyant economic growth in the background during the boom years or the possibility that fiscal policy is tightened in response to the credit boom in place.

may be limited. The newer proposals advocating "financial taxation" make sense on paper, but remain to be tested.

Macroprudential Regulation

So far, the empirical analysis and the case studies seem to suggest that the effectiveness of macroeconomic policies in curbing credit booms is questionable. One reason for this discouraging message could be the high potential costs imposed on economic activity by these far-reaching and relatively blunt policies. A more targeted approach can, in principle, be more effective and reduce the costs associated with policy intervention, although this obviously is not true if one espouses the view that monetary aggregates (and therefore credit) are the major determinant of inflation pressures. Macroprudential policies offer such a targeted approach. Moreover, the externalities that exist between financial institutions and that contribute to the accumulation of vulnerabilities during the boom or amplify the negative shocks during the bust provide a rationale for macroprudential regulation.

Macroprudential policies are policies aimed at limiting system-wide risks in the financial system. In a strict sense, they include prudential tools and regulation to address externalities in the financial system (BIS, 2011; and IMF, 2011a). In a broader sense, however, the objective of macroprudential policies is to smooth financial and credit cycles to prevent systemic crises and cushion their adverse effects. For the purposes of this chapter, the broader interpretation is relevant. From this perspective, the most commonly used macroprudential tools can be grouped into the following three categories:[21]

- *Capital and liquidity requirements.* These measures affect the cost or composition (or both) of the liabilities of financial institutions by increasing their capital and liquidity buffers. For instance, countercyclical capital requirements increase the cost of bank capital, and thus lending, in good times. Dynamic loan-loss provisioning rules, which build up capital buffers in the form of reserves in good times to absorb losses during bad times, also fall into this category. Capital and liquidity requirements can be countercyclical to smooth the credit cycle and can include surcharges for systemically important financial institutions to limit the buildup of systemic risk.

- *Asset concentration and credit growth limits.* These measures alter the composition of the assets of financial institutions by imposing limits on the pace of credit growth or on their concentration in specific assets. Examples include speed limits on credit expansion, limits on foreign currency exposure or foreign-currency-denominated lending, and limits on sectoral concentration of loan portfolios. The aim of these measures is to reduce the exposure of bank portfolios to sectoral shocks and, to the extent that slower credit growth improves average loan quality, to aggregate shocks.

---

[21] Note that tools from different categories can be combined to address specific sources of systemic risk.

- *Loan eligibility criteria.* These measures limit the pool of borrowers that have access to finance to improve the average quality of borrowers. Examples include loan-to-value (LTV) and debt-to-income (DTI) limits. These limits seek to leave the "marginal" borrowers out of the pool. LTVs also safeguard lenders by increasing loan collateral. Eligibility criteria can be tailored to fit a loan portfolio's risk profile. For example, LTV limits can be linked to local house price dynamics or be differentiated based on whether loans are made in foreign currency to unhedged households.

Several obstacles make the econometric analysis of the impact of macroprudential policy on credit booms difficult. First, there are serious data availability and measurement issues. Macroprudential policy frameworks have not been around for very long, and a mere handful of countries have used them regularly. Second, macroprudential policy is often implemented in combination with changes in the macroeconomic stance and involves multiple instruments in the same package. Therefore, attributing specific outcomes to specific instruments is a difficult task. Third, in most cases, policies are implemented in reaction to credit market developments. Hence, endogeneity is a major problem, and this analysis does not attempt to establish causality. However, endogeneity would result in positive coefficients: more credit growth leads to macroprudential tightening. Thus, a significant negative correlation between the use of macroprudential tools and credit booms would suggest that these policies are effective in alleviating booms.

An aggregate measure of macroprudential policy is constructed that includes the sum of the following six measures: differential treatment of deposit accounts, reserve requirements, liquidity requirements, interest rate controls, credit controls, and open foreign exchange position limits.[22] Information on these measures is compiled from various issues of the IMF's *Annual Report on Exchange Arrangements and Exchange Restrictions* and is complemented with information from IMF Article IV reports and responses of country authorities to an IMF questionnaire (see IMF, 2011b).[23] The identified measures have been used more intensely since the mid-1990s (Figure 11.9). Reserve and liquidity requirements, followed by limits on open foreign exchange positions, have been used most frequently.

This exercise yields some promising results, suggesting that macroprudential tools can reduce the incidence of credit booms and decrease the probability that booms end up badly (Tables 11.7 and 11.8).[24] Consistent with the focus of macroprudential tools on financial sector vulnerabilities, the reduction in the

---

[22] Ideally, a variable would be used that indicates the macroprudential policy stance throughout the duration of the boom. Although that can be done with the monetary and fiscal policy variables, there is not enough variation for measuring macroprudential policy in the same way.

[23] Especially in the early years of the sample period, the use of such measures may not reflect macroprudential concerns as they came to be defined in the aftermath of the 2007–09 global financial crisis (for such a definition of macroprudential policy, see BIS, 2011, and IMF, 2011a).

[24] When estimating regressions using the subcomponents of the macroprudential index, we find that credit and interest controls and open foreign exchange position limits enter significantly in most regressions, although their significance is sensitive to the specific combination of variables included.

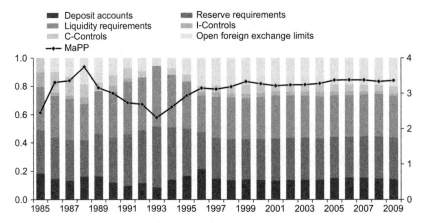

Figure 11.9 Macroprudential Policy Index and Its Components

Sources: IMF, *Annual Report on Exchange Arrangements and Exchange Restrictions*; Article IV reports; and surveys with country teams and country authorities (IMF, 2011b).

Note: Deposit accounts, I-Controls, C-Controls, and MaPP stand for differential treatment of deposit accounts, interest rate controls, credit controls, and macroprudential policy (the composite measure), respectively. Each component shown on the left scale is indicated by the proportion of countries adopting it in a given year. MaPP, shown on the right scale, is constructed as the within-year average of the within-country sum of component dummies.

probability of a bad boom is found primarily for booms that end up in a financial crisis, although the effect on the probability of economic underperformance is not very different. This outcome suggests that macroprudential policy can reduce the risk of a bust while simultaneously reducing the vulnerability of the rest of the economy to troubles in the financial system.[25] These findings are in line with those in Lim and others (2011), who suggest that macroprudential tools, such as LTV and DTI caps, ceilings on credit growth, reserve requirements, and dynamic provisioning rules, can mitigate the procyclicality of credit.

This empirical evidence supports the experience of countries that have used macroprudential policy tools. In general, these tools have been found to perform better in avoiding bad outcomes following credit booms rather than in preventing them altogether. Country experience with the most common macroprudential tools can be summarized as follows:

- *Capital and liquidity requirements.* These measures have been broadly successful in building up buffers to deal with busts. But they have been less successful in curtailing the incidence and duration of credit booms. Tight capital and reserve requirements in Croatia are viewed as having been effective in increasing banks' liquidity and capital buffers. This helped banks weather the global financial crisis, but was less effective in slowing credit growth and capital inflows (Kraft and Galac, 2011; and Ostry and others,

---

[25] The macroprudential policy measure are interacted with the macroeconomic policy variables to control for any complementarities or conflicts between these policies. No significant results are obtained.

2011). Likewise, Peru's reserve requirements on deposits in 2008 helped contain the risks posed by rapid credit growth while shielding the inflation targeting framework (Terrier and others, 2011). Dynamic loan-loss provisioning rules introduced in Spain in 2000 allowed Spanish banks to better absorb the negative shocks and maintain exposures during the crisis. In this way, the rules worked in their intended countercyclical fashion (Jiménez and others, 2011). Yet they did not stop the boom, and reliance on historical series to determine their magnitude may have made the buffers too small for what turned out to be an exceptional boom-bust cycle. In an interesting case targeting a specific class of assets, Brazil raised the risk weight on high-LTV car loans in December 2010 to restrain the rapid growth in this segment. Preliminary data suggest that this move has had its intended effect of raising interest rates on car loans and slowing down the supply of such credit.

• *Asset concentration and credit growth limits.* These measures have had some success in slowing down the pace of credit growth, although often at the expense of building up concentrations of risk elsewhere in the system. For example, although credit growth in Romania remained strong despite a wave of measures, strict foreign exchange exposure limits introduced between September 2005 and January 2007 managed to curb foreign-currency-denominated loan growth. In Croatia, speed limits on credit growth by banks were introduced in 2003 (limiting the annual growth of banks' domestic credits to 16 percent), combined with a penalty in the form of minimum holdings of central bank bills if credit growth exceeded this limit. These measures had some success in reducing the growth rate of bank credit (which fell from 28.7 percent in 2002 to 11.8 percent in 2003) because the penalty for breaching the rule was high. However, the growth of total domestic credit (including credit from nonbanks) barely declined; banks circumvented the rule by booking loans directly on their foreign parent banks and by lending to the private sector through their nonbank subsidiaries (e.g., leasing companies—Kraft and Galac, 2011). This contributed to the buildup of systemic risk in the nonbank financial sector.

• *Loan eligibility criteria.* Experience using these measures is limited, but when implemented they seem to have been effective in curbing the deterioration in lending standards typically associated with credit booms (Dell'Ariccia, Igan, and Laeven, 2008). For example, the resilience of the banking system in Hong Kong SAR during the Asian financial crisis in the late 1990s has been attributed to the introduction of actively managed LTV and DTI restrictions (Wong and others, 2011). Similarly, in Korea, LTV and DTI limits seem to have discouraged speculation in housing markets (Igan and Kang, 2011). In Poland, loan eligibility requirements on foreign-currency-denominated mortgage loans were credited with keeping default rates low during the global financial crisis, in spite of the zloty's significant depreciation against the currencies (euro and Swiss franc) in which these loans were denominated.

As a whole, macroprudential tools show promise in dealing with credit booms and busts (see also Lim and others, 2011, based on the experience of 49 countries since 2000). However, more time and analysis are needed for a full assessment of their effectiveness. Their targeted nature entails a more favorable cost-benefit balance. Yet a potential problem with their targeted nature is that it makes these instruments more susceptible to circumvention and political resistance. Circumvention may end up masking or increasing systemic risks by shifting credit activity into less-regulated intermediaries or to riskier loan types. And these distortions may prove economically important, similar to those documented for credit controls (Kane, 1977; and Borio, 2003, 2009).

Because the losers and winners associated with implementation of a particular macroprudential measure are more evident than when macroeconomic policies are used, it might be easier to gather and organize public opposition to the implementation of certain measures. Tension then arises between a rules-based approach to the application of these measures, to minimize political interference, and a discretionary approach that could better deal with circumvention. As with monetary tightening, cross-border policy coordination could help prevent circumvention and enhance the potential effectiveness of macroprudential policies. For example, the incentives to shift lending to foreign bank branches or less-regulated financial institutions may be reduced when communication and coordinated action among supervisors are strong.

CONCLUSIONS

Prolonged credit booms are a harbinger of financial crises and have real costs. This analysis shows that, even though only a minority of booms end up in crises, those that do can have long-lasting and devastating real effects if left unaddressed. Yet it appears to be difficult to identify bad booms as they emerge; therefore, the cost of intervening too early and curtailing a good boom has to be weighed against the desire to prevent financial crises.

Although the analysis offers some insights into the origins and dynamics of credit booms, from a policy perspective a number of questions remain unaddressed. In part this reflects the limited experience to date with macroprudential policies and the simultaneous use of multiple policy tools, making it hard to disentangle specific policy measures' effectiveness.

First, although monetary policy tightening seems the natural response to rapid credit growth, the analysis finds only weak empirical evidence that it contains booms and their fallout on the economy. This may be partly the result of a statistical bias. But there are several legitimate factors that limit the use and effectiveness of monetary policy in dealing with credit booms, especially in small open economies. In contrast, there is more consistent evidence that macroprudential policy is up to this task, although it is more susceptible to circumvention.

All of the above issues raise important questions about the optimal policy response to credit booms. Our view is that when credit booms coincide with periods of general overheating in the economy, monetary policy should act first and foremost. If the boom lasts and is likely to end up badly or if it occurs in the absence of overheating, then macroprudential policy should come into play. Preferably, macroprudential policy should be used in combination and coordination with macroeconomic policy, especially when macroeconomic policy is already being used to address overheating of the economy.

Second, questions remain about the optimal mix and modality of macroprudential policies, also in light of political economy considerations and the type of supervisory arrangements in a country. Political economy considerations call for a more rules-based approach to setting macroprudential policy to avoid pressure from interest groups to relax regulation during a crisis. But such considerations have to be weighed against the practical problems and unintended effects of a rules-based approach, such as the calibration of rules with rather demanding data requirements and the risk of circumvention in the presence of active earnings management. The design of a macroprudential framework should also consider the capacity and ability of supervisors to enforce such rules so that unintended and potentially dangerous side effects can be avoided.

Third, the optimal macroprudential policy response to credit booms, as well as the optimal policy mix, will likely depend on the type of credit boom. Because of data limitations, this analysis has focused on aggregate credit. It seems natural that policy responses should adapt to and be targeted to the type of credit, but additional analysis is needed to assess the effectiveness of policies to curtail booms that differ in the type of credit.

Fourth, policy coordination, across different authorities and across borders, may increase the effectiveness of monetary tightening and macroprudential policies. Cooperation and a continuous flow of information among national supervisors, especially regarding the activities of institutions that are active across borders, are crucial. Equally important is the coordination of regulations and actions among supervisors of different types of financial institutions. Whether and how national policymakers take into account the effects of their actions on the financial and macroeconomic stability of other countries is a vital issue, calling for further regional and global cooperation in the setup of macroprudential policy frameworks and the conduct of macroeconomic policies.

APPENDIX 11A. TECHNICAL DEFINITION OF A CREDIT BOOM

This analysis focuses on "extraordinary" deviations in the relationship between credit and economic activity. In this context, a credit boom is defined as an episode in which the ratio of credit to GDP grows faster than what is implied by its trend, which follows the normal pace of credit growth in that particular economy. An episode of rapid credit growth is marked as a boom when the deviation from trend exceeds a country- and path-dependent or an ad hoc threshold. More specifically, the credit-to-GDP ratio in each year t is compared with a country-specific, backward-looking, rolling cubic trend estimated during the period between years $t - 10$ and t. The cubic trend lets two inflection points be introduced so that both financial deepening and its reversal are allowed. An episode becomes a boom if either of the following two conditions is satisfied: (1) the deviation from trend is greater than 1.5 times its standard deviation and the annual growth rate of the credit-to-GDP ratio exceeds 10 percent; or (2) the annual growth rate of the credit-to-GDP ratio exceeds 20 percent.

To capture the borderline cases, a more ad hoc rule is used, defining any period during which the annual growth rate of the credit-to-GDP ratio exceeds 10 percent as a boom. The start of the boom is the earliest year in which either (1) the credit-to-GDP ratio exceeds its trend by more than three-fourths of its historical standard deviation while its annual growth rate exceeds 5 percent; or (2) its annual growth rate exceeds 10 percent.

A boom ends as soon as either (1) the growth of the credit-to-GDP ratio turns negative or (2) the credit-to-GDP ratio falls within three-fourths of one standard deviation from its trend and its annual growth rate is lower than 20 percent. Note that, because credit is a stock variable measured at year-end while GDP is a flow variable, the credit-to-GDP ratio is constructed with the geometric average of GDP in years t and $t + 1$. The robustness of the definition is checked by employing different thresholds and comparing the list of booms obtained with the lists reported in previous studies. Although the main insights remain the same, only the empirical findings using the baseline definition are discussed because of space constraints.

There are several advantages and drawbacks to using this methodology. On the positive side, the financial sector is not considered in isolation: by looking at the credit-to-GDP ratio rather than credit itself, the methodology relates credit developments to the size of the economy and accounts for the procyclicality of credit. In addition, only standard information about relevant past credit growth readily available in real time is used to set the benchmark, which is a particularly desirable feature for policymaking. On the negative side, the methodology may erroneously tag an observation as a credit boom when the credit-to-GDP ratio jumps not because of an increase in credit but because of a decrease in GDP. Such cases are checked manually and dropped from the list of booms. Another potential drawback is that the aggregate measure used captures only *bank* credit to the private sector (line 22d from the IMF's *International Financial Statistics*). Although nonbank financial institutions constitute a small portion of financial system assets and provide a negligible amount of credit to the private sector in many countries, credit booms driven by nonbank provision of loans may be missed. The discrepancy between bank credit and total credit is larger in countries with market-based, rather than bank-based, financial systems. Two countries that particularly stand out in this regard are the United Kingdom and the United States. All in all, however, the methodology provides an operationally convenient way to detect credit booms in real time.

TABLE 11A.1

Correlation of Booms across Definitions				
Trigger for boom dummy	(1)	(2)	(3)	(4)
Ad hoc threshold[1]	1			
Backward-looking, rolling, cubic trend[2]	0.99*	1		
Hodrick-Prescott over entire series[3]	0.50*	0.52*	1	
Hodrick-Prescott from t_0 to t^4				
Absolute	0.55*	0.58*	0.63*	1
Relative	0.75*	0.80*	0.47*	0.84*

Source: IMF staff calculations.
* indicates statistical significance at the 1 percent level.
[1]Boom if credit-to-GDP ratio increases by more than 20 percent.
[2]Barajas, Dell'Ariccia, and Levchenko (2008) definition. Baseline used in this chapter.
[3]Mendoza and Terrones (2008) definition.
[4]Gourinchas, Valdes, and Landerretche (2001) definition.

A natural question is how much the methodology used to define and identify the credit boom episodes alters the major empirical regularities underlined during the analysis. As mentioned at the beginning, various methodologies are used in the literature. The methodology used in this chapter is compared with those used in Gourinchas, Valdes, and Landerretche (2001) and in Mendoza and Terrones (2008). In addition, the identification of booms with these trend-based methodologies is checked against an ad hoc rule that deems any growth in the credit-to-GDP ratio above 20 percent as a boom. The correlation between the boom dummies created by these four methodologies is high (Table 11A.1).[26] Hence, the list of episodes identified in this analysis is not very sensitive to the methodology used. In particular, the major booms (e.g., those preceding the Scandinavian and Asian crises) are captured under all methodologies. The differences appear in small and medium booms because thresholds start to become binding.

Perhaps a more important concern is that, depending on which booms each methodology leaves out, the incidence of bad booms may be different. Indeed, in their original analyses, these methodologies arrive at different probabilities of booms being linked to banking crises. Specifically, Gourinchas, Valdes, and Landerretche (2001) look at 80 booms based on absolute and relative (to the credit-to-GDP ratio) deviation from trend—rather than setting the thresholds first, they limit the number of episodes. Using the criterion of calling a boom bad if it is followed by a crisis within three years of its end, 50 percent of absolute booms and 38 percent of relative booms they identify are bad. Mendoza and Terrones (2008) look at credit per capita instead of the credit-to-GDP ratio and identify 58 episodes, with 47 percent ending badly. The differences may also be due to the sample periods and the data, so the methodologies used in

---

[26] Given that we are comparing binary variables constructed as "binned" realizations of an underlying continuous variable, we use a tetrachoric correlation.

TABLE 11A.2

Incidence of Bad Booms across Definitions		
Definition of boom episodes	Number of booms	Followed by banking crises within three years of end (percent)
Ad hoc threshold[1]	112	38
Backward-looking, rolling, cubic trend[2]	175	33
Hodrick-Prescott over entire series[3]	112	37
Hodrick-Prescott from t_0 to t^4		
Absolute	138	43
Relative	60	42

Source: IMF staff calculations.
[1]Boom if credit-to-GDP ratio increases by more than 20 percent.
[2]Barajas, Dell'Ariccia, and Levchenko (2008) definition. Baseline used in this chapter.
[3]Mendoza and Terrones (2008) definition.
[4]Gourinchas, Valdes, and Landerretche (2001) definition.

these two papers are applied to the data set used in this chapter. The bad boom incidences reported in the baseline are actually on the lower end of the distribution (Table 11A.2).

REFERENCES

Abiad, Abdul, Giovanni Dell'Ariccia, and Bin (Grace) Li, 2011, "Creditless Recoveries," IMF Working Paper 11/58 (Washington: International Monetary Fund).

Abiad, Abdul, Enrica Detragiache, and Thierry Tressel, 2008, "A New Database of Financial Reforms," IMF Working Paper 08/266 (Washington: International Monetary Fund).

Adrian, Tobias, and Hyun Song Shin, 2009, "Money, Liquidity, and Monetary Policy," *American Economic Review*, Vol. 99, No. 2, pp. 600–05.

Backé, Peter, Balázs Égert, and Tina Zumer, 2006, "Credit Growth in Central and Eastern Europe: Emerging from Financial Repression to New (Over)Shooting Stars?" Working Paper No. 687 (Frankfurt: European Central Bank).

Bank for International Settlements (BIS), 2011, "Macroprudential Policy Tools and Frameworks," Update to G20 Finance Ministers and Central Bank Governors (Basel). www.bis.org/publ /othp13.pdf.

Barajas, Adolfo, Giovanni Dell'Ariccia, and Andrei Levchenko, 2008, "Credit Booms: The Good, the Bad, and the Ugly" (unpublished; Washington: International Monetary Fund).

Basel Committee on Banking Supervision (BIS), 2010, "Basel III: A Global Regulatory Framework for More Resilient Banks and Banking Systems" (Basel: Bank for International Settlements). http://www.bis.org/publ/bcbs189.htm.

Berger, Allen N., and Gregory F. Udell, 2004, "The Institutional Memory Hypothesis and the Procyclicality of Bank Lending Behavior," *Journal of Financial Intermediation*, Vol. 13, pp. 458–95.

Berger, Helge, Jakob de Haan, and Jan-Egbert Sturm, 2006, "Does Money Matter in the ECB Strategy? New Evidence Based on ECB Communication," CESIFO Working Paper No. 1652 (Munich: Center for Economic Studies).

Bernanke, Ben, and Mark Gertler, 1989, "Agency Costs, Net Worth, and Business Fluctuations," *American Economic Review*, Vol. 79, No. 1, pp. 14–31.

———, 1995, "Inside the Black Box: The Credit Channel of Monetary Policy Transmission," *Journal of Economic Perspectives*, Vol. 9, No. 4, pp. 27–48.

Boissay, Frédéric, Oscar Calvo-Gonzales, and Tomasz Kozluk, 2006, "Is Lending in Central and Eastern Europe Developing Too Fast?" in *Financial Development, Integration and Stability*, ed. by Klaus Liebscher, Josef Christl, Peter Mooslechner, and Doris Ritzberger-Grünwald (Cheltenham, United Kingdom: Edward Elgar Publishing).

Borio, Claudio, 2003, "Towards a Macroprudential Framework for Financial Supervision and Regulation?" *CESifo Economic Studies*, Vol. 49, No. 2, pp. 181–216.

———, 2009, "The Macroprudential Approach to Regulation and Supervision," VoxEU.org, April 14. http://www.voxeu.org/index.php?q=node/3445.

———, and Philippe Lowe, 2002, "Asset Prices, Financial and Monetary Stability: Exploring the Nexus," BIS Working Paper No. 114 (Basel: Bank for International Settlements).

Borio, Claudio, Robert McCauley, and Patrick McGuire, 2011, "Global Credit and Domestic Credit Booms," *BIS Quarterly Review*, September, pp. 43–57.

Borio, Claudio, and Ilhyock Shim, 2007, "What Can (Macro-) Prudential Policy Do to Support Monetary Policy?" BIS Working Paper No. 242 (Basel: Bank for International Settlements).

Borio, Claudio, and Haibin Zhu, 2008, "Capital Regulation, Risk-taking and Monetary Policy: A Missing Link in the Transmission Mechanism?" BIS Working Paper No. 268 (Basel: Bank for International Settlements).

Brzoza-Brzezina, Michał, Tomasz Chmielewski, and Joanna Niedźwiedzińska, 2010, "Substitution between Domestic and Foreign Currency Loans in Central Europe: Do Central Banks Matter?" European Central Bank Working Paper No. 1187 (Frankfurt: European Central Bank).

Caprio, Gerard, Daniela Klingebiel, Luc Laeven, and Guillermo Noguera, 2005, "Appendix: Banking Crisis Database," in *Systemic Financial Crises: Containment and Resolution*, ed. by Patrick Honohan and Luc Laeven (Cambridge, United Kingdom: Cambridge University Press).

Claessens, Stijn, Giovanni Dell'Ariccia, Deniz Igan, and Luc Laeven, 2010, "Cross-Country Experiences and Policy Implications from the Global Financial Crisis," *Economic Policy*, Vol. 25, No. 62, pp. 267–93.

Claessens, Stijn, Michael Keen, and Ceyla Pazarbasioglu, 2010, "Financial Sector Taxation," IMF report with background material presented to the G-20 (Washington: International Monetary Fund).

Claessens, Stijn, Ayhan Kose, and Marco E. Terrones, 2012, "How Do Business and Financial Cycles Interact?" *Journal of International Economics*, Vol. 87, No. 1, pp. 178–90.

Cottarelli, Carlo, Giovanni Dell'Ariccia, and Ivanna Vladkova-Hollar, 2003, "Early Birds, Late Risers, and Sleeping Beauties: Bank Credit Growth to the Private Sector in Central and Eastern Europe and the Balkans," IMF Working Paper 03/213 (Washington: International Monetary Fund).

Crowe, Christopher W., Deniz Igan, Giovanni Dell'Ariccia, and Pau Rabanal, 2011, "How to Deal with Real Estate Booms: Lessons from Country Experiences," IMF Working Paper 11/91 (Washington: International Monetary Fund).

Decressin, Jörg, and Marco E. Terrones, 2011, "Credit Boom-Bust Cycles: Their Triggers and Policy Implications," Box 1.2 in *World Economic Outlook*, September (Washington: International Monetary Fund).

Dell'Ariccia, Giovanni, Deniz Igan, and Luc Laeven, 2008, "Credit Booms and Lending Standards: Evidence from the Subprime Mortgage Market," *Journal of Money, Credit, and Banking*, Vol. 44, March, pp. 367–84.

Dell'Ariccia, Giovanni, and Robert Marquez, 2006, "Lending Booms and Lending Standards," *Journal of Finance*, Vol. 61, No. 5, pp. 2511–46.

De Nicolò, Gianni, Giovanni Dell'Ariccia, Luc Laeven, and Fabian Valencia, 2010, "Monetary Policy and Bank Risk-Taking," Staff Position Note 2010/09 (Washington: International Monetary Fund).

De Nicolò, Gianni, Giovanni Favara, and Lev Ratnovski, 2012, "Externalities and Macroprudential Policy," IMF Staff Discussion Note 12/05 (Washington: International Monetary Fund).

Duenwald, Christoph, Nikolay Gueorguiev, and Andrea Schaechter, 2005, "Too Much of a Good Thing? Credit Booms in Transition Economies," IMF Working Paper 5/128 (Washington: International Monetary Fund).

Eichengreen, Barry, and Kris Mitchener, 2003, "The Great Depression as a Credit Boom Gone Wrong," BIS Working Paper No. 137 (Basel: Bank for International Settlements).

Enoch, Charles, and Inci Ötker-Robe, 2007, *Rapid Credit Growth in Central and Eastern Europe: Endless Boom or Early Warning?* (New York: Palgrave Macmillan).

European Central Bank (ECB), 1999, "The Stability-Oriented Monetary Policy Strategy of the Eurosystem," *ECB Monthly Bulletin*, January, pp. 39–50.

Favara, Giovanni, 2003, "An Empirical Reassessment of the Relationship between Finance and Growth," IMF Working Paper 03/123 (Washington: International Monetary Fund).

Financial Services Authority (FSA), 2009, "The Turner Review: A Regulatory Response to the Global Banking Crisis," March (London: Financial Services Authority). www.fsa.gov.uk /pubs/other/turner_review.pdf.

Gilchrist, Simon, and Egon Zakrajsek, 2008, "Linkages between the Financial and Real Sectors: An Overview," Paper prepared for the Academic Consultants Meeting, Federal Reserve Board, October 3.

Gourinchas, Pierre-Olivier, Rodrigo Valdes, and Oscar Landerretche, 2001, "Lending Booms: Latin America and the World," *Economia*, Vol. 1, No. 2, pp. 47–99.

Hilbers, Paul, Inci Ötker-Robe, Ceyla Pazarbasioglu, and Gudrun Johnsen, 2005, "Assessing and Managing Rapid Credit Growth and the Role of Supervisory and Prudential Policies," IMF Working Paper 05/151 (Washington: International Monetary Fund).

Igan, Deniz, Alain Kabundi, Francisco Nadal De Simone, Marcelo Pinheiro, and Natalia Tamirisa, 2011, "Housing, Credit, and Real Activity Cycles: Characteristics and Comovement," *Journal of Housing Economics*, Vol. 20, No. 3, pp. 210–31.

Igan, Deniz, and Heedon Kang, 2011, "Do Loan-to-Value and Debt-to-Income Limits Work? Evidence from Korea," IMF Working Paper 11/297 (Washington: International Monetary Fund).

Igan, Deniz, and Marcelo Pinheiro, 2011, "Credit Growth and Bank Soundness: Fast and Furious?" IMF Working Paper 11/278 (Washington: International Monetary Fund).

International Monetary Fund (IMF), 2011a, "Macroprudential Policy: An Organizing Framework" (Washington: International Monetary Fund). www.imf.org/external/np/pp /eng/2011/031411.pdf.

———, 2011b, "Macroprudential Policy: An Organizing Framework - Background Paper," (Washington: International Monetary Fund). www.imf.org/external/np/pp/eng/2011 /031411a.pdf.

Jeanne, Olivier, 2008, "Dealing with Credit Booms and Busts: The Case for Prudential Taxation," Remarks at "Building an International Monetary and Financial System for the 21st Century: Agenda for Reform," conference organized by the Reinventing Bretton Woods Committee, New York, November 24–25.

———, and Anton Korinek, 2010, "Managing Credit Booms and Busts: A Pigouvian Taxation Approach," NBER Working Paper No. 16377 (Cambridge, Massachusetts: National Bureau of Economic Research).

Jiménez, Gabriel, Steven Ongena, José-Luis Peydró, and Jesús Saurina, 2011, "Macroprudential Policy, Countercyclical Bank Capital Buffers and Credit Supply: Evidence from the Spanish Dynamic Provisioning Experiments," Working Paper (Madrid: Bank of Spain [Banco de Espana]).

Jordà, Òscar, Moritz Schularick, and Alan M. Taylor, 2011, "Financial Crises, Credit Booms, and External Imbalances: 140 Years of Lessons," *IMF Economic Review*, Vol. 59, June, pp. 340–78.

Kane, Edward J., 1977, "Good Intentions and Unintended Evil: The Case against Selective Credit Allocation," *Journal of Money, Credit, and Banking*, Vol. 9, No. 1, pp. 55–69.

Keen, Michael, and Ruud de Mooij, 2012, "Debt, Taxes, and Banks," IMF Working Paper 12/48 (Washington: International Monetary Fund).

King, Robert G., and Ross Levine, 1993, "Finance and Growth: Schumpeter Might Be Right," *Quarterly Journal of Economics*, Vol. 108, No. 3, pp. 717–37.

Kiyotaki, Nobuhiro, and John Moore, 1997, "Credit Cycles," *Journal of Political Economy*, Vol. 105, No. 2, pp. 211–48.

Kraft, Evan, and Tomislav Galac, 2011, "Macroprudential Regulation of Credit Booms and Busts: The Case of Croatia," Policy Research Working Paper No. 5772 (Washington: World Bank).

Laeven, Luc, and Fabian Valencia, 2010, "Resolution of Banking Crises: The Good, the Bad, and the Ugly," IMF Working Paper 10/46 (Washington: International Monetary Fund).

Leigh, Daniel, Deniz Igan, John Simon, and Petia Topalova, 2012, "Dealing with Household Debt," in *World Economic Outlook*, April (Washington: International Monetary Fund).

Levine, Ross, 2005, "Law, Endowments and Property Rights," *Journal of Economic Perspectives*, Vol. 19, No. 3, pp. 61–88.

———, Norman Loayza, and Thorsten Beck, 1999, "Financial Intermediation and Growth: Causality and Causes," Policy Research Working Paper No. 2059 (Washington: World Bank).

Levine, Ross, and David Renelt, 1992, "A Sensitivity Analysis of Cross-Country Growth Regressions," *American Economic Review*, Vol. 82, No. 4, pp. 942–63.

Lim, Cheng Hoon, Francesco Columba, Alejo Costa, P. Kongsamut, A. Otani, M. Saiyid, T. Wezel, and X. Wu, 2011, "Macroprudential Policy: What Instruments and How to Use Them? Lessons from Country Experiences," IMF Working Paper 11/238 (Washington: International Monetary Fund).

Maddaloni, Angela, and José-Luis Peydró, 2011, "Bank Risk-Taking, Securitization, and Low-Interest Rates: Evidence from the Euro-area and U.S. Lending Standards," *Review of Financial Studies*, Vol. 24, No. 6, pp. 2121–165.

Magud, Nicolas E., Carmen M. Reinhart, and Esteban R. Vesperoni, 2012, "Capital Inflows, Exchange Rate Flexibility, and Credit Booms," IMF Working Paper 12/41 (Washington: International Monetary Fund).

Mendoza, Enrique, and Marco E. Terrones, 2008, "An Anatomy of Credit Booms: Evidence from Macro Aggregates and Micro Data," NBER Working Paper No. 14049 (Cambridge, Massachusetts: National Bureau of Economic Research).

Merrouche, Ourda, and Erlend Nier, 2010, "What Caused the Global Financial Crisis? Evidence on the Drivers of Financial Imbalances 1999–2007," IMF Working Paper 10/265 (Washington: International Monetary Fund).

Mitra, Srobona, Jaromír Beneš, Silvia Iorgova, Kasper Lund-Jensen, Christian Schmieder, and Tiago Severo, 2011, "Toward Operationalizing Macroprudential Policies: When to Act?" in *Global Financial Stability Report*, September (Washington: International Monetary Fund).

Ostry, Jonathan D., Atish Ghosh, Karl Habermeier, Luc Laeven, Marcos Chamon, Mahvash S. Qureshi, and Annamaria Kokenyne, 2011, "Managing Capital Inflows: What Tools to Use?" IMF Staff Discussion Note 11/06 (Washington: International Monetary Fund).

Rajan, Raghuram G., 1994, "Why Bank Credit Policies Fluctuate: A Theory and Some Evidence," *Quarterly Journal of Economics*, Vol. 109, No. 2, pp. 399–441.

———, and Luigi Zingales, 1998, "Financial Dependence and Growth," *American Economic Review*, Vol. 88, No. 3, pp. 559–86.

Rancière, Romain, Aaron Tornell, and Frank Westermann, 2008, "Systemic Crises and Growth," *Quarterly Journal of Economics*, Vol. 123, No. 1, pp. 359–406.

Reinhart, Carmen M., and Kenneth S. Rogoff, 2004, "The Modern History of Exchange Rate Arrangements: A Reinterpretation," *Quarterly Journal of Economics*, Vol. 119, No. 1, pp. 1–48.

———, 2009, "The Aftermath of Financial Crises," NBER Working Paper No. 14656 (Cambridge, Massachusetts: National Bureau of Economic Research).

Ruckes, Martin, 2004, "Bank Competition and Credit Standards," *Review of Financial Studies*, Vol. 17, No. 4, pp. 1073–102.

Schularick, Moritz, and Alan M. Taylor, 2009, "Credit Booms Gone Bust: Monetary Policy, Leverage Cycles and Financial Crises, 1870–2008," CEPR Discussion Paper No. 7570 (London: Centre for Economic Policy Research).

Svensson, Lars E.O., 2003, "In the Right Direction, But Not Enough: The Modification of the Monetary-Policy Strategy of the ECB," Briefing paper for the Committee on Economic and Monetary Affairs (ECON) of the European Parliament.

Terrier, Gilbert, Rodrigo Valdés, Camilo E. Tovar, Jorge Chan-Lau, Carlos Fernández-Valdovinos, Mercedes García-Escribano, Carlos Medeiros, Man-Keung Tang, Mercedes Vera Martin, and Chris Walker, 2011, "Policy Instruments to Lean against the Wind in Latin America," IMF Working Paper 11/159 (Washington: International Monetary Fund).

Terrones, Marco E., 2004, "Are Credit Booms in Emerging Markets a Concern?" in *World Economic Outlook*, April (Washington: International Monetary Fund).

Vandenbussche, Jérôme, Ursula Vogel, and Enrica Detragiache, 2012, "Macroprudential Policies and Housing Prices: A New Database and Empirical Evidence for Central, Eastern, and South-Eastern Europe," IMF Working Paper 12/303 (Washington: International Monetary Fund).

Woodford, Michael, 2008, "How Important Is Money in the Conduct of Monetary Policy?" *Journal of Money, Credit and Banking*, Vol. 40, No. 8, pp. 1561–98.

Wong, Eric, Tom Fong, Ka-fai Li, and Henry Choi, 2011, "Loan-to-Value Ratio as a Macroprudential Tool: Hong Kong's Experience and Cross-Country Evidence," Working Paper No. 01/2011 (Hong Kong SAR: Hong Kong Monetary Authority).

CHAPTER 12

Policies for Macro-Financial Stability: Managing Real Estate Booms and Busts

CHRISTOPHER CROWE, GIOVANNI DELL'ARICCIA, DENIZ IGAN, AND PAU RABANAL

Real estate boom-bust cycles can have far-reaching consequences. These booms are generally accompanied by fast credit growth and sharp increases in leverage, and when the bust comes, debt overhang and deleveraging spirals can threaten financial and macroeconomic stability. Despite these dangers, the traditional policy approach to real estate booms has been one of "benign neglect" (Bernanke, 2002; and Greenspan, 2002), notwithstanding the more proactive approach adopted by a few central banks (Mishkin, 2011). This attitude was based on two main premises. First was the belief that, as with other asset prices, it is extremely difficult to identify unsustainable real estate booms, or "bubbles" (sharp price increases not justified by fundamentals), in a timely manner. Second was the notion that the distortions associated with preventing a boom outweigh the costs of cleaning up after a bust. The 2007–09 global economic and financial crisis has challenged (at least the second of) these assumptions.

The burst of the real estate bubble in the United States triggered the worst financial crisis and the deepest recession since the Great Depression. The crisis quickly spread to other countries, especially those with their own homegrown bubbles. Traditional macroeconomic policy rapidly reached its limits, as monetary policy rates approached the zero bound and sustainability concerns emerged on the fiscal front. And despite the recourse to extraordinary measures (ranging from bank recapitalization to asset purchase programs and quantitative easing), the aftermath of the crisis was characterized by a weak recovery, as debt overhang and financial sector weakness continued to hamper economic growth. Bubbles remain hard to spot with certainty. But this task can be made easier by narrowing the focus to episodes involving sharp increases in credit and leverage, which are, after all, the true source of vulnerability. Although early intervention may engender its own distortions, it may be best to undertake policy action on the basis of a judgment call (as with inflation) if there is a real risk that inaction could result in catastrophe.

The authors would like to thank Franklin Allen, Olivier Blanchard, Stijn Claessens, and Susan Wachter for useful comments and discussions. Mohsan Bilal and Jeanne Verrier provided excellent research assistance.

Yet a call for a more preventive policy action raises more questions than it answers. What kind of indicators should trigger policy intervention to stop a real estate boom? If policymakers were fairly certain that intervention were warranted, what policy tools would be at their disposal? What are their impacts? What are their negative side effects and limitations? What practical issues would limit their use? This chapter explores these questions.

It should be recognized at the outset that a more proactive policy stance can help reduce the risks associated with real estate booms, but will inevitably result in its own costs and distortions. With this in mind, the chapter reaches the following conclusions: Policy efforts should focus on booms that are financed through credit and when leveraged institutions are directly involved because the following busts tend to be more costly. In that context, monetary policy is too blunt and costly a tool to deal with the vulnerabilities associated with increased leverage, unless the boom occurs as a result of or at the same time as broader economic overheating. Fiscal tools may be, in principle, effective. But, in practice, they would likely create distortions and are difficult to use in a cyclical fashion. Macroprudential tools (such as limits on loan-to-value ratios) are the best candidates for dealing with the dangers associated with real estate booms because they can be aimed directly at curbing leverage and strengthening the financial sector. But their careful design is crucial to minimizing circumvention and regulatory arbitrage. Furthermore, they will involve a cost to the extent that some agents find themselves rationed out of credit markets.

The chapter opens with a summary of how real estate boom-bust cycles may threaten financial and macroeconomic stability. Then it discusses different policy options to reduce the risks associated with real estate booms,[1] drawing on several country experiences and the insights from an analytical model.[2] The chapter concludes with a brief discussion of guiding principles for using public policy measures to deal with real estate booms.

THE CASE FOR POLICY ACTION ON REAL ESTATE BOOMS

Before the 2007–09 global crisis, the main policy tenet in dealing with an asset price boom was that it was better to wait for the bust and pick up the pieces afterward than to attempt to prevent the boom ahead of time (admittedly, this was less true in emerging market economies, which often paid close attention to real estate markets). Given this prescription, the characteristics of a particular asset class (such as how purchases are financed and what agents are involved, or whether the asset has consumption value besides investment value) were secondary details. However, if postbust policy intervention is of limited effectiveness and, thus, the costs associated with a bust are large, these details are critical to determining whether it is worth attempting to contain a boom in the first place. From this standpoint, several frictions and externalities make the case for early policy intervention in real estate market booms more strongly than for booms in other asset classes.

---

[1] The focus is on cyclical policies; a discussion of the impact of structural measures is in IMF (2011).
[2] A more detailed analysis of country cases is in Crowe and others (2011).

Leverage and the Link to Crises

From a macroeconomic stability perspective, what matters may be not the boom itself, but how it is funded. Busts tend to be more costly when booms are financed through credit and leveraged institutions are directly involved because the balance sheets of borrowers (and lenders) deteriorate sharply when asset prices fall.[3] The involvement of banks can lead to a credit crunch with negative consequences for real economic activity. In contrast, economic booms with limited leverage and limited bank involvement tend to deflate without major economic disruptions. For example, the bursting of the dot-com bubble was followed by a relatively mild recession, reflecting the minor role played by leverage and bank credit in funding the boom.

Real estate markets are special along both dimensions. The vast majority of home purchases and commercial real estate transactions in advanced economies involve borrowing. And banks and other leveraged players are actively involved in the financing. Moreover, home buyers are allowed leverage ratios orders of magnitude higher than for any other investment activity. A typical mortgage loan carries a loan-to-value ratio of 71 percent on average across a global sample of countries. In contrast, stock market participation by individuals hardly ever relies on borrowed funds. And when it does, loans are subject to margin calls that prevent the buildup of highly leveraged positions.

Highly leveraged housing markets had a prominent role during the 2007–09 crisis. In particular, the decline in U.S. house prices was at the root of the distress in the market for mortgage-backed securities. When house prices started to fall, both speculative buyers and owner-occupiers that were unwilling or unable to repay their mortgages could not roll them over or sell their properties and started to default (Mayer, Pence, and Sherlund, 2008). As uncertainty about the quality of the underlying loans increased, the value of mortgage-backed securities began to decline. Investors holding these securities and their issuers, both often highly leveraged themselves, found it increasingly difficult to obtain financing and some were forced to leave the market. This, in turn, decreased the available funds for mortgage financing, starting a spiral. The role of the boom and associated leverage in explaining defaults is evident in Figure 12.1.

This pattern was not limited to the United States, nor was it new to this crisis. The amplitude of house price upturns before 2007 is statistically associated with the severity of the crisis across countries (Figure 12.2; Claessens and others, 2010). The U.S. market may have been the initial trigger, but the countries that experienced the most severe downturns were those with real estate booms of their own. And, historically, many major banking distress episodes have been associated with boom-bust cycles in property prices (Figure 12.3; Herring and Wachter, 1999; and Reinhart and Rogoff, 2009). Looking at the 12 infamous episodes,

---

[3] In models as in Kiyotaki and Moore (1997), the collateral role of property magnifies swings as real estate cycles become correlated with credit cycles. A two-way amplification process develops between rising house prices and a credit boom during the upswing, and declining prices and a credit crunch during the downturn.

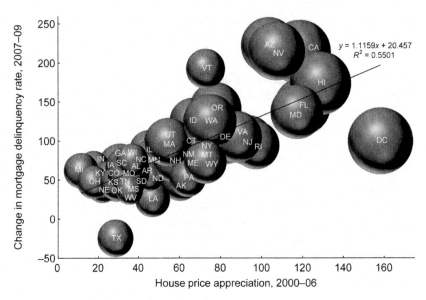

Figure 12.1 Leverage: Linking Booms to Defaults

Sources: Bureau of Economic Analysis; Federal Housing Finance Agency; Mortgage Bankers Association; and U.S. Census Bureau.
Note: Bubble size shows leverage (calculated as mortgage credit outstanding divided by household income) in 2007.

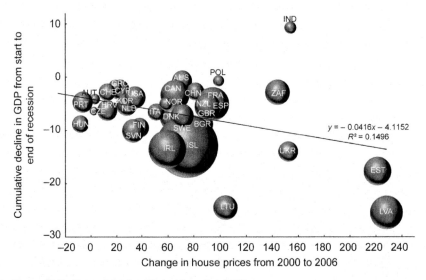

Figure 12.2 House Price Run-Up and Severity of Crisis

Source: Claessens and others, 2010.
Note: Bubble size shows the change in bank credit from 2000 to 2006. AUS = Australia; AUT = Austria; BGR = Bulgaria; CAN = Canada; CHE = Switzerland; CHN = China; CYP = Cyprus; CZE = Czech Republic; DNK = Denmark; ESP = Spain; EST = Estonia; FIN = Finland; FRA = France; GBR = United Kingdom; GRC = Greece; HRV = Croatia; HUN = Hungary; IND = India; IRL = Ireland; ISL = Iceland; ITA = Italy; KOR = Korea; LTU = Lithuania; LVA = Latvia; NLD = Netherlands; NOR = Norway; NZL = New Zealand; POL = Poland; PRT = Portugal; SVN = Slovenia; SWE = Sweden; UKR = Ukraine; USA = United States; ZAF = South Africa.

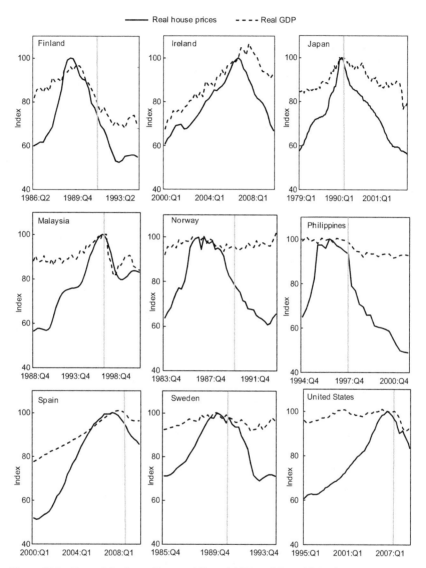

Figure 12.3   House Price Boom-Busts and Financial Crises: Selected Episodes

Sources: IMF, *International Financial Statistics*; IMF staff calculations; and Organization for Economic Co-operation and Development, Global Property Guide.

Note: Crisis beginning dates, shown by the vertical lines, are from Caprio and others (2003), further complemented in Laeven and Valencia (2010). Real GDP series are detrended.

house prices plunged 25 percent in the three-year period from their peak while real GDP dropped by 6 percentage points compared with its level when house prices were at their peak (Figure 12.4).[4]

---

[4] The infamous episodes comprise Spain in the early 1980s; Australia, Denmark, Finland, Norway, and Sweden in the late 1980s; Japan in the early 1990s; Malaysia and the Philippines in the late 1990s; and Ireland, Spain, and the United States in the first decade of the 2000s.

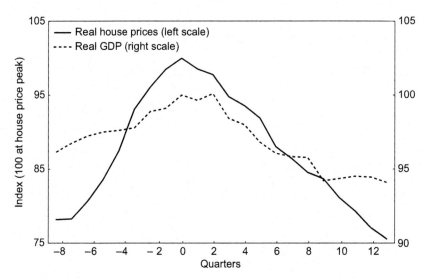

Figure 12.4 House Price Boom-Busts and Financial Crises: Average Damage

Sources: IMF staff calculations; and Organization for Economic Co-operation and Development, Global Property Guide.

Note: The paths of real house prices and real GDP 8 quarters before and 12 quarters after the house price peak (dated 0) for 12 infamous episodes (see text) are shown. Both real house prices and real GDP are indexed to equal 100 at house price peak.

Another distinguishing feature of "bad" real estate boom-bust episodes seems to be coincidence between the boom and the rapid increase in leverage and exposure of households and financial intermediaries. In the 2007 episode, this coincidence occurred in more than half the countries in a 40-country sample (Table 12.1). Almost all the countries with "twin booms" in real estate and credit markets (21 out of 23) ended up suffering from either a financial crisis or a severe drop in the GDP growth rate relative to the country's performance in the 2003–07 period. Eleven of these countries actually suffered from both damage to the financial sector and a sharp drop in economic activity. In contrast, of the seven countries that experienced a real estate boom, but not a credit boom, only two went through a systemic crisis and these countries, on average, had relatively mild recessions.

Wealth and Supply-Side Effects

Real estate is an important, if not the most important, storage of wealth in the economy. Additionally, the majority of households tend to hold wealth in their homes rather than in equities. Typically, in advanced economies fewer than half of households own stock (directly or indirectly) while home ownership rates hover around 65 percent (Guiso, Haliassos, and Jappelli, 2003).[5]

---

[5] Although stock market fluctuations are typically larger, the wealth loss associated with real estate busts tends to be larger because of spillover effects. For instance, during the dot-com bust, the value of American households' equity holdings declined by 44 percent or US$5.4 trillion. The real estate bust that started at the end of 2006 has brought about a 15 percent decline in the value of real estate assets, or US$3.7 trillion. However, total wealth lost stands at US$10 trillion or 13 percent of end-2006 total household assets.

TABLE 12.1

Booms, Crises, and Macroeconomic Performance

Type of boom	Boom followed by financial crisis (percent)[1]	Boom followed by poor performance (percent)[2]	Boom followed by financial crisis *or* poor performance (percent)	Boom followed by financial crisis *and* poor performance (percent)	Number of countries
Real estate[3]	53	77	87	43	30
Credit[4]	67	78	93	52	27
Real estate but not credit	29	71	71	29	7
Credit but not real estate	100	75	100	75	4
Both	61	78	91	48	23
Neither	27	18	45	0	11

Sources: IMF, *International Financial Statistics*; IMF staff calculations; and Organization for Economic Co-operation and Development, Global Property Guide.

[1] A financial crisis is a systemic banking crisis as identified in Laeven and Valencia (2010).

[2] Poor performance is defined as a more than 1 percentage point decline in the real GDP growth rate in 2008–09 compared with the 2003–07 average.

[3] A real estate boom exists if the annual real house price appreciation rate in the upward phase of the housing cycle before the crisis exceeds the country-specific historical annual appreciation rate.

[4] A credit boom exists if the growth rate of bank credit to the private sector in percentage of GDP is more than the arbitrary cut-off of 20 percent or it exceeds the rate implied by a country-specific, backward-looking, cubic time trend by more than one standard deviation.

In addition, the supply-side effects associated with house price dynamics can be substantial. The construction sector, a significant contributor to value added, takes property prices as a signal and adjusts production accordingly. As a result, the interaction between real estate boom-busts and economic activity is not limited to financial crises, but extends to "normal times." In most advanced economies, house price cycles tend to lead credit and business cycles (Igan and others, 2009). This suggests that fluctuations in house prices create ripples in the economy through their impacts on residential investment, consumption, and credit whereas the reverse effect is not as prominent, implying that the housing sector can be a *source* of shocks, or at least there is a two-way relationship between house prices and economic activity (IMF, 2011). In advanced economies, recessions that coincide with house price busts tend to be deeper and last longer than those that do not, and their cumulative losses are three times the damage done during recessions without busts (Table 12.2). Again, by contrast, recessions that occur around equity price busts are not significantly more severe or persistent than those that do not (Claessens, Kose, and Terrones, 2008).

Illiquidity, Opacity, and Network Effects

Boom-bust cycles are an intrinsic feature of real estate markets, reflecting delays in supply responses to demand shocks and the slow pace of price discovery

TABLE 12.2

Recessions with and without House Price Busts			
	Recession without bust	**Recession with bust**	**Recession with severe bust[1]**
Duration (quarters)	3.2	4.5 **	4.6 **
Amplitude (percent)	−2.0	−3.2 *	−4.1 **
Cumulative loss (percent)	−3.5	−10.4 **	−14.0 *

Source: Reproduced from Table 8 in Claessens, Kose, and Terrones (2008).
Note: The sample includes 21 Organization for Economic Cooperation and Development countries. Mean values are shown.
[1]Severe busts are those that are in the top half of all house price bust episodes.
* and ** indicate that the difference between means of recessions with house price busts and recessions without house price busts is significant at the 10 percent and 5 percent levels, respectively.

associated with opaque and infrequent trades as well as illiquidity owing to high transaction costs and the virtual impossibility of short sales. Therefore, real estate prices and construction activity can be expected to display large swings over long periods, even absent the distortions caused by the institutional features of real estate finance and policy actions (Igan and Loungani, 2012).[6]

Network externalities also complicate the picture. Homeowners in financial distress (particularly those with negative equity) have less incentive to maintain their properties and do not internalize the effects of this behavior on their neighbors. Similarly, foreclosures (and the associated empty houses) tend to diminish the value of neighboring properties beyond their effect through fire sales. The double role of real estate as investment and consumption goods may reduce mobility and increase structural unemployment because households in negative equity may be reluctant or unable to sell and take advantage of job opportunities elsewhere. The preferential tax treatment of home ownership exacerbates this problem by creating a wedge between the cost of owning and renting. Hence, a housing bust may weaken the positive association between employment growth and mobility. Indeed, U.S. regions in which house prices declined more, pushing an increasing number of households into negative-equity territory, experienced sharper declines in the mobility rate (defined as the portion of households that move from the region to another region).

POLICY OPTIONS

The 2007–09 crisis has lent some support to the camp favoring early intervention in real estate boom-bust cycles. Policy proved to be of limited effectiveness in cleaning up the mess. In several countries, monetary easing, fiscal stimulus, direct support to the financial sector, and special housing market initiatives helped, but could not prevent the largest recession since the Great Depression. Ultimately,

---

[6]Another factor that could delay adjustment of prices to fundamentals in real estate markets is the existence of a large set of investors with adaptive expectations (Case and Shiller, 2003; and Piazzesi and Schneider, 2009).

there were large costs, including social and human costs caused by foreclosures and job losses associated with the bust. Although the issue remains of distinguishing bubbles—that is, price misalignments relative to economic fundamentals—from large or rapid movements in prices, better yardstick indicators (such as price-income and price-rent ratios, measures of credit growth, and leverage) can be developed to guide the assessment of the risks posed by a run-up in prices and the decision to take action against bad booms.[7] And, similar to other policy decisions, action may have to be taken under considerable uncertainty when the costs of inaction might be prohibitively high.

If we accept the notion that intervention may be warranted even though it is often difficult to separate good from bad booms, which policy lever is best suited to reining in the bad booms? The main risks from real estate boom-bust cycles are associated with increased leverage in both the real (in particular, household) and financial sectors. Thus, policies should, whenever possible, aim at containing these risks rather than containing price increases. In that context, one could think of policies as targeting two main objectives (not to be taken as mutually exclusive): (1) preventing real estate booms and the associated leverage buildup in household and banking sectors altogether, and (2) increasing the resilience of the financial system to a real estate bust. Table 12.3 summarizes available policy measures along with their pros and cons.

It should be recognized at the outset that there is no silver bullet. Each policy will have costs and distortions, and its effectiveness will be limited by loopholes and implementation problems. Broad-reaching measures (such as a change in the monetary policy rate) will be more difficult to circumvent and therefore potentially more effective, but will typically involve greater costs. More-targeted measures (such as maximum loan-to-value ratios) may limit costs, but will be challenged by loopholes, jeopardizing efficacy.

What follows are explorations. The narrative in the chapter focuses on residential real estate. However, several (although not all) of the measures discussed could easily apply to commercial real estate booms as well. The chapter examines the potential role of monetary, fiscal, and macroprudential policies. Supply-side housing policies (such as publicly provided housing and land sales) widely used in a few countries (Hong Kong SAR and Singapore in particular) are not discussed because they would be difficult to export to different institutional settings. The benefits and challenges associated with the various policy options are discussed using case studies of countries with experience in the use of particular measures and, where possible, cross-country evidence. Finally, policy options are also examined through the lens of a stylized theoretical model.

---

[7] Although leverage is the real target, price misalignment ratios can also act as helpful indicators because of the aforementioned two-way relationship between credit and prices. Also, in practice, these ratios can signal vulnerabilities as more households stretch their finances to pay for housing services.

TABLE 12.3

Policy Options to Deal with Real Estate Booms

Macroeconomic Policy	Potential impact	Side effects	Practical issues
Monetary measures			
Interest rates · Reserve requirements (responding to property prices and real estate loan growth)	potential to prevent booms, less so to stop one that is already in progress	inflict damage to economic activity and welfare	identifying "doomed" booms and reacting in time; constraints imposed by monetary regime
Fiscal measures			
Transaction/capital gains taxes linked to real estate cycles	automatically dampen the boom phase	impair already-slow price discovery process	incentive to avoid by misreporting, barter, folding the tax into the mortgage amount
Property taxes charged on market value	(could) limit price increase and volatility	—	little room for cyclical implementation
Abolition of mortgage interest deductibility	reduce incentives for household leverage and house price appreciation	(potentially) inflict damage on the real estate sector by taking away a sectoral advantage	little room for cyclical implementation
Regulatory Policy *Macroprudential measures*			
Differentiated capital requirements for real estate loans · Higher risk weights on real estate loans	increase cost of real estate borrowing while building buffer to cope with the downturn	costs associated with potential credit rationing	may get too complicated to enforce, especially in a cyclical context; effectiveness also limited when capital ratios are already high
Dynamic provisioning for loans collateralized by real estate	increase cost of real estate borrowing while building buffer to cope with the downturn	earnings management	data requirements and calibration
Limits on mortgage credit growth	(could) limit household leverage and house price appreciation	loss of benefits from financial deepening	move lending outside the regulatory periphery
Limits on exposure to real estate sector	(could) limit leverage and price appreciation as well as sensitivity of banks to certain shocks	costs associated with limiting benefits from specialization	shift lending to newcomers for whom exposure limits do not yet bind or are outside the regulatory periphery
Limits on loan-to-value ratio · Limits on debt-to-income ratio	(could) limit household leverage and house price appreciation while decreasing probability of default	costs associated with potential credit rationing	calibration is difficult, circumvention is easy

Sources: IMF country reports; Enoch and Ötker-Robe (2007); Borio and Shim (2007); and IMF staff.

Monetary Policy

Can monetary tightening stop or contain a real estate boom? An increase in the policy rate makes borrowing more expensive and reduces the demand for loans. In addition, higher interest payments lower the affordability index (the ratio of median household income to income necessary to qualify for a typical mortgage loan) and shrink the number of borrowers that qualify for a loan of a certain amount. Indirectly, to the extent that monetary tightening reduces leverage in the financial sector, it may alleviate the financial consequences of a bust even if it does not stop the boom (Adrian and Shin, 2009; De Nicolò and others, 2010).

However, monetary policy is a blunt instrument for this task. First, it affects the entire economy and is likely to involve substantial costs if the boom is limited to the real estate market. Put differently, a reduction in the risk of a real estate boom-bust cycle may come at the cost of a larger output gap and the associated higher unemployment rate (and possibly an inflation rate below the desired target range). Obviously, these concerns are lower when the boom occurs in the context (or as a consequence) of general macroeconomic overheating. Then, the distortions associated with monetary tightening would be minimized. Indeed, when financial constraints are present and real estate is important as collateral, a policy rule reacting to real estate price movements or credit growth (in addition to inflation and the output gap) can trump a traditional Taylor rule but only for booms that occur along with general macroeconomic overheating (see the section below on "Model-Based Evaluation of Policy Options").

A second concern is that, during booms, the expected return on assets (in this case, real estate) can be much higher than what can be affected by a marginal change in the policy rate. It follows that monetary tightening may not directly affect the speculative component of demand. If that is the case, tightening may have the perverse effect of leading borrowers (who would have otherwise qualified for standard mortgages) toward more dangerous forms of loans (such as interest-only, variable-rate loans, and in some cases foreign-currency loans).[8] Moreover, in the presence of free capital mobility, the effectiveness of monetary policy may be limited, especially for exchange rate regimes that are not fully flexible.

Finally, the effectiveness of a change in the policy rate will also depend on the structure of the mortgage market. In systems in which mortgage rates depend primarily on long-term rates, the effectiveness of monetary policy will depend on the relationship between long and short rates.

To a large extent, empirical evidence supports these concerns, leading to the conclusion that monetary policy could, in principle, stop a boom, but at a very high cost. At first glance, there is little evidence across countries that the precrisis monetary stance had much to do with the real estate boom preceding the 2007–09 crisis. Inflationary pressures were broadly contained throughout the period

---

[8] For instance, Brzoza-Brzezina, Chmielewski, and Niedzwiedzinska (2007) find that in the Czech Republic, Hungary, and Poland, monetary tightening led to decreased domestic-currency lending but accelerated foreign-currency-denominated loans.

and the extent of house price booms does not appear to have been correlated with real interest rates or other measures of monetary conditions, except in a subsample of euro area countries (IMF, 2009). This lack of a relationship can be explained in part by the rapid decline in import prices driven by the trade integration of emerging economies—notably China—that may have offset relatively high inflation in nontradables sectors (IMF, 2006). Housing booms were more salient in countries that experienced declines in import prices relative to the general price level. But the relationship between the monetary policy stance and house prices remains weak (albeit more statistically significant) after controlling for this issue (with Taylor residuals based on domestic inflation rather than overall consumer price index inflation). Policymakers would have had to "lean against the wind" dramatically to have had a meaningful impact on real estate prices and credit, with large effects on output and inflation. This intuitive result is confirmed by a panel vector autoregression, which suggests that, at a five-year horizon, a 100-basis-point hike in the policy rate would reduce house price appreciation by only 1 percentage point, compared with a historical average increase of 5 percent per year (see Crowe and others, 2011, for details). But it would also lead to a decline in GDP growth of 0.3 percentage point.

Part of the problem may be that speculation is unlikely to be stemmed by changes in the monetary policy stance. Some evidence indicates that conditions in the more speculative segment of mortgage markets are little affected by changes in the policy rate. For example, in the United States, denial rates (calculated as the proportion of loans originated to applications received) in the market for prime mortgages appear highly related to changes in the federal funds rate, with banks becoming more choosy when the rate increases. In contrast, denial rates for subprime loans (typically more linked to speculative purchases) do not seem to move systematically with monetary policy (Crowe and others, 2011).

Fiscal Tools

In most systems, a variety of fiscal measures (transaction taxes, property taxes, credits, deductibility of interest payments) bear on the decision to invest in real estate. The net result is often socially driven favorable treatment of home ownership (and sometimes housing-related debt).[9] In theory, some of these fiscal tools could be adjusted in a cyclical manner to influence house price volatility while preserving the favorable treatment of homeownership on average during the cycle. However, if the net present value of all future taxes is capitalized in property prices, adjusting taxes countercyclically around the same expected mean would not affect the prices.[10] In practice, moreover, cyclically adjusted fiscal measures may be of limited use. First, the evidence on the relationship between the tax

---

[9] See, for instance, Cremer and Gahvari (1998) for the economics of tax treatment of owner-occupied housing.
[10] Further to this point, adjusting taxes according to the cycle violates the principle of tax smoothing, which minimizes the excess burden of the taxes.

treatment of residential property and real estate cycles is inconclusive. Second, technical and political economy problems may complicate implementation.

At the structural level, the tax treatment of housing does not appear to be related across countries to the amplitude of real estate cycles: during the most recent global house price boom, real house prices increased significantly in some countries with tax systems that are highly favorable to housing (such as Sweden) as well as in countries with relatively unfavorable tax rules (such as France). Similarly, appreciation was muted in countries with both favorable systems (e.g., Portugal) and unfavorable ones (e.g., Japan). Overall, taxation was not the main driver of house price developments during the boom (Keen, Klemm, and Perry, 2010). Furthermore, levels of home ownership (the main excuse for favorable tax treatment of housing) are, if anything, *negatively* (but not significantly) related to the degree to which the tax system is favorable to owning one's own home.

In addition, the scope for the use of fiscal tools in a cyclical setting is likely to be limited. The institutional setup in most countries separates tax policy from monetary and financial regulation policies, making it extremely hard to implement changes in tax policies as part of a cyclical response with financial stability as the main objective. Instead, local governments may use lower property or transaction tax rates to attract residents during good times if the burden were to be a bust is shared with other jurisdictions. The ability of cyclical transaction taxes to contain exuberant behavior in real estate markets may be further compromised if home buyers do not respond to these taxes fully because they consider them to be an acceptable cost for an investment with high returns and consumption value. Also, during a boom phase, the incentives to "ride the bubble" may increase efforts to circumvent the measure by misreporting property values or folding the tax into the overall mortgage amount. Finally, as with most tax measures, the distortions created by a cyclical transaction tax may make it more difficult to evaluate a property, which already tends to be hard, and also may reduce the mobility of households, with potential implications for the labor market.

TRANSACTION TAXES

Transaction taxes that change with real estate conditions may, in theory, be promising for dealing with booms (Allen and Carletti, 2010). But it should be recognized that these taxes induce considerable distortions in real estate markets and, indirectly, in labor markets through their impact on mobility. On the bust side, the use of time-limited tax credits linked to house purchases in the United States and the suspension of the stamp duty in the United Kingdom helped stabilize the housing market. And, especially in the United States, the price stability and revival of activity disappeared with the expiration of the tax breaks (IMF, 2010). On the boom side, China and Hong Kong SAR introduced higher stamp duties to dampen real estate prices and discourage speculation. Their experience, however, indicates that transaction volume responds more than prices do (suggesting that the associated collateral costs are high) and the impact of the introduction of the tax may be transitory.

PROPERTY TAXES

Some evidence from the United States suggests that higher rates of property taxation may help limit housing booms as well as short-run volatility around an upward trend in prices (more details can be found in Crowe and others, 2011). A one-standard deviation ($5 per $1,000 of assessed value) increase in property tax rates is found to be associated with a 0.9 percentage point decline in average annual price growth (compared with annual growth of about 5.6 percent per year). One interpretation of this finding is that property taxes, indirectly taxing imputed rent, may mitigate the effect of other tax treatments favoring home-ownership and perhaps reduce speculative activity in housing markets. Of course, caveats apply in deriving implications from this evidence. First, munic-ipalities often face pressure to reduce tax rates when markets are booming and tax revenues are high. This implies that some of the negative correlation between prices and taxes may be spurious, and challenges the ability to use property taxes as a countercyclical tool.[11] In addition, the results may be specific to the U.S. housing market, the characteristics of which differ markedly from those in many other advanced economies, let alone emerging markets. Moreover, property tax rates clearly did not cause (or prevent) the emergence of a national housing boom in the United States, although they may have limited its impact on some areas, and the impact at the national level of a hypothetical national property tax might be very different from the localized impact of local taxes.

MORTGAGE INTEREST TAX DEDUCTIBILITY

Theoretically, mortgage interest tax deductibility, by encouraging debt financing, may lead to higher household debt and more leveraged loans and, in turn, to more severe financial sector distress during real estate downturns. Empirically, tax reforms that reduce the value of mortgage interest relief have been shown to lead to lower loan-to-value ratios (see Hendershott, Pryce, and White, 2003, for the United Kingdom; and Dunsky and Follain, 2000, for the United States). And they are estimated to cause an immediate decline in house prices of about 10 percent (see Agell, Englund, and Södersten, 1995, for Sweden; and Capozza, Green, and Hendershott, 1996, for the United States). This evidence suggests that a more neutral tax treatment may help make the economy less vulnerable to real estate busts by reducing incentives for leverage and preventing artificially elevated prices and homeownership rates. However, these estimates are based on

---

[11] Also, despite their impact on prices, neither transaction nor property taxes directly get to credit and leverage.

one-off changes, hinting at the difficulties in using mortgage interest tax deductibility rules in a cyclical way. Furthermore, eliminating interest deductibility will not eliminate booms. Before the recent crisis, some countries that tax mortgage interest experienced rapid growth in prices and household debt levels (such as Australia) while others that allow full deductibility did not have as big a boom (such as Switzerland).

Macroprudential Regulation

At least in theory, macroprudential measures, such as higher capital requirements or limits on various aspects of mortgage credit, could be designed to target narrow objectives (for instance, household or bank leverage) and tackle the risks associated with real estate booms more directly and at a lower cost than either monetary or fiscal policy.

Against the benefit of lower cost, macroprudential measures are likely to present two shortcomings. First, they may be easier to circumvent because they target a specific type of contract or group of agents. When circumvented, these measures can be counterproductive, possibly leading to liability structures that are more difficult to resolve or renegotiate in busts. Second, they may be more difficult to implement from a political economy standpoint. Monetary policy decisions have come to be accepted as a necessary evil thanks to central banks' increasing credibility and independence. In contrast, the use of macroprudential measures could be considered an unnecessary intrusion into the functioning of markets. The more direct impact of these measures would also complicate implementation because winners and losers would be more evident than if macroeconomic policies were used (although several countries seem to have dealt effectively with this problem).

This analysis focuses on three specific sets of measures: first, capital requirements or risk weights that change with the real estate cycle; second, dynamic provisioning, that is, the practice of increasing banks' loan loss provisions during the upswing phase of the cycle; and third, the cyclical tightening and easing of eligibility criteria for real estate loans through loan-to-value (LTV) and debt-to-income (DTI) ratios.[12] These macroprudential tools may be able to achieve both objectives: (1) reducing the likelihood or magnitude of a real estate boom (for instance, by imposing measures to limit household leverage), and (2) strengthening the financial system's ability to withstand the effects of a real estate bust (for example, by urging banks to save in good times for rainy days).

A caveat is in order: A major limitation in assessing the effectiveness of macroprudential tools stems from the fact that macroprudential policy frameworks are still in their infancy, and only a handful of countries have actively used them (Table 12.4; Borio and Shim, 2007; CGFS, 2010). And these measures have

---

[12] Other measures not discussed here include cyclical ceilings on portfolio exposure to real estate, speed limits on real estate lending, and restrictions on certain types of loans. These tools have been used even more sparingly.

TABLE 12.4

Survey-Based Assessment of Policy Frameworks as of September 2010 (proportion of respondents giving a particular answer, percent)

	Monetary policy framework		Tax system		Restrictions			Regulatory structure				
	Credit growth explicitly considered?	Property prices explicitly considered?	Transactions tax?	Mortgage interest deductibility?	On which financial institutions can extend mortgage loans?	On types of mortgages?	On loan-to-value ratio?	On debt-to-income ratio?	On mortgage credit growth rate?	Real-estate-specific loan loss provisioning?	Real-estate-specific risk weights?	Full recourse on mortgages?
No	78	64	6	39	50	81	53	50	94	61	56	25
Yes	22	36	94	61	50	19	47	50	6	39	44	75
Directly (not through, e.g., the rent component of CPI)	14	8										
Subject to restrictions			64	44								
Cyclically based										11	11	

Source: Survey of country authorities conducted by IMF staff.

Note: Compiled responses from 36 countries. Country-by-country responses to this brief in-house survey are in Crowe and others, 2011. CPI = consumer price index.

typically been used in combination with macroeconomic policy and direct interventions in the supply side of housing markets (such as in Singapore), further complicating the challenge of attributing outcomes to specific tools.

But much can be learned from case studies. Following the Asian crisis of the late 1990s, some countries in the region took a more heavy-handed approach to dealing with risks posed by real estate booms. Countries in Central and Eastern Europe experimented with various measures to control the rapid growth in bank credit to the private sector in the first decade of the 2000s. Others put in place dynamic provisioning frameworks. Table 12.5 summarizes policy experiences with real estate booms (a detailed account of country cases is in Crowe and others, 2011). On the whole, success stories appear to be few, perhaps reflecting the learning curve in expanding the policy toolkit, improving the design of specific tools, and sorting out implementation challenges. However, when policy succeeded in slowing down a boom and avoiding a systemic crisis in a bust, some macroprudential measures were almost always involved.

HIGHER CAPITAL REQUIREMENTS OR RISK WEIGHTS

Capital regulation has a procyclical effect on the supply of credit. During upswings, better fundamentals reduce the riskiness of a given loan portfolio, improving a bank's capital adequacy ratio and its ability to expand its assets. In a downturn, the opposite happens, possibly leading to deleveraging through fire sales. Countercyclical capital requirements could help reduce this bias. Furthermore, by forcing banks to hold more capital in good times, buffers would be built against future losses (see Gordy and Howells, 2006, and references therein).[13]

For real estate loans, the countercyclical element of capital regulation is largely absent. In most countries, existing rules do not take collateral values into consideration or reflect the heterogeneity among loans backed by real estate, other than the commercial-residential distinction. Under Basel II's standard approach, risk weights for property loans are fixed (50 percent for residential mortgages and 100 percent for commercial property loans). As a result, mortgage loans with predictably different default probabilities (for instance, because of different LTV ratios or exposure to different aggregate shocks) are often bundled in the same risk category and no adjustment is made to account for the real estate cycle.[14] Thus, capital requirements or risk weights linked to real estate price dynamics could

---

[13] The discussion focuses on the price-related measures of capital regulation, but exposure limits would have similar implications working as a quantity-based measure.

[14] Fixed risk weights are applicable only under the standard approach of Basel II. Under the internal-rating-based approach, regulators (and banks) can split loans into subcategories based on several risk indicators and vary risk weights accordingly. A few countries have applied higher risk weights to high-LTV loans (see Table 3 in Crowe and others, 2011, for more on country-by-country policy actions and their outcomes).

TABLE 12.5

Stylized Facts on Policy Responses to Real Estate Booms: Stocktaking

Measure	Issue addressed	Country	Impact
Macroeconomic			
Monetary tightening	Rapid credit growth or real estate boom	Croatia, Iceland, Latvia, Ukraine; Australia, Israel, Korea, Sweden	Not always effective, capital flows and currency switching risk are major limitations
Maintaining a flexible and consistent foreign exchange policy	Rapid credit growth	Czech Republic, Poland	Foreign-exchange-denominated credit growth slowed down in Poland but not in the Czech Republic
Fiscal tightening or removal of incentives for debt financing (e.g., mortgage interest tax relief)	Rapid credit growth or real estate boom	Estonia, Netherlands, Poland, United Kingdom; Lithuania, Spain	Limited effect on house prices, slightly more on household leverage
Additional/higher transaction taxes to limit speculative activity	Real estate boom	China, Hong Kong SAR, Singapore	Some effect on transaction acitivity, but not long lasting
Macroprudential			
Higher/differentiated capital requirements or risk weights by loan type	Rapid credit growth or real estate boom	Bulgaria, Croatia, India, Poland, Norway	Not always effective, some side effects of shifting the risk elsewhere in the system
Tighter/differentiated loan classification and provisioning requirements	Rapid credit growth or real estate boom	Bulgaria, Croatia, Greece, Israel, Ukraine	Limited effect
Dynamic provisioning	Resilience to cyclical downturn/bust	China, Colombia, India, Spain, Uruguay	So far so good on bank distress, small or no impact on credit conditions
Tightening eligibility requirements, e.g., limits on loan-to-value ratios	Real estate boom	China, Hong Kong SAR, Korea, Malaysia, Singapore; Sweden	Short-lived effect on prices and mortgage activity

Sources: Borio and Shim (2007); IMF country reports; Enoch and Ötker-Robe (2007); and IMF staff.

Note: The table gives a snapshot; it is not meant to be a comprehensive and detailed list of cases in which authorities took one or more of the measures listed to address credit/real estate developments. Bolivia and Peru have also put in place a dynamic provisioning framework, and Romania had used a battery of policy measures to address rapid credit growth; yet these countries are not included in the table because of lack of house price data. Dynamic provisioning in China and India is discretionary rather than rules based. In the entries in the "Country" column, countries following a semicolon implemented the measure under question only in the recent bust phase.

help limit the consequences of boom-bust cycles. These measures could build buffers against the losses incurred during busts by forcing banks to hold more capital against real estate loans during booms. And by increasing the cost of credit, they might reduce demand and contain real estate prices themselves.[15] Finally, weights could be fine-tuned to target regional booms.

Implementation Challenges

Several caveats exist in implementing countercyclical capital regulation to curb real estate booms. First, absent more risk-sensitive weights, an across-the-board increase in risk weights (or capital requirements) carries the danger of pushing lenders in the direction of riskier loans.[16] Thus, the introduction of countercyclical risk weights for real estate loans should be accompanied by the implementation of a finer cross-sectional risk classification. Second, as with any other measure that increases the cost of bank credit (when credit is in high demand), countercyclical risk weights may be circumvented through recourse to nonbank intermediaries, foreign banks, and off-balance-sheet activities. Third, these measures will lose effectiveness when actual bank capital ratios are well in excess of regulatory minimums (as often happens during booms). Fourth, although they would improve the resilience of the banking system to busts, tighter requirements are unlikely to have a major effect on credit availability and prices, that is, they are unlikely to reduce vulnerabilities in the real (household) sector. Finally, regulators may be reluctant to allow banks to reduce risk weights during a bust (when borrowers become less creditworthy).

Evidence

The empirical evidence on the effectiveness of these measures is mixed. In an effort to contain the rapid growth in bank credit to the private sector and the associated boom in asset markets, several countries have raised capital requirements or risk weights (or both) on particular groups of real estate loans. Some attempts (such as in Bulgaria, Croatia, Estonia, and Ukraine) failed to stop the boom; others (as in Poland) were at least a partial success.[17]

It is not easy to say why measures taken in one country may have been more effective than those taken elsewhere or the extent to which other developments account for the observed changes. Furthermore, even in countries in which tighter capital requirements appeared to produce some results for controlling the growth of particular groups of loans, real estate price appreciation and overall credit growth remained strong.

---

[15] Obviously, the increase in the cost of borrowing may have a side effect: credit rationing may set in, reducing welfare gains associated with access to finance.

[16] This is essentially the risk-shifting effect identified by models in the spirit of Stiglitz and Weiss (1981).

[17] Evidence on exposure limits is scant. Many countries have constant exposure limits, but there is no apparent relationship between the level of these limits and real estate boom-bust episodes.

DYNAMIC PROVISIONING

Dynamic provisioning (the practice of mandating higher loan loss provisions during upswings and one of the elements in Basel III) can help limit credit cycles.[18] The mechanics and benefits are similar to those of countercyclical capital requirements. Forcing banks to build (in good times) an extra buffer of provisions can help them cope with the potential losses that occur when the cycle turns (see, for example, the case of Spain). However, it is unlikely to cause a major increase in the cost of credit, and thus to stop a boom. That said, one advantage over countercyclical capital requirements is that dynamic provisioning would not be subject to minimums as capital requirements are, so it can be used when capital ratios maintained by banks are already high. Provisioning for property loans could be made a specific function of house price dynamics. In periods of booming prices, banks would be forced to increase provisioning, which they would be allowed to wind down during busts. As with risk weights, provisioning requirements could depend on the geographical allocation of a bank's real estate portfolio.

Implementation Challenges

As noted, this type of measure is primarily targeted at protecting the banking system from the consequences of a bust. Consequently, it is not meant to have a significant impact on credit and to contain other vulnerabilities associated with a boom, such as increases in debt and leverage in the household sector. In addition, practical issues, such as calibration of rules with rather demanding data requirements, and unintended effects, such as earnings management (which may raise issues with tax authorities and securities markets regulators) should be discussed in each country's context, and frameworks should be designed that best fit each country's circumstances. There are also other shortcomings, similar to those of countercyclical risk weights. (Being primarily targeted at commercial banks, dynamic provisioning may be circumvented by intermediaries outside of the regulatory perimeter.) Last, application of the measure only to domestically regulated banks may hurt their competitiveness and shift lending to banks abroad, raising cross-border supervision issues.

Evidence

The experience with these measures suggests that they are effective in strengthening a banking system against the effects of a bust, but do little to stop the boom. Spain led the countries that have adopted countercyclical provisioning and constitutes an interesting case study for a preliminary assessment of its effectiveness. Starting in 2000 and with a major revision in 2004, the Bank of Spain required banks to accumulate additional provisions based on the "latent loss" in their loan portfolios.[19] Dynamic provisioning forced banks to set aside, on average, the

---

[18] As has been the case for capital requirements, procyclicality of regulations governing loan loss provisions was subjected to criticism before the crisis (e.g., Laeven and Majnoni, 2003).
[19] For more details on the Spanish dynamic provisioning framework, see Saurina (2009).

equivalent of 10 percent of their net operating income; yet household leverage grew by a still-high 62 percent in Spain. At the end of 2007, just when the real estate bust started, total accumulated provisions covered 1.3 percent of total consolidated assets, in addition to the 5.8 percent covered by capital and reserves (for some perspective, the value of the housing stock has decreased by roughly 15 percent in real terms). Hence, Spanish banks had an important buffer that strengthened their balance sheets when real estate prices started to decline and the economy slipped into recession. The recession has deepened as the problems in peripheral Europe escalated, making it difficult to say whether the Spanish economy would have suffered even more if dynamic provisioning had not been in place.

LIMITS ON LOAN-TO-VALUE AND DEBT-TO-INCOME RATIOS

A limit on LTV can help prevent the buildup of vulnerabilities on the borrower side (in particular in the household sector). Containing leverage reduces the risks associated with declines in house prices; that is, the lower the leverage, the greater the drop in prices needed to put a borrower into negative equity. In turn, fewer defaults should occur when the bust comes because more borrowers unable to keep up with their mortgages will be able to sell their houses. In addition, in default situations, lenders will be able to obtain higher recovery ratios. On the macro front, a limit on LTV will reduce the risk that a large sector of the real economy ends up with a severe debt overhang. In addition, it will reduce the pool of borrowers that can obtain funding (for a given price) and thus will reduce demand pressures and contain the boom.

Similar to limits on LTV, DTI limits will rein in the purchasing power of individuals, reducing the pressure on real estate prices. Limits on DTI will be effective in containing speculative demand by screening out borrowers who would qualify for a mortgage only on the assumption that the house would be quickly resold. Limits will also reduce vulnerabilities because borrowers will have an "affordability" buffer and will be more resilient to a decline in their income or temporary unemployment.

Implementation Challenges

Careful design of these measures is key to limiting circumvention. For instance, in the Republic of Korea, lower LTV limits for loans with less than three years to maturity spurred a boom in loans originated with maturity of three years and one day. During the housing boom in the United States, the practice of combining two or more loans to avoid mortgage insurance (which kicked in when LTV exceeded 80 percent) became common.[20] An LTV limit applied to a borrower's

---

[20] With these "piggyback" loans, the first lien would cover 80 percent of the home value and the remainder would be split between a second lien and a down payment (which could be as low as zero).

overall exposure would improve effectiveness. Similarly, an obvious way to get around a DTI limit would be to extend sequential loans and report the ratios separately. In Hong Kong SAR, where regulators impose maximum limits on the debt-service ratio (which also takes into account the payments the borrower has to make on nonmortgage loans), supervisors often encounter cases in which lenders choose not to report all outstanding debt obligations.

Circumvention may result in significant costs, possibly resulting in liability structures that can complicate debt resolution during busts (for example, in the United States, holders of second liens often object to restructuring). In addition, circumvention may involve the shifting of risks not only across mortgage loan products, but also to outside the regulatory perimeter, through expansion of credit by nonbank, less-regulated financial institutions or by foreign banks (which may result in increased currency mismatches as the proportion of foreign-currency-denominated loans rises).

As with monetary policy, calibration of these tools involves a learning process. And clear communication strategies must be developed to improve their efficiency. Frequent intervention and excessively sharp changes in the limits may lead to confusing signals and carry the risk of generating policy-induced real estate cycles.

The narrow target of these measures may increase political economy obstacles (as happened in Israel),[21] particularly because the groups more highly affected by LTV and DTI limits tend to be those more in need of credit (poorer and younger individuals). In addition, unlike with more macro measures, the consequences of these limits are immediate and transparent. Nevertheless, several Asian countries successfully introduced various versions of these measures. Beyond these political economy considerations, LTV and DTI limits, by rationing sensitive groups out of credit markets, will also diminish intertemporal consumption smoothing and lower investment efficiency.

Evidence

Establishing a causal link running from LTVs to price and credit dynamics is difficult. At the cross-country level, a major concern is the lack of a time dimension: In many countries, multiple data points are not available. Even when data availability is not a problem, very few countries have time variation in maximum allowable LTV because it has not been an active part of the regulatory agenda. Another issue is that the values reported are simple guidelines for mortgage insurance or prudential concerns—there are no mandatory maximum limits. Hence, because of the feedback loop between mortgage credit availability and house price movements, endogeneity remains a concern.

With these caveats in mind, the scant existing empirical evidence suggests that these limits hold promise. For example, in a simple cross-section of 21 (mostly developed) countries, maximum LTV limits are positively related to house price

---

[21] "Bank of Israel May Increase Housing-Loan Provisions to Slow Rising Prices" 2010 (http://www.bloomberg.com/news/2010-05-24/bank-of-israel-may-increase-housing-loan-provisions-to-slow-rising-prices.html).

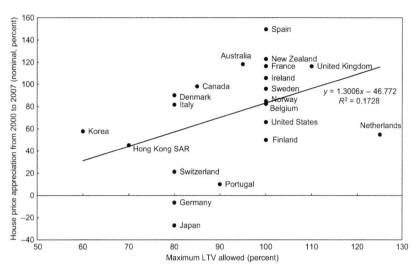

Figure 12.5   Maximum Loan-to-Value Ratio and House Prices

Sources: Bank for International Settlements; Economic Commission for Latin America and the Caribbean; European Mortgage Federation; Inter-American Development Bank; International Union for Housing Finance; International Union of Tenants; national statistics, and central bank statistics; Organization for Economic Cooperation and Development; United Nations Economic Commission for Europe.

Note: Maximum loan to value allowed refers to new mortgage loans and, in most cases, shows the limits above which additional requirements such as mortgage insurance would apply.

appreciation between 2000 and 2007 (Figure 12.5). And rough calculations suggest that a 10 percentage point increase in maximum LTV allowed by regulation is associated with a 13 percent increase in nominal house prices. Regressions on a panel of U.S. states from 1978 to 2008 suggest a weaker association between house price appreciation and a given LTV at loan origination: roughly a 5 percent increase in house prices for a 10 percentage point increase in LTV. Duca, Muellbauer, and Murphy (2010) construct a series for LTV faced by first-time home buyers and estimate a cointegration model of house-price-to-rent ratios at the national level for the United States between 1979 and 2007. Their results suggest a 10 percentage point increase in LTV for first-time home buyers has an impact of 8–11 percent on house prices, assuming rents remain constant.

A review of the experience of countries that experimented with changing mandatory LTV limits in response to real estate market developments also suggests that doing so can be quite effective. For instance, when the Korean authorities introduced LTV limits in September 2002, the month-over-month change in house prices decreased from 3.4 percent to 0.3 percent immediately and remained low until April 2003. Subsequent reductions in LTV ratios were also followed by significant drops in the house price appreciation rate. A similar pattern applies to DTI limits, with the month-over-month change dropping from 2.3 percent in July 2005 to 0.2 percent in August 2005 with the introduction of the measure. Interestingly, the measures had a much smaller (or no) impact on prices in "nonspeculative" areas in which the limits were untouched. The impact on year-over-year changes, however, has been smaller because prices tend to start regaining their faster pace after the first immediate reaction.[22] In Hong Kong SAR, prudent lending practices guided by LTV and DTI limits have been credited with pausing the house price boom briefly in 1994 and guarding the system against the fallout from the crash in 1997 (Wong, Fung, and others, 2004; 2011).

MODEL-BASED EVALUATION OF POLICY OPTIONS

This section provides a quantitative evaluation of the policy trade-offs discussed in the previous sections, using a dynamic stochastic general equilibrium (DSGE) model that incorporates a housing sector and credit markets. DSGE models have become popular tools for analyzing optimal policy under credit market frictions (e.g., Kannan, Rabanal, and Scott, 2009; Angelini, Neri, and Panetta, 2010). But a main disadvantage is that they do not have the capability to replicate the non-linear dynamics often observed in a crisis context, nor can they incorporate bubbles in a tractable way. Hence, the analysis in this section deals with house price fluctuations that come from fundamentals and that reflect the expected present discounted value of rents. That is, these are booms that reflect general macroeconomic overheating. However, even in this context, the analysis supports the view that tools that are narrower in focus (by addressing a specific rigidity) can perform better (Table 12.6).

TABLE 12.6

Performance of Policy Rules in a Dynamic Stochastic General Equilibrium Model

		Type of shock		
		Productivity	Financial	Both
	Original Taylor	8	10	10
Monetary policy	+ reaction to real estate prices	1	5	5
	+ reaction to mortgage credit	3	6	3
	+ reaction to both prices and credit	1	3	3
Fiscal policy	+ constant tax	10	10	9
	+ cyclical tax	7	8	8
	+ both taxes	8	7	7
Macroprudential policy	+ rule on real estate prices	6	3	6
	+ rule on mortgage credit	4	2	1
	+ rule on both prices and credit	4	1	1

Source: IMF staff calculations.
Note: Policy rules are compared with the original Taylor rule and ranked by their welfare costs under each shock scenario. Rank 1 corresponds to the rule that would deliver the largest welfare improvement and is highlighted. When two rules deliver roughly the same improvement, they are assigned the same rank.

---

[22] This pattern, potentially an indication of the difficulty of calibrating these rules in practice, may elicit frequent intervention by policymakers.

The model has conventional New Keynesian features: prices and wages do not adjust immediately. Households make decisions on how much to invest in housing, in addition to choosing their consumption of nondurable goods. To make the model's dynamics more realistic, consumption and residential investment are assumed to adjust slowly, and it is costly for workers to shift from producing consumption goods to building houses, and vice versa. The presence of these nominal and real frictions means that monetary policy can stabilize the economy by affecting interest rates and, hence, spending on both nondurables and housing. Credit is introduced by assuming that some agents are more impatient than others and prefer to consume early by borrowing. The lending rate is modeled as a spread over the policy (or deposit) rate that depends on the balance sheet position of potential borrowers. This assumption generates a feedback loop between credit spreads, house prices, and net worth of households. The spread also depends on a banking sector markup (i.e., a financial shock) and a policy instrument, which may take the form of a macroprudential or a fiscal tool. A main shortcoming is that the banking sector markup is exogenous and independent of the balance sheet of the banks.

The objective is to determine which policy regime is better at stabilizing the economy in the face of pressures on the housing market. The conclusions that can be drawn from this analysis depend crucially on which shocks drive the house price boom. To illustrate the importance of correctly identifying the drivers of the housing boom, policy regimes are examined under two shocks: a financial shock that prompts a relaxation in lending standards, and a positive productivity shock that leads to an increase in income.[23]

Effectiveness of Monetary Policy

Suppose the central bank follows a standard Taylor (1993)-type rule, whereby it raises rates whenever consumer price index inflation is running above target or when the economy is expanding at a faster rate than its fundamentals suggest (i.e., the output gap is positive). This rule can be expanded by including reactions to nominal house price inflation, nominal mortgage credit growth, or both. When the economy is hit by a productivity shock, this augmented rule leads to an improvement in welfare, mostly due to a decline in output gap volatility, especially when the rule responds to house prices. This outcome occurs because the shock reflects a change in one of the fundamentals, income, that drives house prices. For a financial shock, welfare is improved by responding to real estate prices and credit because policy directly targets the source that triggers the feedback loop.

If both productivity and financial shocks are present, reacting to credit is superior to reacting to real estate prices. Reacting to credit is better because the optimal response to credit developments is broadly the same for both shocks, whereas the optimal response to changes in house prices is very

---

[23] Financial and total factor productivity shocks explain a large fraction of the fluctuation in the main U.S. macroeconomic variables (Nolan and Thoenissen, 2009).

different across shocks. It follows that when shocks are difficult to identify, the best option is to directly respond to credit growth because it helps keep in check the push on house prices while at the same time containing the relaxation in credit conditions.

Effectiveness of Fiscal Policy

Taxes on home ownership and housing transactions, in principle, can curb demand for housing and tame exuberance in real estate markets. Consider a property tax imposed on homeowners, to whom the tax receipts are paid back as a lump sum. The policymaker can set two parameters in the tax rule. First, the steady-state level tax rate, and second, the cyclical reaction of the tax rate to house price inflation. In either case, the welfare improvements are small. High property taxes would be needed to have some bite in reducing the volatility of house prices (and the associated accelerator effect), but high taxes would lead to highly distorted prices—hence, the overall small welfare improvement.

Effectiveness of Macroprudential Policy

In the model, policies that can directly affect the spread between lending and deposit rates can help stabilize the cycle. For instance, by lowering the maximum LTV when house prices increase, the supervisory authority can lower the volume of credit, increasing the spread between lending and deposit rates and thus reducing the accelerator effect. To assess the efficacy of this macroprudential rule, the analysis looks at the impulse response to a 1 percent permanent reduction in the steady-state LTV. Initially, interest rate spreads increase 25 basis points, and credit decreases on impact by 0.3 percent.[24] The increase in lending rates leads to a decline in private consumption (0.15 percent), consumer prices (0.02 percent), residential investment (0.2 percent), and real house prices (0.07 percent). The central bank provides support by cutting the policy rate (which equals the deposit rate in this economy), which helps cushion the downturn. Over time, residential investment and house prices return to their initial values and credit is permanently reduced by 1 percent.

The next question is whether welfare can be improved if the LTV is tied linearly to certain observables such as credit growth and house price inflation. Under either shock, the macroprudential instrument brings important welfare gains, mostly because volatility of the output gap is greatly reduced. It turns out that an LTV reacting to nominal credit growth is superior to one linked to house price fluctuations: the macroprudential instrument directly addresses the financial friction in the model, therefore it is optimal to have it react to excessive credit under either or both shocks.

---

[24] BIS (2010) estimates that an increase of 1 percent in bank capital requirements also leads to an increase of 25 basis points in the spread between lending rates and the cost of funds for banks. Therefore, the exercise can also be thought of as increasing capital requirements.

CONCLUSION

Determining the correct policy response to real estate booms is, like many other policymaking decisions, an art more than a science. Of the policy options considered, macroprudential measures appear to be the best candidates for achieving the objective of curbing real estate prices and leverage because of their ability to attack the problem at its source, their adaptability to accommodate the specific circumstances in different locations at different times, and their added benefit of increasing the resilience of the banking system.

Provisional policy recommendations, from the evidence reviewed and the analysis, depend on the characteristics of the real estate boom in question (see Figure 12.6). If property prices are out of sync with income and rent, *and* if leverage is increasing rapidly, taking action is advisable.[25] In deciding which policy option to choose, policymakers should adopt a wider view of the economy and complement targeted measures with broader macroeconomic tightening if the boom is a part of or a reflection of general overheating in the economy.

This leads to the following tentative core principles that could guide policymakers in designing an effective toolkit for dealing with real estate booms:

- Widen the policy perspective to recognize imbalances that do not necessarily show up in traditional measures of inflation targets and output gaps.

- Recognize the local features of real estate markets and use targeted macroprudential tools rather than across-the-board monetary policy responses to respond to excessive and destabilizing movements in prices and activity.

- Complement measures aiming to reduce the risk of bubbles with measures aiming to increase the resilience of the financial system and with well-defined resolution frameworks to hasten the cleanup in the aftermath of bubbles that survive the first line of defense.

- Minimize distortions caused by special treatment of housing and homeownership and strengthen the supply-side response to mitigate the impact of demand shocks in the longer term.

Two important questions will need to be answered when it comes to applying these principles in practice. First, what are the potential complementarities and conflicts between monetary and macroprudential policies and what policy design framework can best accommodate them? Undoubtedly, there is a complex relationship between the objectives of macroeconomic and financial stability and the respective primary objectives of monetary and macroprudential policy. Take, for instance, the option of raising capital requirements for loans secured by real estate, which would increase the cost of borrowing in this segment through interest rate changes, which could also spill over to other types of loans. Any kind of credit rationing that may stem from this move could also alter real activity. Both consequences are in the realm of monetary policy. In turn, recent studies show

---

[25] Additional uncertainty may be involved because leverage can be a lagging indicator. Hence, keeping a close watch on credit origination, including by nonbank financial intermediaries, is warranted.

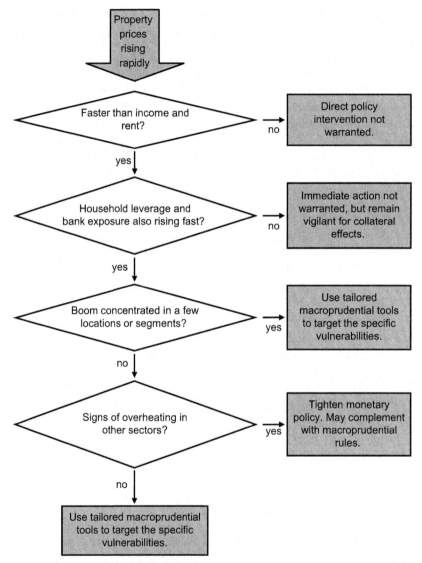

Figure 12.6 Dealing with Real Estate Booms
Sources: IMF country reports; and IMF staff.

that loose monetary policy can fuel risk-taking incentives and a buildup of leverage, which could warrant tighter macroprudential rules. Given these interactions, the best option may be to consider the macroprudential policy framework alongside, not apart from, the monetary policy decision.

Second, should the macroprudential framework be based on discretion or rules? On the one hand, in a discretionary framework the measures could be better calibrated to particular situations and circumvention may be less likely because of the temporary nature of the measure (less incentive, less time to learn). On the other hand, a rules-based framework could be better because political economy problems may be less severe (no fight to put measures in place during a boom), adjustment of private agents' behavior to the new framework may quickly accomplish a certain degree of prudence, and time inconsistency is not an issue. The choice of framework would need to weigh these pros and cons. We leave these questions to future research.

REFERENCES

Adrian, T., and H.S. Shin, 2009, "Money, Liquidity, and Monetary Policy," *American Economic Review*, Vol. 99, No. 2, pp. 600–605.

Agell, J., P. Englund, and J. Södersten, 1995, "Swedish Tax Policy in Theory and Practice," Appendix No. 1 to the Tax Reform Evaluation Report.

Allen, F., and E. Carletti, 2010, "What Should Central Banks Do about Real Estate Prices?" Paper prepared for the Columbia University Center on Capitalism and Society's conference on "Microfoundations for Modern Macroeconomics," New York, November 19–20.

Angelini, P., S. Neri, and F. Panetta, 2010, "Macroeconomic Stabilization Policies: Grafting Macroprudential Tools in a Macroeconomic Framework," Bank of Italy Working Paper (Rome: Bank of Italy).

Bank for International Settlements (BIS), 2010, "Assessing the Macroeconomic Impact of the Transition to Stronger Capital and Liquidity Requirements," Interim Report by the Macroeconomic Assessment Group established by the Financial Stability Board and the Basel Committee on Banking Supervision (Basel: Bank for International Settlements).

Bernanke, B.S., 2002, "Asset Price Bubbles and Monetary Policy," Remarks before the New York Chapter of the National Association for Business Economics, New York, New York, October 15. http://www.federalreserve.gov/boarddocs/speeches/2002/20021015.

Borio, C., and I. Shim, 2007, "What Can (Macro)-Prudential Policy Do to Support Monetary Policy?" BIS Working Paper No. 242 (Basel: Bank for International Settlements).

Brzoza-Brzezina, M., T. Chmielewski, and J. Niedzwiedzinska, 2007, "Substitution between Domestic and Foreign Currency Loans in Central Europe: Do Central Banks Matter?" National Bank of Poland Working Paper (Warsaw: National Bank of Poland).

Capozza, D.R., R.K. Green, and P.H. Hendershott, 1996, "Taxes, Mortgage Borrowing and House Prices," Wisconsin-Madison CULER Working Paper No. 96-06 (Madison, Wisconsin: University of Wisconsin Center for Urban Land Economic Research).

Case, K.E., and R.J. Shiller, 2003, "Is There a Bubble in the Housing Market?" *Brookings Papers on Economic Activity*, Vol. 34, No. 2, pp. 299–362.

Claessens, S., G. Dell'Ariccia, D. Igan, and L. Laeven, 2010, "Cross-Country Experiences and Policy Implications from the Global Financial Crisis," *Economic Policy*, Vol. 25, pp. 267–93.

Claessens, S., M.A. Kose, and M.E. Terrones, 2008, "What Happens during Recessions, Crunches and Busts?" IMF Working Paper 08/274 (Washington: International Monetary Fund).

Committee on the Global Financial System (CGFS), 2010, "Macroprudential Instruments and Frameworks: A Stocktaking of Issues and Experiences," CGFS Paper No. 38 (Basel: Bank for International Settlements).

Cremer, H., and F. Gahvari, 1998, "On Optimal Taxation of Housing," *Journal of Urban Economics*, Vol. 43, No. 3, pp. 315–35.

Crowe, C., G. Dell'Ariccia, D. Igan, and P. Rabanal, 2011, "How to Deal with Real Estate Booms: Lessons from Country Experiences," IMF Working Paper 11/91 (Washington: International Monetary Fund).

De Nicolò, G., G. Dell'Ariccia, L. Laeven, and F. Valencia, 2010, "Monetary Policy and Risk Taking," IMF Staff Position Note 2010/09 (Washington: International Monetary Fund).

Duca, J.V., J. Muellbauer, and A. Murphy, 2010, "House Prices and Credit Constraints: Making Sense of the U.S. Experience," Oxford University Working Paper (Oxford: Oxford University).

Dunsky, R.M., and J.R. Follain, 2000, "Tax-Induced Portfolio Reshuffling: The Case of the Mortgage Interest Deduction," *Real Estate Economics*, Vol. 28, pp. 683–718.

Gordy, M.B., and B. Howells, 2006, "Procyclicality in Basel II: Can We Treat the Disease Without Killing the Patient?" *Journal of Financial Intermediation*, Vol. 15, pp. 395–417.

Greenspan, A., 2002, "Economic Volatility," Remarks at a symposium sponsored by the Federal Reserve Bank of Kansas City, Jackson Hole, Wyoming, August 30. http://www.federalreserve.gov/boarddocs/speeches/2002/20020830/#f2.

Guiso, L., M. Haliassos, and T. Jappelli, 2003, "Household Stockholding in Europe: Where Do We Stand and Where Do We Go?" *Economic Policy*, Vol. 18, No. 36, pp. 123–70.

Hendershott, P.H., G. Pryce, and M. White, 2003, "Household Leverage and the Deductibility of Home Mortgage Interest: Evidence from U.K. House Purchases," *Journal of Housing Research*, Vol. 14, pp. 49–82.

Herring, R.J., and S. Wachter, 1999, "Real Estate Booms and Banking Busts: An International Perspective," Center for Financial Institutions Working Paper 99-27 (Philadelphia: Wharton School Center for Financial Institutions, University of Pennsylvania).

Igan, D., A.N. Kabundi, F. Nadal-De Simone, M. Pinheiro, and N.T. Tamirisa, 2009, "Three Cycles: Housing, Credit, and Real Activity," IMF Working Paper 09/231 (Washington: International Monetary Fund).

Igan, D., and P. Loungani, 2012, "Global Housing Cycles," IMF Working Paper 12/217 (Washington: International Monetary Fund).

International Monetary Fund (IMF), 2006, "How Has Globalization Affected Inflation?" in *World Economic Outlook: Globalization and Inflation* (Washington: International Monetary Fund).

———, 2009, "Lessons for Monetary Policy from Asset Price Fluctuations," in *World Economic Outlook: Sustaining the Recovery* (Washington: International Monetary Fund).

———, 2010, "Box 1.4. Dismal Prospects for the Real Estate Sector" in *World Economic Outlook: Recovery, Risk, and Rebalancing* (Washington: International Monetary Fund).

———, 2011, "Housing Finance and Financial Stability–Back to Basics?" in *Global Financial Stability Report*, April (Washington: International Monetary Fund).

Kannan, P., P. Rabanal, and A. Scott, 2009, "Monetary and Macroprudential Policy Rules in a Model with House Price Booms," IMF Working Paper 09/251(Washington: International Monetary Fund).

Keen, M., A. Klemm, and V. Perry, 2010, "Tax and the Crisis," *Fiscal Studies*, Vol. 31, No. 1, pp. 43–79.

Kiyotaki, N., and J. Moore, 1997, "Credit Cycles," *Journal of Political Economy*, Vol. 105, No. 2, pp. 211–48.

Laeven, L., and G. Majnoni, 2003, "Loan Loss Provisioning and Economic Slowdowns: Too Much, Too Late?" *Journal of Financial Intermediation*, Vol. 12, No. 2, pp. 178–97.

Laeven, L., and F. Valencia, 2010, "Resolution of Banking Crises: The Good, the Bad, and the Ugly," IMF Working Paper 10/146 (Washington: International Monetary Fund).

Mayer, C., K. Pence, and S.M. Sherlund, 2008, "The Rise in Mortgage Defaults," FRB Finance and Economics Discussion Series No. 2008-59 (Washington: Federal Reserve Board).

Mishkin, Frederic S., 2011, "How Should Central Banks Respond to Asset-Price Bubbles? The 'Lean' versus 'Clean' Debate after the GFC," *RBA Bulletin*, June, pp. 59–70.

Nolan, C., and C. Thoenissen, 2009, "Financial Shocks and the U.S. Business Cycle," *Journal of Monetary Economics*, Vol. 56, No. 4, pp. 596–604.

Piazzesi, M., and M. Schneider, 2009, "Momentum Traders in the Housing Market: Survey Evidence and a Search Model," *American Economic Review*, Vol. 99, No. 2, pp. 406–11.

Reinhart, C.M., and K.S. Rogoff, 2009, *This Time Is Different: A Panoramic View of Eight Centuries of Financial Folly* (Princeton, New Jersey: Princeton University Press).

Saurina, J., 2009, "Dynamic Provisioning: The Experience of Spain," Crisis Response Note 7 (Washington: World Bank).

Stiglitz, J.E., and A. Weiss, 1981, "Credit Rationing in Markets with Imperfect Information," *American Economic Review*, Vol. 71, No. 3, pp. 393–410.

Taylor, J.B., 1993, "Discretion versus Policy Rules in Practice," *Carnegie-Rochester Conference Series on Public Policy*, Vol. 39, No. 1, pp. 195–214.

Wong, J., L. Fung, T. Fong, and A. Sze, 2004, "Residential Mortgage Default Risk in Hong Kong," Hong Kong Monetary Authority Working Paper.

Wong, E., T. Fong, K. Li, and H. Choi, 2011, "Loan-to-Value Ratio as a Macroprudential Tool: Hong Kong's Experience and Cross-Country Evidence," Hong Kong Monetary Authority Working Paper No. 01/2011.

CHAPTER 13

Resolution of Banking Crises: The Good, the Bad, and the Ugly

LUC LAEVEN AND FABIÁN VALENCIA

Since 2007, the world has experienced a period of severe financial stress not seen since the time of the Great Depression. This crisis started with the collapse of the subprime residential mortgage market in the United States and spread to the rest of the world through exposure to U.S. real estate assets, often in the form of complex financial derivatives, and a subsequent collapse in global trade. Many economies were severely affected by these adverse shocks, which caused systemic banking crises in a number of countries despite extraordinary policy interventions.

Systemic banking crises are disruptive events not only to financial systems but to the economy as a whole. Such crises are not specific to the recent past or to specific countries— almost no country has avoided the experience and some have had multiple banking crises. Although the banking crises of the past have differed in their underlying causes, triggers, and economic impacts, they share many commonalities. Banking crises are often preceded by prolonged periods of high credit growth and are often associated with large imbalances in the balance sheets of the private sector, such as maturity mismatches or exchange rate risk, that ultimately translate into credit risk for the banking sector.

With the recovery from the 2007–09 crisis under way, some questions naturally arise: What caused the most recent crisis? Why did this crisis lead to varied levels of stress in different countries? How does the cost of this crisis compare with that of previous banking crisis episodes? And how do current policy responses differ from those of the past?

This chapter presents new and comprehensive data on the starting dates and characteristics of systemic banking crises during the period 1970–2009, building on earlier work by Caprio and others (2005), Laeven and Valencia (2008), and Reinhart and Rogoff (2009). In particular, it extends the database presented in Chapter 2, which builds on Laeven and Valencia (2008), to include the episodes following the U.S. mortgage crisis of 2007. The update makes several improvements to the earlier database, including an improved definition of systemic

The authors thank Eugenio Cerutti, Stijn Claessens, Luis Cortavarria-Checkley, Peter Dohlman, Mark Griffiths, Aditya Narain, David Parker, Noel Sacasa, and Johannes Wiegand for comments or discussions, and Jeanne Verrier for outstanding research assistance.

banking crises, the inclusion of crisis ending dates, and broader coverage of crisis management policies. The result is the most up-to-date banking crisis database available.[1]

The new data show that 2007–09 crises and past crises share many common characteristics, both in their underlying causes and in policy responses, yet there are also some striking differences in the economic and fiscal costs associated with the new crises. The economic cost of the new crises is on average much larger than that of past crises, both in output losses and in increases in public debt. The median output loss (computed as the deviation of actual output from its trend) is 25 percent of GDP in the 2007–09 crises, compared with a historical median of 20 percent of GDP, and the median increase in public debt (for the three-year period following the start of the crisis) is 24 percent of GDP in the 2007–09 crises, compared with a historical median of 16 percent of GDP. These differences reflect, in part, an increase in the size of financial systems, the concentration of the 2007–09 crises in high-income countries, and possible differences in the size of the initial shock to the financial system.

At the same time, direct fiscal costs to support the financial sector were smaller this time at 5 percent of GDP, compared with 10 percent of GDP for past crises, as a consequence of relatively swift policy action and the significant indirect support the financial system received through expansionary monetary and fiscal policy, the widespread use of guarantees on liabilities, and direct purchases of assets that helped sustain asset prices.

Policy responses broadly consisted of the same type of containment and resolution tools as used in previous crisis episodes. As in past crises, policymakers used extensive liquidity support and guarantees. However, recapitalization policies were implemented more quickly in the 2007–09 crises. In previous crises it took policymakers about one year from the time that liquidity support became extensive before comprehensive recapitalization measures were implemented; this time recapitalization measures were implemented about the same time that liquidity support became extensive.

Although these extraordinary measures contributed to reducing the real impact of the 2007–09 crises, they also increased the burden of public debt and the size of contingent fiscal liabilities, raising concerns about fiscal sustainability in a number of countries.

The chapter proceeds as follows. The first section presents a brief review of the events that led to the 2007–09 global crises. The second section defines a systemic banking crisis and presents a list of countries that meet this definition. The third section describes the policy responses and contrasts them with past crises. The fourth section presents the cost of the 2007–09 crises and a comparison with past episodes. The final section summarizes the differences between the 2007–09 crises and those of the past.

---

[1] The banking crisis data set is available at http://www.imf.org/external/pubs/cat/longres.aspx?sk =23971.0.

THE 2007–09 GLOBAL CRISIS: A SYNOPSIS

During the decade before the crisis, the United States and several other advanced economies experienced an uninterrupted upward trend in real estate prices, which was particularly pronounced in residential property markets. The origins of this boom are still a source of debate, although there appears to be broad agreement that financial innovation in the form of asset securitization, government policies to increase home ownership, global imbalances, expansionary monetary policy, and weak regulatory oversight played important roles (Obstfeld and Rogoff, 2009; Taylor, 2009; and Key and others, 2010).

The boom in real estate prices was exacerbated by financial institutions' ability to exploit loopholes in capital regulation, allowing banks to increase leverage significantly while maintaining capital requirements. They did so by moving assets off their balance sheets into special purpose vehicles that were subject to weaker capital standards and by increasingly funding themselves short term and in wholesale markets rather than with traditional deposits. These special purpose vehicles were used to invest in risky and illiquid assets (such as mortgages and mortgage derivatives) and were funded in wholesale markets (for example, through asset-backed commercial paper) without the backing of adequate capital. The growing importance of this shadow banking system that was highly dependent on short-term funding, combined with lax regulatory oversight, was a key contributor to the asset price bubble (Gorton, 2008; Brunnermeier, 2009; and Acharya and Richardson, 2009).

Higher asset prices led to a leverage cycle by which increases in home values led to increases in debt. The rise in asset prices decreased measured "value at risk" at financial institutions, creating spare capacity in their balance sheets and leading to an increase in leverage and supply of credit (Adrian and Shin, 2008). A similar mechanism took place in the household sector, as perceived household wealth increased by virtue of rising home values. Easy access to the equity accumulated in their homes led households to increase their leverage substantially. Mian and Sufi (2011) estimate that the average homeowner extracted 25 to 30 cents for every dollar increase in home equity to be used in real outlays. The asset price boom was further fueled by an explosion of subprime mortgage credit in the United States starting in 2002 and reaching a peak in mid-2006 (Dell'Ariccia, Laeven, and Igan, 2008).

The first signs of distress came in early 2007 from losses at U.S. subprime loan originators and institutions holding derivatives of securitized subprime mortgages. However, these first signs were limited to problems in the subprime mortgage market. Later in 2007 these localized signs of distress turned into a global event, with losses spreading to banks in Europe (such as U.K. mortgage lender Northern Rock), and distress was no longer limited to financial institutions with exposure to the U.S. subprime mortgage market.

To alleviate liquidity shortages, the U.S. Federal Reserve reduced the penalty to banks for accessing its discount window, and later that year created the Term Auction Facility. Similarly, a blanket guarantee was issued in the United Kingdom for Northern Rock's existing deposits. Problems intensified in the United States with the bailout of Bear Stearns, and later in the year with the collapse of investment bank Lehman Brothers and the government bailouts of insurer AIG and mortgage lenders Freddie Mac and Fannie Mae. By the end of 2007, many economies around the world suffered from a collapse in international trade, reversals in capital flows, and sizable contractions in real output. However, as the crisis mounted, so did the policy responses, with many countries announcing bank recapitalization packages and other support for the financial sector in late 2008 and early 2009.

Although some aspects of this crisis appeared to be new, such as the role of asset securitization in spreading risks across the financial system, it broadly resembled earlier boom-bust episodes, many of which followed periods of financial liberalization. One common factor among these crises is a substantial rise in private sector indebtedness; infected sectors in addition to banks were the household sector (as in the U.S. crisis in 2007–09 and the Nordic crises of the 1990s), the corporate sector (as in the case of the 1997–98 East Asian financial crisis), or both. As in earlier crisis episodes, asset prices rose sharply while banks decreased reliance on deposits in favor of less stable sources of wholesale funding, and while nonbanking institutions (for instance, finance companies in Thailand in the 1990s, and offshore financial institutions in Latin America in the 1980s and 1990s) grew significantly owing in part to less stringent prudential requirements for nonbanks.

When such crises erupt, they generally trigger losses that spread rapidly throughout the financial system by way of downward pressures on asset prices and interconnectedness among financial institutions. These broad patterns repeated themselves in the 2007–09 crises when losses in the U.S. real estate market triggered general runs on the U.S. shadow banking system, which ultimately hit banks in the United States and elsewhere.

WHICH COUNTRIES HAD SYSTEMIC BANKING CRISES IN 2007–09?

The financial crisis that started in the United States in 2007 spread around the world, affecting banking systems in many other countries. This section defines a systemic banking crisis and identifies which countries experienced one. It also identifies countries that can be considered to have experienced borderline banking crises, and countries that escaped banking crises altogether (either because they staved off a crisis through successful policies or because they were not hit by the negative shock emanating from the United States).

A banking crisis is considered to be systemic if two conditions are met:

- Significant signs of financial distress are exhibited by the banking system (as indicated by significant bank runs, losses in the banking system, and bank liquidations).

- Significant banking policy intervention measures are taken in response to significant losses in the banking system.

The first year that both criteria are met is taken to be the starting year of the banking crisis. Policy interventions in the banking sector are considered to be significant if at least three out of the following six measures were used:[2]

Extensive liquidity support (5 percent of deposits and liabilities to nonresidents). In implementing this definition of systemic interventions, liquidity support is considered to be extensive when the ratio of central bank claims on the financial sector to deposits and foreign liabilities exceeds 5 percent and more than doubles relative to its precrisis level.[3]

Bank-restructuring costs (at least 3 percent of GDP). Direct bank-restructuring costs are defined as the component of gross fiscal outlays directed to restructuring the financial sector, such as recapitalization costs. They exclude asset purchases and direct liquidity assistance from the treasury. Direct restructuring costs are defined to be significant if they exceed 3 percent of GDP.

Significant bank nationalizations. Significant nationalizations are takeovers by the government of systemically important financial institutions and include instances in which the government takes a majority stake in the capital of such institutions.

Significant guarantees put in place. A significant guarantee on bank liabilities indicates that either a full protection of liabilities has been issued or that guarantees have been extended to nondeposit liabilities of banks.[4] Simply raising the level of deposit insurance coverage is not deemed significant.

Significant asset purchases (at least 5 percent of GDP). Asset purchases from financial institutions include those implemented through the treasury or the central bank. Significant asset purchases are those exceeding 5 percent of GDP.[5]

Deposit freezes and bank holidays. Includes the suspension of banking activities for a short period. It can be accompanied by the conversion to a longer-than-contracted maturity of existing deposits in the banking system, or simply the suspension of redemptions for a specified period.

In the past, some countries intervened in their financial sectors using a combination of fewer than three of these measures but on a large scale (for example, by

---

[2] When possible, the magnitude of policy interventions and associated fiscal costs are expressed as ratios to GDP rather than banking system size to control for the ability of a country's economy to support its banking system. This tactic naturally results in higher measured fiscal costs for economies with larger banking systems.

[3] Domestic nondeposit liabilities are excluded from the denominator of this ratio because information on such liabilities is not readily available on a gross basis. For euro area countries, liquidity support is considered to be extensive if in a given half-year the increase in this ratio is at least 5 percentage points. Data on euro area central bank claims are confounded by large volumes of settlements and cross-border claims between banks in the Eurosystem. As a result, the central banks of some euro area countries (notably Germany and Luxembourg) already had large precrisis levels of claims on the financial sector.

[4] Although a quantitative threshold for this criterion is not defined, guarantees in all cases involved significant financial sector commitments relative to the size of the corresponding economies.

[5] Asset purchases also provide liquidity to the system. Therefore, an estimate of total liquidity injected would include schemes such as the Special Liquidity Scheme (185 billion pounds sterling) in the United Kingdom and Norway's Bond Exchange Scheme (230 billion kroner), as well as liquidity provided directly by the treasury.

nationalizing all major banks in the country). Therefore, a sufficient condition for a crisis episode to be deemed systemic occurs when either (1) a country's banking system exhibits significant losses resulting in a share of nonperforming loans above 20 percent or bank closures of at least 20 percent of banking system assets; or (2) fiscal restructuring costs of the banking sector exceed 5 percent of GDP.[6] For the 2007–09 wave of crises, none of these additional criteria are needed to identify systemic events.

Quantitative thresholds to implement this definition of a systemic banking crisis are admittedly arbitrary; therefore, an additional list is maintained of borderline cases that almost meet this definition of a systemic crisis. At the same time, the more quantitative approach is a major improvement over earlier efforts to date banking crises (such as Caprio and others, 2005; Laeven and Valencia, 2008; and Reinhart and Rogoff, 2009), which relied on qualitative approaches to determining banking crises, defining them as situations in which a large fraction of banking system capital has been depleted.

Table 13.1 provides a list of countries that met this chapter's definition during the 2007–09 episode. The exact criteria that are met are also indicated. A separate column on deposit freezes and bank holidays is not included because no episode during this wave of banking crises made use of banking holidays, while deposit freezes were used only for Parex bank in Latvia. In total, 13 systemic banking crises and 10 borderline cases are identified as having occurred since 2007.[7] Table 13A.1 in the appendix presents more detailed information about the policy interventions in these cases.

As in Chapter 2, the starting year of the banking crises in the United Kingdom and the United States is 2007; for all other cases in the 2007–09 wave the starting date is 2008.[8]

Most policy packages announced in countries that do not meet the definition can be seen as preemptive interventions. In a large subset of Group of 20 (G-20) countries, direct policies to support the financial sector were quite modest. For instance, Argentina, Brazil, China, India, Indonesia, Mexico, Saudi Arabia, South Africa, and Turkey did not announce direct financial sector support measures that involved fiscal outlays. Some issued or increased guarantees on bank

---

[6] One concrete historical example is Latvia's 1995 crisis; when banks totaling 40 percent of financial system assets were closed, depositors experienced losses, but few of the interventions listed above were implemented.

[7] This new definition of a systemic banking crisis is somewhat more specific than the one used in Chapter 2, which considered systemic crises to include events with "significant policy interventions." As a consequence, a few cases listed as systemic banking crisis in that previous release would, under this definition, be considered borderline cases: Argentina 1995, Brazil 1990, the Czech Republic 1996, the Philippines 1997, and the United States 1988.

[8] Undoubtedly the most salient events of the U.K. and U.S. financial crises took place in 2008 (such as the bailout of Bear Stearns, the collapse of Lehman Brothers, the takeover of the government-sponsored enterprises, and the Troubled Asset Relief Program in the United States; and the nationalization of the Royal Bank of Scotland in the United Kingdom), but significant signs of financial sector distress and policy actions directed to the financial sector were already observed in 2007 in both cases.

TABLE 13.1

Country	Extensive liquidity support	Significant restructuring costs	Significant asset purchases	Significant guarantees on liabilities	Significant nationalizations
Systemic Banking Crises, 2007–09					
Systemic Cases					
Austria	✓	—	—	✓	✓
Belgium	✓	✓	—	✓	✓
Denmark	✓	—	—	✓	✓
Germany	✓	—	—	✓	✓
Iceland	✓	✓	—	✓	✓
Ireland	✓	✓	—	✓	✓
Latvia	✓	—	—	✓	✓
Luxembourg	✓	✓	—	✓	✓
Mongolia	✓	✓	—	✓	✓
Netherlands	✓	✓	—	✓	✓
Ukraine	✓	✓	—	—	✓
United Kingdom	✓	✓	✓	✓	✓
United States	✓	✓	✓	✓	✓
Borderline Cases					
France	✓	—	—	✓	—
Greece	✓	—	—	✓	—
Hungary	✓	—	—	✓	—
Kazakhstan	✓	✓	—	—	—
Portugal	✓	—	—	✓	—
Russian Fed.	✓	—	—	✓	—
Slovenia	✓	—	—	✓	—
Spain	✓	—	—	✓	—
Sweden	✓	—	—	✓	—
Switzerland	✓	—	✓	—	—

Source: Authors' calculations.

liabilities, creating contingent liabilities for the government. For example, Mexico announced a guarantee on commercial paper up to a limit of 50 billion pesos. Other G-20 countries were more seriously affected by the financial turmoil and reacted more strongly, but ultimately did not intervene at a large enough scale for the crises to be deemed systemic. Appendix Table 13A.2 provides more details about these cases, including the actual use of policy measures. The differences between announced and actually used amounts are striking in a number of cases, with the actual usage of announced packages on average being small.[9]

Chapter 2 includes only the first year of the crisis but does not report an end date for the crisis episode. In this chapter, we expand the database by dating the end of each episode as the year before two conditions hold: real GDP growth and real credit growth are positive for at least two consecutive years. If real GDP and real credit grow in the first two years, the crisis is dated to end the same year it

---

[9] See also Cheasty and Das (2009) for a comparison of announced and used amounts.

starts.[10] Admittedly, this is an oversimplification given the many factors that come into play in a crisis, and the differences in crises and recoveries across the sample. In a number of cases this methodology results in long crisis durations, which sometimes are the consequence of additional shocks affecting the economic performance of the countries. To keep the rule simple, duration is truncated at five years, beginning with the crisis year. As of end-2009, none of the 2007–09 crises had ended according to the definition used in this chapter. The median duration of a crisis for the old episodes is two years. Start and end dates for all episodes are reported in Table 13.2, which also reports output losses (defined in the next section).

POLICY RESPONSES IN THE 2007–09 CRISES: WHAT IS NEW?

Crisis management starts with the containment of liquidity pressures through liquidity support, guarantees on bank liabilities, deposit freezes, or bank holidays. This containment phase is followed by a resolution phase during which a broad range of measures (such as capital injections, asset purchases, and guarantees) are typically taken to restructure banks and reignite economic growth. It is intrinsically difficult to compare the success of crisis resolution policies given differences across countries and time and size of the initial shock to the financial system, the size of the financial system, the quality of institutions, and the intensity and scope of policy interventions. With this caveat, policy responses during the 2007–09 crisis episode are now compared with those of the past.

The policy responses during the 2007–09 crisis episodes were broadly similar to those used in the past. First, liquidity pressures were contained through liquidity support and guarantees on bank liabilities. Like the crises of the past, during which bank holidays and deposit freezes were rarely used as containment policies, no records show the use of bank holidays during the 2007–09 wave of crises, and a deposit freeze was used only in Latvia for deposits in Parex Bank. On the resolution side, a wide array of instruments were used for the 2007–09 crises, including asset purchases, asset guarantees, and equity injections. All these measures were used in the past, but this time they seem to have been put in place more quickly.[11]

One commonality among the 2007–09 banking crises is that they mostly affected advanced economies with large, internationally integrated financial

---

[10] In computing end dates, bank credit to the private sector (in national currency) from *International Financial Statistics* (IFS—line 22d) is used. Bank credit series are deflated using consumer price indices from the IMF's *World Economic Outlook* (WEO). GDP in constant prices (in national currency) also comes from the WEO. When credit data are not available, the end date is determined to be the first year before GDP growth is positive for at least two years. In all cases, the duration of a crisis is truncated at five years, including the first crisis year.

[11] For detailed information about the frequency of policy interventions in past crisis episodes, see Chapter 2.

institutions that were deemed too large or interconnected to fail. The large international networks and cross-border exposures of these financial institutions helped propagate the crisis to other countries. Failure of any of these large financial institutions could have resulted in the failure of other systemically important institutions, either directly by imposing large losses through counterparty exposures or indirectly by causing a panic that could generate bank runs. These exposures prompted large-scale government interventions in the financial sector (including preemptive measures in some countries).

Given that the crisis started in U.S. subprime mortgage market, financial exposure to the United States was a key propagation mechanism of the crisis (Claessens and others, 2010). Figure 13.1 shows foreign claims by nationality of reporting banks, from the Bank for International Settlements' consolidated banking statistics, expressed as percentages of home-country GDP, as of end-2006. Cross-border banking exposure to the United States varied a great deal across countries, ranging from less than 1 percent of GDP for Mexico to 300 percent of GDP for Switzerland. Eight out of ten of the most exposed economies meet the definition of systemic banking crises or are categorized as borderline cases.

Liquidity support was used intensively as a first response to this shock emanating from the United States. Not only was liquidity provision large, as illustrated in Figure 13.2, but it was also made available more broadly through a larger set of instruments and institutions (including nonbank institutions), and under weaker collateral requirements. Examples of unconventional liquidity measures include the U.S. Federal Reserve's decision to grant primary broker-dealers access to the discount window, the widening of collateral accepted by the Federal Reserve and many other central banks, and the purchase of asset-backed securities by the Federal Reserve. These actions were also accompanied in some cases by the introduction of nonconventional facilities to fund nonfinancial companies directly, such as the Federal Reserve's Commercial Paper Facility and the Bank of England's Asset Purchase Facility.

This significant liquidity provision is reflected in a large increase in central bank claims on the financial sector. The median change from the precrisis level to its peak in the ratio of central bank claims on the financial sector to deposits and foreign liabilities amounts to 5.5 percent.[12] This is about half its median in past crisis episodes. For comparison purposes, Figure 13.2 also reports the historical median of liquidity support among high-income countries given that most of the 2007–09 crises occurred in high-income economies (with the exceptions of Latvia, Mongolia, and Ukraine).[13]

---

[12] At its peak this variable reached 9.4 and 14.7 percent for Germany and Luxembourg, respectively, but the increments look small because, even before the crisis, banks in these countries maintained high balances because of cross-border settlements. Liquidity support is computed as the ratio of central bank claims on deposit money banks (line 12 in IFS) to total deposits and liabilities to nonresidents. The denominator is then computed as the sum of demand deposits (line 24), other deposits (line 25), and liabilities to nonresidents (line 26).

[13] There are only five crisis episodes among high-income countries in the historical sample.

TABLE 13.2

Banking Crisis Start and End Dates

Country	Start	End	Output loss (percent)	Country	Start	End	Output loss (percent)	Country	Start	End	Output loss (percent)
Albania[1]	1994	1994	...	Costa Rica	1987	1991	0	Kenya	1985	1985	24
Algeria	1990	1994[3]	41	Costa Rica	1994	1995	0	Kenya	1992	1994	50
Argentina	1980	1982[4]	58	Côte d'Ivoire	1988	1992[3]	45	Korea, Rep.	1997	1998	58
Argentina	1989	1991	13	Croatia[1]	1998	1999	...	Kuwait	1982	1985	143
Argentina[2]	1995	1995	0	Czech Republic[1,2]	1996	2000[3]	...	Kyrgyz Rep.[1]	1995	1999[3]	...
Argentina	2001	2003	71	Denmark	2008	...	36	Latvia[1]	1995	1996	...
Armenia[1]	1994	1994[4]	...	Djibouti	1991	1995[3]	43	Latvia[2]	2008	...	116
Austria	2008	...	17	Dominican Rep.	2003	2004	...	Lebanon	1990	1993	102
Azerbaijan[1]	1995	1995[4]	...	Ecuador	1982	1986[3]	98	Liberia	1991	1995[3]	...
Bangladesh	1987	1987	0	Ecuador	1998	2002	25	Lithuania[1]	1995	1996	...
Belarus[1]	1995	1995	...	Egypt	1980	1980	1	Luxembourg	2008	...	47
Belgium	2008	...	23	El Salvador	1989	1990	0	Macedonia, FYR[1]	1993	1995	0
Benin	1988	1992[3]	15	Equatorial Guinea	1983	1983[4]	0	Madagascar	1988	1988	0
Bolivia	1986	1986	49	Eritrea	1993	1993[4]	...	Malaysia	1997	1999	31
Bolivia	1994	1994	0	Estonia[1]	1992	1994	0	Mali	1987	1991[3]	0
Bosnia and Herzegovina[1]	1992	1996[3]	...	Finland	1991	1995	70	Mauritania	1984	1984	8
Brazil[2]	1990	1994[3]	62	France[2]	2008	...	21	Mexico	1981	1985[3]	27
Brazil	1994	1998	0	Georgia[1]	1991	1995[3]	...	Mexico	1994	1996	14
Bulgaria	1996	1997	60	Germany	2008	...	19	Mongolia	2008	...	0
Burkina Faso	1990	1994	...	Ghana	1982	1983	45	Morocco	1980	1984[3]	22

Country	Start	End	Output loss (percent)
Russian Fed.[2]	2008	...	0
São Tomé & Príncipe	1992	1992[4]	2
Senegal	1988	1991	6
Sierra Leone	1990	1994[3]	34
Slovak Rep.	1998	2002[3]	0
Slovenia[1]	1992	1992	...
Slovenia[2]	2008	...	37
Spain	1977	1981[3]	59
Spain[2]	2008	...	39
Sri Lanka	1989	1991	20
Swaziland	1995	1999[3]	46
Sweden	1991	1995	33
Sweden[2]	2008	...	31
Switzerland[2]	2008	...	0
Tanzania	1987	1988	0
Thailand	1983	1983	25
Thailand	1997	2000	109
Togo	1993	1994	39
Tunisia	1991	1991	1
Turkey	1982	1984	35

Country	Start	End	Output loss
Burundi	1994	1998[3]	121
Cameroon	1987	1991[3]	106
Cameroon	1995	1997	8
Cape Verde	1993	1993	0
Central African Rep.	1976	1976	0
Central African Rep.	1995	1996	9
Chad	1983	1983	0
Chad	1992	1996[3]	0
Chile	1976	1976	20
Chile	1981	1985[3]	9
China	1998	1998	19
Colombia	1982	1982	47
Colombia	1998	2000	43
Congo, Dem. Rep.	1983	1983	1
Congo, Dem. Rep.	1991	1994[3]	130
Congo, Dem. Rep.	1994	1998[3]	79
Congo, Rep.	1992	1994	47
Greece[2]	2008	...	29
Guinea	1985	1985[4]	0
Guinea	1993	1993	0
Guinea-Bissau	1995	1998	30
Guyana	1993	1993	0
Haiti	1994	1998	38
Hungary[1]	1991	1995[3]	0
Hungary[2]	2008	...	42
Iceland	2008	...	42
India	1993	1993	0
Indonesia	1997	2001[3]	69
Ireland	2008	...	110
Israel	1977	1977	76
Jamaica	1996	1998	38
Japan	1997	2001[3]	45
Jordan	1989	1991	106
Kazakhstan[2]	2008	...	0
Mozambique	1987	1991[3]	0
Nepal	1988	1988	0
Netherlands	2008	...	25
Nicaragua	1990	1993	11
Nicaragua	2000	2001	0
Niger	1983	1985	97
Nigeria	1991	1995[3]	0
Norway	1991	1993	5
Panama	1988	1989	85
Paraguay	1995	1995	15
Peru	1983	1983[4]	55
Philippines	1983	1986	92
Philippines[2]	1997	2001[3]	0
Poland[1]	1992	1994	0
Portugal[2]	2008	...	37
Romania[1]	1990	1992[4]	0
Russian Fed.[1]	1998	1998[4]	0
Turkey	2000	2001	37
Uganda	1994	1994	0
Ukraine[1]	1998	1999	0
Ukraine	2008	...	5
United Kingdom	2007	...	24
United States[2]	1988	1988	0
United States	2007	...	25
Uruguay	1981	1985[3]	38
Uruguay	2002	2005	27
Venezuela	1994	1998[3]	1
Vietnam	1997	1997	0
Yemen	1996	1996	16
Zambia	1995	1998	31
Zimbabwe	1995	1999[3]	10

Sources: IMF *World Economic Outlook*; Laeven and Valencia (2008); and authors' calculations.

Note: Output losses are computed as the cumulative difference between actual and trend real GDP, expressed as a percentage of trend real GDP for the period t through $t+3$, where t is the starting year of the crisis. Trend real GDP is computed by applying a Hodrick-Prescott filter ($\lambda = 100$) to the GDP series over $t-20$ through $t-1$.

[1] No output losses are reported for crises in transition economies that took place during the period of transition to market economies.

[2] Borderline cases.

[3] The duration of crises is truncated at five years, starting with the first crisis year.

[4] Credit data missing. For these countries, end dates are based on GDP growth only.

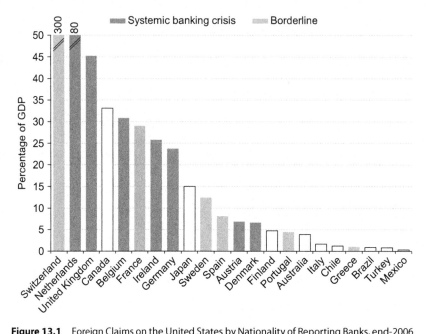

Figure 13.1 Foreign Claims on the United States by Nationality of Reporting Banks, end-2006

Source: Bank for International Settlements.

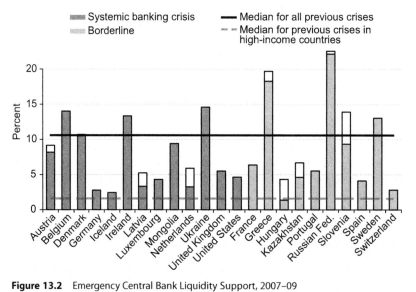

Figure 13.2 Emergency Central Bank Liquidity Support, 2007–09

Sources: Laeven and Valencia, 2008; IMF, *International Financial Statistics*; and authors' calculations.

Note: Total height of each bar represents the ratio of direct liquidity support from the treasury to total deposits and foreign liabilities (2007–09). Shaded portion of each bar represents the change in the ratio of central bank claims on the financial sector to total deposits and liabilities from the year before the crisis to the peak in the ratio. Liquidity data for Iceland were available only through March 2008.

In some cases, liquidity was also provided directly by the treasury, as indicated in Figure 13.2. Slovenia shows the largest increase in liquidity funded by the treasury, amounting to close to 5 percent of deposits and foreign liabilities. Similarly, government deposits at Parex Bank in Latvia were an important source of liquidity assistance for this bank.[14] Liquidity injected in countries labeled as borderline was also significant, particularly for Greece, Russia, and Sweden. For Greece, liquidity support increased steadily starting in September 2009. In Russia, liquidity support subsided quickly after reaching a peak of 22 percent of deposits and foreign liabilities in 2009.

Guarantees on bank liabilities were also widely used during the 2007–09 crisis episodes to restore the confidence of bank liability holders. All crisis countries except Ukraine (and Kazakhstan, Sweden, and Switzerland among borderline cases) extended guarantees on bank liabilities other than raising deposit insurance limits. However, the coverage extended varied widely (Appendix Table 13A.1). Although guarantees on bank liabilities were not uncommon in past crises, asset guarantees were used less frequently in the past. In the 2007–09 crises, asset guarantees were used in some cases, including in Belgium and the United Kingdom. For instance, the Bad Bank Act in Germany, passed in July 2009, provided private banks relief on holdings of illiquid assets by allowing them to transfer assets to a special entity in exchange for government-guaranteed bonds issued by this entity. Although direct fiscal costs for Germany amounted to slightly more than 1 percent of GDP, total guarantees (including those associated with bad bank and financial institutions' debt) reached about 6 percent of GDP.[15]

One measure of the length of a crisis is the time it takes central banks to withdraw liquidity support. As a measure of the time it took to withdraw liquidity support, the number of months between the peak of liquidity support and the month when liquidity support declined to its precrisis level is computed. In earlier crises, emergency liquidity support was withdrawn within 14 months (median). However, this time, as of end-2009 only Denmark, Germany, Hungary, Luxembourg, the Netherlands, and Switzerland saw their liquidity support return to precrisis levels, suggesting that liquidity remained an issue for a prolonged time in the 2007–09 crises.

The overall size of monetary expansion is also considered by computing the change in the monetary base; monetary expansion is found to be significantly higher in the 2007–09 crises compared with past crises. Figure 13.3 shows the change in the monetary base between its peak during the crisis and its level one year before the crisis, expressed in percentage points of GDP.[16] The median monetary

---

[14] Latvia satisfies the threshold used in this chapter's definition of extensive liquidity support once government deposits at Parex are counted.

[15] Because Germany's Bad Bank Act called for asset transfers, they could also be treated as asset purchases. This analysis treats it as guarantees, so Germany is not listed as having met the significant-asset-purchases threshold.

[16] Data on reserve money come from IFS. For euro area countries, reserve money corresponds to the aggregation of currency issued and liabilities to depository corporations, divided by euro area GDP.

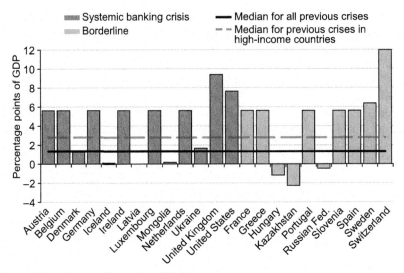

Figure 13.3 Monetary Expansion, 2007–09

Sources: IMF, *International Financial Statistics*; Laeven and Valencia (2008); and authors' calculations.

expansion of about 6 percent in the 2007–09 crises significantly exceeds its historical median of about 1 percent, although it is not that different from its historical
median among high-income countries. Relatively larger financial systems and credibility of monetary policy in high-income economies may explain this difference.

About 70 percent of fiscal outlays correspond to public sector recapitalizations
of financial institutions. Bank recapitalizations, although not more common than
in earlier crisis episodes, were implemented much faster than in the past. The
median difference between the time it took to implement public recapitalization
programs and the time that liquidity support became extensive (that is, when
liquidity support exceeded 5 percent) is zero months for the 2007–09 crises compared with 12 months for past crises (Figure 13.4).[17] Addressing solvency problems with public money is generally a complex and lengthy process because it
requires political consensus and legislation. Policymakers, therefore, often prolong the use of liquidity support and guarantees in the hope that problems in the
banking sector subside. With the 2007–09 crises, though, policymakers acted
with relative speed, at least in some countries.[18]

---

[17] For bank recapitalizations, only "comprehensive" recapitalization packages in which public funds
were used are considered, thereby excluding ad hoc interventions and biasing upward the estimate
of the response time. In the 2007–09 crises, three recapitalization programs targeted specific banks:
Iceland (the three largest banks), Luxembourg (Fortis and Dexia), and Latvia (Parex). The last two are
included in the calculation because of the size of the affected institutions. However, the median does
not change if they are excluded. Iceland is not included because of limited data for computing the date
when liquidity support became extensive.

[18] In many cases, banks were able to raise capital in private markets or from parent banks, which generally took place before public money was used. In addition, many banks were temporarily allowed to
avoid the recognition of market losses and thereby overstate regulatory capital.

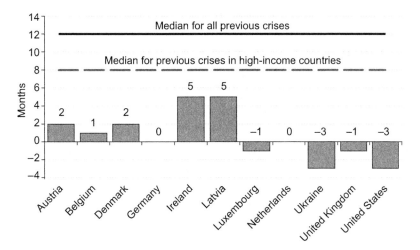

Figure 13.4 Timing of Recapitalization Policies for Countries with Systemic Banking Crises, 2007–09

Sources: Laeven and Valencia (2008); and authors' calculations.

Governments typically acquire stakes in the banking sector as part of government recapitalization programs, and such ownership stakes often end up being held by the government for a prolonged period. Although divestments (or repayments) of government support on average start about one year from the start of the crisis, suggesting that the early repayments from the Troubled Asset Relief Program capital support endeavor witnessed in the United States are not uncommon, government participation in banks has, in many cases, largely exceeded the initially envisioned holding period.[19] In many cases, the public sector retained participation for more than 10 years (in Japan, for instance, as of end-2008 over 30 percent of capital injected in financial institutions following the crisis in 1997 remained to be sold). In some cases, divestment took place by tender, through sales of entire institutions to foreign investors or large domestic banks; in other cases, it took place more gradually through markets.

Bank failures—defined broadly by including institutions that received government assistance—were also significant during the 2007–09 wave of crises. This proportion of failures is striking given that bank failures are rare events in most countries, in part due to regulatory forbearance and too-big-to-fail or -close problems. Relative to the total assets in the banking system, the bank failures in Iceland were by far the most significant, at about 90 percent of total banking assets (Figure 13.5). In Belgium and Greece as well as Iceland, banks that failed or received government assistance represented 80 percent or more of banking system assets. When using the more conservative definition of failure that

---

[19] A comprehensive analysis of guidelines for exit strategies from crises can be found in Blanchard, Cottarelli, and Viñals (2010).

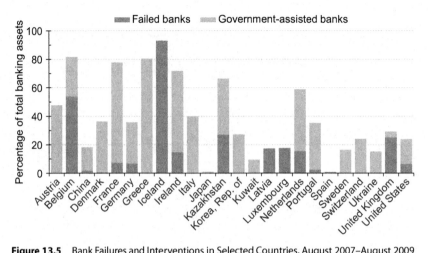

Figure 13.5   Bank Failures and Interventions in Selected Countries, August 2007–August 2009

Source: Authors' calculations based on data from IMF *International Financial Statistics*, European Union, U.S. Federal Deposit Insurance Corporation, and the Deposit Insurance Corporation of Japan.

Note: Government-assisted banks means public capital support resulting in the government holding a minority stake in the bank. Failed banks mean bank closure, bank taken over by government, nationalization, or public capital support resulting in the government becoming a majority shareholder.

excludes government assistance, Iceland is followed by Belgium, Kazakhstan, and the United Kingdom, with failing banks representing 53 percent, 28 percent, and 26 percent, respectively, of the system. With banks holding 80 percent of total banking system assets receiving some form of government assistance, Greece topped the charts. Greece is followed by France and Ireland, with banks holding about 70 percent and 55 percent, respectively, of banking system assets receiving government assistance.

For the United States, for which historical data on bank failures since the 1930s are available, the recent failures that included assistance are unprecedented, with banks holding about one-quarter of the deposit market having failed or received some of form of government assistance since 2007. (See Box 13.1 for a more detailed analysis of historical U.S. bank failures.) Excluding banks that received public assistance, 1989 is by far the worst year on record, with banks holding more than 6 percent of the deposit market failing during the U.S. savings and loan crisis. The United States was clearly not an outlier during the 2007–09 crises, even when using the broader definition of bank failures that includes government assistance. Of course, the U.S. failure list excludes such large financial institutions as Fannie Mae, Freddie Mac, and AIG because they are not banks, although they meet this chapter's definition of failure; therefore, this analysis could be underestimating the magnitude of financial distress in the United States.

A consequence of these dramatic bank failures has been a reorganization of the world's financial map, with large players becoming significantly smaller, freeing up space for new players, particularly in emerging markets. Bank failures during

Box 13.1 U.S. Bank Failures: Past and Present

U.S. bank failures since the 1930s have come in three waves: the Great Depression era of the 1930s, the savings and loan crisis of the 1980s, and the mortgage crisis late in the first decade of the 2000s, with the number of bank failures peaking in the years 1937, 1989, and 2009, respectively. Compared with the earlier bank failure episodes, the 2007–09 wave of bank failures appears more short lived and, at least compared with the savings and loan crisis, less dramatic as measured by the number of failing banks (Figure 13.1.1). Note that 2005 and 2006 were the only years since 1934 that reported no bank failures.

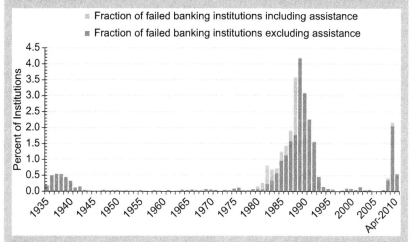

Figure 13.1.1   U.S. Bank Failures: Fraction of Failed Banks, 1934–2010

Source: U.S. Federal Deposit Insurance Corporation.
Note: The data include all failures and assistance transactions across 50 U.S. states and the District of Columbia.

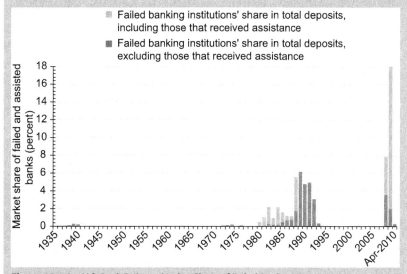

Figure 13.1.2   U.S. Bank Failures: Market Share of Failed Banks, 1934–2010

Source: U.S. Federal Deposit Insurance Corporation.
Note: The data include all failures and assistance transactions across 50 U.S. states and the District of Columbia.

Owing in part to consolidation following financial deregulation starting in the 1980s, the average U.S. bank grew substantially. After accounting for this development, the recent failures look much worse. Failed U.S. banks during the 2007–09 crisis held about 26 percent of the deposit market—that is, when including banks that did not fail but received government assistance, such as Citigroup and Bank of America (Figure 13.1.2). Using this definition of failure, 2009 is by far the worst on record. When excluding banks that received public assistance, 1989 is the worst year on record.

Bank failures during 2007–09 generated similar losses compared with the past, with a median loss rate to the deposit insurance fund on assets of failed banking institutions of 19 percent (Figure 13.1.3). Median losses are relatively stable over the examined period (data on loss rates are available starting in 1986), and roughly the same during the 2007–09 crisis as compared with the savings and loan crisis. The median loss rate peaked in 2008 at 28 percent. Losses to the deposit insurer were significantly lower in 2008, at 0.12 percent of U.S. GDP, than the highest loss on record in 1989 of 0.97 percent of U.S. GDP. Overall, in the particular case of the United States, the failure rate of banks and losses incurred by the government in closing failed banks in the 2007–09 crises were similar to the U.S. banking crisis of the 1980s, with a median loss rate in bank failures of about 20 percent of bank assets.

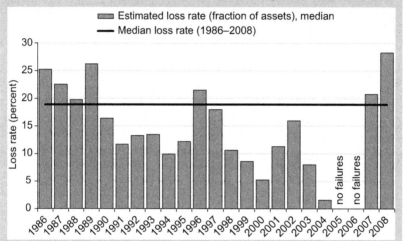

Figure 13.1.3   U.S. Bank Failures: Loss Rates on Assets of Failed Banks, 1986–2008

Source: U.S. Federal Deposit Corporation.
Note: Includes all failures and assistance transactions across 50 U.S. states and the District of Columbia. Total assets are for FDIC-insured commercial banks only. The estimated loss is the difference between the amount disbursed from the Deposit Insurance Fund (DIF) to cover obligations to insured depositors and the amount estimated to be ultimately recovered from the liquidation of the receivership estate. Estimated losses reflect unpaid principal amounts deemed unrecoverable and do not reflect interest that may be due on the DIF's administrative or subrogated claims should its principal be repaid in full.

the 2007–09 wave of crises were particularly dramatic for the United States and some of the countries in Western Europe that, before the crisis, were top-tier players in global banking. Before the crisis, at end-2006, the top 30 banks worldwide had a total stock market capitalization of about US$3.4 trillion, of which 40 percent belonged to U.S. banks, 12 percent to U.K. banks, and 12 percent to Japanese banks (see Table 13.3).[20] Countries with systemic banking crises in

---

[20] A complete list of global top-30 banks in 2006 and 2009 is reported in Appendix Table 13A.4.

TABLE 13.3

Market Capitalization of Top 30 Banks Worldwide, by Nationality				
	Number of banks		Percent of market capitalization	
Country	End-2006	End-2009	End-2006	End-2009
United States	10	5	39.8	20.9
United Kingdom	4	3	12.5	13.9
France	3	3	7.8	8.8
Japan	3	1	11.9	2.5
Netherlands and Belgium[1]	3	0	6.9	0.0
Spain	2	2	6.5	9.5
Switzerland	2	2	7.5	4.9
Canada	1	2	1.8	5.0
Italy	1	2	2.9	5.1
Germany	1	1	2.4	2.1
Australia	0	4	0.0	8.8
Brazil	0	2	0.0	4.4
China	0	2	0.0	12.2
Sweden	0	1	0.0	1.9
Total	**30**	**30**	**100.0**	**100.0**

Source: Bankscope.
Note: Banks used in the calculation are listed in Appendix Table 13A.4.
[1] Includes two Dutch institutions and Fortis, a Dutch-Belgian financial conglomerate.

2007–09 dominated the banking arena in 2006 with a share of close to 60 percent of the total.

The crisis changed the map significantly. Twelve banks dropped from the top-30 list of 2006, of which three were acquired by other institutions. The overall loss in market capitalization of the top-30 banks between 2006 and 2009 was a staggering 52 percent, a figure that even includes a significant stock market recovery during 2009. Excluding banks that were acquired by other institutions, Citigroup had the largest decline in market capitalization; however, at the country level, the Netherlands (including Fortis Bank) experienced the largest average decline, followed by Japan. The latter is surprising given that Japan is not even classified as having had a borderline systemic banking crisis (because, although announced policy interventions in Japan were significant, the actual use of these resources was small).

What did the list of the world's top-30 banks look like at the end of 2009? Four countries were on the list for the first time: Australia, Brazil, China, and Sweden. The Netherlands and Belgium—listed together in Table 13.3 because of jointly owned Fortis Bank—dropped from the top-30 ranking in 2009. The number of U.S. banks on the list fell to five, together holding only 21 percent of the market capitalization of the world's 30 largest banks compared with 40 percent for the 10 U.S. banks on the list in 2006. The United States clearly had the most dramatic change in market capitalization share. Other clear losers included the Netherlands and Japan. In 2006, no emerging market appeared on the list, but at end-2009 banks from Brazil and China together were holding 16 percent of the total market capitalization of top-30 banks worldwide. Other clear winners were Australia and

Canada, whose large banks mostly escaped entanglement in the U.S. mortgage crisis.

HOW COSTLY WERE THE 2007–09 SYSTEMIC BANKING CRISES?

The cost of each crisis is estimated using three metrics: direct fiscal costs, output losses, and the increase in public sector debt relative to GDP. Direct fiscal costs include fiscal outlays committed to the financial sector from the start of the crisis through end-2009 (see Appendix Table 13A.3 for a list of items included), and capture the direct fiscal implications of intervention in the financial sector.[21] Output losses are computed as deviations of actual GDP from its trend, and the increase in public debt is measured as the change in the public-debt-to-GDP ratio during the four-year period beginning with the crisis year.[22] Output losses and the increase in public debt capture the overall real and fiscal implications of the crisis.

The 2007–09 crises were overall more costly in output losses and increases in debt, but less so in direct fiscal outlays compared with the average crisis of the past. However, when the comparison is limited to high-income countries—given that they dominate the new crises sample—output losses are found to be similar to those of the past, increases in public debt are somewhat lower, but direct fiscal outlays are higher (Table 13.4).

The median direct fiscal costs associated with financial sector restructuring for the 2007–09 systemic banking crises amounted to almost 5 percent of GDP, about half its historical median of 10 percent. Figure 13.6 illustrates the direct fiscal costs for the 2007–09 systemic crises, as well as for the borderline cases. Greece, Kazakhstan, Russia, and Slovenia show the highest costs among the borderline cases, although for Slovenia all costs correspond to liquidity support from the treasury in the form of bank deposits. For Greece and Kazakhstan, at least half is also liquidity assistance from the treasury. For Russia, the entire amount cor-

---

[21] As of 2012, it is still early to provide final numbers about recoveries and losses for recent crises, but wherever funds have been recovered, they have been included in Table 13A.3. Also, potential losses arising from contingent liabilities (such as asset guarantees) and schemes funded by the central bank (such as asset purchases) are not included, although losses from those schemes may ultimately have fiscal consequences.

[22] Output losses are computed as the cumulative sum of the differences between actual and trend real GDP over the period t through $t + 3$, expressed as a percentage of trend real GDP, with t being the starting year of the crisis. Trend real GDP is computing by applying a Hodrick-Prescott filter (with $\lambda = 100$) to the log of real GDP series over $t - 20$ through $t - 1$ (or shorter if data are not available, though at least four precrisis observations are required). Real GDP is extrapolated using the trend growth rate during the same period. Real GDP data are from the WEO. For the 2007–09 crisis episodes, GDP projections are based on the April 2010 WEO. The duration of a crisis is truncated at five years, including the first year. Wherever the methodology results in a crisis duration of more than five years, or when data availability impede application of the methodology, the end year is set as the fifth year from the crisis start year.

TABLE 13.4

Summary of the Cost of Banking Crises, 1970–2009

	Direct fiscal cost	Increase in public debt	Output losses
		Median (% of GDP)	
Previous crises (1970–2006)			
Advanced economies	3.7	36.2	32.9
Emerging markets	11.5	12.7	29.4
All	10.0	16.3	19.5
Most recent crises (2007–09)			
Advanced economies	5.9	25.1	24.8
Other economies	4.8	23.9	4.7
All	4.9	23.9	24.5

Sources: Laeven and Valencia (2008); and authors' calculations.
Note: The 2007–09 crises comprise Austria, Belgium, Denmark, Germany, Iceland, Ireland, Latvia, Luxembourg, Mongolia, the Netherlands, Ukraine, the United Kingdom, and the United States.

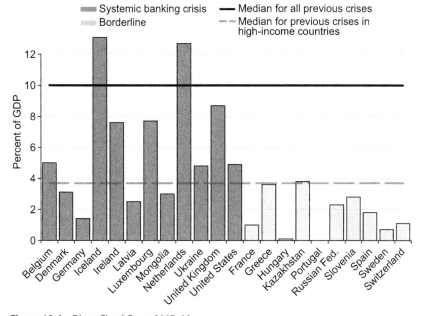

Figure 13.6 Direct Fiscal Costs, 2007–09
Sources: Laeven and Valencia (2008); and authors' calculations.

responds to recapitalization. As one would expect, on average, direct fiscal costs for borderline cases are lower than those for the systemic crises. Iceland has the highest fiscal outlays, at 13 percent of GDP.[23]

---

[23] These costs exclude the obligations (mostly to the United Kingdom and the Netherlands) arising from the Icesave crisis, which in net present value terms, IMF staff estimates to be about 16 percent of GDP.

The lower direct fiscal outlays associated with high-income countries in past crises, relative to all past crises, is regarded as a consequence of the greater flexibility these countries have in supporting their financial systems indirectly through expansionary monetary and fiscal policy and direct purchases of assets that help sustain asset prices. Additionally, some high-income countries opted for sizable contingent liabilities to complement direct fiscal outlays (see Appendix Table 13A.3).

Given that countries can also indirectly support their financial sectors in times of crisis through expansionary fiscal policies that support output and employment, the overall increase in public debt can be used as a broader estimate of the fiscal cost of the crisis. The median debt increase among 2007–09 crises was 24 percent of GDP, about 8 percentage points higher than its historical median of 16 percent. Thus, public debt burdens increased significantly as a consequence of policy measures taken during the crisis.

Figure 13.7 shows the increase in the public debt burden for each crisis country and also reports the historical median of the increase in public debt at crisis times. The increase in public debt that can be attributed to the crisis is approximated by computing the difference between pre- and postcrisis debt projections. For the 2007–09 crises, the fall WEO debt projections from the year before the crisis year are used as precrisis debt figures (i.e., September 2006 WEO for the United Kingdom and the United States and October 2007 WEO for all other 2007–09 crises) and the spring 2010 WEO debt projections for the postcrisis debt figures. For past episodes, the actual change in debt is reported.[24]

Among the 2007–09 borderline cases, France, Greece, Portugal, and Spain exhibited the largest expected increases in debt. Although overall fiscal stimulus packages to counteract the global recession were significant in some of these countries, the direct interventions in the financial sector were not sufficient—as of end-2009—to qualify as systemic banking crises.

Figures 13.6 and 13.7 suggest a large difference between increases in fiscal costs arising from direct support to the financial sector and increases in overall public debt. This difference appears to be positively correlated at about 0.4 with an economy's level of income (Figure 13.8). Given that direct fiscal outlays to support the financial sector generally increase public debt, the difference between the increase in public debt and fiscal costs reflects, in part, the outcome of measures taken to support the real sector. This difference can be partly explained by discretionary fiscal policy and automatic stabilizers. One possible interpretation of this positive correlation is that high-income economies generally face easier financing opportunities than their low-income counterparts, and therefore may choose to complement financial measures with expansionary fiscal measures to

---

[24] The increase in debt is computed as a percentage of GDP during $t - 1$ through $t + 3$, where t is the starting year of the crisis. The choice of sources is guided by the availability of general government debt. When it is not available, central government debt is reported instead. The primary data source is the WEO. When WEO debt data are not available, the OECD Analytical Database and the IMF's Government Finance Statistics are used.

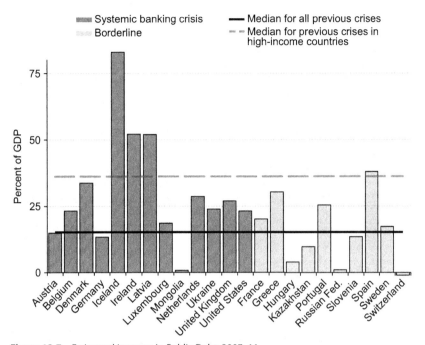

Figure 13.7 Estimated Increase in Public Debt, 2007–11

Sources: Authors' calculations; IMF, *World Economic Outlook*, various years; and Laeven and Valencia (2008).

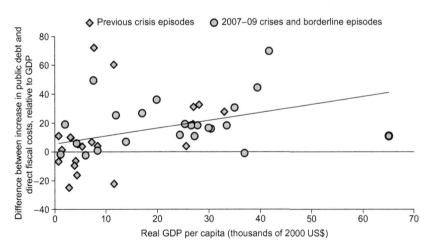

Figure 13.8 Increase in Public Debt and Direct Fiscal Costs

Sources: Authors' calculations; IMF, *World Economic Outlook*; and Laeven and Valencia (2008).
Note: Previous episodes exclude countries that experienced sovereign debt crises, using data from Laeven and Valencia (2008).

deal with banking crises. Clearly, expansionary fiscal policy indirectly supports the financial sector by stimulating aggregate demand, which in turn props up loan demand and lowers the risk of loan defaults.

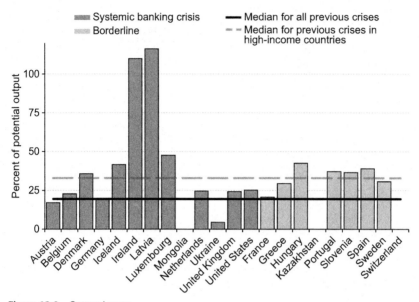

Figure 13.9 Output Losses

Sources: Laeven and Valencia (2008); IMF, *World Economic Outlook*, various years; and authors' calculations.

The fallout from the 2007–09 crises on the real sector was large. The median output loss is estimated to be 25 percent of GDP, which is almost 5 percentage points higher than the historical median loss during previous crises of 20 percent. Output losses are estimated by computing the difference between trend GDP and actual GDP for the four-year period beginning with the crisis year.[25] Therefore, the methodology does not distinguish between permanent and transitory output losses. For the 2007–09 crises, spring 2010 WEO projections are used as actual GDP for the postcrisis years. Figure 13.9 shows the results.[26]

Output losses differ depending on the size of the initial shock, differences across countries in how the shock was propagated through the financial system, and the intensity of policy interventions. The output losses for Ireland and Latvia stand out at more than 100 percent of potential GDP. Losses among borderline cases are also significant, in particular for Hungary, Portugal, and Spain. On average, countries with larger financial systems, and especially those that experienced rapid expansion before the crisis (such as Iceland, Ireland, and Latvia), were hit hardest.

---

[25] Trend GDP is computed applying a Hodrick-Prescott filter to the real GDP series over the 20-year period before the crisis.

[26] The medians reported in Figure 13.9 are based on output losses recomputed for all crisis episodes using the methodology employed in this chapter rather than by relying on estimates of output losses in Laeven and Valencia (2008). They computed the real GDP trend using all available data, using a different horizon for each country. The recomputed output loss estimates are, on average, similar to those in Laeven and Valencia (2008), though they differ for low-income countries and countries affected by large shocks such as wars.

CONCLUSION

This chapter extends the database presented in Chapter 2 on systemic banking crises through end-2009 to include the 2007–09 wave of financial crises following the U.S. mortgage crisis of 2007. The update results in 13 new systemic banking crisis episodes and 10 borderline cases since early 2007. The update makes several improvements to the earlier database, including an improved definition of systemic banking crisis, the inclusion of crisis ending dates, and broader coverage of crisis management policies.

The new data show that the 2007–09 crises and past crises share many commonalities, both in underlying causes and in policy responses. All crises share a containment phase during which liquidity pressures are kept in check through liquidity support and in some cases guarantees on bank liabilities. This phase is followed by a resolution phase during which a broad range of measures are taken to restructure banks and encourage bank lending (including asset purchases, guarantees, and capital injections) to reignite economic growth. These common patterns echo earlier findings summarized in Honohan and Laeven (2005) and Reinhart and Rogoff (2009).

However, the 2007–09 wave of crises also shows some important differences from previous crisis episodes.

- First, the 2007–09 crises were concentrated in advanced economies, in particular those with large and integrated financial systems, unlike many of the boom-bust cycles of the past that centered on emerging market economies. Liquidity shortages at systemically important, globally interconnected financial institutions in these advanced economies prompted large-scale government interventions.

- Second, although the intensity of policy interventions was comparable to past crisis episodes, the speed of intervention and implementation of resolution policies was faster for the 2007–09 crises. This timely response reflects, in part, that most of the crisis-affected countries were high-income countries with strong legal, political, and economic institutions that created an enabling environment for effective and speedy crisis resolutions. Recapitalization policies, in particular, were implemented much sooner than in the past, contributing to lower direct fiscal outlays.

- Third, countries used a much broader range of policy measures compared with past episodes, including unconventional monetary policy measures, asset purchases and guarantees, and significant fiscal stimulus packages. These large-scale public interventions were possible in part because most of the crisis-affected countries were high-income countries with relatively greater institutional quality and credibility of policy actions.

- Fourth, preliminary estimates indicate that the overall economic costs of the 2007–09 crises are higher in output losses and increases in public debt compared with past crises, although fiscal costs associated with financial sector interventions were lower this time.

APPENDIX TABLE 13A.1

Systemic Banking Crisis Policy Responses, 2007–09

Country	Liquidity support (percentage point increase in central bank claims on financial institutions as a ratio of deposits and foreign liabilities)	Gross restructuring costs (recapitalization and other restructuring costs, excluding liquidity and asset purchases, as a percentage of GDP)	Asset purchases and guarantees (funded by treasury and central bank, as a percentage of GDP)	Guarantees on liabilities (significant guarantees on bank liabilities in addition to increasing deposit insurance ceilings)	Nationalizations (state takes control of institutions; year of nationalization in parentheses)
			Systemic Crises		
Austria	8.2	2.1	Guarantees: 0.6	Unlimited coverage to depositors. Bank and nonbank bond issues.	Hypo Group Alpe Adria (2009)
Belgium	14.0	5.0	Guarantees: 7.7	DI raised from €20,000 to €100,000. Deposit-like insurance instruments. Interbank loans and short-term debt. Specific guarantees on Dexia.	Fortis (2008)
Denmark	10.5	2.8	n.a.	Deposits and unsecured claims of Private Contingency Association banks.	Fionia Bank (2009)
Germany	2.8	1.2	Purchases: 0.2	Unlimited coverage of household deposits. Interbank loans and bank debt (capped at €400 billion).	Hypo Real Estate (2008)
Iceland	2.4	13.0	n.a.	Unlimited coverage of domestic deposits.	Kaupthing, Landsbanki, Glitnir, Straumur-Burdaras, SPRON, and Sparisjóðabankinn (2008)
Ireland	13.3	7.6	n.a.	Unlimited coverage until September 29, 2010 of most liabilities of 10 banks.	Anglo Irish Bank (2009)
Latvia	3.3	2.5	n.a.	DI raised to €50,000. Guarantee on Parex Bank syndicated loans.	Parex Bank (2008)
Luxembourg	4.3	7.7	n.a.	DI raised from €20,000 to €100,000. €4.5 billion guarantee on Dexia Bank's debt.	Fortis and Dexia's subsidiaries (2008)
Mongolia	9.4	3.0	n.a.	Unlimited coverage of all deposits.	Zoos Bank (2009)
Netherlands	3.3	6.5	Guarantees: 3.3	DI raised to €100,000. Interbank loans to solvent banks. Fortis bonds (€5 billion) and ING bonds (€10 billion).	ABN-AMRO/Fortis (2008)
Ukraine	14.6	4.8	n.a.	DI raised from 50,000 hryvnia to 150,000 until January, 2011.	Prominvest (2008); Nadra, Inprom, Volodimrski, Dialog, Rodovid, Kiev, Ukrgaz (2009)

Country					
United Kingdom	5.5	5.1	Purchases: 13.4 Guarantees: 14.5	DI raised from £35,000 to 50,000. Guarantee on short- to medium-term debt (capped at £250 billion). Blanket guarantee on Northern Rock and Bradford & Bingley wholesale deposits.	Northern Rock, RBS (2008)
United States	4.6	3.5	Purchases: 9.0	DI raised from $100,000 to $250,000 (until end-2009). Money market funds (capped at $50 billion). Full guarantee on transaction deposits. Newly issued senior unsecured debt.	Fannie Mae, Freddie Mac, AIG (2008)
Borderline Cases					
France	6.4	n.a.	n.a.	DI already higher than new European Union limit. €360 billion in guarantees for refinancing credit institutions. €55 billion of Dexia's debt.	n.a.
Greece	18.3	1.7	n.a.	DI raised from €20,000 to €100,000. Funding guarantees up to €15 billion.	n.a.
Hungary	1.3	0.1	n.a.	Unlimited protection to depositors of small banks.	n.a.
Kazakhstan	4.6	2.4	n.a.	DI raised from 0.7 million tenge to 5 million.	n.a.
Portugal	5.5	n.a.	n.a.	DI raised from €25,000 to €100,000. Debt securities issued by credit institutions (up to 12 percent of GDP).	Banco Portugues de Negócios (small bank) (2008)
Russian Federation	22.2	1.0	n.a.	DI raised from 400,000 rubles to 700,000. Interbank lending for qualifying banks.	n.a.
Slovenia	9.3	n.a.	n.a.	Unlimited protection for all deposits by individuals and small enterprises until end-2010. New debt issued by financial institutions until end-2010.	n.a.
Spain	4.1	n.a.	n.a.	DI raised from €20,000 to €100,000. Credit institutions' new debt issues (capped at €200 billion).	n.a.
Sweden	13.1	0.7	n.a.	DI raised from 250,000 kronor to 500,000. Medium-term debt of banks and mortgage institutions (up to 1.5 trillion kronor).	n.a.
Switzerland	2.8	1.1	Purchases: 6.7	DI raised from 30,000 francs to 100,000 until December 31, 2011.	n.a.

Sources: IMF staff reports; Mayer Brown (2009); official websites; and IMF, *International Financial Statistics*.
Note: — = not available; DI = deposit insurance; n.a. = not applicable.

TABLE 13A.2

Preemptive Crisis Responses in Selected G-20 Countries, 2007–09

Country	Liquidity support (percentage point increase in central bank claims on financial institutions as a ratio of deposits and foreign liabilities, relative to precrisis level)	Gross restructuring costs (recapitalization and other restructuring costs, excluding liquidity and asset purchases, as a percentage of GDP)	Asset purchases and guarantees (funded by treasury and central bank, as a percentage of GDP)	Guarantees on liabilities (significant: guarantees of other liabilities in addition to increasing deposit insurance (DI) ceilings)	Nationalizations (state takes control of institutions; year of nationalization in parentheses)
Australia	n.a.	n.a.	n.a.	Unlimited coverage of deposits (if above 1 million Australian dollars, only those with maturity < five years).	n.a.
Canada	1.8	n.a.	Purchases: 4.4	Temporary insurance on the wholesale term borrowing of deposit-taking institutions. Increased deposit insurance in some provinces.	n.a.
Italy	2.5	0.8	n.a.	n.a.	n.a.
Japan	1.1	< 0.1	Purchases: 1.1 Guarantees: 2.6 (for small and medium enterprises)	n.a.	n.a.
Korea, Republic of	2.1	0.8	Purchases: < 0.1 Guarantees: 1.8 (for small and medium enterprises)	Payment guarantees to Korean banks' external debt (US$100 billion cap).	n.a.

Sources: IMF staff reports; Mayer Brown (2009); official websites; and IMF, *International Financial Statistics.*
Note: n.a. = not applicable.

TABLE 13A.3

Direct Fiscal Outlays, Recoveries to Date, and Asset Guarantees, 2007–09 (percent of GDP)

Country and action	Program	Gross	Recoveries	Net[1]
Austria				
Recapitalizations	Capital injection program	2.1		
Asset purchases	impaired assets and liquidity	2.0		
	Total fiscal outlays	*4.1*		*4.1*
Asset guarantees	*Asset guarantee program*	*0.6*		
Belgium				
Recapitalization	Ethias, Fortis, KBC, and Dexia	4.7		
Other	Capital for Fortis SPV	0.2		
	Total fiscal outlays	*5.0*		*5.0*
Asset guarantees	Asset relief facility	6.0		
	Fortis SPV	1.3		
	Fortis portfolio	0.4		
	Total asset guarantees	*7.7*		*7.7*
Denmark				
Recapitalization	Capital assistance program	2.7		
	Capital injection in Fionia Bank	0.1		
Other	Loan to Fionia Bank	0.3		
	Total fiscal outlays	*3.1*		*3.1*
France				
Recapitalization	SPPE acquisition of subordinated bonds	0.5		
	Second-stage recapitalization (BNP, SG, Dexia)	0.5		
	Total fiscal outlays	*1.0*		*1.0*
Asset guarantees	Financial Security Assurance Inc.	0.3		
Germany				
Recapitalization	Capital injection program	1.2		1.2
Asset purchases	Asset purchase program	0.2		
	Total fiscal outlays	*1.4*		*1.4*
Asset guarantees	Bad Bank Act[2]	6.1		
Greece				
Recapitalization	Capital injection package	1.7		
Other	Liquidity	1.9		
	Total fiscal outlays	*3.6*		*3.6*
Hungary				
Recapitalization	Capital injection in FHB (mortgage lender)	0.1		
Other	Foreign exchange loans to large banks	2.6		
	Total fiscal outlays	*2.7*	*1.6*	*1.1*
Iceland[3]				
Recapitalization	Landsbanki, Kaupthing, and Islandsbanki	13.0		13.0
Ireland				
Recapitalization	Bank of Ireland, Allied Irish Bank, and Anglo Irish	7.6		7.6
Kazakhstan				
Recapitalization	BTA, Halyk, Alliance, and KKB	2.4		
Other	Liquidity through deposits of the development agency	1.3		
	Total fiscal outlays	*3.8*		3.8
Latvia				
Recapitalization	Parex and MLBN	2.5		
Other	Liquidity	2.5		
	Total fiscal outlays	*4.9*		*4.9*
Luxembourg				
Recapitalization	Fortis and Dexia	7.7		7.7
Netherlands				
Recapitalization	Fortis, ING, SNS, and AEGON	6.5		
Other	Loans to Icesave and Icelandic Deposit Insurance	0.2		
	Loan to Fortis	5.9		
	Total fiscal outlays	*12.7*	*5.9*	*6.8*

(Continued)

TABLE 13A.3 (*Continued*)

Direct Fiscal Outlays, Recoveries to Date, and Asset Guarantees, 2007–09 (percent of GDP)

Country and action	Program	Gross	Recoveries	Net[1]
Asset guarantees	ABN AMRO/Fortis mortgage portfolio	6.0		
	ING Alt-A RMBS portfolio	4.8		
	Total asset guarantees	**10.8**		
Mongolia				
Other	Restructuring of Avod Bank	3.0		3.0
Portugal				
Recapitalization		0		0
Russian Fed.	State Mortgage Agency , VTB, Rosselhozbank, Rosagroleasing, VEB	1.0		
	Subordinated loans from VEB	0.9		
	Liquidity through government deposits in commercial banks	0.4		
	Total fiscal outlays	**2.3**		**2.3**
Slovenia				
Liquidity	Public sector deposits in banks (proceeds from bond issue)	2.8		2.8
Spain				
Asset purchases	Purchase of high-quality securities from credit institutions	1.8		1.8
Sweden				
Recapitalization	Recapitalization package	0.2		
Other	Initial contribution to stabilization fund	0.5		
	Total fiscal outlays	**0.7**		**0.7**
Switzerland				
Recapitalization	Mandatory convertible notes UBS	1.1	1.5	−0.4
Ukraine				
Recapitalization	Public recapitalization program	4.8		4.8
United Kingdom				
Recapitalization	RBS, Lloyds, LBG, and Northern Rock	5.0		
Other	Dunfermline Building Society takeover	0.1		
	Deposit compensation	1.8		
	Loans to Northern Rock and Bradford & Bingley	1.9		
	Total fiscal outlays	**8.7**	**1.0**	**7.7**
Asset guarantees	Pool of RBS assets and contingent convertibles	14.5		
United States				
Recapitalization	Capital purchase program	1.4		
	AIG	0.5		
	Targeted investment program	0.3		
	Support to GMAC	0.1		
	Support to Fannie Mae and Freddie Mac	0.8		
Other	Home Affordable Modification Program	0.2		
	Credit Union Homeowners Affordability Relief Program	0.1		
Asset purchases	MBS purchase	1.4		
	Public-private investment program	0.2		
	Total fiscal outlays	**4.9**	**0.6**	**4.3**
Asset guarantees	Citigroup asset guarantee			

Sources: IMF staff reports; official websites; and Mayer Brown (2009).

Note: SPPE = state shareholding company.

[1] Includes repayments up to end-2009 of capital support as well as interest and fees generated from loans and guarantee programs for the cases for which data were available.

[2] Includes total guarantees issued by the Stabilization Fund, which includes items related to the Bad Bank Act as well as debt issued by financial institutions.

[3] The baseline case does not include the increase in debt that would result from the Icesave crisis as part of the fiscal costs. Most disbursements took place at end-2008 and the first half of 2009, so 2009 nominal GDP (from WEO) is used to express the figures as percentage points of GDP.

TABLE 13A.4

Top 30 Banks in the World by Market Capitalization, 2006 and 2009

Market Capitalization (million US$)						Market Capitalization (million US$)			
2006 Rank	Bank Name	Country	2006	2009		2009 Rank	Bank Name	Country	2009
1	Citigroup	United States	286,337	17,016		1	HSBC Holdings	United Kingdom	199,785
2	Bank of America	United States	251,872	68,660		2	China Construction Bank	China	193,240
3	Mitsubishi UFJ Financial Group	Japan	188,034	53,052		3	JP Morgan Chase	United States	148,484
4	HSBC Holdings	United Kingdom	172,938	199,785		4	Banco Santander	Spain	136,918
5	JP Morgan Chase	United States	172,109	148,484		5	Wells Fargo & Co	United States	112,251
6	UBS	Switzerland	156,455	50,242		6	BNP Paribas	France	95,359
7	Banco Santander	Spain	127,400	136,918		7	Goldman Sachs	United States	69,454
8	Wells Fargo & Co	United States	122,056	112,251		8	Ind'l & Commercial Bank of China	China	68,968
9	Wachovia Corp	United States	114,542	Failed		9	Banco Bilbao Vizcaya Argentaria	Spain	68,733
10	Mizuho Financial Group	Japan	114,249	21,423		10	Bank of America	United States	68,660
11	BNP Paribas	France	110,786	95,359		11	Royal Bank of Canada	Canada	64,894
12	ING Groep	Netherlands	106,700	38,077		12	National Australia Bank	Australia	56,732
13	Royal Bank of Scotland	United Kingdom	102,726	26,655		13	UniCredit	Italy	56,538
14	UniCredit	Italy	99,639	56,538		14	Credit Suisse Group	Switzerland	55,706
15	Sumitomo Mitsui Financial	Japan	98,384	27,429		15	Intesa Sanpaolo	Italy	53,771
16	Credit Suisse Group	Switzerland	96,203	55,706		16	Mitsubishi UFJ Financial Group	Japan	53,052
17	Banco Bilbao Vizcaya Argentaria	Spain	93,333	68,733		17	Société Générale	France	52,169
18	Goldman Sachs	United States	91,457	69,454		18	Standard Chartered	United Kingdom	51,268
19	Société Générale	France	85,410	52,169		19	Itau Unibanco Holdings	Brazil	50,722
20	Merrill Lynch & Co	United States	82,235	Failed		20	American Express	United States	50,281
21	Morgan Stanley	United States	80,553	31,307		21	UBS	Switzerland	50,242
22	Deutsche Bank	Germany	80,433	44,201		22	Barclays	United Kingdom	49,295
23	Barclays	United Kingdom	76,734	49,295		23	Commonwealth Bank of Australia	Australia	48,062
24	American Express Company	United States	75,285	50,281		24	Deutsche Bank	Germany	44,201
25	HBOS	United Kingdom	69,158	6,138		25	Banco do Brasil	Brazil	43,382
26	US Bancorp	United States	68,942	39,617		26	Bank of Nova Scotia	Canada	43,190
27	Crédit Agricole	France	68,723	41,302		27	Westpac Banking Corp	Australia	43,137
28	ABN Amro Holdings	Netherlands	64,717	Failed		28	Australia and New Zealand Banking	Australia	42,473
29	Fortis	Belgium/Netherlands	60,674	8,886		29	Crédit Agricole	France	41,302
30	Royal Bank of Canada	Canada	59,686	64,894		30	Nordea Bank	Sweden	41,284
	Total		**3,377,767**	**1,633,871**			**Total**		**2,153,554**

Source: Bankscope.

Note: Shaded ranking positions on 2006 list indicate banks no longer among the top 30 in 2009; shaded ranking positions on 2009 list indicate banks that entered the top 30 list in 2009.

The lower short-run fiscal costs reflect the relatively swift government announcements of recapitalization measures and other actions to restore the health of the financial system. However, the lower costs were also a consequence of the significant indirect support the financial system received through expansionary monetary and fiscal policy, the widespread use of guarantees on liabilities, and direct purchases of assets that helped sustain asset prices. The significant support deployed through monetary and fiscal policies, including coordinated international efforts to ensure adequate foreign exchange liquidity, and timely implementation of measures to address solvency problems in the financial system, contributed significantly to reducing the real impact of the 2007–09 crises. Moreover, the indirect support from macroeconomic stabilization policies also lifted the burden on traditional crisis management policies, ultimately keeping the direct fiscal costs associated with bank recapitalization and other direct interventions into the financial sector lower than they otherwise would have been.

However, in the medium term, these indirect support measures significantly increased the burden of public debt and the size of government contingent liabilities, raising concerns about fiscal sustainability in a number of countries. Moreover, the crisis is still ongoing (as of late 2013) in several countries and its ultimate impact will have to be reassessed in the future. Therefore, it may be premature to hail recent crisis management efforts as being more successful than those of the past.

REFERENCES

Acharya, Viral, and Matthew Richardson, 2009, *Restoring Financial Stability: How to Repair a Failed System* (Hoboken, New Jersey: John Wiley and Sons).

Adrian, Tobias, and Hyun Shin, 2008, "Financial Intermediaries, Financial Stability, and Monetary Policy," Federal Reserve Bank of New York Staff Report 346 (New York: Federal Reserve Bank of New York).

Blanchard, Olivier J., Carlo Cottarelli, and José Viñals, 2010, "Exiting from Crisis Intervention Policies," IMF Policy Paper 10/10 (Washington: International Monetary Fund).

Brunnermeier, Markus, 2009, "Deciphering the Liquidity and Credit Crunch 2007–2008," *Journal of Economic Perspectives*, Vol. 23, pp. 77–100.

Caprio, Gerard, Daniela Klingebiel, Luc Laeven, and Guillermo Noguera, 2005, "Banking Crisis Database," in *Systemic Financial Crises: Containment and Resolution*, ed. by Patrick Honohan and Luc Laeven (Cambridge, United Kingdom: Cambridge University Press).

Cheasty, Adrienne, and Udaibir Das, 2009, "Crisis-Related Measures in the Financial System and Sovereign Balance Sheet Risks," IMF Policy Paper 09/91 (Washington: International Monetary Fund).

Claessens, Stijn, Giovanni Dell'Ariccia, Deniz Igan, and Luc Laeven, 2010, "Cross-Country Experiences and Policy Implications from the Global Financial Crisis," *Economic Policy*, Vol. 62, pp. 267–93.

Dell'Ariccia, Giovanni, Luc Laeven, and Deniz Igan, 2008, "Credit Booms and Lending Standards: Evidence from the Subprime Mortgage Market," IMF Working Paper 08/106 (Washington: International Monetary Fund).

Gorton, Gary, 2008, "The Panic of 2007," NBER Working Paper No. 14358 (Cambridge, Massachusetts: National Bureau of Economic Research).

Honohan, Patrick, and Luc Laeven (eds.), 2005, *Systemic Financial Crises: Containment and Resolution* (Cambridge, United Kingdom: Cambridge University Press).

Keys, Benjamin, Tanmoy Mukherjee, Amit Seru, and Vikrant Vig, 2010, "Did Securitization Lead to Lax Screening? Evidence from Subprime Loans," *Quarterly Journal of Economics*, Vol. 125, pp. 307–62.

Laeven, Luc, and Fabián Valencia, 2008, "Systemic Banking Crises: A New Database," IMF Working Paper 08/224 (Washington: International Monetary Fund).

Mayer Brown, 2009, "Government Interventions in the Wake of the Financial Crisis: The European Response So Far," The Mayer Brown Practices.

Mian, Atif, and Amir Sufi, 2011, "House Prices, Home Equity-Based Borrowing, and the U.S. Household Leverage Crisis," *American Economic Review*, Vol. 101, No. 5, pp. 2132–56.

Obstfeld, Maurice, and Kenneth Rogoff, 2009, "Global Imbalances and the Financial Crisis: Products of Common Causes," CEPR Discussion Paper No. 7606 (London: Centre for Economic Policy Research).

Taylor, John, 2009, *Getting Off Track: How Government Actions and Interventions Caused, Prolonged, and Worsened the Financial Crisis* (Stanford, California: Hoover Press).

Reinhart, Carmen, and Kenneth Rogoff, 2009, *This Time is Different: Eight Centuries of Financial Folly* (Princeton, New Jersey: Princeton University Press).

CHAPTER 14

How Effective Is Fiscal Policy Response in Financial Crises?

EMANUELE BALDACCI, SANJEEV GUPTA, AND
CARLOS MULAS-GRANADOS

Countercyclical fiscal policies—comprising discretionary expansionary budget measures and the operation of automatic stabilizers—have generally helped shorten recessions in advanced economies during crisis episodes (IMF, 2009a, 2010a). The evidence is not as clear in emerging market economies, where procyclical spending biases, narrow automatic stabilizers, and limited credit access have constrained governments' ability to provide fiscal stimulus during adverse economic periods (Kaminsky, Reinhart, and Végh, 2004). Initial fiscal conditions generally play an important role in crisis responses (Alesina and others, 2002) in both advanced and emerging economies. Countries are more likely to adopt countercyclical fiscal policies if sufficient fiscal space existed before the crisis.[1] The success of fiscal policy in restoring growth also depends on the role of accompanying macroeconomic policies and on the design of the fiscal stimulus packages, because the size of multipliers varies across government spending and tax measures.[2]

One of the key findings of the literature is that expansionary fiscal responses lead to sustained economic recoveries after the crisis only when the financial sector's vulnerabilities are addressed without endangering fiscal sustainability (IMF, 2009c). Crisis resolution measures generally entail costly government restructuring of the private sector's balance sheet, including the financial sector, which can have a lasting negative impact on public debt levels. Furthermore, government interventions to boost private sector credit and domestic demand could leave the economy exposed to the risk of high inflation and low private investment growth. Therefore, a potential conflict arises between the size of countercyclical fiscal expansions during downturns and their medium-term growth implications.

The authors wish to thank Fabian Bornhorst, Stijn Claessens, Julio Escolano, Mark Horton, Julie Kozack, Paolo Manasse, Krishna Srinivasan, and Steve Symansky for providing very helpful comments on an earlier version of the chapter. They would also like to acknowledge excellent research assistance from Diego Mesa and John Piotrowski.
[1] Creating fiscal space includes bringing public sector debt to manageable levels and improving the composition of liabilities (e.g., by currency and maturity) in the public sector balance sheet.
[2] Fiscal multipliers are typically largest for government consumption, public investment, and transfers to households, whereas they are relatively smaller for indirect taxes (Spilimbergo, Symansky, and Schindler, 2009). Fiscal multipliers can also vary depending on the cyclical position of the economy (IMF, 2012).

Against this backdrop the contribution of this chapter is twofold. First, it addresses crisis episodes originating in the banking sector that are of a systemic nature (Laeven and Valencia, 2008, 2010) to assess the effectiveness of fiscal policy in restoring growth during times of distress and in sustaining economic expansion in the postcrisis period. Although studies have been carried out to assess policy responses during recessions (Claessens, Kose, and Terrones, 2008; and IMF, 2009a, 2010b) and the role of fiscal policy to stimulate growth and its limits (Feldstein, 2002), detailed evidence on fiscal policy effects during periods of financial distress is lacking.[3] During financial crises, the environment for fiscal policy implementation is made more difficult by the high economic cost associated with the shock. Moreover, financial distress can freeze capital market, making it difficult to access financing for deficit expansion.

Second, it addresses the composition of fiscal policy response to assess its effectiveness during shocks. The composition of fiscal expansions and their impact on crisis length and postcrisis output recovery have not been dealt with in sufficient detail in the literature. However, fiscal policy composition could be expected to play a key role in determining both the likelihood of exiting a crisis and medium-term growth prospects, given that short-term fiscal multipliers differ across fiscal policy instruments. Moreover, tax and spending measures adopted during periods of financial distress can have long-term implications for economic efficiency and productivity growth when the crisis is over and contribute to debt-consolidation success (Galí, Lopez-Salido, and Vallés, 2007; Ghosh and others, 2009; Reinhart and Rogoff, 2009; and Baldacci, Gupta, and Mulas-Granados, 2012).

Therefore, the objective of this chapter is to answer the following questions:

- To what extent does fiscal policy shorten the duration of systemic banking crisis episodes and strengthen economic growth in the medium term?

- Does the composition of the fiscal policy response matter for either crisis duration or postshock growth performance?

The chapter is organized as follows: The first section reviews the relevant literature. The second section describes the data and the econometric approach. The third section presents the empirical results and is followed by robustness tests in the fourth section. The concluding section summarizes the results and discusses the key policy implications.

LITERATURE REVIEW

Fiscal Impact of Banking Crisis

Until recently, the study of financial crises typically focused either on historical experiences of advanced economies (mainly the banking panics before World War II),

---

[3] Aizenman and Jinjarak (2011) provide a general discussion of the fiscal policy response to the 2007–09 financial crisis in advanced and emerging economies. They show the level and composition of the stimulus packages adopted, but no econometric analysis of their impact on crisis length and growth is attempted.

or on more recent episodes in emerging market economies.[4] An important strand of this literature deals with the controversial issue of identifying and classifying different types of episodes that occurred in the 20th century. There are two major references in this area.

First, Reinhart and Rogoff (2008a, 2008b, 2009) mark banking crises as two types of events: bank runs that lead to the closure, merger, or takeover by the public sector of one or more financial institutions; and if there are no runs, the closure, merger, takeover, or large-scale government assistance for an important financial institution that marks the start of a string of similar outcomes for other financial institutions. With these criteria, they identify 66 cases that occurred between 1945 and 2007. They find that banking crises lead to sharp declines in tax revenues, as well as to significant increases in government spending. On average, they find that government debt rises by 86 percent during the three years following a banking crisis, and at the end of this period, growth resumes slowly to reach an average annual rate of 2½ percent in the third year after the crisis is over. Laeven and Valencia (2010) show that these conclusions hold for a wider sample of crisis episodes.

The second major reference is the papers by Laeven and Valencia (2008, 2010, 2012), which introduce a new data set on banking crises, with information on the type of policy responses implemented to resolve these crises in different countries and the related fiscal costs. Under their definition, in a systemic banking crisis, a country's corporate and financial sectors experience a large number of defaults, and financial institutions and corporations face difficulties repaying loans on time. Using this mix of objective data and subjective assessments,[5] they identify 124 systemic banking crises for the period 1970–2007, and estimate that fiscal costs net of recoveries associated with these crises average about 13.3 percent of GDP, while output losses average 20 percent of GDP. In Chapter 13 of this book, Laeven and Valencia explain that direct fiscal costs to support the financial sector were smaller in the recent crisis because of swift policy action and significant indirect support from expansionary monetary and fiscal policy, the widespread use of guarantees on liabilities, and direct purchases of assets.

Many authors have also focused on the origins of banking crises. These studies have typically found that crises tend to erupt when the macroeconomic environment is weak, particularly when growth is low and inflation and interest rates are high (Demirgüç-Kunt and Detragiache, 1998; and Collyns and Kincaid, 2003).[6] Others focus instead on the consequences of these crises, including the study by

---

[4] See Calomiris and Gorton (1991) and Gorton (1988) on pre–World War II banking panics; Reinhart and Rogoff (2008a, 2008b) for an analysis of all post–World War II banking crises in advanced economies; Bordo and others (2001) for an analysis that encompasses both advanced and emerging market economies; and Jácome (2008) on banking crises in Latin America.

[5] Unlike previous work (Caprio and Klingebiel, 1996; and Caprio and others, 2005), they exclude banking system distress that affected isolated banks but was not systemic in nature.

[6] For a review of the literature on the origins of banking crisis, see Lindgren, Garcia, and Saal (1996); Kaminsky and Reinhart (1999); and Dooley and Frankel (2003).

Reinhart and Rogoff (2009) cited above.[7] Claessens, Kose, and Terrones (2008) take the analysis one step further and study recessions caused by credit contractions, those associated with house price declines, and episodes of equity price declines. Their results show that the interaction between macroeconomic and financial variables can play a major role in determining the severity and duration of recessions. Specifically, they find evidence that recessions associated with credit crunches and house price busts tend to be deeper and longer than other recessions.[8]

Policy Responses to Banking Crises

The analysis of policy responses to these crises constitutes another area of interest for scholars.[9] Some studies analyze the types of containment and resolution policies aimed at stabilizing the banking sector during financial crises (Laeven and Valencia, 2008, 2010). Others assess the macroeconomic policy response. Claessens, Kose, and Terrones (2008) and IMF (2009a) find that both monetary and fiscal policy tend to be countercyclical during recessions, credit contractions, and asset price declines, in both advanced and emerging economies. In these episodes, fiscal policy appears to be more accommodative, suggesting a more aggressive countercyclical fiscal stance. They also find that expansionary fiscal policy (proxied by discretionary government consumption) tends to shorten the duration of recessions.[10]

The lessons from these analyses have stimulated other authors to take a more prescriptive approach. For instance, one paper argues that an optimal fiscal package for mitigating the adverse consequences of financial crises should be large, lasting, diversified, contingent, collective, and sustainable (Spilimbergo and others, 2008). Perotti (2011) and DeLong and Summers (2012) also find that in periods of stagnation fiscal policy stimulus can help sustain private sector growth and remove the negative effects on the economy of private sector deleveraging. However, fundamentals matter: Cottarelli and Jaramillo (2012) and Kumar and Woo (2011) show that high debt levels hamper growth; a result confirmed by Panizza and Presbitero (2012). Baldacci and Kumar (2010) highlight that the main channel through which fiscal deficits may reduce long-term growth is higher interest rates, because economic agents anticipate the effect of future taxes to compensate for current deficits and become less confident about debt sustainability. However, fiscal contractions during recessions can harm growth because fiscal multipliers tend to be positive and high during periods of

---

[7] For similar analyses of the real effects of banking crises, see Frydl (1999) and Dell'Ariccia, Detragiache, and Raghuram (2008).

[8] See Spilimbergo and others (2008) for a review of historical episodes of financial crises and the conduct of fiscal policy during the shock period.

[9] For an overview of existing literature on how crisis resolution policies have been used and the trade-offs involved, see Hoelscher and Quintyn (2003) and Honohan and Laeven (2005).

[10] Berg and Ostry (2011) find that the duration of growth spells is also affected by income distribution. Output growth episodes tend to be shorter and less frequent when income inequality is higher.

output decline and financial crises (Baum, Poplawski-Ribeiro, and Weber, 2012; IMF, 2012).

Market Perceptions of High Deficits

The increase in fiscal deficits and public debt linked to fiscal policy expansions during crises has also led to a discussion of financial markets' perceptions of fiscal sustainability. Ardagna (2009) shows that financial markets value fiscal discipline because interest rates on long-term government bonds and stock market prices worsen considerably in periods of fiscal expansion.[11] Alper, Forni, and Gerard (2012) highlight that both fiscal fundamentals and global risk factors are important for credit risk, but in periods of fiscal stress and for countries with high debt, growth prospects also matter. In addition, during financial crises risks tend to spill over to other economies reflecting banking sector links and mutual interdependencies across financial systems (Caceres, Guzzo, and Segoviano, 2010).

Composition of Fiscal Policy

Looking at the composition of fiscal policy, Akitoby and Stratmann (2008) show that financial markets react to the composition of the budget in emerging market economies. For example, revenue-based adjustments lower government spreads more than do expenditure-based adjustments, and debt-financed spending increases sovereign risks.[12] Baldacci, Gupta, and Mulas-Granados (2012) find that when adjustment needs are large, as in many economies in the aftermath of financial crises, debt sustainability is more likely to be accomplished through a combination of expenditure and revenue measures, rather than expenditure cuts only. Baldacci, Gupta, and Mati (2011) also highlight that the composition of fiscal policy affects government spreads, but debt levels matter too. They show that spending on public investment contributes to lower government bond spreads, as long as the fiscal position remains sustainable and the fiscal deficit does not worsen.[13]

Fiscal stimulus is not the only way to support growth during recessions. Automatic stabilizers also play a role and, depending on their design and size, they can contribute to stabilization. Economies with larger automatic stabilizers require, on average, lower fiscal stimulus to generate the same level of support to the economy. Dolls, Fuest, and Peichl (2010) report that automatic stabilizers absorb 38 percent of a proportional income shock in the European Union, compared with 32 percent in the United States. For an unemployment shock, 47 percent of it is absorbed in the European Union, compared with 34 percent in

---

[11] Afonso and Strauch (2004) obtain similar results using events analysis on a sample of European Union countries.

[12] Revenue-based adjustments along with expenditure efficiency measures are also found to sustain fiscal consolidation episodes in emerging market economies (Gupta and others, 2005).

[13] On financial market reactions to fiscal policy initiatives, and how these developments affect corporate bond spreads, see Durbin and Ng (2005) and Cavallo and Valenzuela (2007).

the United States. According to the authors, automatic stabilizers cushion disposable income, leading to demand stabilization of up to 30 percent in the European Union and up to 20 percent in the United States. However, they report large heterogeneity in the size of automatic stabilizers within the European Union (their size is larger in central and northern European economies).

This chapter builds on the literature to assess the relationship between the composition of fiscal policy response during banking crises, the duration of these episodes, and postcrisis economic performance. Although Laeven and Valencia (2008) report multiple measures of containment and resolution policies, they only use one measure of fiscal policy (the budget balance) and their work is not focused on causal analysis. Subsequent empirical work also proxies the fiscal policy response using government consumption and primary balance indicators (IMF, 2009a, 2009b). Instead, this analysis measures the effectiveness of fiscal policy using the different budget categories (on both the revenue side and the spending side) and the observed characteristics of each episode.

FISCAL POLICY DURING BANKING CRISES

This section describes the impact of banking crises on budgets. A data set of banking crises from a panel of 182 countries between 1980 and 2012 is constructed following the criteria established by Laeven and Valencia (2008, 2010). Some 140 episodes of banking crises are identified that occurred in 112 different countries (crises occurred up to four times in some countries, as in Argentina).[14] Laeven and Valencia's database is complemented with additional data from the IMF's *World Economic Outlook* and *Government Finance Statistics*, and the Global Financial Database.[15]

Unlike Laeven and Valencia (2008, 2010, 2012), this analysis not only identifies the start of the crises, but also defines their duration. Laeven and Valencia in Chapter 13 of this book address this shortcoming and provide their own estimation of the duration of the financial crises that they identify.[16] Identifying the duration of banking crises is difficult because there is no single financial indicator that is valid for all crises. Nevertheless, regardless of the origins and the characteristics of each banking crisis, an assumption is made that a crisis ends after two

---

[14] Laeven and Valencia (2008) identify 124 episodes of banking crises, 208 currency crises, and 63 sovereign debt crises. This analysis uses the data set of 124 banking crises and drops 10 of them because of the lack of fiscal data. That leaves 114 cases, to which were added 4 more cases from Laeven and Valencia's other two data sets (initially classified as currency crises or debt crises that later triggered banking crises). Finally, the total sample of 140 cases was achieved by including 22 new observations that Laeven and Valencia (2010) added to their updated database, most of which were advanced economies affected by the 2007–09 financial meltdown in the United States and Europe.

[15] https://www.globalfinancialdata.com/index.html.

[16] They define the end of a crisis as the year before two conditions hold: real GDP growth and real credit growth are positive for at least two consecutive years.

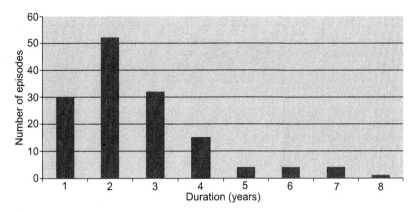

Figure 14.1 Frequency and Duration of Banking Crises

Source: Authors' estimates.

consecutive years of real GDP growth greater than ½ percentage point per year.[17] For the purposes of this chapter this definition allows a link to be made between the crisis duration and the negative output implications of the crisis. This is consistent with the focus on the effects of fiscal policy responses in restoring economic stability.[18] The robustness of the results to a different definition of crisis duration, based on stock market performance, is tested later in this chapter.

The above criteria indicate that banking crises lasted on average for 2.6 years, with 83 percent of the crisis episodes lasting between one and four years, and only one episode lasting eight years (see Figure 14.1). This finding is consistent with the findings of Claessens, Kose, and Terrones (2008), who report an average duration of recessions linked to credit crises of 2½ years. Reinhart and Rogoff (2008a) estimate an average duration for their reduced sample of financial crises of about three years.

Consistent with previous studies, the analysis also finds that banking crises generate large economic costs. Peak-to-trough figures (differences between the worst level of a variable during the crisis and its precrisis value) show that the average GDP growth rate fell by more than 6.2 percentage points during a crisis, general government debt increased by 59 percentage points of GDP, and the budget deficit increased by 3.4 percentage points of GDP (see Figure 14.2).[19]

---

[17] For those episodes of banking crises that are still ongoing, the last year of our sample, 2011, is taken as the final year and IMF projections are used to assess postcrisis GDP growth.

[18] An alternative measure to the one used in the chapter could be the cumulative output loss during the crisis. A strong positive correlation is found between crisis length and output losses during the banking crisis episodes used in the analysis.

[19] Results using alternative measures, such as period changes and period averages, yield similar conclusions, thus, the rest of the chapter focuses on one definition of crisis effects. The robustness of empirical findings to alternative definitions and results still hold. The fiscal balance incorporates the effect of discretionary policy changes (including measures to support the financial system), automatic stabilizers, and other nondiscretionary budget changes. Public debt also incorporates the cost of below-the-line measures to repair the financial system during crises.

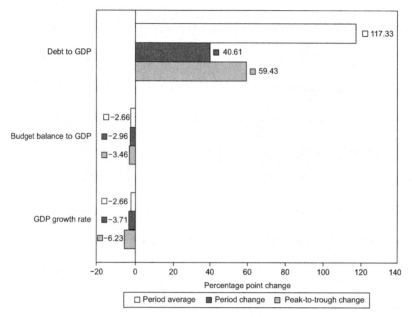

Figure 14.2 Economic Consequences of Banking Crises

Source: Authors' estimates.

Note: "Period" is from the precrisis year to the last year of the crisis.

Period changes (differences between the precrisis year and the last year of the crisis) are calculated to assess the behavior of fiscal variables during crisis episodes.[20] Results for descriptive statistics are expressed as percentages of GDP (Table 14.1).

During banking crises, fiscal deficits increased by almost 3 percentage points and public debt worsened by 40 percentage points of GDP. Total revenues increased by 2 percentage points during the crisis period, despite the heavy fall in tax revenues because they were offset by nontax revenues. But government expenditures rose by more than 5 percentage points of GDP.[21]

THE EFFECTIVENESS OF FISCAL RESPONSE

In a standard Keynesian framework, a fiscal expansion driven by cuts in taxes and increases in public spending would be expected to shorten the duration of

---

[20] The fiscal balance incorporates only "above-the-line" budget measures implemented during the crisis to support the financial sector (e.g., interest rate subsidies) following the Government Finance Statistics methodology. "Below-the-line" measures to help bank recapitalization and support liquidity are included in public sector debt data when governments bear the cost.

[21] The change in government expenditure in part reflects a decline in output, which raises the ratio of spending to GDP. Nonetheless, cyclically adjusted spending also rose in the period, reflecting discretionary fiscal expansion and automatic stabilizers. The rest of the chapter uses fiscal variables expressed as ratios to GDP. The robustness of this assumption is tested by replacing these indicators with cyclically adjusted variables and the results hold.

TABLE 14.1

Period Change in Fiscal Aggregates: Descriptive Statistics					
	Mean	Standard deviation	Minimum	Maximum	Observations
Change in public debt (percent of GDP)	40.60	22.55	11.12	80.34	140
Change in budget balance (percent of GDP)	−2.82	5.75	−31.37	15.45	140
Change in public revenue (percent of GDP)	2.38	13.46	−50.23	41.63	140
Change in tax revenues (percent of total revenues)	−1.97	4.93	−16.45	8.55	140
Change in tax from income (percent of total revenues)	−2.40	4.03	−13.58	11.59	139
Change in tax from goods and services (percent of total revenues)	2.93	1.29	−5.72	13.83	139
Change in nontax revenues (percent of total revenues)	4.37	13.53	−48.75	37.17	140
Change in public expenditure (percent of GDP)	5.20	13.07	−46.95	38.25	140
Change in public consumption (percent of total expend)	2.61	9.50	−34.55	35.21	140
Change in public investment (percent of total expend)	2.58	6.72	−19.21	22.37	140

Source: Authors' estimates based on data from IMF *World Economic Outlook* and *Global Financial Statistics*.

the crisis and sustain medium-term growth. Higher government spending and lower taxes help boost aggregate demand during downturns associated with banking crises, replacing falling private consumption as a growth engine (Arreaza, Sorensen, and Joshua, 1999). Public investment measures can, at least in part, offset the collapse in private investment (Aschauer, 1989). A simple plot of changes in levels of these variables as ratios to GDP against the duration of banking crisis episodes supports these hypotheses.[22] Figure 14.3 and Table 14.2 show a strong positive correlation between higher deficits and shorter crisis duration. However, budget composition changes matter as well as the size of the fiscal package (see Table 14.3). Higher public consumption (as a percentage of total expenditures) and lower income taxes (as a percentage of total revenues) also shorten the duration of banking crises. The contribution of higher public investment in reducing the crisis length is, however, significantly weaker. Instead, its role is much higher in increasing postcrisis economic growth (see Table 14.4); this confirms previous findings pointing to larger multipliers for public investment than public consumption (Spilimbergo, Symansky, and Schindler, 2009).

To test if fiscal expansions reduce the duration of financial crises, and following Laeven and Valencia (2008) an indicator is created labeled *Fiscal Expansion.*

---

[22] As in the previous section, all variables are calculated as the change during the period (from precrisis year to last year of crisis). Public consumption and public investment are computed as shares of total expenditures, and tax revenues from income and goods and services are computed as shares of total revenues.

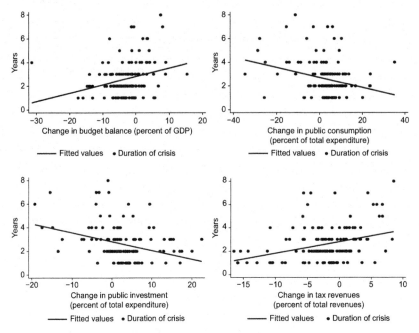

Figure 14.3 Fiscal Policy and Duration of Banking Crises

Source: Authors' estimates.

The following model is used to determine the effect of fiscal policy and other accompanying measures on the duration of banking crises

$$Duration_t = \alpha + \beta_1 \ Fiscal \ Expansion_t + \beta_2 \ Credit \ Boom_{t-1}$$
$$+ \ \beta_3 \ Containment \ (Dep. \ Guarantee)_t + \beta_4 \ Resolution$$
$$(N. \ Banks \ Closed)_t + \beta_5 \ Resolution \ (Gov't \ Intervention)_t + \varepsilon_t$$

in which t refers to the entire span of the banking crisis episode and $t - 1$ refers to the year preceding the onset of the crisis. *Fiscal Expansion* is an indicator of fiscal expansion equal to 1 if the budget balance worsens by more than 1½ percent of GDP in the first three years following the onset of the crisis, and is equal to zero otherwise. *Credit Boom* is a dummy variable equal to 1 if the banking crisis was preceded by an abnormal expansion of credit, and is equal to 0 otherwise; and *Dep Guarantee* is a dummy variable equal to 1 if there was a freeze on deposits or a blanket guarantee in the initial phases of the banking crisis.[23] Finally, two measures of resolution policies are included, captured by the total

---

[23] An attempt was made to include other containment policies defined in Laeven and Valencia (2008), but these factors were strongly correlated to the other exogenous variables.

TABLE 14.2

The Relationship between Government Balance and Duration

	Duration of crisis			
	Coefficient	*t*-statistic	*R*-squared	Observations
Change in the budget balance over crisis episode	0.071***	3.35	0.075	140
Expansionary budget balance (Laeven and Valencia, 2008)	1.033***	−4.16	0.111	140

Source: Authors' estimates.
*** significant at 1 percent; ** significant at 5 percent; * significant at 10 percent.

TABLE 14.3

The Relationship between Composition of the Budget and Duration

	Duration of crisis			
	Coefficient	*t*-statistic	*R*-squared	Observations
Change in total public expenditures over crisis episode	−0.042***	−4.72	0.139	140
Change in public consumption (percent of total expenditures)	−0.042***	−3.33	0.074	140
Change in public investment (percent of total expenditures)	−0.075***	−4.24	0.115	140
Change in total public revenues over crisis episode	0.043***	−5.04	0.155	140
Change in tax revenues (percent of total revenue)	0.099***	4.10	0.109	140
Change in tax from income (percent of total revenues)	0.128***	4.33	0.121	139
Change in tax from goods and services (percent of total revenues)	0.078*	1.82	0.024	139
Change in nontax revenues (percent of total revenues)	−0.042***	−4.84	0.145	140

Source: Authors' estimates.
*** significant at 1 percent; ** significant at 5 percent; * significant at 10 percent.

TABLE 14.4

The Relationship between Composition of the Budget and Post-Growth

	Average Growth (*t* through *t* + 5)			
	Coefficient	*t*-statistic	*R*-squared	Observations
Change in total public expenditures over crisis episode	0.098***	4.57	0.132	140
Change in public consumption (percent of total expenditures)	0.430	1.37	0.014	140
Change in public investment (percent of total expenditures)	0.283***	7.55	0.293	140
Change in total public revenues over crisis episode	0.088***	4.22	0.115	140
Change in tax revenues (percent of total revenues)	0.081	−0.43	0.001	140
Change in tax from income (percent of total revenues)	−0.253***	−3.54	0.084	139
Change in tax from goods and services (percent of total revenues)	0.317***	3.20	0.07	139
Change in nontax revenues (percent of total revenues)	0.081***	3.86	0.097	140

Source: Authors' estimates.
Note: Post-Growth defined as average GDP growth rate during the next five years after end of the crisis.
*** significant at 1 percent; ** significant at 5 percent; * significant at 10 percent.

TABLE 14.5

The Relationship between Fiscal Policy, Resolution Policies, and Duration				
	Duration (ordinary least squares)		Duration (ordered logit)	
	(1)	(2)	(3)	(4)
Change in budget balance (percent of GDP)	0.537***	...	0.083***	...
	−2.98	...	−2.62	...
Expansionary fiscal policy	...	0.665***	...	−0.932***
	...	(−3.03)	...	(−2.63)
Previous credit boom	0.829***	0.755***	1.217***	1.113***
	−4.04	−3.65	−3.67	−3.33
Deposit freeze or guarantee	−0.608***	−0.603***	−0.766**	−0.714**
	(−2.89)	(−2.87)	(−2.32)	(−2.15)
Number of banks closed	−0.163***	−0.147***	−0.394***	−0.374***
	(−3.40)	(−3.03)	(−4.49)	(−4.27)
Government intervention	−0.632***	−0.690***	−0.827**	−0.894**
	(−2.95)	(−3.24)	(−2.39)	(−2.59)
Constant	3.424***	3.728***	...	...
	−15.35	−14.61	...	...
Observations	139	139	139	139
Adjusted R-squared/pseudo R-squared	0.357	0.358	0.155	0.154

Source: Authors' estimates.
*** significant at 1 percent; ** significant at 5 percent; * significant at 10 percent.

N. Banks Closed during the episode and the degree of *Govt Intervention* in the financial sector.[24]

The dependent variable is discrete, and takes values ranging from one year to eight years. A baseline model is estimated in a truncated sample of 140 episodes of banking crises, using ordinary least squares and ordered logit.[25] Results are reported in Table 14.5 and show that fiscal expansions are a decisive factor for reducing the duration of banking crises. Based on these results, the average fiscal policy response in the sample reduces the crisis length by more than two quarters.

The variables capturing the role of the accompanying policies have the expected coefficient signs and are statistically significant. Crises tend to be shorter when fiscal expansions are accompanied by decisive actions to guarantee deposits (reduction in crisis length of two to four quarters) and to close failed banks (reduction in average crisis length of about one year). Crises last about one year longer when preceded by credit booms leading to banking sector vulnerabilities and asset bubbles.[26]

---

[24] See Laeven and Valencia (2008) for the derivation of these variables.

[25] The ordered logit estimation can be seen as a robust analysis method to control for the influence of outliers (e.g., crises with long duration). This equation was also estimated using a Tobit estimator to account for the nonnegativity of the dependent variable. Results were similar to the ordered logit.

[26] Although the model measures the direct impact of various financial crisis responses, the possibility of more complex dynamic interactions between fiscal variables and other accompanying policies in response to shocks is not ruled out. However, attempts to add interaction terms do not yield significant results. The good fit of the estimated model confirms that other factors, including interactions, would not add much to the explanatory power of the equation.

The model is then estimated to capture the role of budget composition:

$$Duration_t = \alpha + \beta_1 \; Fiscal \; Expansion_t + \beta_2 \; Fiscal \; Composition_t$$
$$+ \; \beta_3 \; Credit \; Boom_{t-1} + \beta_4 \; Containment \; (Dep. \; Guarantee)_t$$
$$+ \; \beta_5 \; Resolution \; (N. \; Banks \; Closed)_t + \beta_6 \; Resolution$$
$$(Gov't \; Intervention)_t + \varepsilon_t.$$

Results are reported in Table 14.6 and confirm that a fiscal expansion helps reduce the duration of banking crises.[27] An increase in the share of public consumption in total expenditure reduces the duration of crisis episodes because it stimulates aggregate demand.[28] An increase of 5 percentage points in this composition variable reduces the crisis length by almost three months. The size of the estimated coefficient for public investment is similar, although its statistical significance is weaker. The results further indicate that governments can actually choose between expenditure-based and revenue-based fiscal expansions because a declining share of revenues from income taxes or taxes on goods and services also helps shorten the duration of banking crises. The effect of cuts in goods and services taxes is, however, larger than the impact of income tax reductions because the former affect a wider number of taxpayers with likely larger impacts on consumption decisions.

As in the previous results, the policy control variables are also statistically significant. Crises preceded by credit booms tend to last longer. And those in which bank deposits are guaranteed tend to be shorter. Closing failed banks and strong government intervention are also beneficial to resolving the crisis. All these results are consistent with historical evidence. Overall, the size of the coefficients show that fiscal variables are as important as other accompanying policies in shortening crisis length.

The effectiveness of fiscal policy during banking crises not only contributes to reducing the length of crisis episodes, it also helps create conditions for promoting economic growth following a crisis. The factors affecting average GDP growth rate in the five years following the end of the crisis are estimated using the following specification:[29]

---

[27] These results also hold when the budget balance is used instead of the large fiscal expansion indicator. For the sake of space, results are not reported in the chapter but are available upon request from the authors.

[28] As mentioned earlier, the end of the crisis period is defined on the basis of output growth. This is why fiscal measures associated with aggregate demand boost are effective in shortening crisis duration, consistent with the literature on fiscal multipliers (Spilimbergo, Symansky, and Schindler, 2009). This assumption is also tested for robustness using alternative definitions of crisis end based on financial sector performance. Results reported in the next section show that the findings hold under different definitions of crisis duration.

[29] Because this chapter's focus is on the implications of fiscal responses during shock episodes on post-crisis growth, current fiscal and monetary policy variables are not included in the equation to avoid endogeneity and collinearity among regressors. However, given the potential importance of these factors, the robustness of the results to the inclusion of the coincident fiscal deficit and short-term nominal interest rate is assessed, with the result that conclusions in the text are not affected.

TABLE 14.6

The Relationship between Composition of the Budget, Resolution Policies, and Duration

	Duration of crisis (ordinary least squares)				Duration of crisis (ordered logit)			
	(1)	(2)	(3)	(4)	(1)	(2)	(3)	(4)
Expansionary fiscal policy	-0.602***	-0.629***	-0.585***	-0.654***	-0.880**	-0.898**	0.805**	-0.903**
	(-2.72)	(-2.90)	(-2.75)	(-2.97)	(-2.46)	(-2.53)	(-2.26)	(-2.55)
Change in public consumption (percent of total expenditures)	-0.019*	...	...	...	-0.017	...	...	...
	(-1.70)				(-1.02)			
Change in public investment (percent of total expenditures)	...	-0.035**	...	...	...	-0.041*	...	...
		(-2.22)				(-1.71)		
Change in income tax revenue (percent of total revenues)	...	...	0.086***	...	...	...	0.138***	...
			(-3.4)				(-3.03)	
Change in goods and services tax revenue (percent of total revenues)	...	...	...	0.034	...	...	...	0.063
				(-0.97)				(-1.09)
Previous credit boom	0.728***	0.715***	0.692***	0.741***	1.092***	1.102***	1.087***	1.094**
	(-3.53)	(-3.49)	(-3.45)	(-3.56)	(-3.26)	(-3.29)	(-3.23)	(-3.27)
Deposit freeze or guarantee	-0.614***	-0.514***	-0.479**	-0.609***	-0.724***	-0.605*	-0.583*	-0.745**
	(-2.94)	(-2.44)	(-2.32)	(-2.88)	(-2.18)	(-1.79)	(-1.72)	(-2.23)
Number of banks closed	-0.137***	-0.129***	-0.134***	-0.141***	-0.362***	-0.355***	-0.340***	-0.361***
	(-2.82)	(-2.66)	(-2.85)	(-2.86)	(-4.09)	(-1.79)	(-3.86)	(-4.07)
Government intervention	-0.640***	-0.661***	-0.748***	-0.699***	-0.851***	-0.880**	-1.009***	-0.930***
	(-3.00)	(-3.15)	(-3.63)	(-3.27)	(-2.45)	(-2.54)	(-2.86)	(-2.68)
Constant	3.700***	3.712***	3.867***	3.717***	...	...	...	...
	-14.57	-14.75	-15.48	-14.32				
Observations	139	139	138	138	139	139	138	138
Adjusted R-squared/pseudo R-squared	0.367	0.376	0.407	0.36	0.157	0.161	0.177	0.158

Source: Authors' estimates.

*** significant at 1 percent; ** significant at 5 percent; * significant at 10 percent.

$$PostGrowth_t = \alpha + \beta_1 \; Fiscal \; Expansion_t + \beta_2 \; Fiscal \; Composition_t$$
$$+ \beta_3 \; Credit \; Boom_{t-1} + \beta_4 \; Containment \; (Dep. \; Guarantee)_t$$
$$+ \beta_5 \; Resolution \; (N. \; Banks \; Closed)_t + \beta_6 \; Resolution$$
$$(Gov't \; Intervention)_t + \beta_7 \; Private \; Sector_t + \varepsilon_t.$$

This model includes three new variables under a common vector that captures the underlying conditions for the activity of the *Private Sector*. These variables are expected to have an important effect on medium-term growth. First, the change in private investment during the episode is included as a percentage of total investment to capture the vitality of the private sector in stimulating productivity growth. Second, the cost of financing for companies and households (measured by the average difference between long-term interest rates and interbank interest rates) is included to proxy the cost of capital.[30] Last, a dummy (fresh capital injections) from Valencia and Leaven (2008) is included that equals 1 if new capital injections into the banking sector were made as part of the resolution policies.

Results for the growth equation are reported in Table 14.7 and show that fiscal expansions do not have any statistically significant effect on GDP growth in the period following banking crises.[31] Changing the composition of government spending through higher public consumption is also not statistically significant; however, an increase in public investment or a reduction in the share of income taxes are both positive for medium-term growth because they boost productivity and eliminate distortions that lead to inefficiency.[32]

Variables controlling for the origin of the crisis and the accompanying containment and resolution policies lose statistical significance. However, variables capturing the behavior of the private sector are systematically linked with the expected sign to better economic performance. An increase in the share of private investment, a reduction in the cost of financing, and an increase in fresh capital for the banking sector all have positive impacts on medium-term output growth.

Initial fiscal and economic conditions are key to fiscal policy effectiveness during crises. To isolate the potential nonlinear effects of initial levels of public debt and GDP per capita on fiscal policy performance, a new augmented specification is estimated. Two new dummy variables are included: *Highly Indebted* equals 1 when initial public sector debt as a ratio to GDP is above the sample average; and *High GDP per capita* equals 1 when initial GDP per capita (in purchasing-power-parity dollars) is above the sample average.[33] These variables are included in the equation in isolation and they are also interacted with the indicator of fiscal expansion and the budget composition vector.

---

[30] This variable measures the opportunity cost of investing compared to holding liquidity.

[31] Results are confirmed when using the fiscal balance in the place of the fiscal expansion indicator.

[32] This is consistent with previous studies for a sample of crisis and noncrisis episodes (for example, Alesina and others, 2002). The fiscal mix in noncrisis periods is also found to be a significant driver of medium-term financial implications of fiscal expansions (Ardagna, 2009) and the sustainability of fiscal adjustments in emerging market economies (Gupta and others, 2005).

[33] Using alternative thresholds for these variables yields similar results.

TABLE 14.7

The Relationship between Composition of the Budget, Resolution Policies, and Long-Term Growth

	Average growth (t through t + 5) (ordinary least squares)				Average growth (t through t + 5) (robust)			
	(1)	(2)	(3)	(4)	(1)	(2)	(3)	(4)
Discretionary expansionary fiscal policy	0.072 (−0.14)	−0.326 (−0.58)	−0.072 (−0.12)	0.078 (−0.14)	0.072 (−0.13)	−0.326 (−0.77)	−0.003 (−0.01)	0.131 (−0.27)
Change in public consumption (percent of total expenditures)	0.001 (−0.01)	...	...	...	−0.001 (−0.01)	...	...	...
Change in public investment (percent of total expenditures)	...	0.243*** (−5.93)	...	...	...	0.245*** (−5.54)	...	...
Change in income tax revenue (percent of total revenues)	...	...	−0.170** (−2.30)	...	...	...	−0.169** (−2.41)	...
Change in goods and services tax revenue (percent of total revenues)	...	...	...	0.370*** (−3.96)	...	...	...	0.370*** (−4.15)
Previous credit boom	−0.078 (−0.14)	0.245 (−0.48)	0.026 (−0.05)	−0.102 (−0.19)	−0.078 (−0.14)	0.245 (−0.52)	0.033 (−0.06)	−0.095 (−0.18)
Deposit freeze or guarantee	1.415** (−2.39)	0.855 (−1.6)	1.102* (−1.83)	1.415** (−2.5)	1.415** (−2.55)	0.855** (−1.87)	1.091* (−1.98)	1.413*** (−2.69)
Number of banks closed	0.203 (−1.48)	0.125 (−1.03)	0.174 (−1.3)	0.279** (−2.14)	0.203* (−1.89)	0.125 (−1.45)	0.173 (−1.6)	0.276*** (−2.81)
Government intervention	−0.240 (−0.40)	−0.353 (−0.67)	−0.137 (−0.23)	−0.216 (−0.38)	−0.239 (−0.43)	−0.353 (−0.73)	−0.142 (−0.27)	−0.215 (−0.42)
Change in private investment (percent of total investment)	0.438 (−0.74)	0.830 (−1.58)	0.115 (−0.17)	0.014 (−0.02)	0.438 (−1.38)	0.830*** (−2.98)	0.100 (−0.27)	0.002 (−0.01)
Change in cost of financing[1]	−0.127*** (−3.35)	−0.075** (−2.19)	−0.120*** (−3.23)	−0.124*** (−3.47)	−1.274** (−2.12)	−0.075 (−1.36)	−0.121** (−2.03)	−0.124** (−2.21)
Fresh capital injections into financial sector	1.270** (−2.14)	0.833 (−1.58)	1.159** (−1.99)	1.287** (−2.3)	1.270** (−2.18)	0.833* (−1.85)	1.163** (−2.15)	1.279** (−2.39)
Constant	2.168*** (−2.9)	2.384*** (−3.62)	2.065*** (−2.87)	1.901*** (−2.74)	2.168*** (−3.19)	2.384*** (−4.12)	2.035*** (−2.96)	1.871*** (−3.01)
Observations	139	139	138	138	139	139	138	138
Adjusted R-squared/pseudo R-squared	0.134	0.319	0.168	0.228	0.19	0.363	0.222	0.278

Source: Authors' estimates.

Note: Dependent variable: Average GDP growth in the five years following the end of the crisis.

[1] The cost of financing variable is an average of the lending interest rates and the interbank interest rates.

*** significant at 1 percent; ** significant at 5 percent; * significant at 10 percent.

Consistent with expectations, the positive impact of fiscal expansions and the budget mix on crisis length weakens substantially when initial conditions are poor (Tables 14.8 and 14.9). Countries with higher debt levels and lower per capita income face a higher probability of exiting banking crises later than countries with stronger initial conditions. However, the impact of fiscal expansions on crisis duration is larger once initial economic and fiscal conditions are accounted for: countries with more sustainable public finances have more scope for counter-cyclical fiscal responses during banking crises. Although weak fiscal conditions do not affect postcrisis growth, countries with high initial per capita GDP tend to be associated with better economic performance in the period immediately following the crises. In all cases, controlling for initial fiscal and economic conditions leads to higher effects of the budget composition variables on growth.

ROBUSTNESS ANALYSIS

This section assesses the strength of the above results on the basis of three robustness analyses:

- *A different definition of duration.* In the baseline model, the definition of duration is based on GDP growth recovery, which means that the end of the banking crisis can only be registered when output growth resumes. However, this definition may be inappropriate if the banking sector problems are resolved quickly but GDP growth lags because of other cyclical or structural impediments. The opposite can also be true, in theory, because cyclical growth may resume with persistent weakness in the financial sector; therefore, the baseline definition of duration is potentially biased. As an alternative, the end of the crisis is defined as the first year in which the stock market index returns to its precrisis level. Under this definition, episodes' durations are shorter because the stock market tends to recover faster than real output in the sample. Results of regressions using the alternative definition of crisis length are robust to alternative definitions of duration (see Table 14A.1 in the appendix).[34]

- *A different measure of discretionary fiscal policy.* The index of fiscal expansion created by Laeven and Valencia (2008) and used in the baseline model is appropriate for identifying sizable fiscal expansions (those beyond 1½ percent of GDP). However, this index is incapable of differentiating between fiscal expansions that are discretionary and those that are the unintended result of a dramatic collapse of GDP growth. An indicator of discretionary fiscal policy following Blanchard (1990) is calculated for this analysis.[35]

---

[34] This and other robustness results are available from authors upon request.

[35] Blanchard (1990, p. 12) defined this indicator as follows: "the value of the primary surplus which would have prevailed, were unemployment at the same value as in the previous year, minus the value of the primary surplus in the previous year." Both variables are expressed as a percentage of GDP. When this change was greater than –1½ percent of GDP, the year was labeled as a fiscal expansion (value 1), and zero otherwise.

TABLE 14.8

Robustness Estimations: Explaining Duration and Controlling for Initial Fiscal and Economic Conditions

	Duration of crisis			
	(1)	(2)	(3)	(4)
Expansionary fiscal policy	−0.34	−0.394	−0.322	−0.328
	(−1.16)	(−1.33)	(−1.03)	(−1.09)
Expansionary fiscal policy × Highly indebted (t − 1)	−0.715*	−0.672	−0.696	−0.695
	(−1.68)	(−1.57)	(−1.66)	(−1.57)
Change in public consumption (percent of total expenditures)	−0.050***	...	...	...
	(−2.79)			
Change in public consumption × Highly indebted (t − 1)	0.041*	...	...	...
	(−1.79)			
Change in public investment (percent of total expenditures)	...	−0.059**	...	...
		(−2.38)		
Change in public investment × Highly indebted (t − 1)	...	0.031	...	...
		(−0.97)		
Change in income tax revenue (percent of total revenues)	...	...	0.096***	...
			(−2.70)	
Change in income tax revenue × Highly indebted (t − 1)	...	...	−0.025	...
			(−0.47)	
Change in goods and services tax revenue (percent of total revenues)	...	...	...	0.049
				(−0.84)
Change in goods and services tax revenue × Highly indebted (t − 1)	...	...	...	−0.043
				(−0.58)
Previous credit boom	0.644***	0.668***	0.599***	0.661***
	(−3.1)	(−3.22)	(−2.89)	(−3.07)
Deposit freeze or guarantee	−0.633***	−0.545**	−0.518**	−0.676***
	(−3.01)	(−2.55)	(−2.44)	(−3.12)
Number of banks closed	−0.142***	−0.138***	−0.149***	−0.151***
	(−2.95)	(−2.84)	(−3.04)	(−3.01)
Government intervention	−0.573***	−0.574***	−0.709***	−0.693***
	(−2.68)	(−2.62)	(−3.30)	(−3.16)
Highly indebted (t − 1)	0.948***	0.939***	0.868**	0.872**
	(−2.8)	(−2.76)	(−2.58)	(−2.44)
GDP per capita (t − 1)	−7.28e−06*	−5.65E−06	−5.83E−06	−6.79E−06
	(−1.84)	(−1.43)	(−1.48)	(−1.66)
Constant	3.577***	3.544***	3.771***	3.654***
	(−10.31)	(−10.18)	(−10.73)	(−9.988)
Observations	133	133	132	132
Adjusted R-squared	0.409	0.405	0.423	0.376

Source: Authors' estimates.

*** significant at 1 percent; ** significant at 5 percent; * significant at 10 percent.

TABLE 14.9

Robustness Estimations: Post-Growth and Controlling for Initial Fiscal and Economic Conditions

	Average growth (t through $t + 5$)			
	(1)	(2)	(3)	(4)
Expansionary fiscal policy	−0.476	−0.48	−0.645	−0.514
	(−0.81)	(−0.97)	(−1.11)	(−0.99)
Expansionary fiscal policy × Highly indebted ($t − 1$)	0.684	0.116	0.474	1.078
	(−0.77)	(−0.16)	(−0.57)	(−1.40)
Change in public consumption (percent of total expenditures)	−0.025	...	...	...
	(−0.60)			
Change in public consumption × Highly indebted ($t − 1$)	0.027	...	...	...
	(−0.51)			
Change in public investment (percent of total expenditures)	...	0.264***	...	...
		(−5.36)		
Change in public investment × Highly indebted ($t − 1$)	...	−0.04	...	...
		(−0.64)		
Change in income tax revenue (percent of total revenues)	...	...	−0.155*	...
			(−1.95)	
Change in income tax revenue × Highly indebted ($t − 1$)	...	...	−0.088	...
			(−0.78)	
Change in goods and services tax revenue (percent of total revenues)	...	...	...	0.605***
				(−5.12)
Change in goods and services tax revenue × Highly indebted ($t − 1$)	...	...	...	−0.343**
				(−2.27)
Previous credit boom	0.121	0.355	0.279	0.024
	(−0.25)	(−0.88)	(−0.59)	(−0.05)
Deposit freeze or guarantee	1.256**	0.64	0.855*	1.059**
	(−2.51)	(−1.52)	(−1.73)	(−2.39)
Number of banks closed	0.193*	0.134	0.141	0.278***
	(−1.71)	(−1.43)	(−1.25)	(−2.75)
Government intervention	−0.346	−0.615	−0.205	−0.527
	(−0.69)	(−1.431)	(−0.416)	(−1.190)
Change in private investment (percent of total investment)	0.554	0.772*	0.12	0.122
	(−1.12)	(−1.87)	(−0.22)	(−0.24)
Change in cost of financing[1]	−0.082**	−0.021	−0.074**	−0.062**
	(−2.55)	(−0.77)	(−2.41)	(−2.20)
Fresh capital injections into financial sector	0.917*	0.487	0.776	0.796*
	(−1.82)	(−1.17)	(−1.61)	(−1.8)
Highly indebted ($t − 1$)	0.016	−0.11	0.123	−0.774
	(−0.02)	(−0.18)	(−0.17)	(−1.17)
GDP per capita ($t − 1$)	−7.23E−06	−8.97E−06	−8.41E−06	−8.78E−06
	(−0.77)	(−1.16)	(−0.93)	(−1.06)
Constant	2.758***	3.143***	2.688***	3.125***
	(−3.39)	(−4.65)	(−3.44)	(−4.31)
Observations	133	133	132	132
Adjusted R-squared	0.087	0.375	0.161	0.283

Source: Authors' estimates.
*** significant at 1 percent; ** significant at 5 percent; * significant at 10 percent.
[1] The cost of financing variable is an average of the lending interest rates and the interbank interest rates.

Results are reported in Table 14A.2 in the appendix and show that baseline results are consistent with this new formulation.

- *Testing for endogeneity between duration and fiscal policy.* Because fiscal policy and output growth are correlated, baseline results could be biased as the result of endogeneity as GDP growth enters the definition of crisis length. To control for this factor, a new model is estimated using a two-stage least squares estimator, including all other independent variables and a measure of liquidity support as instruments. Results in Table 14A.3 in the appendix suggest that the main findings hold.

CONCLUSION

This chapter assesses the effects of fiscal policy responses during 140 episodes of systemic banking crises in advanced and emerging market economies. The results indicate that timely countercyclical fiscal expansions (resulting from both discretionary measures and automatic stabilizers), accompanied by actions to deal with financial sector weaknesses, contribute to shortening the length of crisis episodes. During crises caused by financial sector distress, fiscal expansions increase the likelihood of earlier exit from a shock episode. Expansionary fiscal policies reduce the crisis duration by almost one year in the sample. These results hold for different definitions of crisis duration and alternative specification and estimation methods. The findings are consistent with recent studies that highlight the importance of countercyclical macroeconomic policies in response to recessions associated with financial sector problems (Claessens, Kose, and Terrones, 2008; and IMF, 2009a, 2009b).

Initial fiscal conditions matter for fiscal performance during shocks. In countries with high precrisis public debt levels, lack of fiscal space not only constrains the government's ability to implement countercyclical policies, but also undermines the effectiveness of fiscal stimulus and the quality of fiscal performance. In these countries, crises last almost one year longer than they do in low-debt countries and the effect of high public debt on duration offsets the benefits of expansionary fiscal policies. Similar results are found for countries with lower per capita income because poor implementation capacity and high macroeconomic risks limit the scope and the effects of fiscal expansions during crises (Botman and Kumar, 2006). These findings point to the importance of creating fiscal space and enhancing macroeconomic stability in tranquil times to limit the risk of falling into crises and to enhance the effectiveness of policy responses when exogenous shocks hit countries (Tavares and Valkanov, 2001). In emerging market economies, attention needs to be paid to strengthening fiscal institutions, reducing political risks, and improving budget execution capacity to reap the benefits of countercyclical fiscal policies (Baldacci, Gupta, and Mati, 2011).

The composition of fiscal expansions matters for crisis length—a point that has not been studied in the literature. Stimulus packages that rely mostly on measures to support government consumption are more effective in shortening the crisis duration than those based on scaling up public investment. A 10 percentage point increase in the share of public consumption in the budget reduces the crisis length by three to four months. Reducing the share of income taxes is also less effective than lowering taxes on goods and services. These results suggest that tailoring the composition of fiscal response packages is important for enhancing the effectiveness of countercyclical fiscal measures in both advanced and emerging market economies (Spilimbergo and others, 2008; IMF, 2009a).

Initial conditions weigh on output recovery after the crisis though. Crises can have long-term negative effects, damaging human and physical capital, with negative implications for productivity and potential output growth. Early recovery from a crisis is therefore important, both to minimize output losses in the short term and to enhance medium-term growth prospects. The advantages of early recovery call for timely fiscal responses during downturns. However, fiscal policy responses may not be effective when initial fiscal conditions are poor and fiscal space is limited. High public debt levels and past macroeconomic instability limit the scope for countercyclical deficit expansions and hamper the effectiveness of fiscal stimulus measures because markets perceive the higher future fiscal risks embodied in larger deficits (Balduzzi, Corsetti, and Foresi, 1997; and Uribe, 2006).

The quality of the fiscal stimulus package matters most for postcrisis growth resumption. Fiscal responses relying largely on scaling up the share of public investment in the budget show the largest positive effect on medium-term output growth. A 1 percent increase in the share of capital outlays in the budget raises postcrisis growth by about ⅓ of 1 percent per year. Income tax reductions are also associated with positive growth effects.

The results of the short-term and medium-term impacts of fiscal policy during financial crises highlight a potential trade-off between short-term aggregate demand support measures and medium-term productivity growth objectives in fiscal policy responses to shocks. Implementation lags for government investment, which were documented during the 2007–09 crisis, may be, at least in part, responsible for these results. They also point to the need for careful consideration of the composition of fiscal stimulus packages, given that different short-term and medium-term fiscal multipliers can affect fiscal policy performance during the crisis and in its aftermath (Spilimbergo, Symansky, and Schindler, 2009).

The results of the chapter also call for further research. Economic theory predicts that, in normal circumstances, fiscal expansions tend to crowd out private investment and increase the cost of financing for the private sector. However, the empirical findings presented here indicate that an increase in the share of public investment (as a percentage of total public spending) is compatible with an increase in the share of private investment (as a percentage of total investment) during banking crises, and both can make a positive contribution to long-term growth in the subsequent period. This constitutes very preliminary evidence of the crowding-in effects potentially attributed to expansionary fiscal policy in situations of financial stress (Aschauer, 1989). However, a proper test of this hypothesis was beyond the scope of this chapter.

APPENDIX

TABLE 14A.1

Robustness Estimations: A Different Definition of Duration Based on Stock Market Recovery

	Duration of crisis			
	(1)	(2)	(3)	(4)
Expansionary fiscal policy	-0.859***	-0.892***	-0.843***	-0.883***
	(-4.55)	(-4.76)	(-4.57)	(-4.71)
Change in public consumption (percent of total expenditures)	-0.069	...	...	...
	(-1.15)			
Change in public investment (percent of total expenditures)	...	-0.004	...	...
		(-0.27)		
Change in income tax revenue (percent of total revenues)	...	...	0.051**	...
			(-2.31)	
Change in goods and services tax revenue (percent of total revenues)	...	...	...	0.008
				(-0.28)
Previous credit boom	0.384**	0.396**	0.357**	0.386**
	(-2.19)	(-2.24)	(-2.05)	(-2.18)
Deposit freeze or guarantee	-0.21	-0.195	-0.138	-0.216
	(-1.18)	(-1.07)	(-0.77)	(-1.20)
Number of banks closed	-0.070*	-0.074*	-0.069*	-0.0756*
	(-1.69)	(-1.76)	(-1.69)	(-1.81)
Government intervention	-0.373***	-0.399**	-0.442**	-0.415**
	(-2.05)	(-2.20)	(-2.48)	(-2.29)
Constant	2.949***	2.963***	3.057***	2.981***
	(-13.61)	(-13.64)	(-14.13)	(-13.51)
Observations	139	139	138	138
Adjusted R-squared	0.275	0.268	0.297	0.269

Source: Authors' estimates.
*** significant at 1 percent; ** significant at 5 percent; * significant at 10 percent.

TABLE 14A.2

Robustness Estimations: Focusing on Discretionary Expansionary Fiscal Policy

	Duration of crisis			
	(1)	(2)	(3)	(4)
Discretionary expansionary fiscal policy	-0.484**	-0.526**	-0.459**	-0.530**
	(-2.25)	(-2.50)	(-2.20)	(-2.45)
Change in public consumption (percent of total expenditures)	-0.020*	...	...	...
	(-1.81)			
Change in public investment (percent of total expenditures)	...	-0.037**	...	...
		(-2.34)		
Change in income tax revenue (percent of total revenues)	...	...	0.087***	...
			(-3.40)	
Change in goods and services tax revenue (percent of total revenues)	...	...	...	0.034
				(-0.96)
Previous credit boom	0.738***	0.723***	0.705***	0.754***
	(-3.55)	(-3.51)	(-3.48)	(-3.59)
Deposit freeze or guarantee	-0.597***	-0.487**	-0.463**	-0.590***
	(-2.82)	(-2.28)	(-2.20)	(-2.75)
Number of banks closed	-0.145***	-0.137***	-0.142***	-0.151***
	(-2.98)	(-2.81)	(-3.02)	(-3.05)
Government intervention	-0.627***	-0.648***	-0.740***	-0.689***
	(-2.91)	(-3.06)	(-3.55)	(-3.19)
Constant	3.601***	3.618***	3.765***	3.611***
	(-14.55)	(-14.76)	(-15.41)	(-14.22)
Observations	139	139	138	138
Adjusted R-squared	0.356	0.366	0.395	0.347

Source: Authors' estimates.
*** significant at 1 percent; ** significant at 5 percent; * significant at 10 percent.

TABLE 14A.3

Robustness Estimations: Controlling for Endogeneity (two-stage least squares estimations)

	Duration of crisis			
	(1)	(2)	(3)	(4)
Expansionary fiscal policy	-0.602***	-0.629***	-0.585***	-0.654***
	(-2.72)	(-2.90)	(-2.75)	(-2.97)
Change in public consumption (percent of total expenditures)	-0.019*	...	...	...
	(-1.70)			
Change in public investment (percent of total expenditures)	...	-0.035**	...	...
		(-2.22)		
Change in income tax revenue (percent of total revenues)	...	...	0.086***	...
			(-3.41)	
Change in goods and services tax revenue (percent of total revenues)	...	...	...	0.034
				(-0.97)
Previous credit boom	0.728***	0.715***	0.692***	0.741***
	(-3.53)	(-3.49)	(-3.45)	(-3.56)
Deposit freeze or guarantee	-0.614***	-0.514**	-0.479**	-0.609***
	(-2.94)	(-2.44)	(-2.32)	(-2.88)
Number of banks closed	-0.137***	-0.129***	-0.134***	-0.141***
	(-2.82)	(-2.66)	(-2.85)	(-2.86)
Government intervention	-0.640***	-0.661***	-0.748***	-0.699***
	(-3.00)	(-3.15)	(-3.63)	(-3.27)
Constant	3.700***	3.712***	3.867***	3.717***
	(-14.57)	(-14.75)	(-15.48)	(-14.32)
Observations	139	139	138	138
Adjusted R-squared	0.367	0.376	0.407	0.36

Source: Authors' estimates.
Note: Instrumented variable: Expansionary fiscal policy; Instrument: Liquidity Support.
*** significant at 1 percent; ** significant at 5 percent; * significant at 10 percent.

REFERENCES

Afonso, A., and R. Strauch, 2004, "Fiscal Policy Events and Interest Rate Swap Spreads: Evidence from the EU," European Central Bank Working Paper No. 303 (Frankfurt: European Central Bank).

Aizenman, J., and Y. Jinjarak, 2011, "The Role of Fiscal Policy in Response to the Financial Crisis," Background paper for United Nations, World Economic Situation and Prospects 2011. http://www.un.org/en/development/desa/policy/wesp/wesp_archive/2011wesp_bg _paper_aizenman.pdf.

Akitoby, B., and T. Stratmann, 2008, "Fiscal Policy and Financial Markets," *Economic Journal*, Vol. 118, No. 533, pp. 1971–85.

Alesina, A., S. Ardagna, R. Perotti, and F. Schiantarelli, 2002, "Fiscal Policy, Profits, and Investment," *American Economic Review*, Vol. 92, No. 3, pp. 571–89.

Alper, C.E., L. Forni, and M. Gerard, 2012, "Pricing of Sovereign Credit Risk: Evidence from Advanced Economies during the Financial Crisis," IMF Working Paper 12/24 (Washington: International Monetary Fund).

Ardagna, S., 2009, "Financial Markets' Behavior around Episodes of Large Changes in the Fiscal Stance," *European Economic Review*, Vol. 53, No. 1 (January), pp. 37–55.

Arreaza, A., B.E. Sorensen, and O. Yosha, 1999, "Consumption Smoothing through Fiscal Policy in OECD and EU Countries," in *Fiscal Institutions and Fiscal Performance*, ed. by J.M. Poterba and J. von Hagen (Chicago: University of Chicago Press) pp. 59–80.

Aschauer, D.A., 1989, "Does Public Capital Crowd Out Private Capital?" *Journal of Monetary Economics*, Vol. 24, pp. 171–88. http://dx.doi.org/10.1016/0304-3932(89)90002-0.

Baldacci, E., S. Gupta, and A. Mati, 2011, "Political and Fiscal Risk Determinants of Sovereign Spreads in Emerging Markets," *Review of Development Economies*, Vol. 15, No. 2, pp. 251–63. http://dx.doi.org/10.1111/j.1467-9361.2011.00606.x.

Baldacci, E., S. Gupta, and C. Mulas-Granados, 2012, "Reassessing the Fiscal Mix for Successful Debt Reduction," *Economic Policy*, Vol. 71, pp. 365–406.

Baldacci, E., and M. Kumar, 2010, "Fiscal Deficits, Public Debt, and Sovereign Bond Yields," IMF Working Paper 10/184 (Washington: International Monetary Fund).

Balduzzi, P., G. Corsetti, and S. Foresi, 1997, "Yield-Curve Movements and Fiscal Retrenchments," *European Economic Review*, Vol. 41, pp. 1675–85. http://dx.doi.org/10.1016 /S0014-2921(96)00059-1.

Baum, A., M. Poplawski-Ribeiro, and A. Weber, 2012, "Fiscal Multipliers and the State of the Economy," IMF Working Paper 12/286 (Washington: International Monetary Fund).

Berg, A., and J. Ostry, 2011, "Inequality and Unsustainable Growth: Two Sides of the Same Coin?" IMF Staff Discussion Note 11/08 (Washington: International Monetary Fund).

Blanchard, O., 1990, "Suggestions for a New Set of Fiscal Indicators," OECD Working Paper No. 79 (Paris: Organization for Economic Cooperation and Development).

Bordo, M., B. Eichengreen, D. Klingebiel, and M.S. Martínez-Peria, 2001, "Is the Crisis Problem Growing More Severe?" *Economic Policy*, Vol. 16, pp. 51–82. http://dx.doi .org/10.1111/1468-0327.00070.

Botman, D., and M.S. Kumar, 2006, "Fundamental Determinants of the Effects of Fiscal Policy," IMF Working Paper 06/72 (Washington: International Monetary Fund).

Caceres, C., V. Guzzo, and M. Segoviano, 2010, "Sovereign Spreads: Global Risk Aversion, Contagion or Fundamentals?" IMF Working Paper 10/120 (Washington: International Monetary Fund).

Calomiris, C.W., and G. Gorton, 1991, "The Origins of Banking Panics: Models, Facts, and Bank Regulation," in *Financial Markets and Financial Crises*, ed. by R. Glenn Hubbard (Chicago: University of Chicago Press).

Caprio, G. Jr., and D. Klingebiel, 1996, "Bank Insolvencies: Cross Country Experience," World Bank Policy Research Working Paper No. 1620 (Washington: World Bank).

———, L. Laeven, and G. Noguera, 2005, "Banking Crisis Database," in *Systemic Financial Crises: Containment and Resolution*, ed. by Patrick Honohan and Luc Laeven (Cambridge, United Kingdom: Cambridge University Press).

Cavallo, E., and P. Valenzuela, 2007, "The Determinants of Corporate Risk in Emerging Markets: An Option-Adjusted Spread Analysis," IMF Working Paper 07/228 (Washington: International Monetary Fund).

Claessens, S., A. Kose, and M.E. Terrones, 2008, "What Happens during Recessions, Crunches and Busts?" IMF Working Paper 08/274 (Washington: International Monetary Fund).

Collyns, C., and G.R. Kincaid, 2003, "Managing Financial Crises: Recent Experience and Lessons for Latin America," IMF Occasional Paper No. 217 (Washington: International Monetary Fund).

Cottarelli, C., and L. Jaramillo, 2012, " Walking Hand in Hand: Fiscal Policy and Growth in Advanced Economies," IMF Working Paper 12/137 (Washington: International Monetary Fund).

Dell'Ariccia, G., E. Detragiache, and R. Raghuram, 2008, "The Real Effect of Banking Crises," *Journal of Financial Intermediation*, Vol. 17, No. 1, pp. 89–112. http://dx.doi.org/10.1016/j .jfi.2007.06.001.

DeLong, J.B., and L. Summers, 2012, "Fiscal Policy in a Depressed Economy," Paper prepared for the Brookings Panel on Economic Activity, Spring. http://www.brookings.edu/~/media/ Files/Programs/ES/BPEA/2012_spring_bpea_papers/2012_spring_BPEA_delongsummers. pdf.

Demirgüç-Kunt, A., and E. Detragiache, 1998, "The Determinants of Banking Crises in Developed and Developing Countries," *IMF Staff Papers*, Vol. 45, No. 1, pp. 81–109. http: //dx.doi.org/10.2307/3867330.

Dolls, M., C. Fuest, and A. Peichl, 2010, "Automatic Stabilizers and Economic Crisis: U.S. vs. Europe," NBER Working Paper No. 16275 (Cambridge, Massachusetts: National Bureau of Economic Research).

Dooley, M., and J. Frankel, 2003, *Managing Currency Crises in Emerging Markets* (Chicago: University of Chicago Press).

Durbin, E., and D. Ng, 2005, "The Sovereign Ceiling and Emerging Market Corporate Bond Spreads," *Journal of International Money and Finance*, Vol. 24, pp. 631–49. http://dx.doi .org/10.1016/j.jimonfin.2005.03.005.

Feldstein, M., 2002, "Commentary: Is There a Role for Discretionary Fiscal Policy?" in "Rethinking Stabilization Policy, A Symposium Sponsored by the Federal Reserve Bank of Kansas City Jackson Hole, Wyoming, August 29–31, 2002," pp. 151–62.

Frydl, E.J., 1999, "The Length and Cost of Banking Crises," IMF Working Paper 99/30 (Washington: International Monetary Fund).

Galí, J., D. López-Salido, and J. Vallés, 2007, "Understanding the Effects of Government Spending on Consumption," *Journal of the European Economic Association*, Vol. 5, No. 1, pp. 227–70.

Ghosh, A.R., M. Chamon, C. Crowe, J.I. Kim, and J.D. Ostry, 2009, "Coping with the Crisis: Policy Options for Emerging Market Countries," IMF Staff Position Note 09/08 (Washington: International Monetary Fund).

Gorton, G., 1988, "Banking Panics and Business Cycles," *Oxford Economic Papers*, Vol. 40, No. 4, pp. 751–81.

Gupta, S., E. Baldacci, B.E. Clements, and E.R. Tiongson, 2005, "What Sustains Fiscal Consolidations in Emerging Market Countries?" *International Journal of Finance and Economics,* Vol. 10, No. 4, pp. 307–21.

Hoelscher, D., and M. Quintyn, 2003, "Managing Systemic Banking Crises," IMF Occasional Paper No. 224 (Washington: International Monetary Fund).

Honohan, P., and L. Laeven, 2005, *Systemic Financial Crises: Containment and Resolution* (Cambridge, United Kingdom: Cambridge University Press). http://dx.doi.org/10.1017 /CBO9780511528521.

International Monetary Fund, 2009a, "From Recession to Recovery: How Soon and How Strong?" in *World Economic Outlook*, April (Washington: International Monetary Fund).

———, 2009b, "Recessions and Recoveries in Asia, What Can the Past Teach Us about the Present Recession?" *Asia and Pacific Regional Outlook*, April (Washington: International Monetary Fund).

————, 2009c, "The State of Public Finances: Outlook and Medium-Term Policies after the 2008 Crisis" (Washington: International Monetary Fund).

————, 2010a, *From Stimulus to Consolidation: Revenue and Expenditure Policies in Advanced and Emerging Economies* (Washington: International Monetary Fund).

————, 2010b, *World Economic Outlook*, October (Washington: International Monetary Fund).

————, 2012, *Fiscal Monitor: Balancing Fiscal Policy Risks* (Washington: International Monetary Fund).

Jácome, L., 2008, "Central Bank Involvement in Banking Crises in Latin America," IMF Working Paper 08/135 (Washington: International Monetary Fund).

Kaminsky, G., and C. Reinhart, 1999, "The Twin Crises: The Causes of Banking and Balance of Payment Problems," *American Economic Review*, Vol. 89, No. 3, pp. 473–500. http://dx.doi.org/10.1257/aer.89.3.473.

————, and C.A. Végh, 2004, "When It Rains, It Pours: Procyclical Capital Flows and Macroeconomic Policies," NBER Working Paper No. 10780, (Cambridge, Massachusetts: National Bureau of Economic Research).

Kumar, M., and J. Woo, 2010, "Public Debt and Growth," IMF Working Paper 10/174 (Washington: International Monetary Fund).

Laeven, L., and F. Valencia, 2008, "Systemic Banking Crises: A New Database," IMF Working Paper 08/224 (Washington: International Monetary Fund).

————, 2010, "Resolution of Banking Crises: The Good, the Bad, and the Ugly," IMF Working Paper 10/146 (Washington: International Monetary Fund).

————, 2012, "Systemic Banking Crises: An Update," IMF Working Paper 12/163 (Washington: International Monetary Fund).

Lindgren, C.-J., G. Garcia, and M. Saal, 1996, *Bank Soundness and Macroeconomic Policy* (Washington: International Monetary Fund).

Panizza, U., and A.F. Presbitero, 2012, "Public Debt and Economic Growth: Is There a Causal Effect?" POLIS Working Paper 168 (Alexandria, Egypt: Institute of Public Policy and Public Choice).

Perotti, R., 2011, "The 'Austerity Myth': Gain without Pain?" NBER Working Paper No. 17571 (Cambridge, Massachusetts: National Bureau of Economic Research).

Reinhart, C., and K. Rogoff, 2008a, "This Time Is Different: A Panoramic View of Eight Centuries of Financial Crises," NBER Working Paper 13882 (Cambridge, Massachusetts: National Bureau of Economic Research).

————, 2008b, "Banking Crises: An Equal Opportunity Menace," NBER Working Paper 14587 (Cambridge, Massachusetts: National Bureau of Economic Research).

————, 2009, "The Aftermath of Financial Crises," NBER Working Paper 14656 (Cambridge, Massachusetts: National Bureau of Economic Research).

Spilimbergo, A., S. Symansky, O. Blanchard, and C. Cottarelli, 2008, "Fiscal Policy for the Crisis," IMF Staff Position Note 08/01 (Washington: International Monetary Fund).

Spilimbergo, A., S. Symansky, and M. Schindler, 2009, "Fiscal Multipliers," IMF Staff Position Note 09/11 (Washington: International Monetary Fund).

Tavares, J., and R. Valkanov, 2001, "The Neglected Effect of Fiscal Policy on Stock and Bond Returns," EFA 2003 Annual Conference Paper No. 201 (Los Angeles, California: UCLA, Anderson School of Management).

Uribe, M., 2006, "A Fiscal Theory of Sovereign Risk," *Journal of Monetary Economics,* Vol. 53, No. 8. pp. 1857–75. http://dx.doi.org/10.1016/j.jmoneco.2005.09.003.

Policy Measures to Mitigate the Impact of Financial Crises; and the Restructuring of Banks and of Household and Sovereign Debt

Crisis Management and Resolution: Early Lessons from the 2007–09 Financial Crisis

STIJN CLAESSENS, CEYLA PAZARBASIOGLU, LUC LAEVEN,
MARC DOBLER, FABIÁN VALENCIA, OANA NEDELESCU, AND
KATHARINE SEAL

This chapter compares the policy choices in the 2007–09 global financial crisis with those in past episodes and draws some preliminary policy lessons focusing mainly on crisis management tools and techniques.[1] Country experiences in recent and past crises are examined with a particular focus on the extent to which policy choices were affected by initial conditions and the nature of the crisis. The chapter reviews the state of financial and operational restructuring during the 2007–09 crisis, as well as institutional reforms, in the light of lessons from past episodes, and provides policy implications for the near- and long-term agendas.

The 2007–09 crisis was unusual in its speed and breadth and the types of countries affected. Systemic crises—situations of significant stress in the financial sector, followed by significant policy interventions—often affect several countries at the same time. In the past, though, crises have been largely limited to specific regions or types of economies—the Nordic countries in the early 1990s, Latin America in the mid-1990s, Asia in the late 1990s, and the emerging market economies early in the first decade of the 2000s. The recent crisis was unusual in its global nature, affecting countries with a speed and virulence not seen since the Great Depression, with major advanced economies and countries recently acceding to the European Union (EU) most affected.

The chapter is organized as follows: The first section reviews the initial macroeconomic and financial conditions for two sets of countries, one drawn from past crises and the other from the 2007–09 crisis, and documents differences that help explain the choice of policies used by countries in the two samples. The

The authors are grateful for guidance provided by Olivier Blanchard and José Viñals, input from Luis Cortavarria, and very useful comments from internal and external reviewers, including during an informal discussion at the IMF Executive Board.
[1] Dziobek and Pazarbasioglu (1998); Calomiris, Klingebiel, and Laeven (2003); Hoelscher and Quintyn (2003); Honohan and Laeven (2005); Laeven and Valencia (2008); and Reinhart and Rogoff (2009) review the patterns in macroeconomic and financial variables surrounding crises and the policies used in containment and resolution.

second section reviews the policy choices made in the recent crisis countries in light of outcomes to date and shows how the choices involved trade-offs. The third section concludes with lessons on the best mix of policies for crisis management, the adequacy of current resolution toolkits to deal with systemic distress, and the structural reform agenda to reduce systemic risks.

WHAT WAS DIFFERENT IN THE 2007–09 CRISIS?

Initial Macroeconomic and Financial Conditions

The study collected and compared two samples of crises—past (1991–2002) and recent (2007–09)—that, for each country, qualified as a systemic banking crisis (see Appendix 15A). The past crises occurred in 17 countries during the 1991–2002 period. The recent crises were the manifestations of the 2007–09 global financial crisis as it appeared in 12 countries.[2]

Table 15.1 provides precrisis macroeconomic, institutional, and financial data for the two samples of crisis countries (past crises and recent crises), with data as of one year before each crisis started. The past crises were most frequently among emerging and developing economies, whereas the recent crises were mostly among advanced economies. These advanced economies were, at the time, generally considered to have relatively strong institutional frameworks, a condition associated with a lower probability of a crisis. At the same time, financial systems in the sample of recent crisis countries were generally larger than those in countries in the sample of past crises, and larger systems suggest higher costs in the event of a crisis. Past crises, however, often involved twin crises (both a banking and a currency crisis), and many involved an IMF program.

Credit growth and asset appreciation were stronger in the recent crises and accompanied by large external imbalances in some cases. A common precrisis condition in the past episodes was a large current account deficit (Table 15.1). Currency mismatches were often a significant source of vulnerability and losses once the exchange rate came under pressure. In the recent crises, fiscal and current accounts were, on average, close to balance, although there was, as with past crises, ample variation across countries, and global imbalances were large in absolute terms. Currency mismatches were important triggering and amplifying factors in some of the recent cases. Common to all precrisis periods was the presence of credit or asset price bubbles (Laeven and Valencia, 2008; and Reinhart and Rogoff, 2009). More pronounced in the 2007–09 crises were the sharp increases in leverage for households, also reflected in the higher increase in house prices.

---

[2] Past: *Nordic crises*: Finland, Norway, Sweden (all 1991); *Latin American crises*: Brazil (1994), Mexico (1994), and Jamaica (1996); *Asian crises*: Indonesia, Japan, the Republic of Korea, Malaysia, and Thailand (all 1997); and the *emerging markets crises*: Colombia (1998), Ecuador (1998), the Russian Federation (1998), Turkey (2000), Argentina (2001), and Uruguay (2002). Recent (as of end-2009): Austria, Belgium, Denmark, Germany, Iceland, Ireland, Latvia, Luxembourg, the Netherlands, Ukraine, the United Kingdom, and the United States (see Appendix 15A).

TABLE 15.1

Precrisis Indicators

	Past crises		Recent crises	
	All	Advanced	All	Advanced
	18 episodes	4 episodes	12 episodes	10 episodes
	Medians (percent of GDP unless indicated otherwise)[1]			
Institutional and Macroeconomic				
Overall fiscal balance	−0.7	3.0	0.0	0.0
Gross public debt	32.7	28.9	42.0	43.0
Current account	−3.1	−0.6	−0.9	1.8
Private credit growth (median, $t-1$ through $t-4$)	6.1	2.9	8.9	8.9
Real estate prices (median growth, $t-1$ through $t-4$)	−2.8[2]	2.0	5.2	5.2
Stock prices (MSCI in US$, median percent growth, $t-1$ through $t-4$)	18	21	26	26
Stock market capitalization	29	34	86	102
Private bond market capitalization	8	39	45	45
Real GDP growth (percent, $t-1$)	1.9	1.5	3.6	3.2
GDP per capita (constant 2000 US$)	4,520	25,561	27,563	30,425
CPI inflation	7.0	4.6	3.2	3.1
Creditors' rights (4 = best)	2	2.5	3	3
Central bank independence (1 = best)	0.63	0.61	0.83	0.83
Governance[3] (2.5 = best)	0.17	1.68	1.57	1.61
Deposit insurance in place (percent of cases)	50	75	100	100
Financial				
Bank assets	48	80	150	156
Bank credit	43	72	136	160
Bank credit/deposits (percent)	118	126	125	124
Net interest margin (percent of revenues)	5	2	3	2
Size of five largest banks (global assets)	23	76[4]	307	391
Market share of three largest banks	48	97	58	62
Commercial banks/total system assets (percent)	86	76	67	59
Cross-border claims	9	15	91	114
Bank return on equity (percent)	7	1	11	11
Bank Z-score (standard deviations)	6.25	6.25	8.19	8.19
Core capital/assets (percent)	9	5	8	8
Other operating income/average assets (percent)	2	1	1	1
Loans/assets (percent)	49	69	51	47
Liquid assets/customers and short-term funding (percent)	23	32	37	37
Other funding/total liabilities (percent)	1.3	9.6	5.2	5.0

Sources: Thomson Reuters Datastream; Djankov, McLiesh, and Shleifer (2007); the Organization for Economic Co-operation and Development, the World Bank, and IMF *World Economic Outlook* for creditors' rights; Crowe and Meade (2003) for central bank independence; World Bank for governance; Laeven and Valencia (2008) for deposit insurance; and BankScope and Organization for Economic Co-operation and Development for bank profitability. World Bank Financial Structure Database.

Note: CPI = consumer price index; MSCI = Morgan Stanley Capital International stock market index

[1] See Appendix 15A for data sample and crisis dates. All precrisis variables are measured as of one year before the start of the crisis, unless indicated otherwise. Past advanced economies are the Nordic countries and Japan; recent advanced countries are all but Latvia and Ukraine.

[2] Median for advanced economies and Asian crisis episodes.

[3] Aggregate of six dimensions of governance.

[4] Japan only.

Financial systems were much larger and more concentrated in the recent crises, and financial institutions much more complex. Global assets of the five largest banks were typically more than 300 percent of their home country's GDP (Table 15.1). Many of these institutions enjoyed the benefits of being "too important to fail," that is, borrowing at preferential rates, operating with higher levels of leverage, and engaging in riskier activities. These firms were often highly complex in their balancing of business, tax, and regulatory objectives. For efficiency purposes, management would operate through business lines from the center, with liquidity and treasury functions often centralized. Yet, for tax and regulatory reasons, trades and exposures would be booked wherever most profitable or efficient. Hence, the formal and de facto governance structures of many groups would diverge. In consequence, host and, in some cases, even home supervisors with formal oversight authority, were often at best only partially able to identify and assess a group's financial health, including the adequacy of its capital and liquidity arrangements, the nature of risks, and the location of risks within the wider group.

High interconnectedness in the recent crises was enabled by financial innovations, especially securitizations and traded credit derivatives, and the expansion of the role of nonbank financial institutions known as the "shadow banking system." Securitization created assets that were packaged, and then repackaged, into new layers such as collateralized debt obligations, and each new layer further spread risks while reducing the clarity of risk exposures. Credit default swaps led to a separation of credit risks on and off balance sheets, and facilitated the concentration of risks in single entities that went undetected. And although nonbanks were a cause of instability in some of the past crises, the role of the shadow banking system in the recent crises was much more important through banks' use of conduits and collateralized transactions. Nonbank institutions like mortgage lenders, broker-dealers, and money market funds had grown rapidly, and some became systemically important. Large, internationally active financial institutions, large cross-border claims exceeding 90 percent of GDP (six time larger than in past crises), and complex linkages combined to transmit stress rapidly, most notably related to problems in the U.S. subprime mortgage market (Claessens and others, 2010).

As in past precrisis periods, traditional financial system indicators and favorable macroeconomic conditions obscured risks in the run-up to the recent crises. Conventional indicators of financial soundness based on balance sheet data showed precrisis bank profitability, liquidity, and capital to be higher than in the past, at least when comparing across only advanced economies. One exception was the increasing leverage of many large financial institutions, but that was generally thought to be consistent with improvements in risk management that allowed for the more efficient use of capital. An increased reliance on wholesale funding was also not generally considered a concern. Taken together, however, these misinterpretations meant an underestimation both of the risks accumulating outside banks' balance sheets and of large-scale systemic liquidity withdrawals.

The Policy Responses

Policy responses in the recent crises were initially similar to those in past crises, but over time have diverged. Past crisis responses typically involved three phases: first, containment, to deal with acute liquidity stress and to stabilize financial liabilities; second, resolution and balance sheet restructuring, which involves removing insolvent financial institutions from the system and recapitalizing viable ones; and, finally, operational restructuring to restore the financial soundness and profitability of viable institutions and asset management to rehabilitate nonperforming loans. The recent crises followed this pattern through the first phase, but subsequent policy responses were less forceful, at least for the major countries.[3]

The sequence and range of policy responses in the past crises differed in important respects from those in the recent crises. Figure 15.1 provides the timing of interventions by depicting the evolution of liquidity support and the timing of guarantees and recapitalizations by governments around the onset of crises. Figure 15.2 compares the frequency of policies used as of end-2009. (Appendix 15B provides details on timelines and intervention measures.) As in past crises, liquidity support and guarantees were deployed in the early stages, although more extensively relative to GDP. However, this support was followed more rapidly in the recent crises compared with the past crises with recapitalization across the board in many countries, which mitigated the real effects of the crises. After these

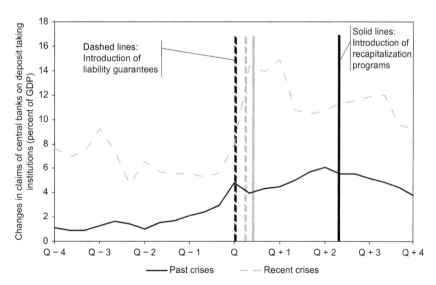

Figure 15.1 Timing of Interventions and Amount of Liquidity Support

Source: Laeven and Valencia, Chapter 2, in this volume.
Note: "Past crises" refers to pre-2007; "Recent crises" refers to crises since 2007. All dates are relative to crisis peaks, with periods referring to quarters before or after.

---

[3] Other papers reviewing policy responses in past and recent crises include Claessens, Klingebiel, and Laeven (2003); Ingves and Lind (2008); Ingves and others (2009); and Panetta and others (2009).

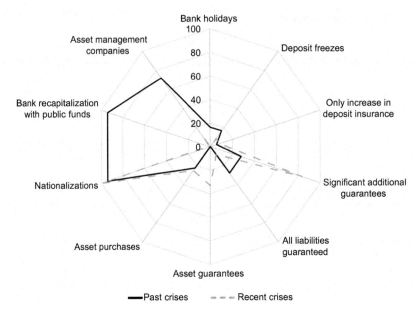

Figure 15.2 Containment and Resolution Policies *(percent of sample countries adopting)*

Source: Laeven and Valencia, Chapter 2, in this volume.

Note: "Past crises" refers to pre-2007 and "Recent crises" refers to crises since 2007.

general interventions, policy approaches in the recent crises became less forceful than those typically followed in the past. In particular, progress with comprehensive operational and asset restructuring was slower.

However, in Iceland, Ireland, and Ukraine, the sequence and types of responses more closely resembled those of past crises, including due diligence on the viability of financial institutions and quality of assets, government recapitalization, removal of nonperforming assets, operational restructuring, and the adoption of IMF programs. The details of policy mixes varied, reflecting differences in the causes and severity of countries' respective crises, including whether they also involved a currency or a sovereign debt crisis, types of defunct assets, and political economy considerations. In Iceland—and to a lesser degree in Ukraine, where foreign exchange exposures were large—wholesale funding runs and withdrawal of foreign capital led to crises and created pressures on currencies, which then reduced the repayment capacity of borrowers. In Ireland, problems were predominantly real estate–related and mostly affected commercial banks.

LIQUIDITY AND OTHER CENTRAL BANK SUPPORT MEASURES

With capital losses, severe funding pressures emerged relatively early on. Losses on securitized assets, reflecting expectations of default and deteriorating economic conditions, quickly appeared on institutions' balance sheets (traded assets are normally marked to market or recorded at fair value). Price declines and ratings downgrades of securitized assets during 2007–08 quickly impacted firms' capital through valuation losses. By end-2007, more than 70 percent of banks' losses came from structured products and securitized positions. Because reputational risks compelled many banks to put previously off balance sheet obligations on their books, liquidity needs rose sharply. Given the large reliance on wholesale funding, liquidity needs spiked across many markets, and interbank market spreads widened dramatically. In tandem, asset prices and solvency positions worsened further.

Central banks responded quickly with liquidity support on a more massive and widespread scale than in the past crises (Stone, Fujita, and Ishi, 2011). They extended the duration of liquidity facilities and eased counterparty and collateral requirements. New facilities were established to alleviate liquidity shortfalls in specific markets. Liquidity support to financial institutions was accompanied or followed by large-scale asset purchases and other unconventional, quantitative interventions. The U.S. Federal Reserve and the Bank of England purchased large amounts of securities. The European Central Bank introduced a covered bond purchase program. Coordinated policy responses, unprecedented in many ways, then followed, including central bank swap facilities. Altogether, central banks' balance sheets expanded much more than in previous crises, and support was more flexible.

Funding strains prompted the provision of guarantees, including to shadow banks, but more selectively than in past crises, when they covered a wide set of liabilities and were mostly in the form of blanket guarantees. In the recent episodes, formal guarantees were largely applied to specific banks (such as Northern Rock in the United Kingdom) or new debt issuance only. With deposit insurance schemes already in place, countries also quickly increased the coverage limits, substantially in some cases.[4] In addition, guarantees were extended to some nonbank financial institutions, notably in the United States, where a run on money market funds, then a $3 trillion industry, led to the provision of guarantees traditionally used to protect bank deposits. Finally, governments made statements expressing their support for the whole sector.

ACCOMMODATIVE MONETARY AND FISCAL POLICIES

Expansionary monetary policies during the recent crises were critical in supporting banks and markets. Monetary policy was relaxed significantly early on by quickly adjusting short-term interest rates to historical lows (Figure 15.3), with major central banks taking coordinated actions. Taking advantage of their reserve currency status, several central banks committed themselves, at least condition-

---

[4] Belgium, Luxembourg, and the Netherlands increased limits from €20,000 to €100,000 as part of an EU-wide decision; the United States more than doubled them; and some countries guaranteed all retail deposits.

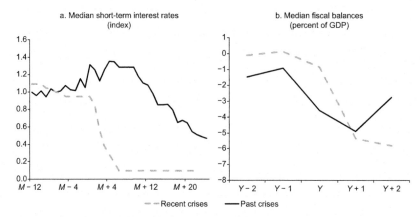

Figure 15.3 Monetary and Fiscal Policies during Crises

Sources: Haver Analytics; IMF, *International Financial Statistics*, and IMF, *World Economic Outlook*.
Note: *M* and *Y* on *x*-axes refer to month and year of the onset of the crisis, respectively.

ally, to maintaining low interest rates for prolonged periods. Those moves were opposite of the efforts of central banks in many past crises in which nominal rates were kept high or sometimes even raised to support currencies. In the recent crises, the low policy rates and ample liquidity often allowed banks to preserve their intermediation margins in spite of higher costs of other funding. Accommodative monetary policy also helped support overall asset values, reduced the risk of an adverse debt-deflation spiral, and limited nonperforming loans, at least initially, thus protecting some of the banks' profit streams and balance sheets despite losses on traded securities.

Accommodative fiscal policies were important to maintaining aggregate demand and asset values, thus indirectly supporting financial institutions. Better initial conditions allowed for larger fiscal deficits than in past crises; most policymakers opted to allow automatic stabilizers to operate, and many undertook countercyclical fiscal measures. By supporting aggregate demand, fiscal stimulus helped reduce expected defaults on bank loans and thus reduced banks' recapitalization needs.[5] This approach also differed from that in past crises, when fiscal policy was often contractionary (Figure 15.3). Furthermore, fiscal policy responses were more coordinated across countries than in the past, further helping to support economies.

CAPITAL SUPPORT

The private sector (including sovereign wealth funds) contributed much to recapitalizing financial institutions in the 2007–09 crises, albeit to varying

---

[5] Fiscal policy has a greater effect on firms that are relatively dependent on external finance (Aghion, Hemous, and Kharroubi, 2009; and Laeven and Valencia, 2011).

degrees across regions. From September 2007 to September 2008, private capital injections for U.S., European, and Asian institutions amounted to 71, 78, and 94 percent, respectively, of announced losses (IMF, 2008) and greatly reduced balance sheet pressures during that period. Also, in some smaller countries, recapitalization came from foreign banks that dominated markets. During the entire 2007–09 crisis period, private investors contributed about 61 percent of capital, but more so in the United States than in the euro area (about 86 percent versus 47 percent).

Changes to accounting and valuation practices also alleviated capital pressures. It was perceived that fair-value accounting might contribute to a fire sale of assets and exacerbate solvency and liquidity concerns. After much political pressure, accounting standards boards allowed banks in October 2008 to reclassify certain assets, including complex structured securities, as held-to-maturity, which meant they could be reported on a historical or amortized cost basis. Also, firms could rely more on their own assumptions and models in valuing assets, including mortgage-backed securities, during illiquid or inactive market conditions. This greater flexibility in valuing assets also limited the need to raise new capital (Huizinga and Laeven, 2009).

Government recapitalizations were, proportionately, much lower than in past crises. Together with accommodating policies that supported asset values and held down losses, the rapid and large private recapitalization meant that government recapitalizations took place at a point when banking solvency was much stronger than in past crises. Government capital support totaled US$441 billion—$245 billion in the United States under the Troubled Asset Relief Program (TARP) and US$196 billion in the European Union—which, at only 5 percent of GDP on average, is about one-third of the amount provided in past crises. However, by aiming to have a rapid effect, avoid stigmatization, and support lending, the government recapitalizations were spread too broadly, forgoing the benefits of separating viable from nonviable institutions.

ASSET RESTRUCTURING

In a typical crisis, nonperforming loans rise steeply, even before its onset, as banks acknowledge the expected deterioration in corporate and household repayment capacity. Although the recent crises broadly exhibited the characteristics of a typical collapse following a boom (Lindgren, Garcia, and Saal, 1996; Dooley and Frankel, 2003; and Reinhart and Rogoff, 2009), the rise in nonperforming loans was much less pronounced (Figure 15.4). Write-downs of impaired assets showed up only gradually and as of mid-2011 were lower than in past crises. This was in part due to the types of assets involved, with the drop in the value of securitized loans occurring earlier than in other crises, before the end of the cycle. Actual defaults followed only when the crisis affected the real economy and corporate sector and household conditions had worsened. Furthermore, corporate sectors were generally not overleveraged.

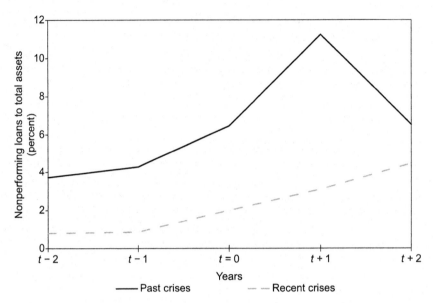

Figure 15.4 Nonperforming Loans in Past and Recent Crises

Sources: BankScope; and IMF, *Global Financial Stability Report*, 2010.
Note: *t* = 0 denotes the year of the onset of the crisis.

Partly for these reasons, asset restructuring was far more limited in the recent crises than in the past. Restructuring refers to two processes. The first is diagnosing the value of a bank's loans and investments, stating the value of its securities at market prices rather than acquisition cost, provisioning for and writing off part of nonpaying loans, and possibly selling off securities and loans, and deleveraging the institution. The second is to ensure that borrowers' financial conditions are sound and their creditworthiness is restored, which typically involves both financial restructuring (extending the maturity of loans, reducing interest rates and amount owed) and operational restructuring (selling of assets, reducing labor and administrative costs, and the like).

In the recent episodes, many countries applied asset restructuring on a case-by-case basis, with government relief provided mainly through guarantees against a large deterioration in asset values; less frequent in the recent crises was the use of "bad banks" (Table 15.2). Asset guarantees require little up-front funding and do not involve immediate loss recognition or recapitalization, unlike purchasing impaired assets at a discount. Given the size and complexity of nonperforming assets—including the many securitized portfolios and mortgages to be restructured—guarantees were often the only, or at least the preferred, option. Also, high government debt levels in some countries may have prevented asset transfers. Although guarantees reduce uncertainty for financial institutions and help with their funding, the government takes on higher contingent costs.

TABLE 15.2

Selected Asset Relief Measures during Recent and Past Crises

Type of measure	Use	Countries	Beneficiaries	Asset types	Amount[1] Billion US$	Amount[1] % of GDP
Asset guaran- tees	Recent crises	Belgium	Dexia (FSAM)	Structured assets	10.5	2.2
			KBC		33.5	7.1
			Fortis		29.4	6.2
		Germany	West LB	Structured assets	7.0[2]	0.2
			Bayern LB		6.7	0.2
			LBBW		21.7[3]	0.6
		Netherlands	ING	RMBS, mortgage loans	35.1[4]	4.4
		United Kingdom	RBS	Pools of assets	524.0	24.0
			Lloyds		483.0	22.2
		United States	Citigroup	Real estate-related	301.0	2.1
			Bank of America		118.0[5]	0.8
"Bad banks"	Recent crises	Belgium	Fortis	Structured assets	28.7	6.0
		Germany	West LB	Toxic and nonstrategic assets	107.8	3.2
		Latvia	Parex	Impaired and nonstrate- gic assets	1.2	5.1
		United Kingdom	Northern Rock	Mortgage loans and other loans	121.0[6]	5.6
			Bradford & Bingley		79.3[6]	3.6
		United States	Bear Stearns	RMBS, CDOs	30.0	0.2
			AIG		52.3[7]	0.4
	Past crises	Sweden	Nordbanken Gotabanken	Real estate–related and corporate loans	11.5	4.3
AMCs / asset pur- chases	Recent crises	Ireland	Banks	Distressed real estate- related (purchased by NAMA)	97.8	44.0
		United States	Government- sponsored entities	New MBS (purchased by asset managers for the Treasury)	197.6	1.4
			Banks	"Legacy" MBS/loans (PPIFs)	14.2	0.1
	Past crises	Thailand	Banks	Bad loans (purchased by TAMC)	17.0	13.7
		Korea, Rep. of	Financial institutions	Bad loans (purchased by KAMCO)	90.0	19.5

Sources: Borio, Vale, and von Peter (2010); Boudghene, Maes, and Schmeicher (2010); European Commission State Aid Register; Fung and others (2004); country authorities; and IMF staff.

Note: AMC = asset management company; CDO = collateralized debt obligation; KAMCO = Korea Asset Management Corporation; MBS = mortgage-backed security; PPIF = Public-Private Investment Funds; RMBS = residential mort- gage-backed security; TAMC = Thai Asset Management Company.

[1] For asset guarantees, amount refers to guaranteed (book) value of portfolio or otherwise as footnoted. For asset purchas- es, amounts generally refer to the book value of assets transferred, that is, before any writedowns, except in cases of mar- ketable securities bought, in which case they refer to the actual market values.

[2] Swap facility.

[3] Includes asset-backed securities portfolio and loan to Sealink portfolio.

[4] Backup facility.

[5] The guarantee was provided in January 2009; however, the arrangement was never implemented and Bank of America paid an exit fee in September 2009.

[6] Refers to the total asset size of the institutions as of January 1, 2010.

[7] Represents lending to AIG special purpose vehicles by the Federal Reserve Bank of New York (FRBNY), which is less than the total assets of the "bad bank" for AIG. The loans from FRBNY were repaid from the liquidation of AIG assets.

During the recent crises in comparison with most past episodes, such as the Nordic and Asian crises, fewer assets were removed from the balance sheets of financial institutions through government asset management companies (AMCs) or other programs (Table 15.2). One important exception was Ireland, where distressed loans with a book value equivalent to 44 percent of GDP were transferred to a government AMC. Other asset-targeted programs, like the U.S. Public Private Investment Program, amounted to only 0.1 percent of GDP. Although the Federal Reserve and other central banks also purchased large amounts of private securities to support targeted markets, those efforts were not directly aimed at asset restructuring.

POLICY CHOICES AND PRELIMINARY LESSONS

This section reviews the outcomes of policies chosen and compares these policies with both good practice and lessons from past crises. It first assesses the costs—using the metrics of output losses, fiscal costs, and increases in government debt—in comparison with past crises. Considering various trade-offs and differences in country circumstances, it then compares recent policy responses with those adopted in the past and with good practice guidelines for resolving crises (see Appendix 15C). It provides some preliminary lessons for effectiveness.

The Costs of Crises

The costs of crises can be assessed in different ways, including their direct fiscal costs, encompassing direct outlays to support the financial system and for resolving nonperforming assets; their broader fiscal costs, measured as the increase in government debt over some chosen horizon (plus the direct fiscal costs); and the real output losses.

The direct fiscal support has been lower than in past crises. The fiscal costs attributable to direct support in the recent crises reached 5 percent of GDP on average as of end-2009, against 15 percent for past crises (Figure 15.5). With the important caveat that the crisis was still unfolding in many countries, especially in EU countries, this lower cost reflected the more accommodative monetary and fiscal policies and the lesser need for and use of government recapitalization. The management of distressed assets was more decentralized than in past crises, a reflection of the more limited nature of government interventions and the greater use of guarantees. Guarantees (including liability guarantees, liquidity, and other contingent support) reduce the need for up-front fiscal outlays, but impose higher contingent fiscal costs. Broader fiscal costs, however, were larger than in past crises. Projected increases in debt for the four-year period after the onset of the crisis are higher for the recent crises (about 25 percent of GDP). These increases come on top of the already-large government debt burdens in many advanced economies.

Output losses were lower than in the past but still significant. At 25 percent of GDP, cumulative over four years, the median output losses were lower than the

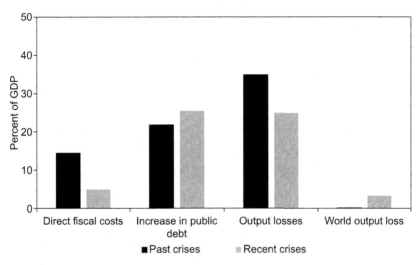

Figure 15.5   Median Costs of Recent and Past Crises

Source: Laeven and Valencia, Chapter 2, in this volume.
Note: Costs are measured as of the end of 2009.

35 percent for past crises, reflecting in great part the beneficial effects of the extraordinary policy measures implemented during the recent crises (and also reflecting the fact that in the recent crises, the affected countries had lower growth trends preceding the crisis).[6] Measured for the whole world, however, output losses from the recent crises were 3.3 percent versus 0.2 percent for the past. That global output losses were larger this time is no surprise given the size of the affected economies and the ensuing spillovers.

Costs relative to output in the recent crises varied greatly across countries but were more comparable relative to banking system assets. For major advanced economies, the direct costs were relatively small, 3 percent to 5 percent of GDP. For some of the smaller countries, however, the direct costs were much larger, up to 17 percent of GDP for Iceland (excluding Icesave) and 25 percent for Ireland (as of end-2010). These countries engaged in larger-scale government recapitalizations and removals of bad assets from banks' balance sheets. Furthermore, their banking systems were relatively larger (as measured by assets as a percentage of GDP). Indeed, as a share of banking assets, the direct costs were more comparable across countries. At the same time, whereas government debt in these smaller countries rose because of recapitalization programs, major countries had larger overall debt increases.

---

[6] Output losses are defined as the deviation of real GDP from its trend (computed as the Hodrick-Prescott-filtered series for the 20-year period ending a year before the crisis) for the four-year period beginning with the first crisis year.

The Policy Choices and Preliminary Lessons

The following discussion offers preliminary lessons and suggestions for further reforms to the policy sequence and mix in crisis management and resolution; the diagnosis of financial institutions; the operational restructuring of weak institutions; the restructuring of assets, in particular of household debt; and measures to restore proper incentives and market discipline.

AN OVERALL ACCOMMODATIVE POLICY MIX SHOULD NOT PRECLUDE DEEP RESTRUCTURING

Responses in the recent crises primarily relied on accommodative monetary and fiscal policy to contain the potential spillovers to the real sector. Affected countries included mostly advanced economies that had the ability to conduct countercyclical monetary and fiscal policy without undue concern, at least initially, about the impact on interest rates, exchange rates, or government debt. The accommodative policies contained the crisis by forestalling sharp increases in interest rates and large currency depreciations (currencies even appreciated in some countries)—which can degrade borrowers' solvency and increase bank losses—and thus by directly and indirectly propping up bank asset quality and values.

This mix of policies may have transferred the costs to the future, however, in the form of higher government debt and possibly slower economic recoveries. Although the complexity of the crises may have justified more emphasis on the restoration of confidence and less extensive restructuring early on, it precluded thorough due diligence of individual banks and might have reduced incentives to restructure assets. Instead of a policy of targeted, diagnosis-based resolution and early asset restructuring, the stance was a muddling-through approach of accounting and regulatory forbearance, guarantees, and implicit government support that delayed addressing nonviable banks and nonperforming assets. The presumption should therefore remain in favor of deep restructuring early on, even when pursuing accommodative general policies.

DIAGNOSIS OF FINANCIAL INSTITUTIONS SHOULD PRECEDE RECAPITALIZATION

Thorough, independent examinations were typically conducted in past crises to assess asset values and the viability of financial institutions in an effort to judge the appropriateness of recapitalization. Nonviable institutions would be closed or viable parts sold off and the rest of the institution liquidated. Once the size of the losses was determined, recapitalization plans for viable institutions would be announced and implemented. This process could take considerable time: in Indonesia, the government announced a blanket guarantee in January 1998, began examinations in August 1998, and implemented recapitalizations in March 1999.

In the recent crises, policymakers in the major advanced economies focused on reducing systemic consequences and therefore often opted for providing quick support to all institutions, including weak and potentially nonviable ones. Governments faced unprecedented complexity, and were hampered by limited information and limited tools for addressing systemic and cross-border entities. Therefore, they rapidly engaged in measures, first ad hoc and then more systematic, to stem contagion and restore market stability. Ad hoc assistance was provided to institutions embodying important counterparty risks (notably, in the United States, to AIG, to specialized municipal bond insurers, and to the two giant government-sponsored housing-related enterprises, Fannie Mae and Freddie Mac; and in Europe to a number of banks).[7]

The more rapid interventions typically did not allow for a separation of viable institutions from less-viable ones. Systematic assessments of institutions were conducted through stress tests and publicly disseminated in the United States and the EU (in May 2009 and July 2010, respectively), but only after initial government recapitalizations.[8] These stress tests restored short-term investor confidence, but their long-term impact was uneven, in part because market participants had mixed views on the credibility of the assumptions used and the remedial actions announced subsequent to the tests. EU authorities were compelled to engage in a new round of stress tests. Furthermore, government support of institutions required little in the way of their operational restructuring, in contrast to earlier crises. In the recent crises in Iceland, Ireland, Latvia, and Ukraine, however, the sequence was more typical: diagnosis, recapitalization, and the removal of nonperforming assets or the creation of bad and good banks.

The lesson is that diagnosis needs to be conducted, including through strict and transparent stress tests, even while accommodative policies are being put in place. Given the circumstances, many governments had no alternative but to apply quick support measures. However, those quick measures should have been immediately followed by forward-looking measures, including asset and operational restructuring. Delaying the restructuring hampered the economic recovery because institutions were weighed down by troubled assets . As a result of residual uncertainty, confidence in many systems was still very dependent on implicit and explicit government and central bank support. Stress tests should have been conducted in many countries, accompanied as needed by credible recapitalization plans, or restructuring of institutions' liabilities, without adding to sovereign debt burdens.

---

[7] In the European Union, key policies were subsequently coordinated (e.g., EU, 2008), followed by agreements to coordinate recapitalization, guarantees, asset insurance, and transfer schemes.

[8] A first round of EU-wide stress tests was conducted in September 2009, but results were not made public.

DEALING WITH DISTRESSED INSTITUTIONS REQUIRES OPERATIONAL RESTRUCTURING

Although most countries imposed limits on compensation to management and shareholders, more-intrusive measures—including cost cutting, downsizing, changes in management, and forced write-downs of shareholder value—were used less than in the past, except where governments took majority ownership of or fully nationalized institutions. Rather, obligations were placed on banks to continue to provide support to the real sector. The less-intrusive measures reflected institutions' stronger solvency and continued majority private ownership, conditions different from those in past crises. But it also reflected the fact that the rapid and broad-based government support was mostly oriented toward financial stability and to limiting adverse short-term impacts.

In EU countries, additional conditions were imposed on state support measures, whereas in the United States both initial and ongoing conditions attached to state support (under the TARP program) were more limited. For those EU institutions that participated, government guarantees on liabilities carried restrictions on balance sheet growth, dividends, and employee compensation. For institutions benefiting from recapitalization and asset relief, significant balance sheet and operational conditions (e.g., restrictions on acquisitions, refocus on core activities, divestments of businesses and assets) were included for competition policy reasons. In the United States, capital assistance under TARP required that institutions be adequately capitalized. As a result, the only restriction imposed on these institutions was on executives' compensation and advance U.S. Treasury permission for any increase in dividend payments.

Bank solvency has improved in many of the countries affected by the 2007–09 crisis, but mainly on the basis of balance sheet restructuring, including recapitalization; the support of abnormally low interest rates, which improve profits from lending and investing; and enormous fiscal stimulus, which supports loan performance. Although interest rates have remained low for some time now in many advanced economies, those conditions cannot be expected to continue. With many financial systems still overextended and subject in the coming years to new regulatory requirements,[9] profitability will be under pressure. For institutions faced with limited prospects, the current incentive structures and competition for profits may again foster risky behavior. Uncertainty about possible further losses and shortages of capital may dissuade others from lending to the real economy and they may instead continue to deleverage. Although it is difficult to distinguish between demand and supply effects in the provision of credit, evidence suggests that recapitalization aids the speed and sustainability of recovery (Laeven and Valencia, 2011).

---

[9] The Basel III agreement on international banking standards reached by the Basel Committee on Banking Supervision calls for a substantial increase in the quantity and quality of capital and liquidity buffers, new regulations and tougher standards for nonbank firms, and other macroprudential rules.

With fewer government levers to do the job, operational restructuring in the major countries depended largely on market pressures. For banks with large government ownership interests, restructuring efforts depended directly on government actions. And over time, the government must sell off its stake. Market pressures will force many other institutions, including those that benefited from government support, to rebuild balance sheets and restructure operations. Regulatory reforms addressing gaps and shortcomings could have helped speed this process along. But the problems were large and complex, market conditions were depressed, and the economic recovery in the advanced economies was still weak. Those challenges underscore the importance of creating appropriate incentives for bank managers and owners and for supervisors and markets to monitor banks and ensure prudent governance.

DEALING WITH DISTRESSED BORROWERS OFTEN LAGGED

Although the across-the-board policies improved conditions at many financial institutions and supported economic activity, they may have reduced the incentives for restructuring the asset side of bank balance sheets. In many markets, asset quality remained uncertain. The prices of various financial assets improved following government support measures, but they remained low in many markets. Incomplete or dubious disclosures of asset quality, attributable in part to accounting changes, hindered market transparency and liquidity. The complexity of the task notwithstanding, asset restructuring was not as far along four years after the start of the crises than it was at similar stages in past crises. In the Asian and Nordic crises, government asset management companies (AMCs) and bad banks were accustomed to removing nonperforming loans—especially real estate loans—from the balance sheets of banks taken over by the authorities, thereby incurring upfront fiscal outlays. In the 2007–09 crisis, reflecting the limited government intervention in institutions, asset restructuring was largely left to the financial institutions themselves in most large advanced economies.

Although loss recognition was not always swift in past crises either, banks nonetheless underwent more rapid dispositions of their problem assets than they did in the 2007–09 crises. The limited use of AMCs in the 2007–09 crises reflects the complex nature of the assets involved, which do not permit easy centralized restructuring. But the chosen alternative route—injection of capital into the banks while leaving nonperforming loans on their balance sheets—poses the risk of continued losses, further weakening banks' profitability and absorbing management capacity. It could also foster forbearance from formal regulations because it extends the government safety net and thereby impedes a full recovery of confidence. These alternative paths—disposal of bad assets versus capital injections with government funds and delay of clean up—are illustrated by the experiences of Sweden and Japan in their past crises (Box 15.1). Sweden took a comprehensive approach to dealing with distressed assets (primarily commercial real estate)

Box 15.1 Bank Restructuring and Asset Management: Sweden and Japan

In Sweden, the authorities responded to the initial signs of financial strain in the fall of 1990 with a series of ad hoc interventions. When these measures failed to restore stability, a new bank resolution agency was established to deal comprehensively with the crisis. The agency evaluated the financial condition of troubled banks on a forward-looking basis, categorized banks as solvent or insolvent, forced shareholders to recapitalize the former, and took control of the latter. Asset management companies (AMCs) were set up for two nationalized banks, and problem assets, conservatively valued—particularly real estate loans—were transferred to the AMCs. The process helped put a floor under real estate prices and facilitated the return of investors. As early as 1993, confidence in the financial system began to recover.

The Swedish experience provides useful lessons for the 2007–09 crises but needs to be placed in context (Klingebiel, 2000). The ultimate fiscal costs were relatively small, totaling only 4 percent of GDP, partly because of a global economic recovery and the competitive benefits of a 30 percent depreciation in the currency. Problem assets were mainly relatively simple commercial and residential real estate loans, and the banks operated domestically rather than cross border. These features, which enabled quick valuation and a centralized approach to restructuring and asset management funded by the state, were not characteristics of the 2007–09 crises.

In Japan. a financial crisis was triggered in 1995 when several regional deposit-takers failed. The authorities responded with emergency liquidity and a government guarantee of bank liabilities. Recapitalization schemes in 1998 and 1999 failed to restore confidence, and although a zero interest rate policy (adopted in February 1999) and quantitative easing (introduced in early 2001 and increased substantially in 2002) ultimately eased liquidity problems, those measures did not address the root causes of the crisis—uncertainty about the solvency of banks. In fall 2002, authorities finally set quantitative targets for the disposal of nonperforming loans and conducted rigorous examinations with more stringent provisioning standards. Along with two AMCs established to underpin asset prices, these measures ultimately helped restore stability.

Their special circumstances notwithstanding, the contrasting experiences of Sweden and Japan offer two key warnings about the management of financial crises: First, delays in recognizing problem loans may exacerbate a financial crisis and postpone recovery. Weak accounting practices and regulatory forbearance may blunt incentives for remedial action, sustain uncertainty about asset values and solvency, and hinder price formation. Second, liquidity provision may mitigate the immediate effects of a systemic crisis but mask fundamental problems in the banking system. Without comprehensive measures to recognize losses and address resulting capital shortfalls, the extended provision of exceptional liquidity may delay necessary restructuring.

Sources: Drees and Pazarbasioglu (1998); Ingves and Lind (2008); Ishi (2009); Syed, Kang, and Tukuoka (2009).

and implemented it quickly. In contrast, by taking much longer, Japan showed that such delays can impose enormous costs.

Unless interventions in the banks include restructuring, especially of household debt, the recovery is likely to lengthen. Before the crisis, households in many countries had accumulated large debts, especially for home purchases; all told, debt amounted to more than 130 percent of disposable income in the United States and more than 160 percent in some European countries. For many households these debts became too onerous to service given the unfavorable economic conditions. Although low interest rates eased the debt-servicing burden and reduced the pressure on lenders to adjust borrowers' debt levels, risks will increase when interest rates return to normal levels. Efforts by banks to reduce the burden of household loans were not enough; likewise, government programs to restructure home mortgage loans were small in scope and largely ineffective as indicated by the recurrent defaults on restructured loans. Restructuring needs to be accelerated through a more effective mix of private and government actions (see Laeven and Laryea, 2009, and Chapter 17 of this volume for some best practices).

REDUCING SYSTEMIC RISKS AND PREVENTING MORAL HAZARD REQUIRE MORE REFORMS

Some of the structural characteristics that contributed to the buildup of systemic risks in financial sectors are still in place today, and moral hazard increased during the crisis. In most countries, the structure of the financial system changed little. In fact, because large banks acquired failing institutions, concentration increased on average—for the twelve 2007–09 crisis countries, the assets of the five largest banks combined rose from 307 percent of GDP before the crisis to 335 percent in 2009—complicating resolution efforts. The large-scale government support provided to institutions and markets—a contingent liability equivalent to one-quarter of GDP at the peak of the crisis—exacerbated perceptions of "too important to fail" (Goldstein and Veron, 2011). Failing firms may be resolved in a number of ways (see Appendix 15D), but in the 2007–09 crises, few creditors were forced to write down claims because of the risk of contagion. The shielding of creditors restored confidence more quickly, but at the cost of more moral hazard and the perpetuation of too-important-to-fail problem (and stretched sovereign balance sheets).

Countries need to implement measures that reduce moral hazard and that lower both the odds of a new systemic crisis and the effects it would have. Governments had to wean banks off their implicit government support, scale down deposit insurance schemes, and restore creditor discipline. For the longer term, they must also begin, through regulations and supervisory actions, to reduce incentives for complexity so as to facilitate restructuring in a crisis and diminish the expectations of bailouts and their adverse effects. Measures need to be well targeted and globally coordinated, yet flexible enough to reflect local factors. Examples include living wills and recovery and resolution plans; restrictions on the types of activity undertaken (such as the Volcker rule in the United States, which limits proprietary trading); a capital charge or levy on institutions commensurate with the systemic risk they create; eliminating government support provided to systemically important banks, including through carefully designed and monitored contingent capital or bail-in instruments, with clear triggers, so that losses are shared fairly; and reining in the proliferation of complex financial instruments. Policymakers will need to be cognizant, however, of possible unintended consequences given that many of these measures remain untested.

The enhanced frameworks and tools adopted by several countries to resolve complex bank, and sometimes nonbank, institutions are only a start; more progress is needed, especially on cross-border resolution. Since the 2007–09 crisis, several countries have adopted more effective resolution regimes for large financial institutions that allow losses to be borne by uninsured creditors, but more countries need to do so.[10] Much is yet to be done toward enhancing supervision of cross-border exposures and related risks. And in all cases, the ability of the new regimes to deal with actual failures of large, cross-border institutions remains an unknown.

CONCLUSIONS

The financial upheavals of 2007–09 exposed serious weaknesses in crisis management and resolution. In many ways, the crisis is ongoing and further analysis is needed, but this chapter provides some preliminary lessons on the basis of experience in 12 countries in the recent crisis and 17 more countries in past crises going back to 1991. The major lessons and the policies requiring urgent attention include those in the following areas:

- *The overall policy mix and sequencing.* Each of the major advanced economies dealt with the 2007–09 crisis differently, and except for the initial period, less decisively from the ways countries dealt with past crises. In the 2007–09 crisis, they quickly enacted accommodative monetary and fiscal policies and sustained them for extended periods. These measures helped reestablish confidence and stabilize economies. But unlike the responses in past crises, the governments made little effort to conduct in-depth diagnoses of banks' balance sheets and follow-on restructuring (removal of bad loans and other assets devalued by the crisis). The resulting persistent weaknesses at banks likely retarded economic recovery. The in-depth restructuring of weak financial institutions and nonperforming assets remain on the agenda in many countries for dealing with the 2007–09 crises. In designing responses

---

[10] In the United Kingdom, the Banking Act 2009 allows for early intervention using a wide array of tools to deal with failing banks. In Germany, a temporary regime was replaced by a permanent resolution framework for systemically important banks. The United States (through the 2010 Dodd-Frank Act) and several European countries (including Belgium) extended resolution regimes to cover systemically important nonbank financial institutions. Although progress is being made in the EU (e.g., in January 2011 the European Commission made proposals for crisis preparedness and cross-border resolution in the European Union, and in September 2012 it was agreed to pursue a banking union), important issues still remain to be agreed upon, including burden sharing, cross-border deposit insurance claims, secrecy laws, and other legal impediments.

to future crises, striking the right balance between containment and restructuring policies is a major policy challenge.

- *Institutional tools for resolution.* In the 2007–09 crisis, countries had little ability to wind down large cross-border banks and systemic nonbank financial institutions in an orderly fashion. The ongoing challenge is to design the framework—the institutional infrastructure—for such resolutions, including principles for burden sharing, to reduce moral hazard and enhance financial stability. Measures need to limit government bailouts proactively by providing greater capital and liquidity buffers and better cost-sharing arrangements with creditors in cases of distress. Establishing the framework is even more urgent today because concentration in the financial sector has increased.

- *The approaches to reducing systemic risks.* The 2007–09 crisis showed that systemic risk had built to cataclysmic levels during the preceding boom. Because the lenses through which markets and supervisors looked for such risk kept it mostly hidden, national and international bodies will need to provide for greater public transparency on exposures and other aspects of systemic risk to facilitate supervisors' work and enhance market discipline. Greater supervisory cooperation, including through supervisory colleges, will be needed. Developing methods for containing the buildup of systemic vulnerabilities will make a systemic crisis less likely and make it easier to deal with should it occur. Measures being considered include those that encourage institutions to reduce complexity or prohibit them from engaging in risky activities. The effectiveness of these measures and trade-offs in the efficient allocation of resources, however, require further analysis.

APPENDIX 15A. DEFINITIONS, DATA SAMPLE, AND FISCAL COSTS OF CRISES

Definition of Systemic Banking Crisis

A systemic crisis is defined as an episode of stress in the banking sector followed by significant policy intervention (Laeven and Valencia, 2010). Because stress is difficult to measure, a crisis is defined to be systemic when any three out of five commonly used crisis resolution policies are applied extensively: liquidity support, restructuring, asset purchases, significant guarantees, and nationalizations.

Sample of Recent and Past Crises

Episodes in 12 countries during the crisis of 2007–09 were identified as meeting the definition of a systemic crisis. Appendix Table 15A.1 shows the policy measures used in each country (all as of end-2009). Some crisis countries

APPENDIX TABLE 15A.1

Recent Crises *(all measures are as of end-2009)*						
Country	Extensive liquidity support	Significant restructuring costs	Significant asset purchases	Significant guarantees on liabilities	Significant nationalizations	Income level[1]
Austria	✓			✓	✓	A
Belgium	✓	✓		✓	✓	A
Denmark	✓			✓	✓	A
Germany	✓			✓	✓	A
Iceland	✓	✓		✓	✓	A
Ireland	✓	✓		✓	✓	A
Latvia	✓			✓	✓	E
Luxembourg	✓	✓		✓	✓	A
Netherlands	✓	✓		✓	✓	A
Ukraine	✓	✓			✓	E
United Kingdom	✓	✓	✓	✓	✓	A
United States	✓	✓	✓	✓	✓	A

Source: Laeven and Valencia, Chapter 2, in this volume.
Note: A = advanced economy; E = emerging market economy.

adopted additional measures after end-2009, some of which are noted in the text. Also, euro area periphery countries faced difficulties since, but interventions were limited as of 2009 and hence were not included in these comparisons.

The following systemic crises in emerging and advanced economies that took place between 1991 and the 2007–09 crises are used for illustrative comparisons: Nordic crises: Finland, Norway, and Sweden (all 1991); Latin American crises: Brazil (1994), Mexico (1994), and Jamaica (1996); Asian crises: Indonesia, Japan, the Republic of Korea, Malaysia, and Thailand (all 1997); and emerging markets crises: Colombia (1998), Ecuador (1998), the Russian Federation (1998), Turkey (2000), Argentina (2001), and Uruguay (2002). Because these crises are a subset of historical cases, summary statistics reported here can differ from those in cited references.

Fiscal Costs of Crises

For the crises that began in 2007, direct fiscal costs consist of fiscal outlays committed to the financial sector through end-2009. For each past crisis, direct fiscal costs are the total fiscal outlays during the episode. See Laeven and Valencia in this volume for country-specific figures.

APPENDIX 15B

Timeline of Events and Policy Responses

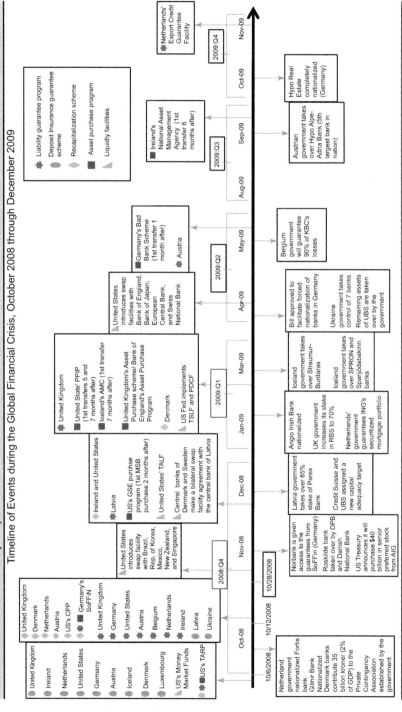

Timeline of Events during the Global Financial Crisis, October 2008 through December 2009

Source: IMF staff.

Note: AMC = asset management company; CPP = capital purchase program; DPB = Det Private Beredskab (Danish Bankers Association); GSE = government-sponsored entity (Fannie Mae and Freddie Mac); PDCF = Primary Dealer Credit Facility; PPIP = public-private investment program; SoFFiN = Special Financial Market Stabilization Funds; TALF = Term Asset-Backed Securities Loan Facility; TARP = Troubled Asset Relief Program; TSLF = Term Securities Lending Facility.

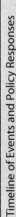

APPENDIX 15C

The ABCs of Crisis Resolution and Experiences in the 2007–09 Crisis

ABCs of Crisis Resolution	Experiences in the 2007–09 Crisis
Leadership and transparency. Appoint a single, accountable body with a clear mandate for financial stability and formal arrangements for cooperation with other agencies. Announce measures and procedures on a timely basis.	**Countries had a variety of different arrangements for coordination among authorities but improvements were needed.** Inadequacies were exposed in all regimes with respect to identifying systemic risks, managing information flows, assigning decision-making responsibility, and communicating transparently and promptly. In most countries, clear responsibilities for financial stability were neither collectively nor individually assigned to agencies. Legislation was drafted or enacted in several countries to set up specific bodies to identify and respond to financial stability risks (such as the Financial Stability Oversight Council in the United States).
International coordination. For crises with cross-border incidence, policy responses should be coordinated as much as possible across the spectrum of measures from intervention on individual institutions through to sector-wide programs and macroeconomic policy responses.	**Crisis containment measures were initially uncoordinated and, although coordination improved at the macro policy level, cross-border resolution remained an issue.** Deposit guarantees were raised to different levels on an uncoordinated basis across countries in the fall of 2008. However, guarantees were soon followed by joint interest rate cuts by several major central banks and a G-20 announcement on coordinated fiscal stimulus. Currency swap lines were provided by the U.S. Federal Reserve to the central banks of 14 countries. The resolution of cross-border firms proved to be very difficult, in most cases leading to uncoordinated decisions and suboptimal outcomes.
Diagnosis and analysis. Comprehensive and intrusive diagnostics of the depth and breadth of problems in the financial sector to identify insolvent banks should be undertaken. Financial institutions should continue to be monitored throughout the crisis, including, where necessary, strengthening regulatory reporting.	**Publishing the results of system-wide stress tests was a new feature of the 2007–09 crisis.** But many firms in the United States and Europe received capital injections from the government sector before the stress tests, suggesting the tests may have been used more as a crisis containment tool to address information asymmetries and uncertainty than as a diagnostic exercise to inform decision makers.
Protection of depositors. In addition to the protection of insured depositors, targeted and credible guarantees of creditors may be necessary to prevent contagion and facilitate the closure of weak banks. Wide creditor guarantees incur risk for the state.	**Targeted guarantees were widely deployed.** All of the 12 sample countries announced measures to enhance protection for retail depositors. Countries either fully guaranteed the majority of retail deposits or increased the coverage of their deposit insurance schemes. Eight out of the 12 countries additionally guaranteed other liabilities such as wholesale deposits. Blanket guarantees for all creditors were adopted only in Ireland whereas they were deployed in half of all previous crises in advanced economies.

As with past crises, the treatment of creditors was inconsistent with previously stated policy, with ongoing moral hazard consequences. Despite a small number of notable exceptions, many large financial institutions had to be nationalized with creditors (other than shareholders) made whole. Studies suggest that the too-big-to-fail subsidy increased as a result of these bailouts.

Conditions attached to recapitalization programs were initially less extensive than those applied during past crises, except in cases in which state-aid rules applied. Limits were placed on compensation to management and shareholders but "traditional" restructuring measures such as cost-cutting measures, downsizing, and forced writedown of shareholders reportedly were less prevalent, at least initially. In EU countries, such conditions were subsequently imposed as part of state aid approval. What was new during the 2007–09 crisis were the conditions placed on banks to extend new lending to support the economy, including targets on net lending to business customers.

Traditional asset management companies were less frequently deployed in the 2007–09 crisis in comparison with past crises. However, the asset management phase of the 2007–09 crisis is arguably still incomplete and AMC's may be less relevant for dealing with complex structured products. Instead asset guarantees were used extensively in the 2007–09 crisis. Asset guarantees were provided on both "good" and "bad" assets and were seemingly deployed primarily as crisis-containment tools to reassure creditors that banks were sufficiently capitalized rather than to restructure banks' balance sheets.

Resolution tools for dealing with failing financial firms were inadequate. Most countries did not have special administration regimes to allow early intervention before insolvency. Resolution options were therefore limited to liquidation, bailout, or nationalization if private sector solutions failed. Special resolution regimes that did exist generally did not extend to nonbank entities. Consequently, the U.S. authorities were unable to prevent Lehman Brothers from going into liquidation after efforts to sell the firm failed, and were forced to nationalize AIG days later.

Corporate insolvency regimes largely proved adequate. The majority of the crisis countries were advanced economies with well-established and funded judicial systems. However, economic recovery is incomplete, with some countries falling back into recessions, and further corporate insolvencies may follow.

Equitable and time-consistent burden sharing. Subject to preserving financial stability, the authorities should ensure consistent treatment of creditors independent of the size, complexity, and ownership of failed firms. This requires effective resolution regimes, intrusive supervision, and effective contingency planning.

Conditionality. Government support should be conditioned on the implementation of measures to address operational failure and ensure proper incentives, including improving banks' risk management; replacing management and owners; rigorous audit followed by prudent writedown of assets; measures to cut costs and eliminate excess capacity; and where necessary, closing or transferring part of an insolvent firm to another firm.

Impaired-asset management. Early action on impaired assets is essential to preventing creditor discipline from further eroding. A variety of institutional arrangements and techniques can be chosen to balance rapid resolution and recovery of the value of impaired assets. Removing nonperforming loans from banks' balance sheets may be necessary to address banks' stock problem.

Resolution regimes. Resolution regimes should be strengthened to ensure that failing financial institutions (including systemically important nonbank financial firms), can be resolved promptly and in ways that minimize risks to financial stability and government sector costs.

Corporate insolvency regimes. Orderly and effective insolvency regimes are needed to ensure predictable and equitable outcomes. Reforms may be needed in crises to establish fast-track procedures to deal with many failures.

Source: IMF staff.

APPENDIX 15D

Resolution Approaches, Restructuring, and Moral Hazard

Type of resolution	Bearer of costs	Implications for moral hazard	Comments
Liquidation of the whole bank, and insured depositors paid off.	Shareholders, uninsured creditors, and the Deposit Guarantee Fund (DGF).	No moral hazard.	This tool was rarely used in the 2007–09 crises (and in past crises) and only for small banks, because of concerns about contagion.
Good/bad bank split of the firm into liabilities that are protected to prevent contagion and to preserve financial stability plus good assets; and other liabilities and "bad assets." The former are sold to another firm and the latter are liquidated.	Shareholders, creditors, the DGF, and the authorities if significant wider liabilities are rescued.	To the extent that all (or most) uninsured creditors are left behind in the liquidation, the effect on moral hazard will be zero (or low). Shareholders and creditors left behind will receive what they would have received in whole-company liquidation (typically zero for shareholders). But if significant noninsured creditors are rescued, for example, wholesale deposits, then moral hazard will rise.	This transaction is called a purchase and assumption in the United States. The rescued liabilities and the good assets are sold to a third party, perhaps via the intermediate step of a bridge bank. This tool was mainly used for small banks in the 2007–09 crisis, with some exceptions.
Recapitalization by the government or **nationalization** of a failing bank.	Shareholders and the authorities. It is very unlikely that the creditors incur losses, unless the recapitalization fails and the firm is subsequently put into insolvency.	Creditors are bailed out, creating significant moral hazard. If shareholders are only diluted or receive compensation, moral hazard will be further exacerbated.	This tool was used extensively in the 2007–09 crisis (as in past crises).
Open bank assistance, which allows a failed firm to survive under original ownership. Assistance can take the form of • subsidized funding • subsidized asset guarantees or asset purchases • liability guarantees.	The authorities and shareholders, depending upon the terms of the assistance. For example, if assets are purchased at less than book value, or asset guarantees include a first-loss piece for the firm, shareholders incur losses.	Significant moral hazard. Creditors will only incur losses if not guaranteed and the firm is subsequently placed into liquidation. Worse still, shareholders remain owners of the firm and may not face significant losses, depending on the degree of subsidy in the government assistance.	These measures were extensively deployed in the 2007–09 crisis. These measures were typically deployed in conjunction with recapitalization by the authorities.

Source: IMF staff.

REFERENCES

Aghion, P., D. Hemous, and E. Kharroubi, 2009, "Credit Constraints, Cyclical Fiscal Policy and Industry Growth," NBER Working Paper No. 15119 (Cambridge, Massachusetts: National Bureau of Economic Research).

Borio, C., B. Vale, and G. von Peter, 2010, "Resolving the Financial Crisis: Are We Heeding the Lessons from the Nordics?" BIS Working Paper No. 311 (Basel: Bank for International Settlements).

Boudghene Y., S. Maes, and M. Schmeicher, 2010, "Asset Relief Measures in the EU—Overview and Issues" (unpublished; Brussels: European Commission Directorate-General for Competition).

Calomiris, C., D. Klingebiel, and L. Laeven, 2003, "Financial Crisis Policies and Resolution Mechanisms: A Taxonomy from Cross-Country Experience," in *Systemic Financial Distress: Containment and Resolution*, ed. by P. Honohan and L. Laeven (Cambridge, United Kingdom: Cambridge University Press).

Claessens, S., G. Dell'Ariccia, D. Igan, and L. Laeven, 2010, "Cross-Country Experience and Policy Implications from the Global Financial Crisis," *Economic Policy*, Vol. 62, pp. 269–93.

Claessens, S., D. Klingebiel, and L. Laeven, 2003, "Financial Restructuring in Banking and Corporate Sector Crises: What Policies to Pursue?" in *Managing Currency Crises in Emerging Markets*, ed. by M. Dooley and J. Frankel (Chicago: University of Chicago Press), pp. 147–80.

Crowe, C., and E. Meade, 2007, "Evolution of Central Bank Governance around the World," *Journal of Economic Perspectives*, Vol. 21, No. 4, pp. 69–90.

Djankov, S., C. McLiesh, and A. Shleifer, 2007, "Private Credit in 129 Countries," *Journal of Financial Economics*, Vol. 84, pp. 299–329.

Dooley, M., and J. Frankel, eds., 2003, *Managing Currency Crises in Emerging Markets*, Proceedings of a National Bureau of Economic Research conference (Chicago: University of Chicago Press).

Drees, B., and C. Pazarbasioglu, 1998, "The Nordic Banking Crises: Pitfalls in Financial Liberalization?" Occasional Paper No. 161 (Washington: International Monetary Fund).

Dziobek, C., and C. Pazarbasioglu, 1998, "Lessons from Systemic Bank Restructuring," Economic Issues Paper 14 (Washington: International Monetary Fund).

European Union (EU), 2008, "Declaration on a Concerted European Action Plan of the Euro Area Countries," Summit of the Euro Area Countries, October 12.

Fung, B., J. George, S. Hohl, and G. Ma, 2004, "Public Asset Management Companies in East Asia: A Comparative Study," Occasional Paper No. 3 (Basel: Bank for International Settlements).

Goldstein, M., and N. Veron, 2011, "Too Big to Fail: The Transatlantic Debate," Working Paper 495 (Brussels: Bruegel).

Hoelscher, D., and M. Quintyn, 2003, "Managing Systemic Banking Crises," IMF Occasional Paper No. 224 (Washington: International Monetary Fund).

Honohan, P., and L. Laeven, eds., 2005, "*Systemic Financial Crises: Containment and Resolution*" (Cambridge, United Kingdom: Cambridge University Press).

Huizinga, H., and L. Laeven, 2009, "Accounting Discretion of Banks during a Financial Crisis," European Bank Center Discussion Paper No. 2009-17 (Tilburg, Netherlands: Tilburg University).

Ishi, K., 2009, "Have the Right Lessons Been Learned from the Banking Crisis of the 1990s?" Attachment II of Sweden: 2009 Article IV Consultation, IMF Country Report 09/247 (Washington: International Monetary Fund).

Ingves, S., and G. Lind, 2008, "Stockholm Solutions," *Finance and Development*, Vol. 45, No. 4.

———, M. Shirakawa, J. Caruana, and G.O. Martinez, 2009, "Lessons Learned from Previous Banking Crises: Sweden, Japan, Spain and Mexico," Group of Thirty, Occasional Paper 79 (Washington: Group of Thirty).

International Monetary Fund (IMF), 2008, *Global Financial Stability Report*, October (Washington: International Monetary Fund).

———, 2010, *Global Financial Stability Report*, October (Washington: International Monetary Fund).

Klingebiel, D., 2000, "The Use of Asset Management Companies in the Resolution of Banking Crises," World Bank Research Working Paper 2294 (Washington: World Bank).

Laeven, L., and T. Laryea, 2009, "Principles of Household Debt Restructuring," Staff Position Note 9/15 (Washington: International Monetary Fund).

Laeven, L. and F. Valencia, 2008, "Systemic Banking Crises: A New Database," IMF Working Paper 08/224 (Washington: International Monetary Fund).

———, 2010, "Resolution of Banking Crises: The Good, the Bad, and the Ugly," IMF Working Paper 10/146 (Washington: International Monetary Fund).

———, 2011, "The Real Effects of Financial Sector Interventions during Crises," Working Paper 11/45 (Washington: International Monetary Fund).

Lindgren, C.-J., G. Garcia, and M.I. Saal, 1996, *Bank Soundness and Macroeconomic Policy* (Washington: International Monetary Fund).

Panetta, F., T. Faeh, G. Grande, C. Ho, M. King, A. Levy, F.M. Signoretti, M. Taboga, and A. Zaghini, 2009, "An Assessment of Financial Sector Rescue Programmes," BIS Paper No. 48 (Basel: Bank for International Settlements).

Reinhart, C., and K. Rogoff, 2009, *This Time Is Different: Eight Centuries of Financial Folly* (Princeton, New Jersey: Princeton University Press).

Stone, M., K. Fujita, and K. Ishi, 2011, "Should Unconventional Balance Sheet Policies Be Added to the Central Bank Toolkit?" Working Paper 11/145 (Washington: International Monetary Fund).

Syed, M., K. Kang and K. Tukuoka, 2009, "Lost Decade in Translation: What Japan's Crisis Could Portend about Recovery from the Great Recession," IMF Working Paper No. 09/282 (Washington: International Monetary Fund).

CHAPTER 16

The Economics of Bank Restructuring: Understanding the Options

AUGUSTIN LANDIER AND KENICHI UEDA

What is the best policy option for rescuing a troubled systemically important bank? Various plans have been proposed, some of which have already been implemented around the world. Examples include capital injections in the form of equity or hybrid securities (such as convertible debt or preferred shares), asset purchases, and temporary nationalizations. However, the various restructuring options are rarely evaluated and compared with each other based on a coherent theoretical framework. This chapter develops such a framework.[1]

Claims often heard in the public debate can be clarified and evaluated using this framework. Should bad assets be sold off before a bank is recapitalized? Should hybrid securities, such as preferred stock or convertible debt, be used rather than common stock in recapitalizations? Is it possible to restructure a bank balance sheet without resorting to a bankruptcy procedure and without involving public money? Is it better when taxpayers participate in a rescue plan to benefit from upside risk?

This chapter makes three main points:

- In principle, restructuring can be done without taxpayer contributions.

- If debt contracts cannot be renegotiated, taxpayer transfers are needed, but some schemes are more expensive than others.

- Once the relevant market imperfections are taken into account, restructuring is likely to require actions on both the liability and the asset sides.

The goal of restructuring is assumed to be to lower the probability of the bank's default with minimal taxpayer burden. The analysis starts with a simple frictionless benchmark, following Modigliani and Miller (1958). It then excludes the possibility of debt renegotiation. This approach illuminates a key conflict

---

The authors are deeply indebted to Olivier Blanchard and Stijn Claessens for numerous discussions. They would also like to thank Ricardo Caballero, Giovanni Dell'Ariccia, Takeo Hoshi, Takatoshi Ito, Nobuhiro Kiyotaki, Thomas Philippon, Philipp Schnabl, and many colleagues at the IMF for their helpful comments.

[1] If a bank is not systemically important, a government should apply standard procedures, such as those defined in the Prompt Corrective Action law in the United States.

between shareholders and debt holders. Later, more realistic assumptions, for example, the costs of financial distress and asymmetric information, are introduced.

In the frictionless framework, debt contracts can be renegotiated easily and the default probability of a bank can be lowered by transforming some debt into equity (debt-for-equity swap). This restructuring preserves the financial value of both debt and equity. Therefore, there is no need for public involvement to decrease the probability of default. In practice, however, restructuring is often difficult because of the speed of events, the dispersion of debt holders, and the potential systemic impact.

When debt contracts cannot be renegotiated, taxpayer transfers are necessary for a restructuring plan to be carried out. The debt holders see the value of their claim go up, thanks to a lower default probability. Absent government transfers, their gain equals the loss in equity value; shareholders would therefore oppose the restructuring.

Transfers vary depending on the plan. The level of transfers reflects the extent to which debt holders benefit from the restructuring. Most options are equivalent to a simple recapitalization in which the bank receives a subsidy conditional on the issuance of common equity. The transfer can be reduced if the proceeds of new issues are used to buy back debt. Restructuring involving asset sales turns out to require more transfers than does recapitalization.

Next the chapter examines how to design restructuring outside the Modigliani and Miller framework. Specifically, cases are examined in which restructuring can bring economic gains; for example, the bank can gain new customers who were previously apprehensive. The potential for private surplus can facilitate restructurings and reduce taxpayer cost. In maximizing the total surplus (i.e., private surplus and social benefits), both the pros and the cons of key strategies emerge. The restructuring plan should include contingent transfers so that a bank manager has an incentive to try to make the bank profitable. Up-front transfers should be minimized to prevent misuse of taxpayer money. Separating bad assets from a bank helps managers focus on standard bank management and can therefore increase productivity. Some assets may be underpriced compared with their fundamental value as a result of lack of liquidity and deep-pocket investors. In such cases, it may be optimal for the government to buy them. However, because the government often lacks the necessary expertise, it is advisable to use private experts to run an asset management fund or a nationalized bank. Finally, from a long-term perspective, managers and shareholders should be sufficiently penalized to prevent future financial crises.

The chapter also investigates the role of asymmetric information—when banks know more about their assets than the public does. In that case, banks are more reluctant to participate in a restructuring plan, so they would demand additional taxpayer transfers for their participation. This is because participating banks may be perceived by the market to have more toxic assets and to need more of a capital buffer. Such negative market perception induces a lower market valuation and higher financing costs. The use of hybrid instruments, such as convertible bonds or preferred shares, mitigates the problem because it does not signal that the issuer is in a dire situation. Asset guarantees turn out to be even more advantageous. To eliminate participation-related transfers, a compulsory program, if feasible, is best. In addition, the government should gather accurate information on underlying assets through rigorous bank examination and use it in designing restructuring options.

In summary, the best course for government is to combine several restructuring options to solve the multifaceted problem. On the one hand, rescue plans determine how the surplus from restructuring is shared among debt holders, equity holders, and taxpayers. On the other hand, the surplus from the restructuring itself varies depending on the plans because different plans change the behavior of the various parties. The best overall strategy involves both asset- and liability-side interventions.

The chapter proceeds as follows. The first section introduces the benchmark Modigliani-Miller framework. The second section assumes no scope for debt renegotiation and compares several restructuring options under a fixed restructuring surplus to achieve the target default probability of a bank. The third section examines, under various frictions, how the restructuring design affects the surplus. The fourth section discusses the willingness of banks to participate in a plan when asset quality is known only by bank managers. The fifth section analyzes other considerations, namely, political constraints and a worst-case scenario in which bankruptcy is inevitable. The penultimate section reports case studies for Switzerland, the United Kingdom, and the United States, and is followed by a conclusion.

A BENCHMARK FRICTIONLESS FRAMEWORK

The exercise begins by analyzing the restructuring of a bank in a simple framework in the spirit of Modigliani and Miller (1958), and shows that the bank can decrease its probability of default to any target level by converting some debt into equity. A restructuring can be carried out in such a way that neither equity holders nor debt holders are financially worse off.

Setup

A bank manages an asset A currently (time 0), which will have a final value A_1 next period (time 1). The final value A_1 is stochastic. It is drawn from a cumulative distribution function F. The capital structure at time 0 is debt with face value D, which needs to be repaid at time 1. Equity has book value E (see Figure 16.1, panel a). Absent restructuring, the probability of default of the bank at time 1, p, is the probability that the next-period value A_1 will be less than the debt obligation D, that is, $p = F(D)$ (see Figure 16.1, panel b).

a. Assets and liabilities of the bank

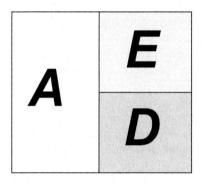

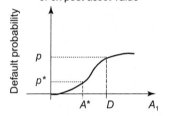
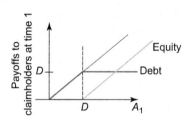

Figure 16.1 A Frictionless Framework

Source: Authors' illustration.

Note: A^* = asset value that achieves target default probablility; A_1 = final asset value; D = debt; E = equity; p = probability of default; p^* = target probability of default.

The assumptions of Modigliani-Miller are that markets are complete and efficient, without any information frictions. Under these assumptions, the sum of the market values of debt and equity is independent of the bank's capital structure and equals the market value of the asset: $V(A) = V(E) + V(D)$ (see Figure 16.1, panel c). This chapter also assumes $D < V(A)$, implying that the bank is not currently insolvent, but it does assume a positive default probability.[2] The market value of debt $V(D)$ is thus smaller than the book value D.

Assuming large social costs associated with default of a systemically important bank, the government's objective can be stated as lowering the default probability or, in practice, achieving a target default probability $p^* = F(A^*)$.[3] A bank-restructuring

---

[2] A more practical definition of insolvency is regulatory insolvency. Under regulatory solvency, certain positive equity is required to be solvent, that is, a bank is solvent if the book value of assets is large enough ($A > D + required\ capital$). However, the thrust of the analysis would not change; thus, a simple condition of solvency, $V(A) > D$, is used throughout this chapter.

[3] The marginal threshold of the realization of A_1 to achieve the target default probability is $A^* = F^{-1}(p^*)$. Put differently, if the debt is restructured to have face value A^*, then the default probability will be p^*. The social costs associated with default are assumed not to be sensitive to the recovery rate of debt in the event of bankruptcy.

problem amounts to finding a way to achieve $p = p^*$ starting from a higher default probability, $p > p^*$.

First Best: Voluntary Debt Restructuring

The government's objective is to decrease the probability of default p while making no one financially worse off. This objective is feasible by a change in the structure of claims, namely, the partial transformation of debt into equity. More specifically, a restructuring that leaves both debt and equity holders indifferent is the conversion of debt D into a combination of lower-face-value debt ($D' = A^*$) and an additional piece of equity with value $V(D) - V(D')$. This is a partial debt-for-equity swap. The new financial stake of the initial debt holders is worth $V(D') + (V(D) - V(D'))$, which is by design unchanged from the original market value of debt $V(D)$. The bank's future cash flows are unchanged; only the sharing rule for these cash flows has changed, so the total value of the bank is unchanged (following the Modigliani-Miller theorem). Because the value of the claims that belong to the initial debt holders is unchanged, the value of the equity of the initial shareholders remains the same as well.

Figure 16.2 illustrates the change in the liability structure induced by this partial debt-for-equity swap that makes the probability of default equal to p^*. The total payment promised to debt holders decreases from D to A^*. This is illustrated by the downward shift of the horizontal line for debt payoff in Figure 16.2. After the restructuring, a fraction of the equity is given to the initial debt holders to compensate them for the decrease in the value of debt. Thus, when the bank does not default, equity accounts for a larger fraction of the asset's payoffs. Graphically, the equity line shifts up. The full conversion of debt into equity against a fraction

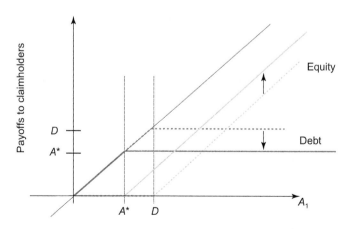

Figure 16.2 Debt-for-Equity Swap

Source: Authors' illustration.

Note: A^* = asset value that achieves target default probability; A_1 = final asset value; D = debt.

of equity would also be a solution to the restructuring problem. Either scheme can be implemented by means of a debt-for-equity swap.[4]

RESTRUCTURING WITH NO DEBT RENEGOTIATION

Although the proposed debt-for-equity swap is the first-best solution, it is often a difficult solution to implement in practice. A major reason is the speed of events, which leaves no time for negotiation. The possibility of a deposit run calls for quick resolution, while the dispersion of bank debt holders requires a lengthy negotiation process. An orderly bankruptcy might be the most efficient way to structure the renegotiation process, but might negatively affect other systemically important institutions. The discussion below assumes that the government wants to avoid such a bankruptcy procedure because of the potential systemic costs.

With no renegotiation of debt contracts and no help from the government, a restructuring that reduces the probability of default increases the value of the debt and thus decreases the value of the equity. Therefore, it will be opposed by shareholders and a restructuring will not happen unless the government provides subsidies in some form or makes participation compulsory. This section examines various possible restructuring options that do not involve renegotiation of the debt contracts. It also assumes that transactions with external parties other than the government are carried out at a fair price (i.e., reflecting expected discounted cash flows) and that markets are efficient. This means that, for these external parties, financial transactions must be zero net present value projects.

Many schemes are equivalent, though not all—some imply a higher recovery rate for debt in case of default than others. Asset sales, for example, are more expensive than subsidies to the issuance of common equity. The optimal scheme is a form of partial insurance on the asset's payoff. Changing the liability side by subsidized debt buyback is an option close to the optimal scheme.

Difficulty of Voluntary Restructuring

Without debt renegotiation and in the absence of transfers from the government, all restructuring that lowers the default probability p would be opposed by equity holders because such restructuring increases the value of debt at the expense of equity (the debt overhang problem; Myers, 1977). Debt holders are better off in every possible scenario—the default probability of a bank becomes lower and the recovery rate in the event of default becomes higher. The value of debt thus increases from $V(D)$ to $V'(D)$ and, without third-party involvement,

---

[4] This scheme is possible only when debt holders and equity holders negotiate freely and reach agreement easily. In practice, this amiability is difficult outside a bankruptcy regime. Zingales (2009) argues that this solution can be achieved by changing the bankruptcy law for banks. Note that in this truly frictionless framework, it is sufficient to prevent default with an ex post debt-for-equity swap that is triggered when the realized asset value is less than the debt obligation, $A_1 < D$. In other words, no ex ante restructuring is needed.

the increase in debt value is precisely compensated for by a decrease in equity value, $V'(E) - V(E) = -(V'(D) - V(D)) < 0$. The worse shape the bank is in initially, the larger $V(D) - V'(D)$ and the larger the loss imposed on shareholders. Shareholders of more distressed banks thus tend to be more reluctant to restructure.

Shareholders need to be either forced or induced in some way through government subsidies to approve such restructuring. Their approval is needed because they have control rights as long as the bank does not default. The transfer needed from the government is equal to the increase in the value of debt, $T = V'(D) - V(D)$. This transfer equals the expected discounted value of immediate and future payoffs from the government. Under this transfer, the value of equity remains unchanged. How this transfer varies across different restructuring schemes is now examined in detail.

Government Subsidy and Debt Recovery

All restructuring schemes that achieve a target default probability p^* must involve a subsidy from the government. The size of this subsidy determines the debt's degree of safety. From this perspective, among the schemes examined, asset sales appear to be the most costly for taxpayers. Whatever the final realization of A, asset sales result in the largest increase in debt recovery and therefore the largest transfer to debt holders. Figure 16.3 gives a preview of the results, illustrating the debt recovery schedule for various realizations of A_1 and various types of restructuring. Restructuring shifts the default threshold to the left (from D to A^*) and changes the payoff to the debt holders in case of default $D < A^*$. This new recovery schedule can vary depending on the restructuring plan (three different slopes in Figure 16.3). Restructuring that creates higher recovery schedules is more costly to taxpayers because it (indirectly) transfers more value to debt holders.

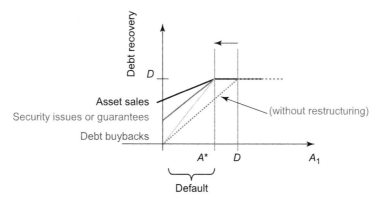

Figure 16.3   Restructuring and Debt Recovery

Source: Authors' illustration.

Note: A^* = asset value that achieves target default probability; A_1 = final asset value; D = debt.

State-Contingent Insurance: Optimal Subsidy

The restructuring scheme that minimizes the transfer from taxpayers is described first. The size of the transfer can be expressed graphically as a function of the asset's realization A_1 (Figure 16.4, panel a). Figure 16.4, panel b, shows the corresponding debt recovery. Because the objective is to decrease the probability of default, improving the recovery of debt in case of default is not needed. Graphically, default occurs in the left part of the figure, $A_1 < A^*$. The government should make no transfer in this region (Figure 16.4, panel a). This leaves debt recovery unchanged from the prerestructuring situation (Figure 16.4, panel b). When the realized asset value A_1 is between A^* and D, the bank needs a transfer $D - A_1$ from the government so that it is able to repay D to debt holders and avoid default. When the realized A_1 is above D, no subsidy is needed to avoid default. In other words, the optimal restructuring is a guarantee under which the government transfers money ex post only when the bank is in default but not far from solvency. This scheme would not provide any transfer to debt holders when default is inevitable ($A_1 < A^*$) or when the bank can repay debt on its own ($A_1 > D$).[5]

The relative cost to taxpayers of various types of restructuring depends on how close the schemes are to implementing this optimal debt-recovery schedule. The optimal scheme might be difficult to implement and calibrate in practice, but it provides three useful insights. First, to decrease the probability of default, the government does not have to subsidize the recovery rate for all the realized value of the assets. It should instead focus on avoiding default only when the bank is close to solvency. Second, it is not necessarily a bad deal that the taxpayers do not receive any upside or even any positive cash flow in exchange for their intervention. Some

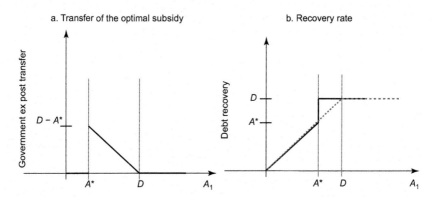

Figure 16.4 Minimizing the Transfer from Taxpayers

Source: Authors' illustration.

Note: A^* = asset value that achieves target default probability; A_1 = final asset value; D = debt.

---

[5] It is assumed that the social benefits from saving a systemically important bank are limited; thus, the government will not transfer funds beyond the upper limit $D - A^*$. However, if there is a need to transfer money to counterparties in case of default, a subsidy that gives higher debt recovery given default $A_1 < A^*$ may be optimal.

of the rescue schemes examined below occasionally provide payments to taxpayers. However, the optimal scheme never provides any payments to taxpayers, but its overall cost to taxpayers is the lowest. Third, more transfers could boost the share price, but a higher share price does not mean a good rescue plan from the point of view of taxpayers.

Recapitalization with Common Equity

One straightforward way of decreasing the default probability is to issue new equity and keep the proceeds as cash, which makes the debt less risky. Bankruptcy occurs then with $prob(A_1 + Cash < D)$, equivalently, $prob(A_1 < D - Cash)$ or $F(D - Cash)$. The minimum amount of cash that has to be raised is such that $p^* = F(D - Cash)$, that is, $Cash = D - A^*$. This is shown as the intercept of the debt-recovery schedule in Figure 16.5. For a given realization of asset value A_1 that forces the bank into default $(A_1 < A^*)$, the debt holders can recover cash in addition to the remaining assets, $D - A^* + A_1$.

Because default occurs less often and the recovery rate is higher, the value of debt increases from $V(D)$ to $V'(D)$. The new equity holders do not make or lose money by investing (efficient markets). Assuming no government subsidy, the gain of debt holders $V'(D) - V(D)$ is obtained at the expense of the old equity holders, who will lose exactly that amount. This implies that the equity holders would oppose the restructuring. Issuance of equity is dilutive for preexisting shareholders, not because an equally large pie is now divided among more shareholders—in fact, the pie is bigger because of the proceeds of the new equity issue—but because the debt holders receive more of the pie.

To make the restructuring acceptable to shareholders, the value of the equity should not decrease. To this end, a possible policy option is for the government

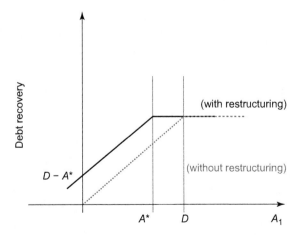

Figure 16.5 Recapitalization

Source: Authors' illustration.
Note: A^* = asset value that achieves target default probability; A_1 = final asset value; D = debt.

to give the bank cash in the amount of $V'(D) - V(D)$ conditional on the bank's issuance of equity of an amount $D - A^* - (V'(D) - V(D))$ at a fair price reflecting the expected discounted value of future payouts to shareholders. With the total new cash $D - A^*$, the probability of default becomes p^*. The market value of the debt jumps by $V'(D) - V(D)$ and the government loses exactly that amount, so that, as planned, shareholder value is unchanged (see Figure 16.5).

Recapitalization by Issuing Preferred Stock or Convertible Debt

Instead of issuing equity, banks could issue hybrid securities such as convertible debt or preferred stock.[6] This would not change the analysis of the previous section. In these cases, the debt-recovery schedule of initial debt holders is the same as in Figure 16.5, implying that the restructuring's impact on preexisting debt value, $V'(D) - V(D)$, and thus the transfer of the taxpayer, is the same as in a recapitalization through the issuance of equity.

To show that the recovery of preexisting debt is the same as in Figure 16.5, two cases are considered separately. In the first case, the new claims do not trigger default. This case applies to preferred stock or convertible debt with a conversion option at the issuer's discretion, given that the dividends do not have to be paid out (preferred stock) or the debt converted into equity (convertible debt) when the bank is unable to pay dividends or coupons. In this case, the capital that needs to be raised to achieve the target default probability $p = p^*$, and thus the recovery schedule of initial debt, remains the same as in the case of recapitalization with common equity. The second case involves the issuance of convertible debt, with the conversion not determined by the issuer (i.e., the conversion is automatic or at the holder's discretion) and seniority equal to that of preexisting debt.[7] The recovery rate is in proportion to total debt (*pari passu*)—so the slope of the recovery is the same as in the equity issue case (see Figure 16.6, panel a). At the same time, the trigger point for defaults after restructuring is set to be A^* as in the equity issuance case. Thus, the recovery of preexisting debt is exactly the same as in the equity issuance case.[8]

To make equity holders willing to accept the restructuring, the government has to compensate them with a conditional transfer identical to the one needed for an equity issuance. Total wealth before and after the restructuring remains the same (conservation of value). That is, the sum of the changes in wealth of initial equity holders, initial debt holders, new claim holders, and taxpayers is zero. Because new claims are issued at a fair price, the new claimholders' wealth is

---

[6] Issuance of new (nonconvertible) debt would increase the default probability and is thus not a possible restructuring scheme.

[7] Conversion options in hybrid securities are further discussed below.

[8] It is more costly for taxpayers to issue convertible subordinated debt (i.e., junior to preexisting debt) with conversion not determined by the issuer. In this case, although the trigger point is still the same as in Figure 16.6, panel a, the preexisting debt holders will be given priority in a default. This extra gain imposes an extra cost on taxpayers.

a. Same seniority convertible

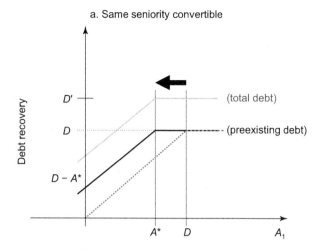

b. Recapitalization with hybrid securities

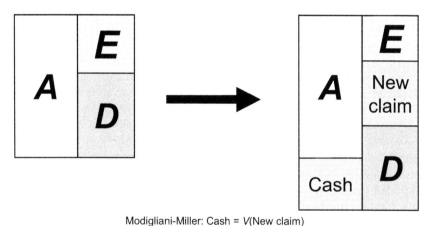

Modigliani-Miller: Cash = V(New claim)

Figure 16.6 Issuance of Convertible Securities

Source: Authors' illustration.

Note: A^* = asset value that achieves target default probability; A_1 = final asset value; D = debt; D' = debt after restructuring. Modigliani and Miller (1958) indicate that Cash = V(New claim) in panel b.

unchanged. Provided the restructuring needs to leave initial equity holders' wealth unchanged, the taxpayer transfer should be equal to the change in debt value. This is the same as in an equity issue.

Subsidized Debt Buybacks

When equity or other securities are issued, banks do not have to keep the proceeds on their balance sheets and might as well use them to buy back some debt. This decreases the taxpayer transfers required to implement $p = p^*$. The bondholders that sell to the bank are not assumed to be naive—they know that the value of the debt will rise as a result of the restructuring and therefore agree to sell only at the fair price that reflects the postrestructuring value of their claim.[9] The fraction α of outstanding debt that needs to be bought is such that $(1 - \alpha)$ $D = A^*$, and the remaining debt contracts are untouched, so the new aggregate face value of the debt is $(1 - \alpha) D = A^*$. After the announcement, the value of the initial debt should increase from $V(D)$ to $V'(D)$, reflecting the lower default probability after the restructuring. Out of this initial debt, a fraction a is bought back by the bank at a value $\alpha V'(D)$, while a fraction $(1 - \alpha)$ remains outstanding, with market value $(1 - \alpha) V'(D)$.

To leave the equity holders indifferent, the government needs to subsidize the buyback. In exchange for the transfer, the bank should be willing to issue equity to buy back a fraction α of the debt. Equivalently, the government can directly buy debt at the postrestructuring market price and convert it into equity at a conversion rate that leaves equity holders indifferent.[10] As in the other schemes, the optimal size of the government transfer is equal to the increase in debt holders' wealth created by the restructuring, $V'(D) - V(D)$. Regardless of whether they keep their bonds or sell them, all initial debt holders receive this gain on a *pro rata* basis. The remaining debt is a fraction $(1 - \alpha)$ of the initial debt. The gains of the remaining debt holders are $(1 - \alpha)$ of the gains of all the initial debt holders. Thus, the transfer by the government can be calculated by rescaling the realized recovery of the remaining debt by a factor $1/(1 - \alpha)$ (the upper line in Figure 16.7). This total implied recovery reflects the restructuring effects on the full initial debt.

This scheme is less costly for taxpayers than a recapitalization in which cash from new issues is kept on the balance sheet. Indeed, this scheme's recovery schedule (upper line of Figure 16.7) is lower than the recovery schedule of the recapitalization in Figure 16.5. Economic intuition suggests that buying back debt and converting it into equity is closer to the first-best solution (i.e., debt-for-equity swap agreed to by debt holders). Altering the liability structure decreases the size of the transfer required from the government (Bulow and Klemperer, 2009).

Simple Asset Guarantees

An alternative way to decrease the default probability to p^* is for the government to offer full or partial insurance on the bank's assets using simple asset guarantees. To limit the cost to the taxpayers, such insurance can have a cap (partial insurance). For instance, to reach a default probability p^*, the government can insure against the value of assets falling below D, with a maximum transfer of $D - A^*$.

---

[9] This is a conservative assumption in evaluating taxpayer transfers, because it implies that the bank is not able to buy back debt secretly and restructure afterward by surprise.

[10] This scheme is equivalent to finding some debt holders that agree to convert into equity at the postrestructuring price, which is higher than the current market price but below the face value.

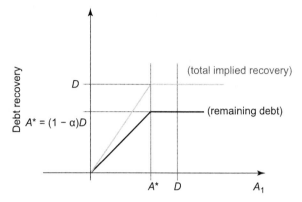

Figure 16.7 Debt Buyback

Source: Authors' illustration.
Note: A^* = asset value that achieves target default probability; A_1 = final asset
value; D = debt; α = fraction of debt bought by bank by issuing new equity.

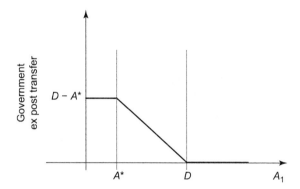

Figure 16.8 Transfer under Capped Asset Guarantee

Source: Authors' illustration.
Note: A^* = asset value that achieves target default probability; A_1 = final asset
value; D = debt.

This guarantees that the bank will be able to repay its debt fully as long as $A_1 \geq A^*$. In contrast to the optimal scheme, however, this transfer will be paid even in the worst cases, $A_1 < A^*$ (see Figure 16.8).

This scheme leaves the equity value unchanged from the prerestructuring situation (all transfers benefit debt holders) and has exactly the same cost for the government as a recapitalization that involves subsidizing new securities issues (equity or hybrids). This outcome occurs because the implied debt recovery is identical to that in Figure 16.5. Compared with the optimal partial insurance scheme discussed previously, this plan is more costly because it makes debt recovery higher in a default. A full insurance scheme (without the transfer cap) would cost taxpayers more because it would involve higher payments in the worst cases, $A_1 < A^*$.

It is always optimal for taxpayers to insure total assets as opposed to a specific subset of them (e.g., mortgage-related debt only). Future payoffs of a subset of assets do not perfectly predict the default of the bank as a whole. Thus, higher transfers (as a precautionary cushion) are necessary to achieve the same default probability.

Caballero's Scheme

Ricardo Caballero (2009) proposes the following: If the bank issues new equity in the amount of $D - A^*$ to private investors, the government provides a loss guarantee for the new equity owners by promising to buy back the new equity at a fixed price in the future. That is, the government distributes free put options to the new equity holders. The floor price can be set by backward induction. Specifically, the government transfer should be set to equal the gains of debt holders, $V'(D) - V(D)$. This makes the current equity holders willing to adopt this scheme because it leaves their wealth unchanged.

With regard to transfer by the government, Caballero's scheme is equivalent to the subsidized recapitalization with common equity (Figure 16.5) because it implements the same debt recovery schedule, $D - A^* + A_1$. It differs from the subsidized equity issues in that it requires no up-front transfer by the government.

Above-Market-Price Asset Sales

Another alternative is to sell a fraction a of the assets to the government at an overvalued price with markup m, that is, $(1 + m) a V(A)$, to achieve the target default probability $p = p^*$ without dilution for shareholders.[11] The proceeds of the sale are again assumed to be kept as cash on the balance sheet. It turns out that the government transfer needed for these asset sales is larger than for all the mechanisms considered so far.

To see this, note that the new assets owned by the bank are cash and remaining old assets, $(1 + m) a V(A) + (1 - a) A$, which have higher expected value and lower risk than the original assets A (see Figure 16.9, panel a). Because default occurs less often than in the do-nothing case, the value of the debt increases by $V'(D) - V(D)$. This jump is larger than in the case of recapitalization with common equity, with the same default probability p^*, because the recovery rate for every realization A_1 is larger.[12] This is illustrated by a simple graph showing that the slope of the recovery schedule in the default zone is now $(1 - a)$ instead of 1

---

[11] The parameters α and m can be picked as the solutions of two equations. The first equation states that the probability of default is p^*, $(1 + m) a V(A) + (1 - a) A^* = D$. The second equation states that the negative net present value of the government's injection covers the increase in the value of debt, $a m V(A) = V'(D;a) - V(D)$. The new value of debt, $V'(D;a)$, depends on the sales fraction a.

[12] The probability of default is equal to $prob((1 - a) A_1 < D - cash)$, equivalently, $prob (A < (D - a V(A))/(1 - a))$. Hence, the required fraction of assets a should solve $(1 - a) A^* = D - a V(A)$. For a given realization of asset value A_1 that makes the bank default $(A_1 < A^*)$, the debt holders recover cash $a V(A)$ and liquidation value $(1 - a) A_1$, that is, $D - (1 - a) (A^* - A_1)$, which is more than in the equity issue case, $D - (A^* - A_1)$.

a. Assets and liabilities after asset sales of a fraction *a*

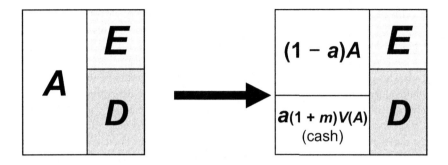

b. Debt recovery after asset sales of a fraction *a*

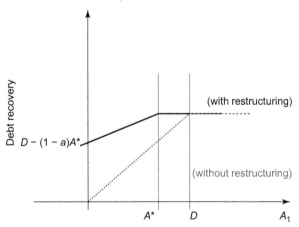

Figure 16.9   Above-Market-Price Asset Sales

Source: Authors' illustration.
Note: A^* = asset value that achieves target default probability; A_1 = final asset value; a = fraction of assets bought by government at an overvalued price; D = debt; E = equity; m = markup on assets.

(see Figure 16.9, panel b). It is irrelevant whether the government or private investors hold the assets, as long as the government subsidizes the price by a markup m so that it provides the subsidy required to compensate equity holders.

Sachs's Proposal

Sachs's (2009) proposal is a variant of asset sales. Instead of using a market price, Sachs proposes to sell a fraction of assets at book value to the government to avoid immediate write-downs, but with a condition that requires the bank to pay the government's losses when the assets are sold off later (recourse condition). Sachs proposes to use newly issued equity to compensate the government for the later losses. More specifically, the government would hold warrants entitling it to receive common stock equal in value to the eventual loss from the sale of the assets. The current equity holders would bear the costs through the dilution.

This plan includes a hidden subsidy from the government to debt holders. The probability of default is indeed now lower and the recovery rate higher. The government does not recover anything unless all debt has been repaid, because the value of the equity is zero in a default. However, equity holders become worse off under this plan. On the one hand, if the asset value turns out to be lower than the book value, equity holders face the same payoff as in the do-nothing case—the government receives the difference between the book value and the realized value. On the other hand, if the asset value turns out to be higher than the book value, the initial equity holders receive only the initial book value. Therefore, the impact of the plan on the value of the equity is negative: equity holders would oppose it.

Combining Several Schemes

A bank-restructuring plan can be designed by combining multiple schemes, such as asset sales with recapitalization. As long as banks have to participate in all schemes or none, the overall transfer matters, but not the origin of the transfer. For example, a higher asset sales price can be compensated for by a lower subsidy to new equity issues. However, if banks can choose to participate in some schemes but not others, subsidies must be chosen optimally on a scheme-by-scheme basis rather than as a whole.

PRIVATE AND SOCIAL SURPLUS FROM RESTRUCTURING

The future cash flows of a bank can be thought of as a pie shared between shareholders and debt holders. Restructuring can increase the size of this pie. To this end, the government needs to pay attention to the various stakeholders' payoffs and incentives. For example, decreasing the probability of default might attract customers who were previously worried about the bank's high probability of failure. This potential private surplus can facilitate restructuring and reduce or even eliminate the need for transfers from taxpayers. Contrary to the clear-cut picture that emerges from the previous section, an optimal restructuring plan is no longer easily identified. Actual plans may need to combine features of various schemes considered so far. For example, relying exclusively on asset guarantees might diminish managerial incentives to optimize ex post asset payoffs, but relying exclusively on ex ante cash injections might create opportunities for managers to increase their own private benefits.

Key Concepts

Costs of Financial Distress

A high probability of default is widely recognized to reduce a firm's total value (the value of equity plus liabilities). A bank is in financial distress when this decrease in value becomes economically significant. The exposition will associate financial distress with a probability of default $p > p^*$. A small fraction of the costs of financial distress is composed of the direct, ex post costs of bankruptcy (e.g., legal fees), but a large fraction is composed of indirect, ex ante costs. For example, depositors, interbank market counterparties, and employees tend to avoid a bank close to bankruptcy. Managerial attention might be diverted to keeping the company afloat rather than managing the business. In addition, some positive-value projects, such as new lending opportunities, may not be undertaken by a financially distressed bank,[13] which reduces the total value of the firm (debt overhang).[14] All in all, lowering the default probability of a bank (from p to p^*) can create some extra value, called the *private restructuring surplus*.

A parsimonious way to introduce the potential gains from restructuring is to assume that when the probability of default is higher than p^*, the ex post payoff of assets becomes less than its potential by an amount C.[15] The restructuring is then a positive-sum game over the surplus C to be shared between debt and equity holders. It is difficult to quantify this surplus for a bank, but the corporate finance literature estimates that for a typical nonfinancial company the costs of financial distress are about 10 percent to 23 percent of ex post firm value (Andrade and Kaplan, 1998). The surplus can be generated if the default probability becomes less than p^*. Because there is a private surplus (C) to share, the incentives to find an agreement through renegotiation are higher than in the frictionless case.

Social Benefits and Government Participation

Restructuring a systemically important bank is likely to bring aggregate economic gains, in particular when it is near collapse.[16] The magnitude of the *social benefit B* determines the upper limit of government's willingness to pay for a restructuring plan. The social benefit depends on how much other banks are affected by the bank's failure (putting the functioning of the payment system at risk) and on how unexpected the default event is.[17]

---

[13] A significant fraction of the value generated by these projects would go to the debt holders, whereas the costs would be fully paid by the equity holders. Because the latter have the control rights, the bank will not finance these projects (Myers, 1977). There is a vast amount of literature on the costs of financial distress and debt overhang, for example, summarized in Tirole (2006).

[14] Liquidity policies aim to reduce the cost of financial distress and may indirectly reduce the probability of default. Examples include accommodating monetary policy (both conventional and unconventional measures), loss guarantees for debt holders, and (implicit) subsidies for new lending. Such policies are outside the scope of this chapter.

[15] In other words, the cumulative density function of default probability F shifts to the right when a restructuring occurs, and becomes $F'(\bullet) = F(\bullet + C)$.

[16] A key risk is the collapse of the decentralized payment system (Rochet and Tirole, 1996).

[17] Government also has a direct stake in the bank, given that it typically provides deposit insurance.

Allowing for government intervention, restructuring a bank becomes a positive-sum game in which the total surplus $S = C + B$ is shared among three parties: equity holders, debt holders, and government. There can be three cases:

- If the private restructuring surplus for a bank is more than the improvement in debt value caused by the restructuring, $C > V'(D) - V(D)$, government intervention is not needed. The government should resist attempts by the other stakeholders to extract a subsidy.

- If government intervention is needed, the government is willing to pay a transfer T as long as the aggregate benefit is bigger than this transfer, $B > T$. The minimum cost for the government to achieve $p = p^*$ is $V'(D) - V(D) - C$, that is, the change in debt value net of the private surplus created by the restructuring.

- If the social benefits are small, $B < V'(D) - V(D) - C$, the aggregate surplus is still positive but too small to leave the debt contract unchanged and make both equity and the government better off. In this case, the government needs to organize renegotiation of the debt contract to reach a mutually beneficial restructuring.

Endogenous Surplus and Restructuring Design

Neither the private nor the social surplus created by decreasing the bank's default probability are purely exogenously given, but are affected by the design of the restructuring plan. Among the various schemes that achieve the target default probability $p = p^*$, those that maximize the restructuring surplus $B + C$ are the most efficient—they will minimize the transfer required from taxpayers—and thus should be pursued.[18] Several relevant frictions are analyzed below, such as the allocation of talent and managerial incentives. These frictions should be taken into account when designing a restructuring plan.

Allocation of Talent

Span of control and attention. To increase bank managers' productivity, it may be useful to remove toxic assets from a bank, either through asset sales or by splitting a bank into a "good" bank and a "bad" bank. Removing distressed assets from the managers' span of control allows them to focus their attention on typical bank operations, without spending much time on bad-asset management, which other specialists, such as vulture-fund managers and bankruptcy lawyers, can handle with more expertise.

---

[18] In fact, the optimal p^* can be determined by maximizing total surplus S as a function of restructuring design, taking into account the optimal bank capital structure, payment-system implications, and macroeconomic consequences.

Expertise. Managerial decisions should be in the hands of agents equipped with the appropriate level of expertise and experience. This concern is particularly relevant when public control is involved in a restructuring. The mechanisms through which managers are appointed and monitored should be carefully designed when the government inherits some control rights. This principle should apply to both banks and asset management companies. In other words, bank restructuring, particularly asset sales, should involve some form of public-private partnership. One way to select managers in a transparent and efficient way (i.e., without leaving them excessive rents) is to auction off the management contracts to a predetermined group of professional investors who meet certain standards of quality.

Moral Hazard (Hidden Actions)

Free cash flow (*looting of subsidies*). Injecting public money up front, before the assets' payoffs are realized, may offer bank managers an unnecessary opportunity to use public money for their private benefit, such as larger bonuses and perks. In addition, shareholders may demand more dividend payments. To reduce this problem, government should try to use ex post rather than ex ante transfers. For example, asset guarantees are immune to this ex ante looting possibility because they do not provide managers and shareholders with an opportunity to misuse public money.

Incentives to run a restructured bank. Bank managers should be given incentives to maximize the final payoff A_1. For example, asset guarantees may reduce managerial incentives to maximize the assets' payoffs A_1 as well as shareholders' incentives to monitor managers. The implications of this concern are thus the opposite of the previous one. The optimal solution depends on the relative importance of both frictions. A reverse problem occurs in Sachs's (2009) proposal, in which assets are bought at face value by the government and banks commit to pay the losses ex post—a full guarantee by banks about ex post payoffs might provide poor incentives to the government or the manager of the asset management company to maximize asset liquidation values.

Concerns about the Future

Positive medium-term effects of convertibles. A restructuring plan should be evaluated not only for its effect on the following period but on subsequent periods as well. The plan can minimize the costs of financial distress in the future by including a plan of action if the bank's outlook were to deteriorate further. In particular, adding a convertible feature to new debt-like claims enhances surplus because it can be seen as an automatic restructuring plan for future periods. Suppose, for example, that a bank raises capital in the initial period through convertible debt, but that the default probability in the future turns out to be higher than expected. In this case, the bank (the issuer) would convert the convertible debt to common equity, thereby reducing the default probability in the future (Stein, 1992).

Long-term impact. To prevent future crises, it is important to recognize the long-term effect of a restructuring plan. The moral hazard problem inherent in too-big-to-fail institutions is increased if the punishment received by managers and equity holders (and then bondholders) was small and transfers from taxpayers were large.

Undervaluation Resulting from Limits of Arbitrage

So far the analysis has assumed efficient markets, such that market valuation $V(A)$ always coincides with the fundamental value of assets, $J(A)$ (i.e., the discounted value of future cash flows). However, the market does not always price assets at their fundamental value. Undervaluation of assets does not necessarily stem from irrational behavior of market participants. It can result from a lack of deep-pocket arbitrageurs. The price of an asset depends on liquidity constraints of market participants and can drop following negative shocks to the liquidity available for funding. Because the government is less constrained, such limits of arbitrage in the market may create a situation in which the market price of the asset $V(A)$ is lower than the pricing by the government $V^{GOV}(A)$. The difference in pricing creates a motive to trade between market participants and the government. The surplus from restructuring a bank should include this arbitrage gain to the government, $V^{GOV}(A) - V(A)$.

If they are indeed undervalued in the market, toxic assets might be bought by the government above the market price but below their fundamental value, with a net gain from the point of view of the taxpayers. The arbitrage gains are largest if the government purchases the most-underpriced assets from banks. The arbitrage gains of the government are smaller if its claims on the banks or on the vehicles holding toxic assets are more debt-like than equity-like. A debt claim's payoff is capped, and therefore does not vary with the underlying asset's final payoff when it is large. By contrast, an equity claim's final payoff keeps increasing with the underlying asset's payoff, allowing the arbitrage to be large. This is also the case for a highly distressed debt instrument that behaves like equity. If the government relies on private investors to purchase toxic assets from banks at their fundamental value, the government may use a part of the potential arbitrage gains $V^{GOV}(A) - V(A)$ as an incentive for private managers to ensure their participation.

When computing the fundamental value of an asset, the same cost of capital should be applied, whether by a private market participant or by the government. It is *not* the cost at which debt can be issued by the entity but the cost that reflects the risks of the specific asset. In the current context, both the government and market participants should value a bank at the same fundamental value $J(A)$—the sum of future profits discounted by the risk premium associated with assets, but without including a liquidity premium associated with the financing constraints of a specific entity. The arbitrage gains, if any, exist because the market participants cannot purchase at this fundamental value as a result of funding-liquidity constraints, not because the fundamental value for the government is different from the fundamental value for the market participants (the cost-of-capital fallacy).

PARTICIPATION ISSUES UNDER ASYMMETRIC INFORMATION

When the asset quality of banks is unknown to market participants but known to managers, participation in a restructuring plan tends to signal negative information about asset quality. This makes banks reluctant to participate in a plan unless persuaded by a high subsidy. This reluctance comes in addition to the reluctance induced by the debt-overhang problem analyzed previously. The additional subsidy required to overcome the signaling problem can be reduced if the plan uses asset guarantees or hybrid securities rather than equity issues. A compulsory program, if feasible, reduces the taxpayer burden. Rigorous bank examination can also mitigate the problem if the results can be communicated credibly to market participants.

Recapitalization with Asymmetric Information on across-Bank Asset Quality

In the presence of asymmetric information, managers have private information on the fundamental quality of their assets $J(A)$.[19] The market values the bank's assets at the average quality $V(A)$. If private information could credibly be made public, high-quality banks would be valued above market value. Otherwise, the information gap remains.

Voluntary Participation

The analysis now turns to inducing banks to participate in a recapitalization plan. Assume there are two types of banks: one with high-quality assets and the other with low-quality assets. The focus is on the case in which even banks with high-quality assets need restructuring. The probabilities of default of low-quality banks (p_L) and high-quality banks (p_H) are both higher than the threshold level, $p_L > p_H > p^*$.[20] The goal of the government is to make sure that both types of systemically important banks achieve the (same) target level of default probability p^* while minimizing taxpayer transfers to those banks.

When banks participate voluntarily in a restructuring plan that involves claims issued to private investors, managers of high-quality banks demand high subsidies from the government because the high-quality bank cannot signal

---

[19] How a bank evaluates securities and business loans is difficult to know. Under the current accounting rules, even securities with market prices do not need to be evaluated at the market price (they can be "marked to model"). Moreover, the composition of assets is also difficult to know, at least in real time.

[20] The assumption is not restrictive. The case in which high-quality banks are healthy (i.e., $p_H < p^*$) can be analyzed in a similar fashion.

their true value. Thus, when issuing new financial claims on assets based on market perception, existing shareholders would bear an unfair burden: Because new claim holders would price the new claims below their fundamental value, the issue would take place at a discount, at the expense of existing shareholders. This discount must be compensated for in the transfers the government provides.

Without a high subsidy, high-quality banks would opt out of the plan. Given this behavior by high-quality banks, even low-quality banks would not participate in the plan. If they participated, their identity would be revealed and their assets would be valued at their true, low level $J(A_L)$. This would further increase the cost of their financial distress.[21]

Therefore, the government needs to pay a high subsidy to induce all banks to participate in the plan. As a result, low-quality banks would be oversubsidized, benefiting from an informational rent. At the same time, high-quality banks would end up overrecapitalized by the plan because they would receive the same treatment as the low-quality banks.[22]

Role of Hybrid Securities

To induce voluntary participation in a plan involving the issuance of new equity, the subsidy from taxpayers would have to be high—the information gap between the fundamental value and the market value of the equity is large for a high-quality bank. Debt would be an ideal claim to issue, because the gap is small as a result of its flat payoff shape.[23] Unfortunately, issuing debt is not useful given that the goal of restructuring is to decrease the default probability. However, hybrid debt-like claims can be used to decrease taxpayer costs because their value is less sensitive to private information than is the value of equity. In addition, hybrid securities such as convertible notes, subordinated debt, and preferred shares can be counted, at least partially, as regulatory capital.

- *Convertible notes* can be seen as essentially "backdoor equity" if the exercise of the conversion option is mandatory or at the discretion of the holder. Convertible notes are a way to issue equity while reducing the information-based cost of equity issues. For a specified period (typically, a few to several years), convertible notes have the payoffs of a debt contract and can be converted after that at the discretion of the holder into a specified number of equity shares. Figure 16.10 illustrates the final payoff of a convertible

---

[21] Negative market perception translates into a high financing cost in the interbank market and even a possible bank run. A similar situation was analyzed first by Majluf and Myers (1984).

[22] Although it is not always possible, the government could save some informational costs by differentiating between two types of banks in a separating equilibrium in which low-quality banks self-select into equity-based recapitalization that does not attract high-quality banks. However, the costs of asymmetric information would not be removed completely because the issuance of equity by low-quality banks occurs at a high financing cost, which would need to be compensated for. A separating equilibrium would require a menu of contracts, which is quite sensitive to distributional assumptions on asset quality among banks and are difficult to implement in practice. We therefore refrain from the analysis.

[23] Debt is said to be less information sensitive, whereas equity is information sensitive.

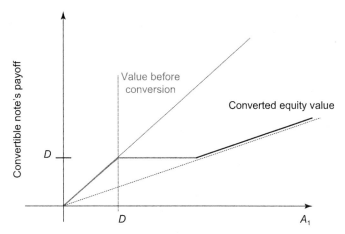

Figure 16.10   Convertible Note

Source: Authors' illustration.

Note: A^* = asset value that achieves target default probability; D = debt.

note, with conversion at time 1 at the holder's discretion. Notations are identical to those in the section titled "Restructuring with No Debt Renegotiation," but the payoff is shown for one unit of the convertible note with a normalized face value of one. The converted equity value of the security is depicted on the right side of the figure. The slope of this part of the payoff line is proportional to the conversion ratio (i.e., the number of shares each convertible note becomes).

Unlike the issuance of additional debt, issuing convertibles allows the probability of default to decrease because the cash raised by issuing the convertible is the value of the debt portion plus the equity portion of the convertibles' future payoffs. If the equity portion is large enough, the amount of cash raised is larger than the promised debt payment D, so the issue decreases the probability of default. The choice of the conversion ratio needs to solve a trade-off: on the one hand, the higher the conversion ratio, the lower the probability of default, because more cash is raised initially; on the other hand, when the conversion ratio is lower, the payoff is flatter overall and therefore less sensitive to information on the final payoff. In line with theory, stock market reactions to convertible issues are typically much less negative than for equity issues. If the conversion is automatic after a certain time, rather than left to the discretion of the holder, the equity feature of the convertible is stronger (everything else equal). Thus the signaling cost is higher.[24]

---

[24] If the option or timing of conversion is at the discretion of the issuer, the issuer will convert in bad times, not in good times, so that the convertible issue will lose its signaling virtues. This contrasts with the benefit under the other objective, because it is clearly a good instrument for a bank in distress, especially from a medium-term perspective (see "Recapitalization by Issuing Preferred Stock or Convertible Debt" earlier in the chapter).

- *Preferred shares* essentially work as a credit line: payments are fixed but can be skipped, in which case they accumulate at a certain rate. This type of claim is clearly less information sensitive than equity is (because payments are fixed) but more sensitive than debt is (the firm can skip payments when in distress). Therefore, the costs to initial shareholders of the bank issuing preferred shares should be lower than for its issuing common equity. Note that features of preferred shares and convertibles (or any hybrids) can be combined in practice.

Optimality of Asset Guarantees or State-Contingent Transfers

The cost of asymmetric information can be mitigated if the government proposes transfers that do not involve the issuance of new securities and that are contingent on the realization of asset values. From the point of view of asymmetric information frictions, among the restructurings considered so far, asset guarantees, either the optimal partial insurance scheme or the second-best capped transfer contingent on default, appear to dominate all restructuring plans involving the issuance of a claim on the assets. If a plan does not ask anything from banks in return, every bank will participate in the plan (no signaling). The government should compute A^* using the payoff distribution of the low-quality bank. By doing so, it overinsures the high-quality banks as in recapitalization cases (they will have a default probability lower than p^*), but there is no need to overtransfer to low-quality banks, unlike under recapitalization cases in which the low-quality banks benefit from an informational rent (subsidy to compensate for the stigma of issuing equity).

Compulsory Programs

The costs associated with asymmetric information stem from the need to ensure that banks voluntarily participate when participation is regarded as a bad signal about the quality of a bank's assets. However, the government does not need to use a voluntary program. Rather, it can use a compulsory program targeting a specific set of banks (e.g., mandatory equity issuance as proposed by Rajan, 2008; and Diamond and others, 2008). By doing so, the government can largely mitigate the asymmetric information problem. A compulsory program, however, may need specific changes in the legislation and might not be feasible when systemic risk is imminent.

Asset Sales with within-Bank Adverse Selection ("Lemons" Problem)

Some bank assets are of higher quality than others, and managers have private information on their quality. If given the opportunity, banks will sell lower-quality assets. The government should factor in this behavior and pay only the price that reflects the anticipated quality of assets, which could be determined by an auction mechanism (Ausubel and Cramton, 2008).

Balance sheet externalities. The price of sold assets determines the book value of bank assets (under mark-to-market accounting) and therefore the compliance of banks with regulatory solvency ratios. If government purchases an asset at the price of low-quality assets, it may force a bank into regulatory insolvency because this bank (as well as all other banks) needs to book all assets at this price. A consequence would be that all banks will write down equity or set limits on asset growth (i.e., credit crunch). This effect in turn may justify subsidized sales prices. However, this argument has no economic motive other than regulatory constraint because rational market participants are aware that banks sell their worst assets.[25]

Correlation between the amount of toxic assets and overall asset quality. If a bank sells more toxic assets to the government than the average bank, market participants will infer that the bank's asset quality is below average.[26] The bank might then be reluctant to participate in the plan as a result of the negative signal.

Use of Government Information

Bank examination. If the government obtains more accurate information about bank assets from a rigorous examination (e.g., a stress test), the government can reduce the cost of any restructuring plan by disclosing the results to inform investors.

Asset guarantee. Asset guarantees without caps on transfers put taxpayers at risk and thus can work as a credible signal that the government is confident about the downside risk of assets. In contrast, a public statement without such a commitment would not be a credible signal. In turn, asset guarantees can convince investors to invest in the bank at a price that may not be dilutive for existing shareholders.

Caballero's scheme and commitment on future policy. Insurance on the stock price of a bank, as in Caballero's (2009) proposal, is another way to send a credible signal about government's confidence in the asset quality of a bank as well as future policies of the government. For example, by guaranteeing the stock price, nationalization with high dilution of shareholder value becomes a more costly option for the government. The higher cost can expunge a possible

---

[25] Regulatory reform is beyond the scope of this chapter. However, we would like to note that if mark-to-market accounting were weakened, the degree of the asymmetric information problem would increase. To mitigate the regulatory distortion, it would be better to design countercyclical capital-ratio regulation while keeping mark-to-market accounting.

[26] Philippon and Schnabl (2009) analyze a case in which the asset quality and future profits are uncorrelated. Then, the problem regarding the asymmetric information on asset quality and the problem of revealing future profit opportunities are distinct from each other. If the government uses only one tool (e.g., asset purchase or recapitalization), there can be a preferable policy—recapitalization with common equity in their analysis.

time-inconsistency problem of the government on ex post nationalization of the bank. This, in turn, can make equity more valuable.

OTHER CONSIDERATIONS

Political Constraints

Opportunity cost for the government. If the government has limited overall resources, it should take into account the restrictions that the restructuring scheme puts on other investments. In addition, given political pressures and fiscal rules, the cost of mobilizing liquid resources immediately may be high (see discussions in Johnson and Kwak, 2009). In this case, preference might be given to mechanisms such as asset insurance or Caballero's scheme (insurance on new stock issues), which involve only ex post transfers. However, a credible plan for honoring these transfers should be in place.

Political influence on management. If government continues to be a major shareholder for a long period, a general problem for state-owned enterprises would emerge. Voting-rights holders are supposed to monitor management, but the government is not equipped for this function. Mismanagement would be likely to occur often because government lacks expertise and might be subject to political pressures concerning the bank's lending policy. This would discourage the bank from participating in a restructuring plan, if voluntary. Recapitalization using hybrid instruments, without voting rights, would be less likely to induce this type of mismanagement. If there is little chance of selling public stakes quickly, one way to avoid the inefficiency resulting from public control is to have government hold common equity without voting rights. However, with a large disparity between control rights and cash flow rights, another type of mismanagement may arise. For example, other shareholders might use their de facto control power to misuse the bank's profits at the expense of the taxpayers (tunneling). In addition, even without voting rights, government (or parliament) could influence—at least partially—managerial decisions if a bank participates in any government-led restructuring plan.

If Bankruptcy Is Inevitable

If the realized asset value is less than the threshold level ($A_1 < A^*$), the optimal response of government may be to let the bank go bankrupt—A^* should be chosen that way ex ante by weighing the trade-off between benefits and costs. In particular, if the bank is under heavy liquidity pressure in the market or from depositors, other options may not be readily available. Still, government should make the bankruptcy less destructive. For a typical distressed firm, private equity funds or rival firms would take over immediately. However, there is often little time for those types of investors to conduct due diligence for a bank, partly because banks are highly leveraged and may collapse before the due diligence is completed. Moreover, bank assets are much more opaque compared with the assets of firms in other industries, so due diligence requires more time, likely a half year or more.

To carry out an orderly resolution, temporary nationalization is inevitable.[27] This strategy essentially mimics a private solution for a severely distressed firm in other industries (e.g., by a vulture fund). By holding a large share of common equity, government can control the bank's management. In particular, the government can acquire all the necessary information to assess asset values and liquidity conditions more accurately and quickly. As the majority owner, government is in a strong position to ask debt holders and other stakeholders to share the burden. As a consequence, government can limit the taxpayers' burden, expedite the resolution process, and sell the bank to private investors.

If temporary nationalization is unavoidable, further discussion is needed about the scope of debt to be honored, in addition to deposits covered under deposit insurance or any other instruments covered under various insurance schemes. Even without any prearrangement, to save the payment system—at least in the short term—transaction-purpose instruments, for example, interbank market borrowings, should be honored. There is less justification for honoring long-term debt. However, further discussion is needed on other transaction-purpose instruments, such as bank guarantees on securities backed by credit card debt and accounts payable.

CASE STUDIES

Switzerland: Good Bank/Bad Bank Split in the Case of UBS as of May 2009

Information on Bank Asset Quality and Participation

The Swiss case in fall 2008 was relatively straightforward. Switzerland has only two systemically important banks. Only one of them, UBS, had substantial exposure to U.S. subprime mortgage securities by fall 2008. Therefore, the Swiss authorities focused their restructuring efforts on UBS. UBS voluntarily participated in the plan. Credit Suisse was initially offered the opportunity to participate in the same plan but declined.[28]

Overview

The plan was a combination of asset sales to an asset management fund (the bad bank) and recapitalization by convertible notes. Almost all transfers were up front. UBS is not liable for future losses on transferred assets but kept a partial

---

[27] This solution is the norm for smaller banks. See also cases for systemically important banks in Japan, in particular, Long-Term Credit Bank and Nippon Credit Bank (Hoshi and Kashyap, 2008).

[28] Credit Suisse raised US$10 billion in new capital by selling equities and hybrids to private sources (including a sovereign wealth fund).

share of its upside. There are two potential sources of subsidies: (1) the price of transferred assets could be higher than the fundamental value of the assets net of the buyback option's value, and (2) the issuance price of convertible notes could be above fundamental value.

Asset-Side Restructuring: Asset Sales

In October 2008, the Swiss authorities and UBS removed toxic assets by creating a special purpose vehicle (StabFund) to hold them under the Swiss National Bank.[29] The StabFund was to be the bad bank, and the remainder of UBS was supposed to become the good bank. Up to US$60 billion in toxic assets was allowed to be removed from UBS, whose assets totaled almost US$2 trillion at that time. UBS provided 10 percent of asset value (i.e., up to US$6 billion) for the equity of the bad bank but immediately transferred the equity ownership to the Swiss government for US$1. The US$6 billion would cover the first 10 percent of losses of the StabFund. The Swiss National Bank lent the StabFund additional funding, up to US$54 billion at the London interbank offered rate (LIBOR) plus 250 basis points. The future loss of the StabFund would not be charged to UBS (nonrecourse condition), but UBS retained some upside option.[30] In the end, UBS transferred only $39 billion of its assets to the StabFund. The price was set by an independent valuation process.

Liability-Side Restructuring: Recapitalization

Although the asset side of UBS was improved by asset sales as described above, the original plan did not include restructuring of the liability side, but UBS did end up being recapitalized. UBS received capital of US$6 billion from the Swiss government by issuing mandatory convertible notes at 12.5 percent interest. The proceeds were intended to finance the same amount of UBS's equity injection in the StabFund, which was immediately valued at US$1. If UBS had injected the equity to the StabFund up to the limit of US$6 billion, there would have been no increase in the capital of UBS. However, because UBS ended up transferring only about US$4 billion to the StabFund, UBS was able to retain US$2 billion worth of capital in net. See Figure 16.11 for a schematic of the plan.

Corporate Governance

UBS shareholders had already suffered through voluntary recapitalization in April 2008 by new equity issuance (rights issue) without any public help. The old

---

[29] The assets purchased were primarily U.S. and European residential and commercial mortgage-backed securities.

[30] Once this loan is fully repaid by the StabFund, UBS can exercise its option to repurchase the fund equity by paying the Swiss National Bank US$1 billion plus 50 percent of the equity value at the time of exercise in excess of US$1 billion.

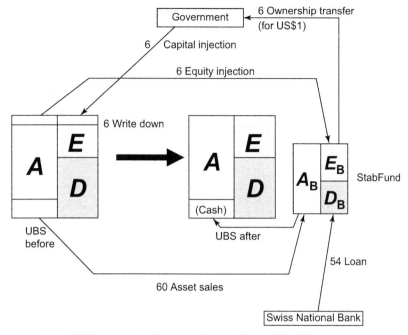

Figure 16.11 UBS Restructuring (announced plan, *billions of U.S. dollars*)

Source: Authors' illustration.
Note: *A* = assets; *D* = debt; *E* = equity.

management also had to exit in April 2008, at the annual general meeting of the shareholders, when UBS asked for the rights issue.[31]

United Kingdom: Recapitalization and Asset Guarantee for RBS and Lloyds-HBOS as of May 2009

Overview

The U.K. case combines recapitalization and asset guarantees. The initial state-financed recapitalization in fall 2008 of the Royal Bank of Scotland (RBS) and Lloyds-HBOS appeared to be an emergency rescue rather than a preventive measure because it occurred after the realization of large valuation losses. However, asset protection introduced in January 2009 was a preventive measure to avoid future defaults. The government also asked the banks to continue lending to homeowners and small businesses.

Liability-Side Restructuring: Recapitalization

By fall 2008, it was clear that RBS and HBOS were in trouble. In October 2008, the U.K. authorities decided to offer a recapitalization scheme to systemically

---

[31] The first-round recapitalization by UBS was in October 2007 by convertible note issues to a sovereign wealth fund of Singapore and a private investor from the Middle East.

important banks, targeting RBS and newly merged Lloyds-HBOS.[32] The government injected capital with preferred shares and ended up owning 58 percent (£20 billion) of RBS and about 44 percent (£17 billion) of Lloyds-HBOS.

Asset Guarantees Combined with Government Ownership

In January 2009, additional measures were taken. A large portion of RBS's and Lloyds-HBOS's assets were guaranteed (under the Asset Protection Scheme): £325 billion (14.5 percent) of end-2008 assets for RBS and £260 billion (23.4 percent) of end-2008 assets for Lloyds-HBOS.[33] If the valuation of assets were to fall below a particular threshold,[34] the government would compensate the loss up to 90 percent.

The asset guarantee was not offered for free. The insurance fees were to be paid in preferred shares. For Lloyds-HBOS, the government would own close to 50 percent of the total economic stake. For RBS, in addition to insurance fees, the government announced an extra injection of capital through preferred shares. The government's economic stake would rise to more than 80 percent. With the conversion of preferred shares to common equity, the voting rights share of the government for RBS became about 70 percent.

Corporate Governance

As the majority shareholder, the government needs to monitor bank management. In the October 2008 plan, the government obtained the right to appoint new independent nonexecutive directors. In addition, the government limited executive compensation and dividend payouts.

United States: The Geithner Plan as of May 2009[35]

In the United States, the relative asset quality of systemically important banks was not fully known in fall 2008. The authorities needed to take into account this lack of information when they designed the first-round rescue plan at that time.

---

[32] RBS raised capital using a rights issue in April 2008 without government help. Lloyds was relatively healthy before acquiring troubled HBOS. In October 2008, as a liquidity measure, the government introduced the Credit Guarantee Scheme, which applied to a wider set of banks. This provided insurance for debt holders, thereby lowering banks' financing costs. In January 2009, the Asset-Backed Securities Guarantee Scheme was introduced to complement the Credit Guarantee Scheme because the latter excluded nonstructured instruments. This second scheme essentially aimed to facilitate new mortgage lending, given that it guaranteed the value of originally AAA-rated mortgage-backed securities issued only after January 2008.

[33] As an expansion of monetary policy (i.e., liquidity injection), the Asset Purchase Facility was introduced in January. It was funded by the treasury and established within the Bank of England. The Bank of England used it to improve corporate credit liquidity and to meet the inflation target.

[34] This was tailored to each bank. The first-loss amounts (i.e., threshold) were £19.5 billion (6 percent) of protected assets for RBS and £25 billion (9.6 percent) of protected assets for Lloyds-HBOS.

[35] Actual implementation of TARP funds evolved further. However, this chapter records discussions on proposed plans as of May 2009, when this chapter originally was completed after numerous iterations from January 2009.

Given the information problem, the treasury encouraged many banks to participate in a recapitalization program. Banks could receive cash by offering preferred shares to the treasury. The recapitalization was across the board with few conditions.[36] The recapitalization was accomplished under the Capital Purchase Program as a part of the Troubled Assets Relief Program (Paulson Plan) in October and November 2008.[37]

An exception was made for Citibank in November 2008 because of an urgent situation. Citibank received additional recapitalization as well as asset guarantees from the treasury, the FDIC, and the Federal Reserve. In January 2009, both measures were formalized as the Targeted Investment Program and Asset Guarantee Program, respectively, and extended to Bank of America. Terms and conditions were determined on a case-by-case basis.

The Geithner Plan: Restructuring Based on Better Information

Overview

In February 2009, the U.S. Treasury announced a comprehensive bank-restructuring plan, the Financial Stability Plan (Geithner Plan). The plan tried first to evaluate the asset quality of systemically important banks through a specific examination of their assets' risks (stress test or Supervisory Capital Assessment Program).[38] This evaluation was compulsory for the 19 largest banks. Then the plan combined recapitalization (Capital Assistance Program) and asset purchase using private money (Public-Private Investment Program). These programs were voluntary in principle but semivoluntary in practice because banks had to meet the required capital criteria. In addition, the plan included several conditions to prevent misuse of public money and to facilitate lending. The plan also encouraged banks to lend, especially to small businesses and communities, and to support homeowners, especially those facing foreclosure.

Information Gathering and Communication

In early May 2009, the treasury reported the detailed results of the comprehensive stress test, the Supervisory Capital Assessment Program, which is a forward-looking examination of bank solvency, identifying how much capital was needed to cope with future adverse shocks to the asset quality of each bank. The stress test evaluated the future downside risk more rigorously than a typical bank examination. The results confirmed that the largest banks were not insolvent and

[36] Some conditions (e.g., limit to executive compensation) were applied after recapitalization.
[37] As a liquidity measure, new debt holders of Federal Deposit Insurance Corporation (FDIC) member banks were temporarily insured by the FDIC under the Temporary Liquidity Guarantee Program. Moreover, the Federal Reserve began lending up to $200 billion on a nonrecourse basis to holders of certain AAA-rated asset-backed securities (ABS) backed by newly and recently originated consumer and small business loans (Term Asset-Backed Securities Loan Facility). Banks were given incentives to increase new lending given that they would not face the downside risk of valuation loss in the ABS.
[38] The authorities also planned to increase balance sheet transparency and disclosure.

determined how much extra capital was needed, if any, for each bank to weather a future adverse shock.

Liability-Side Restructuring: Recapitalization

Banks were required to raise the extra capital identified by the stress test. This compulsory feature eliminated the signaling problem described earlier in this chapter. Banks could raise capital through private markets or by participating in the Capital Assistance Program. In this program, banks would receive capital from the government by issuing preferred shares that would automatically convert into common equity after seven years. An earlier conversion could be made at the issuer's discretion with the approval of the regulator. The use of such hybrid securities minimizes the future cost of financial distress should asset values deteriorate further (as discussed previously). The investment of the treasury is managed under a separate entity (Financial Stability Trust).

Asset-Side Restructuring: Asset Sales

Under the asset sales scheme (Public-Private Investment Program), the government solicited private investors for the purchase of troubled (legacy) loans and securities from banks. Slightly different schemes were provided for loans than for securities. However, the key idea was to use private expertise and solicit it by guaranteeing against the future losses and providing subsidized loans.

Several funds were to be set up to purchase legacy loans. Each fund was to buy pools of legacy loans sold by banks. The price would be determined by competitive bidding by funds. In addition, inexpensive financing was to be available—each fund would receive 50 percent equity participation from the treasury without voting rights and could also issue debt guaranteed by the FDIC (leverage ratio up to 6). The FDIC was to supervise the funds.

In addition, several funds were to be set up to purchase legacy securities from banks. Eligible securities were nonagency residential-mortgage-backed securities that were originally AAA rated and outstanding commercial mortgage-backed securities and ABS that were rated AAA. The treasury again was to provide a 50 percent equity stake without voting rights and lend money to each fund at up to a 2-to-1 leverage ratio. These were to be nonrecourse loans: If the asset values turned out to be very low, funds could default on the treasury, and fund managers would not have any responsibility other than their losses on their own investment in the funds.

The fact that the plan involved a government transfer is in line with this chapter's analysis of noncompulsory plans—a transfer is needed to convince banks to participate. Private sector involvement would lower the fiscal costs by using private sector money as well as private sector expertise. Further evaluation of the plan requires assessment of whether it minimized the level of the government transfer, given the recapitalization objective. For this, it is necessary to evaluate how close the plan was to an optimal compensation scheme. There are two dimensions to consider. The first is the moral hazard problem in running the asset management funds. The inexpensive government-sponsored leverage was necessary to encourage private investors to take risks, but the risk taking might have become excessive, more than optimal. The second consideration is the calibration of the subsidy necessary to secure the participation of high-quality managers. A difficulty with the plan was estimating how the public subsidy was to be shared between the banks and the fund managers (as Spence, 2009, stressed). It has been argued that the optimal subsidies could have been calibrated using an auction to sell the management and cash flow rights (Bebchuk, 2009). This would have required thorough preselection of qualified managers but might also have set the equilibrium transfer to the banks at an amount less than intended, which could have discouraged banks from participating in the plan.

Corporate Governance

To address potential moral hazard problems, the plan required banks to restrict executive compensation, dividends, stock repurchases, and acquisitions. At the same time, the plan prohibited political interference in investment decisions, and the Treasury made all contracts public.

CONCLUSION

When designing a restructuring plan for a systemically important bank, a key issue is limiting transfers from taxpayers. Limiting such transfers prevents unnecessary subsidies to debt holders and maximizes the economic value created by the restructuring. There is no magic bullet. Table 16.1 summarizes the pros and cons of various policy options. Some of the key findings are the following:

- In a Modigliani-Miller (1958) framework in which cash flows are independent of capital structure, restructuring is theoretically possible by converting some debt into equity. However, this is difficult in practice.

- If debt contracts are not changed, all restructuring involves transfers from the government. A plan subsidizing common equity issues and buying back debt is close to optimal. Subsidized asset sales are more costly to taxpayers because debt holders benefit more.

- The precise design of a restructuring should take into account the value created or destroyed because of changes in the participants' behavior. Managers' expertise and incentives are concerns that should be addressed in restructuring.

- If assets are undervalued as a result of liquidity or "lemons" problems, the government can make profits by buying assets above market value but below fundamental value. A caveat is that such undervaluation is difficult to assess.

- Asymmetric information on the value of future payoffs makes equity holders even more reluctant to support restructurings involving new-claim issues.

TABLE 16.1

Pros and Cons of Various Policy Options[1]

	Constant surplus		Endogenous surplus[2]			Future concerns[2]		Other concerns	
	First best	(Honoring debt contracts)	Talent allocation	Moral hazard	Adverse selection[3]	Near future distress	Long-run view punishment	Regulatory requirement	Up-front taxpayer cost
	(1)	(2)	(3)	(4)	(5)	(6)	(7)	(8)	(9)
Nonstate-contingent measures	…	…	…	…	…	…	…	…	…
Debt-for-equity swap	+	n.a.	n.a.	n.a.	n.a.	n.a.	n.a.	+	–
Recapitalization (with debt reduction)	…	…	…	…	…	…	…	…	…
With common equity	n.a.	+	…	…	–	…	…	+	–
With convertible notes	…	…	…	…	…	…	…	…	…
(Holder converts or mandatory)	n.a.	+	…	…	…	+	…	+	–
(Issuer converts)	n.a.	+	…	…	–	+	…	+	–
With preferred share	n.a.	+	…	…	…	…	…	+	–
With subordinated debt	n.a.	+	…	…	…	…	…	+	–
Asset purchase (Either via asset management company or good bank/bad bank)	n.a.	–	+	…	…	…	…	–	–
State-contingent measures	…	…	…	…	…	…	…	…	…
Limited loss guarantee on assets for banks	n.a.	+	…	–	+	…	+	…	+
Loss guarantee on liability for liability holders	n.a.	+	…	–	+	…	+	…	+

Recapitalization with loss guarantee on equity	n.a.	+	...	...	...	+	+	+
Only for new equity holders (Caballero)	...	...	...	...	...	+	...	...
Good/bad bank split with recourse condition	n.a.	–	+	–	+	+	–	+
With loss paid by equity of good bank (Sachs)	...	...	...	...	...	...	...	...

[1] + indicates the restructuring plans that are worth considering; – indicates those that should be avoided.

[2] Assessment is made for the cases without renegotiating the debt contracts.

[3] Assessment is based on voluntary plans. Compulsory plans can eliminate this problem. Also, the government can mitigate this problem with rigorous bank examination.

A restructuring impasse can be avoided through (1) conducting stress tests with credibly publicized results, (2) using compulsory rather than voluntary schemes, (3) providing contingent guarantees for banks to avoid new-claim issues, or (4) making banks issue low-information-sensitive claims such as convertible debt or preferred stocks.

• From a long-term perspective, it is important that managers and shareholders of bailed-out banks be punished in a way that discourages excessive future risk taking.

Overall, the restructuring of a systemically important bank should combine several solutions to resolve multiple concerns and trade-offs on a case-by-case basis. In fact, the case studies are in line with this analysis. Although different schemes were used in Switzerland, the United Kingdom, and the United States, all of them employed measures both on the asset side (e.g., sales of toxic assets) and on the liability side (e.g., recapitalization with preferred shares). In addition, the speed of events appeared to be a major friction when the restructuring plans were designed. However, there may be room for improvement. In particular, the costs to taxpayers and the final beneficiaries of the subsidies should be more transparent in all plans. Treatment of managers and shareholders could be less favorable.

A restructuring plan cannot be judged by the stock market reaction. That reaction depends on the gap between ex ante anticipations and the announced plan—anticipated transfers may be larger or smaller than those in the announced plan. Moreover, even if the announcement comes as a surprise, a stock price increase may not be good news. On the one hand, it may suggest an increase in surplus, both private (e.g., reduction in the cost of financial distress) and social (e.g., stabilization of the financial system). On the other hand, it may also suggest too high a transfer to shareholders from taxpayers. A good compulsory plan may clearly be associated with a decrease in stock prices because shareholders are forced to take some responsibility.

In the long run, various frictions can and should be reduced to make the restructuring of systemic banks less complex and less costly. Specifically, a better legal framework should be designed so that the renegotiation of debt can be handled more quickly and with a smaller threat of systemic meltdown. For example, opacity can be reduced by more timely and in-depth disclosure requirements for bank asset information and counterparty exposures. Regulation can give banks more incentives to include conversion clauses in their long-term debt contracts so that such debt will automatically convert into equity in a distress situation.

REFERENCES

Andrade, Gregory, and Steven Kaplan, 1998, "How Costly Is Financial (Not Economic) Distress? Evidence from Highly Leveraged Transactions that Became Distressed," *Journal of Finance*, Vol. 53, No. 5, pp. 1443–93.

Ausubel, Lawrence M., and Peter Cramton, 2008, "Auction Design Critical for Rescue Plan," *The Economists' Voice*, Vol. 5, No. 5, Article 5.

Bebchuk, Lucian A., 2009, "Buying Troubled Assets," *Yale Journal on Regulations*, Vol. 26, No. 2, pp. 343–58.

Bulow, Jeremy, and Paul Klemperer, 2009, "Reorganising the Banks: Focus on the Liabilities, Not the Assets," *VOX,* March 21.

Caballero, Ricardo J., 2009, "A (Mostly) Private Capital Assistance Program (CAP)," *RGE Monitor*, March 17.

Diamond, Douglas, Steve Kaplan, Anil Kashyap, Raghuram Rajan, and Richard Thaler, 2008, "Fixing the Paulson Plan," *Wall Street Journal*, September 26–28.

Hoshi, Takeo, and Anil K. Kashyap, 2008, "Will the U.S. Bank Recapitalization Succeed? Lessons from Japan," NBER Working Paper No. 14401 (Cambridge, Massachusetts: National Bureau of Economic Research).

Johnson, Simon, and James Kwak, 2009, "Geithner's Plan Isn't Money in the Bank," *Los Angeles Times*, March 24.

Majluf, Nicholas S., and Stewart C. Myers, 1984, "Corporate Financing and Investment Decisions When Firms Have Information that Investors Do Not Have," *Journal of Financial Economics*, Vol. 13, pp. 187–221.

Modigliani, Franco, and Merton Miller, 1958, "The Cost of Capital, Corporate Finance, and the Theory of Investment," *American Economic Review*, Vol. 48, pp. 261–97.

Myers, Stewart C., 1977, "Determinants of Corporate Borrowing," *Journal of Financial Economics*, Vol. 5, pp. 147–75.

Philippon, Thomas, and Philipp Schnabl, 2009, "Constrained-Efficient Mechanisms against Debt Overhang" (unpublished; New York: New York University).

Rajan, Raghuram, 2008, "Desperate Times Need the Right Measures," *Financial Times*, September 19.

Rochet, Jean-Charles, and Jean Tirole, 1996, "Payment Systems Research and Public Policy Risk, Efficiency, and Innovation," *Journal of Money, Credit and Banking*, Vol. 28, No. 4, Part 2, pp. 733–62.

Sachs, Jeffrey, 2009, "A Proposal on How to Clean the Banks," *Huffington Post*, February 12.

Spence, Michael, 2009, "The Geithner Plan: Criticisms Are off the Mark," *Financial Times*, April 7.

Stein, Jeremy, 1992, "Convertible Bonds as Backdoor Equity Financing," *Journal of Financial Economics,* Vol. 32, pp. 3–21.

Tirole, Jean, 2006, *The Theory of Corporate Finance* (Princeton, New Jersey: Princeton University Press).

Zingales, Luigi, 2009, "Yes, We Can, Secretary Geithner," *The Economists' Voice*, Vol. 6, No. 2, Article 3.

CHAPTER 17

Principles of Household Debt Restructuring

Luc Laeven and Thomas Laryea

Household indebtedness reached historically high and likely unsustainable levels in several countries hit by the 2007–09 financial crisis (Figure 17.1). In some countries the indebtedness stemmed from excessive credit booms in the run-up to the crisis, and was exacerbated by sharp declines in house prices. In other countries, where foreign-currency-denominated loans were prevalent, it was also the result of a balance sheet effect triggered by currency depreciation.

Household debt overhang and debt-servicing problems feed into different but connected downward spirals.[1] First, they weaken bank balance sheets through an increase in nonperforming loans, which, in turn, may lead to a reduction in credit availability, putting further pressure on house prices and prices of other asset classes. The resulting decrease in wealth and collateral value further worsens the household debt problem. Second, household debt problems can negatively affect consumption, which may turn into lower growth and higher unemployment, compressing household income and further feeding into both downward spirals.

At times of financial crisis, governments often contemplate debt restructuring to deal with social problems that arise when households are no longer able to repay their loans. These problems can be particularly pronounced when the distressed debt involves household mortgage loans (Figure 17.2). Although governments with fiscal space may decide to pursue restructuring policies on the basis of social considerations, the design of such debt-restructuring programs should be based on sound economic principles.

The authors thank Jochen Andritzky, Tam Bayoumi, Olivier Blanchard, Stijn Claessens, Luis Cortavarria-Checkley, Giovanni Dell'Ariccia, Karl Driessen, Sean Hagan, Antonio Ignacio Garcia Pascual, David Hoelscher, Yan Liu, Mauro Mecagni, James Morsink, Martin Muhleisen, Ceyla Pazarbasioglu, Catriona Purfield, Nadia Rendak, Guillermo Tolosa, Fabián Valencia, Tessa van der Willigen, Johannes Wiegand, and members of the interdepartmental Debt Restructuring Working Group for helpful discussions and comments.
[1] Debt overhang is a situation in which a borrower's debt exceeds his or her future capacity to repay. The debt overhang problem has been analyzed for firms by Myers (1977). Krugman (1988), among others, provides an analysis for sovereign debt.

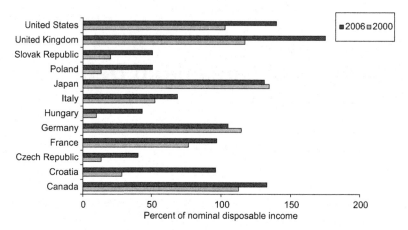

Figure 17.1 Household Indebtedness in 2000 and 2006

Sources: Organization for Economic Co-operation and Development statistics; and IMF staff calculations.

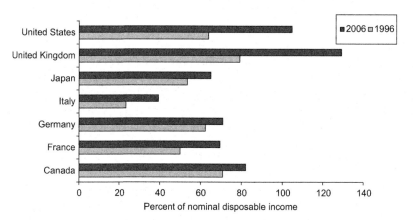

Figure 17.2 Household Mortgage Indebtedness in 1996 and 2006

Sources: Organization for Economic Co-operation and Development statistics; and IMF staff calculations.

This chapter assesses the case for government intervention in household debt restructuring and proposes a template for a household debt-restructuring program that could be adapted to individual country circumstances.[2]

---

[2] The analysis does not address the weakening supply of credit or temporary liquidity problems of households, nor does it address efforts to support asset prices or banking sector resolution. The chapter also does not deal with complexities associated with the link between household debt and structured credit products (for example, through securitization) as in some advanced economies. A complete analysis that would address these other problems could alter the design of the debt-restructuring strategy and call for additional policy measures not covered by the chapter.

THE CASE FOR GOVERNMENT INTERVENTION

Resolving the debt overhang problem requires the economy as a whole to bear some costs associated with the resolution of distressed loans. The purpose of policy is to minimize the inefficiencies associated with resolving the problem. Any government intervention will involve distortions; however, the question is whether the benefits of intervention exceed its costs. Moreover, if intervention involves government financing, the extent of intervention should be constrained by the degree of fiscal space available and the potential negative impact of the intervention on public debt sustainability.

Two sets of issues may interfere with a market-driven solution and can justify more proactive policy than simply letting the courts and normal bankruptcy procedures, together with voluntary loan workouts, attempt to address the problem. First, a crisis affecting the household sector, such as the one faced by a number of countries in 2007–09, may involve a very large number of bankruptcy cases—even larger in absolute numbers than corporate sector bankruptcies. A timely resolution of these bankruptcies through the court system would not be feasible even for countries with the highest institutional capacity and the most efficient legal systems (Table 17.1).[3] Additionally, voluntary loan workouts can give rise to attrition problems, with delays that are optimal for the individual negotiators but not for the economy as a whole. Delays and the potential gridlock problems of market-driven solutions, the legal costs involved, and the associated destruction of wealth call for a more organized resolution strategy.

Household debt restructuring can also be warranted to address the externalities that arise when massive loan defaults by households result in unnecessary and costly liquidations, including foreclosures on real estate. These problems are particularly severe when homeowners possess negative equity in their homes. Although financial institutions initiated voluntary restructuring schemes in several countries (e.g., Lithuania, Mexico, and the United States[4]) to avoid collateral

---

[3] Table 17.1 indicates the legal costs and time associated with typical corporate (not individual) bankruptcy proceedings in selected economies, highlighting the variation in such costs across countries. These data are compiled in normal times. The noted delays would be expected to be significantly longer in the context of wide-scale corporate insolvencies associated with systemic crises. No similar data on personal insolvency proceedings is available.

[4] Since the burst of the U.S. housing bubble in 2007, the U.S. federal government has introduced or sponsored several initiatives to prevent rising foreclosures, including the FHA-Secure program announced in August 2007 and the Hope for Homeowners (H4H) program started on October 1, 2008. These efforts met with very limited success in stemming foreclosures, largely because they targeted severely delinquent borrowers who without more generous support were not able to service their mortgage payments. In March 2009, the U.S. Treasury introduced a more comprehensive initiative aimed at mitigating mortgage foreclosures, the Homeowners Affordability and Stability Plan. The program establishes guidelines for affordable loan modifications and refinancing aimed at reducing monthly payments to sustainable levels and provided incentives for loan modifications for borrowers, lenders, and other participants of the mortgage market, including through the personal bankruptcy mechanism as the last resort. It also contained other measures to support the housing market, including through increased funding commitments to the government-sponsored agencies, renter assistance, grants for innovative local programs to reduce foreclosures, and counseling for the most heavily indebted borrowers.

TABLE 17.1

Cost of Corporate Bankruptcy Proceedings in Selected Economies, 2009			
Country	Time (years)	Cost (percent of estate)	Recovery rate (cents on the dollar)
Argentina	2.8	12.0	29.8
Austria	1.1	18.0	71.5
Brazil	4.0	12.0	17.1
Bulgaria	3.3	9.0	32.1
Estonia	3.0	9.0	37.5
France	1.9	9.0	44.7
Germany	1.2	8.0	52.2
Hungary	2.0	15.0	38.4
Iceland	1.0	4.0	76.6
Italy	1.8	22.0	56.6
Japan	0.6	4.0	92.5
Latvia	3.0	13.0	29.0
Lithuania	1.7	7.0	48.0
Romania	3.3	9.0	29.5
Spain	1.0	15.0	73.2
Sweden	2.0	9.0	75.1
Thailand	2.7	36.0	42.4
Turkey	3.3	15.0	20.2
Ukraine	2.9	42.0	9.1
United Kingdom	1.0	6.0	84.2
United States	1.5	7.0	76.7

Source: World Bank Doing Business database, 2009.
Note: This table summarizes weaknesses in existing corporate bankruptcy law and the main procedural and administrative bottlenecks in the bankruptcy process. Data are based on a prototype firm (a hotel) and refer to bankruptcy proceedings for firms rather than households.

execution, financial institutions do not fully internalize the negative externalities generated by such unnecessary liquidations. House prices will not stabilize so long as there is an expectation of continuing house price deflation, exacerbated by widespread foreclosures. In addition, foreclosures can have a negative effect on neighborhood values. Essentially, this can be seen as a multiple equilibria situation: in one equilibrium, debt overhang is resolved more rapidly, leading to stabilization of house prices and resumption of growth; in the other, debt overhang lingers, resulting in further declines in house prices and contributing to a worsening of the recession.

In addition to taking into account the capacity of the legal and institutional system to handle wide-scale, case-by-case restructuring, the argument for government intervention depends on the dimension of the debt problem, both from the perspective of the debtors (households) and the creditors (banks). If the scale of distressed household debt is relatively small or banks are sufficiently sound, coordination problems are not overwhelming, and foreclosures are not widespread enough to create significant negative externalities, then the problem can be left to private sector borrower-creditor debt renegotiations. Box 17.1 summarizes some operational guidelines for assessing the scale of the problem. Government intervention is needed when both the scale of distressed household debt is sufficiently

BOX 17.1 Assessing the Size of the Problem: Some Operational Suggestions

A practical issue in deciding whether household debt restructuring may be needed is determining how to assess the size of the problem. This exercise involves collecting and analyzing data on several possible dimensions of distressed household debt.

Current picture. A comprehensive assessment requires information on the outstanding amount of nonperforming (gross) household debt, both in nominal terms and as a percentage of the total loan portfolio of banks, as well as data on that debt by type of credit (mortgages, credit cards, car loans, and other consumer credit), currency, amounts and number of days past due, and collateral values (accounting values according to the bank records). These stock data statically frame the problem, allowing it to be usefully compared with the broader picture of all household debt, whether performing or nonperforming. In addition, if data are available, indicators such as loan-to-value (LTV) ratios, loan-to-disposable income (LTDI) ratios, and original and current debt-service-to-disposable-income may allow household borrowers to be grouped according to their current financial condition.

Evolution over time. The transition in credit quality for household claims in distress, that is, how quickly household debt is deteriorating from "watch status" to the various nonperforming categories (substandard, doubtful, and loss), based on the length of time loans are overdue, must be assessed. The trend over time of total household debt in distress (in absolute amounts and appropriately scaled) and the evolution of the shares of debt in different credit quality categories (particularly the incidence of "loss" credits) allows an assessment to be made of whether the problem is becoming wider and deeper, or may become so in the future, or is instead relatively stable. In addition, information on real estate prices may help determine to what extent "negative equity" (an LTV ratio greater than one) of mortgage loans is, or is expected to become, a problem for household borrowers and lenders. However, it should be kept in mind that the definition of nonperforming loan categories may differ somewhat across countries. In addition, in crisis situations with rapidly rising unemployment and falling house prices, past trends may be a poor guide for future developments.

Distribution across financial institutions. Of immediate interest, from both a financial stability and a contingent liability standpoint, is how concentrated the problem is among individual banks. At least two dimensions matter. The first dimension is whether the institutions most affected are those that play a systemic role in the payments and settlement system, or in other key financial segments such as the interbank market in which exposures could act as a channel for further spillover effects. The second dimension is whether the institutions affected have enough cushion—provisions, loan loss reserves, and overall capitalization—to absorb the losses without violating prudential capital requirements or other supervisory norms that would trigger corrective action.

Impact on financial institutions. The impact of restructuring strategies on the financial institutions must be gauged. This evaluation requires, for example, determining the likely impact of reduced rates or lengthened maturities for distressed claims undergoing restructuring on financial institutions' cash flows, liquidity, and earnings. Similar exercises would involve assessing the impact of additional provisioning on profitability and capitalization of the institutions most affected, and the dependence of their earnings on continued household debt service. These exercises are typically conducted in collaboration with banking experts, the supervisory authorities, and the involved lending institutions.

Note: This box was prepared primarily by Mauro Mecagni (IMF, Strategy, Policy, and Review Department).

large to have macro implications and banks in distress are paralyzed by insufficient capital to absorb expected losses, lack of internal capacity to carry out individualized restructurings, or by coordination failures. The capacity of the legal and institutional framework to support individualized restructuring will also be a factor informing government intervention.

Whether government intervention in the form of financial support is feasible and credible depends on its impact on public debt sustainability and the available fiscal space. If government bank-recapitalization programs are also envisaged, authorities need to consider any overlap between the costs of debt restructuring and the costs of bank recapitalization when assessing the impact of government intervention on public debt. Debt restructuring, by generating writedowns in asset values on banks' balance sheets, will negatively affect the capital position of banks, and will thus most likely have to be accompanied by a bank recapitalization program. Such a recapitalization program will need to be calibrated in the amount necessary to bring the banks back to solvency after debt restructuring.

DESIGN OF GOVERNMENT INTERVENTION IN HOUSEHOLD DEBT RESTRUCTURING

When considering the extent and nature of government intervention in household debt restructuring, two broad approaches, which are not mutually exclusive, can be envisioned.

Under the first approach, the government establishes the legal and institutional framework that supports case-by-case restructuring. If operation of the framework is sufficiently predictable, the process will also catalyze restructurings that take place out of court. A reasonably effective legal system for credit enforcement, including through foreclosure, is necessary to support extension of credit in the economy and to bring debtors to the negotiating table if restructuring is warranted. However, the wealth destruction and extreme liquidity pressures that can arise in systemic crises can be exacerbated by wide-scale resort to credit enforcement measures. In particular, as discussed above, widespread foreclosure of mortgaged property can further depress house prices. Therefore, it is important that an effective court-supervised insolvency framework be in place for individual debtors, providing for multicreditor restructuring through the following key legal features: (1) an automatic stay on creditor enforcement and debtor payments should be enforced during the insolvency proceedings; (2) if the debt is secured, but the market value of the collateral (including the value of the household property securing a mortgage) is below the value of the loan, the court has the power to restructure the amount of the deficiency as unsecured debt; (3) the modification of loan terms should take into account the payment capacity of the debtor; and (4) a "fresh start" should be provided through discharge of financially responsible debtors from the liability for unsustainable debts at the end of the liquidation or rehabilitation period.[5]

Case-by-case debt renegotiations between creditors and debtors can result in an adjustment in loans on a voluntary basis to reduce debt payments through some combination of interest rate reductions, principal amount reductions, and maturity extensions. These three methods of debt reduction are often mixed to improve incentives for both lenders and borrowers to participate. For example, interest rate reductions alone, while attractive for the borrower, may severely reduce the cash flow position of the lender. Maturity extensions allow the adverse impact on the cash flow of the lender to be spread over a longer period, thereby making interest rate reductions more affordable to the lender. In addition to putting in place the relevant legal and institutional framework, the government can play an important role in facilitating case-by-case workouts by creating proper incentives and removing impediments to loan restructuring. For example, government can enhance participation by supporting nonbinding guidelines for private-sector-led restructuring.

A second approach involves the establishment of a government-sponsored debt-restructuring program that includes some form of financial support. Such a program could cover a certain group of borrowers or loans, or could include all loans.[6] Government support could take a multitude of forms. The government could provide financial support to the banks that restructure household loans, or it could establish a separate asset management company to purchase and resolve distressed assets. Furthermore, the government can provide direct support to the households through some form of subsidy, such as debt forgiveness, interest or exchange rate subsidies, or tax incentives.

When household debt overhang is widespread and severe, and the capacity of the banking system to restructure loans is limited, voluntary workouts that rely on case-by-case restructuring of loans become a less attractive option, making a comprehensive debt-restructuring program a more effective approach. At the same time, comprehensive debt-restructuring programs risk being too generous by offering restructuring to borrowers who would have been able and willing to make payments on their debt without restructuring. Ideally, debt-restructuring programs should be designed to lead to a "separating equilibrium" in which only

---

[5] In addition, debt-counseling services can be an effective tool for encouraging individuals to address their debt problems at an early stage by providing them with professional advice on their legal rights and responsibilities and on applicable procedures for negotiation. The insolvency law can facilitate the use of these services by making their use a condition to debtors filing for rehabilitation in insolvency proceedings. For a general discussion of key principles of individual insolvency law, see INSOL International (2001).

[6] Examples of government-sponsored debt-restructuring programs that targeted certain groups of loans are the 1933 Home Owners Loan Corporation program in the United States, the 1998 Punto Final program in Mexico, the 2000 debt-restructuring program in Uruguay, the 2002 credit card debt program in the Republic of Korea, and the 2008 IndyMac loan modification program in the United States. See Appendix 17A for a brief description of previous country episodes of household debt restructuring.

borrowers that are unable to repay their debt take advantage of the program. The degree of government intervention depends on the scale of the problem, the ability of debtors and creditors to absorb losses, and the fiscal space of the government.

Any government-sponsored debt-restructuring program should help restore the viability of individual borrowers while minimizing the direct fiscal cost, reducing the risk of bank failures, and establishing the basis for the recovery of the real sector. These multiple goals may not be fully compatible, and policy choices may need to be made about where to strike the balance. The design of a debt-restructuring program should incorporate a number of basic features:[7]

- *Objective.* The primary objective is to turn troubled loans into performing loans, while mitigating the moral hazard created by offering debtors the opportunity to not repay on the loan's original terms. The program could be directed to reducing the debt-service requirements of borrowers who have experienced increases in their scheduled loan repayments as a result of adverse interest rate or foreign exchange rate shocks, or to address the buildup of a substantial amount of nonperforming loans.

- *Scope.* The program should, where feasible, be selective and target borrowers who cannot meet their debt-service obligations but whose ability to service their debt is likely to be restored upon restructuring. The restructuring program could be designed to compensate the targeted group of borrowers either partially or in full—but in any case at a sufficient level to restore sustainable debt levels and the servicing capacity of borrowers. Defining criteria for such selectivity and reliably applying the criteria could be a major challenge, especially if data are unreliable and political or social considerations are pressing factors. Public funding, if used, would need to be sufficient to cover all qualifying participants. Conversely, the scope of the program could be subject to the public funding envelope.

- *Proportionality.* The degree of government intervention in the program should depend on the scale of the problem, the capacity of creditors and debtors to absorb losses, and the fiscal space of the government. Intervention should not impinge on government debt sustainability, and burden sharing between creditors and debtors should depend on their ability to absorb losses.

- *Participation.* Participation should be on a voluntary basis. Banks should be induced, not forced, to restructure their debts with borrowers.[8] Compulsory

---

[7] These basic features are designed on the model of a single main creditor for each household debtor and thus does not address creditor coordination and inter-creditor equity issues that would arise in countries in which multiple creditors of household debtors are prevalent.
[8] However, banks' participation may be enhanced by making it mandatory for banks that receive public funds, for example, in the context of a government-orchestrated bank-restructuring program.

restructuring, outside of the court-supervised insolvency process, will give rise to legal challenges and should be avoided.[9]

- *Simplicity.* Given the large number of loans involved in household debt restructuring, program design should be based on simple rules and verifiable information to speed up restructuring and reduce the potential for abuse. These rules should be based on analysis of the structure of banks' household loan portfolios. If it is not available already, banks will need to share with the government the necessary information to conduct such analysis should public funds be used to support the program.

- *Transparency and accountability.* The program should include mechanisms that allow the authorities to monitor restructuring progress to ensure the accountability of the program participants, and to make adjustments to the program if necessary. Mechanisms such as ongoing reporting and audit requirements are especially important if public funds are used because they would help safeguard the integrity of the program and make the most effective use of taxpayer money.

IMPLEMENTING A GOVERNMENT-SPONSORED DEBT-RESTRUCTURING PROGRAM

Before embarking on a government-sponsored debt-restructuring program for the household sector, several factors must be taken into account, including ongoing efforts to restructure loans by banks and the dynamic impact on the quality of banks' loan portfolios. Close coordination with key market players may help to identify the need for and size of public intervention. Also, loan restructuring could set perverse incentives for borrowers in the future, negatively affecting the level of nonperforming assets. To avoid multiple rounds of debt restructuring, government-sponsored debt-restructuring programs should generally not be introduced before macroeconomic policies have stabilized the economy and a bank recapitalization program has been put in place to restore the banking sector to health, taking into account prospective losses from debt restructuring. Debt restructuring should not be regarded as an instrument that can displace sound macroeconomic policies.

The advantage of a restructuring program that provides systematic loan modifications for a large pool of borrowers is that it offers a streamlined approach that can take advantage of economies of scale. Economies of scale reduce coordination costs, thereby enhancing participation by a large number of banks and

---

[9] Compulsory loan-restructuring programs have been rare. In the corporate debt context, Uruguay introduced a framework for compulsory restructuring of small loans in June 2000 to deal with large-scale debt overhang in the corporate sector. Under the program, loan maturities were extended under gradually increasing repayment schedules. Compulsory restructuring decreases the bargaining power of banks in the debt-restructuring process, which could be beneficial in circumstances in which banks have capacity to restructure but are recalcitrant. However, the risk of legal challenge and the potential to damage the credit culture likely outweigh the potential benefits of compulsory restructuring.

borrowers. At the same time, it should be realized that any debt relief generates moral hazard by offering debtors the opportunity to avoid repaying on the loan's original terms. If possible, design should mitigate such moral hazard and lead to a separating equilibrium in which only borrowers who are unable to repay their debt take advantage of the program. Depending on the financial situation of households, conditions can be attached to participation in the program. Conditions can include penalties that would present a disincentive for borrower defaults on restructured loans. For instance, borrowers may be required to allow banks to deduct direct loan repayments from their paychecks and incur the penalty of the original loan terms being restored if they default on the restructured terms. Alternatively, participation could require up-front cash payments, although such penalties may not be an option if households are already cash strapped. Beneficiaries could also be reported to the central credit register (if one exists) as restructured borrowers, limiting the scope for new loans. Above all, the borrowers' capacity to repay has to be a key element of design.

A government-sponsored debt-restructuring program may include a combination of the following additional elements:

Incentives for borrowers. In general, borrowers will recognize the benefit of restructuring. Government incentives may on occasion be warranted to overcome obstacles to borrowers seeking restructuring; for example, it may be individually efficient for borrowers with significant negative equity to walk away from their mortgages, but costly to the economy as a whole. In such cases, the government might give incentives to borrowers to restructure loans on a voluntary basis through loan subsidies on restructured debt (such as subsidized interest rates for borrowers,[10] subsidized refinancing, guarantees of payments,[11] subsidized write-offs, and insurance against future exchange rate or interest rate changes). For distressed mortgages, the government might also subsidize conversion of part of the debt into a more equity-like instrument, such as a shared-appreciation mortgage, so that repayment depends on the value of the house when sold (possibly accompanied by the government sharing in the upside).

Incentives for lenders. Government incentives may include tax credits for restructured loans, low interest rate credit lines to banks, or the tying of the restructuring to a government-sponsored bank recapitalization program.[12] Although the government may consider giving banks incentives to restructure loans by temporarily easing provisioning requirements on restructured loans, or by imposing unusually stringent provisioning on nonrestructured debt, such

---

[10] See the description in Appendix 17A of the Punto Final program adopted by Mexico in 1998.

[11] See the description in Appendix 17A of the Homeowners Support Mortgage Scheme introduced by the U.K. Treasury in early December 2008.

[12] Many countries allow their banks to upgrade restructured loans that were classified as loss or doubtful before restructuring into the substandard category after a new debt profile has been prepared on the basis of the borrower's more realistic repayment capacity. After a certain number of payments on the basis of the new schedule have been made (international practice varies between 6 and 12 monthly payments), these restructured loans can often be upgraded further.

measures are to be avoided. Experience suggests that formal forbearance may work only in the framework of a comprehensive and credible bank-restructuring program that requires capital injections from bank shareholders. Nonetheless, in view of the potential for moral hazard and conflicts of interest, regulatory forbearance is risky even in the context of a bank-restructuring program. Thus, banking authorities should use this resource very cautiously and only in exceptional circumstances.[13]

Legal and institutional reforms. The utility of a debt-restructuring program is increased if backed up by an effective legal, institutional, and regulatory framework for the enforcement of creditor rights. In particular, an effective personal bankruptcy framework for addressing collective enforcement of creditor claims and rehabilitation of debtors may also be useful if multiple creditors are present. Although use of credit enforcement tools on a case-by-case basis would not be feasible for resolving large-scale defaults on household debt that may arise in a systemic crisis, the credible threat of their use as a last resort is important for setting markers for the behavior of debtors and creditors.

Specific measures to address loans denominated in foreign currency. When distressed household debt is largely denominated in foreign currency, consideration could be given to converting the debt into local currency. However, such conversion gives rise to a number of problems. In principle, local-currency conversion eliminates borrowers' exposure to exchange rate flexibility, though its effects on the banking system will be country specific and depend on the net open currency positions of financial institutions. That said, conversion is likely to be prohibitively expensive for the banks and their borrowers, especially in systems with high levels of foreign-currency-denominated loans, unless the costs of conversion are transferred to the government.[14] In addition, local-currency conversion may have adverse side effects on foreign exchange markets as lenders demand foreign currency to rebalance their portfolios. Then, for conversion to be an option, the foreign currency mismatch at financial institutions needs to be solved first, which requires the availability of foreign-currency-denominated liquid assets. Public support could be granted to banks in the form of dollar-denominated or indexed restructuring bonds to reduce the currency mismatch that arises on banks' balance sheets after loans are converted into local currency, though the feasibility of such bonds depends on country circumstances, including the degree of dollarization of

---

[13] Although not best practice, some countries have eased provisioning requirements when faced with a surge in nonperforming loans. See Appendix 17A for instances in the Republic of Korea (2002) and Taiwan Province of China (2005).

[14] In November 2008, Hungarian commercial banks, faced with increased credit risk in their loan portfolios denominated in foreign currency as the result of a sharp depreciation of the local currency, signed a gentleman's agreement with the ministry of finance on a foreign-currency loan workout program that included the option to convert foreign currency loans into Hungarian-forint-denominated loans. The conversion part of the program was not taken up by borrowers because of the perceived cost of conversion implied by domestic interest rates that are much higher than interest rates on foreign currency loans.

the economy.[15] In particular, such bonds may not be sufficiently liquid to resolve funding problems at banks. In any case, forced conversion—for example, through legislative fiat—should be avoided.[16] Forced conversion would give rise to legal challenges, may lead to a run on the currency as banks try to rebalance their portfolios, and would undermine the overall creditworthiness of a country.

Administrative measures as last resort. If the size of the debt problem is overwhelming and other tools, including government financial support, are ineffective, administrative measures may be used as a last resort. Administrative measures include the imposition of a standard way of modifying distressed loans (possibly differentiated according to local market conditions) and a payment moratorium or foreclosure ban on distressed loans. A debt-payment moratorium is particularly problematic because it interferes with contracts, negatively affecting the market's perception of the quality of future contract enforcement, and would not address underlying debt overhang problems. Similarly, the imposition of an administrative ban on foreclosures does not solve the underlying debt overhang problems and could generate incentives to default by reducing the associated penalty, thereby exacerbating spillover effects on bank balance sheets. Other administrative measures, such as deposit freezes or the imposition of capital controls, should be avoided when possible, given the high economic costs they impose on future financial intermediation.

OTHER POLICY RESPONSES

Government-sponsored debt-restructuring programs are only one mechanism for restructuring household debt. The key advantage of these programs is simplicity and speed—recognizing loan losses up front thus providing immediate relief to borrowers. At the same time, debt restructuring does not directly impose losses on borrowers, thereby posing incentive problems, including moral hazard. However, these issues can be mitigated to some degree by targeting a select group of borrowers and through burden sharing with borrowers.

Household debt restructuring may also be facilitated indirectly through mechanisms supporting the financial health of banks such as recapitalizations and government purchases of distressed loans,[17] for example, by transferring distressed loans to asset management companies (AMCs) better equipped to resolve these

---

[15] Such foreign-currency-denominated restructuring bonds have been used before in Bulgaria (1994, 1997, 1999), Korea (1998), Mexico (1995–96), Poland (1991), and Uruguay (1982–84), while foreign-currency-indexed restructuring bonds have been used in Indonesia (1998–2000) and Nicaragua (2000–01). However, in all these countries, these bonds were issued as part of more general bank-restructuring programs rather than household debt-restructuring programs. See Hoelscher (2006) for further details.

[16] The 2002 Argentine asymmetric pesification is an example of a forced debt-conversion program that imposed significant losses on banks and depositors, with profoundly negative implications for financial intermediation and future economic growth. See Appendix 17A.

[17] An example of a government program that involved government purchases of distressed loans is the U.S. Home Owners Loan Corporation (HOLC) established in 1933. See Appendix 17A.

loans. A positive feature of recapitalization is that—depending on its political support—bank-specific public support can be provided more selectively, and can be based on the strength of the financial institution, taking into account prospective losses resulting from the resolution of distressed assets. The transfer of distressed loans to an AMC may facilitate household debt restructuring (while providing incentives to banks to recognize losses). However, such transfers are not without problems, including the risk of transferring assets at above-market prices, thus bailing out existing bank shareholders; offering support beyond that necessary to restore the debt viability of borrowers; and political and legal challenges in asset resolution. The experience with AMCs has been mixed, and their success depends largely on the legal and institutional environment.[18]

Countries typically apply a combination of these resolution strategies—with some directed toward financial institutions and others more geared toward borrowers—and in the process often incur substantial fiscal costs.[19] The mix of policy responses will ultimately be crisis specific and depend on a variety of factors, including the nature and depth of the financial crisis, and specific country circumstances.

APPENDIX 17A. BRIEF SUMMARIES OF PREVIOUS EPISODES OF HOUSEHOLD DEBT RESTRUCTURING[20]

United States (1933)

In 1933, at the onset of the U.S. Great Depression, the Home Owners Loan Corporation (HOLC) was established to prevent mortgage foreclosures. HOLC bought distressed mortgages from banks in exchange for bonds with federal guarantees on interest and principal. It then restructured these mortgages to make them more affordable to borrowers and developed methods of working with borrowers who became delinquent or unemployed, including assisting them with job searches. Eligible mortgages included those with an appraised value of $20,000 or less ($321,791 in 2008 dollars). Approximately 40 percent of those eligible for the program applied; half of the applications were rejected or withdrawn. Of the 1 million loans HOLC issued, 200,000 homes were acquired from borrowers

---

[18] Although a detailed analysis of the pros and cons of using an AMC as a debt-restructuring tool is beyond the scope of this chapter, in addition to valuation of the assets to be transferred, other key issues that need to be addressed in setting up and operating an AMC include (1) whether the AMC is fully financed by the government or through a combination of government and other (e.g., official and private sector) financing; (2) risk- and loss-sharing arrangements if the AMC has more than one shareholder; and (3) the governance and decision-making structure of the AMC.

[19] For a more extensive overview of how crisis resolution policies have been used in past financial crises and the trade-offs involved, see Hoelscher and Quintyn (2003), and Honohan and Laeven (2005).

[20] Some of the cases described in this appendix touch on the issues that go beyond the intended coverage of the chapter. Table 17A.1 presents data on selected household indicators for each case study (except the recent cases of Hungary [2008], the United Kingdom [2008], and the United States [2008]).

who were unable to pay their mortgages. HOLC ended up making a relatively small profit when it was liquidated in 1951, in part because declining interest rates and the government guarantee allowed it to borrow inexpensively.

Mexico (1998)

Following the unsuccessful FOBAPROA bank-restructuring program initiated in 1995, the government of Mexico initiated the Punto Final program in December 1998. The program was a government-led debt-relief program targeted at mortgage holders, agribusiness, and small and medium enterprises. The program offered large subsidies (up to 60 percent of book value of the loan) to bank debtors to pay back their loans. The discounts depended on the sector, the amount of the loan, and whether the bank restarted lending to the sector. For every three pesos of new loans extended by the bank, the government would assume an additional one peso of discount. The program thus combined loss sharing between the government and the banks with an incentive to restart lending. The program was successful in providing rapid debt relief but at very large cost to taxpayers.

Uruguay (2000)

In Uruguay, a debt-restructuring scheme approved in June 2000 offered a framework for the systemic and compulsory restructuring of small loans (up to US$50,000) by extending loan maturities and introducing gradually increasing payment schedules, and a largely voluntary scheme for large borrower workouts, with strong incentives for both banks and borrowers to reach restructuring agreements. Incentives to encourage creditor participation included (1) a flexible classification system for restructured loans to encourage banks to recognize implicit losses and (2) a reclassification as a loss with a 100 percent provisioning requirement for the failure to restructure a nonperforming loan within the timeframe provided by the scheme.

Republic of Korea (2002)

A rapid expansion of the credit card market in Korea, encouraged by lax lending standards and other factors, resulted in a distressed credit card market with rising delinquencies in 2002 (Kang and Ma, 2007). Credit card debt as percentage of GDP reached 15 percent in 2002. The credit card crisis spilled over to commercial banks because the banks were heavily exposed to troubled credit card issuers through credit lines. Korean commercial banks' lending to one single large troubled credit card issuer stood at 38 percent of creditor banks' combined equity. Nevertheless, Korea's commercial banks were generally able to absorb the losses for their credit card units without broader repercussions because affected units were generally merged into the respective parent banks. The stand-alone credit card companies were more severely affected by the crisis. The principal way of dealing with the bad credit card debt was to write off the loans. Other resolution methods included sales to third parties and debt-to-equity conversions of credit card issuers' debt. In addition, Korean authorities allowed issuers to roll over delinquent credit card loans, a practice known as "re-aging." This form of regulatory forbearance eased the burden of provisions and charge-offs of these loans for issuers.

Argentina (2002)

The 2002 Argentine asymmetric pesification is an example of what not to do. In response to the crisis, in January 2002 Argentina introduced a heterodox economic program that included an external debt moratorium, an end to convertibility, and the introduction of a dual exchange regime. In February, the exchange regime was unified, the maturities of time deposits extended (the *corralón*), and bank balance sheets de-dollarized at asymmetric rates—Arg$1 per U.S. dollar on the asset side, and Arg$1.4 per U.S. dollar on the liability side. The assets and liabilities of the banks were also subjected to asymmetric indexation: deposits were indexed to the rate of consumer price inflation whereas certain loans were indexed to wage inflation.

This policy framework imposed significant losses on banks and depositors. The fiscal cost amounted to about 15 percent of GDP, largely due to fiscal outlays accruing to the banks;[21] the losses suffered by banks far exceeded the entire net worth of the banking system. The deposit freeze and conversion resulted in a loss of depositor confidence and the collapse of financial intermediation. The conversion of deposits meant a dollar value erosion of 40 percent. Banks also lost because many of the creditworthy borrowers worrying about a further change in the government's decision opted to pay off their loans. This left the banks with a smaller, lower-quality loan book. Most banks reported significant reductions in both staff and branches and remained cautious in expanding credit. The conversion led to a severe undercapitalization of the banking system. Moreover, depositors took advantage of exceptions and loopholes in the system, using judicial rulings to release frozen deposits at the market exchange rate. In this environment, a large number of banks were weakened and became dependent on the central bank liquidity window, accounting for 13 percent of total assets in 2003. The crisis had profound effects on the portfolio of the banking system. Private sector credit fell sharply, reflecting the collapse in credit demand and the repayments by existing borrowers. By 2003, loans to the private sector declined to 15 percent of total assets (US$8.4 billion) and exposure to the public sector increased to 50 percent of total assets.

Taiwan Province of China (2005)

Rapid expansion of credit card debt resulted in a distressed credit card market, although credit card losses mostly affected small and specialized institutions. The

---

[21] A large fraction of this fiscal cost included subsidies to banks to compensate for the asymmetric pesification and asymmetric indexation.

ratio of nonperforming loans (NPLs) to total loans for cash cards peaked at about 8 percent in 2006 (up from about 2 percent a year earlier), and for credit cards at about 3.5 percent (up from about 3 percent a year earlier). The system-wide NPL ratio was not visibly affected and continued the downward trend that started when Taiwan POC's financial sector reform program began in 2000. Although the system-wide NPL ratio was not severely affected by the nonperforming card loans, there was a negative impact on the profitability of domestic banks. The average return on equity of domestic banks dropped to –0.41 percent at end-2006 (from 4.58 percent at end-2005), and the average return on assets dropped to –0.03 percent at end-2006 (from 0.31 percent at end-2005). To facilitate renegotiation of debt between credit card issuers and debtors, the authorities initiated a personal-debt-restructuring program offering better repayment terms, covering 30 percent of outstanding credit card balances. Restructured loans were largely reclassified as performing, effectively granting issuers regulatory forbearance.

United States (2008)

A prolonged credit boom, supported by low interest rates and lax underwriting standards, and the expectation of rising house prices, came to a halt in 2007. The bursting of the U.S. housing bubble led to rising foreclosures, which further depressed house prices. Foreclosures were increasing because of household debt overhang,[22] coordination failures in arranging preforeclosure workouts, and legal impediments to loan workouts.[23] The U.S. federal government introduced or sponsored a number of homeowner rescue programs, starting with the FHA-Secure program[24] announced in August 2007, and the Hope for Homeowners

---

[22] About 10 million U.S. homeowners reportedly had negative equity, and more than half of subprime borrowers had debt-to-income ratios exceeding 38 percent, a level below which loans are generally deemed affordable in the United States.

[23] Including no-recourse mortgages that allow "under water" borrowers to walk away from affordable loans; bankruptcy law that does not allow modification of unaffordable mortgages on principal residences; and lack of safe harbor for loan modifications that leaves servicers open to lawsuits from disgruntled investors.

[24] FHA-Secure, introduced on August 31, 2007, and significantly amended on May 7, 2008, offered stressed homeowners an opportunity to refinance into FHA-insured loans. The lender had to agree to write the loan off (via a "short refinancing") for an amount not to exceed 97 or 90 percent of the current appraised home value, depending on the borrower's recent payment record. The 97 percent LTV applied to borrowers who had not missed more than two monthly payments (individually or consecutively) during the previous year, and 90 percent to borrowers who had missed up to three monthly payments. The payments on the new loan were not to exceed 31 percent of income, and the total of all debt payments (home and nonhome) were not to exceed 43 percent. Delinquent borrowers had to pay a 2.25 percent up-front mortgage insurance premium and 55 basis points annually, while current borrowers paid 1.50 and 0.50 percent. The program, however, was not successful in overcoming the difficulties identified in this chapter. The number of FHA-Secure refinancings was disappointing, and it was phased out at the end of 2008.

(H4H) program,[25] which was activated on October 1, 2008. These efforts met with very limited success in stemming foreclosures (for further details, see Kiff and Klyuev, 2009).

In addition, the Federal Deposit Insurance Corporation (FDIC) introduced a streamlined modification program for the mortgage loans it picked up from failed mortgage lender-servicer IndyMac.[26] A similar program for Fannie Mae– and Freddie Mac–guaranteed mortgages was also introduced by the Federal Housing Finance Agency.[27] They both use a stepwise decision process focusing on affordability, not negative equity.

Several large U.S. banks designed voluntary workouts of distressed mortgages. For example, Citigroup announced in early November 2008 that it would modify terms on mortgages for borrowers with debt-to-income ratios in excess of 40 percent. Modifications included a lowering of the interest rate, an extension of the terms of the loans, and as a last resort, a reduction in principal.

Also, some states imposed foreclosure moratoriums, typically three to six months long, but these were just temporary palliatives unlikely to be effective in the long run in the absence of a more comprehensive approach.

---

[25] The H4H program improved on FHA-Secure by covering severely delinquent borrowers and providing incentives for second-lien write-offs. It applies to mortgages on primary residences originated before January 2, 2008, and to borrowers whose current mortgage payments exceed 31 percent of gross income. The lender has to agree to write the loan off for an amount not to exceed 96.5 percent of the current appraised value, and waive all prepayment penalties and late payment fees. This "short refinancing" is funded by a new 30- or 40-year, fixed-rate, FHA-insured loan with payments that are at or below 31 percent of income, and all debt payments (home and nonhome) must be at or below 43 percent. For borrowers with higher debt loads, the debt-to-income ratio can be expanded to 38 percent but, in this case, the new principal amount cannot exceed 90 percent of current appraised value. The first lien holder also pays a 3 percent up-front FHA insurance premium, and the homeowner pays a 1.50 percent annual premium. In addition, if the homeowner sells the house or refinances the new mortgage, the Department of Housing and Urban Development gets back some of the "instant" equity (100 percent in the first year, declining to 50 percent after five years), plus, if the property is sold, 50 percent of any net house price appreciation. Also, borrowers are prohibited from taking out new subordinated liens during the first five years, except when necessary to ensure maintenance of property standards.

[26] Under the IndyMac loan-modification program, eligible mortgages were modified into sustainable mortgages at a permanently reduced interest rate to achieve sustainable payments at a 38 percent debt-to-income ratio. The loan modification was available for borrowers on a first mortgage on their primary residence owned or securitized and serviced by IndyMac if the borrower was seriously delinquent or in default. The loan modification did not involve fees or other charges for the borrower. The IndyMac scheme is an example of a voluntary loan workout scheme.

[27] First, they only consider for modification loans that are seriously delinquent (60 days or more for the FDIC program and 90 days for the FHFA program), to borrowers who own and occupy the property and who have not filed for bankruptcy. The programs then attempt to find the modification with the minimum net present value impact that achieves a 38 percent debt-to-income ratio. The sequential process used by the FDIC program starts by capitalizing the arrearage into the unpaid balance, and if the resulting payment puts the borrower's DTI above 38 percent, interest rate reductions and amortization term extensions are offered. If the DTI is still above 38 percent, principal forbearance is applied, involving converting a portion of the unpaid balance into a zero interest note due when the mortgage is paid off. Seriously delinquent loans, for which these modifications are insufficient to achieve the DTI targets, can still be considered on a case-by-case basis.

TABLE 17A.1

Household Indicators before and after Debt Restructuring											
	United States (1933)		Mexico (1998)		Uruguay (2000)		Korea, Rep. of (2002)		Argentina (2002)		Taiwan Province of China (2005)	
	1932	1936	1997	2001	1999	2003	2001	2005	2001	2005	2004	2008
Household income growth (%)	−25.8	15.1	5.2	−1.2	−3.3	2.3	3.1	3.7	−5.4	8.1	…	…
Consumption growth (%)	−21.5	9.7	6.5	2.5	−1.5	2.0	4.9	3.6	−5.7	8.9	4.5	1.3
Unemployment rate (%)	22.7	14.2	3.7	2.8	11.3	15.4	4.0	3.7	20.7	10.1	4.4	3.9
Private debt/GDP (%)	45.4	32.1	24.5	14.5	49.8	46.4	92.7	100.3	20.8	11.7	…	…

Source: IMF staff estimates.

Hungary (2008)

In November 2008, Hungarian commercial banks—faced with increased credit risk in their loan portfolios denominated in foreign currency due to a sharp depreciation of the local currency—signed a gentleman's agreement with the Ministry of Finance on a foreign-currency loan workout program.[28]

The workout provided borrowers with the following options: The first option was to apply to have their foreign-currency loans converted to forint-denominated loans. If they did so before the end of the year, they would not be charged additional fees. The second option was to ask for an extension of the loan duration free of charge if there was a significant increase in their monthly repayments. The third option was to ask for a temporary easing of repayment obligations, especially for borrowers who became unemployed. The key elements of the restructuring (the rate of loan conversion into the local currency and interest rates charged on restructured loans) were left to be determined by the parties involved. The conversion part of the program was not taken up because of high domestic interest rates.

In addition, the government was preparing legislation that would allow for temporary government guarantees (up to two years) on mortgage payments for those who became unemployed. Guarantees were available for mortgages outstanding up to 20 million Hungarian forint on primary residences only, and required that a minimum payment of 10,000 forint a month be maintained by the borrower.

United Kingdom (2008)

In early December 2008, the U.K. Treasury announced the Homeowners Support Mortgage Scheme to reduce the number of home foreclosures. Under the scheme, U.K. homeowners struggling to make mortgage payments could defer a portion of their payments by up to two years. Borrowers with mortgages up to £400,000

---

[28] Reportedly, the agreement was signed somewhat reluctantly by the largest nine commercial banks, after the Ministry of Finance had stated it would introduce legislation to the same effect.

and with savings lower than £16,000 were eligible to roll up mortgage payments into the principal, and pay off the principal when conditions improved. The U.K. Treasury was to guarantee the deferred interest payments for those banks participating in the scheme. Most of the country's largest lenders agreed to participate in the program.

Table 17A.1 summarizes household indicators for each of the case studies, except for the recent episodes in Hungary, the United Kingdom, and the United States.

REFERENCES

Hoelscher, David, 2006, *Bank Restructuring and Resolution* (Washington: International Monetary Fund).

———, and Marc Quintyn, 2003, *Managing Systemic Financial Crises,* IMF Occasional Paper No. 224 (Washington: International Monetary Fund).

Honohan, Patrick, and Luc Laeven, 2005, *Systemic Financial Crises: Containment and Resolution* (Cambridge, United Kingdom: Cambridge University Press).

INSOL International, 2001, "Consumer Debt Report: Report of Findings and Recommendations," May.

Kang, Tae Soo, and Guanon Ma, 2007, "Recent Episodes of Credit Card Distress in Asia," *BIS Quarterly Review,* June. http://www.bis.org/repofficepubl/arpresearch_fs_200706.01 .pdf?noframes=1.

Kiff, J., and V. Klyuev, 2009, "Foreclosure Mitigation Efforts in the United States: Approaches and Challenges," IMF Staff Position Note 09/02 (Washington: International Monetary Fund).

Krugman, P., 1988, "Market-Based Debt-Reduction Schemes," NBER Working Paper No. W2587 (Cambridge, Massachusetts: National Bureau of Economic Research).

Myers, S., 1977, "Determinants of Corporate Borrowing," *Journal of Financial Economics,* Vol. 5, pp. 147–75.

CHAPTER 18

Dealing with Household Debt

Deniz Igan, Daniel Leigh, John Simon, and Petia Topalova

Household debt soared in the years leading up to the Great Recession. In advanced economies, during the five years preceding 2007, the ratio of household debt to income rose by an average of 39 percentage points, to 138 percent. In Denmark, Iceland, Ireland, the Netherlands, and Norway, debt peaked at more than 200 percent of household income. A surge in household debt to historic highs also occurred in emerging market economies such as Estonia, Hungary, Latvia, and Lithuania. The concurrent boom in both house prices and the stock market meant that household debt relative to assets held broadly stable, which masked households' growing exposure to a sharp fall in asset prices (Figure 18.1).

When house prices declined, ushering in the global financial crisis, many households saw their wealth shrink relative to their debt and, with less income and more unemployment, found it harder to meet mortgage payments. By the end of 2011, real house prices had fallen from their peak by about 41 percent in Ireland, 29 percent in Iceland, 23 percent in Spain and the United States, and 21 percent in Denmark. Household defaults, underwater mortgages (for which the loan balance exceeds the house value), foreclosures, and fire sales became endemic in a number of economies. Household deleveraging by paying off debts or defaulting on them began in some countries. It was most pronounced in the United States, where about two-thirds of the debt reduction reflected defaults (McKinsey, 2012).

What does this imply for economic performance? Some studies suggest that many economies' total gross debt levels are excessive and need to decline.[1] For example, two influential reports by McKinsey (2010, 2012) emphasize that to "clear the way" for economic growth, advanced economies need to reverse the recent surge in total gross debt. Yet others suggest that the recent rise in debt is not necessarily a reason for concern. For example, Fatás (2012) argues that the McKinsey reports' focus on gross debt is "very misleading" because what matters for countries is net wealth, not gross debt.[2] A high level of private sector debt as

The authors thank Edda Rós Karlsdóttir and Franek Rozwadowski for extensive contributions and Shan Chen and Angela Espiritu for excellent research assistance.
[1] Sovereign debt rose sharply in advanced economies as a result of the crisis, and overall gross debt has reached levels not seen in half a century.
[2] To illustrate this point, Fatás (2012) refers to Japan, where the gross-debt-to-GDP ratio is exceptionally high but where, reflecting years of current account surpluses, the economy is a net creditor to the rest of the world. Similarly, the elevated Japanese gross government debt stock is balanced by large private sector assets.

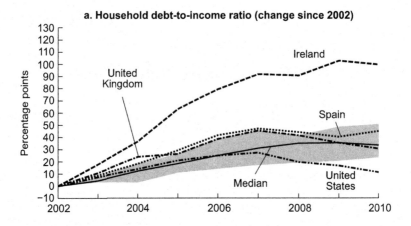

a. Household debt-to-income ratio (change since 2002)

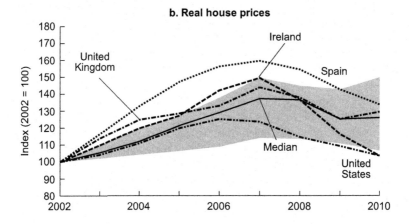

b. Real house prices

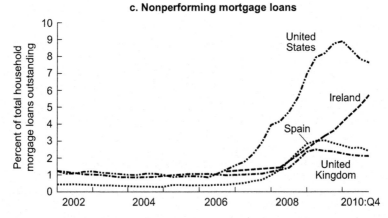

c. Nonperforming mortgage loans

Figure 18.1 Household Debt, House Prices, and Nonperforming Mortgage Loans, 2002–10

Sources: Eurostat; Haver Analytics; Federal Reserve Bank of New York; Reserve Bank of Australia; Bank of Spain; U.K. Council of Mortgage Lenders; Central Bank of Ireland; Chapter 3 of April 2011 *Global Financial Stability Report*; and IMF staff calculations.

Note: The shaded areas in panels a and b denote the interquartile range of the change in the household debt-to-income ratio since 2002 and the real house price index, respectively. Nonperforming loans are loans more than 90 days in arrears.

a share of the economy is also often interpreted as a sign of financial development, which, in turn, is beneficial for long-term growth (e.g., Rajan and Zingales, 1998). Similarly, Krugman (2011) notes that because gross debt is "(mostly) money we owe to ourselves," it is not immediately obvious why it should matter. However, Krugman also cautions that gross debt can become a problem because of distributional and incentives concerns. Overall, there is no accepted wisdom about whether and how gross debt may restrain economic activity.

This chapter contributes to the debate about gross debt by focusing on the household sector. Previous studies focused more on deleveraging by other sectors.[3] In particular, it addresses the following questions:

- What is the relationship between household debt and the depth of economic downturns? Are busts that are preceded by larger run-ups in gross household debt typically more severe?

- Why might gross household debt be a problem? What are the theoretical mechanisms by which gross household debt and deleveraging may restrain economic activity?[4]

- What can governments do to support growth when household debt becomes a problem? In particular, what policies have been effective in reducing the extent of household debt overhang and in averting unnecessary household defaults, foreclosures, and fire sales? How effective have recent initiatives been?[5]

To address these questions, a statistical analysis is conducted of the relationship between household debt and the depth of economic downturns. The purpose is to provide prima facie evidence rather than to establish causality. The analysis focuses on housing busts, given the important role of the housing market in triggering the Great Recession, but also considers recessions more generally. It then reviews the theoretical reasons for why household debt might constrain economic activity. Finally, selected case studies are used to investigate which government policies have been effective in dealing with excessive household debt. The episodes considered are the United States in the 1930s and late in the first decade of the 2000s, Hungary and Iceland late in the first decade of the 2000s, Colombia in 1999, and the Scandinavian countries in the early 1990s. In each case, a housing

---

[3] For example, see IMF (2010), which assesses the implications of sovereign deleveraging (fiscal consolidation). Because deleveraging by various sectors—household, bank, corporate, and sovereign—will have different implications for economic activity, each is worth studying in its own right.

[4] A related question is what level of household debt is optimal, but such an assessment is beyond the scope of this chapter.

[5] This chapter does not investigate which policies can help prevent the excessive buildup of household debt before the bust, an issue that is addressed in other studies. These two sets of policies are not mutually exclusive. For example, policies that prevent an excessive buildup in household debt during a boom can alleviate the consequences of a bust. See Crowe and others (2011), IMF (2011a), Dell'Ariccia and others (2012), and Chapters 11 and 12 in this volume for policies designed to avert real estate price booms and restrain rapid growth in private sector debt.

bust preceded or coincided with a substantial increase in household debt, but the policy responses were very different.

These are the chapter's main findings:

- Housing busts preceded by larger run-ups in gross household debt are associated with significantly larger contractions in economic activity. The declines in household consumption and real GDP are substantially larger, unemployment rises more, and the reduction in economic activity persists for at least five years. A similar pattern holds for recessions more generally: recessions preceded by larger increases in household debt are more severe.

- The larger declines in economic activity are not simply a reflection of the larger drops in house prices and the associated destruction of household wealth. The severity of the contraction seems to be explained by the combination of house price declines and prebust leverage. In particular, household consumption falls by more than four times the amount that can be explained by the fall in house prices in high-debt economies. Nor is the larger contraction simply driven by financial crises. The relationship between household debt and the contraction in consumption also holds for economies that did not experience a banking crisis around the time of the housing bust.

- Macroeconomic policies are a crucial element of forestalling excessive contractions in economic activity during episodes of household deleveraging. For example, monetary easing in economies in which mortgages typically have variable interest rates, as in the Scandinavian countries, can quickly reduce mortgage payments and avert household defaults. Similarly, fiscal transfers to households through social safety nets can boost households' incomes and improve their ability to service debt, as in the Scandinavian countries. Furthermore, such automatic transfers can help prevent self-reinforcing cycles of rising defaults, declining house prices, and lower aggregate demand. Macroeconomic stimulus, however, has its limits. The zero lower bound on nominal interest rates can prevent sufficient rate cuts, and high government debt may constrain the scope for deficit-financed transfers.

- Government policies targeted at reducing the level of household debt relative to household assets and debt service relative to household repayment capacity can—at limited fiscal cost—substantially mitigate the negative effects of household deleveraging on economic activity. In particular, bold and well-designed household-debt-restructuring programs, such as those implemented in the United States in the 1930s and in Iceland more recently, can significantly reduce the number of household defaults and foreclosures. In so doing, these programs help prevent self-reinforcing cycles of declining house prices and lower aggregate demand.

The first section of this chapter conducts a statistical analysis to shed light on the relationship between the rise in household debt during a boom and the severity of the subsequent bust. It also reviews the theoretical literature to identify the channels through which shifts in household gross debt can have a negative effect on economic activity. The second section provides case studies of government policies aimed at mitigating the negative effects of household debt during housing busts. The last section discusses the implications of these findings for economies facing household deleveraging.

HOW HOUSEHOLD DEBT CAN CONSTRAIN ECONOMIC ACTIVITY

This section reviews the role of gross household debt in amplifying slumps by analyzing the experience of advanced economies since 1980. It also discusses the theoretical reasons gross household debt can deepen and prolong economic contractions.

Stylized Facts: Household Debt and Housing Busts

Are housing busts more severe when they are preceded by large increases in gross household debt? To answer this question, some stylized facts are provided about what happens when a housing bust occurs in two groups of economies. The first has a housing boom but no increase in household debt. The other has a housing boom and a large increase in household debt. The focus is on housing busts, given how prevalent they were in advanced economies during the Great Recession.[6] But the results for recessions in general are also reported, regardless of whether they are associated with housing busts. The discussion starts by summarizing the ways in which different economies fared during the Great Recession depending on the size of their household debt buildup. A more refined statistical approach is then used to consider the broader historical experience with housing busts and recessions and to distinguish the role of household debt from the roles of financial crises and house price declines.

The Great Recession

The Great Recession was particularly severe in economies that had larger buildups in household debt before the crisis. As Figure 18.2 shows, the consumption loss in 2010 relative to the precrisis trend was greater for economies that had larger increases in the gross household-debt-to-income ratio during 2002–06.[7] The consumption loss in 2010 is the gap between the log level of real household consumption in 2010 and the projected real household consumption that year based on the precrisis trend. The precrisis trend is, in turn, defined as the extrapolation of the log level of real household consumption based on a linear trend estimated

---

[6] Housing-related debt (mortgages) comprises about 70 percent of gross household debt in advanced economies. The remainder consists mainly of credit card debt and auto loans.

[7] See Appendix 18A for data sources. Glick and Lansing (2010) report a similar finding for a smaller cross-section of advanced economies.

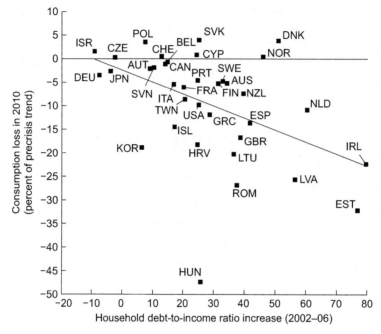

Figure 18.2 The Great Recession: Consumption Loss versus Precrisis Rise in Household Debt

Sources: Eurostat; Haver Analytics; and IMF staff calculations.

Note: AUS: Australia; AUT: Austria; BEL: Belgium; CAN: Canada; CHE: Switzerland; CYP: Cyprus; CZE: Czech Republic; DEU: Germany; DNK: Denmark; ESP: Spain; EST: Estonia; FIN: Finland; FRA: France; GBR: United Kingdom; GRC: Greece; HRV: Croatia; HUN: Hungary; IRL: Ireland; ISL: Iceland; ISR: Israel; ITA: Italy; JPN: Japan; KOR: Republic of Korea; LTU: Lithuania; LVA: Latvia; NLD: Netherlands; NOR: Norway; NZL: New Zealand; POL: Poland; PRT: Portugal; ROM: Romania; SVK: Slovak Republic; SVN: Slovenia; SWE: Sweden; TWN: Taiwan Province of China; USA: United States.

from 1996 through 2004, following the methodology of IMF (2009). The estimation of the precrisis trend ends several years before the crisis so that it is not contaminated by the possibility of an unsustainable boom during the run-up to the crisis or a precrisis slowdown. The slope of the regression line is –0.26, implying that for each additional 10 percentage point rise in household debt before the crisis, the consumption loss was larger by 2.6 percentage points, a substantial (and statistically significant) relationship.[8]

---

[8] The sharper fall in consumption in high-debt-growth economies does not simply reflect the occurrence of banking crises. The relationship between household debt accumulation and the depth of the Great Recession remains similar and statistically significant after excluding the 18 economies that experienced banking crises at some point during 2007–11, based on the banking crises identified by Laeven and Valencia (2010). The sharper contraction in consumption also does not simply reflect a bigger precrisis consumption boom. The finding of a strong inverse relationship between the precrisis debt run-up and the severity of the recession is similar and statistically significant when controlling for the precrisis boom in consumption.

Historical Experience

Is the Great Recession part of a broader historical pattern—specifically, are busts that are preceded by larger run-ups in gross household debt usually more severe? To answer this question, statistical techniques are used to relate the buildup in household debt during the boom to the nature of economic activity during the bust. Given the data available on gross household debt, the focus is on a sample of 24 Organization for Economic Cooperation and Development (OECD) economies and Taiwan Province of China during 1980–2011. First, housing busts are identified based on the turning points (peaks) in nominal house prices compiled by Claessens, Kose, and Terrones (2010).[9] In the sample of 25 economies, 99 housing busts occurred. Next, the housing busts are divided into two groups: those that involved a large run-up in the household-debt-to-income ratio during the three years leading up to the bust and those that did not.[10] The two groups are referred to as "high-debt" and "low-debt" busts, respectively. Other measures of leverage (such as debt-to-assets and debt-to-net-worth ratios) are not widely available for this multicountry sample. Finally, measures of economic activity are regressed on the housing bust dummies for the two groups using a methodology similar to that of Cerra and Saxena (2008), among others. Given the focus on the household sector, the analysis starts by considering the behavior of household consumption and then reports results for GDP and its components, unemployment, and house prices.

Specifically, changes in the log of real household consumption are regressed on its lagged values (to capture the normal fluctuations of consumption) as well as on contemporaneous and lagged values of the housing bust dummies. Including lags allows household consumption to respond with a delay to housing busts.[11] To test whether the severity of housing busts differs between the two groups, the housing bust dummy is interacted with a dummy variable that indicates whether the bust was in the high-debt group or the low-debt group. The specification also includes a full set of time fixed effects to account for common shocks, such as shifts in oil prices, and economy-specific fixed effects to account for differences in the economies' normal growth rates. The estimated responses are cumulated to recover the evolution of the level of household consumption following a housing bust. The figures that follow show the estimated response of consumption and a one standard error band around the estimated response.

---

[9] Claessens, Kose, and Terrones (2010) identify turning points in nominal house prices using the Harding and Pagan (2002) algorithm.

[10] For the baseline specification, a "large" increase in debt is defined as an increase above the median of all busts, but, as the robustness analysis in Appendix 18B reports, the results do not depend on this precise threshold. The median is an increase of 6.7 percentage points of household income during the three years leading up to the bust, and there is wide variation in the size of the increase. For example, the household-debt-to-income ratio rose by 17 percentage points during the period leading up to the U.K. housing bust of 1989 and by 68 percentage points before the Irish housing bust of 2006.

[11] Appendix 18B provides further details on the estimation methodology.

The regression results suggest that housing busts preceded by larger run-ups in household debt tend to be followed by more severe and longer-lasting declines in household consumption. Panel a of Figure 18.3 shows that the decline in real household consumption is 4.3 percent after five years for the high-debt group and only 0.4 percent for the low-debt group. The difference between the two samples is 3.9 percentage points and is statistically significant at the 1 percent level, as reported in Appendix 18B. These results survive a variety of robustness tests, including different estimation approaches (such as generalized method of moments), alternative specifications (changing the lag length), and dropping outliers (as identified by Cook's distance). (See Appendix 18B on the robustness checks.)

Housing busts preceded by larger run-ups in household leverage result in more contraction of general economic activity. Figure 18.3 shows that real GDP typically falls more and unemployment rises more for the high-debt busts. Net exports typically make a more positive contribution to GDP—partially offsetting the fall in domestic demand—but this reflects a greater decline in imports rather than a boom in exports.[12]

A logical question is whether the larger decline in household spending simply reflects larger declines in house prices. Panel a of Figure 18.4 shows that real house prices do indeed fall significantly more after highly leveraged busts. The fall in real house prices is 10.8 percentage points larger in the high-debt busts than in the low-debt busts, and the difference between the two samples is significant at the 1 percent level. However, this larger fall in house prices cannot plausibly explain the greater decline in household consumption. Real consumption declines by more than 3.9 percentage points more in the high-debt busts, implying an elasticity of about 0.4, well above the range of housing wealth consumption elasticities in the literature (0.05–0.1; 0.075 is used in Figure 18.4). Based on this literature, the fall in house prices therefore explains at most one-quarter of the decline in household consumption. To further establish that the decline in consumption reflects more than just house price declines, the analysis is repeated while replacing the housing bust dummy variable with the percentage decrease in house prices. The results suggest that for the same fall in real house prices (1 percent), real household consumption falls by about twice as much during high-debt busts as during low-debt busts. Therefore, it seems to be the combination of house price declines and prebust leverage that explains the severity of the contraction of household consumption.

Moreover, household deleveraging tends to be more pronounced following busts preceded by a larger run-up in household debt. In particular, the household-debt-to-income ratio declines by 5.4 percentage points following a high-debt housing bust (Figure 18.5). The decline is statistically significant. In contrast, there is no decline in the debt-to-income ratio following low-debt

---

[12] Estimation results for investment also show a larger fall for the high-debt busts. Estimation results for residential investment (for which data are less widely available) also show a larger fall for the high-debt busts, but the responses are not precisely estimated because of the smaller sample size.

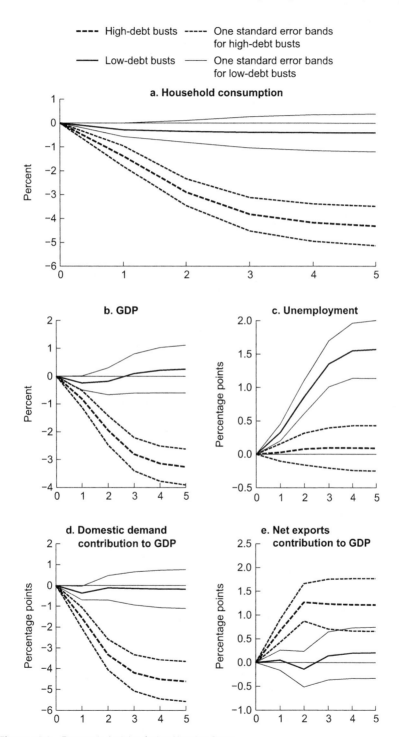

Figure 18.3 Economic Activity during Housing Busts

Source: IMF staff calculations.

Note: Year 0 denotes the year of the housing bust. High- and low-debt busts are defined, respectively, as above and below
the median increase in the household debt-to-income ratio during the three years preceding the bust.

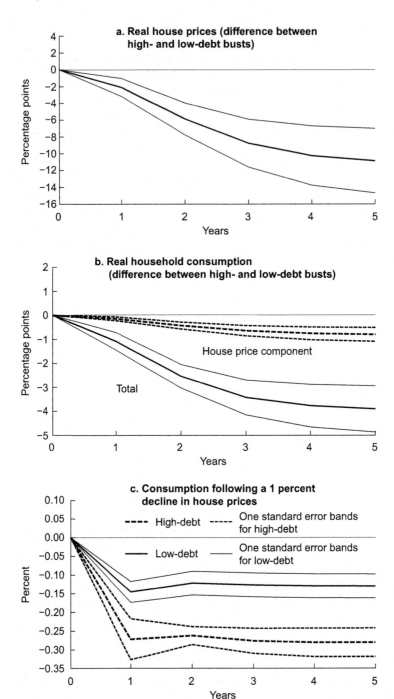

Figure 18.4 Housing Wealth and Household Consumption

Source: IMF staff calculations.

Note: Year 0 denotes the year of the housing bust. High- and low-debt are defined, respectively, as above and below the median increase in the household debt-to-income ratio during the three years preceding the full in house price.

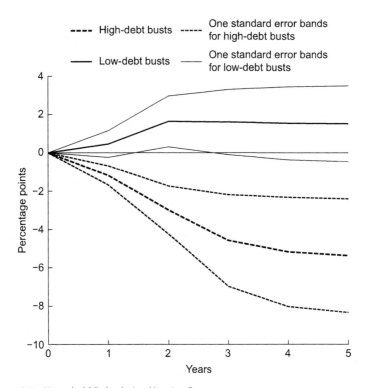

Figure 18.5   Household Debt during Housing Busts

Source: IMF staff calculations.

Note: Year 0 denotes the year of the housing bust. High- and low-debt busts are defined, respectively, as above and below
the median increase in the household debt-to-income ratio during the three years preceding the bust.

housing busts. Instead, there is a small and statistically insignificant increase. This finding suggests that part of the stronger contraction in economic activity following high-debt housing busts is due to a more intense household deleveraging process.

It is important to establish whether the results are driven by financial crises. The contractionary effects of such crises have already been investigated by previous studies (among others, Cerra and Saxena, 2008; IMF, 2009; and Reinhart and Rogoff, 2009). The analysis finds that the results are not driven by the global financial crisis—similar results apply when the sample ends in 2006, as reported in Appendix 18B. Moreover, similar results are found when the analysis is repeated but focuses only on housing busts that were not preceded or followed by a systemic banking crisis, as identified by Laeven and Valencia (2010), within a two-year window on either side of the housing bust. For this limited set of housing busts, those preceded by a larger accumulation of household debt are followed by deeper and more prolonged downturns (Figure 18.6). Therefore, the results are not simply the result of banking crises.

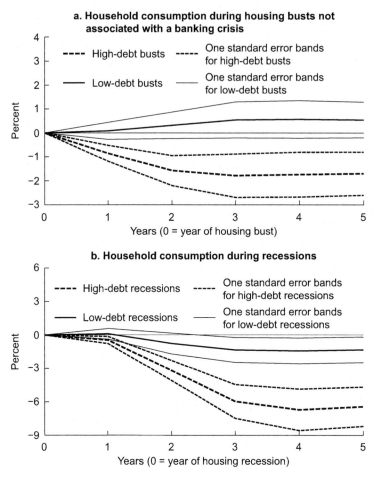

Figure 18.6 Household Consumption

Source: IMF staff calculations.

Note: Systemic banking crisis indicators are from the updated Laeven and Valencia (2010) database. High- and low-debt busts are defined, respectively, as above and below the median increase in the household debt-to-income ratio during the three years preceding the housing bust. High- and low-debt recessions are defined, respectively, as above and below the median increase in the household debt-to-income ratio during the three years preceding the recession.

Finally, it is worth investigating whether high household debt also exacerbates the effects of other adverse shocks. The analysis is thus repeated replacing the housing bust dummies with recession dummies. The recession dummies are constructed based on the list of recession dates provided by Howard, Martin, and Wilson (2011). Figure 18.6 (panel b) also shows that recessions preceded by a larger run-up in household debt do indeed tend to be more severe and protracted.

Overall, this analysis suggests that when households accumulate more debt during a boom, the subsequent bust features a more severe contraction in economic activity. These findings for OECD economies are consistent with those of Mian, Rao, and Sufi (2011) for the United States. These authors use detailed U.S. county-level data for the Great Recession to identify the causal effect of household debt. They conclude that the greater decline in consumption after 2007 in U.S. counties that accumulated more debt during 2002–06 is too large to be explained by the larger fall in house prices in those counties.[13] This conclusion is consistent with the cross-country evidence in Figure 18.4. They also find evidence of more rapid household deleveraging in high-debt U.S. counties, which underscores the role of deleveraging and is consistent with the cross-country evidence in Figure 18.5. In related work, Mian and Sufi (2011) show that a higher level of household debt in 2007 is associated with sharper declines in spending on consumer durables, residential investment, and employment (Figure 18.7). Based on their findings, they conclude that the decline in aggregate demand driven by household balance sheet weakness explains the majority of the job losses in the United States during the Great Recession (Mian and Sufi, 2012).

The findings are also broadly consistent with the more general finding in the literature that recessions preceded by economy-wide credit booms—which may or may not coincide with household credit booms—tend to be deeper and more protracted than other recessions (e.g., Claessens, Kose, and Terrones, 2010; and Jordà, Schularick, and Taylor, 2011). This conclusion is also consistent with evidence that consumption volatility is positively correlated with household debt (Isaksen and others, 2011).

Why Does Household Debt Matter?

Evidence has been found that downturns are more severe when preceded by larger increases in household debt. This subsection discusses how the pattern fits with the predictions of theoretical models. A natural starting point is to consider a closed economy with no government debt. In such an economy, net private debt must be zero, because one person's debt is another's asset. Some people may accumulate debt, but this would simply represent "money we owe to ourselves" (Krugman, 2011) with no obvious macroeconomic implications. Nevertheless, even when changes in gross household debt simply are accompanied by change in economy-wide net debt, those changes can influence macroeconomic performance by amplifying the effects of shocks. In particular, a number of theoretical models predict that buildups in household debt drive deep and prolonged downturns.[14]

---

[13] In particular, by comparing house price declines with consumption declines in counties with high and low levels of household debt, they obtain an implicit elasticity of consumption relative to house prices of 0.3 to 0.7, which is well above the range of estimates in the literature. This outcome suggests that only 14 to 30 percent of the greater decline in consumption in high-debt counties was due to the larger falls in house prices in those counties.

[14] In an open economy, gross household debt can have additional effects. In particular, a reduction in household debt could signal a transfer of resources from domestic to foreign households, resulting in even larger macroeconomic effects than in a closed economy.

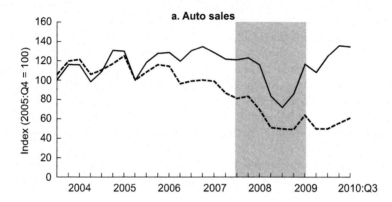

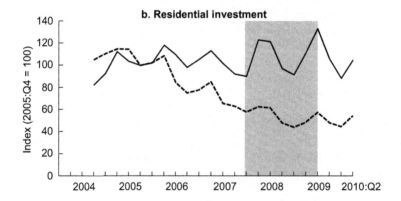

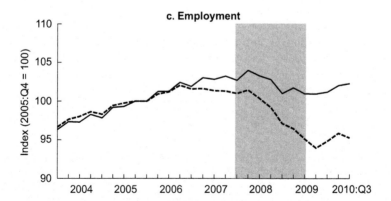

FIGURE 18.7 Economic Activity during the Great Recession in the United States

Source: Mian and Sufi (2011).

Note: Shaded area indicates U.S. recession based on National Bureau of Economic Research dates.

The main channels through which household debt can amplify downturns and weaken recoveries are now discussed, highlighting the policy implications. In particular, the circumstances under which government intervention can improve on a purely market-driven outcome are explained.

Differences between Borrowers and Lenders

The accumulation of household debt amplifies slumps in a number of recent models that differentiate between borrowers and lenders and include liquidity constraints. A key feature of these models is the idea that the distribution of debt within an economy matters (Eggertsson and Krugman, 2010; Guerrieri and Lorenzoni, 2011; and Hall, 2011).[15] As Tobin (1980, p. 10) argues, "the population is not distributed between debtors and creditors randomly. Debtors have borrowed for good reasons, most of which indicate a high marginal propensity to spend from wealth or from current income or from any other liquid resources they can command."[16] Indeed, household debt increased more at the lower ends of the income and wealth distribution during the first decade of the 2000s in the United States (Kumhof and Rancière, 2010).

A shock to the borrowing capacity of debtors with high marginal propensities to consume that forces them to reduce their debt could then lead to a decline in aggregate activity. Deleveraging could stem from a realization that house prices were overvalued (as in Buiter, 2010; and Eggertsson and Krugman, 2010), a tightening in credit standards (Guerrieri and Lorenzoni, 2011), a sharp revision in income expectations, or an increase in economic uncertainty (Fisher, 1933; and Minsky, 1986). Here, a sufficiently large fall in the interest rate could induce creditor households to spend more, thus offsetting the decline in spending by the debtors. But, as these models show, the presence of the zero lower bound on nominal interest rates or other price rigidities can prevent these creditor households from picking up the slack. This feature is particularly relevant today because policy rates are near zero in many advanced economies.

Consumption may be further depressed following shocks in the presence of uncertainty, given the need for precautionary saving (Guerrieri and Lorenzoni, 2011; and Carroll, Slacalek, and Sommer, 2012). The cut in household consumption would then be particularly abrupt, "undershooting" its long-term level (as it appears to have done in the United States late in the first decade of the 2000s; Glick and Lansing, 2009). Such a sharp contraction in aggregate consumption would provide a rationale for temporarily pursuing expansionary macroeconomic

---

[15] In an earlier theoretical sketch, King (1994) discusses how differences in the marginal propensity to consume between borrowing and lending households can generate an aggregate downturn when household leverage is high.

[16] Differences in the propensity to consume can arise for a number of reasons. Life-cycle motives have been emphasized as a source of differences in saving behavior across cohorts (Modigliani, 1986, among others). Others have focused on the role of time preferences, introducing a class of relatively impatient agents (Iacoviello, 2005; and Eggertsson and Krugman, 2010). Dynan, Skinner, and Zeldes (2004) find a strong positive relationship between personal saving rates and lifetime income, suggesting that the rich consume a smaller proportion of their income than the poor.

policies, including fiscal stimulus targeted at financially constrained households (Eggertsson and Krugman, 2010; and Carroll, Slacalek, and Sommer, 2012) and household debt restructuring (Rogoff, 2011).

Negative Price Effects from Fire Sales

A further negative effect on economic activity of high household debt in the presence of a shock, postulated by numerous models, comes from the forced sale of durable goods (Shleifer and Vishny, 1992; Mayer, 1995; Lorenzoni, 2008; and Krishnamurthy, 2010). For example, a rise in unemployment reduces households' ability to service their debt, foreshadowing increases in household defaults, foreclosures, and creditors selling foreclosed properties at distressed, or fire-sale, prices. Estimates suggest that a single foreclosure lowers the price of a neighboring property by about 1 percent, but that the effects, if there is a wave of foreclosures, can be much larger, with estimates of price declines reaching almost 30 percent (Campbell, Giglio, and Pathak, 2011). The associated negative price effects, in turn, reduce economic activity through a number of self-reinforcing contractionary spirals. These include negative wealth effects, a reduction in collateral value, a negative impact on bank balance sheets, and a credit crunch. As Shleifer and Vishny (2010) explain, fire sales undermine the ability of financial institutions and firms to lend and borrow by reducing their net worth, and this reduction in credit supply can reduce productivity-enhancing investment. These externalities—banks and households ignoring the social cost of defaults and fire sales—may justify policy intervention aimed at stopping household defaults, foreclosures, and fire sales.

The recent case of the United States illustrates the risk of house prices undershooting their equilibrium values during a housing bust on the back of fire sales. The IMF staff notes that "distress sales are the main driving force behind the recent declines in house prices—in fact, excluding distress sales, house prices had stopped falling" and that "there is a risk of house price undershooting" (IMF, 2011c, p. 20).[17]

Inefficiencies and Deadweight Losses from Debt Overhang and Foreclosures

A further problem is that household debt overhang can give rise to various inefficiencies. For firms, debt overhang is a situation in which existing debt is so great that it constrains the ability to raise funds to finance profitable investment projects (Myers, 1977). Similarly, homeowners with debt overhang may invest little in their properties. They may, for example, forgo investments that improve the net present value of their homes, such as home improvements and maintenance expenditures. This effect could be large. Based on detailed household-level U.S. data, Melzer (2010) finds that homeowners with debt overhang (negative equity)

---

[17] As of end-2011, U.S. house prices were at or below the levels implied by regression-based estimates and some historical valuation ratios. Slok (2012) and *The Economist* (2011) also report that U.S. house prices were undervalued.

spend 30 percent less on home improvements and maintenance than home-owners without debt overhang, other things equal. Although privately renegotiating the debt contract between the borrower and the lender could alleviate debt overhang problems, renegotiation is often costly and difficult to achieve outside bankruptcy because of free-rider problems or contract complications (Foote and others, 2010).

Foreclosures and bankruptcy can be an inefficient way of resolving households' inability to service their mortgage debt, giving rise to significant "deadweight losses" (BGFRS, 2012). These deadweight losses stem from the neglect and deterioration of properties that sit vacant for months and their negative effect on neighborhoods' social cohesion and crime (Immergluck and Smith, 2005, 2006). Deadweight losses are also caused by the delays associated with the resolution of a large number of bankruptcies through the court system.

Overall, debt overhang and the deadweight losses of foreclosures can further depress the recovery of house prices and economic activity. These problems make a case for government involvement to lower the cost of restructuring debt, facilitate the writing down of household debt, and help prevent foreclosures (Philippon, 2009).

DEALING WITH HOUSEHOLD DEBT: CASE STUDIES

Having established that household debt can amplify slumps and weaken recoveries, the chapter now investigates how governments have responded during episodes of household deleveraging. The discussion starts by reviewing four broad policy approaches that can, in principle, allow government intervention to improve on a purely market-driven outcome. These approaches are not mutually exclusive and can be complementary. Each has benefits and limitations. The approach a government decides to use is likely to reflect institutional and political features of the economy, the available policy space, and the size of the household debt problem.

- *Temporary macroeconomic policy stimulus.* As discussed above, household deleveraging following a balance sheet shock can result in an abrupt contraction in household consumption to well below the long-term level (undershooting). The costs of the associated contraction in economic activity can be mitigated by an offsetting temporary macroeconomic policy stimulus. In an economy with credit-constrained households, this prospect provides a rationale for temporarily pursuing expansionary fiscal policy, including through government spending targeted at financially constrained households (Eggertsson and Krugman, 2010; and Carroll, Slacalek, and Sommer, 2012).[18] For example, simulations of policy models developed at six policy

---

[18] The presence of financially constrained households with high marginal propensities to consume out of disposable income increases the effectiveness of fiscal policy changes—it renders the economy non-Ricardian—in a wide range of models (see Coenen and others, 2012, for a discussion). The presence of the zero lower bound on interest rates further amplifies the multipliers associated with temporary fiscal policy changes (Woodford, 2010).

institutions suggest that, in the environment of the Great Recession, a temporary (two-year) transfer of 1 percent of GDP to financially constrained households would raise GDP by 1.3 percent and 1.1 percent in the United States and the European Union, respectively (Coenen and others, 2012).[19] Financing the temporary transfer by a lump-sum tax on all households rather than by issuing government debt would result in a "balanced-budget" boost to GDP of 0.8 and 0.9 percent, respectively, in the United States and the European Union. Monetary stimulus can also provide relief to indebted households by easing the debt-service burden, especially in countries in which mortgages have variable rates, such as Spain and the United Kingdom. In the United States, the macroeconomic policy response since the start of the Great Recession was forceful, going much beyond that of several other countries. It included efforts by the Federal Reserve to lower long-term interest rates, particularly in the key mortgage-backed security segment relevant for the housing market. Macroeconomic stimulus, however, has its limits. High government debt may constrain the available fiscal space for a deficit-financed transfer, and the zero lower bound on nominal interest rates can prevent real interest rates from adjusting enough to allow creditor households to pick up the economic slack caused by lower consumption by borrowers.

- *Automatic support to households through the social safety net.* A social safety net can automatically provide targeted transfers to households with distressed balance sheets and high marginal propensities to consume, without the need for additional policy deliberation. For example, unemployment insurance can support people's ability to service their debt after becoming unemployed, thus reducing the risk of household deleveraging through default and the associated negative externalities.[20] However, as with discretionary fiscal stimulus, allowing automatic stabilizers to operate fully requires fiscal space.[21]

- *Assistance to the financial sector.* When the problem of household sector debt is so severe that arrears and defaults threaten to disrupt the operation

---

[19] The six policy institutions are the U.S. Federal Reserve Board, the European Central Bank, the European Commission, the OECD, the Bank of Canada, and the IMF. The simulations assume that policy interest rates are constrained by the zero lower bound—a key feature of major advanced economies as of 2012—and that the central bank does not tighten monetary policy in response to the fiscal expansion. See Coenen and others (2012) for further details.

[20] The generosity and duration of the associated welfare payments differ by country. In Sweden, for example, workers are eligible for unemployment insurance for up to 450 days, although at declining replacement rates after 200 days. By contrast, in the United States, unemployment insurance is normally limited to 26 weeks, and extended benefits are provided during periods of high unemployment. The maximum duration of unemployment insurance was extended to 99 weeks (693 days) in February 2009, and this extension was renewed in February 2012.

[21] Furthermore, to provide targeted support in a timely manner, the safety net needs to be in place before household debt becomes a problem.

of the banking sector, government intervention may be warranted. Household defaults can undermine the ability of financial institutions and firms to lend and borrow by reducing their net worth, and this reduction in credit supply can reduce productive investment (Shleifer and Vishny, 2010). A number of policies, including recapitalizations and government purchases of distressed assets, can prevent such a tightening in credit availability.[22] Such support mitigates the effects of household balance sheet distress on the financial sector. The U.S. Troubled Asset Relief Program established in 2008 was based, in part, on such considerations. Similarly, in Ireland, the National Asset Management Agency was created in 2009 to take over distressed loans from the banking sector. Moreover, assistance to the financial sector can enable banks to engage in voluntary debt restructuring with households. However, strong capital buffers may be insufficient to encourage banks to restructure household debt on a large scale, as was evident in the United States in the aftermath of the Great Recession. In addition, this approach does not prevent unnecessary household defaults, defined as those that occur as a result of temporary liquidity problems. Finally, financial support to lenders facing widespread defaults by their debtors must be designed carefully to avoid moral hazard—indirectly encouraging risky lending practices in the future.

- *Support for household debt restructuring.* The government may choose to tackle the problem of household debt directly by setting up frameworks for voluntary out-of-court household debt restructuring—including write-downs—or by initiating government-sponsored debt-restructuring programs. Such programs can help restore the ability of borrowers to service their debt, thus preventing the contractionary effects of unnecessary foreclosures and excessive asset price declines. To the extent that the programs involve transfers to financially constrained households from less financially constrained agents, the programs can also boost GDP in a way comparable to the balanced-budget fiscal transfer discussed above. These programs can also have a limited fiscal cost. For example, as indicated later on, the programs may involve the government buying distressed mortgages from banks, restructuring them to make them more affordable, and later reselling them, with the revenue offsetting the initial cost. Such programs also sometimes focus on facilitating case-by-case restructuring by improving the institutional and legal framework for debt renegotiation between the lender and the borrower, which has no fiscal cost. However, the success of these programs depends on a combination of careful design and implementation.[23] In particular, these programs must address the risk of moral hazard when

---

[22] See Honohan and Laeven (2005) for a discussion of the various policies used for the resolution of financial crises.

[23] Laeven and Laryea (2009) discuss in detail the principles that should guide government-sponsored household-debt-restructuring programs.

debtors are offered the opportunity to avoid complying with their loan's original terms.

Any government intervention will introduce distortions and lead to some redistribution of resources within the economy and over time. The question is whether the benefits of intervention exceed the costs. Moreover, if intervention has a budgetary impact, the extent of intervention should be constrained by the degree of available fiscal space. The various approaches discussed above differ in the extent of redistribution involved and the associated winners and losers. For example, the presence and generosity of a social safety net reflect a society's preferences about redistribution and inequality. Government support for the banking sector and household-debt-restructuring programs may involve clearer winners than, say, monetary policy stimulus or an income tax cut. The social friction that such redistribution may cause could limit its political feasibility. Mian, Sufi, and Trebbi (2012) discuss the political tug-of-war between creditors and debtors and find that political systems tend to become more polarized in the wake of financial crises. They also argue that collective action problems—struggling mortgage holders may be less well organized politically than banks—can hamper efforts to implement household debt restructuring. Moreover, all policies that respond to the consequences of excessive household debt need to be carefully designed to minimize the potential for moral hazard and excessive risk taking by both borrowers and lenders in the future.

To examine in practice how the above policies can mitigate the problems associated with household debt, the effectiveness of government action during several episodes of household deleveraging are investigated. The examination focuses on policies that support household debt restructuring directly because of the large amount of existing literature on the other policy approaches. For example, there is a large literature on the determinants and effects of fiscal and monetary policy. There are also a number of studies on international experience with financial sector policies.

The episodes considered are the United States in the 1930s and late in the first decade of the 2000s, Hungary and Iceland late in the first decade of the 2000s, Colombia in 1999, and three Scandinavian countries (Finland, Norway, Sweden) in the 1990s. In each of these cases, a housing bust was preceded by or coincided with a substantial increase in household debt, but the policy response was different.[24] The discussion starts by summarizing the factors that led to the buildup in household debt and what triggered household deleveraging. The government response is reviewed next, focusing on policies that directly address the negative

---

[24] The real estate bust in Japan in the 1990s is not discussed because household leverage relative to both safe and liquid assets was low at the time and household deleveraging was not a key feature of the episode. As Nakagawa and Yasui (2009) explain, "The finances of Japanese households were not severely damaged by the mid-1990s bursting of the bubble. Banks, however, with their large accumulation of household deposits on the liability side of their balance sheets, were victims of their large holdings of defaulted corporate loans and the resulting capital deterioration during the bust; in response, banks tightened credit significantly during this period" (p. 82).

effect of household debt on economic activity. Finally, the lessons to be learned from the case studies are summarized.[25]

FACTORS UNDERLYING THE BUILDUP IN HOUSEHOLD DEBT

In each of these episodes, a loosening of credit constraints allowed households to increase their debt. This increase in credit availability was associated with financial innovation and liberalization and declining lending standards. A wave of household optimism about future income and wealth prospects also played a role and, together with the greater credit availability, helped stoke the housing and stock market booms.

The United States in the 1920s—the "roaring twenties"—illustrates the role of rising credit availability and consumer optimism in driving household debt. Technological innovation brought new consumer products such as automobiles and radios into widespread use. Financial innovation made it easier for households to obtain credit to buy such consumer durables and to obtain mortgage loans. Installment plans for the purchase of major consumer durables became particularly widespread (Olney, 1999). General Motors led the way with the establishment of the General Motors Acceptance Corporation in 1919 to make loans for the purchase of its automobiles. By 1927, two-thirds of new cars and household appliances were purchased on installment. Consumer debt doubled from 4.5 percent of personal income in 1920 to 9.0 percent of personal income in 1929. Over the same period, mortgage debt rose from 11 percent of GNP to 28 percent, partly as the result of new forms of lending such as high-leverage home mortgage loans and early forms of securitization (Snowden, 2010). Reflecting the economic expansion and optimism that house values would continue rising, asset prices boomed.[26] Real house prices rose by 19 percent from 1921 to 1925,[27] while the stock market rose by 265 percent from 1921 to 1929.

---

[25] Other economies also implemented measures to address household indebtedness directly. For example, in the United Kingdom, the Homeowners Mortgage Support Scheme aimed to ease homeowners' debt service temporarily with a government guarantee of deferred interest payments; the Mortgage Rescue Scheme attempted to protect the most vulnerable from foreclosure; and the expansion of the Support for Mortgage Interest provided more households with help in meeting their interest payments. Reforms implemented in Ireland included modernizing the bankruptcy regime by making it less onerous and facilitating voluntary out-of-court arrangements between borrowers and lenders of both secured and unsecured debt. In Latvia, the authorities' efforts focused on strengthening the framework for market-based debt resolution (Erbenova, Liu, and Saxegaard, 2011).

[26] Regarding the reasons for this optimism, Harriss (1951) explains that "In the twenties, as in every period of favorable economic conditions, mortgage debt was entered into by individuals with confidence that the burden could be supported without undue difficulty . . . over long periods the value of land and improvements had often risen enough to support the widely held belief that the borrower's equity would grow through the years, even though it was small to begin with" (p. 7).

[27] In certain areas, such as Manhattan and Florida, the increase was much higher (30 to 40 percent).

Rising credit availability resulting from financial liberalization and declining lending standards also helped drive up household debt in the more recent cases considered in this chapter. In the Scandinavian countries, extensive price and quantity restrictions on financial products ended during the 1980s. Colombia implemented a wave of capital account and financial liberalization in the early 1990s. This rapid deregulation substantially encouraged competition for customers, which, in combination with strong tax incentives to invest in housing and optimism regarding asset values, led to a household debt boom in these economies.[28] Similarly, following Iceland's privatization and liberalization of the banking system in 2003, household borrowing constraints were eased substantially.[29] It became possible, for the first time, to refinance mortgages and withdraw equity. Loan-to-value (LTV) ratios were raised as high as 90 percent by the state-owned Housing Financing Fund, and even further by the newly private banks as they competed for market share. In Hungary, pent-up demand combined with the prospect of membership in the European Union triggered a credit boom as outstanding household debt grew from a mere 7 percent of GDP in 1999 to 33 percent in 2007. The first part of this credit boom episode was also characterized by a house price rally, driven by generous housing subsidies. In the United States in the first decade of the 2000s, an expansion of credit supply to households that had previously been unable to obtain loans included increased recourse to private-label securitization and the emergence of so-called exotic mortgages, such as interest-only loans, negative amortization loans, and "NINJA" (no income, no job, no assets) loans.

Factors That Triggered Household Deleveraging

The collapse of the asset price boom, and the associated collapse in household wealth, triggered household deleveraging in all of the historical episodes considered here. The U.S. house price boom of the 1920s ended in 1925, when house prices peaked. Foreclosure rates rose steadily thereafter (Figure 18.8), from 3 foreclosures per 1,000 mortgaged properties in 1926 to 13 per 1,000 by 1933. Another shock to household wealth came with the stock market crash of October 1929, which ushered in the Great Depression. A housing bust also occurred in the Scandinavian countries in the late 1980s and in Colombia in the mid-1990s. Similarly, the end of a house price boom and a collapse in stock prices severely dented household wealth in Iceland and the United States at the start of the Great Recession. In all these cases, household deleveraging started soon after the col-

---

[28] In Finland, the ratio of household debt to disposable income rose from 50 percent in 1980 to 90 percent in 1989; in Sweden it rose from 95 percent to 130 percent. In Colombia bank credit to the private sector rose from 32 percent of GDP in 1991 to 40 percent in 1997.

[29] Financial markets in Iceland were highly regulated until the 1980s. Liberalization began in the 1980s and accelerated during the 1990s, not least because of obligations and opportunities created by the decision to join the European Economic Area in 1994. Iceland's three new large banks were progressively privatized between the late 1990s and 2003, amid widespread accusations of political favoritism (OECD, 2009).

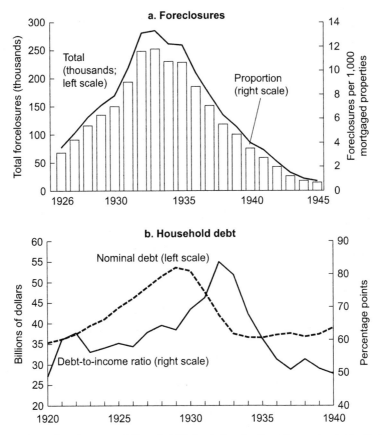

Figure 18.8 Foreclosures and Household Debt during the Great Depression in the United States

Source: IMF staff calculations.

lapse in asset prices. In addition, a tightening of available credit associated with banking crises triggered further household deleveraging during these episodes. The distress in household balance sheets due to the collapse of their wealth spread quickly to financial intermediaries' balance sheets, resulting in tighter lending standards and forcing even more household deleveraging.

Iceland's experience in 2008 provides a particularly grim illustration of how a collapse in asset prices and economic prospects, combined with a massive banking crisis, leads to household overindebtedness and a need for deleveraging. Iceland's three largest banks fell within one week in October 2008. Household balance sheets then came under severe stress from a number of factors (Figure 18.9). First, the collapse in confidence triggered sharp asset price declines, which unwound previous net wealth gains. At the same time, massive inflation and the large depreciation of the krona during 2008–09 triggered a sharp rise in household debt because practically all loans were indexed to the consumer price index (CPI) or

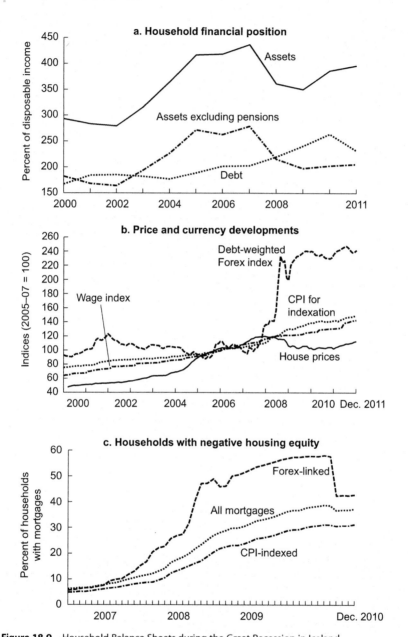

Figure 18.9 Household Balance Sheets during the Great Recession in Iceland

Sources: Central Bank of Iceland; Statistics Iceland; and IMF staff estimates.
Note: In panel a, pension assets are corrected for an estimated tax of 25 percent. CPI = consumer price index; Forex = foreign exchange.

the exchange rate. CPI-indexed mortgages with LTV ratios above 70 percent were driven under water by a combination of 26 percent inflation and an 11 percent drop in house prices. Likewise, with the krona depreciating by 77 percent, exchange-rate-indexed mortgages with LTV ratios above 40 percent went under water. Inflation and depreciation also swelled debt-service payments, just as disposable income stagnated. The combination of debt overhang and debt-servicing problems was devastating. By the end of 2008, 20 percent of homeowners with mortgages had negative equity in their homes (peaking at 38 percent in 2010), while nearly a quarter had debt-service payments greater than 40 percent of their disposable income.

The Policy Response

Having summarized the factors that drove up household debt and triggered household deleveraging, the discussion now turns to the policies that governments pursued to mitigate the negative effects on economic activity. Each episode starts with an overview of the policies implemented and of the political context in which they were introduced. The discussion then considers how effective the policies were in addressing the negative effects of household debt on economic activity. In particular, the review investigates whether the policies helped prevent foreclosures (by restructuring a large share of mortgages), provided transfers to credit-constrained households with a high marginal propensity to consume, and reduced debt overhang. At the same time, the small number of episodes considered and the lack of counterfactual experiences complicate quantifying the effect of these policies on macroeconomic aggregates, such as real GDP.

The discussion starts with two cases that illustrate broadly successful approaches to dealing with household debt—the United States during the Great Depression and Iceland since the Great Recession. These cases are then contrasted with less successful episodes—Colombia in the 1990s and Hungary and the United States since the Great Recession. Finally, the Scandinavian countries during the 1990s are considered, when, despite a large increase in household debt, the authorities did not adopt discretionary household-debt-restructuring policies.

The United States during the Great Depression

This episode exemplifies a bold and broadly successful government-supported household-debt-restructuring program designed to prevent foreclosures, the U.S. Home Owners' Loan Corporation (HOLC). HOLC was established in 1933 because a series of earlier initiatives designed to stop the rising number of foreclosures had achieved little (see Figure 18.8), and social pressure for large-scale intervention was high.[30] As Harriss (1951) explains, "The tremendous social costs imposed by these conditions of deep depression are vividly and movingly revealed in the files of the Home Owners' Loan Corporation. Demands for direct action by the government were insistent and nearly unanimous" (p. 9). In April 1933, a newly elected President Franklin Roosevelt urged

---

[30] The earlier policies included a number of state initiatives to impose moratoriums on foreclosures and the Federal Home Loan Bank (FHLB) Act of 1932, designed to increase bank lending by providing funding for liquidity-constrained banks. The FHLB Act accepted only 3 out of 41,000 applications within its first two years.

Congress to pass legislation that would prevent foreclosures, and HOLC was established that summer.[31]

To prevent mortgage foreclosures, HOLC bought distressed mortgages from banks in exchange for bonds with federal guarantees on interest and principal. It then restructured these mortgages to make them more affordable to borrowers and developed methods of working with borrowers who became delinquent or unemployed, including assisting with job searches. HOLC bought about 1 million distressed mortgages that were at risk of foreclosure, or about one in five of all mortgages. Of these 1 million mortgages, about 200,000 ended up foreclosing when the borrowers defaulted on their renegotiated mortgages. The HOLC program helped protect the remaining 800,000 mortgages from foreclosure, corresponding to 16 percent of all mortgages (Table 18.1).[32] HOLC mortgage purchases amounted to $4.75 billion (8.4 percent of 1933 GDP), and the mortgages were sold over time, yielding a nominal profit by the time the HOLC program was liquidated in 1951. The HOLC program's success in preventing foreclosures at a limited fiscal cost may explain why academics and public figures called for an HOLC-style approach during the Great Recession.

A key feature of HOLC was the effective transfer of funds to credit-constrained households with distressed balance sheets and high marginal propensities to consume, which mitigated the negative effects on aggregate demand discussed above. The objective, emphasized by President Roosevelt in a message to Congress, was to relieve "the small home owner . . . of the burden of excessive interest and principal payments incurred during the period of higher values and higher earning power" (Harriss, 1951, p. 9). Accordingly, HOLC extended mortgage terms from a typical length of 5 to 10 years, often at variable rates, to fixed-rate 15-year terms, which were sometimes extended to 20 years (Green and Wachter, 2005). By making mortgage payments more affordable, it effectively transferred funds to households with distressed mortgages that had higher marginal propensities to consume and away from lenders with presumably lower marginal propensities to consume.[33] In a number of cases, HOLC also wrote off part of the principal to ensure that no loan exceeded 80 percent of the appraised value of the house, thus mitigating the negative effects of debt overhang discussed above.

Iceland during the Great Recession

Iceland's case illustrates how a multipronged approach can provide debt relief to a large share of households and stem the rise in defaults. Iceland's bold policy

---

[31] Household debt had been falling in nominal terms since 1929 because of defaults but continued to rise as a share of households' shrinking incomes until 1933 (see Figure 18.8).

[32] Fishback and others (2010) and Courtemanche and Snowden (2011) offer evidence that this action provided relief to the housing market by supporting home values and home ownership.

[33] HOLC also changed adjustable-rate, interest-only mortgages to fixed-rate, fully amortizing mortgages. This change reduced uncertainty about future debt-service obligations and resulted in less need for precautionary saving and helped homeowners avoid a large lump-sum payment at the loan's maturity.

TABLE 18.1

Government-Supported, Out-of-Court, Debt-Restructuring Programs in Selected Case Studies

Program	Beneficiaries	Debt Modifications	Incentives and Burden Sharing	Take-Up (percent of mortgages, unless otherwise specified)
United States 1929				
Home Owners' Loan Corporation	Households already in default (or at-risk mortgages held by financial institutions in distress)	Repayment burdens further reduced by extending loan terms and lowering interest rates. Principal reductions to a maximum loan-to-value (LTV) ratio of 80 percent.	Moral hazard avoided because program was limited to those already in default. Participation was voluntary, but lenders were offered payouts above the amount they could recover in foreclosure. Eligibility criteria ensured that the borrower could service the new loan and limited the potential losses to be borne by taxpayers. Burden of principal reductions was shared between lenders and the government. Government bore risk on restructured mortgages.	Total households: 25 million Households with a mortgage: 5 million Eligible mortgages: 50 percent Applications: 38 percent Approved applications: 20 percent Foreclosures avoided: 800,000 Total authorization: $4.8 billion (8.5 percent of gross national product—GNP) Total restructurings: $3.1 billion (5.5 percent of GNP)
Iceland 2008				
Payment Smoothing	Households with consumer price index (CPI)-linked and foreign exchange (FX)-linked mortgages and car loans	Debt service reduced through rescheduling and maturity extension.	CPI-linked mortgages: Statutory requirement FX-linked loans: Agreement between government and lenders	Total households: 130,000 Households with a mortgage: 85,000 *Indicators of distress (excluding impact of measures):*[1] Households with negative equity (2010): 40 percent Households with debt service exceeding 40 percent of disposable income (2010): 30 percent Mortgages in default (2010): 15 percent *Take-up:* CPI- and FX-payment smoothing: 50–60 percent
Sector Agreement (bank- administered voluntary restructuring)	Households with multiple creditors and debt-service difficulties but able to service mortgages amounting to at least 70 percent of the value of the house	Debt service scaled down to capacity to pay. Debt reduced to 100 percent of collateral value if household remains current on reduced payments for three years.	Government fostered agreement among largest lenders. Voluntary participation. If agreement not reached, debtors may apply to the Debtor's Ombudsman (DO) or the courts. The burden of restructuring the loans falls on the lenders.	Approved and in-process restructurings: Sector Agreement: 1.6 percent Debtor's Ombudsman (DO): 3.9 percent Write-Down for Deeply Underwater Households: 14.9 percent

(Continued)

TABLE 18.1 (Continued)

Government-Supported, Out-of-Court, Debt-Restructuring Programs in Selected Case Studies

Program	Beneficiaries	Debt Modifications	Incentives and Burden Sharing	Take-Up (percent of mortgages, unless otherwise specified)
DO-Administered Voluntary Restructuring	Similar to Sector Agreement, but reached less wealthy households. Aimed at households seeking advice and support in dealing with creditors.	Similar to Sector Agreement, but allowed deeper temporary reduction in debt service. Procedures more tailored and complex than under Sector Agreement.	Statutory framework that leads to court-administered restructuring in the event that negotiations are unsuccessful. The burden of restructuring the loans falls on the lenders.	
Mortgage Write-down for Deeply Underwater Households	Households with LTV ratios above 110 percent as of December 2010	Principal reduced to 110 percent of the value of the debtor's pledgeable assets.	Agreement between mortgage lenders and government. Participation voluntary, but lenders signed on because the written-down value exceeded the recovery likely through bankruptcy. Moral hazard avoided because the program was limited to those with an LTV ratio above 110 percent in December 2010. The burden of restructuring the loans fell on the lenders.	
United States 2009				
Home Affordable Modification Program (HAMP)[2]	Households in default	Focused on reducing repayment burdens through (1) interest rate reductions, (2) term extensions, (3) forbearance, and (4) since October 2010, principal reduction for loans outside the government-sponsored enterprises (Fannie Mae, Freddie Mac).	Voluntary participation (except for receivers of Troubled Asset Relief Program funds). Principal write-offs not often used, increasing the likelihood that the modified loan will re-default. Restructuring initiated by servicers (not lenders) who have very little financial incentive to participate. Securitization and junior-claim holders create conflicts of interest and exacerbate asymmetric information costs.	Total number of households: 114 million Households with a mortgage: 51 million Households with negative equity: 23 percent Targeted reach: 6–8 percent Trial modifications: 4 percent Permanent modifications: 1.9 percent Total committed: $29.9 billion (0.2 percent of GDP) Total amount used: $2.3 billion[3]

Hungary 2011				
September 2011	Borrowers in good standing with FX-denominated mortgages	Principal write-down through the ability to prepay mortgages at a preferential exchange rate.	Mandated by statute. Burden of writedown borne by lenders alone. Prepayment requirement limits ability of borrowers to participate.	Number of households: ≈ 4 million; Households with a mortgage: 800,000; Mortgages in arrears: 90,000; Technically eligible: 90 percent; Practically eligible: 25 percent; Preliminary take-up: 15 percent
Colombia 1999				
1999	Mortgage holders	Banks forced to retake underwater property and treat loan as fully repaid. Repayment burden lowered through interest rate reduction.	Participation mandated by court ruling. Moral hazard and loss of confidence led to credit crunch.	Number of households: ≈ 10 million; Households with a mortgage: ≈ 700,000; Mortgages in arrears: 126,000 (peak in 2002); Repossessed homes: 43,000 (1999–2003); Eligible borrowers: ≈ 100 percent

Sources: Central Bank of Iceland; Daily TARP Update for December 30, 2011, Federal Reserve Board; Fogafin (2009); Forero (2004); Harriss (1951); Icelandic Association of Financial Services; IMF (2011b, 2011c); Karlsdóttir, Kristinsson, and Rozwadowski (forthcoming); MHA (2012); U.S. OCC (2011); Ólafsson and Vignisdóttir (2012); and authors' calculations.

[1] Near-universal indexation caused the indicators of distress to peak in 2010, two years after the crash.

[2] HAMP is the flagship debt-restructuring program. As discussed in the text, there are other initiatives under the Making Home Affordable (MHA) program. The description of the program and cited numbers are as of the end of 2011.

[3] Source is Daily TARP Update for December 30, 2011 (Washington: U.S. Treasury). This reflects the amount obligated for all MHA initiatives. The total amount obligated for all housing programs under the Troubled Asset Relief Program is $45.6 billion.

response was motivated by the sheer scale of its household debt problem (see Figure 18.9) and intense social pressure for government intervention. In some of the largest protests ever seen in Iceland, thousands of people took to the streets demanding debt writedowns. During a two-year period, the government provided a framework for dealing with household debt in the context of an IMF-supported program.

The approach to resolving the household debt problem had several elements. At the outset, stopgap measures offered near-term relief to ensure that families did not lose their homes owing to temporary problems and to prevent a spike in foreclosures leading to a housing market meltdown. The measures included a moratorium on foreclosures, a temporary suspension of debt service for exchange-rate- and CPI-indexed loans, and rescheduling (payment smoothing) of these loans. About half the households with eligible loans took advantage of payment smoothing, which reduced current debt-service payments by 15–20 percent and 30–40 percent for CPI-indexed and foreign-exchange-indexed loans, respectively.

At a later stage, households were given the option of restructuring their loans out of court by negotiating with their lenders directly or with the help of a newly created Office of the Debtor's Ombudsman acting on their behalf. The negotiations were on a case-by-case basis but used templates developed through dialogue between the government and the financial institutions. The templates provided for substantial writedowns designed to align secured debt with the supporting collateral, and debt service with the ability to repay. The case-by-case negotiations safeguarded property rights and reduced moral hazard, but they took time. As of January 2012, only 35 percent of the case-by-case applications for debt restructuring had been processed. To speed things up, a debt-forgiveness plan was introduced, which writes down deeply underwater mortgages to 110 percent of the household's pledgeable assets. In addition, a large share of mortgage holders received a sizable interest rate subsidy over a two-year period, financed through temporary levies on the financial sector.[34]

Iceland's financial institutions had both the incentive and the financial capacity to participate. After the spectacular collapse of the country's banking system, the three large new banks that were assembled from the wreckage acquired their loan portfolios at fair value that took into account the need for writedowns. This gave the banks the financial room to bear the costs of writedowns, and they frequently took the initiative. Much of the cost of debt restructuring was borne indirectly by foreign creditors, who took significant losses when the banks collapsed. Aligning households' incentives to participate was more complicated. The combination of indexation, inflation, and falling house prices meant that the longer households waited, the larger the writedown. The unconditional moratorium on foreclosures and the suspension of debt service also reduced the incentive to resolve debt problems, and frequent revisions of the debt-restructuring

---

[34] For a full discussion of household debt restructuring in Iceland, see Karlsdóttir, Kristinsson, and Rozwadowski (forthcoming).

framework created an expectation of ever more generous offers. It was only when a comprehensive framework was put in place with a clear expiration date that debt writedowns finally took off. As of January 2012, 15–20 percent of all mortgages had either been—or were in the process of being—written down (see Table 18.1).

Although the jury is still out on Iceland's approach to household debt, the policy response seemed to address the main channels through which household debt can exert a drag on the economy. A spike in foreclosures was averted by the temporary moratorium and the concerted effort to find durable solutions to the household debt problem. By enabling households to reduce their debt and debt service, the debt-restructuring framework transferred resources to agents with relatively high marginal propensities to consume. The financial-sector-financed interest subsidy played a similar role. Finally, the write-down of a substantial portion of excess household debt (that is, in excess of household assets) mitigated the problems associated with debt overhang. The extent to which the Icelandic approach was able to achieve the ultimate goal of putting households back on their feet, while minimizing moral hazard, remains to be seen.

Colombia during the 1990s

This episode illustrates how household-debt-resolution measures that put the burden on a fragile banking sector can lead to a credit crunch. Following the sudden stop in capital inflows in 1997 triggered by the Asian and Russian crises, and the associated rise in interest rates, household defaults increased sharply and mortgage lenders suffered substantial losses (Fogafin, 2009). With their mortgage obligations increasing significantly while house prices collapsed and unemployment rose, many borrowers took their case to the courts (Forero, 2004). In response, the authorities conducted a bank restructuring program in 1999, and the constitutional court passed a series of rulings that aimed to lower households' mortgage debt burden and prevent foreclosures. In particular, the court ruled that mortgages were no longer full-recourse loans—households now had the option of walking away from their mortgage debt. The court also declared the capitalization of interest on delinquent loans unconstitutional.

These reforms represented a substantial transfer of funds to households with distressed balance sheets—those likely to have high marginal propensities to consume—but imposed heavy losses on the fragile financial sector. The reforms also encouraged strategic default by households that would otherwise have repaid their loans, which further exacerbated lenders' losses.[35] Moreover, the court rulings weakened confidence regarding respect for private contracts and creditor rights. A severe and persistent credit crunch followed, and mortgage credit picked up only in 2005.

---

[35] To compensate lenders for losses incurred by the court ruling, the national deposit insurance company established a line of credit with favorable rates for lenders in 2000.

Hungary during the Great Recession

This episode illustrates how a compulsory program that is poorly targeted and puts the burden of debt restructuring on a fragile banking sector can jeopardize the stability of the financial system without achieving the desired economic objectives.

Hungarian households' indebtedness in foreign currency was among the highest in eastern Europe, although total household debt peaked at a relatively modest level, 40 percent of GDP, and was concentrated in roughly 800,000 households (or 20 percent of the total).[36] With the sharp depreciation of the Hungarian forint after the start of the global financial crisis, concerns that the rising debt service was undermining private consumption compelled the authorities to help foreign-currency-indebted households.[37] After a series of failed efforts to provide relief (such as a temporary moratorium on foreclosures and a voluntary workout initiative), the government introduced a compulsory debt-restructuring program in September 2011, without prior consultation with stakeholders. During a fixed window (roughly five months), banks were forced to allow customers to repay their mortgages at a preferential exchange rate, roughly 30 percent below market rates. All losses from the implied debt reduction would be borne by the banks alone.

The compulsory debt-restructuring program appears to have achieved high participation based on preliminary estimates—about 15 percent of all mortgages (see Table 18.1). However, it had three core limitations. First, it was poorly targeted as far as reaching constrained households with high marginal propensities to consume. Only well-off households can repay outstanding mortgage balances with a one-time forint payment, thereby limiting redistribution toward consumers with high marginal propensities to consume. Second, the compulsory program placed the full burden of the losses on the banks, some of which were ill prepared to absorb such losses. And finally, the implicit retroactive revision of private contracts without consulting the banking sector hurt the overall investment climate.

The United States since the Great Recession

This episode, which is still ongoing as of late 2012, illustrates how difficult it is to achieve comprehensive household debt restructuring in the face of a complex mortgage market and political constraints. In the years since their inception, the key programs have reached far fewer households than initially envisaged. These shortfalls led the authorities to adopt additional measures in February 2012 to alleviate the pressure on household balance sheets.

Since the start of the Great Recession, a number of U.S. policymakers have advocated a bold household-debt-restructuring program modeled on the HOLC

---

[36] By the time the crisis arrived in 2008, 100 percent of all new lending and 50 percent of household loans outstanding were in Swiss francs and collateralized by housing.

[37] As IMF (2011b) explains, debt service for holders of foreign-currency-denominated loans increased by more than 50 percent.

of the Great Depression.[38] However, support for such large-scale government intervention in the housing market has, so far, been limited.[39] Instead, the authorities implemented a number of more modest policies.[40] The focus of this discussion is on the Home Affordable Modification Program (HAMP), the flagship mortgage-debt-restructuring initiative targeted at households in default or at risk of default. Announced in February 2009, HAMP's goal was to stabilize the housing market and help struggling homeowners get relief by making mortgages more affordable through the modification of first-lien loans. The program was amended in October 2010 to allow principal write-downs under the Principal Reduction Alternative and further enhanced in 2012, as discussed below. HAMP is part of the Making Home Affordable (MHA) initiative, which helps struggling homeowners get mortgage relief through a variety of programs that aid in modification, refinancing, deferred payment, and foreclosure alternatives. Other options under the MHA initiative include the Home Affordable Refinance Program (HARP), which also aims to reduce monthly mortgage payments. However, households already in default are excluded from HARP, and the impact on preventing foreclosures is likely to be more limited.[41]

HAMP had significant ambitions but as of late 2012 had achieved far fewer modifications than envisaged. Millions of households remained at risk of losing their homes. The stock of properties in foreclosure at the end of 2011 stood at about 2.4 million—a nearly fivefold increase over the precrisis level—and the so-called shadow inventory of distressed mortgages suggested that this number could

---

[38] Specific proposals for household debt policies along the lines of HOLC include those of Blinder (2008) and Hubbard and Mayer (2008). Blinder (2008) proposed an HOLC-style program to refinance 1 million to 2 million distressed mortgages for owner-occupied residences by borrowing and lending about $300 billion. Hubbard and Mayer (2008) proposed lowering repayment amounts and preventing foreclosures and estimated that this would stimulate consumption by approximately $120 billion a year, or 0.8 percent of GDP a year. Approximately half of this effect was estimated to come through the wealth effect—higher house prices due to fewer foreclosures—and half through the transfer of resources to constrained households ("HOLC effect"). See Hubbard and Mayer (2008) and Hubbard (2011). Analysis accompanying IMF (2011c, Chapter II) suggests that, for each 1 million foreclosures avoided, U.S. GDP would rise 0.3 to 0.4 percentage point.

[39] The case of "cramdowns" illustrates how political constraints affected the policy response. As IMF (2011c) explains, the authorities viewed allowing mortgages to be modified in courts (cramdowns) as a useful way to encourage voluntary modifications at no fiscal cost, but noted that a proposal for such a policy had failed to garner sufficient political support in 2009. Mian, Sufi, and Trebbi (2012) argue that creditors' greater ability to organize politically and influence government policy may be the reason they were better able to protect their interests during the aftermath of the 2007–09 financial crisis: "Debtors, on the other hand, were numerous and diffused, therefore suffering from typical collective action problems" (p. 20).

[40] Early attempts to fix the household debt problem were the Federal Housing Administration (FHA) Secure program, the Hope Now Alliance, the Federal Deposit Insurance Corporation's Mod in a Box, and Hope for Homeowners.

[41] The MHA initiative also includes the FHA's Short Refinance Program for borrowers with negative equity, the Home Affordable Unemployment Program, the Home Affordable Foreclosure Alternatives Program, the Second Lien Modification Program, and the Housing Finance Agency Innovation Fund for the Hardest Hit Housing Markets.

rise significantly. Meanwhile, the number of permanently modified mortgages amounted to 951,000, or 1.9 percent of all mortgages (see Table 18.1).[42] By contrast, some 20 percent of mortgages were modified by the Depression-era HOLC program, and HAMP's targeted reach was 3 million to 4 million homeowners (MHA, 2010).[43] By the same token, the amount disbursed under MHA as of December 2011 was only $2.3 billion, well below the allocation of $30 billion (0.2 percent of GDP).

Issues with HAMP's design help explain this disappointing performance. The specific issues are as follows:

- Limited incentives for the parties to participate in the program and tight eligibility criteria for borrowers resulted in low take-up. The initial legislation made creditor cooperation completely voluntary, thereby enabling many creditors to opt out of the program. Loan servicers had little incentive to initiate a costly renegotiation process given that they are already compensated for some legal costs when delinquent loans enter foreclosure.[44] The high probability of re-default may lead lenders and investors to prefer forbearance and foreclosure to modification (Adelino, Gerardi, and Willen, 2009). Securitization presents additional coordination and legal problems. In addition, conflicts of interest may arise, for example, when second-lien holders forestall debt restructuring (IMF, 2011c). Several factors also hamper borrower participation. For instance, many of the expenses related to the outstanding loan, such as late fees and accrued interest, get folded into the new, modified loan. Finally, many distressed borrowers are effectively locked out of the program because of tight eligibility requirements. The unemployed are ineligible to apply for HAMP (they are eligible for a different initiative under MHA that is designed for the unemployed), and households that suffered large income losses often fail to meet the postmodification debt-to-income requirements, especially without principal reduction. Overall, therefore, the program transfers only limited funds to distressed homeowners.

---

[42] As MHA (2012) explains, as of January 2012, 1.79 million trials had been started, but only 951,000 of these trials succeeded in becoming "permanent." (The trial period allows the loan servicer to test the borrower's ability to make the modified loan payment before finalizing the loan modification.) Note that some 200,000 of these modifications were subsequently canceled, leaving 769,000 active permanent modifications.

[43] In a report on the implementation of the HAMP program, the Office of the Special Inspector General for the Troubled Asset Relief Program (SIGTARP) clarified that "Treasury has stated that its 3 to 4 million homeowner goal is not tied to how many homeowners actually receive sustainable relief and avoid foreclosure, but rather that 3 to 4 million homeowners will receive offers for a trial modification" (SIGTARP, 2010). The report criticizes measuring trial modification offers—rather than foreclosures avoided through permanent modifications—as "simply not particularly meaningful."

[44] As Kiff and Klyuev (2009) explain, a servicer's primary duty is to collect mortgage payments from borrowers and pass them to the mortgage holders (trusts, in the case of securitized loans). Servicers also manage the escrow accounts they hold on behalf of borrowers to pay property taxes and insurance, and they employ various loss-mitigation techniques should the borrower default. Servicers are paid a fee for this work.

- HAMP has not reduced monthly mortgage payments enough to restore affordability in many cases. HAMP includes strict step-by-step instructions for modifying a loan, with the primary methods being interest rate reductions, term extensions, and forbearance. Certain exceptions to this step-by-step process are allowed. Non-GSE loans with LTV ratios above 115 percent may also be eligible for principal reductions under the Principal Reduction Alternative.[45] As of end-2011, 11 percent of HAMP permanent modifications included a principal write-down.[46] The nonparticipation by GSEs, which hold about 60 percent of all outstanding mortgages, helps explain this low take-up. Importantly, the modifications focus on bringing a narrow definition of the mortgage repayment burden down to 31 percent of monthly gross income rather than the total repayment burden (including other installment loans and second mortgages). As a result, most borrowers remain seriously constrained even after the modifications, with after-modification total debt-repayment burdens averaging 60 percent of monthly gross income and the after-modification LTV ratio sometimes actually increasing (MHA, 2012). This helps explain the high re-default rate on the modified loans, which averaged 27 percent after 18 months and as high as 41 percent if the monthly payment reduction was less than or equal to 20 percent (MHA, 2012).

In response to these shortcomings, the authorities adopted additional measures to alleviate the pressure on household balance sheets. In February 2012, the authorities announced an expansion of HAMP, including broader eligibility and a tripling of the incentives for lenders to offer principal reductions. In addition, the program was extended by one year. However, participation of the GSEs in the program remains subject to approval by the Federal Housing Finance Agency. Principal reductions are likely to reduce foreclosure rates and, if implemented on a large scale, would support house prices substantially—helping to eliminate the overall uncertainty weighing on the housing market via the shadow inventory.[47]

Scandinavia during the 1990s

The Scandinavian countries illustrate how institutional features, such as a large social safety net, may influence governments' adoption of discretionary household-debt-restructuring policies. In contrast to the cases discussed above, these episodes featured few government initiatives directly targeted at household debt.

---

[45] The GSEs—government-sponsored enterprises—are the Federal National Mortgage Association (Fannie Mae) and the Federal Home Loan Mortgage Corporation (Freddie Mac).

[46] As MHA (2012) explains, 47,000 permanent modifications received principal writedowns (p. 4), which is equivalent to 11 percent of the 432,000 permanent modifications between October 2010 and December 2011.

[47] Other measures include a pilot sale of foreclosed properties for conversion to rental housing. Turning properties into rentals should help reduce the negative impact of foreclosures on house prices. The authorities also called on Congress to broaden access to refinancing under HARP for both GSE-backed and non-GSE mortgages; these measures would support the recovery of the housing market. In particular, they would allow non-GSE loans to be refinanced through a streamlined program operated by the FHA.

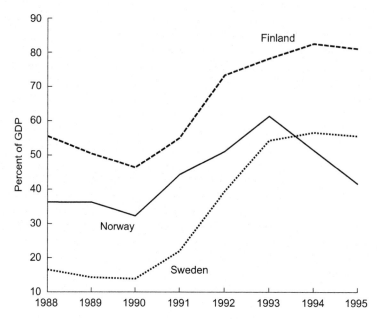

Figure 18.10 Government Debt in the Scandinavian Countries, 1988–95
Source: IMF staff calculations.

After house prices peaked in the late 1980s and the subsequent onset of banking crises in these economies, the primary discretionary policy responses of the Scandinavian governments consisted of support for the financial system.

These countries did not initiate any household-debt-restructuring measures, but their large existing social safety nets supported household incomes and households' ability to service their debt. The large safety nets are a result of a tradition of providing many public services, mainly as a way to promote equality in these economies.[48] For example, unemployment benefits as a percentage of previous wages averaged 65 percent in Finland, Norway, and Sweden in 1991, well above the 47 percent average in other OECD economies (OECD, 1995). In Sweden, the wage-replacement ratio was 83 percent. This government-provided insurance, along with other social safety net benefits, substantially mitigated the impact of job loss on households with distressed balance sheets and supported their ability to pay their mortgages. At the same time, the automatic transfer programs combined with the recession resulted in a substantial rise in government debt. The government debt-to-GDP ratio rose from an average of 31 percent in 1990 to 64 percent in 1994 (Figure 18.10).[49] In response, the authorities implemented cuts

---

[48] For example, IMF (1991) explains that in Norway, "the Government has traditionally sought to provide many basic services in the areas of health and education publicly, mainly as a way to promote equity but also for reasons of social policy. In addition, efforts to redistribute incomes and reduce regional differences have led to an extensive transfer system" (p. 19).

[49] The rise in government debt was also a result of financial support to the banking sector and discretionary fiscal stimulus aimed at reducing unemployment.

to social welfare payments in the mid- to late 1990s as part of a multiyear fiscal consolidation (Devries and others, 2011).

In addition, the variable mortgage rates prevalent in these economies allowed lower interest rates to pass through quickly to lower mortgage payments. The decline in short-term interest rates after the Scandinavian countries abandoned the exchange rate peg to the European currency unit in November 1992 was substantial. For example, the abandonment of the exchange rate peg allowed a cumulative 4 percentage point reduction in short-term interest rates in Sweden (IMF, 1993). By contrast, households in economies where mortgage rates tend to be fixed over multiyear terms often need to apply for a new mortgage (refinance) to reap the benefit of lower prevailing rates, a process that can be hampered by lower house values and negative equity.

LESSONS FROM THE CASE STUDIES

This investigation of the initiatives implemented by governments to address the problem of household debt during episodes of household deleveraging leads to the following policy lessons:

- Bold household-debt-restructuring programs, such as those implemented in the United States in the 1930s and in Iceland in the aftermath of the global crisis, can significantly reduce the number of household defaults and foreclosures and substantially reduce debt-repayment burdens. In so doing, these programs help prevent self-reinforcing cycles of declining house prices and lower aggregate demand. The Icelandic experience also highlights the importance of a comprehensive framework, with clear communication to the public and an explicit time frame. It was only after such a framework was put in place that the process of household debt restructuring took off.

- Ensuring the strength of the banking sector is crucial during the period of household deleveraging. In Iceland, because the new banks had acquired their loan portfolios at fair value, far-reaching household debt restructuring could proceed without affecting bank capital. This also gave banks incentives to initiate negotiations with borrowers. In contrast, in Colombia in the 1990s and in Hungary late in the first decade of the 2000s, insufficiently capitalized banking sectors could not absorb the losses associated with mandatory household debt restructuring. This resulted in a disruption of credit supply.

- Existing institutional features may influence whether governments implement discretionary policy initiatives to tackle the problems associated with household debt. In the Scandinavian countries, despite a significant buildup in household debt before the housing bust of the late 1980s, the authorities introduced few new policies targeted at household debt. This chapter argues that this lack of a policy response may reflect the existence of substantial automatic fiscal stabilizers through the social safety net, in addition to variable mortgage interest rates that quickly transmitted monetary policy stimulus to homeowners.

- An important element in the design of targeted policies is sufficient incentives for borrowers and lenders to participate. For example, debt-restructuring initiatives need to offer creditors and debtors a viable alternative to default and foreclosure. The experience of the United States during the Great Depression demonstrates how specific provisions can be implemented to ensure that lenders willingly accept the government-supported modifications. In contrast, the United States since the Great Recession, a situation in which loan modifications may open the door to potential litigation by investors, illustrates how poorly designed household-debt-restructuring efforts can result in low participation.

- Government support for household-debt-restructuring programs involves clear winners and losers. The friction caused by such redistribution may be one reason such policies have rarely been used in the past, except when the magnitude of the problem was substantial and the ensuing social and political pressures considerable.

SUMMARY AND IMPLICATIONS

Housing busts preceded by larger run-ups in gross household debt are associated with deeper slumps, weaker recoveries, and more pronounced household deleveraging. The decline in economic activity is too large to be simply a reflection of a greater fall in house prices. And it is not driven by the occurrence of banking crises alone. Rather, it is the combination of the house price decline and prebust leverage that seems to explain the severity of the contraction. These stylized facts are consistent with the predictions of theoretical models in which household debt and deleveraging drive deep and prolonged slumps.

Macroeconomic policies are a crucial element of efforts to avert excessive contractions in economic activity during episodes of household deleveraging. For example, fiscal transfers to unemployed households through the social safety net can boost their incomes and improve their ability to service debt, as in the Scandinavian economies in the 1990s. Monetary easing in economies in which mortgages typically have variable interest rates can quickly reduce mortgage payments and prevent household defaults. Support to the financial sector can address the risk that household balance sheet distress will affect banks' willingness to supply credit. Macroeconomic stimulus, however, has its limits. The zero lower bound on nominal interest rates can prevent sufficient rate cuts, and high government debt may constrain the scope for deficit-financed transfers.

Targeted household-debt-restructuring policies can deliver significant benefits. Such policies can, at a relatively low fiscal cost, substantially mitigate the negative impact of household deleveraging on economic activity. In particular, bold household-debt-restructuring programs, such as those implemented in the United States in the 1930s and in Iceland after the Great Recession, can reduce the number of household defaults and foreclosures and alleviate debt-repayment burdens. In so doing, these programs help prevent self-reinforcing cycles of declining house prices and lower aggregate demand. Such policies are particularly relevant for economies with limited scope for expansionary macroeconomic policies and in which the financial sector has already received government support.

However, the success of these programs depends on careful design. Overly restrictive eligibility criteria or poorly structured incentives can lead to programs having a fraction of their intended effect. Conversely, overly broad programs can have serious side effects and undermine the health of the financial sector.

APPENDIX 18A. DATA CONSTRUCTION AND SOURCES

Data on household balance sheets were collected from a variety of sources. The main source is the Organization for Economic Cooperation and Development (OECD) Financial Accounts Database. The data set contains detailed information on households' financial assets and liabilities for 33 economies, spanning the period 1950–2010, though the series for most of the economies begin in the 1990s. This chapter's focus is the household sector's total financial liabilities. For several economies, the series on total financial liabilities were extended back using data from national sources (Finland, Italy, the Republic of Korea, New Zealand, Norway, Sweden, the United Kingdom, and the United States). Household financial liabilities series for Australia, Belgium, France, Germany, Greece, the Netherlands, and Portugal going back to 1980 were obtained from Cecchetti, Mohanty, and Zampolli (2011). More recent data on household balance sheets for several non-OECD countries (Bulgaria, Latvia, Lithuania, and Romania) were obtained from Eurostat. Data for the United States before 1950 come from the U.S. Bureau of Economic Analysis and from *Historical Statistics of the United States;* for Iceland, data on household liabilities are from national sources.

The remainder of the series used in the chapter draw mostly on the IMF World Economic Outlook (WEO), World Bank World Development Indicators, OECD. Stat, and Haver Analytics databases. In particular, household disposable income, house prices, and unemployment rates are taken from OECD.Stat and spliced with Haver Analytics data to extend coverage. House price information for Colombia and Hungary is from the *Global Property Guide;* for Iceland, the housing price index is from national sources. Macroeconomic variables, such as real and nominal GDP, private consumption, investment, and so on are from the WEO database.

Housing bust indicators are obtained from Claessens, Kose, and Terrones (2010), who use the Harding and Pagan (2002) algorithm to determine turning points in the log level of nominal house prices. Recession indicators are from Howard, Martin, and Wilson (2011), who define a recession as two consecutive quarters of negative growth. Because the empirical analysis relies on annual data, the recession or housing bust is assigned to the year of the first quarter of the recession or house price peak, respectively. Financial crisis indicators are from Laeven and Valencia (2010).

APPENDIX 18B. STATISTICAL METHODOLOGY AND ROBUSTNESS CHECKS

This appendix provides further details on the statistical methods used in the first section of the chapter and the robustness of the associated regression results.

Model Specification and Estimation

The baseline specification is a cross-section and time-fixed-effects panel data model estimated for 24 Organization for Economic Cooperation and Development economies and Taiwan Province of China during 1980–2011:

$$\Delta Y_{it} = \mu_i + \lambda_t + \sum_{j=0}^{2} \beta_j \Delta Y_{i,t-j} + \sum_{s=0}^{2} \beta_s Bust_{i,t-s}$$

$$+ \sum_{s=0}^{2} \gamma_s \left\{ Bust_{i,t-s} \times HiDebt_{i,t-s-1} \right\} \qquad (18B.1)$$

$$+ \sum_{s=0}^{2} \delta_s HiDebt_{i,t-s-1} + v_{i,t}$$

in which ΔY_{it} denotes the change in the variable of interest. The analysis starts with the log of real household consumption and then examines the components of GDP, unemployment, household debt, and house prices. The term *Bust* denotes a housing bust dummy that takes the value of 1 at the start of a housing bust; *HiDebt* is a dummy variable that takes the value of 1 if the rise in the household-debt-to-income ratio in the three years before the bust was "high." In the baseline specification, the rise is defined as high if it was above the median for all housing busts across all economies. A number of robustness checks are conducted on this definition of "high," and find similar results (see below). Country and time fixed effects are included to allow for global shocks and country-specific trends. The estimates of equation (18B.1) are cumulated to obtain estimates of the response of the level of the variable of interest (Y) along with the standard error (clustered by economy) using the delta method.

Robustness Checks

As Table 18B.1 shows, the finding that housing busts preceded by large build-ups in household debt tend to be more severe holds up to a number of robustness checks. Each robustness check focuses on the severity of the housing bust for the high- and low-debt groups as measured by the decline in real household consumption five years after the bust.[50] The robustness tests include the following:

---

[50] Similar results are obtained at horizons of less than five years, but these are not reported, given space constraints.

TABLE 18B.1

Real Consumption Following Housing Busts: Robustness			
	High debt	**Low debt**	**Difference**
Baseline	−4.312***	−0.407	−3.905***
	(0.827)	(0.790)	(0.963)
Alternative samples			
Excluding the Great Recession	−4.098***	−0.425	−3.673**
	(0.987)	(1.068)	(1.294)
Excluding financial crises	−1.701*	0.540	−2.241**
	(0.902)	(0.741)	(1.089)
Excluding outliers	−2.978***	−0.131	−2.847***
	(0.755)	(0.730)	(0.952)
Alternative statistical models			
Generalized method of moments	−4.142***	−0.284	−3.857**
	(0.997)	(1.019)	(1.305)
Four lags of dependent variable	−2.124**	0.976	−3.100**
	(1.072)	(1.273)	(1.310)
Alternative definitions of high versus low debt			
Above vs below median (percent increase in debt)	−3.661**	−0.548	−3.113***
	(0.779)	(0.844)	(0.914)
Top vs bottom quartile (percentage points increase in debt)	−5.709**	−1.068	−4.641**
	(1.610)	(1.252)	(2.368)

Source: IMF staff calculations.
Note: Standard errors in parentheses. ***,**, and * indicate significance at the 1, 5, and 10 percent level, respectively.

- *Definition of "high-debt" group.* The baseline places a housing bust in the high-debt group if it was preceded by an above-median rise in the household-debt-to-income ratio during the three years leading up to the bust. The results do not depend on whether the rise is defined in absolute terms (percentage point increase in the ratio) or in relative terms (proportionate increase in percent). The results are also similar if "high debt" is defined as being in the top quartile and "low debt" as being in the bottom quartile of the increase in the debt-to-income ratio.

- *Time sample.* The results are not driven by the Great Recession. Ending the sample in 2006 produces similar results.

- *Outliers and specification.* The results regarding the more severe contraction in economic activity are robust to the exclusion of outliers using Cook's distance. (This involves excluding outlier data points with large residuals or high influence.)

- *Number of lags.* The results are also similar if a dynamic specification is used with four lags instead of the two lags in the baseline specification.

- *Alternative estimation procedure.* The results are also similar if the estimation is undertaken using the Arellano-Bond (1991) estimator. This procedure addresses the possibility of bias because country fixed effects are correlated with the lagged dependent variables in the autoregressive equation.

REFERENCES

Adelino, Manuel, Kristopher Gerardi, and Paul Willen, 2009, "Why Don't Lenders Renegotiate More Home Mortgages? Redefaults, Self-Cures, and Securitization," NBER Working Paper No. 15159 (Cambridge, Massachusetts: National Bureau of Economic Research).

Arellano, Manuel, and Stephen Bond, 1991, "Some Tests of Specification for Panel Data: Monte Carlo Evidence and an Application to Employment Equations," *Review of Economic Studies*, Vol. 58, pp. 277–97.

Blinder, Alan S., 2008, "From the New Deal, a Way Out of a Mess," *The New York Times*, February 24.

Board of Governors of the Federal Reserve System (BGFRS), 2012, "The U.S. Housing Market: Current Conditions and Policy Considerations," Staff white paper (Washington, January).

Buiter, Willem H., 2010, "Housing Wealth Isn't Wealth," *Economics—The Open-Access, Open-Assessment E-Journal*, Vol. 4, No. 22, pp. 1–29.

Campbell, John, Stefano Giglio, and Parag Pathak, 2011, "Forced Sales and House Prices," *American Economic Review*, Vol. 101, No. 5, pp. 2108–31.

Carroll, Christopher, Jiri Slacalek, and Martin Sommer, 2012, "Dissecting Saving Dynamics: Measuring Credit, Wealth and Precautionary Effects," IMF Working Paper 12/219 (Washington: International Monetary Fund).

Cecchetti, Stephen G., M.S. Mohanty, and Fabrizio Zampolli, 2011, "The Real Effects of Debt," BIS Working Paper No. 352 (Basel: Bank for International Settlements).

Cerra, Valerie, and Sweta Saxena, 2008, "Growth Dynamics: The Myth of Economic Recovery," *American Economic Review*, Vol. 98, No. 1, pp. 439–57.

Claessens, Stijn, Ayhan Kose, and Marco Terrones, 2010, "Financial Cycles: What? How? When?" in *NBER International Seminar on Macroeconomics,* ed. by Richard Clarida and Francesco Giavazzi (Chicago: University of Chicago Press) pp. 303–43.

Coenen, Günter, Christopher J. Erceg, Charles Freedman, Davide Furceri, Michael Kumhof, René Lalonde, Douglas Laxton, Jesper Lindé, Annabelle Mourougane, Dirk Muir, Susanna Mursula, Carlos de Resende, John Roberts, Werner Roeger, Stephen Snudden, Mathias Trabandt, and Jan in't Veld, 2012, "Effects of Fiscal Stimulus in Structural Models," *American Economic Journal: Macroeconomics*, Vol. 4, No. 1, pp. 22–68.

Courtemanche, Charles, and Kenneth Snowden, 2011, "Repairing a Mortgage Crisis: HOLC Lending and Its Impact on Local Housing Markets," *Journal of Economic History*, Vol. 71, No. 2, pp. 307–37.

Crowe, Christopher W., Giovanni Dell'Ariccia, Deniz Igan, and Pau Rabanal, 2011, "Policies for Macrofinancial Stability: Options to Deal with Real Estate Booms," IMF Staff Discussion Note 11/02 (Washington: International Monetary Fund).

Dell'Ariccia, Giovanni, Deniz Igan, Luc Laeven, Hui Tong, Bas Bakker, and Jerome Vandenbussche, 2012, "Policies for Macrofinancial Stability: Options to Deal with Credit Booms," IMF Staff Discussion Note 12/06 (Washington: International Monetary Fund).

Devries, Pete, Jaime Guajardo, Daniel Leigh, and Andrea Pescatori, 2011, "A New Action-Based Dataset of Fiscal Consolidation in OECD Countries," IMF Working Paper 11/128 (Washington: International Monetary Fund).

Dynan, Karen, Jonathan Skinner, and Stephen P. Zeldes, 2004, "Do the Rich Save More?" *Journal of Political Economy*, Vol. 112, No. 2, pp. 397–444.

The Economist, 2011, "The Bursting of the Global Housing Bubble Is Only Halfway Through," November 26. www.economist.com/node/21540231.

Eggertsson, Gauti B., and Paul Krugman, 2010, "Debt, Deleveraging, and the Liquidity Trap: A Fisher-Minsky-Koo Approach," *Quarterly Journal of Economics*, Vol. 127, No. 3, pp. 1469–513.

Erbenova, Michaela, Yan Liu, and Magnus Saxegaard, 2011, "Corporate and Household Debt Distress in Latvia: Strengthening the Incentives for a Market-Based Approach to Debt Resolution," IMF Working Paper 11/85 (Washington: International Monetary Fund).

Fatás, Antonio, 2012, "No Need to Deleverage Gross Debt." *Antonio Fatas and Ilian Mihov on the Global Economy* (blog). http://fatasmihov.blogspot.com/2012/01/no-need-to-deleverage -gross-debt.html.

Fishback, Price V., Alfonso Flores-Lagunes, William Horrace, Shawn Kantor, and Jaret Treber, 2010, "The Influence of the Home Owners' Loan Corporation on Housing Markets during the 1930s," *Review of Financial Studies*, Vol. 24, No. 6, pp. 1782–813.

Fisher, Irving, 1933, "The Debt-Deflation Theory of Great Depressions," *Econometrica*, Vol. 1, No. 4, pp. 337–47.

Fondo de Garantías de Instituciones Financieras (Fogafin), ed., 2009, Crisis Financiera Colombiana en los Años Noventa: Origen, Resolución y Lecciones Institucionales, Universidad Externado de Colombia (Bogotá).

Foote, Christopher, Kristopher Gerardi, Lorenz Goette, and Paul Willen, 2010, "Reducing Foreclosures: No Easy Answers," *NBER Macroeconomics Annual* 2009, Vol. 24, pp. 89–138.

Forero, Efrain, 2004, "Evolution of the Mortgage System in Colombia: From the UPAC to the UVR1 System," Paper presented at the XLI Conferencia Interamericana para la Vivienda, Panama City, August 11–13, 2003.

Glick, Reuven, and Kevin J. Lansing, 2009, "U.S. Household Deleveraging and Future Consumption Growth," *FRBSF Economic Letter*, May 15.

———, 2010, "Global Household Leverage, House Prices, and Consumption," *FRBSF Economic Letter*, January 11.

Green, Richard K., and Susan M. Wachter, 2005, "The American Mortgage in Historical and International Context," *Journal of Economic Perspectives*, Vol. 19, No. 4, pp. 93–114.

Guerrieri, Veronica, and Guido Lorenzoni, 2011, "Credit Crises, Precautionary Savings and the Liquidity Trap," NBER Working Paper No. 17583 (Cambridge, Massachusetts: National Bureau of Economic Research).

Hall, Robert E., 2011, "The Long Slump," *American Economic Review*, Vol. 101 (April), pp. 431–69.

Harding, Don, and Adrian Pagan, 2002, "Dissecting the Cycle: A Methodological Investigation," *Journal of Monetary Economics*, Vol. 49, No. 2, pp. 365–81.

Harriss, C. Lowell, 1951, "Background of Home Owners' Loan Corporation Legislation," in *History and Policies of the Home Owners' Loan Corporation* (Cambridge, Massachusetts: National Bureau of Economic Research).

Honohan, Patrick, and Luc Laeven, eds., 2005, *Systemic Financial Crises: Containment and Resolution* (Cambridge, United Kingdom: Cambridge University Press).

Howard, Greg, Robert Martin, and Beth Ann Wilson, 2011, "Are Recoveries from Banking and Financial Crises Really So Different?" Board of Governors of the Federal Reserve System International Finance Discussion Paper No. 1037 (Washington, November).

Hubbard, Glenn, 2011, "Q&A for Hubbard-Mayer Mortgage Refinancing Proposal." www .glennhubbard.net/papers/369-qaa-for-hubbard-mayer-mortgage-refinancing-proposal .html.

———, and Chris Mayer, 2008, "First, Let's Stabilize Home Prices," *Wall Street Journal*, October 2. http://online.wsj.com/article/SB122291076983796813.html.

Iacoviello, Matteo, 2005, "House Prices, Borrowing Constraints, and Monetary Policy in the Business Cycle," *American Economic Review*, Vol. 95, No. 3, pp. 739–64.

Igan, Deniz, and Prakash Loungani, 2012, "Global Housing Cycles," IMF Working Paper 12/217 (Washington: International Monetary Fund).

Immergluck, Dan, and Geoff Smith, 2005, "There Goes the Neighborhood: The Effect of Single-Family Mortgage Foreclosures on Property Values" (Chicago: Woodstock Institute).

———, 2006, "The Impact of Single Family Mortgage Foreclosures on Neighborhood Crime," *Housing Studies*, Vol. 21, No. 6, pp. 851–66.

International Monetary Fund (IMF), 1991, *Recent Economic Developments*, Norway (Washington).

———, 1993, *Recent Economic Developments*, Sweden (Washington).

————, 2009, "What's the Damage? Medium-Term Output Dynamics after Financial Crises," in *World Economic Outlook*, September (Washington).

————, 2010, "Will It Hurt? Macroeconomic Effects of Fiscal Consolidation," in *World Economic Outlook*, October (Washington).

————, 2011a, "Towards Operationalizing Macroprudential Policies: When to Act?" in *Global Financial Stability Report*, September (Washington).

————, 2011b, *Hungary: Staff Report for the 2010 Article IV Consultation and Proposal for Post-Program Monitoring* (Washington).

————, 2011c, *United States: Staff Report for the 2011 Article IV Consultation*, Country Report No. 11/201 (Washington).

Isaksen, Jacob, Paul Lassenius Kramp, Louise Funch Sørensen, and Søren Vester Sørensen, 2011, "Household Balance Sheets and Debt—An International Country Study," Danmarks Nationalbank, Monetary Review, 4th Quarter 2011.

Jordà, Òscar, Moritz H.P. Schularick, and Alan M. Taylor, 2011, "When Credit Bites Back: Leverage, Business Cycles, and Crises," NBER Working Paper No. 17621 (Cambridge, Massachusetts: National Bureau of Economic Research).

Karlsdóttir, Edda Rós, Yngvi Örn Kristinsson, and Franek Rozwadowski, forthcoming, "Responses to Household Financial Distress in Iceland," IMF Working Paper (Washington: International Monetary Fund).

Kiff, John, and Vladimir Klyuev, 2009, "Foreclosure Mitigation Efforts in the United States: Approaches and Challenges," IMF Staff Position Note 09/02 (Washington: International Monetary Fund).

King, Mervyn, 1994, "Debt Deflation: Theory and Evidence," *European Economic Review*, Vol. 38, No. 3–4, pp. 419–45.

Krishnamurthy, Arvind, 2010, "Amplification Mechanisms in Liquidity Crises," *American Economic Journal: Macroeconomics*, Vol. 2, No. 3, pp. 1–30.

Krugman, Paul, 2011, "Debt Is (Mostly) Money We Owe to Ourselves." *The Conscience of a Liberal* (blog), *New York Times*. http://krugman.blogs.nytimes.com/2011/12/28/debt-is-mostly-money-we-owe-to-ourselves.

Kumhof, Michael, and Romain Rancière, 2010, "Leveraging Inequality," *Finance & Development*, Vol. 47, No. 4, pp. 28–31.

Laeven, Luc, and Thomas Laryea, 2009, "Principles of Household Debt Restructuring," IMF Staff Position Note 09/15 (Washington: International Monetary Fund).

Laeven, Luc, and Fabian Valencia, 2010, "Resolution of Banking Crises: The Good, the Bad, and the Ugly," IMF Working Paper 10/146 (Washington: International Monetary Fund).

Lorenzoni, Guido, 2008, "Inefficient Credit Booms," *Review of Economic Studies*, Vol. 75, No. 3, pp. 809–33.

Making Home Affordable Program (MHA), 2010, "Refinements to Existing Administration Programs Designed to Help Unemployed, Underwater Borrowers While Helping Administration Meet Its Goals" (Washington: Department of the Treasury, Department of Housing and Urban Development, and White House). www.makinghomeaffordable.gov/about-mha/latest-news/Pages/pr_03262010.aspx.

————, 2012, "January 2012 Making Home Affordable Report and Servicer Assessments for Fourth Quarter 2011" (Washington: Department of the Treasury, Department of Housing and Urban Development, and White House). www.treasury.gov/initiatives/financial-stability/results/MHA-Reports/Pages/default.aspx.

Mayer, Christopher J., 1995, "A Model of Negotiated Sales Applied to Real Estate Auctions," *Journal of Urban Economics*, Vol. 38, No. 1, pp. 1–22.

McKinsey Global Institute (McKinsey), 2010, *Debt and Deleveraging: The Global Credit Bubble and Its Economic Consequences* (Seoul, San Francisco, London, and Washington).

————, 2012, *Debt and Deleveraging: Uneven Progress on the Path to Growth* (Seoul, San Francisco, London, and Washington).

Melzer, Brian, 2010, "Debt Overhang: Reduced Investment by Homeowners with Negative Equity," Kellogg School of Management Working Paper (Chicago: Kellogg School of Management).

Mian, Atif, Kamalesh Rao, and Amir Sufi, 2011, "Household Balance Sheets, Consumption, and the Economic Slump," Working Paper (Chicago: University of Chicago Booth School of Business).

Mian, Atif, and Amir Sufi, 2011, "Consumers and the Economy, Part II: Household Debt and the Weak U.S. Recovery," *FRBSF Economic Letter*, January 18.

———, 2012, "What Explains High Unemployment? The Aggregate Demand Channel," NBER Working Paper No. 17830 (Cambridge, Massachusetts: National Bureau of Economic Research).

———, and Francesco Trebbi, 2010, "The Political Economy of the U.S. Mortgage Default Crisis," *American Economic Review*, Vol. 95, pp. 587–611.

———, 2012, "Resolving Debt Overhang: Political Constraints in the Aftermath of Financial Crises," NBER Working Paper No. 17831 (Cambridge, Massachusetts: National Bureau of Economic Research).

Minsky, Hyman, 1986, *Stabilizing an Unstable Economy* (New Haven, Connecticut: Yale University Press).

Modigliani, Franco, 1986, "Life Cycle, Individual Thrift, and the Wealth of Nations," *American Economic Review*, Vol. 76, No. 3, pp. 297–313.

Myers, Stewart C., 1977, "Determinants of Corporate Borrowing," *Journal of Financial Economics*, Vol. 5, No. 2, pp. 147–75.

Nakagawa, Shinobu, and Yosuke Yasui, 2009, "A Note on Japanese Household Debt: International Comparison and Implications for Financial Stability," BIS Paper No. 46 (Basel: Bank for International Settlements).

Ólafsson, Tjörvi, and Karen Á. Vignisdóttir, 2012, "Households' Position in the Financial Crisis in Iceland," Central Bank of Iceland Working Paper wp59 (Reykjavik: Central Bank of Iceland).

Olney, Martha L., 1999, "Avoiding Default: The Role of Credit in the Consumption Collapse of 1930," *Quarterly Journal of Economics*, Vol. 114, No. 1, pp. 319–35.

Organization for Economic Cooperation and Development (OECD), 1995, "Economic Survey, Sweden" (Paris).

———, 2009, "Economic Survey, Iceland" (Paris).

Philippon, Thomas, 2009, "The Macroeconomics of Debt Overhang," Paper presented at the 10th Jacques Polak Annual Research Conference, "Financial Frictions and Macroeconomic Adjustment," Washington, November 5–6.

Rajan, Raghuram, and Luigi Zingales, 1998, "Financial Dependence and Growth," *American Economic Review*, Vol. 88 (June), pp. 559–86.

Reinhart, Carmen M., and Kenneth Rogoff, 2009, *This Time Is Different: Eight Centuries of Financial Folly* (Princeton, New Jersey: Princeton University Press).

Rogoff, Kenneth, 2011, "Understanding the Second Great Contraction: An Interview with Kenneth Rogoff," *McKinsey Quarterly* (October). www.mckinseyquarterly.com/Understanding_the_Second_Great_Contraction_An_interview_with_Kenneth_Rogoff_2871.

Shleifer, Andrei, and Robert W. Vishny, 1992, "Liquidation Values and Debt Capacity: A Market Equilibrium Approach," *Journal of Finance*, Vol. 47, No. 4, pp. 1343–66.

———, 2010, "Fire Sales in Finance and Macroeconomics," NBER Working Paper No. 16642 (Cambridge, Massachusetts: National Bureau of Economic Research).

Slok, Torsten, 2012, "Global Home Prices—Several Countries Still Overvalued," Presentation, Deutsche Bank Securities (New York).

Snowden, Kenneth, Jr., 2010, "The Anatomy of a Residential Mortgage Crisis: A Look Back to the 1930s," in *The Panic of 2008: Causes, Consequences and Proposals for Reform*, ed. by Lawrence Mitchell and Arthur Wilmarth (Northampton, Massachusetts: Edward Elgar).

Special Inspector General for the Troubled Asset Relief Program (SIGTARP), 2010, "Factors Affecting Implementation of the Home Affordable Modification Program," SIGTARP-10-005 (Washington, March 25).

Tobin, James, 1980, *Asset Accumulation and Economic Activity: Reflections on Contemporary Macroeconomic Theory* (Oxford: Basil Blackwell).

U.S. Office of the Comptroller of the Currency (OCC), 2011, *Mortgage Metrics Report*, Third Quarter (Washington).

Woodford, Michael, 2010, "Simple Analytics of the Government Expenditure Multiplier," NBER Working Paper No. 15714 (Cambridge, Massachusetts: National Bureau of Economic Research).

CHAPTER 19

Restructuring Sovereign Debt: Lessons from Recent History

UDAIBIR S. DAS, MICHAEL G. PAPAIOANNOU,
AND CHRISTOPH TREBESCH

With the advent of the global financial crisis in 2008, the issue of restructuring sovereign debt returned as a key concern to governments and market participants. However, there still appears to be limited understanding of how restructurings work in actual practice, and detailed historical insights are often missing. This chapter provides an up-to date overview of the process of restructuring sovereign debt in developing economies and emerging markets based on the broad survey by Das, Papaioannou, and Trebesch (2012). The main contribution of the chapter is to distill a set of stylized facts and lessons learned from emerging market restructuring episodes from the late 1990s (following the Brady exchange, see Box 19.1) through 2010. The existing literature includes an increasing number of studies on individual country cases, but very little on cross-country experiences for all major sovereign debt restructurings since the late 1990s.

The first section of this chapter sets the stage by providing an overview and addressing some basic questions: What is a sovereign debt restructuring and how is it defined in relation to concepts such as "default" and "credit event"? How often was sovereign debt restructured in recent decades? What are the determinants of default and debt restructurings?

The second section focuses on procedural aspects of debt restructuring in detail: What are the required operational steps in preparing and implementing a sovereign debt exchange? How did governments communicate with their creditor banks and bondholders? What are the most common debt-restructuring vehicles, in particular the Paris Club and the London Club? And how do modern-day sovereign bond exchanges work in practice? To answer these questions the section describes main insights from the existing literature and draws on newly available data.

The third section summarizes the main characteristics of emerging market sovereign debt restructurings between 1998 and 2010. Among others, the following questions are addressed: What are the typical pitfalls in the restructuring process? How long does it take to restructure sovereign bonds or loans? How frequent are creditor holdouts and litigation? What was the scope of debt relief, or "haircuts," in past restructurings? How do domestic debt restructurings differ from external debt restructurings? And which legal clauses and remedies matter most when sovereign debt is restructured? The existing literature provides limited evidence on these practical questions.

The chapter concludes by discussing the financial stability considerations and other spillover concerns of a sovereign debt restructuring. How do restructurings affect growth or private credit? How quickly did countries reenter capital markets after a debt crisis? What is the evidence of spillovers to the domestic financial sector? These questions are addressed by summarizing the related literature, particularly insights provided by the research of the past few years.

The findings and stylized facts should not be interpreted as providing a full analysis of the underlying causes of restructurings or of their macroeconomic consequences. Instead, the discussion provides new descriptive evidence and historical data in a field in which data are notoriously scarce. It should also be underscored that these insights are based on developing-economy experiences and may not apply to advanced economies or to sovereigns reliant on financing from interconnected financial systems. Nevertheless, the facts summarized here may be relevant for a broader audience interested in debt crises, their resolution, and outcomes.

OVERVIEW AND BASIC CONCEPTS

Definitions and General Considerations

While there is no universally accepted definition, a sovereign debt restructuring can be defined as an exchange of outstanding sovereign debt instruments, such as loans or bonds, for new debt instruments or cash through a formal process. Sovereign debt here refers to debt issued or guaranteed by the government of a sovereign state. One can generally distinguish two main elements in a debt restructuring: debt rescheduling, defined as a lengthening of maturities of the old debt, possibly involving lower interest rates; and debt reduction, defined as a reduction in the face (nominal) value of the old instruments. Both types of debt operations involve a "haircut," that is, a loss in the present value of creditor claims.

Rating agencies, such as Standard & Poor's (2006), typically define distressed debt exchanges as restructurings at terms less favorable than the original bond or loan terms. However, it is important to distinguish distressed-debt exchanges from routine liability management operations aimed at improving the profile of public debt, such as debt swaps, which could occur in normal times (Papaioannou, 2009).

Default events and debt restructurings are closely related but not identical. A default is the failure of a government to make a principal or interest payment on time (beyond the grace period).[1] Defaults can be partial (i.e., when only parts of the country's debt are not being serviced) or complete (a halt of all debt payments to creditors). In most cases, restructurings occur after defaults, and are known as

---

[1] Different loan agreements may have different definitions of "events of default."

postdefault restructurings. However, recent years have also seen a number of pre-emptive debt restructurings, in which outstanding debt instruments are exchanged before the government misses any payments.

The related concept of a "credit event" has gained increasing attention and is mostly used in the context of credit default swaps, which have grown in importance since early in the first decade of the 2000s. Not all sovereign debt restructurings automatically trigger a credit event. Debt exchanges that are not forced upon creditors or debt exchanges in normal times may not constitute a credit event. More specifically, the International Swaps and Derivatives Association (ISDA) considers a restructuring to be a credit event only if (1) it occurs as a result of deterioration in the creditworthiness or financial condition of the sovereign, and (2) it is "binding on all holders" (i.e., applies in mandatory form to all bond-holders of a series).[2] These criteria apply irrespective of whether the debt restructuring is pre- or postdefault.

How Often Was Sovereign Debt Restructured?

According to a new database by Trebesch (2011), sovereign debt–restructuring episodes have occurred throughout the world, with more than 600 individual cases in 95 countries since 1950. Of these, 186 were debt restructurings with private creditors (foreign banks and bondholders) and more than 450 involved restructurings with the Paris Club (government to government debt). Restructuring in low-income countries often proceeded differently from those in emerging markets, including through official-debt-relief initiatives, which makes their experience less relevant for emerging markets. Das, Papaioannou, and Trebesch (2012) provide a detailed classification of all sovereign debt restructurings that took place between 1950 and 2010. Of the 186 debt exchanges with foreign private creditors:

- 18 were sovereign bond restructurings, and 168 affected bank loans;
- 57 involved a cut in face value (debt reduction), while 129 consisted only of a lengthening of maturities (debt rescheduling);
- 109 cases occurred postdefault, and 77 were preemptive; and
- only 26 involved cash buybacks. Most buyback operations were implemented in the context of debt-relief initiatives in poor, highly indebted countries, and involved discounts of 80 percent or more.

Bond restructurings reentered the sovereign debt universe only after the Brady Plan of the mid-1990s (see Box 19.1 later in this chapter). Since 1998, with the debt crises in Pakistan, the Russian Federation, and Ukraine, 18 sovereign bond exchanges with foreign bondholders have occurred. In addition to the 186 debt restructurings with external creditors, there have been several bond restructurings aimed at domestic creditors. These include Ukraine (1998), Russia (1998),

---

[2] Although most credit default swap contracts rely on the form ISDA agreement (and, therefore, would rely on ISDA's determination of a credit event), bilateral contracts in some instances can be different.

Argentina (2001), Uruguay (2003), the Dominican Republic (2005), and Jamaica (2010). Some of these exchanges were implemented in parallel with debt restructurings with foreign creditors.

Determinants of Restructurings and Defaults

A wide range of factors have contributed to default. Most defaults and restructuring episodes were triggered by one or more of the following factors: a worsening of the terms of trade; an increase in international borrowing costs (e.g., caused by tighter monetary policy in creditor countries); consistently poor macroeconomic policies, leading to a buildup of vulnerabilities; or a crisis in a systemic country that causes contagion across goods and financial markets (Sturzenegger and Zettelmeyer, 2006; and Manasse and Roubini 2009).

Additional factors include macroeconomic volatility (Catão and Kapur, 2006), banking crises and related contingent liabilities (Reinhart and Rogoff, 2011), and political and institutional factors (Kohlscheen, 2007; and van Rijckeghem and Weder, 2009). From a historical perspective, Reinhart, Rogoff, and Savastano (2003) identify the occurrence of past defaults as a main predictor of missed payments and restructuring events. They argue that some debtor countries may be "debt intolerant," in that they are less able to sustain high levels of debt as a ratio of GDP without defaulting.

Market perception, too, may have influenced the timing and occurrence of sovereign debt restructurings. When markets perceive a government as being less likely to repay in the future, its borrowing costs can rise rapidly and, therefore, its likelihood of default. Common risk indicators include secondary market bond and sovereign credit default swap spreads, as well as changes in sovereign ratings. Under extreme circumstances, a sudden change in investor perceptions may even act as a default trigger. Debt crises and restructurings can be self-fulfilling and caused by contagion (Cole and Kehoe, 2000). In case of a "debt run" or the effective exclusion from capital markets, countries may have no alternative other than to halt payments. This risk is especially high when governments face large rollover risks (Detragiache and Spilimbergo, 2001).

The structure of the debt portfolio has also affected the likelihood and timing of default and debt negotiation. Factors that determine the debt profile (e.g., currency composition, fixed vs. floating interest rate, maturity, and creditor composition) may have implications for liquidity and solvency conditions and thus may influence the decision to restructure. However, sovereign debt portfolio risks are not always easy to assess, especially at times of generalized financial stress and heightened risk aversion. The decision to restructure often depends on a combination of factors, and the following considerations are broadly valid regarding each of these factors:

- *Currency composition.* Debt issued in foreign currency makes sovereigns vulnerable to exchange rate shocks and currency mismatches because governments typically collect most of their revenue in domestic currency.

- *Floating rate debt.* A high share of floating rate debt can increase the likelihood of severe debt distress caused by the impact of interest rate shocks on countries' average borrowing costs.

- *Maturity structure.* Longer average maturity lessens rollover risks, thereby lowering the likelihood of debt distress when credit markets shut down.

- *Creditor composition.* In addition to being more challenging politically, restructuring of mostly domestically held (as opposed to externally held) debt may lead to a pileup of contingent liabilities and bank bailouts. A decision to restructure may also depend on the share of debt held by official (bilateral) creditors or multilateral creditors because these creditors may be approached in a different way than banks or private sector bondholders (see next section).

The Process of Restructuring Sovereign Debt

This section presents key elements in the process of restructuring sovereign bonds and loans. For illustration, Figure 19.1 provides a stylized timeline from the start of distress to the final restructuring. The restructuring episode is triggered by a default on debt payments or the announcement of a debt restructuring. Thereafter, the government usually embarks on some form of negotiations with its creditors, either bilaterally or with the help of advisors. The key purpose of the debt renegotiation is to agree on the terms of a debt exchange that will provide some form of debt relief and solve the distress situation. The negotiations are also often used as forums for communicating key financial data and the government's fiscal and debt-management plans.

The negotiation or "preparation" phase can take months or even years and usually goes hand-in-hand with a macroeconomic adjustment program and an evaluation of the country's financial situation. Among the first steps a country needs to undertake when considering a debt restructuring is to verify its total debt claims, which means understanding the characteristics of the government's

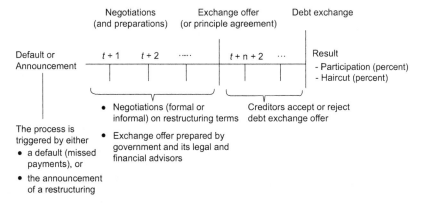

Figure 19.1 Stylized Timeline of a Sovereign Debt Restructuring

Source: Das, Papaioannou, and Trebesch (2012).

outstanding loans, bonds, and other debt instruments, including their legal and financial features.

Lim, Medeiros, and Xiao (2005) suggest verifying the following key characteristics:

- The face and market value of bonds or loans;
- The amortization schedule (bullet versus amortization, and the existence of a sinking fund);
- Interest rate and coupons (fixed versus flexible, and the existence of step-up or linked features);
- Currency (local or foreign) of denomination of the instruments;
- Enhancements, including embedded options or collateral; and
- Legal clauses, including collective action clauses (CACs) and nondefault clauses, and the ability to include exit consents (see the section titled "Financial Stability Implications of Debt Restructuring" for details).

The verification of claims allows countries to assess their debt stocks, debt-service profiles, and the value of the debt instruments. This information lays the foundation for the next crucial procedural step, a detailed debt-sustainability analysis, which provides an indication of the financing gap, the necessary macroeconomic adjustment effort, and the degree of required debt relief. On this basis, governments typically develop a set of restructuring scenarios and prepare a final restructuring proposal, often with the support of legal and financial advisors.

After the restructuring offer is presented to creditors, the creditors have to decide whether to accept or reject the offer. In most cases, a successful exchange requires a certain minimum threshold of acceptance by creditors. Creditor coordination problems and holdout risks are thus likely to be most acute during this period.

In most crisis cases, restructurings mark the end of a debt crisis episode, because the exchange of old for new debt puts the economy back on the path of debt sustainability. However, restructurings do not always put an end to debt distress. Some countries continue to incur arrears after a completed restructuring process and many examples can be found in which sovereigns implemented a series of subsequent restructurings, in particular during the 1980s debt crisis.

The next subsections briefly review the evidence on debt-restructuring processes for each type of creditor involved. Specifically, it summarizes the experience of restructuring processes with regard to bilateral (government to government) debt renegotiated under the Paris Club umbrella; commercial bank debt (London Club); and bond debt (sovereign bond restructurings). A more detailed presentation on debt-restructuring processes for these creditor groups is provided in Rieffel (2003).

Table 19.1 summarizes the differences in negotiation settings across creditors. Note that the restructuring of supplier and trade credits is not discussed in detail

TABLE 19.1

Overview of Debt-Restructuring Vehicles by Type of Creditor					
Sovereign Debt Restructuring by Type of Creditor					
Creditor	Commercial Banks	Bondholders	Bilateral (governments)	Multilateral (World Bank, IMF)	Suppliers, Trade Creditors
Restructuring vehicle	London Club (creditor committees)	Exchange offers	Paris Club	Preferential treatment; debt relief only for poorest countries	ad hoc

because it usually takes place on an ad hoc basis or is excluded from the restructuring exercise. The Heavily Indebted Poor Countries (HIPC) Initiative and the Multilateral Debt Relief Initiative to coordinate debt relief to the poorest countries are also not discussed (for more details on these two initiatives, see IMF and World Bank, 2009).

RESTRUCTURING BILATERAL DEBT: THE PARIS CLUB

The Paris Club is the main institutional framework for restructuring external bilateral sovereign debt, that is, public and publicly guaranteed debt that debtor countries owe to other governments. The origins of the Paris Club date back to 1956, when Argentina met its sovereign creditors in Paris in an effort to prevent an imminent default. With the 1980s debt crisis, the Paris Club became one of the key vehicles for resolving debt crises around the world and has since arranged more than 400 restructuring agreements.

In essence, the Paris Club is an informal group of creditors and an ad hoc negotiation forum. Like the Bank Advisory Committees (of the London Club; see next subsection), the Paris Club has neither legal status nor statutory rules of procedure. However, it has a small secretariat based in Paris and follows a set of established negotiation rules. The Paris Club members are the governments of 19 of the largest world economies, plus additional creditor governments that are invited to participate in the negotiations on a case-by-case basis, depending on whether they have relevant claims on the debtor in question.[3]

A country that wants to restructure its debt with the Paris Club has to approach the Club's secretariat and demonstrate its payment difficulties and need for debt relief based on its economic and financial situation. Debtor countries are also required to agree to a structural adjustment program with the IMF. Once a country satisfies these criteria, it meets and negotiates with a group of its creditors at the Paris Club so as to come to an agreement on broad restructuring terms.

---

[3] As of 2012, the permanent members of the Paris Club are Australia, Austria, Belgium, Canada, Denmark, Finland, France, Germany, Ireland, Italy, Japan, the Netherlands, Norway, the Russian Federation, Spain, Sweden, Switzerland, the United Kingdom, and the United States.

This final agreement (the "agreed minutes") is not legally binding, but establishes the minimum debt-relief conditions that will guide the bilateral negotiations required for the bilateral agreements to become effective.[4]

Usually, the level of debt relief granted in Paris Club restructuring depends on whether the country is a low-income country (LIC), and is often based on the financing gap identified in the related IMF program. Since the 1980s, the trend with regard to LICs has been toward granting more debt relief under increasingly concessional terms. The scope of maximum debt cancellation increased from 33 percent in 1988 (Toronto terms) to 67 percent in 1994 (Naples terms). In 1996, with the establishment of the HIPC initiative, concessional treatment became a standard practice of the Club, with cancellations reaching up to 80 percent in 1996 (Lyons terms) and up to 90 percent in 1999 (Cologne terms). In addition, the Paris Club adopted the "Evian approach" in 2003, offering debt relief to countries other than HIPCs. A key novelty of the Evian approach was its focus on long-term debt sustainability rather than exclusively on short-term debt relief. Thereby, the Paris Club formally recognized that non-HIPC countries may also face solvency problems.

A key principle of the Paris Club is the "comparability of treatment" clause contained in each agreement. The clause calls for equal burden sharing across all creditor groups, private creditors (banks, bondholders, and suppliers) in particular, but also by other official bilateral creditor countries that are not members of the Paris Club. In practice, this means that the scope of debt relief granted by Paris Club creditors will determine how much debt relief other creditors should also grant the country in question. As highlighted by IMF (2001b, p. 43), "comparability of treatment is more an art than a science" and ultimately the Paris Club must judge whether any agreement with banks or bondholders has comparable terms. However, a clear breach of the comparability clause can potentially lead to a cancellation of the Paris Club agreement and, in consequence, jeopardize the financing of the related IMF program.

Thus, the Club's comparability of treatment rule significantly affects the leeway in negotiations with banks or bondholders because Paris Club agreements often precede restructurings with other creditors. Two examples are the Eurobond exchanges of Pakistan in 1999 and the Dominican Republic in 2005, which were, at least in part, motivated by the comparability of treatment clause. In Pakistan's case, for example, only a small share of external debt was owed to private creditors. The Eurobond restructuring only had a volume of about 1 percent of GDP and was thus too small to have a sizable impact on debt sustainability. Despite this, the Paris Club required the government of Pakistan to show signs of "progress" in bondholder negotiations (Sturzenegger and Zettelmeyer, 2006, p. 141).

---

[4] For example, Iraq received 100 percent debt relief from Cyprus, Malta, the Slovak Republic, and the United States under bilateral agreements, although the agreed minutes required only 80 percent debt relief.

Restructuring Bank Loans: The London Club

The process of debt renegotiations between governments and commercial banks is typically labeled as "London Club" restructuring. Despite its name, the London Club is neither a statutory institution based in London nor a well-organized club.[5] Instead, the term loosely describes the case-by-case restructuring routine developed between major Western banks and developing country governments in the late 1970s and early 1980s.

The core element of the London Club process was the Bank Advisory Committee (BAC), or Creditor Committee. Each BAC was a group of 5–20 representative banks that negotiated on behalf of all banks affected by the restructuring. The key aim of the BACs was to overcome coordination problems among hundreds of individual banks and to bundle restructuring expertise in the hands of large banks and their legal and financial advisors.

The members of the BACs were usually senior officials of those banks with the largest exposure to the sovereign.[6] However, as highlighted by Reed (1987), these large banking committees represented only 25–35 percent of a country's total external debt to commercial banks in the 1980s and 1990s. The rest was held by an often fragmented group of banks in a variety of countries.

London Club negotiations tended to proceed as follows: In the early stage of financial distress, a debtor government contacted its one or two major bank creditors asking them to organize and chair a steering committee. During the 1970s and 1980s, it was easy for the government to identify its major creditors because most lending took place via syndicated loans and barely any trading occurred on secondary markets. Also, banks were well informed about who held the debt, so that communication was easier than in dispersed bond markets.

Once the committee of major bankers was established, the banking representatives would meet the country's government officials on a regular basis, often at monthly or weekly intervals. These negotiations typically covered the full spectrum of crisis resolution measures, including the provision of new financing, short-term liquidity support via rollovers or credit lines, as well as the restructuring of loans with maturity prolongation, outright reductions in face value, or both. The BACs were thus a key vehicle for addressing both the liquidity and solvency problems of sovereigns in distress.[7]

---

[5] As highlighted by Rieffel (2003, p. 108) the origins of the "London Club" label remain obscure. The term is to some degree misleading because most meetings of Bank Advisory Committees during the 1980s and 1990s took place in New York, not in London.

[6] Restructuring experience was also a criterion, as shown in the case of Algeria 1996. Although Japanese banks had the largest exposure, the French bank Société Générale was asked to head the committee given that Japanese banks were not experienced in heading steering committees and could not fully rely on their own workout negotiators.

[7] Much of the work was done by legal advisors and subcommittees that focused on particular aspects of a deal. There were subcommittees for processing economic data and surveillance, subcommittees responsible for communicating with the Bretton Woods institutions, and subcommittees specially negotiating trade financing or interbank credit lines.

A key milestone for debt restructurings in the London Club process was the "agreement in principle," which was signed between the representative BAC banks and government officials, once the main restructuring terms had been agreed upon. After the principle agreement had been signed, the terms were sent to all other banks for approval. In this step, unanimity was required for the successful finalization of a restructuring.[8]

Holdouts and intra-creditor disputes were a major problem in the era of bank debt restructuring of the 1980s and 1990s. According to data collected in Trebesch (2010), about 30 percent of London Club restructurings suffered from intra-creditor disputes that led to delays of three months or more in implementing the deal. In most cases, holdout problems were caused by groups of smaller banks, such as regional banks in the United States. However, in some cases, major creditors also refused to participate in agreements arranged by a representative group (e.g., Bankers Trust in Algeria in 1992, Lloyds Bank in Argentina in 1982, and Citibank in Chile in 1987 and in the Philippines in 1986). A further repeated problem was disagreement about the composition and leadership of creditor committees (e.g., in Algeria in 1994, the Dominican Republic in 1983, and South Africa in 1985).

In addition, the implementation of bank loan restructurings was plagued by technical and legal hurdles. The Yugoslav debt deal of 1983 is just one example of a technically very challenging restructuring. Reportedly, the deal required signatures on some 30,000 documents in up to eight international financial centers (see Das, Papaioannou, and Trebesch, 2012). Legal and technical issues also led to significant delays in finalizing deals, such as in Mexico in 1984–85 and in Vietnam's Brady deal negotiations in the mid-1990s. See Box 19.1.

More recent experience with bank debt restructuring has been mixed. Pakistan's (1999) and the Dominican Republic's (2005) restructurings were implemented quickly and took just a few meetings with major bank representatives. In contrast, the bank loan restructurings in Iraq (2006) and Serbia and Montenegro (2004) took much longer and were more disputed. Iraq, for example, faced a creditor group composed of banks, trade creditors, suppliers, and an array of individual companies and investors. Ultimately, the government had to settle more than 13,000 individual claims on Saddam Hussein–era debt, a process that took more than two years.[9] A further example of a troublesome restructuring is the Russian London Club deal of 1998–2000. The domestic debt restructuring committee of 19 international banks was effectively dissolved in 1999 because creditors moved to exchange their debt on a bilateral basis. The process of external

---

[8] This was often not an easy goal, because deals sometimes involved up to 1,000 banks, small and large, in many countries. Typically, each member of the steering committee would manage the reconciliation with a group of banks not in the committee, so as to convince them to sign up for the deal (Rieffel, 2003, p. 122). This was not always successful.

[9] Iraq reopened the private debt exchange of 2006 (so-called 688) in 2008 to try to cover the rest of the private creditors. The new process was called 688-08 and covered the remaining stock of debt. The cash buyback agreement was reportedly quite successful, with significant debt forgiveness. However, some debt remained unresolved.

BOX 19.1 The Brady Plan

By the late 1980s, many developing economies had been in default for nearly a decade. They had settled on a chain of rescheduling agreements with their bank creditors, granting short-term liquidity relief but no cuts in face value. The Brady Plan constituted a major policy shift, because the official sector started to encourage outright debt reduction so as to restore debtor solvency. The plan was first announced by U.S. Treasury Secretary Nicholas Brady in March 1989 and was later widely supported, including by the IMF and the World Bank.

The main elements of the Brady Plan were the following:

- *Exchange of bank loans into sovereign bonds.* The Brady Plan foresaw the exchange of outstanding bank loans into new sovereign bonds, which were partly collateralized by U.S. Treasury bonds. The issuance of new tradable instruments amounting to several billion U.S. dollars created a liquid secondary market for EM sovereign bonds, which had last existed during the interwar years. The Brady Plan can thus be seen as the start of modern-era sovereign bond trading.
- *Menu approach.* Participating creditors were offered a menu of options allowing them to choose between different new instruments, including discount bonds with a cut in face value, and par bonds with long maturities and below-market interest rates but no debt reduction. Banks could also choose to provide new money to the issuing countries, in which case they were offered new instruments with better terms, for example, higher coupons or shorter maturities.
- *Capitalization of arrears.* Interest arrears to commercial banks were partly written off but also partly capitalized into new short-term floating rate bonds.

In total, 17 Brady deals were implemented on a country-by-country basis, starting with Mexico in September 1989 and ending with the last Brady-type agreements in Côte d'Ivoire and Vietnam in 1997. Most Brady countries were in Latin America—Argentina, Bolivia, Brazil, Costa Rica, the Dominican Republic, Ecuador, Mexico, Panama, Peru, Uruguay, and Venezuela. The other six countries were Bulgaria, Côte d'Ivoire, Jordan, Nigeria, the Philippines, Poland, and Vietnam.[a]

The Brady Plan is widely regarded as a success. Debtor countries put an end to the "lost decade" of the 1980s debt crisis and normalized their relations with creditors for the first time after years of protracted debt renegotiations. The agreements also fostered a new wave of capital inflows to emerging markets. Sovereigns were able to re-access capital markets, stock markets rallied, and countries saw an increase in growth and investment, as documented by Arslanalp and Henry (2005). Based on their analysis, Arslanalp and Henry argue that debt relief can be efficient, particularly in countries that face debt overhang problems and that feature strong institutions and a viable private sector economy, thus attracting foreign investment flows.

However, not all hopes connected to the Brady Plan were fulfilled. As highlighted by Chuhan and Sturzenegger (2005), the step-up of interest payments inherent in some of the new bonds threatened the debt sustainability of some debtors 10 years later, thus contributing to renewed default risks. And the belief that Brady bonds were "undefaultable" turned out to be wrong. Ecuador was the first country to restructure its Brady bonds, in 2000, followed by Uruguay (2003), Argentina (2005), and Côte d'Ivoire (2010).

---

[a]Morocco was also supposed to implement a restructuring under the umbrella of the Brady initiative in the early 1990s; however, the government did not fulfill the requirements of a related IMF agreement, so the Brady restructuring did not occur.

bond restructuring was also delayed by many months, partly due to disagreements with a group of mutual funds and hedge funds that held up to 15 percent of debt but that were not represented in the BAC (see Trebesch, 2010, for details).

All in all, however, the BAC process can be regarded as a successful debt-restructuring vehicle. The 1980s and 1990s saw more than 100 debt restructurings under the London Club umbrella (virtually all sovereign debt exchange operations of the time) and most were implemented without major hurdles or conflict.

Sovereign Bond Exchanges

The initial steps in preparing a bond exchange involve gaining a full understanding of the details of all outstanding bonds, including knowing who holds the bonds and possibly who bought credit default swaps on them. Typically, debtor governments also contact legal and financial advisors early on. Legal advisors may provide insights on possible legal hurdles of a restructuring, summarize the legal characteristics of bonds, and may help in drafting the bond exchange documentation and terms of the new bonds. Financial advisors can help identify and reach out to bondholders, and they can play an important role in designing the financial terms of the exchange, such as computing different bond exchange options, drafting "carrot" and "stick" features (see below), and assessing the required scope of debt relief. Similarly, member countries also frequently contact the IMF for advice on bond restructuring.

Bondholder Structure

The key difference between sovereign bond and bank debt restructurings is the creditor structure, which tends to be much more dispersed for sovereign bonds, especially if bonds were sold to retail investors. Some bond restructurings, such as those of Argentina in 2005 and Ukraine in 2000, affected thousands of individual creditors, with an estimated 600,000 and 100,000 retail investors, respectively. Thousands of minor bondholders were also involved in the bond exchanges in Dominica (2004), Pakistan (1999), Uruguay (2003), and Seychelles (2009).

However, bondholder numbers are not always large. In cases like Jamaica (2010), Belize (2007), Grenada (2005), and Ecuador (2000), sovereign bonds were held mostly by a relatively small group of institutional investors. Even more concentrated was the creditor structure in the restructuring of Moldova (2002), where one creditor held 78 percent of the outstanding Eurobonds.

Bondholder Communication and Negotiation

With dispersed creditor structures, identifying bondholders and communicating with them can be difficult, especially if they are retail investors. The main challenge is that bond trading occurs over the counter and no central agency registers the holders of bonds at each moment. Governments undergoing bond restructurings, therefore, need to identify the holders of bonds to initiate a dialogue with them.

In some cases, bondholder consultations have been so extensive that the exchange offers were jointly developed with bondholder representatives. This was the case in Uruguay (2003), but creditor consultations were also wide-ranging in other debt-restructuring cases such as Pakistan (1999), Ukraine (2000), Moldova (2002), Grenada (2005), Belize (2007), Seychelles (2009), and Jamaica (2010). Road shows are a popular communication strategy: senior country officials present the proposed debt exchange to investors and ask for feedback, as was done, for example, by the government of the Dominican Republic in 2004. Official press releases and clearly visible notices in leading financial newspapers are another popular way to keep investors informed.

On the creditor side, large, representative bondholder groups were formed only in a minority of cases, notably in Argentina (2005), Grenada (2005), and Belize (2007).[10] Among these, the Global Committee of Argentina Bondholders was the most visible, claiming to represent more than 50 percent of the outstanding private bonds of Argentina, but it was never formally recognized by the Argentinean government. In Grenada (2005) and Belize (2007), creditor committees consisted of only a few major financial institutions (7 and 14, respectively), but they represented 50 percent or more of the outstanding private debt.

Bond Exchange Offers

One of the key objectives in designing an exchange offer is to achieve a high participation rate by bondholders. Most exchange offers, therefore, contain "carrot" features or "sweeteners" that generate incentives for participation (see the detailed overview in Andritzky, 2006). Sweeteners can take the form of up-front cash repayments, advantageous legal features of the new bonds, or add-ons to the new instruments, such as the GDP-linked warrants in the 2005 Argentine exchange. Liquidity risk can also generate incentives. Many governments exchange an array of old instruments for a small set of new bonds, as in Jamaica, where 356 bonds were replaced by 25 new instruments. These new bonds are likely to trade as benchmark bonds with higher liquidity, making them more attractive for bondholders who hold less-liquid claims. Regulatory sweeteners can also be used, particularly with regard to local bondholders. Argentina, for example, tried to convince domestic banks to participate in its 2005 exchange by allowing them to value the new instruments at par when fulfilling liquidity or capital adequacy requirements.

Another strategy for generating participation incentives is to design a menu of exchange options, allowing investors to choose among different new instruments when tendering their old claims, thus accounting for differing preferences across creditors. Lim, Medeiros, and Xiao (2005) underline that retail investors tend to

---

[10] There were small bondholder groups in the Dominican Republic (2005) and Seychelles (2009) representing only a minority of bondholders. In Ecuador (1999), the government convened the "Creditor Consultative Group" consisting of eight major debt investors; however, it held only two meetings.

prefer new bonds with no face value reduction (cut in principal) and are more willing to accept long maturity and low coupons. In contrast, many institutional investors that mark to market appear to prefer bonds with a principal haircut but a combination of shorter maturities and higher coupons.

Exchange offers can also contain "sticks," which are intended to make the outstanding bonds less attractive. Sticks can be agreed upon by participating creditors via an exit consent, a legal vehicle that allows the removal of clauses from the old bonds, such as cross-acceleration clauses or the listing requirement. These actions effectively reduce the value of the old bond and central bank acceptance as eligible collateral after the exchange, thereby encouraging bondholders to accept the offer. The case evidence provided by Andritzky (2006); Enderlein, Trebesch, and von Daniels (2012); Rieffel (2003); and Roubini and Setser (2004) indicates that it is crucial to strike the right balance between stick and carrot features in preparing an exchange offer.

Once the offer is officially launched, the debtor government usually announces an exchange deadline as well as a minimum participation threshold for an exchange to take place. This minimum threshold has ranged between 75 percent and 85 percent of outstanding bonds in most cases (see Andritzky, 2010, for an overview). Sturzenegger and Zettelmeyer (2006) show that bondholders tend to wait until the last few days before the deadline to accept an offer. To encourage early participation, therefore, sweeteners are sometimes offered only until a certain deadline (e.g., in Uruguay 2003).[11] To achieve higher participation, the exchange deadline is often extended by a few days or weeks. Extensions occurred in all three of Ukraine's debt-exchange offers (1998, 1999, and 2000) and in Dominica in 2004, for which the deadline of its bond exchange was extended twice and by more than four months. Another way to spur higher participation is by using legal means, especially collective action clauses that ease the restructuring of bonds.

STYLIZED FACTS ABOUT RECENT DEBT-RESTRUCTURING EPISODES

This section discusses sovereign debt-restructuring episodes in EMs, focusing closely on restructurings that took place between 1998 and 2010. After summarizing the main characteristics across debt-restructuring cases, such as haircut size and the duration of renegotiation, domestic debt restructurings are compared with foreign debt restructurings and the relevance of legal clauses in exchange operations is reviewed.

---

[11] The same logic applied in some of the London Club debt renegotiations. Argentina, for example, introduced "early participation fees" in 1987. Banks accepting the government's restructuring offer within 30 days were given a 3/8 percent fee, but only 1/8 percent thereafter.

Main Characteristics of Debt Restructurings since 1998

Table 19.2 provides an overview of the main bank and bond debt exchanges in emerging market economies involving foreign creditors that took place since the Brady deal, sorted by the date the restructuring was announced. The following stylized facts can be gleaned from the literature and the data cited therein:

Emerging market sovereign bond restructurings since 1998 were implemented relatively quickly. Of the 18 episodes listed in Table 19.2, seven restructurings took one year or less to complete. More generally, however, the duration of renegotiations varies widely: In some cases, such as Pakistan (1999), Uruguay (2003), and Jamaica (2010), restructuring occurred at record speed, in only three or four months. Other restructurings, such as Argentina (2001–05), took years to resolve. However, as shown by Trebesch (2010) the average duration of renegotiation has decreased compared with earlier decades: bond debt exchanges since 1998 took an average of only 13 months, which is less than half the average duration of bank debt restructurings in the 1980s and 1990s, which took more than 30 months, on average.

The extent of creditor losses (haircuts) shows a large variation, ranging from an estimated 5 percent (the Dominican Republic, 2005) to a nearly 90 percent (Iraq, 2006) reduction in net present value. The reported estimates are taken from a data set by Cruces and Trebesch (forthcoming) and can be interpreted as measuring the loss realized in the exchange from the perspective of a participating creditor. Specifically, the reported values are computed by averaging the loss across all instruments exchanged. Cruces and Trebesch (forthcoming) follow the methodology suggested by Sturzenegger and Zettelmeyer (2006, 2007), which compares the present value of new debt instruments in the exchange with the present value of the old outstanding debt (including past due interest) discounted at imputed exit yields.

The number of debt-restructuring episodes with face value reduction (nominal debt writedowns) has increased notably since the late 1980s. A reason for the increase in frequency of face value reductions is that bank and bond debt exchanges often have come to involve a menu of options, which explicitly includes the face value reduction option.

Postdefault restructuring cases on average show a higher net present value haircut than preemptive restructuring cases (Asonuma and Trebesch, 2012).[12] Postdefault cases also take longer to resolve, on average.

The restructurings varied in complexity. Some restructurings involved only one or two individual bonds, while others, such as Argentina (2005) and Uruguay (2003), exchanged dozens of different instruments.

Domestic versus External Debt Restructurings

Recent case studies show that the negotiation process and the basic restructuring mechanics are very similar in a comparison of domestic debt restructurings to external

---

[12] This is consistent with Finger and Mecagni (2007).

TABLE 19.2

Characteristics of Main Sovereign Debt Restructurings with Foreign Banks and Bondholders, 1998–2010

Case	Preemptive or postdefault?	Default date	Announcement of restructuring	Start of negotiations	Final exchange offer	Date of exchange	Total duration (months)	Debt exchanged (million US$)	Cut in face value (percent)	Haircut estimate (Cruces/Trebesch) (percent)	Discount rate (Cruces/Trebesch)	Outstanding instruments exchanged	New instruments
Pakistan (bank loans)	Postdefault	Aug-98	Aug-98	Mar-99	May-99	Jul-99	11	777	0.0	11.6	0.132	trade credits and debt arrears	1 loan
Pakistan (ext. bonds)	Preemptive	…	Aug-99	Sep-99	Nov-99	Dec-99	4	610	0.0	15.0	0.146	3 Eurobonds	1 Eurobond
Ukraine (ext. bonds)	Preemptive	…	Dec-99	Jan-00	Feb-00	Apr-00	4	1,598	0.9	18.0	0.163	3 bonds, 1 loan	1 Eurobond
Ecuador (ext. bonds)	Postdefault	Aug-99	Jul-98	Sep-99	Jul-00	Aug-00	25	6,700	33.9	38.3	0.173	4 Brady bonds, 2 Eurobonds	2 Eurobonds
Russian Fed. (bank loans)	Postdefault	Dec-98	Sep-98	May-99	Feb-00	Aug-00	23	31,943	36.4	50.8	0.125	PRINs, IANs, debt arrears	1 Eurobond
Moldova (ext. bonds)	Preemptive	…	Jun-02	Jun-02	Aug-02	Oct-02	4	40	0.0	36.9	0.193	1 Eurobond	1 Eurobond
Uruguay (ext. bonds)	Preemptive	…	Mar-03	Mar-03	Apr-03	May-03	2	3,127	0.0	9.8	0.090	18 ext. bonds	18 + 3 new benchmark bonds
Serbia and Montenegro (loans)	Postdefault	since 1990s	Dec-00	Sep-01	Jun-04	Jul-04	44 (since announcement)	2,700	59.3	70.9	0.097	bank loans, arrears	1 Eurobond
Dominican Rep. (bonds/loans)	Postdefault	Jul-03	Jun-03	Dec-03	Apr-04	Sep-04	15	144	15.0	54.0	0.092	2 bonds, short- and medium-term loans	3 bonds
Argentina (ext. bonds)	Postdefault	Jan-02	Oct-01	Mar-03	Jan-05	Apr-05	42	60,572	29.4	76.8	0.104	66 US$ and Arg$ denominated bonds	5 US$ and Arg$ denominated bonds

Dominican Rep. (ext. bonds)	Preemptive	…	Apr-04	Jan-05	Apr-05	May-05	13	1,100	0.0	4.7	0.095	2 bonds	2 bonds
Dominican Rep. (bank loans)	Postdefault	Feb-05	Apr-04	Aug-04	Jun-05	Oct-05	18	180	0.0	11.3	0.097	bank loans, arrears	1 loan
Grenada (bonds/loans)	Preemptive	…	Oct-04	Dec-04	Sep-05	Nov-05	13	210	0.0	33.9	0.097	5 ext. bonds, 8 dom. bonds, 2 ext. loans	1 US$ bond and 1 EC$ bond
Iraq (bank/commercial loans)	Postdefault	since 2003	in 2004	Jul-05	Jul-05	Jan-06	20 (since announcement)	17,710	81.5	89.4	0.123	loans, supplier credit, arrears	mostly cash, 1 US$ bond, 1 Loan
Belize (bonds/loans)	Preemptive		Aug-06	Aug-06	Dec-06	Feb-07	6	516	0.0	23.7	0.096	7 bonds, 8 loans	1 bond
Ecuador (bond buy-back)	Postdefault	Dec-08	Jan-09	no negotiation	Apr-09	June/Nov-09	12	3,190	68.6	67.7	0.130	2 Eurobonds	none (cash settlement)
Seychelles (ext. bonds)	Postdefault	Jul-08	Mar-09	Mar-09	Dec-09	Feb-10	19	320	50.0	56.2	0.107	1 ext. bond, 2 ext. loans, notes	1 bond
Côte d'Ivoire (ext. bonds)	Postdefault	Mar-00	Aug-09	Aug-09	Mar-10	Apr-10	21 (since announcement)	2,940	20.0	55.2	0.099	2 Brady bonds, arrears	1 bond

Sources: Cruces and Trebesch, 2011; Trebesch, 2011, and sources cited therein. The data on preemptive vs. postdefault restructurings are from Asonuma and Trebesch, 2012.

Note: Arg$ = Argentine peso; dom. = domestic; EC$ = Eastern Caribbean dollar; ext. = external; IAN = interest arrear note; PRIN = principle. Debt exchanged refers to effective old debt exchanged in the deal, not eligible debt. Similarly, only old and new instruments that were actually exchanged are listed.

debt restructurings (Sturzennegger and Zettelmeyer, 2006; and Erce, 2012). However, there are also important differences. One difference is that domestic debt is adjudicated domestically, often leaving litigation in domestic courts as the only recourse available to investors. A second difference is that investors in domestic instruments are normally mostly residents (i.e., domestic banks, insurance companies, and pension funds), in which case a restructuring of domestic debt instruments will directly affect the balance sheets of domestic financial institutions and can affect the country's overall financial stability. Finally, exchange rate considerations and currency mismatches play a lesser role in domestic debt than in external debt restructurings.[13]

Another difference is the duration of renegotiations. Since 1998, domestic debt restructurings have been implemented more quickly than external debt restructurings. Argentina's domestic debt was restructured in November 2001, but the external bond exchange took four more years. Russia's domestic GKO bonds were restructured within six months (between August 1998 and March 1999), whereas the restructuring of external bank loans took until 2000 to complete. In Ukraine, the domestic debt exchange was implemented in less than two months, with separate offers for resident and nonresident holders (see Sturzenegger and Zettelmeyer, 2006, for details). In Jamaica, the restructuring of a sizable stock of domestically issued debt took about two months.

In addition, in some instances domestic debt has been treated differently from external debt during restructurings. In Belize (2007), the government restructured only the external bonds. In Ecuador (1998–2000), the authorities restructured both short- and long-term bonds held by nonresidents, but not medium- and long-term domestic debt. In a similar vein, Ecuador's (2008–09) default and debt buyback only affected two outstanding international bonds, but no domestic debt. The opposite occurred in Jamaica's (2010) restructuring, which excluded externally issued Eurobonds.

New Evidence on Creditor Coordination Problems

The problem of creditor holdouts and litigation is widely seen as the main reason for delayed and inefficient debt restructurings. In a typical holdout scenario, a creditor will refuse to participate in a restructuring offer in an effort to enforce better terms later on, possibly by suing the sovereign in a court in London or New York. This type of free-riding behavior and other forms of creditor coordination failures are seen as increasingly important stumbling blocks, mainly due to the shift from bank to bond financing in emerging markets (e.g., Krueger, 2002). Intuitively, large bondholder groups may find it harder to coordinate and agree on a deal, compared with a small group of commercial banks in the London Club process.

However, as shown above, bond restructurings since the 1990s have been implemented more quickly than the bank debt exchanges of the 1980s. In addition, participation rates in sovereign bond exchanges have been very high, on

---

[13] Domestic debt can also be denominated in foreign currency.

average, surpassing 90 percent in most sovereign bond exchanges since 1998 (Das, Papaioannou, and Trebesch, 2012).[14] Trebesch (2010) shows that there is no robust evidence that creditor characteristics play a dominant role in the duration of debt restructurings. He finds no correlation between the duration of renegotiations and the number of creditors involved. In addition, his case archive shows that troublesome holdouts have remained the exception, and that there is no evidence of an increasing trend in inter-creditor disputes since the 1980s. It is sometimes forgotten that London Club restructurings were frequently plagued by creditor coordination problems as well (see the previous section on London Club debt exchanges).

The number of creditor litigation cases in the context of sovereign defaults or restructurings has increased as the result of changes in legal doctrine and the emergence of the so-called vulture creditors. But the total number remains low, with 108 individual occurrences of litigation since 1980 (Schumacher, Trebesch and Enderlein, 2013). One reason for the low number of cases is the costly nature of holdout strategies and litigation and the need for specialized knowledge to carry out these strategies. At the same time, the study finds that the intensity of lawsuits has increased, meaning that the duration of cases has gone up, as have the amounts under litigation, and the number of attachment attempts.

Moreover, there are outlier cases, in which creditor coordination problems did pose a serious problem. The global bond exchange in Argentina (2005) and the restructuring in Dominica (2004) had large shares of holdout creditors, and the countries had difficulties re-accessing international capital markets after the exchange.[15] These countries dealt with holdouts differently. Dominica gradually convinced individual creditors to accept its original exchange offer in the years between 2004 and 2007. Argentina, by contrast, launched a new public exchange offer in April 2010, which achieved a 66 percent participation rate, thereby bringing the total participation rate to 92 percent (Hornbeck, 2010). Many of the remaining 8 percent holdouts, including distressed debt funds, continue their litigation efforts to this day (as of late 2012).

Legal Remedies and Clauses

A bond's governing law plays a major role in a debt restructuring because it pre-defines the contractual provisions for restructuring as well as the jurisdiction for potential litigation. A large majority of outstanding emerging market bonds issued in international markets are under New York law, with English law the second most common. The picture is different for the European Union (EU) countries

---

[14] Bi, Chamon, and Zettelmeyer (2011) develop a related model that rationalizes why coordination failures in past bond exchanges have been the exception and not the rule and why participation rates have typically been very high, even with dispersed bondholders.

[15] In Dominica, the holdouts were mainly linked to three institutions, whereas in Argentina they included thousands of investors, including many retail bondholders. The latter were hard to identify and prone to litigation, and asked for special treatment.

where, since 2003, government bonds have predominantly been issued under domestic laws. An important dimension in which the governing law makes a difference is that it gives a sovereign broader scope to seek to alter the substantive terms of its sovereign debt contracts by changing relevant laws of the sovereign.

Although the inclusion of collective action clauses (CACs) has been the norm under English law, their use has widened in recent years.[16] It is often argued that the presence of CACs can facilitate creditor-debtor negotiations in a restructuring situation, because they reduce the hurdle of having to achieve unanimity on a restructuring agreement (via the majority restructuring clause) and can limit the potential threat of litigation from holdout creditors.[17]

Mexico was the first country to include CACs in its sovereign bond issue in the New York market in February 2003.[18] Other countries quickly followed suit, including Uruguay and Brazil (April 2003), the Republic of Korea and South Africa (May), Belize (June), Italy (July), and Turkey (September). Since then, the inclusion of CACs in New York law bonds has become the norm. During the same period, EU countries agreed to update their bond documentation on internationally issued bonds to include CACs (ECFIN, 2004).[19]

The triggering of CACs in past debt-restructuring episodes was not common, and in the cases in which they were triggered the results were mixed. One example of a successful application is Ukraine (2000), where the authorities took advantage of CACs in the three Eurobonds governed under Luxembourg law. Use of the CACs helped in the implementation of the restructuring and eliminated potential holdout problems.[20] Also in the cases of Moldova (2002) and Uruguay (2003), CACs under English law contributed to quick restructurings. CACs were also embedded in some of the instruments exchanged by Dominica (2004)[21] and Argentina (2005), but they did not prevent the serious holdout problems both countries faced after restructuring.

Exit consents proved to be another type of legal provision with important implications for debt restructuring. Exit consents were first used in Ecuador's 2000

---

[16] In general, CACs cover the following two broad categories: (1) "majority restructuring" provisions, which allow a qualified majority of bondholders of an issuance to change the bond's financial terms and to bind in all other holders of that issuance, either before or after default; and (2) "majority enforcement" provisions, which can limit the ability of a minority of bondholders to enforce their rights following a default.

[17] On some occasions (e.g., Uruguay and Jamaica), explicit announcements of minimum participation thresholds were used to solve coordination problems.

[18] In addition to the IMF, the official sector (e.g., the Group of Ten [1996, 2002], the G-7, and the U.S. Treasury) promoted the more widespread use of CACs (Taylor, 2002).

[19] Although CACs gained considerable attention in the EU public debate, their inclusion in domestic bonds in continental Europe continues to be the exception rather than the rule.

[20] Holders of these bonds were invited to tender their instruments, and at the same time to grant an irrevocable proxy vote to be cast at bondholder meetings. This ensured that bondholders who had tendered proxies could not change their minds and reject the proposed amendments at the meetings without incurring substantial civil liability (see IMF, 2001a, for details).

[21] CACs were included in two Dominican bonds issued in the late 1990s for which Citibank and RBTT Merchant Bank acted as trustees.

exchange of a sovereign bond issued under New York law (Buchheit and Gulati, 2000). The terms of the exchange offer required each participating bond-holder to also agree to a list of amendments of nonpayment terms. The Uruguay (2003) exit consents were mainly aimed at avoiding litigation and limited the possibility of attaching any future payments on the new bonds via a court ruling (waiver of sovereign immunity). In comparison, Ecuador requested amendments on a broader range of terms.[22] The use of exit consents in Ecuador was perceived as part of a "take-it or leave-it" strategy, whereas in Uruguay, participants could opt out of the exit consents (IMF, 2003, p. 23).[23] Use of other clauses (e.g., aggregation, acceleration, cross-default, and cross-acceleration) in restructuring episodes since 1998 has been limited.

Nonpayment terms were amended in the bond restructurings of Dominica (2004), the Dominican Republic (2005), Argentina (2005), and Belize (2007). The exchange prospectus of Argentina, for example, points out that the country might delist the old securities. However, as of January 2012, this delisting had not taken place. Furthermore, it should be underscored that exit consents under New York law have generally withstood legal challenges in U.S. courts. For example, U.S. courts have refused to invalidate exit consents that removed important bondholder rights and protections in a few corporate restructurings, including financial covenants (see IMF, 2001a, for more details).

IMPLICATIONS FOR THE REAL AND FINANCIAL SECTORS

Macroeconomic Implications of Debt Restructuring

How did financial and macroeconomic conditions evolve around debt-restructuring episodes? This question is briefly addressed by plotting median values of a set of variables for a six-year interval around debt-restructuring years. The result is shown in Figure 19.2, with exact annual figures shown in the appendix of Das, Papaioannou, and Trebesch (2012). When interpreting these figures, it is important to highlight once more that a restructuring can occur many years after a country's first payment default. In fact, restructuring episodes often mark the end of a crisis and not its beginning (Levy-Yeyati and Panizza, 2011).

---

[22] Specifically, these terms included "the deletion of the requirement that all payment defaults must be cured as a condition to any annulment of acceleration, the provision that restricts Ecuador from purchasing any of the Brady bonds while a payment default is continuing, the negative pledge covenant, and the covenant to maintain the listing of the defaulted instruments on the Luxembourg Stock Exchange" (IMF, 2001a, p. 35).

[23] Ultimately, more than 90 percent of participants in the Uruguay exchange approved the use of exit consents. Only one small Brady bond did not reach the minimum approval rate of 50 percent of bonds outstanding necessary to activate the exit consents (see Uruguay "Article IV Consultation and Third Review under the Stand-By Arrangement 2003" available at http://www.imf.org/external/pubs/ft/scr/2003/cr03247.pdf).

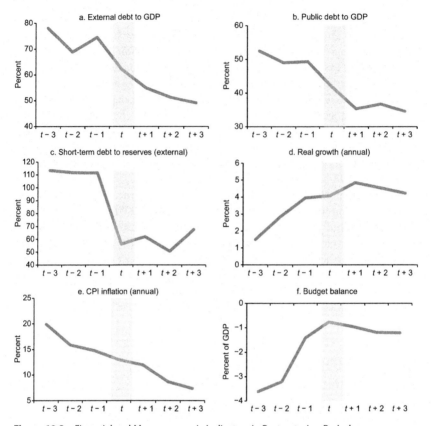

Figure 19.2 Financial and Macroeconomic Indicators in Restructuring Periods

Sources: Economist Intelligence Unit country data; IMF International Financial Statistics database; and World Bank Global Development Finance and World Development Indicator data set.

Note: The sample covers 44 "final restructurings" with banks and bondholders since the 1980s and excludes low-income and heavily indebted poor countries as defined by the World Bank. External debt to GDP covers both public and private external debt. CPI = consumer price index.

As expected, restructuring periods are associated with a notable drop in total public debt as a percentage of GDP, from a median of more than 50 percent to about 35 percent, as well as an even stronger decline in the ratio of total external debt to GDP, from a median close to 80 percent to less than 50 percent. The ratio of external short-term debt to reserves also shows a steep drop from a median of more than 110 percent to slightly more than 55 percent in a single year.

Moreover, macroeconomic conditions also improved after restructuring. Median real growth was only about 1.5 percent three years before final agreements, but stayed consistently above 4 percent during the three years following the exchange.[24] In a similar vein, median inflation decreased from about 20 percent

---

[24] Reinhart and Rogoff (2008) find that output declines associated with domestic debt default appear to be worse than for external debt crises. On average, the output decline in the year before a domestic default is 4 percent, compared with only 1.2 percent in the year before an external default.

three years before restructuring to just 7.5 percent three years after restructuring. However, the median budget balance improved substantially before restructuring (Figure 19.2, panel f).

However, the costs and consequences of defaults and debt restructurings should be carefully considered and compared with the alternative of not restructuring. There appeared to be reputational spillovers from sovereign default and restructurings on other parts of the economy, in particular foreign direct investment and access to credit. Countries that undergo debt restructurings typically see a drop in private sector access to external credit, of up to 40 percent in each year with ongoing debt renegotiations (Arteta and Hale, 2008; and Das, Papaioannou, and Trebesch, 2010). Other research suggests a drop in foreign direct investment flows of up to 2 percent of GDP per year (Fuentes and Saravia, 2010). However, causality is difficult to establish, so these results should be interpreted with caution.

Credit ratings also deteriorate notably before a default, and improve only slowly in the aftermath of debt restructuring. Figure 19.3 shows the evolution of Moody's ratings across nine bond restructuring episodes (for which ratings data were available). Ratings decline markedly, by more than four notches in the three years before a sovereign default event, and start to recover after restructuring, but gained only an average of 1.7 notches in the three subsequent years. After one year, most sovereign bonds retained a C– rating (i.e., having a poor standing and subject to very high credit risk). It is also evident that restructurings rarely come as a surprise. All sovereigns in the list had low ratings in the speculative range one year before the default or restructuring event. One notable outlier is Uruguay,

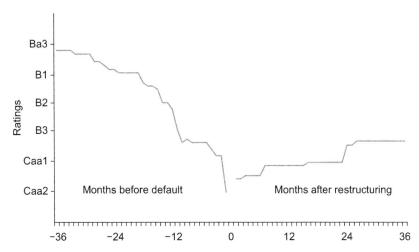

Figure 19.3 Ratings Evolution during Sovereign Restructuring Episodes

Sources: Moody's; and authors' calculations.

Note: Ratings evolution over time, averaged across the following nine bond restructuring episodes: Pakistan (1999), Ecuador (1999 and 2008), Argentina (2001), Moldova (2002), Uruguay (2003), the Dominican Republic (2005), Belize (2006), and Jamaica (2010).

which had investment grade status (Baa3) up to March 2002 and restructured its debt only 14 months later.

Although largely dependent on the specifics of individual cases, market access has typically been restored in a relatively short period after debt restructuring. Gelos, Sandleris, and Sahay (2011) show that most defaulters regain access to new credit within two years of a crisis. The authors also show that the period of exclusion from capital markets during the more recent restructuring episodes has considerably shortened compared with the 1980s. Argentina's restructuring perhaps remains the most extreme—as of 2012, the country had not been able to access the global markets since its 2001 default. Ecuador also suffered a protracted loss of access to international financial markets; it took the country five years after restructuring to regain access.

However, postrestructuring access could come at a cost. Research points out that defaults affect risk spreads only in the first and second year after the restructuring (Borensztein and Panizza, 2009). Other work, however, shows that the impact on market access postrestructuring may depend significantly on the outcome of the restructuring process. Cruces and Trebesch (forthcoming) show that larger haircuts are associated with much larger postrestructuring bond spreads, after controlling for fundamentals and for country and time fixed effects. The effect decreases over time but is still significant in years six and seven after the restructuring. The authors find evidence that haircut size is also highly correlated with the duration of capital market exclusion.

Financial Stability Implications of Debt Restructuring

Sovereign restructuring episodes can have an adverse impact on the financial sector of a debtor country for several reasons. First, the asset side of banks' balance sheets may have to take a direct hit from the loss of value of the restructured assets, such as sovereign bonds. Second, on the liability side, banks can experience deposit withdrawals and the interruption of interbank credit lines. These issues can negatively affect their ability to mobilize resources at a time of stress. Finally, restructuring episodes have also triggered interest rate hikes, thereby increasing the cost of banks' funding and affecting their income positions. Together, these factors may impair the financial position of domestic institutions to such a degree that financial stability is threatened and pressures for bank recapitalization and official sector bailouts are increased.

Recent history confirms that debt restructurings have adversely affected domestic financial sectors. Two main examples are the defaults of Russia and Ecuador, which contributed to the effective collapse of the domestic banking systems in these countries. In Russia, the large Moscow-based commercial banks were affected most owing to their significant exposures to domestic treasury bills and to currency mismatches on their balance sheets. This combination resulted in insolvency and the default of some banks on their external obligations. In Ecuador, the sovereign default had been preceded by a systemic banking crisis (accompanied by liquidation of five financial institutions), yet the restructuring process led to a further significant dent in banks' capital.

In the Jamaica (2010) restructuring, concerns about financial sector stability prompted the government to adopt a preventive financial sector contingency plan. Specifically, with the help of international financial institutions, the government introduced a facility to provide temporary liquidity support to solvent banks that might be affected by sovereign restructuring. As it turned out, there were no requests for such liquidity assistance.

A final observation is that debt restructuring in one country can have cross-border implications. Banks and financial institutions exposed to sovereign risks in a country that undergoes restructuring could transmit the shock across borders, either directly by loss of value of government securities or indirectly through their exposure to the banking sector of that country. Among the larger restructuring episodes, German banks and funds were most heavily exposed to the Russian default of 1998, and U.S. financial institutions and European retail investors were most affected by the Argentine default and debt exchange of 2001–05.

CONCLUSION

This chapter reviews historical experience with debt-restructuring episodes and summarizes a number of lessons based on emerging market economy experience since 1990. A number of factors are identified that appear to have played a role in determining the outcomes of the restructuring process:

- "Twin restructurings" of external and domestic debt seem to have become the norm.

- Despite lengthy negotiations and delays in many debt-restructuring cases, creditor coordination and holdouts have not generally been a major problem. However, the number and intensity of creditor litigation cases has been on the rise.

- Bond restructurings, on average, have been implemented more quickly than bank debt exchanges, and participation rates have often exceeded 90 percent, even with dispersed bondholders.

- Some features embodied in bond contracts (e.g., CACs and other legal clauses) appear to have facilitated debt crisis resolution, but their presence alone did not guarantee a smooth restructuring process.

- Macroeconomic indicators tended to improve in the immediate years after debt restructurings. Credit ratings also tended to recover, although at a slow pace.

- Depending on the country's circumstances, market access could be restored relatively quickly after restructuring. However, postrestructuring access could come at a cost because defaults affect credit risk spreads. Larger haircuts were associated with larger postrestructuring bond spreads, with the effect slowly decreasing over time.

- Debt restructurings in some cases were associated with spillovers into the financial sector, but at least in one of those cases a backstopping mechanism was established to minimize the impact.

Although the analyzed debt exchanges relate to EM economies, these experiences may also prove useful to any distressed country, including advanced economies.

REFERENCES

Andritzky, Jochen, 2006, *Sovereign Default Risk Devaluation: Implications of Debt Crises and Bond Restructurings* (New York: Springer).

———, 2010, "The Return of Investment of Sovereign Restructurings," unpublished.

Arslanalp, Serkan, and Peter Blair Henry, 2005, "Is Debt Relief Efficient?" *Journal of Finance*, Vol. 60, No. 2, pp. 1017–51.

Arteta, Carlos, and Galina Hale, 2008, "Sovereign Debt Crises and Credit to the Private Sector," *Journal of International Economics*, Vol. 74, No. 1, pp. 53–69.

Asonuma, Tamon, and Christoph Trebesch, 2012, "Preemptive versus Post-Default Debt Restructurings," unpublished.

Bi, Ran, Marcos Chamon, and Jeromin Zettelmeyer, 2011, "The Problem that Wasn't: Coordination Failures in Sovereign Debt Restructurings," IMF Working Paper 11/265 (Washington: International Monetary Fund).

Borensztein, Eduardo and Ugo Panizza, 2009, "The Costs of Sovereign Default," *IMF Staff Papers*, Vol. 56, No. 4, pp. 683–741.

Buchheit, Lee C., and Mitu G. Gulati, 2000, "Exit Consents in Sovereign Bond Exchanges," *UCLA Law Review*, Vol. 48, pp. 1–31.

Catão, Luis, and Sandeep Kapur, 2006, "Volatility and the Debt-Intolerance Paradox," *IMF Staff Papers*, Vol. 53, No. 2, pp. 195–218.

Chuhan, Punan, and Federico Sturzenegger, 2005, "Default Episodes in the 1980s and 1990s: What Have We Learned," in *Managing Economic Volatility and Crises: A Practitioner's Guide*, ed. by Joshua Aizenman and Brian Pinto (Cambridge, Massachusetts: Cambridge University Press) pp. 471–519.

Cole, Harold, and Timothy Kehoe, 2000, "Self-Fulfilling Debt Crises," *Review of Economic Studies*, Vol. 67, No. 1, pp. 91–116.

Cruces, Juan, and Christoph Trebesch, forthcoming, "Sovereign Defaults: The Price of Haircuts," *American Economic Journal: Macroeconomics*.

Das, Udaibir S., Michael G. Papaioannou, and Christoph Trebesch, 2010, "Sovereign Default Risk and Private Sector Access to Capital in Emerging Markets," IMF Working Paper 10/10 (Washington: International Monetary Fund).

———, 2012, "Sovereign Debt Restructurings 1950–2010: Literature Survey, Data, and Stylized Facts," IMF Working Paper 12/203 (Washington: International Monetary Fund).

Detragiache, Enrica, and Antonio Spilimbergo, 2001, "Crises and Liquidity: Evidence and Interpretation," IMF Working Paper No. 01/2 (Washington: International Monetary Fund).

Economic and Financial Committee (ECFIN), 2004, "Implementation of the EU Commitment on Collective Action Clauses in Documentation of International Debt Issuance." ECFIN /CEFCPE(2004)REP/50483 final (Brussels). http://europa.eu/efc/sub_committee/pdf/cacs _en.pdf.

Enderlein, Henrik, Christoph Trebesch, and Laura von Daniels, 2012, "Sovereign Debt Disputes: A Database on Government Coerciveness during Debt Crises," *Journal of International Money and Finance*, Vol. 31, No. 2, pp. 250–66.

Erce, Aitor, 2012, "Selective Sovereign Defaults," Globalization and Monetary Policy Institute Working Paper 127, Federal Reserve Bank of Dallas.

Finger, Harald, and Mauro Mecagni, 2007, "Sovereign Debt Restructuring and Debt Sustainability: An Analysis of Recent Cross-Country Experience," IMF Occasional Paper 255 (Washington: International Monetary Fun).

Fuentes, Miguel, and Diego Saravia, 2010, "Sovereign Defaulters: Do International Capital Markets Punish Them?" *Journal of Development Economics*, Vol. 91, No. 2, pp. 336–47.

Gelos, Gaston R., Guido Sandleris, and Ratna Sahay, 2011, "Sovereign Borrowing by Developing Countries: What Determines Market Access?" *Journal of International Economics*, Vol. 83, No. 2, pp. 243–54.

Group of Ten, 1996, "The Resolution of Sovereign Liquidity Crises" (Washington). www.bis .org/publ/gten03.pdf.

———, 2002, "Report of the G-10 Working Group on Contractual Clauses" (Washington). www.bis.org/publ/gten08.pdf.

Hornbeck, Jeff, 2010. "Argentina's Defaulted Sovereign Debt: Dealing with the 'Holdouts'" (Washington: Congressional Research Service). http://fpc.state.gov/documents/organization /142740.pdf.

International Monetary Fund (IMF), 2001a, "Involving the Private Sector in the Resolution of Financial Crises—Restructuring International Sovereign Bonds," (Washington: International Monetary Fund). http://www.imf.org/external/pubs/ft/series/03/IPS.pdf

———, 2001b, "Official Financing for Developing Countries," (Washington: International Monetary Fund), http://www.imf.org/external/pubs/cat/longres.cfm?sk=14803.0.

———, 2003, "Reviewing the Process for Sovereign Debt Restructuring within the Existing Legal Framework," (Washington: International Monetary Fund). http://www.imf.org/external /np/pdr/sdrm/2003/080103.htm.

——— and World Bank, 2009, "Heavily Indebted Poor Countries Initiative (HIPC) and Multilateral Debt Relief Initiative (MDRI). Status of Implementation" (Washington). http: //www.imf.org/external/pp/longres.aspx?id=4365.

Kharas, Homi, Brian Pinto, and Sergei Ulatov, 2001, "An Analysis of Russia's 1998 Meltdown: Fundamentals and Market Signals," *Brookings Papers on Economic Activity*, Vol. 37, No. 1, pp. 1–68.

Kohlscheen, Emanuel, 2007, "Why Are There Serial Defaulters? Evidence from Constitutions," *Journal of Law and Economics,* Vol. 50, No. 4, pp. 713–30.

Krueger, Anne, 2002, *A New Approach to Sovereign Debt Restructuring* (Washington: International Monetary Fund). http://www.imf.org/external/pubs/ft/exrp/sdrm/eng/index .htm.

Levy-Yeyati, Eduardo, and Ugo Panizza, 2011, "The Elusive Cost of Sovereign Defaults," *Journal of Development Economics*, Vol. 94, No. 1, pp. 95–105.

Lim, Chen Hoon, Carlos Medeiros, and Yingbin Xiao, 2005, "Quantitative Assessments of Sovereign Bond Restructurings," International Capital Markets Department (unpublished; Washington: International Monetary Fund).

Manasse, Paolo, and Nouriel Roubini, 2009, "'Rules of Thumb'" for Sovereign Debt Crises," *Journal of International Economics*, Vol. 78, No. 2, pp. 192–205.

Papaioannou, Michael G., 2009, "Exchange Rate Risk Measurement and Management: Issues and Approaches for Public Debt Managers," *South-Eastern Europe Journal of Economics* Vol. 7, No. 1, pp. 7–34.

Reed, John S., 1987, "The Role of External Private Capital Flows," in *Growth-Oriented Adjustment Programs*, ed. by Vittorio Corbo, Morris Goldstein, and Mohsin Khan (Washington: IMF and World Bank).

Reinhart, Carmen, and Kenneth Rogoff, 2008, *This Time Is Different: Eight Centuries of Financial Folly* (Princeton, New Jersey: Princeton University Press).

———, 2011, "From Financial Crash to Debt Crisis," *American Economic Review*, Vol. 10, No. 5, pp. 1676–706.

———, and Miguel Savastano, 2003, "Debt Intolerance," *Brookings Papers on Economic Activity*, Vol. 2003, No. 1, pp. 1–70.

Rieffel, Lex, 2003, *Restructuring Sovereign Debt: The Case for Ad Hoc Machinery* (Washington: Brookings Institution Press).

Roubini, Nouriel, and Brad Setser, 2004, *Bailouts or Bail-ins? Responding to Financial Crises in Emerging Economies* (Washington: Peterson Institute for International Economics).

Schumacher, Julian, Christoph Trebesch, and Henrik Enderlein, 2013, "Sovereign Defaults in Court: The Rise of Creditor Litigation 1976–2010" (unpublished; Berlin: Hertie School of Governance). http://ssrn.com/abstract=2189997.

Standard & Poor's, 2006, "Sovereign Defaults and Rating Transition Data: 2006 Update." http://www2.standardandpoors.com/spf/pdf/fixedincome/KR_sovereign _SovDefaultsTransitionData2006.pdf .

Sturzenegger, Federico, and Jeromin Zettelmeyer, 2006, *Debt Defaults and Lessons from a Decade of Crises* (Cambridge, Massachusetts: MIT Press).

———, 2007, "Creditors Losses versus Debt Relief: Results from a Decade of Sovereign Debt Crises," *Journal of the European Economic Association,* Vol. 5, No. 2-3, pp. 343–51.

Taylor, John, 2002, "Sovereign Debt Restructuring: A U.S. Perspective," Treasury News. http://www.treas.gov/press/releases/po2056.htm.

Trebesch, Christoph, 2010, "Delays in Sovereign Debt Restructurings" (unpublished; University of Munich).

———, 2011, "Sovereign Debt Restructurings 1950–2010: A New Database" (unpublished; University of Munich).

van Rijckeghem, Caroline, and Beatrice Weder, 2009, "Political Institutions and Debt Crises," *Public Choice,* Vol. 138, No. 3, pp. 387–408.

Index

Note: Boxes are denoted by b; figures by f; notes by n; and tables by t.

CPSIA information can be obtained
at www.ICGtesting.com
Printed in the USA
BVOW11*2109060616

450939BV00002B/2/P